'Five percent of offenders commit fifty percent of crimes. Beyond that, what *else* do we know? This book is the authoritative source for the newest information on reoffending, rearrest, reconviction, reincarceration, specialisation, versatility, life-course-persistent offending, escalation or de-escalation, risk assessment, psychopathic personality, desistence, and most important of all, what works to reduce recidivism.'

Terrie E Moffitt, Nannerl O. Keohane University Professor, Duke University, USA

'A small group of offenders are accountable for the majority of crime, and our capacity to explain, predict, and prevent recidivism is of the utmost importance for society. David Farrington and Georgia Zara, leading scholars in the field, provide a penetrating analysis of the most important issues in recidivism research. Deeply informative and clearly written, this groundbreaking book provides a fresh and invigorating perspective on criminal recidivism. Engaging and level-headed, this absorbing and very accessible account of recidivism covers all key knowledge bases on criminal reoffending, including prediction, risk assessment instruments, psychopaths, sex offenders, treatment, and much more. It's an outstanding and invaluable resource for all those who deal with offenders, both in research and practice.'

Adrian Raine, Richard Perry University Professor, Departments of Criminology, Psychiatry, and Psychology, University of Pennsylvania, USA

'This book is an impressive overview of scientific knowledge on criminal recidivism and its correlates, including relevant European data on this topic. I particularly like Zara and Farrington's integration of general quantitative results and their qualitative description of persistent offender's life stories. Crime researchers and Criminal Justice practitioners will find in this book the most solid scientific basis for their analyses and practical interventions.'

Santiago Redondo, Professor of Criminology, Faculty of Psychology, University of Barcelona, Spain

'This volume addresses critical questions for criminal justice policymakers, academics and students of criminology: Why do people continue to commit crime and what can be done to stop them? The depth and range provided by the authors in answering these critical questions make this book a truly impressive contribution.'

Darrick Jolliffe, Professor of Criminology, University of Greenwich, UK

CRIMINAL RECIDIVISM

Criminal Recidivism intends to fill a gap in the criminological psychology literature by examining the processes underlying persistent criminal careers. This book aims to investigate criminal recidivism, and why, how and for how long an individual continues to commit crimes, whilst also reviewing knowledge about risk assessment and the role of psychopathy (including neurocriminological factors) in encouraging recidivism. It also focuses on the recidivism of sex offenders and on what works in reducing reoffending.

At an empirical level, this book attempts to explain criminal persistence and recidivism using longitudinal data from the Cambridge Study in Delinquent Development (CSDD). At a psycho-criminological level it joins together quantitative and qualitative analyses, making its content a practical guide to explain, predict and intervene to reduce the risk of criminal recidivism. The authors present quantitative analyses of criminal careers, as well as qualitative life histories of chronic offenders, in order to bring home the reality and consequences of a life of crime.

The book is aimed not only at advanced students and academics in psychology, criminology, probation studies, social sciences, psychiatry, sociology, political science and penology, but also at decision-makers, policy officials and practitioners within the realm of crime intervention and prevention, and also at forensic experts, judges and lawyers.

Georgia Zara, Ph.D., is Associate Professor of Criminological Psychology at the Department of Psychology, University of Turin, Italy, and is Head and Programme Leader of the Higher Degree in Criminological and Forensic Psychology in the same department.

David P. Farrington, OBE, is Emeritus Professor of Psychological Criminology and Leverhulme Trust Emeritus Fellow in the Institute of Criminology, Cambridge University. He received the Stockholm Prize in Criminology in 2013.

CRIMINAL RECIDIVISM

Explanation, prediction and prevention

Georgia Zara and David P. Farrington

LONDON AND NEW YORK

First published 2016
by Routledge
2 Park Square, Milton Park, Abingdon, Oxon OX14 4RN

and by Routledge
711 Third Avenue, New York, NY 10017

Routledge is an imprint of the Taylor & Francis Group, an informa business

© 2016 Georgia Zara and David P. Farrington

The right of Georgia Zara and David P. Farrington to be identified as authors of this work has been asserted by them in accordance with sections 77 and 78 of the Copyright, Designs and Patents Act 1988.

All rights reserved. No part of this book may be reprinted or reproduced or utilised in any form or by any electronic, mechanical, or other means, now known or hereafter invented, including photocopying and recording, or in any information storage or retrieval system, without permission in writing from the publishers.

Trademark notice: Product or corporate names may be trademarks or registered trademarks, and are used only for identification and explanation without intent to infringe.

British Library Cataloguing-in-Publication Data
A catalogue record for this book is available from the British Library

Library of Congress Cataloging-in-Publication Data
Zara, Georgia.
Criminal recidivism : explanation, prediction and prevention / Georgia Zara and David P. Farrington.
    pages cm
Includes bibliographical references.
1. Recidivism. 2. Criminals–Rehabilitation. 3. Criminal psychology.
I. Farrington, David P. II. Title.
HV6049.Z37 2015
364.3–dc23   2015002391

ISBN: 978-1-84392-707-5 (hbk)
ISBN: 978-1-84392-706-8 (pbk)
ISBN: 978-0-203-08345-1 (ebk)

Typeset in Bembo by Sunrise Setting Ltd, Torquay, UK

DEDICATION

This book is dedicated to Professor Donald J. West, for his pioneering work in founding the Cambridge Study in Delinquent Development and in directing the study for its first two decades.

CONTENTS

List of figures   x
List of tables   xi
Foreword by Rolf Loeber   xiii
Acknowledgements   xv
About the authors   xvii

  Introduction   1

1 Criminal recidivism   4

2 Criminal careers, recidivists and chronic offenders   30

3 Chronic offenders and their life stories   67

4 Risk assessment   148

5 Psychopathy   231

6 Sex offending   282

7 Evidence-based intervention and treatment   310

8 Conclusions   333

References   338
Index   389

LIST OF FIGURES

Figures

1.1	Reconviction frequency rate for different follow-up periods	11
1.2	European countries with and without national recidivism studies	14
5.1	The life course of man 421	265

Image

2.1	David Farrington in the Institute of Criminology's Archive Room (IoC, Cambridge University, March 2010)	38

LIST OF TABLES

1.1	Reconviction rate, frequency and severity rates for different follow-up periods	10
1.2	Percentage of prisoners reconvicted at x years after release	16
1.3	Main differences in offender characteristics in the three datasets	17
2.1	Changes in official offending with age	46
2.2	Age of onset versus criminal career measures	47
2.3	Total number of offences committed	47
2.4	Types of offences committed at different ages	48
2.5	Description of the CSDD offending sample versus criminal careers	50
2.6	Age of onset versus criminal career measures	51
2.7	Frequency of offending versus criminal careers and incarceration	51
2.8	Criminal careers and incarceration for one-timers, recidivists and chronic offenders	52
2.9	Categories of official offenders	52
2.10	Risk factors at ages 8–10 predicting recidivists versus one-time offenders	55
2.11	Risk factors at ages 12–14 predicting recidivists versus one-time offenders	56
2.12	Risk factors at ages 16–18 predicting recidivists versus one-time offenders	57
2.13	Risk factors at age 32 correlating with recidivists versus one-time offenders at age 32	57
2.14	Mean-level comparisons across the offending groups for some criminal career outcomes	60
2.15	Logistic regressions on chronic offenders	61

2.16	(a) Chronic offender mean-level comparisons. (b) Variety Index by chronic offending comparisons	63
2.17	Logistic regression predicting violent offenders (Yes/No)	64
2.18	CSDD recidivism probabilities through the first 11 convictions	65
3.1	Summary of the criminal career of the eight chronic offenders	137
4.1	Risk assessment instruments: AJ instruments for assessing the risk of general and sex violence in adults	166
4.2	Risk assessment instruments: 'Atypical' SPJ for assessing the risk of general and sex violence in adults	179
4.3	Risk assessment instruments: SPJ instruments for assessing the risk of general and sex violence in adults	180
4.4	Risk assessment instruments: AJ instruments for assessing the risk of domestic violence and Intimate Partner Violence (IPV) in adults	188
4.5	Risk assessment instruments: SPJ instruments for assessing the risk of domestic violence and Intimate Partner Violence (IPV) in adults	193
4.6	Risk assessment instruments: AJ instruments for assessing the risk of antisocial behaviour in young people	200
4.7	Risk assessment instruments: SPJ instruments for assessing the risk of antisocial behaviour in young people	202
4.8	Structured Personality Scale and Structured Personality Inventory for assessing personality in problematic young people	211
4.9	2 × 2 prediction table	222
5.1	PCL:SV scores versus the onset of offending in the CSDD	248
5.2	Descriptive PCL:SV scores for the entire CSDD sample	250
5.3	Antisocial personality scales	251
5.4	PCL:SV scores versus antisocial personality at age 10	253
5.5	PCL:SV scores versus antisocial personality at age 14	254
5.6	PCL:SV scores versus antisocial personality at age 18	255
5.7	PCL:SV scores versus antisocial personality at age 32	255
5.8	Correlations of antisocial personality at four ages and PCL:SV scores	256
5.9	Early predictors of psychopathy at age 48	260
5.10	PCL:SV scores versus convictions	262
5.11	PCL:SV scores versus offending	263
5.12	PCL:SV scores versus criminal recidivism	264
7.1	Predictors of the risk of persisting and chronic offending based on the RNR model	328

FOREWORD

Ever since Marvin Wolfgang, Robert Figlio and Thorsten Sellin published *Delinquency in a Birth Cohort* in 1972, the study of criminal recidivism as evident from justice records of rearrest, reconviction and reincarceration, has become a central focus of developmental and life-course criminology. From this interest also grew the study of persistence in offending as evident from self-reported delinquency studies. With the focus on recidivism and persistence has come criminologists' increasing attention to prospectively identify chronic recidivist offenders among all offenders, the costs of recidivist offenders to society and the causes of recidivism as opposed to the causes of desistance from offending. In addition, criminologists have increasingly focused on the impact of the justice system on recidivism, particularly the criminogenic aspects of system intervention, and, by means of randomised controlled trials, they have sought to establish the effectiveness of alternative ways to reduce recidivism.

Georgia Zara and David P. Farrington's present book is very timely and welcome in the annals of recidivism studies and is a groundbreaking example of how to combine quantitative and qualitative data-based analyses on longitudinal data (i.e. the Cambridge Study in Delinquent Development), with an overview of European and North American studies on recidivism, optimal screening devices to ascertain risk for recidivism among active offenders and a focus on interventions to reduce recidivism and thereby decrease prison populations. Because different offence categories have different recidivism probabilities, the volume covers violence, sexual offences and psychopathy.

To my knowledge, no other book to date critically appraises all these important aspects of recidivism. The volume has several surprising and important findings, such as that the majority of serious offences were not committed by those with a serious offence earlier in their delinquency career, and that offence seriousness does not predict recidivism risk very well. The book also shows that recidivism intervals can sometimes be very long, and that, nevertheless, recidivism can be predicted on the basis of several well-replicated factors. And, importantly, case histories of highly recidivist chronic offenders provide new insights about human development, general antisocial tendencies and cumulative exposure to numerous risk factors. However, the authors rightly point to the fact that numerous youth are exposed to many of the risk factors for recidivism but do not become career criminals. Further, the volume contributes in a major way to knowledge about which justice interventions increase recidivism and which interventions reduce reoffending.

Anyone who wants to understand better the delinquency recidivism rates in different European countries, with different justice practices, can learn from advances in research and practice that are chronicled in this volume. Most importantly, the volume explores the rich data from the Cambridge Study in Delinquent Development with its unparalleled high cooperation rate over five decades and the highly complete data, which buttress many of the important conclusions drawn in this volume. The authors can be congratulated for writing this volume on recidivism which, I anticipate, will have a crucial and persisting impact on developmental and life-course criminology studies.

Rolf Loeber
University of Pittsburgh
December 2014

ACKNOWLEDGEMENTS

The age 8–10 data collection of the CSDD was funded by the Home Office and directed by Professor Donald West. The age 32 and age 48 social interviews with the males were funded by the Home Office and directed by Professor David Farrington. The medical interviews with the males at age 48 were funded by the UK National Programme on Forensic Mental Health and co-directed by Professor Jeremy Coid and Professor David Farrington. Part of this work, specifically in the analysis of risk assessment, was supported by PRIN (Ministry of Research and University, Italy) Prot. 2010RP5RNM_004.

We are grateful to Professor Monica Bucciarelli (Department of Psychology, University of Turin, Italy) for her inputs on the psychology of reasoning, to Dr Franco Cauda (Department of Psychology, University of Turin, Italy and member of the GCS-fMRI Group) for his comments on the neuroscientific analysis of the neurocriminology section, to Professor Franco Freilone (Department of Psychology, University of Turin, Italy) for his relevant comments on the psychopathy chapter, and to Professor Luisa Puddu (Department of Education and Psychology, University of Florence) for her observations about the psycho-forensic aspects analysed in some chapters of the book.

We are also grateful to Dr Tara McGee (Griffith University School of Criminology and Criminal Justice, Australia), who was especially collaborative in helping to gather some of the information for the case histories of the chronic offenders, and to Dr. Delphine Theobald (Institute of Psychiatry, King's College London, UK), who was particularly supportive during much of the time devoted to writing this book. A special thank you goes to David Pickup for his patient and attentive observations about the style, structure and content of this volume.

Some of the tables in Chapter 2 were originally presented in a Home Office report (Farrington *et al.*, 2006), and we have permission to reproduce these tables under the UK Open Government Licence, administered by the National Archives.

We are very grateful to John Wiley & Sons Ltd for permission to reproduce material in Table 5.9.

We are very grateful to the Institute of Criminology, Cambridge University, for technical support during the preparation of this volume, and to Maureen Brown for excellent secretarial assistance. A special thank you goes to Anna Evans for her help with the scanned material of the CSDD cases. We are also very grateful to our Publisher Routledge for their patient, competent and attentive assistance, and especially to Heidi Lee, Editorial Assistant, and to Karen Greening for the organisation of the galleyproofs.

Georgia Zara and David P. Farrington
December 2014

ABOUT THE AUTHORS

Georgia Zara, Ph.D., is an Associate Professor of Criminological Psychology at the Department of Psychology, University of Turin, Italy, and is Head and Programme Leader of the Higher Degree in Criminological and Forensic Psychology in the same Department. She has been a Visiting Scholar of the Institute of Criminology, Cambridge University, UK since 2003. She is also a Chartered Psychologist of the British Psychological Society, a Criminologist, and has been appointed an Honorary Judge in Turin's Surveillance Court. Her major research interests are criminal careers, criminal persistence and recidivism, neurocriminology, psychopathy, and violent and sexual offending.

David P. Farrington, OBE, is Emeritus Professor of Psychological Criminology and Leverhulme Trust Emeritus Fellow in the Institute of Criminology, Cambridge University. He received the Stockholm Prize in Criminology in 2013. He is Chair of the ASC Division of Developmental and Life-Course Criminology. His major research interest is in developmental criminology, and he is Director of the Cambridge Study in Delinquent Development, a prospective longitudinal survey of over 400 London males from age 8 to age 56. In addition to over 600 published journal articles and book chapters on criminological and psychological topics, he has published nearly 100 books, monographs and government reports.

INTRODUCTION

This book aims to review and advance knowledge about criminal recidivism. An offender is a recidivist if he or she continues to offend. Generally, the most important recidivist offenders are those who are the most persistent, who commit large numbers of offences over long time periods. The most prolific of these are termed 'chronic' offenders.

The study of criminal recidivism falls within the study of criminal careers. A criminal career is defined as a longitudinal sequence of offences. It has a beginning (onset), a continuation or persistence, and an end (desistance). During their careers, offenders commit crimes at a certain rate or frequency, and they commit different types of crimes (leading to specialisation, versatility, escalation or de-escalation). Longitudinal data is essential for studying criminal careers.

Chapter 1 introduces the topic of criminal recidivism and reviews different definitions and methods of measurement, for example, focusing on reoffending, rearrest, reconviction or reincarceration during a particular follow-up period. It also reviews how recidivism varies after different types of sentences. There is a particular focus on recidivism studies in Europe and on the results obtained in these. The financial cost of recidivism is also addressed, and the topic of desistance is discussed.

This volume is largely based on international evidence from a wide range of empirical studies and especially focuses on results obtained in the Cambridge Study in Delinquent Development (CSDD). This is a prospective longitudinal study of the development of offending and antisocial behaviour of 411 inner-city males who were first contacted at age 8 in 1961–2. The main aims of this survey were to investigate to what extent the onset of antisocial behaviour and offending could be predicted in advance, how juvenile offending began, why it did or did not continue into adulthood, and why adult crime often ended when males reached their twenties. Continuity and discontinuity in offending, and the effects of life events on the development of the criminal career were also investigated. These males have now been followed up to age 48 in face-to-face interviews and up to age 56 in criminal records.

Chapter 2 reviews knowledge about criminal careers and developmental and life-course theories of offending. It pays particular attention to 'life-course-persistent' offenders. The CSDD is described and findings on official criminal careers up to age 50 are presented. There is a particular focus on knowledge gained about the probability of recidivism, persistence in offending, recidivists, and chronic offenders with ten or more convictions. Risk factors that predict recidivists compared with one-time offenders, and the predictors of chronic offenders, are also investigated.

Scientists studying the patterning of criminal recidivism have consistently recognised that a small group of offenders is responsible for the majority of crimes. In the CSDD up to age 56, 31 of the males (7.7 per cent) had 10 or more convictions, and they accounted for 485 of the 909 crimes leading to conviction (53.4 per cent). Of these males, eight had at least 15 convictions and a criminal career lasting at least 30 years. Chapter 3 presents the detailed life histories of these eight highly chronic offenders. This examination allows for a more integrative quantitative and qualitative explanation of why individuals start offending, why they continue offending, and why these chronic offenders persisted while others desisted from their criminal careers.

Chapter 4 reviews knowledge about risk assessment, especially focusing on the prediction of recidivism. It describes four generations of risk assessment instruments: unstructured clinical judgment (first), static actuarial prediction (second), risk/needs assessment and the inclusion of dynamic risk factors (third), and finally risk/needs assessment combined with structured professional judgement and case management (fourth). This chapter also includes detailed descriptions and reviews of risk assessment instruments. The risk assessment methodology, and those instruments which are used within the forensic and mental health settings to assess the risk of future reoffending and violence, are widely discussed because they constitute 'need to know information' for criminologists, psychologists and forensic psychiatrists, lawyers and judges, and practitioners who deal on a daily basis with assessing the risk and making decisions based on risk assessment reports and evaluation.

There exists a number of hazards associated with determining how to intervene effectively to reduce recidivism: the risk of underestimating the future harm to potential victims and to society (*false negatives*) and the risk of overestimating the likelihood of an offender reoffending (*false positives*). The appropriate balance between these competing social costs can only be achieved by widening our scientific knowledge and understanding those factors and processes underlying criminal recidivism. Chapter 4 discusses false negatives, false positives, and other risk assessment issues such as sensitivity, specificity, and the area under the ROC curve.

Chapter 5 focuses on psychopathy, and begins by reviewing the nature, history, and diagnostic criteria for psychopathy. It also discusses the measurement of psychopathy using the Psychopathy Checklist instruments, and the extent to which the concept of psychopathy should include antisocial behaviour or should focus only on psychopathic personality features (such as high impulsiveness, low empathy, callousness, deceitfulness and egocentricity). This chapter then specifies how psychopathy is related to offending and recidivism, and investigates the early predictors of psychopathy, especially focusing on results obtained in the CSDD. It concludes by detailing knowledge gained from neurocriminology.

Chapter 6 reviews knowledge about the recidivism of sex offenders, which is generally lower than for other types of offences. It discusses legislation introduced by the US and British governments designed to reduce recidivism, as well as risk assessment and the prediction of recidivism of sex offenders. This chapter also specifies types of sex offenders and changes in sex offending with age. There is also some discussion of the treatment of sex offenders, especially using cognitive-behavioural techniques.

Chapter 7 discusses what works in reducing recidivism, and it is, paraphrasing Bertrand Russell's (1916) quote, that researchers must look into the resolution of criminal recidivism before being able to speak of desistance and successful interventions. Generally, deterrent methods such as 'scared straight', boot camps, and severe punishment do not work, while cognitive-behavioural techniques in particular are effective. This chapter discusses the need for interventions to be based on an understanding of recidivism, and pays special attention to psychopathic and sex offenders.

The 'risk-need-responsivity' principle is important in designing interventions. The assumption that criminal behaviour can be predicted with a certain degree of accuracy is at the heart of these principles that suggest that treatment should focus on the higher risk offenders (*risk principle*), that criminogenic needs should play a predominant role in the design and delivery of treatment (*need principle*), and that treatment should be provided for offenders in general, and for violent and sexual offenders specifically (*responsivity principle*) in a manner that responds to the offender's cognitive, emotional and life style. Not all programmes are equally effective, and not all offenders respond appropriately to interventions, even when they are evidence-based. Treatment programmes should be tailored to the level of offenders' criminogenic risks, and should take into account the fact that the 'one size fits all' approach has proved to be utterly inappropriate.

Chapter 8 summarises the main conclusions of the book. Theories of recidivism need to be tested in prospective longitudinal studies. Detailed case histories can provide insightful information about human development. Recidivism, and particularly sexual recidivism, can be predicted. The most useful risk assessment instruments include risk and needs assessment, structured professional judgement and case management. Psychopathy is related to chronic offending. There are effective methods of reducing recidivism, but more randomised trials are needed. The financial costs and benefits of treatment should be measured and compared.

1
CRIMINAL RECIDIVISM

Criminal behaviour and violence have constantly been regarded as a threat to the development of a civilised society, and have been socially and legally condemned in every historical period. Social and research evidence shows that most people are law-abiding citizens; they have respect for the law and run their lives in accordance with social rules and community values. However, every country has a share of individuals who act illegally, challenging the law and disregarding other people's rights and needs. Describing them is a complex task in so far as the offending population is characterised by heterogeneity.

Not all offenders commit crime with the same frequency; most of them get involved only in a *one-off* criminal occasion and then switch back to a prosocial life for ever after. Some persist and recidivate into a pattern of systematic criminal behaviour. When reoffending, not all of them relapse with the same crime; some commit different types of crime from the ones they were convicted for.

Persistent offenders are consistently recognised within the scientific literature as a small proportion of people who commit a disproportionate amount of crime; they are responsible for the major share of the crimes committed, and often reoffend at a high frequency during their criminal careers. Continuing offenders are defined as *recidivists*. Little is known about who these offenders really are, and why they are the way they are. Nonetheless, research evidence shows that there is continuity and relative stability in offending, and within the persisting offending population, it is possible to find some homogeneity in the personal, familial, social and criminal career features, and officially these individuals are likely to report numerous criminal convictions for different offences committed (Farrington *et al.*, 2009).

The key to addressing a problem is to start with defining what the problem is and how it is seen differently from different perspectives, and being aware that one must accept the realistic fact that, as Werner Heisenberg (1962) said, 'what we observe is not nature itself, but nature exposed to our method of questioning'.

What makes a behaviour a crime? What makes an individual a persistent or a recidivist offender? If an individual breaks the law but they are never discovered, are they criminals in front of the law? How many offences does a person have to commit in order to become a persistent offender? How many offences that lead to official records does a person have to be prosecuted and/or convicted for in order to be a recidivist?

These are some of the key questions addressed here. The focus of this chapter is to explore criminal recidivism via its definitions, measures and methodological approaches. A look at is given to some preliminary conceptual definitions and distinctions between what is unofficial and official in delinquent development over time. Two main distinctions may help to set the background of this chapter, and both have been widely recognised as important dimensions of criminal careers.

Criminal persistence is the name given to the pattern of criminal and antisocial continuity, without the requirement for the offender to be officially detected, reported, apprehended, arrested, prosecuted, convicted or imprisoned. So an individual could theoretically be persistent without being a *known offender*, in the sense that their crimes may either never be detected or their responsibility for them may never be established or proven. This constitutes the *hidden* dimension of criminality. Thus, some individuals continue to commit crimes during their life and avoid being apprehended or convicted.

Recidivism is the official criminal involvement (based on criminal records) of a person who, after having been convicted for a previous offence, commits a new crime for which they incur another conviction. The new crime does not have to be of the same nature. It follows that recidivism is the name given to the pattern of new crimes being committed by known offenders. Thus, some offenders continue to offend and commit more crimes despite the experience of one or more prior convictions. In more comprehensive terms recidivism is the process involved in continuing offending, and in delaying desistance from a criminal career.

While the authors are aware of the importance of eradicating (or reducing to a minimum) any political biases and controlling for stigmatisation, and are against any form of determinism in science, available scientific findings on recidivism imply that, to a certain degree of accuracy, future behaviour can be predicted, and criminal persistence can be prevented. Everything in the end is a question of *how* rather than *whether* a systematic study of recidivism can be conducted.

Two levels of analysis are involved. The first level targets persistence and recidivism and how they are defined and measured. The obstacles that are routinely met in criminological investigations are related to ethical reservations and data confidentiality, dissimilarity in coding criminal statistics and whether the most accurate way of classifying recidivism would be by considering either:

(1) the time passed after the imposition of the sanction or release from custody: the shorter the time, the lower the risk of recidivism; or
(2) the types of data employed, e.g. official vs. self-reported offences; rearrests vs. reconvictions; court reappearances vs. reincarcerations; persistence (unofficial criminal careers) vs. recidivism (official criminal careers).

The second level of analysis involves a deeper understanding of the risk causes and risk processes related to recidivism, which might help in deciding how to allocate intervention resources where they are most needed. By exploring the risk processes involved in pursuing a criminal career, we attempt to shed some light on *what to know* so as to be scientifically and empirically furnished with evidence-based information to grasp the revolving door of reoffending, and to address *when* and *with whom to intervene*. Within this perspective, targeting recidivism aims not only to break the cycle of crime continuity (which has caused, in societies, a long legacy of suffering, loss of human potential and damage), but also to save young people and adults from a life of crime. Through this aim, more offenders can be helped to desist from a criminal career; more families can be protected from victimisation; citizens can look again at their community with a sense of trust because something that could be done to prevent criminal recidivism has started to be enacted.

The remainder of this chapter will focus on the first level of analysis: defining and measuring persistence and recidivism.

Recidivism defined

In scientific terms recidivism still depends on its etymological origins,[1] and in criminology it includes the concept of relapsing into a criminal path. Any scientific analysis of criminal recidivism cannot be addressed independently of the data set it relies upon. Criminal recidivism in its general sense refers to those activities and behaviours which, being against the law, are enacted by an already convicted offender.

However, despite many researchers having focused attention on studying recidivism and measuring it, no consensus has been reached about what recidivism is, its definition and its measures. Hence there is also a need for a more systematic, accurate, clarifying and consistently integrative theoretical approach to recidivism.

The traditional way of studying criminal recidivism, by employing criminal statistics, criminal records, self-reported data or victimisation information, has proved to be biased or, at best, partial. A precise figure for the rate of recidivism in Western society cannot be ascertained; much crime goes unreported (the *dark figure*); some offenders are never caught (the *grey figure*); the courts, for many reasons, do not always convict offenders, not least because of lack of evidence (the *bias of impunity*). What makes it even more problematic is that rates of recidivism depend on how it is defined and measured.

Recidivism is defined in different ways, using diverse criteria and starting points. Following the research literature (Maltz, 1984), common meanings of recidivism include:

(1) rearrest, which also includes reoffending despite having a prior criminal record;
(2) reincarceration, which includes return of released offenders to custody or to jail;
(3) reconviction for a new offence.

In some situations recidivism is also considered as the failure to complete educational or vocational courses or treatment programmes in or out of prison/jail custody, or during probation, and also the failure to respond to parole conditions accordingly, or the probation revocation, or unsatisfactory termination or rule violation. This variety in recidivism definitions does not allow for an always comparable analysis of data and studies.

Reoffending

Reoffending is the most commonly used term internationally employed for recidivism – where a person, who has received some form of criminal justice sanction (such as conviction or caution), commits another offence within a set time period. Greenfeld (1985) stated that approximately two-thirds of all criminal offenders are recidivists, though this estimate is likely to differ depending on how recidivism is conceptualised and measured. Even though recidivism rates differ depending on whether the focus is on behaviour during the incarceration term, or on behaviour during the post-release phase, or on successful completion of probation or parole, or failure or interruption of programmes, among the above different ways of defining recidivism the most used indicators of it are rearrest, revocation of parole or probation, reincarceration and reconviction (Champion, 1994).

Rearrest

Rearrest – where a person is arrested for a further offence – is probably the most frequently used parameter to measure recidivism rates, especially among probationers or parolees. However, rearrest is a misleading indicator, especially when it is not dependent on new offences committed, but on behaviour that shows no adherence to the rehabilitative regime endorsed. Probationers or parolees, or released inmates, may be in the wrong places at the wrong times or may be seen talking to suspicious people in the proximity of an area that constitutes a crime scene. In circumstances such as these they are likely to be arrested, but are often released later after the police have done all the necessary investigations and discovered that these individuals have alibis or can account for their time when the crime was committed. Rearrests can even occur as a result of revoking parole or probation for technical reasons (such as a curfew), or for not observing probation or parole conditions. Rearrests do not necessarily lead to reconvictions, which are instead the direct result of new crimes committed that are proven in court as having really occurred beyond a reasonable doubt. Reconviction seems, to a certain extent, a more reliable indicator of recidivism.

Reincarceration

Reincarceration is the circumstance in which a probationer or parolee, who has broken the conditions of his or her regime, returns to prison or is placed in a city or county jail for a short period. Reincarceration can be required either for a reconviction for a new criminal offence or for rearrest for a parole revocation. These diverse conditions that could lead to the same legal response arguably make reincarceration an unreliable measure of recidivism because it fails to 'distinguish between the true lawbreaker and the technical rule violator' (Champion, 1994, 90; see also Delaware Executive Department, 1984).

Variations in definitions and measures make studies on reoffending, rearrest or reconviction non-comparable unless some methodological adjustments are made. Researchers should keep under consideration alternative possible ways of thinking about recidivism, because of different aims relating to alternative assessments of criminal continuity. If rehabilitation is the goal of the probation or parole programme, then programme failure seems an appropriate measure of recidivism rates. If control and community protection are the programme goals, then success might consist in the identification and revocation of offenders who have committed new crime. If order, surveillance and security are the goals, then the police who are in charge see an arrest as a 'success', whereas criminologists may see it as a 'failure'. As Petersilia (1987, 89) suggested, 'if community safety is the primary goal, then perhaps an arrest and revocation should be seen as a success and not as a failure'. Recidivism becomes relevant when the rehabilitative values of the programmes are considered. However, the rehabilitative values are often confused with the ability to exercise crime control successfully, rather than true rehabilitation (Petersilia, 1987).

Reconviction

Reconviction – where a person is convicted in court for another offence within a specified follow-up time period – is viewed as the definitive definition of recidivism. It can also be defined as a *proven re-offence* where a person is convicted in court or receives some other form of criminal justice sanction, for an offence committed within a specified follow-up period that is disposed of within either the follow-up period or a later waiting period.[2]

When an offender, who has committed a new offence while on probation or on parole, or an individual who after release from prison commits a new crime, and when for these cases the court has established the offender's criminal liability and determined that the offender is guilty beyond a reasonable doubt, it is suitable to speak of recidivism, not least if the conclusive decision is formalised and pronounced by the court. Generally, official records are gathered from either the police or courts. These sources however underestimate the true level of reoffending because only a proportion of crime is detected and sanctioned, and not all crimes and sanctions are recorded on one central system. As Brody (1976) suggested, reconviction relies on the accurate recording of official data. In England and Wales, for instance, there were two sources of data: the Offender Index (OI), which was discontinued, and the Police National Computer (PNC). However, studies evaluating the reliability of these official data yielded differences in reconviction rates (Friendship *et al.*, 2001). It is likely that, when assessing past criminal history, and deriving risk of reconviction, the most reliable method is to use a combination of data sets in order to provide a more complete picture. Brody (1976) also emphasised that differences in law enforcement attitudes and policing in England and Wales may affect reconviction rates, causing significant rate variations that are often referred to as local factors.

Despite reconviction being described as a proxy for reoffending (Lloyd et al., 1994), official reconviction data are still a gross underestimate of reoffending (Maguire, 1997). Other methods of measuring reoffending, such as self-reports, rely on offenders being truthful about their offending behaviour and are therefore likely to be unreliable or at best biased. The combination of official and self-reported data is usually a more reliable method (Farrington, 1973, 1985; Farrington et al., 2003, 2013; Jolliffe & Farrington, 2014), not least because it allows information from different sources to be used to fill some of the gaps.

A specific look at reconvictions in England and Wales

The adult reconviction rate[3] for adults in England and Wales, from the 2008 cohort, was 40.1 per cent. The 2009 reoffending rate[4] for juveniles was 36.9 per cent, which indicates a 3.3 percentage point fall since 2000.

The *Compendium*[5] *of Reoffending Statistics for England and Wales* (Ministry of Justice, 2011) reports a consistent statistical series, between 1971 and 2006, for measuring reoffending. *Reoffending* is what unanimously and internationally refers to recidivism: it implies, as indicated above, the condition of a person who, having received some form of criminal justice sanction (such as a conviction or a caution), commits another offence. In the National Statistics publication, the rate of reoffending is the percentage of adults who are discharged from custody or start a court order under probation supervision between January and March and who are reconvicted at court within one year.

In the Ministry of Justice's *Compendium* (2011), reoffending rate refers to the reconviction rate as it only includes court convictions. The aim was to analyse the number of offenders who were reconvicted after different follow-up years. The *Compendium* (Ministry of Justice, 2011, 3–4) shows that, of the offenders (n = 42,721) who were discharged from custody or commenced a court order between January and March 2000:

- 20 per cent had been reconvicted within three months;
- 43 per cent within a year;
- 55 per cent within two years;
- 68 per cent within five years;
- 74 per cent had been reconvicted within nine years.

These findings also suggest that the reconviction frequency (number of offences) was higher the longer the follow-up period. As shown in Table 1.1, after one year the reconviction frequency for 100 offenders was 185.1, compared with a rate of

TABLE 1.1 Reconviction rate, frequency and severity rates for different follow-up periods ($n = 42,721$)

Follow-up period	Reconviction rate	Reconviction frequency	Reconviction frequency of reoffenders	Reconviction severity rate
3 months	19.9%	50.3	252.3	0.2
6 months	30.8%	98.9	320.6	0.4
9 months	37.9%	142.6	376.5	0.6
1 year	43.0%	185.1	430.2	0.8
2 years	55.2%	347.5	628.9	1.6
3 years	61.9%	498.5	805.4	2.5
4 years	65.8%	632.9	961.3	3.1
5 years	68.4%	741.7	1,083.5	3.8
6 years	70.4%	833.9	1,184.8	4.4
7 years	71.8%	912.3	1,270.4	5.0
8 years	73.0%	986.4	1,351.1	5.5
9 years	74.0%	1,057.5	1,429.8	6.0

Note: Adapted from Ministry of Justice (2011, 91).

1,057.5 after nine years. Over half of those offenders who were reconvicted within the nine-year follow-up period were convicted within the first year, but the number of offences in the first year was only about one-sixth of the number in nine years.

The *reconviction severity rate*[6] is the number of serious offences that result in a new conviction, at court within 18 months, per 100 offenders, while the reconvictions frequency rate for reoffenders indicates the number of offences that lead to a conviction per 100 reoffenders.

The severity rate shows the number of the most serious offences committed by offenders released from custody or commencing court orders during a one-year follow-up period. It is not therefore meant to be a complete count of all serious offences.

Most serious offences involve *violence against the person* (e.g. murder, attempted murder, manslaughter, infanticide, child destruction, wounding or other act endangering life, grievous bodily harm, etc.); *sexual offences* (e.g. sexual assault on a male (previously indecent assault on a male), rape, sexual assault on female (previously indecent assault on a female), sexual activity – male and female – including with a child under 13 (previously unlawful intercourse with a girl under 13), abuse of children through prostitution and pornography (previously child prostitution and pornography), trafficking for sexual exploitation), *taking and driving away and related offences*, etc.

The chart in Figure 1.1 shows that offenders continue to be reconvicted, and for a significant number of offences, after the first year, even though it is also shown that the number of reconvictions tends to decline each following year.

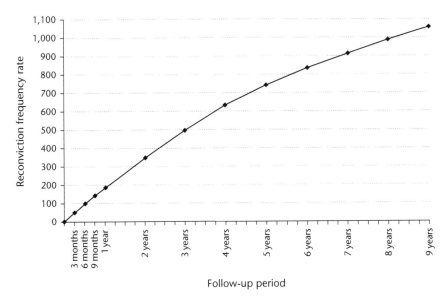

FIGURE 1.1 Reconviction frequency rate for different follow-up periods

Note: Adapted from Ministry of Justice (2011, 92).

Even in the ninth year 4 per cent of offenders who were not reconvicted up to this point were reconvicted thereafter. It may be plausible to speculate that a number of offenders who have not been reconvicted within the nine-year window still may be reconvicted after this period. Moreover, the most severe offences were committed in the second and third years of the follow-up period (Ministry of Justice, 2011), which may suggest that serious offences may require more time than non-severe offences not only to be committed but also to be processed by the criminal justice system, and then convicted.

The report suggests that, despite the fact that those offenders who were reconvicted in the first year committed the majority of convicted offences in future years, this was not the case for the serious offences. The majority of severe re-offences were not committed by those who had already committed a severe offence in the first year. These findings are as insightful as they are counterintuitive: the severity of the offence is not directly associated with an increased risk of recidivism. Scientific evidence, supporting these findings, goes back a long way. For instance, Soothill and Gibbens (1978) followed up offenders involved in rape, incest and unlawful sexual intercourse with girls under 13, who were charged with at least one of these offences and who appeared in higher courts in England and Wales in either 1951 or 1961. The follow-up period for possible reconviction was the end of March 1974. Differential periods of risk (i.e. period after conviction or release from custody) were taken into account, with the shortest being one year and the longest one 23 years. The important finding that emerged is that a sizeable proportion of these offenders were reconvicted a long time after the usual follow-up period of three to five years. Moreover, it was suggested that the reconvictions that occurred after this considerable time period were serious, including sexual or violent offences.

These findings also support those reached by a previous study on the recidivism rates of a 22-year-cohort of rapists (Soothill et al., 1976), and sustain the view that the probability of recidivism for sexual offending seems to remain high after five years from release (Christiansen et al., 1965). However, what was surprising was that, for those offenders with three or more convictions, the likelihood of recidivism did not increase with time. These offenders were in fact not reconvicted for these type of offences after five years. The most serious offenders in Soothill et al.'s study (1976), even after a 10-year follow-up period, were those with a maximum of two previous convictions, which normal follow-ups would miss because of their intermittent criminal careers.

These findings do not contrast with more recent studies on sex offending recidivism, in so far as they had anticipated that there is 'something special about recidivism rates of these sexual offenders' (Soothill & Gibbens, 1978, 275). If reconvicted, many sex offenders are likely to reappear before the court after considerable time spent at liberty, but those who reappear are not the most prolific offenders. As will be investigated later in this volume (see Chapter 6), contrary to the stereotype that sex offenders are persistent criminals, the majority of them are not organised and efficient career criminals. On the other hand, clinical analyses suggest that 'the unduly aggressive individual or the sexually maladjusted have a long-lasting "Achilles heel" normally held in check by compensatory satisfactions of pressures but liable to re-emerge in times of stress' (Soothill et al., 1976, 66–7).

An analysis published by the Ministry of Justice (2013) updated the findings presented in the 2011 *Compendium*, and employed a matching methodology to allow for multiple comparisons of the impact of a range of adult sentences on reoffending. The assessment of the impact of a sentence on reoffending requires looking at the reoffending rate for that sentence in integration by creating matched offender groups for each sentencing comparison, based on the information about the offenders. The statistical method is named 'propensity score matching' (PSM[7]) which is a quasi-experimental approach that, despite not being as robust as a Randomised Controlled Trial (RCT), allows for controlling of differences in the offender's characteristics between two sentencing groups. The aim is to make the two groups as similar as possible so that the only systematic difference between the groups is that one received one type of sentence and the other another type of sentence. By minimising the other differences between groups, sentences become more comparable. The 2013 *Compendium* included the following comparisons:

- *Court orders* (e.g. community orders and suspended sentence orders) compared with immediate custody (less than 12 months);
- *Immediate custody* (1 to 4 years) compared with immediate custody (less than 12 months);
- *Immediate custody* (less than or equal to 6 months) compared with immediate custody (more than 6 to less than 12 months).

The key findings suggest that offenders sentenced to less than 12 months in custody had a higher one-year reoffending rate and committed more re-offences per offender than similar, matched offenders receiving: a *community order* (e.g. of 6.4 percentage points for 2010); a *suspended sentence order* (e.g. of 8.6 percentage points for 2010); a *court order* (either a community order or a suspended order) (e.g. of 6.8 percentage points for 2010).

Those offenders who were sentenced to less than 12 months in custody also reported a higher reoffending rate and committed more re-offences per offender than offenders given an immediate custodial sentence of between 1 and 4 years, with a difference of 12 percentage points for 2010. This difference may be partially explained by the fact that offenders, who are released from custodial sentences of less than 12 months, are not currently subject to supervision by the Probation Service upon release. Government proposals in the Offender Rehabilitation Bill were to extend supervision to all offenders released from custody. This has now become law in the Offender Rehabilitation Act 2014.

A further analysis on the reoffending rate at the end of the sentence shows that, for *court orders*, the end-of-sentence reoffending rate in 2010 was 22.4 per cent, which was lower than the proven reoffending rate of 34.1 per cent. The end of the sentence measure includes all offenders whose orders terminate for a positive reason. In the proven reoffending rate, reoffending is measured from the start of a court order or from the point of release from custody, and also includes those offenders whose court order terminated for a negative reason. Thus, it is not surprising to witness this difference.

For *short prison sentences* of less than 12 months, the end-of-sentence reoffending rate in 2010 was 51.3 per cent, which is lower than the proven reoffending rate of 57.6 per cent. Similarly as for court orders, this difference can be explained with the fact that the proven reoffending measure includes all offenders released from a prison sentence of less than 12 months, whereas the end-of-sentence measure only includes the subset of offenders who had not returned to custody prior to the end of the sentence. Consequently, it is expected to find this difference between the end-of-sentence reoffending and the proven reoffending rates for those receiving short custodial sentences.

Criminal recidivism in Europe

Recidivism in European countries is likely to reflect different legal systems and criminal laws adopted in each country, making interpretation of reoffending and conviction data and comparison between countries complex, and not always possible. No systematic review is yet available of recidivism rates in Europe. As Wartna and Nijssen (2006a) suggested, over recent decades the computerisation of police and judiciary data has opened up opportunities for large-scale recidivism research. Within the scope of this type of research, the WODC – the research bureau of the Ministry of Justice in the Netherlands – made an inventory of the studies that were carried out in Europe. It appears that at least 14 countries, as shown in Figure 1.2, have recently carried out a recidivism study on a national scale. Steps are being taken to bring these countries together and to explore the possibility of making international comparisons of reconviction rates.

A questionnaire on recidivism research was sent out to 41 European countries. The topics touched upon in the questions were related to the prevalence of nation-wide recidivism research, the types of data that were collected and the research design and methods used in the studies. Thirty-three countries participated in the survey and sent in their replies. However, 19 EU states, including Belgium, Italy, Portugal and Spain, reported that national research on recidivism of any kind was lacking in their countries, and the reasons varied from lack of research funds to lack of experience in doing this type of research. For instance, no systematic study has been ever carried out to assess the level of reconviction rates in Italy.

Figure 1.2 shows the European countries in which there are national statistics in one form or another, and it appears that 14 countries have carried out a study on a

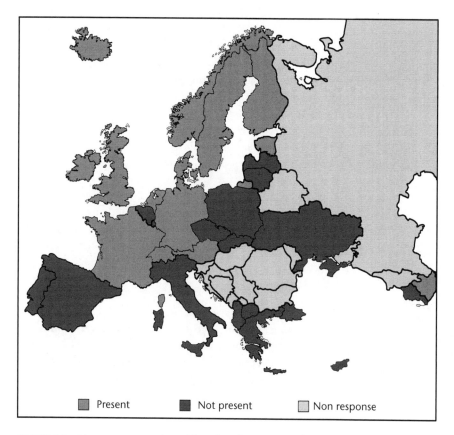

FIGURE 1.2 European countries with and without national recidivism studies

Note: Adapted from Wartna and Nijssen (2006a, 1).

national scale. The representatives of those countries have tried to formulate an international standard for recidivism research and for making cross-national comparisons (Wartna & Nijssen, 2006a). Gathering EU data and information would allow international comparisons to be made, and enable researchers to figure out the differences between the work done in each country.

The 14[8] EU countries involved in this study addressed national research on recidivism: 11 used records on court appearances, and 'reconviction' was the basis for identifying recidivism. None of these national studies was based on self-reported data. It is interesting to mention that in a considerable number of countries automated databases have started to be used in recidivism research. In some European countries the data gathered have already been used to make some statistical predictions. England and Wales are leading in this area, as they are also particularly interested in developing risk assessment procedures to predict the likelihood of recidivism. They are also advanced in promoting an integrative system that takes into account information on criminogenic needs. Their first risk assessment tool on population data was in 1998. Similar work is done in the Netherlands. In Finland and Northern Ireland these types of data are starting to be used in order to generate predictive statistics, while in Denmark, Ireland, Scotland and Sweden this is an option taken into consideration. The assumption that reconviction data should be analysed in association with socio-demographic data on the offenders, such as employment, education, health, and so on, has already been tested in Denmark, Finland, Iceland, Norway and Sweden. In the *Compendium of Reoffending Statistics and Analysis* (Ministry of Justice, 2010c), it is shown that surveying prisoner crime reduction in England and Wales allowed for a comprehensive examination of the offenders' needs. It was evident that the reconviction rates were considerably higher for those offenders who had experienced emotional, psychological, sexual and physical violence as children, who were expelled from school and/or left school without any qualification, who reported being unemployed until the year before imprisonment, who had abused drugs and alcohol prior to custody, and who suffered from mental problems and reported being treated for them. While raw data of reoffending rates and criminogenic needs between EU countries should not be used for a direct international comparison of risk processes of recidivism, it is essential to create scientific shared areas of intervention within Europe.

Table 1.2 shows the reconviction rates of prisoners released in several European countries and the USA. Despite the shared definition of recidivism in each EU country being 'having a new conviction', this does not solve the problem of non-comparability. Does reconviction mean the same thing in all the countries considered? Wartna and Nijssen (2006b) think that unlikely, as their juridical universes are doubtless not identical. The figures reported in Table 1.2 indicate that there are slight differences in age ranges of the prisoners from the six countries.

Age is recognised as a robust predictor of recidivism. Hence the age range in the convicted offenders examined in the study by Wartna and Nijssen (2006b) may have affected the reconviction rates of the different countries involved (see Table 1.2). That is, if a country is, for instance, more restrictive in the imposition

TABLE 1.2 Percentage of prisoners reconvicted at x years after release

Country	Release period	N	Age range	Imprisonment rate*	1	2	3	4 (X)	5	6	7	8
Netherlands	1996–9	69,602	18 and up	85	43.4	55.5	62.0	66.0	67.0	71.1	72.9	74.1
Scotland	1999	5,738	16 and up	120	46.0	60.0	67.0	71.0				
England & Wales	2001	14,569	18 and up	127		58.2						
France	1996–7	2,859	13 and up	89					51.9			
N. Ireland	2001	703	17 and up	52		45.0						
Iceland	1994–8	1,176	18 and up	44			37.0		53.0			
Switzerland	1988	6,393	18 and up	79	12.0	26.0	34.0	40.0	45.0	48.2		
USA (15 states)	1994	33,796	18 and up	600	21.5	36.4	46.9					

Note: Adapted from Wartna and Nijssen (2006b, 14).
*Approximate figures per 100,000 population from the International Centre for Prison Studies, World Prison Brief.

of an unsuspended prison sentence, it is likely that 'only high-risk offenders will be sent to prison and it would be natural for that particular country to have higher reconviction rates' (Wartna & Nijssen, 2006b, 12).

Considering the 'imprisonment rate', i.e. the number of prisoners per 100,000 of the national population, the United States is far less selective in sending people to prison than is Europe. This might explain why reconviction rates for the USA are lower than for the UK and Holland. It does not explain though the outcome for Switzerland, France, Northern Ireland and Iceland. The provisional self-evident conclusion that can be drawn from these data is that for these countries both the imprisonment rates and the reconviction rates are notably low. However, no study is available to offer any explanations about why this is so.

Furthermore, no comparative empirical analyses are available on reconviction rates amongst European states. The only source of information is the Ministry of Justice's report (2011) which offers a synthetic overview of the situation of England and Wales in comparison with Scotland, and then with the Netherlands. While in England and Wales recidivism[9] is defined as an offence committed in the follow-up period (either one or two years), which is proved by a court conviction within the follow-up period, in Scotland the definition of recidivism is a further court conviction during the follow-up period (two years). In the Netherlands, recidivism is defined as an offence committed in the follow-up period (two years) which is registered with the public prosecutor, whether or not it has been ratified (disposed). Even though the data are not fully comparable between these different countries, the analysis helps to identify the possible main differences in offender characteristics once the data sets are reconciled, and it may suggest ways in which countries could move towards more comparable statistics on reoffending.

Table 1.3 shows that offenders in Scotland were on average much older and were more likely to be first-time offenders. Offenders in England and Wales had a more extensive criminal history, indicated by a higher average number of offenders with previous contacts in comparison with their Dutch counterparts.[10] In Scotland the percentage of male offenders was particularly high, while the proportion of offenders younger than age 22 was smaller in comparison with the counterparts. This may explain the smaller number of offenders with more than

TABLE 1.3 Main differences in offender characteristics in the three datasets

	England & Wales	*Scotland*	*Netherlands*
% of offenders who are male	85.4	88.4	86.9
% of offenders aged under 22	36.3	17.2	35.4
Average offender age	29.7	33.8	29.9
% of first-time offenders	12.4	19.7	n.a.
% with more than 5 previous contacts	65.0	49.3	56.4
Average no. of previous contacts	22.8	14.4	10.2

Note: Adapted from Ministry of Justice (2011, 108).

five previous police or court contacts: the younger the offender the shorter the criminal career.

Despite the need for a more systematic analysis of recidivism in Europe, states have only just started working in this direction. Diversities in the juridical systems, and in the administration of sentences, may be responsible for much of the delay in setting in motion a specialised intra-European taskforce to strengthen international approaches to reducing recidivism.

It is not unusual for criminologists to recognise the importance of exchanging knowledge among experts in this field; it is also not so unusual to believe that this process should speed up the realisation of planned projects and help scientists across the world to set up their own national recidivism research (Tavares & Thomas, 2009). Nevertheless, it may still be difficult to translate these intentions into an active taskforce that would involve the whole of Europe, not least before the variations in the criminal justice systems across countries have been reduced. Some progress could be made only if the EU states started to compare data, research, projects, with the aim of harmonising definitions of recidivism and reoffending rates. Europe cannot continue to leave this area of research untouched by not having a joint international framework for intervention and prevention. The cost of crime is unsustainable. The last part of this chapter looks closely at this aspect.

The cost of criminal recidivism

> Not everything that counts can be counted, and not everything that can be counted counts
>
> *(Albert Einstein, in Calaprice, 2011, 482)*

Crime, particularly when persistent, has devastating effects on the victims, the communities, the offenders and their families too, which go, in fact, beyond what can be actually measured. While the individual and familial influences on offending are becoming clearer as scientific research offers more and more insightful explanations of the criminogenic process involved in criminal careers, the burden that crime imposes on the life of individuals and communities is even greater than 30 years ago.

Whilst the general level of crime seems to have declined over the past 20 years, the research finding that deserves special attention is that not only do more people seem to enter the antisocial and criminal threshold earlier (as early as age 10) (Farrington, 2007a; Loeber & Farrington, 2001), but also more individuals are likely to progress into a criminal career, and desist from it only after a long and escalating criminal pattern (as long as 25–30 years in crime) (Farrington & Welsh, 2007; Rutter *et al.*, 1998; Zara, 2005, 2006).

Research findings across Western countries show that young people, aged between 10 and 17 years old, are more likely to offend than adults, with the consequence that they account for a disproportionate amount of crime (Cooper & Roe, 2012).

An understanding of the extent, nature and continuity of youth crime into adulthood is still incomplete. An estimate of the magnitude of youth crime by Budd and colleagues (2005), based on a national self-reported offending survey in 2003, indicated that 35 per cent of offences were committed by young people aged 10 to 17. A drawback of this estimate was the inclusion of low-level offences that in other analyses are not regarded as a crime.

Cooper and Roe (2012) carried out a study to explore patterns of offending in young people and to estimate how much crime could be attributable to them. Their analysis used data on proven offending from the Police National Computer (PNC), which contains information on age of proven offenders in police recorded criminal statistics. Between 2009 and 2010 the analysis estimated that young people, between age 10 and 17, were responsible for over a million of police recorded crimes: about one in four incidents were attributable to young people. This estimate cannot go unnoticed given that young people (aged 10–17) account for approximately one in ten of the population above the age of criminal responsibility, which is 10 in England and Wales. Young people were found to be responsible for 23 per cent of police recorded crime in 2009/10, with young women responsible for 5 or less per cent for each offence type, except shoplifting for which their involvement in the offence was higher than for young men (11 per cent compared to 9 per cent). *Acquisitive offences* accounted for a higher proportion of crime committed by young people, in comparison with adults (58 per cent compared with 51 per cent), who were more likely to be involved in violence (22 per cent compared with 15 per cent). *Acquisitive offence or crime* refers to offences where the offender derives material gain from the crime (e.g. robbery, burglary, offences against vehicles, other theft, including shoplifting, fraud, and forgery). However, Cooper and Roe (2012) indicated that this analysis may under-represent police-recorded crime by young people because youth, whenever possible, are diverted from the criminal justice system and are less likely to be formally sanctioned.

Criminal career research clearly demonstrates that the earlier the antisocial onset, the higher the risk of a long and serious criminal involvement (Piquero *et al.*, 2007). Recidivism is very costly because it involves not only the cost of previous interventions but also the price of failure. A great proportion of new crime each year is committed by people who have been through the criminal justice system before. The burden of crime should not just be estimated by focusing on the amount of crime committed each year in a country, but also by looking at how many of the new offences are committed by previous offenders who continue into their life of crime. More than ever, governments in Western society, especially in Europe (cf. the latest governmental programmes in France, Italy or the UK to address the matter of reoffending), are concerned with the implementation of bills and programmes in order to reduce and to prevent persistent offending, so as to guarantee a safer society and to regain the community's trust in justice.

In 2000 the Home Office issued a report (Brand & Price, 2000) about the economic and social costs of crime. A wide range of sources were used, which provided information from the insurance industries, the criminal justice system and survey data and contributed to estimates of the different economic and social impacts of each type of offence. This report estimated that the total cost of all crime in the United Kingdom was, in 1999–2000, about £60 billion (Brand & Price, 2000). Eight years later another report put the total cost of UK crime at more than £72 billion (Mulheirn et al., 2010). However, as Mulheirn and colleagues (2010) say, this figure is far from being comprehensive because it does not include costs such as fear of crime, quality-of-life impacts, drug crime, low-level disorder, undiscovered fraud, lost productivity or the opportunity costs of crime.

Looking at recorded crime in England, Wales and Northern Ireland, a report (Sinclair & Taylor, 2008) suggests that in 2007 the cost was around £15 billion, equivalent to approximately £275 for every person. Violent crimes against the person, including murder and serious assault, had the highest economic and social costs, being nearly £155 per person; this estimate is significantly lower than the Home Office one because this report focused only on recorded crime.

Apart from the cost of crime, further spending has to be put into the process of convicting offenders and keeping them in prison. HM Prison Service indicated that the costs per prisoner per year for different groups of prisons in 2000/01 were:

- male Young Offender Institution (15–17 year olds) – £47,500;
- high security prison – £41,500;
- female local prison – £30,700;
- male local prison – £23,700;
- male category C (training) prison – £18,200;
- male open prison – £17,500.

The cost per offender per year within a Secure Training Centre (15–17-year-old males) was put at £130,000 per year.

Most prison places are filled up by individuals on long-term sentences, because short-term prisoners tend to be released after only a few months of their sentence. The vast majority of sentences themselves are below 6 months. In 2006, just 14 per cent of short sentences were 6–12 months in length, with 86 per cent lasting up to 6 months (House of Commons Justice Committee, 2008, 32). Prisoners on short-term sentences account for only 11 per cent of the total prison population at any one time (Ministry of Justice, 2007), or about 9,000 offenders in prison, costing around £400 million per year to incarcerate.

What is particularly interesting in terms of recidivism is that short-term prisoners have disproportionately high reconviction rates, apart from contributing to a significant proportion of the criminal justice system costs associated with custodial sentences. The standard two-year reconviction rate for this group is between 70 and 75 per cent (Cunliffe & Shepherd, 2007), and 60 per cent go on to reoffend within just 12 months of release (Mulheirn et al., 2010).

Even though these figures do not specifically state the cost of criminal recidivism, and many of the costs of reoffending by ex-prisoners are not quantifiable, we can infer that the cost of recidivism is very high, as a consequence of the replication of costs imposed by the commission of crime in the first place. Reoffending is a key contributor to the high cost of crime, driving the record levels of investment in police, prison and probation services across England and Wales in recent years (Mulheirn et al., 2010). After a fall in reconviction rates in the 1980s, rates rose throughout the 1990s: in 1993, 53 per cent of prisoners were reconvicted within two years; by 2004, 65 per cent of those leaving prison were reconvicted within two years (Dugan, 2008). While reconviction rates have drifted slightly downwards over the past few years, they remain obstinately high: the two-year reoffending rate for 2006 was around 60 per cent (Mulheirn et al., 2010, 18).

The report on reducing reoffending by ex-prisoners, by the Social Exclusion Unit (2002, 5), indicated that, of those individuals reconvicted within two years following release, each will actually have received on average three further convictions. The report referred to conviction as a guilty judgment, within the criminal justice system, for an offence committed by the defendant. Home Office researchers estimate that each offence leading to reconviction costs the criminal justice system on average £13,000. It is also estimated that five recorded offences are committed for each reconviction, meaning that, during their time at liberty, a reoffending ex-prisoner is likely to be responsible for crime costing the criminal justice system an average of £65,000. This estimate is only partial in so far as those offences leading to conviction involve the criminal justice system costs, while offences that do not lead to conviction do not. The Social Exclusion Unit (2002) stated that '[p]rolific offenders will cost even more. [. . .] The average cost of a prison sentence imposed at a Crown Court is roughly £30,500, made up of court and other legal costs. The costs of actually keeping prisoners within prison vary significantly, but average £37,500 per year' (p. 7). At a conservative estimate, released prisoners are responsible for at least 1 million crimes per year (18 per cent of recorded, notifiable crimes). This estimate does not take into account the amount of unrecorded crime that ex-prisoners, reconvicted or otherwise, will have committed.

The Social Exclusion Unit (2002) reports that offending by ex-prisoners costs the British criminal justice system at least £11 billion a year, 'around 14 billion in today's prices' (Mulheirn et al., 2010, 18).

The cost of crime does not simply equal the calculation of the damage that follows from a committed offence, but is the ongoing process that starts before the criminal onset takes place, and continues after the commission of an offence; it includes the offenders and their families; the victims and their families; the community in general and the citizens' sense of security in particular (Dubourg et al., 2005). This is directly proportional to how many times crimes are repeated by the same offenders. The general perception is that the sense of security in many European countries has been hampered by bleak pieces of news indicating that more inmates or ex-convicted individuals are reoffenders; that there is a rise in the under-18 reoffending rate; that young offenders are more likely to reoffend than older offenders. Both official statistics and research findings seem to confirm these trends, and the reoffending statistics call out for attention and a plan of investigation.

According to a recent research report on the burden of crime in the EU (a comparative analysis of the European Crime and Safety Survey, EUICS, 2005, 22) and of the ICVS (International Crime Victim Survey) data, the level of common crime in Europe reached its limit around 1995 and has shown a steady decline over the past ten years. Along with a trend of crime in Europe falling back to the levels of 1990, common crimes have recently also shown declining trends in the USA, Canada, Australia and other industrialised countries (cf. Van Kesteren et al., 2000). The decline seems to be dependent on changing demographics and increases in public and private security measures, rather than being the result of effective intervention policies targeted at reducing recidivism. Within the 15 EU countries at the time of the EU ICS report (2005),[11] the proportion of the population aged 15 to 24 years decreased from 14.1 per cent in 1993 to 12.2 per cent in 2004.

A proportion of the crime drop could, in fact, be explained, according to Farrell (2013), by the *security hypothesis*: changes in the level and quality of security could be seen as a discouraging force for debutant offenders, whose criminal activities might vanish as soon as their first failure in forcing an alarmed window or a door lock took place. For instance, the proportion of cars in England and Wales *without* immobilisers fell from 77 per cent to 22 per cent between 1991 and 2006, and those without central locking from 60 per cent to 12 per cent: this may account for the majority of the decline of car and other vehicle theft (Farrell et al., 2008). Certainly change in life style and in routine activities may have contributed to a shift towards other forms of offending, especially with the rise of the internet, which has coincided with the decline in street crimes and direct assaults of victims. It may be that the opportunities offered by the internet have encouraged online offending that is less routinely identified, more difficult to record, and also perceived as less risky and less criminal, contributing to a sense of diminished responsibility for what is done to victims through a 'pc screen' (Farrell et al., 2008, 2011). Because not all Member States use the standard definition, it is difficult to analyse violent crime accurately (e.g. violence against the person such as physical assault, robbery and sexual offences, including rape and sexual assault). However, the general trend at the EU level registers a decline of about 6 per cent in the number of these offences recorded between 2007 and 2010, but a rise in the level of domestic burglary (Clarke, 2013).

Researchers are puzzled by these trends, whose explanations may include the waxing gap between actual and recorded crime, the intensification of *e*-crime, the resistance by victims in reporting to the authority the offence endured.

Critical remarks on persisting offending

Offenders who persist in their criminal careers put society at a great risk because they represent the faults occurring either in the criminal system or in the intervention programmes, or both. Preventing persistent crime can be effective and successful only if programmes are based on scientific evidence and substantive findings that in turn will aid policy-makers in allocating crime-fighting resources necessary for primary and secondary prevention. Despite the enormous increase in the awareness of the human, psychological, economic, and social costs imposed by repeated and continuous criminal and violent behaviour on victims, very little research attention is given to recidivism from an integrated and multidisciplinary perspective that goes beyond the count of criminal statistics, and looks at early predictors of late criminal behaviour.

As Friendship and colleagues (2002, 442) described, reconviction has traditionally been evaluated as a dichotomous event (*all or nothing*). The same could be advanced about recidivism: the ultimate manifestation of criminal continuity is having committed a new offence and having been convicted; otherwise there is no recidivism. An 'either or' method to assess recidivism is limited, at least for two reasons. The first involves a dismissal of the concept of individual differences and of the human dimension underlying behaviour. The second does not take into consideration the degree of continuity, the variations in reoffending during the life-course, the frequency or the severity of subsequent reoffending. Moreover, a dichotomous variable (reconvicted/not reconvicted) is typically assessed within a specific fixed period. In England and Wales the conventional period for reconviction studies is two years, even though it has been established that, depending on the offender groups, longer follow-up periods are likely to be more reliable. For instance, for sex offenders the longer the follow-up the higher the base rate of sexual reconviction, especially for those sex offenders discharged from prison who have not been involved in a specific treatment (Friendship & Thornton, 2001). Apparently sex offenders have a longer life span of committing sex offences than general reoffenders. The assumption that the risk of reoffending for released sex offenders persists for many years is supported by Cann et al. (2004). Hence, longitudinal analyses can be the gold standard in criminological research, and can allow for a direct observation of change and continuity in delinquent development.

Another aspect that challenges a dichotomous view of recidivism is the nature of reoffending. For these reasons we address the following questions.

When assessing recidivism rates, should a commission of a new offence, but of a different nature, be included in the computation of re-offences and then of reconvictions? Or should one just consider re-offences of the same nature?

Even though crime is a feature of society, and economists believe that society will never rid itself of crime, research findings show that something could be done to interrupt the continuity of the criminal legacy, only if we understand how to intervene, how early and with whom. Governments, especially including those in Europe and North America, are promising direct measures to tackle crime and contain its consequences. A great proportion of new crime each year is committed by people who have been through the criminal justice system before. Despite these alarming findings, the first and most obvious conclusion, looking at evaluations in the field of criminology or criminal justice, concerns the dearth of systematic studies on criminal recidivism. Following the *integrated cognitive antisocial potential theory* introduced by Farrington (2005b), it is suggested that the commission of crimes depends partly on the individual, partly on the situation, and especially on the interaction between the individual and the situation. To the extent that crime is multi-determined, and that the causes of persistent crime differ from those of one-time offending, the only methodological technique which allows for the exploration of criminal continuity is the longitudinal approach. There exists the controversial view that if individuals perceive great risks from the imposition of law restrictions and sanctions, they will be unlikely to engage in future criminal behaviour. The *paradox of incapacitation* – the fact that the probability of persistence in offending increases steadily after each conviction – challenges three views:

(1) offenders desist and 'grow out of crime' by default, because the process of natural ageing of the organism leaves the individual less energetic to be involved in risk-taking activities;
(2) deterrence will imbue in offenders the rational calculation that the cost of punishment is enormous and not worth the risk;
(3) retribution, detention or incapacitation will prevent criminal continuation, and hence recidivism.

The widely shared common view that penalty increases and harsher sentences have deterrent effects is juxtaposed with the available research findings that suggest that there is little credible evidence that changes in sanctions affect crime rates. The process of crime and punishment is indeed more complex and unpredictable. As Michael Tonry stated,

> deterrence research is incapable of taking into account whether and to what extent purported policy changes are implemented, whether and to what extent their adoption or implementation is perceived by would-be offenders, and whether and to what extent offenders are susceptible to influence by perceived changes in legal threats. At the very least, macro-level research on deterrent effects should test the null hypothesis of no effect rather than the price theory assumption that offenders' behavior will change in response to changes in legal threats.
>
> *(Tonry, 2008, 280)*

Waiting for a *criminal burnout effect*, or increasing the severity of punishment, and incapacitating offenders or locking them away in prison, does not reduce criminal recidivism or provide deterrent benefits, nor are general intervention programmes simply based, for instance, on enhancing the offender's self-esteem and self-confidence. If criminal statistics allow for determining the base-rate of reoffending in different European countries and in Europe as a whole, only longitudinal data allow for observing the acceleration/deceleration pattern of offending, the variation in frequency (i.e. incidence rates), the aggravation in offence types, the risk mechanisms involved and the potential for criminal continuation or desistance from crime. These are but the first steps to start moving towards an integrated investigation that will allow for a more comprehensive understanding of what can be done to predict and prevent criminal recidivism, and foster desistance.

While research on desistance is relevant to recidivism, we do not have space in this book to review desistance research in detail. Nevertheless, we will mention some key studies and summarise some key findings here. Kazemian and Farrington (2010) have published a detailed review of knowledge about desistance.

Desistance is a fundamental feature of criminal careers, but it is not necessarily the opposite of recidivism. Recidivism is usually measured within a particular follow-up period (often two years), whereas desistance refers to the cessation or termination of offending. A person who does not commit any offences during a short follow-up period may nevertheless offend later (Soothill & Gibbens, 1978; see also Soothill et al., 2008, 2009). Of all those who offend at a particular age, some will be desisters, some will be recidivists in the short term and some will be delayed recidivists. Also, our interest is especially in the most frequent and persistent offenders, not merely in all those who recidivate. Of all those who recidivate, some will be infrequent offenders and others will be frequent offenders; some will have short criminal careers and others will have long criminal careers. The predictors and correlates of persistent or frequent offending are not necessarily the opposite of the predictors and correlates of desistance.

According to Gottfredson and Hirschi (1990, 141) reductions in offending over time are 'due to the inexorable aging of the organism'. However, Loeber and LeBlanc (1990) argued that desistance does not occur 'merely as a function of individual's chronological age' (p. 452).

The debate about the assumption that offenders simply grow out of crime naturally, as they age, is not supported by MacLeod et al. (2012). Their findings suggest that the most important factor in desistance is neither ageing nor sentence type, but getting convicted. It seems that conviction is the trigger for desistance, in so far as, if offenders were convicted for more of their offences (if the probability of conviction after an offence was increased), crime would be reduced (MacLeod et al., 2012). According to their estimates, 'reducing the recidivism probability for the high risk offenders by 10 per cent, from 0.84 to 0.76, would result in a 34 per cent reduction in their future offending and, on reaching the steady state, a 14 per cent reduction in overall crime' (MacLeod et al., 2012, 182). These calculations are made by assuming that all high-risk offenders participate in treatment programmes, so that a 10 per cent recidivism reduction can be foreseen and maintained. It is however possible that in real life the results would be different, not least because it is very unlikely that all high-risk and high-need offenders would participate in treatment programmes.

While some researchers recognise the impact of 'natural' desistance according to the age-crime curve, MacLeod and colleagues (2012) speak of desistance in terms of a *termination process* and introduce a desistance probability. Their approach explains that the aggregate decline in criminal offending with age does not require any change in the individual offending frequency, because the decline is caused by the declining participation in offending, rather than by a deceleration in offending amongst the known population of offenders.

The original motive for stopping offending may be the motivation to change oneself, or the birth of a child, or the experience of a marriage, or a new stable job. What makes the offending interruption last to the point of true desistance is a renovated strength to adhere to a prosocial ethos and to have a psychological and social scaffolding that sustains and reinforces this decision, so that any other alternative (e.g. a relapse into offending) becomes not only unbearable but practically impossible. This is why researchers should concentrate not only on what constitutes the trigger towards stopping a life of crime, but on the process that has to unfold for true desistance to take place. A trigger could be a new conviction, with the offender facing future months away from home, in detention, and witnessing the disruption of their lives, rather than the offender making a reasoned choice to stop. What is important is what the offender makes of that trigger, and how it operates to modify social adjustment.

In respect of intervention, it is important to explore when (if ever) an *ex-offender* becomes indistinguishable from a non-offender in the probability of future offending (Kurlychek *et al.*, 2006, 2007; Farrington, 2007a). There is no point in incapacitating those offenders who are going to desist anyway, and waste scarce prison space by locking them up.

Research findings (Farrington, 2007a) show that the probability of future reoffending is likely to depend on criminal career features such as the previous frequency of offending, the seriousness of the previous offence, and the time since the last offence (see Chapter 6). These aspects are extremely relevant in terms of offenders' rehabilitation and integration, and community re-entry. Risk assessment practice should serve the aim of exploring the extent to which ex-offenders have become indistinguishable from non-offenders, so that ex-offenders should not be discriminated against (e.g. in employment). Risk assessment, as will be explained in Chapter 4, should then be developed on the basis of knowledge about criminal career development, which implies an understanding of the predictors of termination, deceleration and residual career length.

This latter aspect is in fact the *crucial knot* that makes desistance a very complicated process to unfold. It was Farrington (1997) who emphasised that only the death of the offender guarantees that the criminal career has finally reached its ultimate and conclusive stage (*true desistance*).

As recidivist offenders are defined as those who have at least two convictions (see Chapter 2), the focus then moves to which length of period of non-offending should be acceptable to define offenders as desisters, and hence similar to non-offenders in their probability of offending. The answer to this debate would involve an understanding of the extent to which redemption times are likely to occur in criminal career offenders. Blumstein and Nakamura (2009) define *redemption times* as when the hazard of a new crime of an ex-offender falls close to the hazard of the first crime of those individuals who do not have any prior conviction.

Desistance is often used both as an empirical variable and as an underlying theoretical construct (Farrington, 2007). As an empirical variable, desistance refers to the observed termination of offending. As a theoretical construct, desistance often refers to decreases in the underlying frequency, variety or seriousness of offending. In Farrington's terms (2007c), desistance could involve a discontinuous transition from the state of *being an offender* to the state of *being a non-offender*. *Discontinuous change* is comparable to the concept of *knifing off* (Maruna & Roy, 2007). *Continuous change* suggests that desistance involves a constant decrease in the underlying antisocial potential or antisocial propensity that leads to a measured decrease in the frequency, variety or seriousness of offending. How discontinuous should the change be in order to speak of criminal interruption (or *intermittency*)? And how continuous should the change in the underlying process be in order to speak of *true desistance*?

Mathematical models suggest that the probability of termination increases with the time interval since the last offence (Barnett *et al.*, 1989). However, while it could be possible to assume that a high-rate offender had stopped committing crimes when a long period of time has passed without reoffending, it becomes more difficult to distinguish termination from the time period between offences for low-rate offenders. Farrington (2007a) suggests that, in order to measure accurately which type of discontinuity in offending it is, what should be calculated is a decrease in the frequency, variety or seriousness of offending.

Certainly, in the study of desistance both self-reported and official measures are essential, as well as agreement between the two measures. For example, Nagin *et al.* (1995) identified 'adolescence-limited' offenders as those who had no convictions after age 21. However, these males continued to commit offences according to their self-reports and continued to use drugs, drink heavily and get into fights.

Desistance, as in any process that is assessed by the quality of change in the individual's life, can be assisted by social institutions and protective factors. Change is meaningful in so far as *cognitive shifts* foster a cognitive and emotional transformation within the person, and in the way of functioning in the social world.

Lösel (2011, 2012) and Kazemian and Farrington (2010) indicate that a marriage to a prosocial partner, and the quality of the relationship, stable employment, the arrival of a child, the involvement in a prosocial network of peers, and prosocial recreational activities, all represent typical examples of major turning points in life that contribute, with other personal and social resources, to desistance (Bottoms *et al.*, 2004; Farrington 2007c; Kazemian, 2007; Laub & Sampson 2007; Lösel & Bender 2003; Maruna 2001; Theobald & Farrington, 2009).

These turning points represent the *respectability package* that Giordano and her colleagues (2002) refer to in their work on cognitive transformation. Changes in individual and life circumstances are instrumental in favouring desistance, but it is not clear whether these factors are in fact causal. Kazemian and Farrington (2010) advocate that turning points and life events are not randomly assigned among individuals and therefore it becomes 'difficult to assess whether these events are causes or correlates of desistance' (p. 42). Further studies are necessary to explore which factors contribute to convert redemption times into turning points that address change and sustain a transformed life free from crime. Ideally, effective interventions to foster desistance should be diversified, depending on different ages or stages of criminal careers, and also because predictors of desistance seem to vary across different periods of the life-course (Farrington & Hawkins, 1991). Randomised experiments are the best methods to test the effectiveness of interventions and of criminal sanctions (Farrington & Welsh, 2005, 2006) in fostering desistance.

This volume aims to address those criminogenic dimensions that research evidence indicates as being directly linked to criminal persistence and recidivism. Despite criminal persistence and recidivism being both widely recognised as important dimensions of criminal careers, it is still puzzling to be confronted with the query of *why and how do individuals continue to offend?*

Many studies have in fact devoted their attention to the onset of a criminal career (Farrington & Moitra, 1985; Loeber & Farrington, 2001; Lynam, 1996; Moffitt & Caspi, 2001), while others have analysed the process involved in desistance from crime (Bushway *et al.*, 2003; Kazemian, 2007; Laub & Sampson, 2001; Maruna, 2001). These studies tend to be based on comparative analyses, official data collection and victim surveys, which are interesting but limited to known criminality, and only a part of criminal development.

This volume focuses on persistent criminal careers, and on those risk processes that sustain them. The chapters that follow will explore the complexity of risk causes and risk processes that contribute specifically to criminal recidivism and how to assess them.

Notes

1 *Recidivism* is a term derived in 1880 from the French language *récidiver* – to fall back or (the habit) of relapsing, which was originally linked to the medieval Latin *recidivare* – to relapse into sin, and from the Latin *recidīvus*, falling back (*Chambers*, 1988).
2 Cf. Ministry of Justice's report on adult reconviction from the 2009 cohort for England and Wales (2011, 5).
3 Cf. Ministry of Justice (2010a). This latest published report contains reoffending statistics for the first quarter of 2008 and statistics are available from 2000 to 2008. It is an annual report that contains reoffending statistics covering adults discharged from custody or commencing a court order under probation supervision in the first quarter of each year.
4 Cf. Ministry of Justice (2010b). This latest published report contains reoffending statistics for the first quarter of 2008 and statistics are available from 2000 to 2008. It is an annual report, which contains reoffending statistics covering juveniles discharged from custody or commencing a non-custodial court disposal or given a reprimand or warning in the first quarter of each year.
5 The *Compendium of Reoffending Statistics and Analysis* is a new Ministry of Justice publication, which contains a selection of papers summarising analyses carried out within the Ministry of Justice on reoffending statistics. It includes comparisons between different disposal types, reoffending rates by individual prisons, breakdowns of published data, long-term reoffending rates and international comparisons.
6 The severity rate is based on the list of offences published in the National Statistics adult reoffending publication and the rate is constructed using offences based on the list for the purposes of the National Probation Serious Further Offence (SFO) Review Process. The severity list includes grievous bodily harm offences, which do not entail a mandatory review under the current Probation SFO Review Process (Ministry of Justice, 2011, 78).

7 As reported in the 2013 Compendium, propensity score matching (PSM) 'constructs statistical comparison groups of offenders based on the probability of receiving one of the sentences in each comparison, using observed offender and offence characteristics. The probability is represented as a *propensity score*, which is a value between 0 and 1. Offenders given one type of sentence (e.g. *treatment sentence*) are matched to offenders receiving the other sentence type (e.g. *control sentence*) where the propensity scores of each offender are similar. After matching, the average treatment effect of receiving one sentence rather than the other is calculated as the difference in the mean re-offending rates between the two sentences' (*Ministry of Justice Statistics Bulletin*, 2013, 8).
8 Austria, Denmark, England & Wales, Finland, France, Germany, Iceland, Ireland, Northern Ireland, Norway, Scotland, Sweden, Switzerland, the Netherlands.
9 Differences in recidivism definitions can be found in the Ministry of Justice's report (2011, 102).
10 Some of this will be explained by the fact that this analysis was based on the January–March sample, which contains a higher proportion of prolific offenders than a full-year sample. Definitions of previous contacts have not been reconciled between countries, so it is only of limited use here (cf. Ministry of Justice's report, 2011, 107).
11 For a comprehensive and updated source for reviewing all the EU statistics related to crime and justice in Europe see: epp.eurostat.cec.eu.int.

2
CRIMINAL CAREERS, RECIDIVISTS AND CHRONIC OFFENDERS

> Science . . . is not interested in the unique event; the unique belongs to history, not to science.
>
> *(Guilford, 1936, 676)*

A criminal career is defined as a patterning of antisocial, delinquent, criminal and violent behaviour that characterises the individual development over the life-course (Blumstein *et al.*, 1986); hence, it should be explored longitudinally (as Guilford already recognised in his psychological study). A criminal career includes a time orderly sequence of events that helps researchers to focus on the time before or after an offence is committed:

- *onset* is the beginning of a criminal career, i.e. the first time an antisocial act takes place;
- *duration* is the length of criminal involvement;
- *antisocial escalation* or *aggravation* is the orderly switching from petty crimes to more serious offences, with increasing time spent in engaging in criminal activities, and its opposite is *de-escalation*;
- *desistance* is the abstention from offending for a prolonged period of time that should be seen as a process rather than a discrete event.

The interruption of a criminal career involves both deceleration (i.e. committing crime less frequently) and of de-escalation (i.e. committing less serious crime). Both these processes constitute a preparation for what may occur to be a *reconversion* into a prosocial life, that differs from a *false desistance* and *intermittent desistance*.

The *criminal career paradigm* (Piquero *et al.*, 2003) recognises that individuals get involved in criminal activities at a particular age, engage in crimes at an individual rate, commit different types of offences, and at a certain point in life desist from offending. The need to study the offending development from its onset is crucial in terms of prevention and intervention. From a preventive perspective, knowledge about the likelihood of offending, given certain risk factors and certain life conditions, will promote a risk and protective factor approach. From an intervention perspective, knowledge of the risk processes involved will allow for a more comprehensive development of programmes targeting both stable risk factors and dynamic criminogenic factors directly responsible for a criminal career. The key aspect of criminal careers is that the likelihood of engaging in illegal activities is not driven exclusively or predominantly by criminal opportunities. As Blumstein and colleagues (1982, 5) noted, "the career concept is intended only as a means of structuring the longitudinal sequence of criminal events associated with an individual in a systematic way". Exploring individual changes in criminal activities over time primarily addresses how the antisocial potential becomes the actuality of criminal actions in different situations, in some places and at certain times instead of others.

The criminal career paradigm addresses the need to explore *why* and *when* some people start offending, and others not, in so far as *becoming an offender* reflects *between-individual differences*. It also emphasises the importance of examining *why* and *how* some people persist in offending, *if* and *why* offending becomes more frequent, more serious, and more specialised over time, *why* and *when* people desist from offending. *Committing offences* reflects *within-individual differences*.

Continuity in offending

Psycho-criminological scientists have always been interested not only in what causes an individual to begin offending, but especially in disentangling the first causes of criminal persistence. Risk causes vary depending on the individuals: on their developmental stage, on their vulnerability, on the mediation or moderation of other factors that may enhance or buffer the risk impact. Criminal recidivism is a post-hoc process in the sense that it is manifest only after an offence has occurred, and it is influenced by many different variables that directly or indirectly contribute to the continuation of criminal events in the life-course of an individual. Longitudinal data are essential in investigating criminal careers in general, and criminal recidivism in particular; they allow for a better understanding of the pattern of risk continuity or discontinuity along the life-course, and facilitate the identification of those life events that may be negative turning points into a criminal pattern.

The central element is that antisocial behaviour is likely to become more serious depending on its precocious onset, its continuity and the more intertwined the offender is with a highly criminogenic background. Residual career length (RCL) and residual number of offences (RNO) not only provide information about the time likely to be invested in further criminal activities, but also offer evidence about the likelihood of offending persistence, recidivism and antisocial escalation.

Research findings suggest that criminal persistence is highly dependent on antisocial onset, so that the earlier the onset the longer the criminal career. Early antisocial onset is also recognised as the most robust factor for criminal aggravation, so an early onset ignites a process of escalation from trivial to more severe forms of offending. An individual who begins to offend early has a longer residual criminal career to invest in, compared with an individual who starts later in life. Within this residual time of potential offending, an individual may get involved in shoplifting at age 14, move towards burglary at age 16, then to robbery at age 18, and escalate into assault, violence and homicide in adulthood. The emphasis on predicting a sequential offending pattern has an empirical foundation. Evidence-based findings with such cases show that individuals enmeshed into a criminal career become more consistent over time (see Chapter 3).

Persistence in offending is at the basis of criminal recidivism. Scientists (Hodgins, 2007; Loeber & Farrington, 1998a; Moffitt, 1993) studying the patterning of criminal recidivism have consistently recognised that a small group of offenders are responsible for the majority of crimes. This small fraction of offenders, defined as chronics, represent about 5–8 per cent of the population, commit a large proportion of all crimes and are involved in a considerable number of antisocial and violent acts.

Developmental and life-course theories (Farrington, 2005a) make different predictions about different categories of offending, and research evidence has significantly showed that this subset of individuals is heterogeneous in their criminal involvement, in their types of offences, and in the duration of their criminal careers. Psycho-criminological studies refer to persistent offenders by talking about chronic offenders, reoffenders or recidivists interchangeably.

- *Are these groups similar in kind and degree of offending?*
- *Or do they deserve a different analysis to see the criminogenic patterns behind their criminal careers?*

Moffitt (1993) promoted the dual taxonomy which contrasted adolescence-limited offenders (ALs) with life-course persistent offenders (LCPs). This taxonomy assumes that the offending population is comprised of more than one group of offenders, each with distinct features and reasons for starting and continuing offending. The hypothesis of a single, unitary process of offending, as suggested by Gottfredson and Hirschi (1990), Sampson and Laub (2005) and Thornberry and Krohn (2003, 2005), is therefore questionable.

The adolescence-limited offenders begin to offend during adolescence; their delinquency is a physiological expression of adolescent turmoil and the maturity gap. The causes of their offending lie in the discrepancy between 'wants and means', and peer pressure. The maturity gap is shaped by individual perceptions of physical and social standards to aspire to, and by the desire for autonomy and status. Delinquent peers provide one of the most robust factors in promoting offending. The peer context is set up by a pro-delinquency attitude, with the perception of success attributed to their delinquent friends, and belittling the scholastic achievements of prosocial peers. The actual involvement in delinquent activities and the time spent with peers are directly proportional to the interest manifested in being a member of the group and being recognised as such. This associative context offers opportunities to learn from as well as to imitate delinquent models. Co-offending is likely to be the manner by which adolescents offend, given that the most frequent activities in which ALs are involved, such as vandalism, theft and shoplifting, drug use and school violence, require the assistance of others. ALs desist around early adulthood with the transition to more mature roles and a more stable status, and some academic or job achievements, and satisfactory amicable or intimate relationships, give them a new scope and stability in life.

Empirical evidence suggests that criminal activities differ over time, not only in types of offences but also in types of offenders. Adolescent delinquents are likely to offend transitorily and temporarily; their delinquency is normative; their crimes tend to be minor and status oriented; their recovery is expected without particular problems. Prosocial functioning is regularly achieved because their pre-delinquent development is unproblematic, and likely to be embedded in a conventional and stable family, and sustained within a scholastic commitment which is nonetheless perceived as an overwhelming and tedious duty. There may be cases in which their recovery is delayed because of some experiences that ensnare them into a compromising transition to prosocial adjustment. Some examples of snares are criminal records, incarceration, addiction to drugs or alcohol, and pregnancy for girls (Piquero & Moffitt, 2005).

Life-course-persistent offenders (LCPs) constitute a specific kind of offenders. The most relevant aspects of their criminal career are their earlier onset and a long and serious criminal career. The criminal involvement of LCPs is likely to be characterised by lone offending, and not having the need of peer assistance to commit their crimes. It may be instead that they provide the delinquent roles for adolescence-limited peers to imitate, who see them as a successful model of status, power and money. They may recruit inexperienced offenders into a life of crime (Reiss & Farrington, 1991).

According to the taxonomy, the 'nature and nurture' interplay is relevant to explain the development of antisocial continuity in the life-course of these children. Their risk emerges from inherited or acquired neuropsychological variation, manifested in deficits in cognitive abilities, difficult temperament, lack of self-control, impulsiveness, hyperactivity and aggressiveness. Their family milieu is also an important contributor to their antisocial development, and it is characterised by poor parenting, conflicts, poverty, disrupted families and harsh discipline. The difficult relational background goes beyond family boundaries though, and also affects how the child relates to teachers and peers, with expanding consequences at many levels of social functioning, and for lengthy periods of time. The relational and social setting of LCPs is often complicated by teenage parenting, scholastic failures and unemployment. Moffitt's developmental taxonomy anticipates that LCPs are often involved in a pattern of antisocial continuity from childhood to adulthood, so that the longer their involvement the more likely the escalation of their offending over time, through a change in the antisocial phenotype (*heterotypic continuity*) (Moffitt, 2006): age-graded changes in opportunities will influence, and hence alter, the expression of the antisocial potential (Farrington, 2005b; Lussier *et al.*, 2009).

The antisocial behaviour of LCPs is a function of a process defined as *cumulative continuity*, in which current antisocial behaviour plays the role of a stepping-stone towards a process of escalating into ever more serious crimes, by enhancing the probability of future antisocial involvement, and reducing the opportunity to desist. Therefore, these offenders are more likely to be responsible for a great number of offences over the life-course. The combination of neuropsychological risk and environmental risk provides the conditions for antisocial persistence. That is not to assume that there is no room for change, and that *absolute stability* is the disconsolate response for the LCP offenders. Rather, what should be considered is that LCPs are expected to be characterised by *relative stability*, i.e. individual idiosyncrasies will remain more or less stable across the life-course. In general, the worst offenders at one age will tend to be the worst offenders at a later age, even though all offenders will tend to improve as they get older.

Research findings have suggested the presence of two other groups to add to the ALs and LCPs: abstainers and late onset offenders. These other groups do not follow the conventional route to delinquency, and exhibit specific psychological and relational characteristics. The identification of these other offending groups sustains the hypothesis of individual differences that influence how similar people adjust to life in a variety of ways, despite a shared environment, and how different people cope with life similarly, despite a completely divergent background. 'Most prior criminal career research treats offenders as homogeneous, but different types of people may have different types of careers' (Farrington, 1999, 156). The message is clear: what is needed is research on what are the most important offender typologies, and on their diverse developmental pathways to criminal careers.

The *abstainers* are adolescents who entirely refrain from delinquent and antisocial activities. Moffitt's (2006) account is that they are excluded from peer groups and social activities because of some personal characteristics that are unappealing or uninteresting to their peers, which reinforce isolation and hence abstention from offending. Chen and Adams (2010), using data from the National Longitudinal Study of Adolescent Health (Add Health), tested the hypothesis of delinquency abstention, and particularly the association between exclusion from friendship networks and delinquency. Their findings did not strongly support the assumption of delinquency abstention as a process of isolation and peer rejection.

In order to test Moffitt's assumption about abstention, Piquero *et al.* (2005) employed data from the 1997 National Longitudinal Survey of Youth. Their findings only partly supported the hypothesis, and provided mixed evidence regarding the personal characteristics associated with delinquency abstention and involvement in deviant and antisocial peer networks. In their sample, the adolescent abstainers were a small group, and females were slightly over-represented in it. Abstainers, especially males, reported a high level of teacher attachment, fitted the profile of a good and compliant student, and had, if any, few delinquent friends. However, they did not seem to have those psychological characteristics of being depressed or sad that in Moffitt's hypothesis significantly contributed to their marginalisation from social situations. Contrary to expectation, it seemed that those teens who appeared sad and depressed were more involved in delinquent acts than their counterparts, and perhaps as a way of compensating for their sense of psychological uneasiness, they joined delinquent peers in order to avoid social rejection and loneliness. In Piquero's and colleagues' (2005) study the abstainers did not appear to be socially inept and isolated, but instead they were more likely to be involved in relationships with prosocial friends, having some resources to avoid the *teenage delinquent social scene*. However, it may be important to follow abstainers as they enter adulthood, in so far as they may constitute those individuals who become late starters.

Some researchers (Eggleston & Laub, 2002; Zara & Farrington, 2006) have shed some light on the phenomenon of late onset offending. Despite being considered a relatively rare aspect by some (Wolfgang et al., 1987) or a methodological artefact by others (Moffitt, 2006), adult onset offending deserves some attention, not least because of the higher proportion of individuals now beginning to offend late in their lives. In a study conducted by Zara and Farrington (2009), using data from the Cambridge Study in Delinquent Development (CSDD), late onset offenders were individuals who started offending only in adulthood at age 21 and onwards. The late starters in Zara and Farrington's study (2010) were characterised by nervousness, anxiety, lack of friends in childhood, neuroticism in adolescence, and lack of sexual experiences in early adulthood; these features, combined with a pattern of anxiety and nervousness, changed, in the course of development, from exercising a protective impact against delinquent models to negatively affecting the quality of adjustment to adult life.

Overall, the nervous children in the CSDD resemble the inhibited children in Caspi and Silva's work (1995) who were shy and fearful already from age 3 and had difficulty in concentrating on tasks when involved in novel settings. While in adulthood these children were characterised by an over-controlled, restrained behavioural style, and a non-assertive personality, the nervous and anxious children in Zara and Farrington's study were likely in adulthood to begin a criminal career. This discrepancy in findings between the two studies is just an apparent one, and it could be explained by the fact that in Caspi and Silva's study the analysis was carried out for a period of 15 years (from ages 3 to 18), while in the CSDD study the longitudinal span included data from ages 8–10 to 48–50. At age 18 the CSDD late onset offenders were characterised by neuroticism and anxiety, which still played an inhibitory and over-controlling role, and had difficulty in achieving a gratifying sexual life; they were then quite similar to the cautious, socially feeble and submissive inhibited children at age 18 described by Caspi and Silva (1995).

Social isolation may be a quite effortless behavioural preference for a nervous and shy child aged 8–10, and for an anxious adolescent. However, life may become more difficult later on, especially when the individual faces the adult world outside of the family (protective) cocoon. Family factors seemed to have only temporarily reduced the levels of social impairment in those nervous and anxious children who later became offenders. If this were the case, as it appears to be, it could not be so unlikely that an isolated, neurotic and anxious individual would begin offending later in life, as a response to social stress, uncertainties and adversities. This is not to say that anxious or nervous children are destined for a life of crime, but we can gain new insight into how children with certain psychological or temperamental characteristics could find themselves in high-risk situations (Moffitt & Caspi, 2007).

In conclusion, nervousness, anxiety and neuroticism might have protected individuals from offending at an early age, because they were not aggressive or involved with other children in antisocial, daring or risk-taking activities. However, their protective effects wore off in adulthood, presenting different risks for social outcomes and mental health. Further research is needed to establish the precise causal mechanisms linking early psychological factors, family conditions and future criminal behaviour.

The criminal career development in the Cambridge Study in Delinquent Development (CSDD)

The aim of this chapter is to first describe the Cambridge Study in Delinquent Development (CSDD) data, to explore the criminogenic reality of the sample and to see how the assumptions about types of offenders could be tested and could explain continuity in offending and persistence. This examination will allow for a more integrative quantitative and qualitative explanation of why individuals start offending, why they continue offending, and why some offenders persist while others desist from a criminal career. Some attention will also be devoted to some case studies of persistent criminals from the CSDD (see Chapter 3).

The CSDD sample was originally composed of 411 males first studied at age 8 in 1961. It is a longitudinal prospective survey of the development of antisocial behaviour and offending in a sample of inner-city boys from London, who were mostly born in 1953. It is a unique project in criminology, and it is the only longitudinal project that includes more than five personal interviews over a 40-year-follow-up period. It is a remarkable source of scientific information, which offers an incomparable and unparalleled opportunity to study criminal recidivism, not least because it is one of the few projects including personal interviews with hundreds of people in three successive generations.

This chapter describes the findings regarding criminal careers up to age 50, looking at both officially recorded convictions and self-reported offending, at childhood and family background, at scholastic achievements and the working life, and at life success or failure.

Epistemological perspective

The CSDD in its original design was not intended to test one particular theory of delinquency. The rationale behind it was in fact to test a variety of hypotheses about causes and correlates of offending, about many different processes and mechanisms involved in linking risk factors and antisocial behaviour, and about the underlying pattern (e.g. antisocial potential) involved in the development of a criminal career. The *raison d'être* behind this multidisciplinary nature is that, when the scientific enterprise is based on different streams of thought within various disciplines, and when competing perspectives are taken into account, the research is likely to gain in depth, completeness, and quality.

Farrington (1988) assumed that in studying the causes of offending the endeavour should be to develop "an explicit scientific theory that yields unambiguous quantitative predictors that can be tested against empirical data" (p. 159). In 1992, in line with Catalano and Hawkins (1996), Farrington recognised that, in order to achieve increased and sound explanatory power, scientists ought to integrate perspectives from several theories and empirical approaches. Farrington (1992) proposed a tentative theory, as he defined it then, of the development of delinquency. After many years of hypotheses testing, data collection and analyses, an integrative theory was developed and presented to explain the results of the CSDD (Farrington, 2005b). The Integrated Cognitive Antisocial Potential (ICAP) theory explicitly distinguishes between the development of underlying antisocial tendencies and potential and the actual occurrence of antisocial acts (Zara, 2010b). *Antisocial potential* (AP) is the central construct underlying offending, and has been defined as the potential to be translated into antisocial behaviour and the commission of antisocial acts. The choice of the word potential, instead of predisposition, proneness or propensity, was based on the interest in using a term free from biological or deterministic connotations. The assumption is that AP is an unobservable underlying hypothetical construct, and that changes that occur in AP could be observed indirectly through the modification of other factors (e.g. antisocial attitudes) that can be empirically measured. Thus, behavioural manifestations of offending reflect this underlying construct, and it is assumed that the translation of AP into antisocial and criminal acts depends on cognitive (thinking and decision-making) processes, as well as opportunities and potential victims. It was suggested that AP could be measured by antisocial attitudes and so could be more easily separated from antisocial behaviour.

AP is thought to reach its peak during the teen years, causing both a high prevalence and a frequency of offending during this period of life (Loeber & Farrington, 1998a, b; Paternoster *et al.*, 1997). Changes in behaviour with age are explained by changes in risk and situational factors, which trigger and activate changes in AP.

Age-appropriate behavioural manifestations of antisocial tendencies mostly depend on changes in situational factors; these age-appropriate manifestations help to explain the onset sequences of antisocial and offending behaviour (Farrington, 2005a; Sampson & Laub, 2005; Wikström, 2005). It follows that antisocial onset sequences are not only age-appropriate (an 8-year-old boy would have some difficulty in doing a bank robbery), but also that certain types of behaviour may promote, facilitate or act as a kind of stepping stone to others. Vandalism is likely to be carried out before shoplifting; shoplifting tends to occur before burglary; burglary takes place before robbery; violence is more likely to take place following a process of escalation and aggravation in a criminal career. Longitudinal data are needed to explore this patterning of antisocial potential along the life-course.

The scientific breadth of the CSDD

At an empirical level, longitudinal data are needed to test explanations of criminal persistence and recidivism, and their causes and risk-mechanisms from a multidimensional perspective. At a methodological level longitudinal data allow for bringing together quantitative and qualitative analyses, and developing a practical guide to predict persistence and to intervene to reduce the risk of criminal recidivism. At an intervention level longitudinal data facilitate the collection of sufficiently reliable and valid data to create a checklist to assess the risk for persistence and recidivism that can constitute a practical guideline for practitioners and help them to tailor their interventions to individual offenders.

The CSDD was first directed for twenty years by Donald J. West. In 1969 David P. Farrington started working on it, and in 1982 Farrington (see Image 2.1) began directing the CSDD. Jeremy W. Coid started as a co-director in 1999. The study has been funded primarily by the Home Office and secondly by the Department of Health.

The focus of the CSDD was three-fold: continuity and discontinuity in behavioural development; the effects of risk factors and life events on individual development; and predicting future behaviour and adjustment to life.

The CSDD has a unique combination of features:

a. It is a prospective longitudinal survey.
b. The focus of interest is on delinquency and criminal development.

IMAGE 2.1 David Farrington in the Institute of Criminology's Archive Room (IoC, Cambridge University, March 2010)

c. Many variables were measured before the youths were officially convicted, to avoid the problem of retrospective bias.
d. The study has involved frequent personal contacts (nine face-to-face interviews) with a group of boys, their parents, their teachers and their peers, so records were supplemented by interview, test and questionnaire data.
e. A fairly representative sample of urban working-class youths was followed up, rather than extreme groups of (predicted or identified) delinquents and non-delinquents, so that all degrees of antisocial behaviour and delinquency were present.
f. The officially delinquent minority became gradually differentiated from their non-delinquent peers, avoiding the problem of selection of control groups.
g. Both official and self-report measures of offending were used. Self-reports were collected repeatedly from age 14 to age 48.
h. The study has an exceptionally low attrition rate, with 93 per cent of the sample reinterviewed at age 48.
i. The study has collected information and data on the original CSDD males who are termed *second generation* (G2); on *first generation* (G1) family members, i.e. parents; on *parallel generation* members, i.e. partners and spouses; and on *third generation* (G3) members, i.e. children.
j. The most recent data collection is a follow-up of the children of the study males, aged at least 18, and 551 out of the 653 eligible children have been interviewed (84 per cent). The purpose of this *Third Generation Follow-Up* was to establish how far risk factors that were significantly related to criminal careers in the past still have an influential impact on the onset and maintenance of modern criminal behaviour (Farrington *et al.*, 2014). This set of data also provides unique information on the intergenerational transmission of offending, on antisocial problems, and on mental and psychological difficulties among three generations of people, opening up the possibility of analysing criminal persistence and recidivism from a wider perspective including the continuation of antisociality and psychopathy from one generation to the next.
k. Multiple and different variables from different sources were measured, making it possible to test many hypotheses about delinquency, to investigate the relative importance of differentiated variables, and to study the significance of some variables while controlling for others.
l. Other advantages in measuring variables from different sources are that they help to determine whether observed relationships reflect real associations between theoretical constructs or measurement biases, to establish validity and reliability, and permit the reduction of measurement error by combining variables from different sources.

Historical background when the CSDD began in 1961

From a criminological perspective, 1961 represents a turning point year: the CSDD began. The national social, cultural and political context when (1961) and where

(Great Britain, and specifically London) the CSDD study took place was quite interesting for many reasons.

Year 1961

The Prime Minister of Great Britain was Harold Macmillan of the Conservative Party. Throughout 1961 many events had direct and indirect social and political influences upon what was then Britain and its Empire. In January John F. Kennedy became USA President. In February the Beatles had their first performance at the Cavern Club in Liverpool. In March the black and white £5 note ceased to be legal tender. On 20 March the Shakespeare Memorial Theatre, Stratford-upon-Avon, became the Royal Shakespeare Theatre and its company became the Royal Shakespeare Company. In April there was the failed US invasion of Cuba at the Bay of Pigs. Also Sierra Leone became independent of the UK, the first of many independences that occurred in 1961, reflecting the break-up of the British Empire. On 1 May, betting shops were legalised, on 2 May, the United Kingdom became a member of the Organisation for Economic Co-operation and Development (OECD), and on 6 May the Tottenham Hotspur team won both the league and the cup final. On 15 May the world witnessed the birth of modern genetics, and on 28 May Amnesty International was founded. On 10 August, Britain applied for membership of the EEC. Between 13 and 31 August the Berlin Wall was built. On 12 October the death penalty was abolished in New Zealand. It was still in force in the UK.

On 8 November there was a referendum relating to Sunday opening of public houses in Wales, and some counties voted to stay *dry*. On 4 December, National Health Service birth control pills were made available by the Health Minister Enoch Powell. On 11 December, the Vietnam War started.

The social structure of the sample

The 411 London boys in the CSDD, mostly born in 1953, have been the most famous sample in psycho-criminological longitudinal research. These 411 males constituted a traditional White, urban working-class sample of British origin, most of whom had lived in the area for many years and often for several generations (West, 1969). At the time when the boys were first contacted, 1961–2, they were living in a working-class area of London. Three hundred and ninety-nine of these boys came from six primary schools which were located within a mile of the CSDD Research Office, which was established for the purpose of the investigation. The other 12 boys were selected from a local school for children with special needs, and were included in the sample so as to make it more representative of the population of the boys living in the area. The homes of the boys and their families were situated in an area of about 1.75 × 1.5 miles. The area was heavily built-up, crossed by busy arterial roads with shops and by main railway lines. The side streets accommodated a good deal of light industry, and housed a quite dense population.

The street market was active on six days a week and was a focal thriving force of the area. Many bars, where English beers were sold, were open at lunchtime and in the evening; they represented a popular social focus for working-class social life.

When the study began, a rehousing programme was in full swing, but some depressing, barrack-like housing blocks, built at the turn of the century, were still in use. Initially, however, a third of the CSDD sample were still (in the early 1960s) living in accommodation with no indoor bathroom. Residents' accounts of living in one of the better and more imaginative new London estates (*Providence*) have been published by Parker (1983). The passage of time brought changes. The old "rag and bone" yards served by horses and carts collecting scrap metal disappeared. In the 1960s the shops were still lacking quality merchandise, the local cinema was gone, and in keeping with national trends a McDonald's restaurant had been opened. Signs of gentrification appeared in some streets where old houses had been refurbished, new and well-designed doors and windows had been installed, and middle-class enclaves had been established.

The inhabitants of some of the worst estates felt the need to keep large dogs for protection. The derelict areas from past demolitions were grassed over and often used as children's playgrounds, but they were contaminated with filth and, at times, with dog dirt. The atmosphere mixed a sense of renovation and a sense of despair. The streets were increasingly polluted with car exhaust fumes. The neighbourhood had an officially reported juvenile delinquency level slightly higher than the national average, and much higher than in the privileged so-called *leafy suburbs*. At the south end of the area was one of the busiest of the London magistrates' courts where some celebrated leaders of criminal mobs had appeared.

The working-class ethos

Within this overall picture of a working-class ethos, bereft of cultural interests and educational values, there was noticeable variation in personal standards, with some families living in squalor, with certain houses not having a bathroom and hot water, others struggling to keep up appearances under tough conditions, and others making some attempt to appear comfortably off with a profusion of household appliances and modern furnishings (Piquero *et al.*, 2007).

A television set was present in every household, even in the most deprived ones. The funeral ceremony was an opportunity for families to show their sorrowful tribute for the loss by lavish spending, which was most likely paid with the help of insurance.

The boys' mothers who worked were mostly part-time office cleaners, travelling in the early morning to the City of London. Few parents envisaged their sons going on to further education. Many others were satisfied for them to take up unskilled jobs like their fathers and brothers, while others wanted them to become apprenticed to a trade. Even the relatively well-off, however, had no aspirations to take on the responsibility of mortgages and own their houses.

Schools

There were no private schools in the neighbourhood and all the primary schools were coeducational, with usually 40 pupils per class. It is likely that these schools were unattractive to ambitious teachers: the academic aspirations of children were low and the neighbourhood was unappealing. Standards of literacy among the pupils, as measured by tests on the CSDD sample, were significantly below the London average for 10 year olds. As a possible reflection of nutritional as well as intellectual deficits, the CSDD boys were also significantly below the national average in height for their age.

Recreational facilities for children were limited. Soccer and swimming were promoted by some of the schools, but the activities of local youth clubs were generally somewhat regimented or run by religious organisations, and were not attractive for many of the boys. The schools differed in their regimes. For instance, Piquero and colleagues (2007) described the opposite educational and scholastic style of some headteachers. One school had a particularly disciplinary headteacher who believed in dividing pupils of similar age into distinct groups according to their academic achievements. Another school was run by a more paternalistic headteacher who tried to promote good relationships with parents, and attempted to create a climate of communication and sharing education perspectives for the next generation. No evidence was found that these differences in scholastic regimes had any significant long-term impact on delinquency potential (Piquero et al., 2007).

The local state-supported primary schools attended by the CSDD boys were in keeping with the character of their surroundings: forbidding-looking Victorian structures encircled by concrete play areas. One of the schools was set among rows of grim-looking nineteenth-century terraced houses lacking any open space. Another was close to a major new housing development that was gradually engulfing the neighbouring streets. Another was close to a confluence of major roads and local shops and served nearby families from both old Victorian mansion blocks and a newly built housing estate.

Ethnicity of the sample

Three hundred and fifty-seven boys (87 per cent of the sample) were of British origin and White in appearance, and were brought up by parents who themselves grew up in England, Wales or Scotland. Of the remaining 54 boys, 12 were Black, having at least one parent of West Indian, usually, or African origin. The other 42 boys were White and of non-British origin: 14 had at least one parent from North or South Ireland, 12 had parents from Cyprus, and the other 16 had at least one parent from another Western industrialised country (Australia, France, Germany, Malta, Poland, Portugal, Spain or Sweden). The ethnicity of the CSDD sample, of course, reflected the ethnicity of families living in that area at that time.

In line with the *Registrar General's Scales*, the social class of the sample was a derived classification achieved by mapping occupation and employment status to class categories.[1] On the basis of the fathers' occupational status, when aged 8, 387 boys (94 per cent of the sample) could be described as working-class (categories III, IV or V on the Registrar General's Scales, describing skilled, partly-skilled or unskilled manual workers), in comparison with the national figure of 78 per cent at that time. The majority of the boys were living in conventional two-parent families, with two operative (but not always biological) parents present. At ages 8–9, only 25 boys (6 per cent) had no operative father and four boys (1 per cent) had no operative mother.

The original sample was limited to males from a working-class urban area because of the high prevalence of juvenile convictions (about a quarter) among them compared to juvenile convictions of females. The sample size was set at 400 because this was considered large enough for allowing statistical comparisons between about 100 convicted and about 300 unconvicted boys, but small enough to interview each boy and his family and build up intensive case histories, and also to allow a manageable follow-up of individual and family development. National and international representative samples of many thousands provide excellent bases for generalisations and statistical analyses, but with such numbers it is difficult to collect anything other than easily available official information and build up detailed case histories of individuals.

At age 18 it was possible to interview 389 males out of 410 alive (95 per cent); at age 32, 378 males out of 403 alive (94 per cent) were interviewed; and at age 48, 365 males out of 394 alive (93 per cent) were interviewed. When the men reached the age of 48, the structure of CSDD sample had undergone the following changes: 17 men had died (of whom 13 were convicted); five men were not traced and 24 men refused to be interviewed.

CSDD: an extensive and unique set of data

Multiple constructs and variables were measured at different ages, many variables were triangulated, with constructs based on combinations of variables, and sources of information were compared to test for reliability and validity. Individual, biological (e.g. heart rate), familial, scholastic, relational and socio-economic factors were measured. This vast array of data and information has provided researchers with a unique opportunity to understand the complexity of factors involved in delinquent development, and to explore how and why some males from a criminogenic background offend, while others do not; why some persist while others desist; and why some start offending early in their life, while others start only in adulthood.

The boys in the CSDD were tested in their schools at ages 8, 10 and 14, and interviewed in the research office when they were aged 16, 18 and 21. At ages 25, 32 and 48 they were interviewed in their homes by young male or female social science graduates. At most ages the aim was to interview the entire sample; there were some exceptions at ages 21 and 25 when only subsamples were involved. The tests administered in schools measured individual characteristics such as intelligence (verbal and non-verbal), attainment, personality and psychomotor impulsiveness. The information gathered during the interviews focused on topics such as living conditions, employment histories, relationships with female partners and children, injuries and illnesses, leisure activities such as drinking, drug use, physical fighting and offending behaviour.

In order to build up a comprehensive picture of these individuals and their psychosocial reality, interviews with their parents and later with their partners or spouses were also carried out. Female psychiatric social workers interviewed their parents in their homes; these interviews took place about once a year from when the boys were aged 8 until ages 14–15, the last year of compulsory education. The mother was most of the times the primary informant, although about three-quarters of the fathers were interviewed at some stage. The information that the parents were able to furnish included the boy's level of daring or nervousness, family income and family size, parental unemployment histories, their histories of psychiatric treatment, their child-rearing practices, including attitudes, discipline and parental disharmony, their level of supervision of the boy, and his temporary or permanent separation from them.

The teachers completed questionnaires when the boys were aged 8, 10, 12 and 14. The information collected included the boys' troublesome and aggressive behaviour at school, their restlessness and poor concentration, their school achievement and their truancy. Information about the delinquency rates of secondary schools was obtained from the local education authority. Also their peers rated the boys, when they were attending primary school, about topics such as their daring, dishonesty, troublesomeness and popularity.

The offending groups in the CSDD

In order to be able to trace findings of guilt of the males, of their biological parents and siblings, their wives or female partners, and those people who associated with them in offending (their co-offenders), searches included various steps, and the collaboration of Scotland Yard in London. Between 1964 and 1979, paper records were consulted in the CRO/NIS at Scotland Yard. In 1979, the records were transferred on to microfiche, and microfiche records were then consulted in the central Criminal Record Office or National Identification Service (CRO/NIS) at Scotland Yard until 1994. As Farrington et al. (2013) described in detail, up to 1994, when most of the males were aged 41, searches were carried out via the CRO/NIS to try to identify records of convictions of the CSDD males and of their relatives. In the case of 18 males who had emigrated outside Great Britain and Ireland by age 32, applications were made to search their criminal records in the eight countries where they had settled, and searches were actually carried out successfully in five countries. From 1995 the microfiche collection was discontinued, and all convictions were recorded on the Police National Computer (PNC). There was only limited copying of old records to the PNC, generally when a person received a new conviction.

Additional searches of criminal records of the CSDD males occurred in July 2002 and December 2004 in the PNC, when most of the males were aged 51. Another search of the PNC was completed in March 2011, when most males were aged 57. This chapter reports findings on offending up to age 50.

Table 2.1 summarises the number of males first convicted at each age, taking into account dates of emigration and death, the number of different males convicted, the number of recidivists and the number of convictions at each age. Out of 404 men at risk, 167 men became offenders; that figure excludes the seven emigrated men mentioned above. It is significant to emphasise that the cumulative prevalence of convictions in the CSDD up to age 50 is 41 percent, while the national prevalence of convictions of males in England and Wales, born in 1953 up to age 45, is 33 per cent (Prime et al., 2001). However, these two figures are not entirely comparable. For instance, in the CSDD all motoring offences were excluded from the analysis (unless otherwise indicated) but they were included in the national figure. Moreover, the national figure includes convictions of visitors and immigrants, who would not be part of the 1953 birth cohort. Despite these differences, it is evident that the cumulative prevalence of convictions of males in this sample is higher than the national figure. Between ages 10 and 16 inclusive (the years of juvenile delinquency in England and Wales at that time), 86 males (21 per cent) were convicted. It is interesting to observe that while up to age 16 first offenders outnumbered recidivists, after that age that proportion changed, highlighting the involvement of many more recidivists in criminal behaviour.

The number of convictions peaked at age 17, with 69 offences committed and 46 different offenders involved. The number of first-time offenders peaked between ages 13 and 17, when 83 of the 167 offenders started their antisocial career. With age, the number of first-time offenders declined, and there were only three new offenders between ages 37 and 40, and another three new offenders after age 40.

Table 2.2 shows the pattern of offending based on the age of onset, showing that the earlier the onset the longer the duration of the criminal career, and the higher the percentage of reoffending involved. Of the 167 who were convicted, 118 were recidivists (70.7 per cent).

A search of conviction records (based on the Police National Computer) took place when all of the men were aged at least 50, at the end of 2004. Convictions were counted only if they were for offences usually recorded in the Criminal Record Office (CRO), thus excluding petty crimes such as common assault, drunkenness and all motoring offences. Offences were defined as illegal acts leading to convictions, and only offences committed on different days were counted. As Farrington and colleagues (2006) explained, the rationale behind this rule was to guarantee that each separate criminal incident could yield only one offence. The most common offences included were thefts, burglaries and unauthorised takings of vehicles. There were also quite a few offences of violence, robbery, vandalism, fraud and drug abuse. The total official number of offences committed by the CSDD sample was 808 offences; 759 of which (94 per cent) were committed by reoffenders. Official cautions were nationally recorded from 1995 and were therefore included from then. In order not to rely just on official criminal records, self-reports of offending were gathered from the males at every age from age 14 (for details, see Farrington, 1989).

Table 2.3 summarises the total number of offences committed, and the number of men who committed each number of offences, indicating that at one extreme

TABLE 2.1 Changes in official offending with age

Age	No. males at risk	No. first convicted offenders	No. convicted offenders	No. recidivist offenders	No. convictions
10	409	6	6	0	7
11	409	6	8	2	10
12	409	8	12	4	15
13	409	15	22	7	28
14	409	19	34	15	49
15	408	17	33	16	46
16	408	15	33	18	59
17	407	17	46	29	69
18	405	8	43	35	64
19	404	9	40	31	52
20	403	9	31	22	50
21	403	2	20	18	23
22	400	3	26	23	40
23	399	2	11	9	12
24	398	2	15	13	20
25	398	3	15	12	20
26	398	4	14	10	16
27	397	0	12	12	18
28	397	2	13	11	15
29	397	0	14	14	19
30	397	1	11	10	13
31	397	4	10	6	10
32	396	2	8	6	10
33	396	3	9	6	9
34	396	2	11	9	13
35	396	2	12	10	14
36	396	0	6	6	7
37	396	1	9	8	12
38	394	0	7	7	7
39	394	1	3	2	3
40	394	1	8	7	8
41	393	0	5	5	8
42	392	0	7	7	7
43	392	0	11	11	13
44	392	1	9	8	9
45	391	1	8	7	11
46	390	0	8	8	11
47	389	1	3	2	3
48	387	0	0	0	0
49	387	0	1	1	1
50	386	0	5	5	7
Total		167			808

Note: No. of males at risk: excluding dead and emigrated/not searched. Figures at age 50 are incomplete and include three offences committed at age 51.

Source: Adapted from Farrington *et al*. (2006, 20).

TABLE 2.2 Age of onset versus criminal career measures

Age first offence	No. offenders	% recidivist	Total no. offences	Av. no. offences	Av. age last offence	Av. career duration	Av. duration (excl. 0)
10–13	35	91.4	316	9.0	25.4	12.8	14.0
14–16	51	84.3	304	6.0	28.5	13.0	15.5
17–20	43	65.1	113	2.6	25.1	6.4	9.9
21–30	19	36.8	38	2.0	28.8	3.8	10.2
31–50	19	42.1	37	1.9	38.8	2.8	6.6
Total	167	70.7	808	4.8	28.2	9.1	12.8

Note: Average duration in years. Excl. 0 = Excluding one-time offenders.

Source: Adapted from Farrington *et al.* (2006, 25).

TABLE 2.3 Total number of offences committed

No. offences	No. men	Cum. no. men	Cum. % men	Cum. % offenders	Cum. no. offences	Cum. % offences
1	49	167	40.8	100.0	808	100.0
2	30	118	28.9	70.7	759	93.9
3	19	88	21.5	52.7	699	86.5
4	13	69	16.9	41.3	642	79.5
5	12	56	13.7	33.5	590	73.0
6	7	44	10.8	26.3	530	65.6
7	3	37	9.0	22.2	488	60.4
8	4	34	8.3	20.4	467	57.8
9	2	30	7.3	18.0	435	53.8
10	4	28	6.8	16.8	417	51.6
11	5	24	5.9	14.4	377	46.7
12	4	19	4.6	11.4	322	39.9
13	1	15	3.7	9.0	274	33.9
14	1	14	3.4	8.4	261	32.3
15	1	13	3.2	7.8	247	30.6
16	2	12	2.9	7.2	232	28.7
17	2	10	2.4	6.0	206	24.8
18	3	8	2.0	4.8	166	20.5
19	1	5	1.2	3.0	112	13.9
20	1	4	1.0	2.4	93	11.5
21	1	3	0.7	1.8	73	9.0
23	1	2	0.5	1.2	52	6.4
29	1	1	0.2	0.6	29	3.6
Total	167	167	409	167	808	808

Note: Cum. = Cumulative.

Source: Adapted from Farrington *et al.* (2006, 24).

there are 49 men who only committed one offence, while at the other extreme of the offending spectrum there are 28 men involved in offending at least ten times in their life-course, with one man who committed 29 offences leading to conviction. This table also shows the cumulative numbers of both men and offences, which helps to indicate who committed the most offences. One hundred and eighteen men were involved in more than two offences. A small proportion of offenders (28 men, 7 per cent of all men, and 17 per cent of offenders) were responsible for more than half of all CSDD offences (417 out of 808 offences).

Table 2.4 shows the types of offences committed at different ages, which have been divided into 18 categories. The most common offences were burglary, with 62 offenders and 130 offences, and vehicle theft.

TABLE 2.4 Types of offences committed at different ages

Type	Age						Total	
	10–15	16–20	21–25	26–30	31–40	41–50	No. offences	No. offenders
BURG	38	54	18	10	8	2	130	62
TOMV	19	62	16	9	2	2	110	62
TFMV	15	14	5	3	1	0	38	29
SL	19	8	7	4	18	10	66	38
TFMA	8	5	1	3	0	0	17	12
TFWK	0	14	2	2	4	0	22	20
OTH	23	30	13	5	3	4	78	54
FRAUD	2	16	13	9	10	10	60	36
REC	6	11	6	7	5	0	35	28
SUSP	10	14	3	3	0	0	30	22
ROB	2	7	4	4	1	0	18	9
ASST	4	14	11	9	14	13	65	42
THR	1	12	6	5	7	4	35	24
OW	2	10	2	3	2	7	26	22
SEX	4	2	0	0	5	2	13	10
DRUG	0	10	5	2	3	8	28	15
VAND	2	11	3	3	10	8	37	27
Total	155	294	115	81	93	70	808	167
MOT	0	7	5	7	10	13	42	25

Note: BURG = burglary, TOMV = theft of motor vehicle, TFMV = theft from motor vehicle, SL = shoplifting, TFMA = theft from machine, TFWK = theft from work, OTH = other theft, REC = receiving, SUSP = suspected person, ROB = robbery, ASST = assault, THR = threats, OW = offensive weapon, VAND = vandalism, MOT = motoring offence (driving while disqualified, drunk driving), which was not counted.

Source: Adapted from Farrington et al. (2006, 21).

Persistence in crime in the CSDD

The concept of persistence implies continuity in behaviour, and hence criminal recidivism. The questions that arise involve a specific analysis of who are those males who reoffend and why. Recidivist offenders are more likely to have an early antisocial onset; tend to commit a variety of offences; are versatile in their offending; are likely to commit violent offences. They are closer to the LCPs defined in Moffitt's dual taxonomy. Wolfgang and colleagues (1972) suggested that a small percentage of individuals are responsible for a large share of the convictions within a targeted sample of offenders. These men, in line with Moffitt's taxonomy (1993), and according to Wolfgang and colleagues' work (1972), are considered life-course persistent or chronic offenders.

From now on, we use the term *recidivists* to define CSDD reoffenders as those individuals who had at least two convictions (from 2 up to 9 convictions), independently of the gravity and seriousness of their offences, and the term *chronics* to define those offenders who were convicted at least ten times (10 up to 29 convictions). The remainder of the chapter will look at both types of offenders.

Are recidivist offenders and chronic offenders like any other offenders?

Recidivist offenders

Criminal recidivism can be defined as the process involved in continuing offending and in delaying desistance from a criminal career. The traditional way of studying criminal recidivism, by employing criminal statistics, criminal records or self-reported data, has proved to be biased or, at best, partial. Recidivism is one of the most complex dimensions of a criminal career, and scientists need to be careful about using simple models just because they may be related to the available data in a more straightforward manner.

The data from the CSDD provide a comprehensive set of information to analyse persistence in offending over an extended period of time, and to explore to what extent variety in criminal convictions up to age 50 could be predicted by childhood and adolescent risk, and also sustained by more proximal risk factors and negative life events in adult life.

As previously shown in Table 2.2, out of 404 men at risk, 167 men became offenders (41.3 per cent), of whom 118 had at least two convictions (70.7 per cent). Among these 118 recidivist offenders, 28 were chronic offenders. The criminal careers and incarceration data for one-time offenders, recidivists and chronic offenders are shown in Table 2.5. The average career duration according to number of convictions up to age 50 is also shown. The CSDD offenders had an average criminal career duration of 9.1 years, which began at age 19.11 and so far, ended at age 28.18. A small fraction of males (7 per cent) were chronic offenders, and accounted for over half of the officially recorded criminal incidents. Each of these men had at least 10 convictions, and 24 of them were sent to prison, with an average time period served of 1.86 years. The vast majority of men who served time in prison were those offenders who committed at least five offences. Chronic offenders had an average career duration of over 21 years, with an onset at age 14.

The one-time offenders, of course, had an average career length of 0. The recidivist offenders, who had at least two convictions had a career duration of 12.84 years. Their career started on average at age 17.49 and ended at age 30.33. On average, they spent 1.37 years in prison. The chronic offenders, who had ten or more convictions, had an average career length of 21.37 years, from age 13.78 to age 35.15 on average. Their average time spent in prison was 1.86 years.

Only 44 of the 167 (26 per cent) offenders were ever sent to prison, borstal, a youth institution or a detention centre. The maximum time served in detention was 15.84 years. Among those who experienced imprisonment, two were one-time offenders, and their average time spent in prison was 0.85 years; 42 were recidivists, of whom 24 were chronic offenders.

Table 2.6 summarises the pattern of offending based on the age of onset. It is clear that those men with an early antisocial onset were more likely to become recidivists. 91.4 per cent of men with a first offence and conviction at age 10–13 were recidivists, committed a total number of 316 offences and their career duration was on average 12.84 years. Their last offence was committed on average at age 25. If one looks at the other young age range of onset (14–16), 84.3 per cent of them became recidivists. Putting together these two groups

TABLE 2.5 Description of the CSDD offending sample versus criminal careers

	Offenders $n = 167$	One-timers $n = 49$	Recidives[†] $n = 118$	Chronics $n = 28$
Av. age onset	19.11	23.00	17.49	13.78
Av. age last offence	28.18	23.00	30.33	35.15
Av. CC duration*	9.07	–	12.84	21.37
Min. CC duration	.00	–	.00	3.44
Max. CC duration**	41.42	–	41.42	41.42
Active CC duration	8.82	–	12.48	20.09
No. men incarcerated	44	2	42	24
% incarcerated	26.3	4.1	35.6	85.7
Av. time served	1.34	.85	1.37	1.86
Min. time served	.04	.72	.04	.17
Max. time served	15.84	.97	15.84	15.84

Note: Recidives = those who had two or more convictions. Chronics = those who had at least 10 convictions. Active CC duration = excluding time served. Average time served was based only on those men who were incarcerated. Six men were incarcerated only after their last conviction.
† = Includes also the 28 offenders who are chronics.
* = Time served in years.
** = One male was first convicted just after his tenth birthday and finally at age 51.

TABLE 2.6 Age of onset versus criminal career measures

Age first offence	No. offenders	% recidivist	Total no. offences	Av. no. offences	Av. age last offence	Av. career duration	Av. duration (excl. 0)
10–13	35	91.4	316	9.0	25.4	12.8	14.0
14–16	51	84.3	304	6.0	28.5	13.0	15.5
17–20	43	65.1	113	2.6	25.1	6.4	9.9
21–30	19	36.8	38	2.0	28.8	3.8	10.2
31–50	19	42.1	37	1.9	38.8	2.8	6.6
Total	167	70.7	808	4.8	28.2	9.1	12.8

Note: Average duration in years. Excl. 0 = Excluding one-time offenders.

Source: Adapted from Farrington et al. (2006, 25).

TABLE 2.7 Frequency of offending versus criminal careers and incarceration

No. offences	No. men	Av. age first offence	Av. age last offence	Av. career duration	No. men incarcerated	% incarcerated	Av. time served (Total)
1	49	23.0	23.0	0.0	2	4.1	0.9
2	30	18.7	24.5	5.8	2	6.7	2.3
3–4	32	19.2	29.2	10.1	4	12.5	0.3
5–9	28	17.9	33.0	15.0	12	42.9	0.6
10–14	15	14.3	34.7	20.4	11	73.3	1.0
15+	13	13.2	35.7	22.5	13	100.0	2.6
Total	167	19.1	28.2	9.1	44	26.3	1.3

Note: Average ages, durations and time served in years. Numbers may not exactly add because of rounding. Average time served was based only on those who were incarcerated.

Source: Adapted from Farrington et al. (2006, 26).

with juvenile onsets, they were responsible for 77 per cent of all offences in the CSDD (620 out of 808).

Looking closely at the recidivist group ($n = 118$), and disaggregating the data by the number of offences committed, it can be seen, in Tables 2.7 and 2.8, that the more offences that were committed, the earlier the age of first offences, and the higher the number of men incarcerated. It is not surprising that the percentage of men who experienced imprisonment increased with the number of offences committed, from 4.1 per cent for those who committed only one offence to 73.3 per cent for those involved in 10–14 offences, and all of those who had 15 or more convictions.

In the CSDD the cumulative prevalence of custodial sentences up to age 50 was 11 per cent (44/404), while the comparable national figure for males up to age 45 was 8 per cent (Prime et al., 2001). Based on Farrington and colleagues' analysis

(2006) Table 2.9 describes the main categories of official offenders and the percentage of those still alive in each category who were interviewed. Of the 167 offenders, 154 were still alive and 93 per cent of them were reinterviewed.

Up to age 20, 129 men (32 per cent) were convicted; 108 men were convicted at age 21 or older, but only 38 men were first convicted only from age 21 onwards. Later analyses show that 53 men were desisters, that is to say that they were convicted before age 21 but not subsequently.

TABLE 2.8 Criminal careers and incarceration for one-timers, recidivists and chronic offenders

No. offences	No. men	Av. age first offence	Av. age last offence	Av. career duration	No. men incarcerated	% incarcerated	Av. time served (Total)
1	49	23.0	23.0	0.0	2	4.5	0.8
2–9	90	18.6	28.8	10.2	18	20.0	0.7
10+	28	13.8	35.1	21.4	24	85.7	1.9
Total	167	19.1	28.2	9.1	44	26.3	1.3

TABLE 2.9 Categories of official offenders

Category	No. men	No. alive	No. interviewed	% inter-viewed
Not convicted	237	233	216	93
Convicted	167	154	143	93
Not convicted up to 20	275	269	247	92
Convicted up to 20	129	118	112	95
Not convicted at 21+	289	284	263	93
Convicted at 21+	108	103	96	93
Convicted only up to 20	53	51	47	92
Convicted only at 21+	38	36	31	86
Convicted before and after 21	70	67	65	97
Not convicted 42–47	135	125	117	94
Convicted 42–47	32	29	26	90
One-time offenders	49	45	42	93
Recidivists	118	109	101	93
Non-chronic offenders	139	128	119	93
Chronic offenders	28	26	24	92
Non-incarcerated offenders	123	114	106	93
Incarcerated offenders	44	40	37	93
Career duration < 15 years	77	70	64	91
Career duration 15 years+	41	39	37	95

Note: % interviewed out of those alive.

Source: Adapted from Farrington *et al.* (2006, 28).

A risk-focused approach

The identification of those risk variables directly responsible for persisting in offending is at the core of prevention and treatment. The term risk factor will always mean a variable that predicts a high probability of offending. Much knowledge is shared on the effects of risk factors on early onset offending, their cumulative impact over time, and their stronger and long-lasting impact with time exposure. The extensive psychological literature provides evidence that early risk factors and experiences affect life development and long-term behaviour.

Longitudinal studies have consistently shown that a constellation of risk factors predict a constellation of childhood antisocial behaviours and also a constellation of adult antisocial behaviours (Robins, 1979). These risk factors are individual, familial and social.

Behavioural problems in childhood cast a long shadow. They often emerge in problematic families, where there exists parental disharmony, with at least one parent having a criminal record, and where the child is likely to experience physical neglect, separation from parents, and inconsistent, poor and harsh parenting. Furthermore, these risk factors tend to have a cumulative effect, and the likelihood of an early antisocial onset increases progressively as an individual experiences an increasing number of adverse influences in childhood. It is also suggested that many of these risk factors may interact (Farrington, 1982, 1994, 2002a, 2003, 2012), and may have different effects at different stages of life. This means that between-individual differences underline the sensitivity of an individual to a specific risk factor or to a constellation of risk factors.

Table 2.10 shows to what extent recidivists and one-time offenders at age 50 possessed key risk factors at age 8–10. It also shows that recidivists differ significantly from one-time offenders on many risk factors analysed.

For this analysis, each variable in each age-range (8–10; 12–14; 16–18; 32) was dichotomised, as far as possible, into the 'worst' quarter of males (e.g. the quarter with the highest level of vulnerability) versus the remainder. The rationale behind this was to compare the importance of different risk variables and also to allow for a 'risk factor approach' (Farrington, 2002b, 2005a, b). While prospective prediction (e.g. the percentage of high-risk children who become persistent offenders) is usually poor, and many children at risk turn out to have successful lives, retrospective prediction (e.g. the percentage of persistent offenders who were high-risk children) is fairly accurate. This leads to strengthening the empirical attention to cumulative, interactive, sequential and delayed effects of risk factors. For example, the probability of becoming a persistent offender increases with the number of risk factors (Farrington, 2002a), almost independently of which particular risk factors are included (Farrington, 2007a).

Antisociality, at age 8–10, considered one of the most crucial personality dimensions, significantly doubled the risk of persistence. Also those boys who were identified by teachers as troublesome tended to become persistent offenders later in life. When the boys were juveniles (at age 8–10), a combined measure of vulnerability was developed, based on having a convicted parent, low family income, large family size (five or more children), poor child-rearing, and low non-verbal IQ (90 or less). Thirty-six per cent of recidivists had high vulnerability scores compared with 12 per cent of one-time offenders. Reporting high level of background vulnerability almost quadrupled the risk of persisting in a criminal career.

Large family size (a large number of children in the family) is a relatively strong and highly replicable predictor of delinquency (Ellis, 1988). If a boy had four or more siblings by his tenth birthday, this tripled the risk of becoming a persistent offender. Low family income almost quadrupled the risk of reoffending. As West and Farrington (1973) indicated, low parental income was closely related to a constellation of other parental circumstances such as poor child-rearing, harsh attitude, parental disharmony, large family size and poor parental supervision that can make it difficult to create a favourable home background for the development of children. Research findings (Haas et al., 2004; Theobald et al., 2013) show that a child who grows up in a family characterised by a strong emotional, educational and situational instability is more likely to manifest dysfunctional behaviour and difficulties in adjusting to life. Previous analyses of the CSDD have suggested that those children who grew up in poor housing, which was characterised by dilapidated surroundings, were also more likely to witness parental disharmony and also to be physically neglected and experience harsh discipline. Though there is not any clear indication of causality, it is likely that certain living conditions reflect the quality of family interaction and stability, which then impacts the quality of individual well-being. When the children were aged 8–10, marital disharmony among their parents was another robust predictor of offending persistence, quadruplicating the risk of reoffending.

Many different types of child-rearing methods, measured early in life, predict a child's delinquency. The most important dimensions of child-rearing are discipline or parental reinforcement, parental praise of the child, warmth or coldness of emotional relationships, parental interest in education, parental disagreement and child neglect. Parental discipline refers to how parents react to a child's behaviour. It is clear that harsh or punitive discipline (involving physical punishment) increases the risk of persistence in offending almost four times. Low parental reinforcement (not praising) good behaviour is also a predictor of persistence in offending later in life. The quality of parenting is a consistent influence on the emotional and behavioural development of a child (Scott, 2005, 2010; Scott et al., 2001, 2010). Patterson (1982) and Patterson and colleagues (1975, 1989, 2004) have demonstrated that the relationship between parenting and child behaviour is bidirectional, and that child temperament and reactivity are likely to affect the quality of parenting, which in turn has an influence on how the child behaves. It is likely that these factors have a pervasive effect over the life of a child, influencing his or her present and often limiting the prospects for a different future. This may be so because of the stability of some of these factors over time, which sheds some light on the fact that early antisocial behaviour has one of the highest patterns of continuity into adulthood of all the measured human features except intelligence (Scott, 2004).

TABLE 2.10 Risk factors at ages 8–10 predicting recidivists versus one-time offenders

Risk variables	Recidivists n = 118	One-time offenders n = 49	Odds ratio	95% (CI)
Ages 8–10	%	%		
Individual factors				
Antisocial	43.2	26.5	2.108	1.014–4.380
Daring	47.4	32.7	1.863	.927–3.744
Psychomotor impulsivity	33.9	32.7	1.058	.521–2.148
Dishonesty	41.2	25.0	2.105	.925–4.653
Troublesomeness	40.7	22.4	2.369	1.102–5.091
Difficult to discipline	32.5	32.7	.992	.487–2.021
Lacks concentration	29.9	26.5	1.182	.560–2.496
Vulnerable	35.6	12.2	3.961	1.557–10.074
Low junior school attainment	39.1	28.9	1.580	.746–3.344
Parental quality				
Poor child-rearing	38.5	12.8	4.284	1.674–10.961
Disagreement between parents	49.0	25.5	2.804	1.309–6.009
Low parental interest in education	29.2	6.4	6.062	1.751–20.994
Low praise by parents	16.5	2.1	9.093	1.173–70.515
Harsh attitude of parents	43.5	17.0	3.756	1.605–8.793
Physical neglect	23.9	14.6	1.058	.521–2.148
Criminogenic family				
Criminal parent	44.1	32.7	1.625	.808–3.269
Delinquent sibling	74.0	74.5	.974	.438–2.164
Family problems				
Large family size	42.4	20.4	2.868	1.308–6.286
Low family income	37.3	12.2	4.261	1.678–10.823
Marital disharmony	41.4	14.9	4.039	1.647–9.906
Behaviour problems of siblings	55.7	37.0	2.142	1.042–4.403

At ages 12–14, many risk variables have a significant and independent association with criminal recidivism (Table 2.11). At a family level, coming from a large family where the child is poorly raised and lacks supervision, and that is characterised by marital disharmony, and where the father is unemployed, are all conditions that increase the risk of becoming future recidivists in comparison with one-time offenders. At an individual level, features such as antisociality, being unpopular, holding an anti-police attitude, lacking concentration and daring are robust risk factors for recidivism. Being involved with delinquent peers, truancy, stealing outside home and self-reporting delinquency are behaviours that contribute to a pattern of antisocial continuity and future recidivism.

As shown in Table 2.12, recidivists in the CSDD were more likely than one-time offenders at age 16–18 to be antisocial, to be heavy drinkers and gamblers, to

TABLE 2.11 Risk factors at ages 12–14 predicting recidivists versus one-time offenders

Risk variables	Recidivists n = 118	One-time offenders n = 49	Odds ratio	95% (CI)
Ages 12–14	%	%		
Individual factors				
Antisociality	50.8	16.3	5.302	2.291–12.270
Lying	52.5	26.5	3.066	1.478–6.361
Anti-police attitude	41.9	22.9	2.424	1.126–5.218
Daring	23.7	8.2	3.500	1.157–10.589
Lacks concentration/restless	47.5	18.4	4.014	1.789–9.009
Parental quality and family problems				
Poor child-rearing	44.3	12.8	5.444	2.130–13.914
Marital disharmony	36.1	11.1	4.528	1.614–12.708
Large family size	34.8	20.4	2.080	.941–4.600
Father unemployment	25.5	4.5	7.200	1.619–32.022
Behavioural factors				
School leaving age	81.4	61.2	2.764	1.321–5.782
Self-reported delinquency	43.6	22.9	2.599	1.208–5.591
Stealing by boy outside home	36.4	17.8	2.643	1.111–6.289
Delinquent friends	47.9	18.8	3.978	1.769–8.947
Unpopularity	24.6	12.3	2.335	.902–6.047
Truancy	36.4	12.2	4.109	1.617–10.443

hold an anti-police attitude, to be involved in unstable jobs or be unemployed. They also self-reported delinquency and violence.

In adulthood, at age 32, the most consistent correlates of recidivism, discriminating recividivists from one-time offenders, concerned areas of social maladjustment such as gambling and antisociality, heavy drinking, holding an anti-police attitude, a high level of unemployment and high level of life failure. Life success was a measure based on nine criteria: successful accommodation; successful employment; successful cohabitation; successful with children; not involved in fights in the last five years; not a substance abuser; no self-reported offences in the last five years (other than theft from work or tax evasion); GHQ^2 score (of 4 or less), and no convictions for offences committed in the last five years. Life failure was significantly correlated with recidivism, almost tripling the risk of criminal persistence. Table 2.13 shows the results of these analyses. As expected, recidivists were more likely to have experienced cumulative risk along the course of their life.

Longitudinal data allow for an exploration of the two types of continuity: homotypic and heterotypic. *Homotypic continuity* can be seen as a continuation of behavioural problems from early childhood. It involves a strong correlation between a problem or disorder (e.g. antisociality) at one point in time and the same problem at a further point in time. *Heterotypic continuity* implies continuity of an antisocial potential that underlies diverse phenotypic behaviours. It describes the

TABLE 2.12 Risk factors at ages 16–18 predicting recidivists versus one-time offenders

Risk variables Ages 16–18	Recidivists n = 118 %	One-time offenders n = 49 %	Odds ratio	95% (CI)
Antisocial	58.8	19.1	6.019	2.660–13.621
Heavy beer drinker	41.2	25.5	2.046	.962–4.350
EPI neuroticism	30.2	40.8	.627	.313–1.254
No exam taken or passed	76.3	48.9	3.362	1.642–6.884
Heavy gambling	38.6	12.8	4.295	1.685–10.952
Group activity	30.7	17.0	2.160	.915–5.096
Unskilled manual job	36.3	8.5	6.122	2.050–18.279
Unstable job record	43.9	23.9	2.486	1.149–5.379
Anti-police attitude	44.3	18.4	3.542	1.573–7.972
Poor relationship with parents	36.0	17.0	2.738	1.169–6.415
Drug user	48.2	29.8	.617	.383–.996
Self-reported delinquency	50.9	27.7	2.709	1.296–5.661
Self-reported violence	42.1	17.0	3.545	1.520–8.268
High unemployment	42.1	15.2	4.052	1.670–9.830

TABLE 2.13 Risk factors at age 32 correlating with recidivists versus one-time offenders at age 32

Risk variables	Recidivists n = 118 %	One-time offenders n = 49 %	Odds ratio	95% (CI)
Renting	73.8	42.2	3.861	1.857–8.027
Antisocial attitude	57.0	22.2	4.641	2.085–10.332
Child elsewhere	41.4	14.3	3.059	1.142–8.190
Cannabis use	36.8	17.8	2.692	1.139–6.363
Heavy drinking	37.7	17.8	2.803	1.187–6.619
Heavy gambling	36.8	20.0	2.328	1.015–5.341
Unemployed	24.5	6.7	4.550	1.301–15.914
Not in a relationship	30.8	13.3	2.899	1.118–7.513
Anti-foreigner attitude	42.1	22.2	2.540	1.141–5.658
Poor relationship with own mother	20.0	5.9	4.000	.866–18.473
Anti-establishment attitude	51.4	33.3	2.115	1.023–4.374
Involved in fights	59.4	35.6	2.656	1.289–5.473
Unstable job record	38.5	22.2	2.188	.977–4.899
Short time in jobs	35.2	8.9	5.577	1.853–16.788
Binge drinking	57.5	40.0	2.033	1.000–4.136
Heavy smoker	47.6	26.7	2.495	1.161–5.365
Self-reported delinquency	43.0	26.7	2.074	.966–4.450
Combined life failure	50.5	26.7	2.802	1.308–6.001
Multiple drug use other than cannabis	22.6	6.7	4.098	1.166–14.396
Inked into crime	35.0	11.1	4.299	1.559–11.850

relationship between a problem at one point in the life cycle and a continued dysfunctioning at another point in time, but with different behavioural manifestations.

When one observes delinquent development in the life-course, one may detect that homotypic continuity between childhood, adolescent and adult antisocial behaviour is stronger *looking backwards* (from adulthood or adolescence, to childhood) than it is *looking forwards*. This assumption can often lead to the conclusion that desistance from antisociality has occurred. Empirical evidence sustains this conclusion (Cicchetti & Cohen, 1995). In fact, despite the important role played by early antisocial behaviour in forecasting adult antisocial behaviour, *most* antisocial children do not become antisocial adults (Robins, 1978). However, it may actually be an indication of undetected heterotypic continuity, since research has also consistently shown that factors for antisocial disorder and criminal offending are often entangled in a patterning of underlying risk over time (Babinski *et al.*, 1999; Pajer, 1998; Pogarsky, 2004; Storm-Mathisen & Vaglum, 1994). Criminal behaviour is in fact one of many different manifestations of a syndrome of antisociality that is pervasive in an individual life and influences not only behaviour but also ways of relating to people, of taking social and professional responsibilities, of building up a family life, and of educating children. These aspects are evident in the lives of many of the CSDD men (G2), and in many of their children (G3) (see Chapter 3).

Chronic offenders

Researchers who are interested in exploring the patterning of offending in a criminal career recognise that a small group of offenders are responsible for a large share of crimes. These offenders are defined as chronics. The definition of chronic offenders is not consistent across studies. It is expected that chronic offenders have longer criminal careers, are more likely to have an early onset, are more likely to have a later age for their last conviction, are more likely to have committed a violent crime and are more likely to have engaged in a heterogeneous variety of crimes. Wolfgang and colleagues' (1972) designation of chronic offenders included those individuals with five or more offences prior to age 18, and found that a small percentage (6 per cent) of the 1945 Philadelphia Birth Cohort was responsible for over 50 per cent of the criminal acts. They basically defined chronic offenders as the small fraction of a cohort who account for just over 50 per cent of all offences. This definition of chronicity however, is arbitrary and it is unknown whether other definitions of chronicity, based on more objective criteria, would identify the same individuals and/or lead to similar substantive conclusions (Blumstein *et al.*, 1985). The CSDD provides an opportunity to study the chronicity question and its dimensions.

Chronicity in offending is often confused with violent offending. While those individuals who commit a large number of offences in their criminal career are more likely to also commit a violent crime (Farrington, 1991b), it is not obvious that chronic offenders are necessarily more violent than other offenders (Farrington & West, 1993). Research findings actually show that in general offenders are more likely to relapse into a non-violent than a violent crime, and this result is also applicable to chronic offenders. What makes a chronic offender more likely to commit violence is the length of his involvement in a pattern of maladjustment and offending, the continuity of offending, and the variety of offences committed as the criminal career lasts longer.

Piquero and colleagues (2007) studied chronic offenders in the CSDD, defined according to five or more convictions up to age 40. However, they then concluded that the five plus designation of offending chronicity 'appears more arbitrary than a true reflection of the persistent population in the CSDD' (Piquero et al., 2007, 138). For the chronic offenders the 'average number of years between the first and fifth convictions was 6.35 years, with minimum and maximum values of 1 and 23 years, respectively'[3] (Piquero et al., 2007, 131). In their analysis, these 53 chronic offenders accumulated many offences, the majority of which were thefts and burglaries. Being a chronic offender significantly predicted whether an offender would commit a violent crime. When Piquero and colleagues (2007) checked for the type of crimes committed by each of the CSDD men in their first five convictions, the offending careers of those chronic offenders who accumulated their five offences in just one year were marked by non-violent crimes. This is an analysis of only five males.

Following this suggestion, in the present analysis of the CSDD data it was decided to employ a more conservative designation of offending chronicity, so that (*high*) chronic offenders here means those individuals who committed at least ten offences in independent offending events, and for which the individual has incurred at least ten convictions, leaving the cut-off of five up to nine convictions for *ordinary* chronics, and the cut-off of two to four convictions for *below* chronics. In line with previous analyses of the CSDD conducted by Farrington and colleagues (2006), this inclusive criterion was chosen on the basis of offending continuity and not on the seriousness and gravity of crime. By using such a conservative criterion for inclusion, it was likely that those males identified as chronic were really representing a true subgroup of persisters, *highly* involved in offending frequency, length of criminal careers and numbers of convictions.

The CSDD offending groups are represented by one-time offenders ($n = 49$), below chronics ($n = 62$), ordinary chronics ($n = 28$) and high chronics ($n = 28$) (see Table 2.14).

High chronics are more likely to have longer criminal careers, over 21 years on average, an earlier age of onset, and more offences and convictions, on average over 14.

In the CSDD, the 28 chronic offenders were responsible for 417 offences (excluding motoring offences) (51.6 per cent) out of the 808 total offences of the entire sample. Their offences were more heterogeneous rather than specialised in any specific or violent type of crime. However, further analyses show that the concentration of violent offences, including sex offences, was higher among the chronic group.

Man 781 was born, like the majority of the men in the study, in 1953. He started his criminal career very early, at age 12.21, and continued offending until his adulthood. His last offence was committed at age 36.87, so that his career was

TABLE 2.14 Mean-level comparisons across the offending groups for some criminal career outcomes

	One-timers $n = 49$	Below chronics $n = 62$	Ordinary chronics $n = 28$	High chronics $n = 28$
Av. age onset	23.00	18.97	17.93	13.78
Av. age last offence	23.00	26.97	32.96	35.15
Av. CC duration*	–	7.99	15.02	21.37
Min. CC duration	–	.00	.76	3.44
Max. CC duration	–	31.91	35.61	41.42
Active CC length	–	7.99	14.81	20.09
Av. convictions	1.00	2.73	6.18	14.89

Note: * = Included time served in years. Active CC length excluded time served.

spread over a duration of 24.66 years. He spent some time in prison (two months). His career was more versatile than specialised, even though he committed a series of violent offences ($n = 5$), from assault at age 13 to causing actual bodily harm at age 36, and also committed a sex crime (indecent assault on a female) at age 34. He met all the criteria for being considered a high chronic offender, incurring 17 convictions by age 50. Chapter 3 presents more detailed case histories of eight high chronic offenders.

We carried out two logistic regression models predicting who were more likely to become chronic offenders or other offenders by age 50 (see Table 2.15). In both models chronic offenders were those offenders with at least 10 convictions. However, in the first model we considered 'ordinary' chronics, those who were persistent and incurred from five to nine convictions; in the second model, we designated as "other offenders", those individuals who reported from one up to nine convictions. The predictors in both models were: age of onset, age of last offence, violence, sex offence and robbery.

As would be expected, an early onset and a late age of the last offence, signifying a longer criminal career duration, were significant in both models, and their effects were strong. Interestingly, violent offending, measured by violence, sex crime and robbery, did not significantly predict chronicity independently of career length. In other words, chronic offenders are likely to be frequent and prolific rather than violent offenders. When an active offender is prolific (i.e. committing a considerable number of crimes) it is in fact quite unlikely that he would commit violence in any particular offending event in which he is involved. Violence, when detected, is more likely than other offences to be followed by incarceration (see the case history in Chapter 3 of man 941). Thus, if chronicity was significantly related to violence, it would be unlikely that chronic offenders would be as prolific as they are. On the other hand, the most plausible assumption is that what characterised chronicity is the variety of offending and high frequency, rather than specialisation in serious offending.

TABLE 2.15 Logistic regressions on chronic offenders

Model 1: predicting high chronic offenders versus ordinary chronics

Predictors	LRCS change*	B	SE(B)	Wald	β	95%CI
Age of onset	11.983**	−.435	.156	7.768	.647	.477−.879
Age of last offence	4.020*	.061	.032	3.647	1.063	.998−1.132
Constant				2.145		
Nagelkerke R-Square	0.331					

Model 2: predicting chronic offenders versus other offenders

Predictors	LRCS change*	B	SE(B)	Wald	β	95%CI
Age of onset	37.078***	−.614	.140	19.236	.541	.412−.712
Age of last offence	29.308***	.128	.028	20.801	1.137	1.076−1.201
Constant				2.145		
Nagelkerke R-Square	0.551					

Note: Model 1: Chronics = 10 plus convictions. Ordinary chronics = 5−9 convictions. Chronics are the reference group in this model. Model 2: Chronics = 10 plus convictions. Other offenders = 1−9 convictions. Chronics are the reference group in this model. Non-significant predictors excluded by the model: sex crime, violence, robbery.
*$p < .05$, **$p < .01$, ***$p < .0001$.

Another aspect in the study of criminal development that deserves attention is to explore whether offenders specialise in their offending or are more likely to be versatile. A versatile criminal career includes the commission of a variety of types of offences during the antisocial life-course.

Looking at the Criminal Justice Act 2003 (Categories of Offences) − Order 2004 two main categories could be considered: crimes against the person and crimes against property. The first includes any offence against a person such as assault, violence, sex abuse, homicide, etc. The second category includes any offence against other people's property including theft and vandalism. Research findings have shown that there is little evidence of specialisation in specific types of offences (e.g. burglary, robbery, sex crime, etc.). This suggests that there are few specialist offenders and only minor specialisation in a few selected types of crimes (e.g. car theft) superimposed on a great deal of versatility (Farrington et al., 1988b). It seems that offenders are more likely to concentrate their antisocial activity within a larger offending domain (e.g. property crimes rather than violent ones) (Cohen, 1986; Piquero et al., 2007), even though the most active and frequent offenders switch within and across categories.

In the CSDD 18 types of crimes were originally identified. A Variety Index (VI) was developed, which is a count of the number of different crime types (out of 18 different types) engaged in by the offender. Higher values indicate a higher number of different offences committed (Piquero et al., 2007). It is assumed that the VI would be influenced by both the age of onset and the duration of the criminal career: the earlier the antisocial onset the longer the career. Thus it could be stated that the higher the number of offences committed, the larger the diversity of crime types and also the higher the probability of engaging in violence in the life-course. This assumption is in contrast with the common belief that persistent and chronic offenders are more likely to be specifically involved in dangerous and violent offences, hence reporting lower values of VI and a more specialised criminal career.

Farrington (1998) studied the predictors, causes and correlates of male violence, from childhood aggression to adult male violence (Farrington, 1991b), and found that violent offences were committed at random in criminal careers. There is little specialisation in violence and the likelihood of engaging in violence is higher for frequent offenders because of their longer criminal career and the higher number of offences that they commit. Their dangerousness is because of their offending frequency and extensive quantity of offences committed, so that with the increasing numbers of crimes committed they are more likely to also accumulate a violent or a sex conviction. Analyses of the CSDD data show that violence is more rare than common, and that the offenders are less likely to specialise in violence.

We conducted a series of analyses employing the offending cut-off of five up to nine convictions to identify ordinary chronic offenders, and ten or more convictions for identifying high chronics. Twenty-eight individuals, who had between five and nine convictions, were identified. Another 28 individuals who committed between 10 and 29 offences were identified. These offenders were compared with two other groups: one-timers ($n = 49$) and below chronics (those with two to four convictions) ($n = 62$).

A series of comparisons were carried out, where means were presented for career length, age at first conviction, age at last conviction, early onset (first conviction prior to age 14), the fraction of the group that had at least one violent offence and the mean number of violent convictions per member of the group. Those offenders who met the designation for chronicity exhibited the most extreme offending across all the measures. In other words, the CSDD ordinary chronic and high chronic offenders had longer criminal careers, were more likely to exhibit an early onset of offending (before age 14), were more likely to have a later age at the last conviction, were more likely to be involved in early offending, were more likely to commit a violent offence along the course of their criminal career and accumulated many more violent convictions than the other offender groups. Following Piquero and colleagues' approach (2007), we carried out some Tukey's B post-hoc comparison tests, which indicated that the high chronic offenders were always significantly different from the other offender groups on all of the comparisons. Table 2.16(a) shows these results.

High chronic offenders were significantly more likely to be involved in a number of different crime types (having a Variety Index – VI – of 6.96) compared to

TABLE 2.16 (a) Chronic offender mean-level comparisons

Group	n	Mean career length	Mean age at first conv'n	Mean age at last conv'n	% early onset	% violent offender	Mean violent conv'ns
(1) One-timer	49	0.00	23.00	23.00	8.6	12.2	0.12
(2) Below chronic	62	7.99	18.97	26.97	28.6	32.3	0.40
(3) Ordinary chronic	28	15.02	17.93	32.96	20.0	39.3	0.50
(4) High chronic	28	21.37	13.78	35.15	42.9	50.0	1.18
F-value		52.550**	11.485*	11.339*	13.304*	9.556*	4.904*

Note: *$p < .05$; **$p < .01$.

Tukey's B Test[a]		1/2/3/4	4/2,3/1	3,4/1,2	4/2,3/1	2,3,4/1	4/1,2,3

(b) Variety Index by chronic offending comparisons

Offence type[b]	One-timers (n = 49)	Below chronics (n = 62)	Ordinary chronics (n = 28)	High chronics (n = 28)	F-values
Shoplifting	8.2%	16.1%	32.1%	53.6%	12.864*
Burglary	14.3%	19.4%	67.9%	85.7%	33.015**
Robbery	0.0%	1.6%	10.7%	17.9%	4.036*
Violence	12.2%	32.3%	39.3%	50.0%	9.556*
Variety Index[c]	1	2.32	4.43	6.96	194.514**

Notes: In this updated analysis conviction records between ages 10 and 50 were employed to examine chronicity.
One-timers = 1 offence; below chronics = 2–4 offences; ordinary chronics = 5–9 offences; high chronics = 10+ offences. Early onset = first offence between ages 10 and 14.
a Tukey's B post-hoc tests of significance should be interpreted in the following manner: 1/2/3/4 indicates that the four groups are significantly different from one another; 4/2,3/1 indicates that group 4 is significantly different from groups 1, 2 and 3, but groups 2 and 3 are not significantly different from one another.
b For the four crime types listed (shoplifting, burglary, robbery and violence), the percentage listed indicates the percentage of individuals in each of the offender groups who have committed this crime type at least once over their criminal career.
c The Variety Index is a count of the number of different crime types (out of 18 different crime types) engaged in by the offender. Higher values indicate a higher number of different crime types committed.
*$p < .05$; **$p < .01$.
Source: See Piquero et al. (2007, 130), for previous analyses with conviction records up to age 40.

ordinary chronics (4.43 different crime types) or below chronic offenders (2.32 different crime types), and one-timers (1 crime type). Looking at chronicity as a whole, ordinary chronic and high chronic offenders were also more likely to be involved in theft offences, shoplifting, burglary, robbery and violence than the other two offender groups (see Table 2.16(b)).

Two logistic regression analyses were carried out in order to test which criminal career variables were more significant in predicting violent offending (see Table 2.17). In the first model the variables were heterogeneity in offending type, measured by VI, career length, age of onset and total convictions. The aim was to explore those variables that are more focused on the type of offending. In the second model, early onset and chronicity were the other variables tested. The aim was to explore the predictability power of variables that relate to the type of offenders.

In the first model reported in Table 2.17, career length and the Variety Index were independent and significant predictors of engaging in violent offending. Unexpectedly, violent offenders have relatively late onsets. Violence emerges as a behavioural escalating occurrence within a long and heterogeneous criminal career. In the second model reported in Table 2.17, high chronic offender status, using the conservative cut-off of 10 plus offences versus the rest of the offenders (up to nine offences), emerged as a significant, robust and positive predictor of violence.

The bivariate correlation between chronicity and early onset was $-.325$, $p < .01$, and between chronicity and the Variety Index was $.616$, $p < .01$, suggesting that chronic offenders start early and engage in more versatile offending activity, which increases the likelihood of also getting involved in violence at some point in their criminal career.

TABLE 2.17 Logistic regression predicting violent offenders (Yes/No)

Model 1						
Predictors	LRCS change*	B	SE(B)	Wald	β	95%CI
Career length	22.877***	.054	.023	5.710	1.055	1.010–1.103
Variety Index (VI)	2.887*	.250	.111	5.057	1.284	1.033–1.596
Age of onset	4.749**	.059	.027	4.875	1.061	1.007–1.118
Constant			.753			
Nagelkerke R-Square	0.236					
Model 2						
Predictors	LRCS change*	B	SE(B)	Wald	β	95%CI
Chronicity	5.633*	1.014	.424	5.723	2.757	1.201–6.327
Constant			.539			
Nagelkerke R-Square			.047			

Note: *p < .05, **p < .01, ***p < .0001.

Recidivism probability

The recidivism probability is the probability of committing another offence (after each offence). Previous recidivism probability analyses showed that after the fourth offence the recidivism probabilities became stable and were likely to reflect the persisting offending pattern of a small group of offenders (Piquero et al., 2007). A similar analysis on the updated CSDD data to age 50 confirms this tendency in so far as the flattening and stability of recidivism seems to start at offence 4 and, with a slight increase, remains stable up to offence 11. Between offences 4 and 11, the average recidivism probability is 85.2 per cent. This result would perhaps be more insightful when contrasted with the probability of non-recidivism, which is on average 14.8 per cent. Table 2.18 reports the recidivism probabilities through the first 11 convictions.

From offence 12 up to offence 29 the recidivism probabilities are based on smaller and smaller numbers, and they show a slender decrease. For instance, the probability of reoffending is 79.2 per cent at offence 12 and 78.9 at offence 13.

Preventing continuity in delinquency is more possible now as scientific evidence is available about the factors that cause, maintain and aggravate criminal behaviour or protect against its beginning or continuation. The prevention, at an early stage, of delinquent development is made feasible by current knowledge about the developmental progression of a criminal career, and about the intertwined influences of childhood and adolescent factors upon adult life. One of the keys to developmental prevention (Jonkman et al., 2008) is to design programmes aimed to target, eliminate or at least control risk factors that, in the long run,

TABLE 2.18 CSDD recidivism probabilities through the first 11 convictions

Offence no.	Recidivism probabilities	
1	0.406	(167/411)
2	0.706	(118/167)
3	0.746	(88/118)
4	0.784	(69/88)
5	0.812	(56/69)
6	0.786	(44/56)
7	0.841	(37/44)
8	0.919	(34/37)
9	0.882	(30/34)
10	0.933	(28/30)
11	0.857	(24/28)

Note: Average recidivism probability between offences 4 and 11 is 85.2%.

Source: Updated from Piquero et al. (2007, 133).

increase the probability of children becoming adult criminals, and to promote and enhance those protective factors that serve as a counterbalance to compensate for more stable risk factors. Chapter 7 reviews methods of preventing and treating recidivism, and attempts to offer a more comprehensive perspective on interventions targeted at preventing personal and social maladjustment, and at stopping individuals from persisting in a life of crime and violence.

A clearer understanding of the risk mechanisms and criminogenic needs involved in criminal recidivism and chronicity could certainly have helped intervention. Chapter 3 directs the attention to the life development of eight CSDD chronic offenders and on how their criminal careers unfolded along a pattern characterised by family disruption, parental negligence, emotional solitude, social deprivation and psychological desperation.

Notes

1 Leete and Fox (1977). OPCS (1980, 1991).
2 GHQ = General Health Questionnaire (Goldberg, 1978) was designed to detect non-psychotic psychiatric illness (anxiety/depression) (see also Ch. 3 in this book). For more details, see Farrington *et al.* (1988a, 167); Farrington *et al.* (2006).
3 Some chronic offenders offend well past a fifth offence. The average time between the first and last conviction among those with five or more convictions was a little over 15 years (median = 15 years).

3
CHRONIC OFFENDERS AND THEIR LIFE STORIES

> The object of our study is a single human being.
>
> *(Stagner, 1937, p. viii)*

Farrington (1997, 363) describes how crime appears 'to be only one element of a larger syndrome of antisocial behaviour which arises in childhood and usually persists into adulthood'. Research findings are consistent in demonstrating that those individuals who are persistently involved in delinquent behaviour also exhibit difficulties in adjusting to other areas of their life that lead to familial conflicts, family disruption and marital breakdown (Lussier *et al.*, 2009; Maughan & Rutter, 2001; Theobald & Farrington, 2009, 2011, 2012), domestic violence (Piquero *et al.*, 2006), unemployment (Laub & Sampson, 2001; Moffitt *et al.*, 2002), drug abuse and heavy alcohol use (McCollister *et al.*, 2010), neuropsychological and emotional impairments (Raine, 2013), and mental problems and personality disorders (Farrington, 1991a; Freilone, 2011).

Criminal acts are committed by people who are individuals with their personal story, who have (or have not any more) at least two parents, who have been experiencing joyful and traumatic events, who have opportunities of social atonement, and who have rejected or who are not ready to follow a path of social reintegration. In many instances, their life stories remain untold in so far as they are not relevant in measuring their official criminal careers. In other words, juridical and forensic studies are more interested in focusing on the actual criminal events that take place in the offenders' antisocial pathways and the law's responses to them. Criminological psychology research attempts to complete the gap, and to build up a more comprehensive picture of those individuals who offend, and do it persistently to the extent that their criminal career is 'chronic', i.e. pervasive and overwhelming. What appears to be relevant is often what is underneath the external and outer behaviour: we know that it is there even if it is not directly visible. The aim is to see, from a longitudinal perspective, those factors and life events that might have contributed to how the life of these chronic offenders has progressed and evolved around a criminogenic core.

If the aim of the analysis were to look at offending as a sequence of criminal acts, then it would have been sufficient to simply look at what the person did, when, in which temporal order and at the official disciplinary or retributive responses they received from the law and criminal justice system. But, if the aim of research is to understand the evolution and transformation of criminal careers, and especially to understand those criminogenic needs that can be targeted to reduce the likelihood to relapse again in crime, then the analysis should go beyond the criminal conduct *per se*, and see who the person is, and how they function socially and psychologically, in order to plan preventive intervention and individualised treatment. Criminogenic needs constitute the psychological and dynamic ingredients of criminal behaviour, and antisocial maladjustment. As Latessa and Lowenkamp (2005) put it, they are crime-producing factors that are strongly correlated with risk, but at the same time they can be modified and reduced in response to adequate treatment and intervention timing (see also Chapters 6 and 7).

> We should enter the violent person's subjective world, not just [. . .] to offer treatment, but to anticipate the nature of the risks they embody both to themselves and to society. To explain is not to exculpate, but understanding is the first step in the prevention of violence.
>
> *(Fonagy, 2003, 191)*

The men involved in the CSDD are individuals who have embarked on a life of crime following different antisocial pathways. Their life stories are unique in so far as they express individual differences and specific criminogenic needs. Their criminal careers are similar to those of many other offenders who have an early antisocial onset, and who have continued offending along their life-course. What seems to emerge as remarkable is that their delinquent development did not appear in a psychological or familial vacuum, but it is intertwined with the social and existential milieu in which they were brought up, and within a system of rules that guides and governs human behaviour and interpersonal interactions.

The aim of this chapter is to focus on the case histories of a sample of eight CSDD chronic offenders, who had an active and prolific criminal career, marked by at least 15 convictions. The reason for focusing attention on chronic offenders lies in the interest of examining those criminogenic processes that sustain and reinforce offending, over and above the evidence of the accumulation of loss, failure and disappointment that a life in crime is destined to have. The case histories are based on information in the files which may in some cases be based on opinion rather than fact.

Each case will be introduced, and the description of their criminal careers will follow the methodological pattern used in the CSDD. The information about the lives of these chronic offenders, as for every CSDD man, was collected at different times of their life development. For instance, information that included childhood data, when the boys were aged 8–10, was collected in 1961–4, while information that related to their teenage years (12–14) was collected in 1965–8. The males were interviewed at age 16 in 1969–70, at age 18 in 1971–3, at age 21 in 1974–6, at age 32 in 1984–6, and at age 48 in 2000–4. The interviews at ages 32 and 48 were approved by the Institute of Psychiatry Ethics Committee.

The boy's parents, who were mostly born in the 1920s, were interviewed by psychiatric social workers about once a year from when the boy was 8 until he was 14–15. The teachers filled in questionnaires about the boys at ages 8, 10, 12 and 14, and the boys were rated by their peers at ages 8 and 10. Along with all the other information gathered since age 8–10 from their parents, teachers, peers, institutional and criminal records, each man was interviewed at various stages. As indicated in Chapter 2 of this book, and described in previous work (Farrington, 2003; Piquero et al., 2007; West & Farrington, 1973, 1977), these males were interviewed nine times, at ages 8, 10, 14, 16, 18, 21, 25, 32 and 48. At all ages, with the exception of ages 21 and 25, the aim was to interview all the males who were still alive. Up to age 56, 31 males were known to have died, of whom 23 had been convicted.

It was always possible to interview a high proportion of those still alive: 405 (99 per cent) at age 14, 397 (97 per cent) at age 16, 389 (95 per cent) at age 18, 378 (94 per cent) at age 32, and 365 (93 per cent) at age 48. By age 48, 17 males had died, 5 could not be traced, and 24 refused, which meant that 365 out of 394 who were alive were interviewed. At age 21, the aim was to interview all the convicted males and an equal number of randomly chosen unconvicted males, and 218 of the 241 target males (90 per cent) were interviewed. At age 25, only 85 males were interviewed.

In adulthood, at ages 32 and 48, their partners or wives were also interviewed. Most of these men participated with interest and collaborated readily with the interviews. They felt special because they knew that we were following up all the boys in their school class. In those cases in which some refused to be involved again in an interview, their partners or family members offered their collaboration or gave some useful information.

Apart from the data gathered through the social and medical interviews, and the SCID-II screening questionnaire for assessing the ten DSM personality disorders, the health and clinical dimensions of these chronic offenders were assessed by using CAGE, GHQ and PCL:SV.

The *CAGE questionnaire* (Mayfield et al., 1974) is a combination of four questions that can be used for the screening of individuals for alcoholism. A total of two or more positive answers indicates a positive history of alcoholism or problem drinking. Farrington and colleagues (2006) considered that the level of a drinking history could be seen as high when at least three of the four criteria were met:

1. Have you ever felt annoyed by criticism of your drinking?
2. Have you ever had guilty feelings about drinking?
3. Have you ever started off the day with a drink?
4. Have you ever thought you should cut down on drinking?

The *General Health Questionnaire* (GHQ) (Goldberg, 1978) was developed in England as a screening instrument to identify psychological distress in adults in primary care settings, and to detect non-psychotic psychiatric illness (anxiety/depression): a satisfactory level of mental health was, in the CSDD, considered equivalent to a score of 4 or less. The CAGE and GHQ were administered in the CSDD at ages 32 and 48.

The *Psychopathy Checklist: Screening Version* (PCL:SV) (Hart et al., 1995) was used when the CSDD males were aged 48. The scores on the 12-item PCL-SV ranged from 0 to 17 (out of a possible maximum of 24) (see Chapter 5). Most chronic offenders involved in this study (see Chapter 2) scored 10 or more on the PCL:SV (Farrington, 2007b). Factor I of the PCL:SV measures affective/interpersonal personality problems, while Factor II measures an irresponsible/antisocial life style.

As described in Chapter 2, the criminal career records of the eight chronic offenders were based on the CRO/NIS data from 1979 to 1994, and on PNC data from 1995. The last search of the PNC was completed in March 2011, taking the criminal records up to age 56. The chronic criminal careers analysed in this chapter include these updated official records.

The minimum age of criminal responsibility in England and Wales is 10. The Criminal Record Office contained records of all relatively serious offences committed in Great Britain and Ireland and also acted as a repository for records of minor juvenile offences committed in London. Convictions in the CSDD were only counted if they were for *standard list* (*more serious*) offences (Farrington et al., 2013). Minor crimes such as traffic infractions and simple drunkenness were excluded from the analysis. The most common offences included were thefts, burglaries and unauthorised takings of vehicles, although there were also quite a few offences of violence, vandalism, fraud and drug abuse (see Chapter 2). There were 18 categories of offences (see Table 2.4). Some serious motoring offences, such as driving while disqualified, were included in the records but were not included in the analyses in Chapter 2.

Up to age 56, 27 males had 11 or more convictions (including motoring offences), and 15 of these had 15 or more convictions. Of those with 15 or more convictions, eight had an official criminal career lasting at least 30 years between the first and the last conviction. These are the eight cases that are described in this chapter. With 15 or more convictions and a criminal career lasting at least 30 years, they are the most chronic official offenders in this sample. All of these eight men were White and of British or Irish origin.

Could these men have become prosocial persons rather than chronic offenders?

This is a question that many professionals are often asked to answer, and which touches upon the core issue of primary prevention. Looking back at the lives of these chronic offenders everything appears to have fallen into a systematic pattern in which one event seems almost inevitably the precursor of another one, as in a chain that could not resolve itself in something other than offending, and offending persistently. However, research evidence has shown that when looking forward, it is difficult, if not impossible, to establish with a total degree of accuracy what is going to happen or what that person will become.

How early can future criminal behaviour be predicted?

Such a question attracts the attention of researchers because it challenges the idea of the infallible prediction of human behaviour. As will be argued later (Chapter 4), the accuracy of any prediction is never perfect, and 'black swans' (Taleb, 2007) are a reminder of those extraordinary events that can redirect or change the course of human decisions, choices and behaviour.

> You may have heard the world is made up of atoms and molecules, but it's really made up of stories. When you sit with an individual that's been here, you can give quantitative data a qualitative overlay.
> *(William Turner[1])*

The stories that follow describe the development of criminal careers and their transformation over time. They provide an understanding of those factors, criminogenic needs and risk processes that seem to have played a significant role in the onset and maintenance of the offending pattern.

Criminal behaviour does not occur in a social and legal vacuum, so psychological, relational, professional and social functioning gathers significance within a world in which a person relates to others and interacts with them. Therefore, social malfunctioning takes many forms, lasts for long or short periods, impacts at various levels and with diverse degrees of intensity depending on the person, on their extent of vulnerability, their resilience and, at the same time, it requires differentiated forms of intervention to respond to specific circumstances and individual differences.

The chronic offenders described below provide a picture of the complexity of variables involved in a persistent criminal career, and feature the uniqueness of each case history, tainted by disappointments, emotional rejection, ambivalent and insecure parental attachment, solitude and aggressiveness. Many of the risk factors and processes were common to many other offenders, but what was unique is how these men were affected by these factors, and how entangled into a criminogenic net they were, to make it so difficult for them not to follow what appeared to be their preordained pathway.

In each of the cases examined, offending seems the least problematic aspect of their existence, despite being the most evident, and it is perhaps the feature that is easiest to tackle.

There is substantial clinical evidence to suggest that recovering from chronic experiences of marginalisation, family disruption, abusive parenting and overwhelming material poverty, along with a life emotionally and intellectually impoverished, takes a life time of intense effort, and, in some extreme cases, it becomes almost impossible to repair the damage. Furthermore, the process of recovering cannot happen suddenly or spontaneously; it is more likely to take place if the person is helped to gain some mastery and control over their own life.

What represents an impediment to recovery is a pervasive suffering, a rooted sense of powerlessness and a fatalistic sense of unchangeability. It is by modifying mental states and building up a secure and stable structure to contain the emotional and behavioural consequences of the stress, strain and despair aroused by life events that chronic and persistent offenders could start a process of change in their self-perceptions and relationships that encourage behavioural and social change.

Case 590 – Jordan

Jordan[2] was born in 1953. His parents had five children. The family accommodation consisted of a large rambling maisonette in a pub, which was difficult to keep clean, and especially to live in also because of the deteriorated interiors.

Jordan's mother

Jordan's biological mother came from the North of England; she was the oldest of five children, but was brought up by her paternal aunt from age 5 until age 16, apparently because her mother did not want her. As far as she knew, no mental or physical illnesses were present in her family. She was an intelligent and nice-looking woman, poised and friendly, easy to interview, not at all defensive and quite willing to help with the study, and apparently glad to discuss her marriage and her children. She attended a technical college, passing commercial typing and shorthand examinations. She expressed herself well, had a good vocabulary, and was alert and quick to see a point.

She did not know her younger brothers, having drifted apart from them. Apparently, they did not approve of her divorce from her first husband (Jordan's father). The problem of Jordan's parents' separation emerged as quite as a surprise. Jordan's mother left for a few weeks, and having such a difficult relationship with her husband, decided to make the separation permanent. She worked with her previous husband in the pub, and she held some nice memories of him. Jordan's parents were very unhappy in their relationship, staying together for ten years mainly because of the children. Jordan's mother did not remember giving her children any formal and complete explanation of why she left, and she suggested that she had not seen any repercussions from her disappearance in her children. On the other hand, the father was always present and looked after the children on his own, until he got married again one year later. In fact both parents remarried a brother and a sister, so they shared the same in-laws.

Jordan's biological mother visited the children whenever she could. But after the divorce Jordan and his siblings saw their biological mother only occasionally, even though they received cards and some money at Christmas. When she was interviewed, the mother was quite cooperative and she mentioned that to have the children with her would be at that moment too much of a strain. She did not deny the possibility in the future of having them with her, but it never happened. She had a new baby girl with her second husband, a veterinary surgeon, and lived in a pleasant middle-class home, with plenty of books around, and in a moderate state of comfort. She was happy with her new life, though she missed her children. She remembered Jordan as a normal and thriving little boy, but given her new life it was perhaps uncomfortable for her to go further down her family memory lane.

Jordan's father

Jordan's father, who had been convicted, was the manager of a busy pub and off licence. He was a burly, rather fat, tense man, quite good, but tired-looking. He was willing to cooperate in the study, but at the first meeting it was difficult for the psychiatric social worker to get much information from him because he was keener to talk about his overall philosophy of life, his politics, his attitude to child-rearing, and things in general, rather than responding to specific questions related to the study. He was reticent to speak about his upbringing. He was the third of five siblings (having one brother and three sisters); his parents separated and he and two of his siblings were admitted to a home, where he stayed until age 14. During that time his mother visited him, despite her poor health, but he did not see much of his father. Despite this, he held some happy memories of his father as a quite kind man who was very busy working at a cinema.

Jordan's father was very unhappy at school, did not do well and frequently truanted. He thought that schooling was too strict and he was constantly beaten. However, he still believed in corporal punishment, and thought that schools were not strict enough nowadays. No particular illnesses in the family were documented. However, it emerged that his mother was quite an abusive and persecutory woman, obsessed mainly with sex and with her own health: she was always cleaning up, sometimes in the middle of the night. He thought of his mother as a sort of neurotic person, and described his father as disgruntled, always worrying about his wife's health. Jordan's father lived for a while with step-parents.

Jordan's biological parents divorced when he was aged 5, after a year of separation, and the children's custody was given to the father. The father said that to be left alone to look after his children was not too difficult as he could work from home, where he had the pub and the off licence business. He described his daily routine as intense, and apparently he never went to bed before 3 a.m., after he had bathed and fed the children, did the washing up, the ironing and all the house chores. He had regrets about not having had enough time with the children.

Jordan's father got married again after the divorce, and seemed very happy in his second marriage; he admitted that his second wife had been a great support. His new wife had become a good stepmother to the children and they were very fond of her, and paid attention to what she said. The climate in the family was quite pleasant; neither father nor stepmother was punitive, and they were reasonably firm, though having so much to do with the pub activity it was very difficult for them to be consistent, calm and coherent in their behaviour.

Jordan's stepmother

Jordan's stepmother, who actually was a real acting mother for him and his siblings, remembered her childhood as a quite happy one, and appeared contented about her present life. Her parents were in good physical and mental health. She was a very nice, vivacious and alert young woman, most cooperative and friendly. She was first interviewed when Jordan was 9 years old, and she was expecting a baby at the end of that year, and was very happy about this.

Jordan's siblings

Jordan had an older sister called Vera, who lived away in hospital because she was epileptic and seriously mentally disabled, and, although she could be looked after as an outpatient, Jordan's father thought that it was better for the whole family to leave Vera in the care of the hospital. Jordan had also another older sister Jenny. He had a paternal half-brother Leon and a half-sister Wilma, and also a maternal half-sister Stephanie. Unfortunately no specific information was available about his siblings. In one of the last interviews, Jordan mentioned that he did not keep in touch with any of them, apart from Leon, but their contacts were seldom and by letters. The general comments by Jordan's father and stepmother about their children were positive and they did not point to any particular problem. Their children were attending school regularly, with Jenny showing a positive attitude in education, while Jordan was a little bit too afraid to do well and always interested in the marks he received. The performance anxiety seemed to be a constant problem for Jordan during his school years, affecting his self-esteem and trust in his own abilities. Jordan's parents' only concern was related to the area they lived in, which was not, in their opinion, always safe, and with Jenny becoming interested in boys they were particularly worried about who she started to go out with. This was the main reason why they wanted to move.

Jordan: childhood

Jordan's behaviour in childhood was not particularly problematic, and his level of antisociality at age 10 was low, but in adolescence, at around age 14, it started to be evidently high. The disciplinary climate in his family was quite unstable; there was an authoritarian attitude towards children's education, mixed with ambivalent messages. Nonetheless, the father was quite involved in Jordan's leisure activities, at least when his job allowed him to spare some time to stay with his family.

Jordan was a boy who got on with everyone, and mixed well with adults too. Jordan's father described him as a bit on the callous side and that he never really noticed how people felt. The father thought that Jordan was not sensitive, and that he took everything in a 'matter of fact' way. His stepmother described Jordan as easy to handle, and although he did as he was told, he had his 'own moments'. Jordan did not show much affection himself, but he liked a good deal of it shown to him. Jordan in fact liked to be made a big fuss of, and his stepmother supposed that this was to make up for what he had lost in his emotional and familial upbringing. When Jordan was slightly unwell or hurt he needed a great deal of attention from his parents. The sudden separation from his biological mother may have been very traumatic for Jordan, as it occurred without anticipation and preparation for the physical and emotional detachment which suddenly overran his life.

Jordan's school reports when he was 9 years old suggested that his English was good and quite neat, and that his imaginative work and reading were good too. He was also good at history, geography and natural history. In arithmetic, he was capable even though occasionally careless. He was described as a helpful and cheerful member of the class, but he needed to concentrate a little harder.

Jordan: adolescence

In adolescence, both biological parents thought that Jordan was very sensible, though a matter-of-fact boy, and independent. Jordan became disinterested in school work, and his school reports were poor. He seemed unable to sustain effort and this was evident in his behaviour, attitude and his readiness to give up his paper round. The complaints from school were that Jordan tended to show off, and that he wanted to impress other boys. This was Jordan's method of courting popularity. He truanted from school by forging a note from his parents: this happened at least once and possibly three times. His parents asked the school to keep an eye on this matter. Even when recognising the seriousness of the problem it was as though his father and stepmother (who from now on will be called the parents) delegated the disciplinary role to the school. This attempt to put on the school the responsibility of checking and controlling Jordan's behaviour might have contributed to creating more opportunity for ambivalent messages and reactions.

One of Jordan's father's difficulties seemed to have been in deciding where to set limits, or perhaps how far and at what point he should intervene. It was as if the father hoped that the school would play a more authoritarian role, perhaps even fulfil this function for him, so he was disappointed that in his view he received so little support on this aspect of Jordan's education. Jordan's father was very preoccupied and too distracted with the practical problems of his job and accommodation to have time to fix another appointment to meet for other CSDD interviews. There was no further contact between Jordan and his natural mother.

It was difficult to assess the relationship that Jordan had with his father, but given the demands and pressure that the job put on the father, the time that the father could spend at home and with Jordan was minimal. The stepmother, on the other hand, kept a fairly sharp eye on Jordan's development. Smartness, tidiness and outward appearances were generally important to her, but she was not rated by the psychiatric social worker as a controlling woman. She may have felt rather undervalued by Jordan, but still she tried to make allowances for him.

When Jordan was 14, both parents, but particularly Jordan's father, expressed concern about Jordan. At this point Jordan did not have any idea of what he wanted to do with himself or his life. His father clearly felt that Jordan's whole attitude to life was casual in the extreme and he was concerned about the boy's future. His parents thought that moving home could lead to finally separating Jordan from the companions who had a bad influence on him, but, in fact, the problems with Jordan tended to increase immediately after the move. The parents complained about his rebellious behaviour, and his refusal to be back home at the time they considered reasonable, i.e. 10.30 p.m. They complained too of Jordan's moodiness, his laziness and swings of behaviour, which made him at some times relatively mature and responsible, and at other times extremely childish, for example insisting on playing with his young sibling's toys and reading their comics, and trying to join in their games, and only succeeding in provoking them. Furthermore, both at home and at school, his behaviour was marked by aimlessness, even more than in previous years. The school report emphasised a totally disinterested attitude in all aspects of school activities. According to his teachers and mother, Jordan often lied to hide or justify his behaviour.

Jordan went out frequently, going out every day with anyone who called, and was involved with delinquent friends. He also held an anti-police attitude. Jordan became a quite aggressive adolescent, often involved in daring or risk-taking activities, and self-reported (at ages 14 and 16) high levels of involvement in delinquency. He also manifested some concentration problems. When Jordan was 14, he went before the juvenile court charged with being in charge of a motor scooter without having a licence. It had been stolen and hidden by a friend who was already on probation but Jordan was not involved in the actual theft.

Jordan was given a conditional discharge. His father and stepmother had been concerned with Jordan's behaviour for some time, but this event seemed to be, in their view, the only brush with the law. His parents' reaction to Jordan's court appearance was to encourage him to find other friends. However, they were a bit vague about his friends, in so far as they did not seem to know much about them, apart from the fact that they were not a positive influence on their son. Nevertheless, they had not forbidden him to see these boys, or set up plans to divert Jordan's attention and interests towards other boys, or even made some attempt to keep a close check on his activities.

Jordan left school rather precipitously when he was 15. At that time, the minimum school leaving age was 15. This outcome seemed to reflect confusion and lack of communication. The parents had originally signed for Jordan to remain in school until age 16 and seemed rather prepared to be firm on this, despite very bad school reports and the boy's own eagerness to leave.

After Jordan left school, he had various short-term employments until he was 18. His work history was confused and it was difficult to reconstruct it in a logical and chronological order. He was an office boy, then worked in quality control for an import food company, for which he did some training in sampling the look, taste and smell of food; rewiring and splicing films at a cinema centre; and packing and loading in a furniture removal shop. He was a pump attendant in a garage; and a switch-board operator in a solicitor's office. At times, he also worked all day on a Saturday in a second-hand furniture shop. Jordan expected to become a publican like his father. According to his parents, the general situation with Jordan had improved, especially since he applied for a job as a clerk for a computer firm, in which there was scope for future prospects.

He seemed to have settled down well, and in some ways his parents felt that he was more adult and more balanced in his behaviour since he left school. He had become more careful about his appearance and seemed prepared to work overtime and be taking a fair amount of interest in the job generally. His stepmother felt that, simply being fully occupied, there was much less likelihood of him being drawn into trouble. Jordan appeared a fairly self-contained boy; he had a number of friends but no particular interests or pursuits. He was happy to spend evenings watching television, and Sunday afternoon at the cinema.

Up to age 19, Jordan was a soldier in the Army, but he described this experience as terrible, and after the first year (when he was posted in Cyprus, Gibraltar, Morocco and Malta), the second year was hell. He was based in England, but spent six months in Ireland. He was then dishonourably discharged because of possessing and supplying drugs.

Jordan: young adulthood

At age 19, his level of antisociality continued to be high. Jordan was a frequent consumer of cannabis and other drugs, and often drove after drinking. He held an anti-establishment attitude, was an active football hooligan and had some gambling problems. Jordan was a quite impulsive person, and this might have influenced his involvement in antisocial activities, which were quite heterogeneous and constituted a pattern of continuity throughout his adult life-course. His self-reported delinquency and violence continued to be high at age 19.

Jordan was interviewed at age 19. His general health was good. Even though he already realised that smoking had affected his health, he smoked about 105 cigarettes per week, and had started smoking regularly at age 16. He had some uneasiness with his sleep, and he recollected that, even when he was younger, at times, he woke up in the night and could not get back to sleep again quickly. When aged 16, he had a tonsillectomy and stayed at home for three weeks; he also had a broken arm, and at age 18 had a broken bone in his right hand because of his involvement in a fight. In his spare time, Jordan enjoyed football and going to nightclubs.

Jordan recounted his antisocial experiences, which included a great deal of stealing, especially cars. He also did shoplifting, but he had not done it in the last couple of years. He had many casual girlfriends, and the longest length of time he had gone out with a girl was six months. Jordan had his first sexual intercourse at age 16. One of his girlfriends got pregnant but Jordan disclosed that she married someone else. He knew that the child was his because before she went to Ireland she was living just at the back of the camp where he was based. He had been going out with her for some months, while her boyfriend was in Ireland. When her husband-to-be came back, they got married; she had the baby about seven months after.

During the interview, it seemed that Jordan used the interviewer as an audience to vent all his anxiety over his experience in Ireland. His responses to various parts of the interview schedule were coloured by this experience; it seemed that he wanted to relate everything to that: drug taking, sex, family, fighting and crime.

When Jordan was 21, he was again interviewed. At this stage, he was officially unemployed, and his job pattern was quite unstable. He had left his job as a barman in the family's pub, where he had worked for almost one year, after a disagreement with his father. He was then employed as a caretaker and handyman, but he left this job because of poor attendance. He then started to work as a roofer's labourer.

Jordan recounted his family situation and his parents' separation at length. He had a good relationship with his stepmother, whom he treated as his natural mother; she was very young, but 'I'd call her my right mum'.

Jordan left home at age 21 to go to live with his girlfriend who became pregnant but he did not use the money his father gave to him to organise an abortion. He continued to smoke almost compulsively and drank quite heavily. He went out every single evening in the week, and he had a casual and promiscuous sexual life. In other words, he admitted to not having changed his social habits despite living with his girlfriend. He got into numerous fights, two of which were particularly vicious because someone was seriously hurt; no weapon was used, just fists. It seemed that he was more involved in antisocial activities in early adulthood than before.

In the previous interviews, Jordan recounted his convictions, aggrandising them with his fantasy. At age 21, it seemed that Jordan was more genuine in expressing his feelings and sharing information about his life. The impression he gave to the interviewer was of a cooperative and truthful person, with the tendency to exaggerate especially about his fights. He looked much older than his age. He was a single man living with his common-law wife, with whom he had a child. His relationship with his partner was tumultuous, and some indication of this emerged from the fact that he often used physical violence against her. He separated from her for about eight months, and he then returned home because the child had difficulties in accepting Jordan's absence. However he remained with them for only three weeks, leaving again after a serious row with his partner.

Jordan: adulthood

When Jordan was 26 years old, he was reinterviewed. He was working for a roofing and tiling firm, and was happy with it. At this time, Jordan was separated from his previous partner, who had also another child from her previous relationship. The cause of their separation was the constant and violent rows. The last time together involved some physical contact, when her partner stubbed a cigarette in his face.

Jordan's life style continued to be casual and irresponsible. He still went out every night of the week, either to the pub, a karate club, playing football or parties. He consumed large amounts of alcohol and cannabis, and sometimes used cocaine. He could not be in a stable relationship with a particular woman. His involvement in fights was always central in the description of his social activities. He had 17 fights in the previous two years, five of which were very vicious to the extent that two of his opponents, as Jordan described them, were hospitalised.

The impression Jordan gave to the interviewer was of a total hedonist, who drank heavily, regularly took drugs, was sexually promiscuous and did whatever suited him. Jordan had a child. He went to see the child just when he felt like it and he had regularly broken arrangements to take the child out. He paid his ex-cohabitee a small amount of money per week, even though he earned enough to give more. Jordan lived with two mates with whom he did drug dealing, and shared the same life style, and disliked responsibilities. They were regularly getting into trouble; mainly fights and drug dealing. Jordan's frequent activity, that he called 'walk-ins', involved entering open doors mainly of private residences and stealing whatever was at hand, and this was a recurrent enjoyment for him. He had a great collection of what he called 'trophies' and he was very proud of showing them to any audience.

In adulthood, his aggressiveness and antisociality levels, measured at age 32, were still high, as was his consumption of cannabis. Jordan reported a high level of anxiety and depression as measured by the General Health questionnaire. His drinking habits were similar to previous years, and he admitted that he drank a lot just to be social, and he did not think that he should cut down on his drinking. He continued to use large amounts of drugs.

Jordan was reinterviewed when he was 32. He was living in a flat that he rented through a housing association; he was not particularly satisfied with it because of the noise around and the neighbours. By this stage, Jordan had three daughters from his previous marriage who were living elsewhere. Jordan lived in the flat with his second wife, and they had a daughter together. Jordan described his relationship with his second wife in positive terms, despite the episodes of physical violence that broke the quality of their relationship. When asked whether they would still be together in five years' time, he responded that he did not know that, but he knew that they would always remain friends. He explained that they both came from split families, and this might have influenced the quality of their own marriage in the long term.

When Jordan was aged 48, he was interviewed again, in his one-bedroom flat. By this time he had separated from his second wife. Jordan described his childhood as happy, growing up in a strict but fair family atmosphere. He did not keep in touch with his two older sisters and his half-sister, but he kept in contact with his half-brother by writing to him.

The flat was rented from the local authority; it was not a very large place, but just about right in space. There were some problems with this accommodation due to the fact that, in the previous year, they had a fire, and the place was still dirty, neglected, poorly furnished, and lacking heating. Jordan was again single, after two marriages that did not work, and he lived in the flat on his own. He was unemployed when the interview took place. His previous job was in building, putting up steel frames. He claimed benefits and job seeker's allowance during the whole unemployment period.

His children, four daughters, lived somewhere else with his previous wives, and he never had any contact with at least two of them. Moreover, Jordan was not able to give specific information about his children, about whether they had any particular problems or difficulties or needs. He clearly had little contact with them.

Jordan was unusual in terms of how badly his life had turned out. He described his life as a disaster: he had a nervous breakdown after he accidentally shot a fellow soldier when he was in the Army. Jordan had a major car crash and a severe beating by 'squaddies', and his face was haggard and broken. In spite of his unhappy life, Jordan was an intelligent and likeable person, which made his circumstances even more dramatic, because it was hard to know why his life had turned out the way it did.

Jordan had been a heroin addict for 20 years, and had been in and out of court and prison almost all his life. He was now clear in admitting that he had had a drug addiction for a very long time, and that he had suffered from four overdoses. However, Jordan described his general health as satisfactory. He was unemployed and stated that he lived on benefits, but he had no explanation about how he could afford his drugs. He was admitted to a detox/rehabilitation clinic, and met the counsellor every week. The treatment had not been very successful. Jordan wanted to start a new life, and he mentioned that he would be going into rehabilitation again soon. He wanted to get off heroin but, given his previous failures in this matter, it would be very unlikely that he could succeed without changing his attitude and life style.

The PCL:SV was administered to him; his level of psychopathy was 15, with 5 points weighted on Factor I (affective/interpersonal) and 10 on Factor II (irresponsible/antisocial life style). This is a very high psychopathy score.

Jordan's level of life failure was quite high. His criminal career started when he was aged 13, and lasted until he was almost 47 years old. His first offence was taking and driving away a motor vehicle, in which three other co-offenders were involved. The length of his criminal career was 33 years, of which over five years was spent in prison. He was convicted for 24 offences, and his *index variety of offences* was 10, indicating that he committed 10 different types of offences out of 18, one of which was violent. Only one of these 24 offences was a serious motoring offence. His most serious appearances were for armed robbery, though he tried to play down his role in it, and antique theft. He frequently appeared in court for cannabis possession. Jordan died at age 53 from heroin abuse.

Case 301 – Callum

Callum was born in 1953. His family was composed of his mother and father and three children. Callum was the middle one; he had two sisters. Both parents were child-centred and warmhearted. The children did not show any particular difficulties or problems. An important aspect of the family life that emerged as relevant for the way Callum reacted to events and behaved in the years to come was that there was very inconsistent discipline at home: at sometimes an overindulging and overprotective atmosphere and at other times a threatening and punitive one. There was no doubt that the children often struggled between the different standards of their parents. The mother thought that the father was erratic, harsh and also spoiling. The father thought that the mother was for a stricter life, and less anxious than him, so that at times she told him not to worry. They disagreed over the children, but in the end they sorted things out together. The parents wanted a great deal of reassurance, especially the father who was very concerned about the rise in delinquency, and was anxious to show his children off, and to be reassured by the psychiatric social worker that his children were lovely.

In 1962, they lived in a fully equipped three-bedroom flat in a working-class area. The flat was nicely decorated, and material standards were excellent, with plentiful toys, TV and radio, and a record player, but there was a certain amount of anxiety, and a parental attitude inclined to philosophizing about the rights and wrongs of life. Callum's parents complained that living in a flat was the worst evil for the children. They had neighbours who complained about the noise and who were unsociable. The family felt constricted and restricted in space, and they were very anxious to move out and to have a garden and more space.

Callum's mother

Callum's mother, who had been convicted, was a very pleasant woman, much more intelligent and down to earth than her husband. She did not know her parents well because at age 6 she had been evacuated with her sister to the country, first to a lady's house, and then to a widow's house where she was happy and stayed until she was 13. She said she had learned a lot about good manners while in service. She described her family as very ordinary and rough, and the climate in her family as unhappy. Her parents never came to visit her while she was evacuated. She left school at 14, and became a waitress. The minimum school leaving age was 14 for the parents' generation. Then she worked as a packer and supervisor and stayed in this job until her marriage when she was 18. She was quite happy to be a wife and a mother. She seemed very fond of her children, and tried to offer them a less restrictive way of life than their father did.

Callum's mother often acted as a stabilizer to any excesses that the father indulged in. After some very stressful periods, when the marriage was so bad that the mother wanted to leave, her husband straightened himself out a little through the acquisition of a paper stand which, in addition to a job in the market, permitted the family to have some financial stability in the short term. Material standards were excellent, the home was comfortable and well equipped, with a new cocktail bar and new carpets, and it was newly decorated. However, the marriage was full of stress and the mother at times had thoughts of leaving her husband, who she described as domineering, and also abusive and violent when drunk. She thought that he was suffering from inferiority feelings partly because of his childhood poverty and his short height. In 1963, she said that her husband was as bad as ever and that she suggested he should see a psychiatrist, but he refused this idea completely. She left him and the children in 1963.

Callum's father

Callum's father, who had been convicted, was too anxious to do the right thing for his children. He came from a very poor East End working-class family of 20 children (though four died at birth). They knew a lot about hardship, but later they managed to have their own house, with a yard and their own chickens. Despite poverty, there was a strong familial bond, and a friendly neighbourhood feeling. Callum's father was very attached to his mother, and he mentioned that when young he had an inferiority complex on account of his short height and small size. He recounted how frightening it was for him when he was in the Army. There was an occasion when he had a 24-hour pass to go to West England; he escaped into London. He was absent without leave for two days. He was court-marshalled and finally discharged on medical grounds. He was almost illiterate and felt rather inferior about it. His wife was a quite good-looking woman, and he felt very proud about her.

Callum's father was a porter in a market, and his income fluctuated since the job was somewhat seasonal. His wife helped him, but since the birth of their young daughter, she decided that having regular house management was better than having a higher income. According to Callum's mother, his father was a compulsive worrier, and every little thing that he took up and worried over made him blow up into a tremendous outburst of emotions. He could be very obsessional about small matters, and could get irritable about them to the extent that it was difficult for him to control himself. He had a very sociable character but could be very critical of everyone else, and was very strict with the children, giving long lectures to them. The father was very concerned about the children's education and obsessed about appearances to the extent that he was terrified of what people might think of him as a husband and as a father. He was capable of outbursts of violent temper.

The father's hyper-talkativeness and his attitude were sometimes felt to be oppressive by the children, especially by Callum who, in the early interviews, when he was 9, 10 and 11 years old, was quite reticent about speaking in front of his father. Nevertheless the presence of the father was important for the children, and even if their mother was absent, the family (father and children) were close to each other. In 1964 the father was terribly distressed and trying to keep his family together after his wife left. Some arrangements to look after the children were made with the help of friends and neighbours, so that not everything was left to the eldest daughter. However, he suffered from severe depression and was in hospital for a time. The children were taken into care, but as soon as he could the father managed to get them back, at least during the weekends.

Callum's siblings

Sarah was Callum's older sister. She was a very pretty child, not shy, very well mannered, and she related well to other people. She was a very patient and calm child, and she could sit for hours doing needlework. She used to cling to her mother, but she was very helpful around the house. She could do anything for Callum, and she even helped him to get his clothes ready. When her younger sister was born, she got depressed and she did not want to do anything anymore. Nevertheless, she managed to get over that and went back to her helpful and peaceful mood again. However, when she was 11 years old, she became a problematic child. She started biting her nails and being very nervous, taking everything very seriously. She became worried and frightened of her father, and was going often to a friend's house to stay because the atmosphere there was easy and free, and she enjoyed herself more. Her mother started to become very anxious about Sarah when she wanted to go out frequently and to go clubbing.

After her parents' separation, Sarah felt the responsibility of looking after the house and family, so as to allow her father to get some more work and earn more money, which the family needed. The worry and the climate of preoccupation in the house was making the father ill and when he got into a very serious mental state Sarah decided that it was better to stay at home. She was an excellent manager and everything in the maisonette was in perfect order. She left school when she was 16, admitting that she did not have any career ambition. She investigated the possibility of further education classes, and doing an evening course in shorthand and typing. She did not envisage going out to work for a number of years but wanted to be qualified. Wanda was the youngest daughter, and she was mostly looked after by her older sister.

Callum: childhood

Callum showed no sign of any particular disturbance, did not have particular fears, and was not moody. However, he often found himself wandering around for hours, alone or with other boys. Once, when he was aged 7 he kept on walking with other boys until they were found lost in the opposite part of the city. He was described as a boy who did not tell deliberate lies, and he did not do something he kept quiet about, and he said everything to his father. At age 9, he was described by his parents as having a quick temper, and having an answer for everything, but was never openly defiant, and yet turned a deaf ear when called upon to take responsibility for things done or not done. Some indicators of antisociality and daring were manifest from an early age. Callum showed a high level of neuroticism at age 10, he did not like to be made fun of, and he could not take a joke, he had a quick temper, but without completely losing control.

Callum liked school for his friends but not for learning. He liked to do things on his own, but needed pushing over routine work. He had some reading problems, and his parents were very concerned about them, and the mother did a lot to help Callum learn how to spell. Callum's father was very concerned about his son's negligence towards school, learning and homework. He tried to explain to Callum that education and learning were necessary to have a quality life, but Callum used to answer to this remark as follows: 'Dad, I'm stupid, like you.' The father felt very distraught about it because he was convinced that Callum was wasting all his opportunities. The father was in fact working hard at the market stall in order to offer his children a better life than the one he had himself.

Callum's parents asked, several times, for some support from the headmaster; they felt that they did not get enough support. Both parents, especially the father, who was the more anxious of the two, and showed also some nervousness, needed some reassurance over the boy's normality. Callum was rated dishonest by his peers, and used to pilfer from home and to steal from elsewhere, despite his parents making him take things back; his parents did not even like him swapping things. Callum was given some freedom to go fishing, and to meet friends, and his school reports improved, with him doing well at sports too. He taught himself to swim and was very proud of this. His father was proud about Callum's ability to make things, and enjoying sport, and described his son as 'soldier mad'.

Callum: adolescence

His parents separated when Callum was 10 years old, and he and his siblings stayed with the father. Callum got along very well with his father, and with his sisters, while he had some problems with his mother. He continued to be antisocial, aggressive and to hold a bullying attitude throughout his adolescence. Callum lost his left eye when he was 14 years old; he was not particularly bothered by this, and was not inconvenienced in any way by this unfortunate accident. The circumstances in which it happened were not clear.

After leaving school, at the age of 15, Callum started working in a greengrocer's shop. He left the job after an argument with the boss. He could not find a job that he liked, and his father thought that his son got depressed because he was bored and had little to do. The father was worried about his son but believed that all the problems would disappear once Callum had a full occupation, and his father found him a job in the market. Until he was about 18, Callum worked in the market; he enjoyed the job very much. He also had Saturday work with a local fruitier. The father was very proud of how his son had responded to the Saturday job.

When Callum was interviewed at age 15, he told the interviewer that he was involved with other boys in getting into places; two of his co-offenders had previous convictions. He explained that, at first, this kind of activity was exciting, but he said that he would not get involved again because of the bother that followed afterwards. His father explained his son's problems with the law by the fact that he was an easily led boy.

Callum: young adulthood

Callum was reinterviewed when he was 18. He described his experiences of getting into group fights between ages 15 and 17: he remembered approximately 35 of them. His description of some of the fights was quite vivid, underlining the rather aggressive dynamics that escalated in a quite short period. He mentioned a fight he had in a pub that occurred around six months previously. Everything started because a girl burnt him on his arm with a cigarette, and did not apologise. Callum complained about the lack of apology, and her boyfriend started arguing. Subsequently many people were seriously hurt and had to be taken to hospital; one person nearly died, and another had 18 stitches in his head. Callum was hit with a bottle on his nose and his mate was hurt on his arm: they abandoned the fight because his mate was losing a lot of blood. Callum and his mate were quite adamant about fighting their own case in court. He admitted that he never carried any weapon or tool when he went out, unless he knew that he was going to get into a fight. In those cases he went equipped (e.g. with an iron bar, hammer, knife, gun, etc.). Callum mentioned that, since he grew up (at age 18), he had tried to avoid being involved in any fights. The fights he got involved in were group ones, and only on one occasion did he have a personal fight to protect his sister. It is possible that impulsivity might have triggered his problems in fighting, and reinforced his anti-police attitude.

At age 18 it emerged that he was involved in gambling, and had some debt problems. The most serious contact he had with the police was when the police searched him for weapons. However, he admitted that on about three occasions he went around 'smashing up phone booths, smashing up windows, breaking into cars and things like that (when he was going round in groups)'. When he was asked why (he did those things), he replied that 'it's something to do isn't it – when you are bored and walking around the streets. There's nothing to do – nowhere to go – that's all.' He spent a year in detention, where Callum was described by the governor as 'bone idle and afraid of hard work; a rather surly young man who displayed a very contemptuous attitude towards authority on reception'.

Callum: adulthood

When Callum was interviewed at age 26, he was described as a person with an aggressive and sullen personality. He became a car salesman but he was obliged to leave because he spent 12 months on remand for a robbery. Other employments included being a salesman, a sales assistant, a shop assistant and a shelf filler.

When he was aged 32, Callum was interviewed again, when he had been out of prison for just a couple of weeks. His general health conditions appeared to be consistent and similar to previous years. He had a foot problem because of an accident that occurred when he was 20: his foot was run over. However, it seemed that much more than usual Callum had some preoccupations, losing confidence in himself, and getting panicky for no good reason. He admitted that he had not seen his mother for a long time because of arguments over money, and he hinted that he was estranged from both his parents because of his criminal behaviour. He had not been in contact with his sisters and stepbrother (from his mother's side) either.

He was living in a terraced house that he had bought and that he was finishing paying for. Callum showed some pride over the fact that there was 'only a couple of thousand pounds outstanding on the mortgage'. He lived there with his wife and his stepson aged 17. Callum had a child, aged 7, from a previous relationship with a common-law wife. The child was living with the boy's mother. His relationship with his wife was not going very well; he suspected that she was having an affair, and she was colluding with her son against him.

The family arrangements were influenced when Callum's stepson was involved in some antisocial activities, and was arrested for theft. Callum and his wife separated soon after. Callum remembered that, before he went to prison, they got along very well, arguing, as far as he remembered, only five times per year. Throughout his interview at age 32, Callum's attitude towards his wife was very hostile.

He was quite evasive over his moving out and back to London. His job and business explanations had probably more to do with illegal activities rather than legitimate ones. When Callum was asked about his main job, he spontaneously responded that he was 'a bank robber, ain't I, or that's what they say I am'. On the question about whether he was very criminal, there seemed to be some competing forces in Callum's mind. On the one hand, he always tried to imply how the police harassed him, but on the other hand, he flaunted information about all the crimes he had allegedly committed. He described himself as tough, and he was much more so when he was younger, a sort of likeable rogue; he mentioned that a doctor described him as psychopathic. The interviewer described him as an affable person. He was employed as a car salesman before going into prison. He had a very rich life style before, and now there was not a steady income. He recognised that the family were not starving, and it was his wife who had the money.

He felt very guilty admitting that every day he started off the day with a drink. He lost some sleep over some preoccupation, felt less affection and warmth for those people near him, and was less able than before to concentrate on things he wanted to do, because he felt constantly under strain.

Callum was also involved in a scandal, which involved receiving stolen goods, one of which included a watch given to him by a male friend, with whom he had a homosexual relationship. His friend apparently stole it from a pop singer with whom he had contact. Callum's wife learned about her husband's bisexuality, and this contributed to their divorce. Callum seemed to live something of a 'Walter Mitty' existence, especially when he spoke about a possible new robbery he was planning to do, if he felt like it, or alternatively he might settle down. He enjoyed speaking about himself.

Callum's antisociality continued to be high, as did his alcoholism (measured by the CAGE test), and he reported a high level of anxiety and depression (on the GHQ). He admitted to consuming large quantities of alcohol, such as that in one evening he managed to drink one bottle of vodka, two bottles of wine, and three pints of lager. Drinking became for him a concern and he mentioned going to a clinic in Miami. He had continued to use cannabis every day over the past five years, but he had stopped taking cocaine and heroin. He was still involved in betting. Callum also had a high level of life failure as measured by the *Life Success Scale* (Farrington *et al.*, 2006; see also Chapter 2).

At age 49, Callum was reinterviewed in his rented council two-bedroom flat. At the beginning, he was quite unpleasant and aggressive, denying his identity and pretending to be a different person. However, he then showed some interest, but was vague in some parts of the interview and unfocused in others. Callum described his childhood as unhappy; he mentioned that he was brought up by his father, who sometimes used strict 'belt and stick' measures with him, and the discipline he received was terrorizing. Friends featured in his social life, and Callum described them as 'someone you like being around'. About his present life, Callum lamented that there were some problems in the area because of gangs hanging around for drug dealing, creating some disturbance.

The presence of his wife may have influenced the responses Callum gave. It seemed that she preferred that the full excesses of her husband's behaviour were best kept secret to avoid extra trouble with the court. She tried her best to discourage her husband from associating with his ex-schoolfriends, probably because she felt that they were the causes of her husband's problems.

Callum mentioned that the relationship with his wife was going very well, but they rowed, quite often, when he was drunk. He admitted that his drinking was affecting his life and his relationship with his wife and wanted to do something about it. Callum and his wife often disagreed about how to educate the son. The son was dyslexic and had gambling problems, which complicated an already difficult behavioural pattern characterised by disobedience, temper tantrums and restlessness.

Callum was self-employed, working in the market, selling fruit and vegetables. He appeared to be happy with this job. Despite working, he also claimed benefits. He had some heart problems, which started recently around age 47. Callum also spent six weeks in a 'drying out' clinic. He described himself as a very 'hyper' person, with a lot of energy to invest somewhere.

He had a history of 30 years of drug taking, but he wanted to stay off cocaine, though he still used cannabis. He recounted that at age 45 he was sent to prison for assault. He explained that he used aggression and attacked the person because he was provoked, so that the court sentence was, in his estimation, harsh.

Callum was a chronic offender, who started his criminal career at age 14 and committed his last official offence at age 58. He spent just over one year in prison in total. The length of his criminal involvement was 43 years. He committed 23 official offences, of which just one was a serious motoring offence, and his *index variety* was 9, including 4 convictions for violence and sex crimes. The first offence he committed was burglary (breaking and entering), and he did it with two co-offenders.

Case 941 – Jasper

Jasper was born in 1953. His family was composed of two parents and four children, two boys and two girls. Jasper was the second child.

The family situation where Jasper grew up was difficult, not least because of the financial troubles the family had, and the unhealthy conditions of their council flat.

They had a good deal of dissatisfaction over the housing situation, and it seemed that this had an effect on the quality of the marriage of Jasper's parents, and also contributed to some of the friction in the family relationships between brothers and sisters.

The home had constant trouble with leaking roofs, gaps in walls and skirting boards, crumbling brickwork and rising damp. The accommodation was in a state of general dilapidation, and stayed like this for years. The family was offered, on at least three occasions, another flat, but these flats were all declined, for different reasons, some also related to heating conditions: the open coal fires, which were likely to be present in the new accommodation, were considered unsafe, and the new accommodation proposed (e.g. a three-bedroom ground floor flat) was considered to be not spacious enough. Thus, they spent a good deal of money and energy over the years to improve their home; internally there was no evidence of neglect. Because of all the money spent to try to improve their living conditions, the family had not been able to afford a holiday for the last nine years. The burden of this situation was aggravated by the fact that there were few opportunities for the children to play outside, because of the amount of traffic in the street, and also because of the neighbour's complaints about the noise disturbance. Jasper's mother admitted that she was very tired about the whole situation. She explained that the house was for them a constant financial drain, and she was resentful about this.

Jasper's mother

Jasper's mother suffered from anxiety, and there was evidently a degree of nervous tension. She was a heavy smoker. In 1968 she had a major operation, from which she was still recovering, and this prevented her from working. She was suffering from a cancerous hip and arthritis, and was not allowed out of the house except in a wheelchair or in a car. Her older daughter was looking after her.

Jasper's father

Jasper's father, who had been convicted, had an elementary education, and left school when he was 11 years old. He worked from when he was 15 until he was 19 as a builder, a van boy, and as a driver. Then he went into the Army and stayed there for five years. Jasper's father seemed rather strict towards his children, in comparison with his wife. At times, he appeared to be rather critical towards his wife about her way of handling the children, and especially Jasper. The father would have liked the children to be able to do things and get some results, and he believed that his wife was responsible for the children's disobedience. The father was less tolerant and less accepting of Jasper's difficulties in settling at school, and became very concerned about Jasper's restlessness.

Jasper's father worked as a long-distance lorry driver, and seemed not to spend much time at home, so the children were left unattended, which did not help to inculcate in them a sense of discipline in a climate of family warmth and sharing. Like his wife, he was a heavy smoker.

Jasper's siblings

Jesminda, Jasper's eldest sister, worked as a Telex operator and was planning to go to Canada to work, having obtained a job there. Jesminda was described by her mother in positive terms as an independent girl, even though the mother thought that some elements of selfishness were present in her. Evidence of this selfishness was seen in the fact that Jesminda cut herself off from the family and was more interested in satisfying her own needs. She spent all her money on herself and her own room, and gave little support to the family, whose financial conditions were evidently quite tight.

Dalbert was Jasper's younger brother, who had some problems at school, was assessed as ESN (educationally subnormal), and was transferred to different schools at least twice. Dalbert was unhappy at school, because of some experiences of being bullied and blackmailed. He had truanted extensively in the past, either simply not turning up to classes or arriving late. The mother felt helpless because, since she went out to work, she did not have enough time to look after Dalbert extensively, and could not monitor properly his comings and goings. At one point, it seemed that the mother had changed her job or even given up working altogether to supervise him more. It appeared that Dalbert's school attendance improved considerably then.

Dalbert left school at age 16 and took employment as a cleaner in a furniture shop where he remained for three weeks before being dismissed for being late for work. He found employment in a meat firm, but stayed there only three weeks and then left of his own accord. His subsequent employment included unskilled jobs. He was a concern for his mother, not least because he was persisting in committing minor offences with his motor scooter, and became involved in some more serious activities, until he was charged for housebreaking, for which he was placed on a supervision order.

Calisto was younger than Jasper. Lori was the little one in the family, and she was much younger than Jasper.

Jasper: childhood

Jasper seemed to have a pleasant outward-going nature and talked quite freely about things and himself. Jasper's early life, at age 8–10, was characterised by poor living conditions, coming from a large family. His siblings had some behavioural problems, and his parents had criminal records. Jasper had a poor verbal IQ, and had low attainment at school. His peers rated him as highly dishonest.

Jasper was a regular smoker at age 13, and he had his first sexual experience before age 15. While his living conditions stayed the same (poor and difficult) his level of antisociality emerged clearly at age 14. He was involved in bullying and was a frequent liar. He was highly neurotic and started to develop a strong anti-police attitude. He was very aggressive, daring, lacked concentration, frequently truanted from school and had a high level of self-reported delinquency. Despite all this, he was very popular among his mates. When aged 15, he did a paper round: he gave some money to his parents and spent the rest on clothes and smoking.

Jasper had numerous friends as well as a girlfriend. He was troublesome and his attendance was assessed as 'appalling'. He had not done any work during the school year and he was very difficult to handle by the teachers. However, Jasper was seen as charming when he wanted to be so. The school did not receive any support or collaboration from his parents. The parents were sent a second warning about Jasper's non-attendance at school. Jasper was first summoned into court a month later, but he did not appear, and the case was adjourned several times until he appeared and no order was made. Another school report was then sent to the court. Jasper was described in this report as a youth of average general health and mental ability, who found much of the school work hard. Moreover, the school report described Jasper as a boy with variable behaviour in class, indifferent to teachers, and overbearing to other children, and who liked to indulge in bullying. It was written that Jasper was completely indifferent and disinterested in school work generally. He could in fact be easily discouraged but read quite well, and was attending a special remedial class. His behaviour in and out of the class was good, and his attitude towards his teachers was pleasant. Jasper was seen as a dreamy person.

Jasper: adolescence

Originally the father signed for Jasper to remain at school until 16, but when Jasper became restless and anxious to start working it was not difficult to persuade his father to allow him to leave school at the minimum age of 15. Apart from his non-attendance at school, Jasper's behaviour was generally socially appropriate until his first offence, which was committed when he was aged 15. He was involved, with a co-offender, in a robbery.

Jasper wanted initially to become a driver like his father, but both parents were convinced that the employment prospects in this field were very limited, and persuaded Jasper to change his interest. He left school at age 15; subsequently he worked in a number of different jobs, but then he settled down to be a chain-man on a building site, and he was quite happy about this.

In adolescence (especially between ages 15 and 16) Jasper used to spend a lot of his time hanging around in a gang and being 'in and out of the nick for breaking windows or doing something like that'. Jasper used to play the whole thing down as though it was a joke which got out of hand. The probation officer wrote in his report that it seemed that Jasper played a minor part in the robbery offence, but Jasper was obviously and evidently compliant. Between ages 16 and 18, Jasper was involved in some car accidents while driving. He was significantly antisocial, and developed a strong anti-police attitude, which seemed to mellow through the years. He often went out with his mates, drank considerable amounts of alcohol and at the same time continued to drive a car. He also consumed drugs. His involvement in various fights after drinking was an exciting aspect of his social life, and a way of dealing with his anger. Jasper started to have some debts, as well as poor job stability and long unemployment. His relationship with his parents remained conflictual over the years. However, after his father left home when Jasper was about age 16, his relationship with his father improved subsequently.

Jasper and his partner, whom he married years later, had their first child when Jasper was aged 19; their situation became complicated because they did not have a place to live. The possibility of staying with Jasper's mother was also problematical; Jasper's mother was registered as physically handicapped, and her daughter was looking after her, but she threatened to leave if Jasper and his family continued to live with them and if the accommodation arrangements did not change. This atmosphere of intimidation was a serious preoccupation for Jasper's mother especially because the risk for the other two younger children of being received into care had to be taken into consideration. Jasper's mother agreed to let Jasper and his family stay when he was 19.

Jasper's mother's accommodation was composed of a kitchen, a small dining room and five other rooms, one of which was very damp, with crumbling walls. It was mentioned that the Health Department had told them not to use that room. There was no bathroom in the house, and they had only an outside toilet. At this time, the living arrangements involved the other son Dalbert sleeping there for a while. Jasper's mother slept in the room downstairs because of her physical condition, while Jasper and his family shared a room with Jasper's younger brother and sister. Also this room was damp and very cold. The overcrowding and the lack of privacy made the conditions intolerable for all of them. The father was not living with them any longer.

Jasper: young adulthood

This description of the persisting unhealthy living conditions of this family helps to build up a picture in which Jasper had to struggle to find a sense of satisfaction with what he faced daily. When interviewed at age 19, Jasper mentioned his constant rows with his sister, which created a very heavy atmosphere at home and with his girlfriend also.

Furthermore, Jasper's job records indicated a quite erratic work situation, characterised by continual changes of job after a short period of being employed in each of them. At the age of 19 Jasper was still buying and selling cars, but the business was not going very well after a successful start, in which his money made was mostly spent on drinking. He was disqualified for drunk driving, so he was trying to respect the court order not to drive.

Jasper showed great concern for his mother's health, but also some admiration for her strength to get on with her life. Probably, being a young adult, he was more aware of her sacrifices to try to keep the family together, even after her husband left. When Jasper was interviewed again, when he was 21 years old, he admitted spending a lot of his spare time going to the pub or staying at home watching TV, and he played football on Sundays.

He was aware of his antisocial behaviour, which also included some burglary, robbery, theft from cars, theft from work, shoplifting and motoring offences, and when asked to say something about it, he stated that

> about 50 times well you know, I've done so many offences it would be pointless me going through them all. [. . .] I was a lunatic driver (with the motor scooter) [. . .]. I got pulled about 8 times during a period of about 6 months. I got 39 charges altogether. [. . .]. Actually, I was pleased about it (the fines). I got £35 in fines, which was good, mind you I was only juvenile I was going to juvenile courts they are not heavy there you know [. . .]. I got off very fairly light and altogether I got 6 months disqualification.

Jasper mentioned that he started getting his motoring offences when he drove while disqualified, when he was aged around 17, and he continued to do this for many years afterwards.

Jasper believed that when he was drunk he was less violent, got on better with people and thought more of them than when he was sober. There were numerous times when Jasper got into serious fights, and in trouble with the police, although he described himself as a person who 'really I don't look for trouble at all'. He mentioned that he used to carry a sheath knife every night of the week for about six months: 'Not really – not with the intent to fight anybody with it. Well I used to carry a knife around – but every young bloke does I suppose. (I stopped) when I was about 16 and a half like I wasn't worried – all I was worried about was my scooter. Never used a weapon at all.'

About his relationship with the police he mentioned that he was beaten up sometimes when he was a juvenile (15–16 years old), and again when he was over 18, after Jasper and his mate broke some windows.

> [. . .] they (the police) gave me a good hiding once. They won't mark you, they won't hit you in the face and give you a black eye or anything like that. If they do mark you when they get you in court and you try to press charges they say he tried to escape and he flew at one of our officers so . . . they have always got a remedy you can't beat them. [. . .] Never hit a policeman. I don't give them a lot of aggravation – no I wouldn't fancy going to court for that.

Jasper also said that the police attitude towards him was somehow biased: 'that's the trouble they still know me and they're always going past my house and they say "Hello Jasper, keeping out of motors" and all that and I say – "get stuffed"'.

Jasper: adulthood

When Jasper was almost 24, he got married to his cohabitee of five years; they had two children, a girl and a boy. At age 25, Jasper described his sexual life as active, having numerous promiscuous and unsafe sexual relationships with different girlfriends.

When Jasper was interviewed at age 25, the interviewer described him as a powerful man, very popular with ladies. Despite having left school without any qualifications, he was quite an intelligent person and was doing well at work: he worked his way up from apprentice to foreman. He got on well with the directors of the firm and was promised a directorship in the near future. He was frequently a guest at his employers' country home and this may have triggered in him the wish to improve his life conditions by joining the ranks of organised crime. Jasper said that he was envious of and fascinated by their wealth.

Jasper was then sent to prison for robbery. In prison he was locked up in a cell with two other inmates for 23 hours. Jasper recounted that he realised then that money was not so important, and that his wife and children meant everything to him. When he was 25, the interviewer believed that Jasper was going to make every possible effort to go straight. However, his tendency to get involved in aggressive incidents was still strong, making it very unlikely that he would remain free from other convictions.

Jasper was reinterviewed again when he was 32. He was extremely friendly and very pleased to talk about himself at length; he enjoyed attention-seeking and being the centre of attention. Jasper was also a very big person, and could be an awesome adversary when furious. Violence was an instrumental tool in his repertoire of relational and social skills, enabling him to resolve his frustrations using physical force, and permitting him to express his emotions. However, Jasper's disarming honesty gave the impression that he got involved in fights not just for the enjoyment of the pain inflicted, but because he thought he had a reason, however silly that could be. Jasper fought with fists or boots, not weapons.

Jasper got married again after divorcing his previous wife. At age 32, Jasper and his wife-to-be were expecting a baby. His previous children were living elsewhere with their mother, but he kept in regular contact with them. The wedding preparations were interrupted by Jasper being involved in a criminal damage offence, over a revenge issue. The police intervention helped him somehow, because he realised that revenge was not worthwhile, otherwise he would have gone ahead and killed the man who, in his account, tried to run him over with a car. Jasper, this time, spoke positively about the police, mentioning that they treated him well, and made favourable comments. His life style continued to be similar during his adulthood, although he was trying to keep out of trouble and settle down. It was evident that Jasper's criminal pattern was still active even after many years of antisocial involvement, court appearances and convictions. At age 32, he was still involved in fights and some damage accidents because of revenge feelings.

Jasper was very pleased with his current job as a car driver, while his wife was not working. Jasper had always manifested his passion for cars, having some practical knowledge of them. His relationship with his wife was going quite well, despite some times when they had rows during which they shouted at and insulted each other, and threw things around and at each other. Despite all this and also despite his infidelity, Jasper thought that their relationship could last, because they enjoyed each other's company and laughed together.

Jasper's social life was not so different from the life he had previously, and from the one many men in his situation had: in his spare time, he went out to the pub and drank a lot, but also he went out with his wife. In all he had five children; three were living in foster families, and two with other family members.

While his older daughter and a youngest son were not having any particular problems, a middle child was constantly restless since age 1 and, allegedly, until he was a young adult; at age 2, the boy started to have sleep disturbance; at age 6 he started to have temper tantrums, and from age 10 the boy started lying, stealing outside home and disobeying (age 12), truanting and fighting (age 13). No information was given about the other two children.

What was striking about Jasper was his consistency in being antisocial all his life, with some signs of prosociality. Jasper continued to be very aggressive, impulsive and antisocial, with an open admission of an extremely high level of self-reported drug use, delinquency and violence. He consumed large amounts of cannabis and alcohol. His job record was consistently unstable, with a very irregular working life. These features of a consistent antisocial syndrome contributed to Jasper's life failure.

Jasper was reinterviewed when he was age 47. He was very interesting to interview, likeable, extremely helpful and open. Jasper led a very criminal and unstable life. He was incapable of moderation in all aspects of his life, be it work, drink, committing offences, or getting into fights, but he sounded an honest and open person in that he could talk about himself without reservation and limitation, sounding fairly intelligent and self-aware of his situation. He had a car business and his wife was running a nail and beauty salon. He was living in a very nice three-bedroom house, in a quiet street; he mentioned that he was paying a mortgage for it. It seemed that Jasper was living an active and full life, despite some of his antisocial habits still affecting him and his health.

Jasper recognised that his health problems (stomach ulcers and irritable bowel syndrome; he had to stay in the hospital for one week for ulcer problems) were probably related to his stressful life style including heavy drinking and unhealthy eating. He became aware that it was necessary to take better care of himself but, at the same time, he mentioned that he could not slow down. When asked about his past, Jasper described his childhood as being very poor, and he remembered that the disciplinary climate at home was tough, with his father beating him.

Over the past few years, Jasper recognised that he had calmed down in the sense that he admitted preferring his liberty rather than money, and appeared to be very happy with his third wife, apart from some rows characterised by shouting episodes and denigrating comments. At times, when the arguments were extremely bad, Jasper and his wife slept in separate beds.

Some friends featured in his present life, and for him a friend was a person who was there when you were in trouble. His criminal career started at the age of 15 and ended at age 55, lasting over 40 years, and included time served in prison, which amounted to over five years. Jasper's first offence was robbery, which he committed with one co-offender. He had committed 15 official offences, with a heterogeneous criminal pattern, which had an *index variety* of 10. Only two of these offences were serious motoring offences. His level of psychopathy, measured by the PCL:SV, was 7, with just one item scored on the affective/interpersonal factor, and six on the irresponsible/antisocial life style.

Case 402 – Lachlan

> To lay there on the beach and smell.
> the wonderful smell of the salty sea
> which no liar can you tell.
> The sea is the life for me. [. . .]'
>
> *(From 'The sea', by Lachlan, 1966)*

Lachlan was born in 1953. He was the second of seven children in the family. Originally, there were eight children, but one child died of pneumonia in infancy.

The family lived in a terraced council four-bedroom house, in a dilapidated, rough delinquent area. Before going to prison, the father had decorated the home, bought a fridge and a sink unit; he installed a central heating system but then abandoned it because it was not working properly. The mother took pride in the home; she did her best to keep it tidy and clean, but it was damp, and the scullery needed redecorating because it looked grubby and the plastic was peeling off.

The family had a history of debt and rent arrears, and during the course of the different interviews it emerged that the mother was having some trouble managing the finances, although she received a great deal of help from social agencies. The mother was not considered a bad manager but as a person who had to feed seven children on a very small allowance. They also lived on NAB (National Assistance Board) allowances when the father was in prison.

Because of the structural conditions of the building and the dampness of the place, it was very difficult to maintain a good standard of living for the children, also because the place was small for the number of children. The parents were not so interested in the education of their children, and the eldest daughters had helped in the house since a young age. Lachlan experienced parental separation by age 10, because of his father's imprisonment and his mother's hospitalisation; this may explain the lack of supervision that he and his siblings experienced.

Lachlan's mother

The mother came from a remote part of Scotland and was one of eight siblings of a loving family. She went into service at age 14 and appeared to be a rather soft and dependent clinging sort of person who must have missed the support of her husband, having to carry on looking after the family, and felt that the children got out of hand with her husband being away a lot. She died of cancer when Lachlan was 12.

Lachlan's father

Lachlan's father, who had many convictions, was a good-looking man, tall and fit. He was polite and collaborative, and was described by the interviewer as a professional criminal. The father came from a neglectful family and went into the Army at a very young age. He was the elder of two siblings, but had 19 stepbrothers and stepsisters from his parents' previous marriages. At the time of the first interview in the early 1960s, he was in prison for receiving secondhand cars. He had been in difficulties with the law before and had been put on probation for two years.

Lachlan's father left the Army at age 16 and started as a professional boxer. He then worked with the National Brigade but he became sickened with war and left. He also went to Nigeria to do some engineering work on a bush station. His working situation was then very isolated and he drank heavily while he was abroad. Lachlan's father was away all week for work and returned home just at weekends. His distance from home was another fact of emotional instability in the life of his children.

The father was described by his wife as devoted to the family, but highly independent and anti-authoritarian, anti-welfare, very obstinate and with a closed mind. The father was described by the psychiatric social worker as a man who seemed to know his children reasonably well and had some understanding of their problems. However, after his wife died, there seemed to be a feeling of abdication of his responsibilities both in his tendency to be 'up and off', and in the way he left so much responsibility to his oldest daughter, while at the same time recognising that she should carry on with her own life. The impression was not of a totally neglectful father. He seemed concerned but on the whole free from any marked anxieties about his family. Restlessness was the strongest characteristic in his personality.

The father started different businesses and he said that the difficulty of any project he undertook was a major attraction for him. He was bored by success and tended to sell out as soon as he noticed that things were going well. For instance, he told the psychiatric social worker that he spent 16 weeks in Portugal, going 'on spec', and built up a quite thriving import business from the contacts he made there. Once the business was established he lost interest and sold it. He was interested in his children, and did not have any trouble in controlling them. However, he was not informed about the problems his children had during his absence. He did not know about the antisocial involvement of his eldest son Jadrien, who did not go to school during his absence, leaving him illiterate like his sister. He thought that Lachlan was a good boy, and that he was boastful to cover up his shyness. The father was instead more worried about Tasmin, the eldest daughter, who was illiterate, and who was extremely dedicated to him and the family, to the extent that he felt uneasy about it and thought that she should have a life of her own.

Lachlan's father suffered from 'black-outs' and possible brain injury. He suffered from headaches, from which he suffered terribly since a crash in the Air Force in which he was the only person not injured. These headache attacks apparently ceased when he went to prison and kept fit. The impression the father gave was of a person who was not dominant or controlling, even though there were some aspects of his personality which he had not revealed.

Lachlan's siblings

All the siblings, except one, were at home under the care of the eldest daughter who took over the mother's role after her death. The father left absolute control to his daughter and never contradicted her decisions in order not to undermine her role.

Jadrien, the eldest boy, was behind in school and left school prematurely without getting any qualifications, instead remaining illiterate. At age 16 he was on probation for taking and driving away a motor-bike, but he also had a previous charge for larceny. He was remarkably dependent on his father, referred all decisions to him, even when, as a young adult, he was old enough to have more autonomy. Jadrien used to praise his father to colleagues and contacts in a way that might have seemed appropriate in a small boy. At age 18, Jadrien started working as a warehouseman and it seemed that he was settling down. His fiancée had a baby, an event that Jadrien kept from his parents until it happened. He even tried to convince his parents that he did not know about the pregnancy himself.

Tasmin seemed to have taken over the mother's role. She was almost friendless, and seemed not to feel the urge to break out of her isolation; she went out only with her father, despite being encouraged by him to go out on her own. Tasmin and Harriet had problems at school, and went before the court for school non-attendance. Harriet was on a two-year supervision order; she suffered from temper fits and convulsions. At age 16, she was an apprentice hairdresser. Abilia, named after her dead sister, was backward at school, and at age 13 she was still attending school but barely literate.

Steven had some behavioural problems, was a bully, very rough with other boys, and had also some trouble with the police. Since age 10, he was always made to sit in front of the class at school as otherwise he disrupted the class and caused disturbances for other children. When aged 12 he started to go to the same school as Lachlan, and they were close companions, even though he was totally unlike his brother in personality. According to his father, Steven was much more like himself: the pace-maker in the family so far as difficult and obstreperous behaviour was concerned. It was Steven who dared Lachlan on to do things which Lachlan would not even dream of attempting doing. Alden was the youngest boy, and at age 7 he already had frequent absences from school.

Lachlan: childhood

Lachlan was described as a shy boy, passive and inactive. He was a healthy boy who in early childhood was backward in his speech when he was 6, but there was a spontaneous recovery without the need of any treatment. When his mother was interviewed, when Lachlan was 10, she said that he had many nervous or behavioural disorders, and he was inclined to be cheeky with his mother. The father saw him as a very amenable boy, quiet and withdrawn, and, from his description, it emerged that Lachlan was quite solitary. His closest relationship seemed to be with his younger brother, Steven, towards whom he had a protective attitude. Lachlan's major occupation was reading and writing short stories and poetry, but this was a very private world of his and he preferred that no one saw his work. At age 10, Lachlan was described as a wanderer, and basically absorbed in his own inner world.

Lachlan and Steven, when they were respectively 14 and 12, during the Spring term truanted 40 times, and had long periods of absence from school. The father did not perceive this as a serious problem since the school never notified him of it, and he thought that Steven was the main driver of the truancy. In one of these long absences, a schoolfriend of Lachlan received a letter from a certain lady, saying that Lachlan had been run over two weeks ago and died of his wounds. The school felt that the letter might have been written by Lachlan himself and the headmaster checked with the police but they had no record of the accident. The letter was clearly a hoax. Even though he was not involved in activities of pilfering at home, Lachlan was involved in frequent stealing from elsewhere, at age 10.

The father described Lachlan as easily led, particularly by his brother. He seemed to have only a few enduring relationships, an aspect that the father explained by the fact that his son was not bothered about friends. However, the psychiatric social worker reported that Lachlan seemed to not have a problem in making friends, because a lot of friends knocked at his house looking for him. He always liked to be the leader. Despite his absences, Lachlan did well at school and English was his main subject. He had some of his work published in the school magazine, and although he was not sure what to do in the future, he certainly wanted to stay at school until the end.

Lachlan: adolescence

When Lachlan was 14, he came before the court and was found guilty of unlawful possession of lead; he was put on probation for one year. The father was convinced of his innocence and believed that the conviction would blot Lachlan's character. It was difficult for the psychiatrist to get an understanding of the relationship between Lachlan and his father. Lachlan continued to be hesitant in his manner, withdrawn, anxious and apprehensive in the presence of his father. Lachlan showed, from an early age, some antisocial and daring behaviour, and impulsiveness. Altogether he seemed to be a very passive, rather lost boy. An overall assessment of Lachlan indicated that he had a high level of vulnerability. Vulnerability was assessed by a combined measure developed by West and Farrington (1973) based on low family income, large family size, a convicted parent, poor child-rearing and low nonverbal IQ (for a more detailed description see also Chapter 2 of this book).

His father was involved in offending and had served some time in prison, and also his siblings showed some behavioural problems and were involved in criminal activities. Lachlan's older brother was often involved in serious trouble with the police. One of his sisters had some trouble with the police too, and was arrested for forgery.

Lachlan continued to act antisocially, showed an anti-police attitude, and was involved with delinquent friends. He started smoking early, at age 13, and had sexual experiences from age 15. He started to manifest some forms of nervousness, and reported a high level of anxiety. He self-reported violence, burglary, vandalism, shoplifting and theft from a machine at ages 14 and 16, and was rated as highly aggressive and daring by teachers. Lachlan was often involved in truancy.

Lachlan left school without passing any examinations. In his own words he explained that, after his mother had died, when he was about 12 years old, he had to contribute to the family management because his father was in prison and they did not have enough money. Otherwise, he wanted to stay at school and continue doing some examinations; he would have been interested in studying English, Mathematics, and History. He felt that too much responsibility was thrown on him, and he believed that this was the origin of his own problems with the law. He completed his schooling at age 15 and then became a resident hotel porter, and enjoyed the job. Unfortunately the hotel closed down nine months later. After then he had some periods of unemployment coupled with working on various building sites. He held some unskilled manual jobs, but his job record was unstable. He admitted having problems in keeping up his interest in the jobs, and reported that he soon got bored, and found it hard to settle down. As a young adult, he started having debts and getting involved in smoking cannabis, using drugs frequently and having a pro-drug attitude.

At age 18, antisociality continued to be a feature of his attitude towards the world and others, and as a way of behaving. During the interview, held at a Detention Centre, when he was 18, he showed a remarkably depressed attitude towards his life. Though he did not like to be in detention, he was not looking forward to his release because he felt that, once he was out, he would be easily led again by his antisocial companions. Lachlan, when describing his delinquency, always looked for an excuse for his behaviour, and tended to explain it by his weakness and inability to avoid being led into trouble by his mates.

The Assistant Governor of the Remand Centre where Lachlan was sent at age 19 mentioned that it took some time for Lachlan to settle down and that at the beginning there was a period of delinquent behaviour and a bad attitude to authority. However, during the latter part of his stay, Lachlan's behaviour started to improve and he made good progress, and he professed that he had learnt his lesson. Lachlan was described as an alert and confident young man who could do well if he put his mind to it, and who was quite intelligent in conversation and could put his points across well. However, with his background, it was thought that Lachlan would require a great deal of supportive help from his probation officer. The chaplain was also interviewed, to give his opinion about Lachlan. He described Lachlan as 'a lonely person with little sense of direction, no real friend, no real reason for living. A person who needs an incredible amount of support.'

Lachlan: young adulthood

From an early age it emerged that this young man appeared to be embarking on a life of crime, following in his father's footsteps. Given his ability and social skills, Lachlan could have done differently and well with appropriate guidance and support. However, with no fixed abode and initially without any contact with anyone apart from the social worker, Lachlan's opportunities were bound to be somewhat limited. Lachlan's father married a woman much younger than him, and the contacts with his son were not consistent. There was a final hope that Lachlan would maintain contact with his father on release from detention but this did not happen. Furthermore, the hurdle of not having anywhere to live after release represented for Lachlan another complication; he did not know about his father's whereabouts, and he had not kept in contact with his brothers and sisters. In the report of his time in prison it was stated that, unless Lachlan got himself into a stable environment on release, it was very likely that he could finish up relapsing into crime and being incarcerated again. Unfortunately, this assessment was to reflect what happened in Lachlan's life.

When Lachlan was aged 20, he was considered to be a polite young man who had been a model prisoner during the induction time; he performed reasonably well since his reception on the wing. He appeared to be intelligent, quite mature and able to do well if he put his mind to it. The assessment report of Lachlan's situation at age 20, during his time in prison, where he stayed in custody awaiting trial on a robbery charge, suggested that he seemed to be capable of doing much better outside than he had done in the past. His upbringing was characterised by frustrations, losses and a deprived adolescence that to some extent may have given rise to his unsatisfactory way of life.

Lachlan: adulthood

At age 32, Lachlan showed a high level of aggression, and reported a high level of alcoholism as measured by the CAGE instrument. He was involved in heavy gambling, reported long periods of unemployment, and was involved in casual work. He held a significant anti-establishment attitude, and was often involved in fights. Lachlan's level of life failure was high.

Lachlan's onset of offending was at age 14, and he had an active criminal career, with 18 offences, that included also four serious motoring offences. He committed his last offence at age 54. His criminal career lasted over 40 years, and included time served in prison, which amounted to over 15 years. He was a persistent and chronic offender. The *index variety* was 8, indicating that he committed 8 types of different offences. The PCL:SV was administered to him; his level of psychopathy was 14, with 4 points on Factor I (affective/interpersonal) and 10 on Factor II (irresponsible/antisocial). This is a high score.

Case 252 – Paul

Paul was born in 1954. He came from a large family of two parents and eight other biological siblings who were alive when the family was enrolled in the CSDD in 1962, and a stepbrother. Some other children in the family died from illness or stillbirth. The family of Paul was extremely problematic, with constant marital problems, which were embedded in an intermittent state of debts and poverty. The family was known to the social services and health committees for years on account of the children's difficulties and periodical financial crises.

The family lived in a terraced house, with three bedrooms, requisitioned by the local authority, in a working-class area. The interior of the house was average, and was kept reasonably clean and tidy. It was an overcrowded home, and the children had to share rooms. Paul's parents always had trouble paying the rent and their habit was to clear the arrears in a lump sum.

The marital situation was disharmonious, going from bad to worse over the years, and the general feeling of the children was that they wanted to distance themselves from their mother. The social services had attempted to work with the family in order to modify the parents' style and behaviour with their children, but any attempt led to failure and provoked further distrust towards the health and social services. Particularly, it was considered a priority to organise supportive work with the mother as the epicentre of the gross family disturbance. The conditions of this family were assessed by the health department as physically neglected, children were at times unkempt and the management of the family by the mother was slightly too casual.

Paul's mother

Paul's mother, who had been convicted, was the dominating factor in the household, while his father had a passive and a laid-back attitude in the family affairs. The mother had great difficulty in accepting and trusting social workers, even though she had begun over the years to make appropriate use of social work help, both to solve marital problems and to control some of her own more destructive aspects.

In 1962, when Paul's mother was contacted, she was initially not very collaborative, and had refused any previous contacts with the CSDD project. The reasons were motivated by the fact that she had done it all before with the hospital and the approved school authorities when some of the children had been admitted. It was too frustrating to talk about her family situation, which she saw as a collection of failures; she did not feel like going through the history again.

Furthermore, she heard about the study from a neighbour, with whom she did not have a very good relationship, and this reinforced her initial dismissive attitude. She then had second thoughts, and said that she would give it a trial. Her collaboration grew gradually, from being very reticent in the first interviews and not wanting to give information about the hospital records of some of her children's mental and health problems, to being more collaborative and revealing some interesting events in the family life.

Paul's mother was the oldest of seven children: she had four brothers and two sisters. Paul's mother's mother suffered from a breakdown following national service, having screaming fits and black outs during the war, and was involved in some homicidal attacks, in which it was not clear whether she was the victim or the attacker. Paul's mother's father was reputed to be very well off, and he may have left some money when he died.

The mother was a dark and overweight lady, who had all her teeth out. She was aggressive, physically violent and emotionally manipulative. Relationally, she was very difficult, talkative, bossy and overruled everybody. In conversation, she interrupted and quarrelled a lot. She controlled her family, especially her sons, and while she was giving them affection and warmth, she also weakened them. She was an anxious and overprotective mother, who was prepared to battle to protect the children from any outside interference. She had a great deal to put up with but her emotional instability interfered constantly in her manner of relating to others, especially her children, towards whom she had ambivalent feelings. She was overwhelmed by the family ordeal. She once left a toddler at the clinic and forgot about him, and did not go back for him later.

Paul's mother married his father relatively young, but the family lived with Paul's maternal grandmother for another five years. The circumstances of her previous marriage were unclear, and it was hidden from her children along with any information about her two children.

Her son Tacey was from her previous marriage, which was the result of an impetuous choice of wanting to be independent from her father and lasted only a few months. She hid from Tacey his background, and this was another cause of severe conflicts when he discovered the truth about his natural father. Tacey was a very disturbed child and she was very keen for him to have ECT (electroconvulsive therapy) and tried insistently to persuade the doctors to give it to him: 'he needs quietening down, he is too violent'. She regarded ECT as a disciplinary and educational measure. She was, indeed, ambivalent and incoherent in the way she educated her children. For instance, at first she denied any difficulties with one of the older sons (Kerwin) and dismissed his offences, considering them isolated incidents. Finally, she was able to see the problematic side of her son's life and agreed to accept the specialised arrangements which could be made by the Education Department to help her son. She constantly clashed with any proposal or plan to help her children; she opposed any professional advice offered to unburden her load of family responsibility.

The mother was described by other agencies as an untrustworthy woman, thought to be a bad influence in the district. She did not like the neighbourhood, and she said that the neighbours were unsociable. She had many unhappy memories of the street, and she wished she could move out. She found a job to provide money to look after her house and keep the property clean.

Paul's mother was working at home as a lampshade maker and she had started to work as a night cleaner, so her earnings would be greater. While she frequently played bingo and was quite successful in winning large sums, there seemed to be an undisclosed source of income in the house. They had the telephone, all modern gadgets, a station wagon and the mother had her own cheque book and spent money freely. There was some suspicion that she also had some side activities, taking in delinquent girls, frequently pregnant, and receiving money for this.

She was always on the verge of a breakdown, not only because of the continuous and escalating problems in which all the family were submerged, but especially from her difficulty in making a coherent and long-lasting decision. When she was age 40, when her husband returned home after a period of separation, she had a miscarriage, which was going to be surgically aborted anyway; at the same time, she had an attack of quinsy, described as inflammation of the tonsils and surrounding tissues with the formation of abscesses. Some of her physical problems might have also worsened by her constantly alarmed mental state.

Paul's father

Paul's father; who had been convicted, had received an elementary education and left school at age 15. He remembered little or nothing about his parents; they separated when he was one year old, and he was put in a home, first in a residential nursery and later in a residential school where he stayed from age 5 to age 15. He stated that he was very happy in the residential school, but he made no permanent friends with other children or adults. He changed houses many times, and there was never one single adult who took care of him and to whom he was attached. He regarded his maternal grandparents as his own parents, and was very unhappy indeed when his maternal grandfather died; this was a real loss to him. There was no relationship with his parents and no lasting relationship with a parent substitute. Paul's father was visited from time to time by his paternal grandfather and his mistress. Paul's father knew he had brothers and sisters but he did not know their whereabouts or how many there were. He thought his wife was still in touch with his paternal grandfather but he had not seen this man for a while. He did at one time try to trace his mother but without much success, other than finding that she was still alive.

Paul's father was described as a feminine, passive, weak and gentle person, who at the same time was malicious and a 'stirrer', beaten down by the force of his wife's personality. He was a withdrawn character and deadpan in his humour. He spoke with some warmth and understanding of his wife, mentioning that she had a difficult temperament, was always flaring up, and was 'pig headed' just like her maternal grandfather. One of the difficulties was that she made decisions without asking him, and was very impulsive. He felt excluded and diminished in his role as a father figure. His passivity, however, appeared less intense later on in the family life, when he had to handle the situation of the new baby boy, Sanders, because his wife started to work again, and she often worked at night.

Paul's father was quite informed about his children's conditions at home and at school; he was recognised by the interviewer as a participating father, concerned for his children, especially the younger ones who needed more attention, and he was considered a reasonably warm parental presence. However, despite being interested in his children, he lacked depth of feeling. He was not a shadowy father, and according to the psychiatric social worker, he was probably far more important and consistent with the children than his wife.

Paul's father had been employed in various jobs in the London area, though it was very difficult to trace his job records. He mentioned that he had served as an infantryman for five years, when he started working for short periods mostly as a cleaner. He mentioned two more little jobs he did which brought his wage up. Very little was known about the family income, but it seemed obvious that something was going on under the surface, and some of the extra money that was available was of an uncertain provenance.

Paul's father had been involved in various criminal acts, including theft, which he belittled, considering that his behaviour was as a snapper up of unconsidered or simple trifles. However, what emerged quite extensively during the various meetings with the father by the different professionals who encountered and spoke to him, was a man who had a very anti-authority, anti-establishment and dishonest attitude.

Family dysfunction

Paul's family was multi-problematic at many levels. His parents' marriage was unsatisfying to both parties, and yet since it had lasted for many years, and as Paul's parents lived together for three years before marrying, it must be presumed that the marriage had some significance for them. The mother claimed that there was only some marital strife since the onset of Tacey's illness, but as there was jealousy and conflicts between the parents, over Tacey and Kerwin, the illness may have triggered off an acute rivalry and condemnation. Tacey was born from the mother's previous marriage; he was accepted by his stepfather, but it was likely that some resentment was still present and the family climate was altered by this unspoken and censored matter.

The parents seemed to keep apart from each other, and the main discussions and rows were about the children. When, on some occasions, the mother and father were interviewed together, it was difficult to get a picture of how they interacted as parents with their children. It emerged as a very fragmented dynamic in which the father took a back seat, while the mother was the central motor of decisions made over the family and the children, and if anyone had to leave home that one should be her husband. The mother, in her husband's view, was very lax and easy with the children, always shouting at and threatening them; she was unable to stick to the rules she herself proposed and wanted to impose without much effectiveness. The father, in his wife's view, was lacking vigilance because he was never present, and appeared disinterested and detached. There was a serious problem of disciplinary inconsistency, with laxity on one side and unconvincing firmness on the other.

Tacey and Kerwin, Paul's older brothers, were the major source of conflict between his parents, as Tacey was the son from her first marriage and Kerwin was their first son. The wife always took Tacey's side and was overprotective towards him, while considering Kerwin a chronic and inveterate liar, who could not be trusted in any way. The husband took the side of Kerwin, denying his son's criminal records, justifying his troubles as getting into bad company that made him go astray and do wrong. The father also minimised Kerwin's difficulties in keeping his employment. For instance, when he was committed to a Borstal, Kerwin ran away to take a job as a fisherman; he was traced by the police and taken to court. The father saw this episode as an example of Kerwin's enterprise and versatility: 'he'll turn his hands to anything'. On the other hand, the father believed that Tacey was overdependent on his mother, and that he was better off in the hospital. The father in fact suggested, while Tacey was in hospital, that during his time there he acquired some autonomy. On the contrary, when at home, according to his stepfather, Tacey always deteriorated. It was difficult to understand what was meant by deterioration, because everything seemed to be reduced to Tacey's nerves. Tacey was in fact considered by his stepfather the 'pet lamb' in the family.

In 1964, the marriage reached such an unsustainable state that the husband moved out for a short time. Paul's mother applied to the court for a legal separation but then she reconsidered the situation and accepted to take her husband back. While away, the husband sent some money, but it was not clear what arrangement they had about the money. In 1965, at the time of the next interview, they were still living at home. The quality of the marriage was still frantic and conflictual, and the wife was contemplating returning to the court for a separation order to be made. This strained marriage continued in the years to come.

Paul's siblings

Tacey was the oldest sibling, and had some serious health and mental problems. When he was a young adult he took an overdose, which required his urgent admission to hospital, to add to the other regular hospital admissions. Tacey was in fact very florid (schizophrenic), and a psychopath, who spent long periods in hospital. At age 20, he completed a training course to become a painter and decorator. There had been considerable improvement in his mental health, though there were still occasions when he got depressed and moody, and at times he did not feel well enough to go out. He spent months without needing to go to the hospital, and was discharged from the outpatient clinic. According to his mother, Tacey was better when off tablets than on them. Between 1965 and 1966, he made two suicide attempts. During this period he did not work, despite the doctor signing that he was fit for work again.

Kerwin was the perfect con man, utterly without conscience at home and outside his family. He had an average IQ, and no special abilities or disabilities. He was short and obese, but physically healthy. He lived in a fantasy world, and was childish and immature. At school his attendance was erratic, and though his behaviour in class was not offensive or insolent, he needed to be told several times before he did what was asked. He seemed not to want to learn, and he had no desire or energy to do any kind of school work. Out of the classroom he required constant supervision. His attitude towards other children was friendly, but other children seemed to reject his company; he romanced and never gave up trying to get into people's good books even when he was rebuffed. As a result of social rejections, he mixed with a more irresponsible group of youths who were older than him. With adults he had established a better relationship, appearing quite at ease in conversation and speaking freely about himself, even though he did not take matters seriously, showing a very irresponsible side of himself.

Kerwin went into the Army but he was discharged because he was assessed as unsuitable. He was involved in different types of offences, and at age 19 he was convicted for larceny and was put on probation. Several of his sentences were for demanding with menaces, and in one specific case he was preying on a homosexual. While on probation, he committed new offences; he admitted that he was a compulsive thief. There was a unanimous opinion by the social services, which dealt with the family for years, about Kerwin being very problematic and antisocial, and too immature to acquire the independence he aspired to and being unable to manage. He tried to disengage himself from his family by accepting jobs away from home for a short period, and then coming back there with, every time, an extra baggage of frustration and renewed sense of failure.

Juliet was partially deaf. She was placed in a school for deaf children, and she was working quite well. Her mother was quite unhappy about this, but she was quite an able lip-reader and her father denied that her deafness was a real source of embarrassment to her.

The younger children were not a problem, but they were resentful. Dacia was quite troublesome at school, while Salena was even more problematic; she was suspended from school and ultimately transferred to an ESN school where she functioned better. Sybil attended a Special Investigation Clinic for poor growth and bedwetting; she made some improvements but her school attendance was extremely poor. Damario had Down's syndrome. He attended an ESN school but he died when he was age 6. Another baby girl died of spina bifida.

Sanders was the next child. His mother did not have any problem in accepting him, but she had some difficulties in showing maternal feeling towards him. His physical care was shared between various members of the family. When she returned to night-work, one of the older boys was asked to give Sanders a bottle in the night. The mother justified the need to go to work because of the need for money. Margot was the youngest in the family. She was an extremely managing, dominant child, sturdy and demanding.

Paul: childhood

Paul, born in 1954, was a maladjusted child. He was described by his mother as a very good baby, never waking up at night, and there were some signs of his being under-active, which were interpreted as positive considering the other problems his parents had with his older siblings. He was clean and dry at 18 months, but later he became enuretic like many of his siblings.

However, in the years that followed, Paul presented many problems and, from age 11, he was at the point where he could not be taught in a normal classroom situation. He demanded absolute individual attention; he had a reading level of a boy aged 7, and was below average ability. His mother, however, was resistant to the idea of any assessment despite recommendations made by school, social and health authorities for him to be visited by some specialists.

At age 8–10, Paul was a boy of below average intelligence and had a low verbal IQ; he was quite nervous and had a high level of neuroticism, which was also manifested by him having a withdrawn and passive attitude. Paul was also impulsive, lacked concentration and rated as unpopular by his peers. His childhood was characterised by a harsh parental attitude, and an ambivalent and inconsistent parental attitude to education. His parents were not interested in Paul's education, did not show particular interest in his scholastic results and never praised him. His child-rearing was extremely poor, not only materially but emotionally as well. Paul was, for all his childhood, poorly supervised and spent a great deal of time with his older brother who was an already active antisocial youth. Some of his siblings had behavioural, physical health and mental problems. His father and his brothers had a prolific criminal career, which was likely to have had an influence on Paul's own social adjustment.

There were some significant signs that created the foundation of the direction that his future life took. Paul was a very vulnerable child, and his level of vulnerability continued to be high all his life. When he was 12 years old, he was put on a waiting list for a maladjusted day school. His mother denied his problems, and maintained that it was the school to be blamed. Paul was bullied and picked on by the rougher boys, and he constantly made excuses not to go to school. According to his mother, he was always 'rock bottom'. His father considered him an easily led boy, who got into bad company, which persuaded him to do wrong. Paul and his brother Kerwin stole heavily at home. Paul's behavioural problems, aggravated by his below average cognitive abilities, became persistent despite the many attempts to help him by probation officers, school authorities and social workers. Paul truanted often from school, and he also wandered in late at night, sometimes being away from home until 11 p.m.

At age 12–14, Paul's level of antisociality became more evident and his involvement in fights outside home was very frequent. He was involved in bullying, but from his records it seemed that he was more a victim of bullying than being a bully himself. His family conditions did not improve, the home was still overcrowded, with a poor level of child-rearing, and a very strong marital disharmony between his parents. Paul was a frequent liar both at home and outside, and he was getting involved with some delinquent friends. He was aggressive, and self-reported frequent involvement in delinquent and violent activities. He continued to lack concentration, truanted frequently from school, and was a particularly anxious and nervous boy.

Paul: adolescence

Paul left school when he was aged 15, and then he had some unskilled and casual jobs, such as a butcher's boy, and a washer in a restaurant, but he left on his own accord after six weeks. When interviewed in 1970, he stated that he was unemployed. Based on the age 18 interview, there was also some suggestion of Paul working as a security officer when he was aged 17. He then got a job as a van boy, but it was impossible to have any more details of Paul's occupational status at this stage, because he refused to give any details about his employer and about the job itself. In 1970, he started to work as a bingo caller, and with his earnings he contributed some money to his mother for his keep. Paul left after a few weeks and then he was employed in a market until 1971.

At age 16–18, Paul's involvement in aggressive group fights was frequent, given his activities in gangs; his levels of aggressiveness and antisociality were high. Accordingly, his self-reported delinquency and violence were symptomatic of this, though Paul tried to hide or diminish the seriousness of his delinquency participation in many offences. Paul was an abuser of cannabis and alcohol, and he often drove under their effects, especially the latter, which could also explain his involvement in fights. Paul's mental condition was somehow feeble and he had a high level of neuroticism (on the EPI), and high antisociality. He was sexually promiscuous.

At age 17, he took a car without the consent of the owner and was stopped by the police; it was also found that Paul was unlicensed and uninsured. He was sentenced to a Borstal youth institution. In the initial assessment, he was described as a very suspicious person and someone who felt that everyone was against him. It might have been the anxious protection of his mother that made him frightened and tending to run away. Discussing his life, it emerged that he had suffered deeply from his home situation, for having an older brother who was constantly in and out of a psychiatric hospital, for having a domineering mother and a passive father. Paul had some 'resentful' feelings about his mentally disturbed brother, finding it hard to understand that he should be the one in the family to go out to work to keep his brother. It seemed that he never had many friends, although he believed that those with whom he was involved were 'real friends with the usual loyalties'. Paul was reluctant to talk about the stealing of the car, but he said that he was picked up by three homosexuals who persuaded him to spend the night in their flat. At night, when one of them made an approach, he fled and needed a car for this. He put down that the reason for his offence was desperation.

Paul was described by the Borstal governor as a quiet, immature, inadequate and naïve young man who obviously did not trust the authorities interviewing him, and he could not see that the Borstal could help him in any way, but it would just make things worse for him. Paul made some progress after a poor start; he had a difficult time with his peers. Although Paul had managed to overcome many of the problems that caused him too much pain, he remained, on occasions, inadequate and unable to cope with situations that involved taking responsibility for his behaviour. Paul was also unable to understand that his attitude and behaviour could affect the quality of his interaction with other people, and how others responded to him.

At a meeting with a psychologist, Paul responded to the situation in an almost mechanical manner, with very little spontaneity. In routine testing he proved to be of below average intelligence, with comparably poor scores on tests of educational attainment. He was also described as a person who felt inferior and craved attention, being very vague and withdrawn, and who tended to run away, but with an element of cunning. He continued to have difficulties in establishing and maintaining meaningful relationships, although his relationship with his personnel officer improved during his period in detention. His father visited him regularly, and offered him a home on discharge. It was recognised that an area in which Paul would need much help was to come to terms with the fact that his mother was a very intrusive and interfering figure in his life; he had to learn how to cope with her, rather than run away and commit offences.

After he was discharged, Paul had frequent spells of unemployment between casual work, and continued to live with his parents. Their home conditions were still poor and the situation there was difficult, not least because of the number of people living there. Paul had in all 13 brothers and sisters, most of whom were residing at home, which created a very overcrowded situation and not only in terms of physical space (three bedrooms). The atmosphere was very tense and conflictual. In some reports, it was noted that Paul was permanently running away and he was recorded as a missing person. Paul in fact frequently left and stayed at other premises for some days, and then went back to his parents' home. His parents considered him to be mentally retarded, and were constantly fearing a repetition of his absenteeism from home.

Paul was arrested at age 18 and committed to stand trial with the charge that being a male person he did persistently importune (male) people passing by for an immoral purpose, while he was waiting for a girl he knew and who worked as a prostitute. He pleaded guilty, but later he decided to change his plea, and was granted legal aid and assisted by a solicitor. It was not clear why Paul pleaded guilty in the first instance, but given the nature of the (homosexual) charge one could understand why he then changed his plea. In the supervision records, the officer who supervised Paul could not make sense of what Paul said about the event. Paul mentioned that on that occasion he met a girl, who was a prostitute, in the hope that she could take him to her flat, and he intimated that she could have had intercourse with him, but that he would not have paid for it.

Paul was a self-confessed homosexual, and associated with other individuals who were homosexual. He spent most of his spare time going to the pub and discos, being with friends and drinking, and going out with his girlfriend.

Paul externalised his aggressiveness: he admitted having been involved in acts of vandalism and many fights, some of which were also violent, but he said that he was never a member of a gang. He said that he had never carried weapons with him, though in some fights he used objects that were around like, for instance, a chair: 'If I go into a pub and somebody picks up a bottle, I think if I don't watch it the bottle's going to get me. So I pick up the nearest thing as well. It may seem cruel or that but I don't fancy getting a bottle across my head.' His mates carried 'a chopper' but he never did.

Paul's antisocial behaviour was very prolific and he committed different types of offences both as a juvenile and as an adult, but he only admitted some of them, and in a sort of random way, without being able to place them in the temporal order and sequence in which they actually happened. A possible explanation of this difficulty of systematically listing them may be the number of criminal involvements.

He admitted some of his court appearances, drunk and disorderly acts, breaking and entering, and also that he had done quite a few wrong things, which he managed to get away with, that he did not want to mention:

> I'm too shrewd for them, I'm as shrewd as I can, sort of thing. The trouble is every time they've got me sort of thing, they haven't really got nothing to get me on sort of things. [. . .]. They (the Police) thought I was involved with all this (a robbery). But I weren't (his brother was). [. . .]. It was a bit rough sort of thing cause they tried to involve all the family. Well it wasn't nothing to do with us. They come around asking questions. [. . .]. My brother has a bad name so they look at me and think 'Ah here's another one'. I suppose if you've broke the law they've got to do their job. They know my face cause they know my brother.

Paul: young adulthood

As a young man, aged 19, Paul was interviewed again. A quite complex picture emerged of his character, since his account of his conviction records bore little relation to the official records. He said he had not been found guilty for indictable offences but only had an acquittal for one offence and one conviction for a non-indictable offence. It was evident that Paul tried on various occasions to project an image of himself that was different from what appeared in the records. He tried to hide his experience of being institutionalised twice because such an admission would have involved, in his view, a loss of reputation and tarnished his self-esteem. He was frequently lying but not perhaps consciously, since Paul was, at times, unable to distinguish between reality and fantasy, or to string sentences together; his eye movements were not fully controlled. He looked strange, as if the world was moving too fast for him.

Paul: adulthood

At the beginning of an interview when he was aged 32, Paul seemed to have quite a menacing or controlled gaze, while at the same time looking rather vacant. He talked briefly about his life, claiming to be an unloved child, and describing a terrible episode of being locked in a cupboard for three days by his brothers; in his account of the sad events that affected him deeply he included his experiences of being 'in and out' of prison all his life. He described his childhood as very unhappy, mentioning the strict discipline in the house, and often being beaten. These events were likely to have had a strong impact upon his mental health. He talked of his parents with some ambivalent feelings; he mentioned that his relationship with his mother was very good, while with his father he could not 'see eye to eye'. It seemed that Paul did not recover from his traumatic childhood, and was still seeing himself as a victim.

At age 32, Paul's home arrangements were not quite clear; he was sharing council accommodation with some friends, to whom he and his wife paid a contribution. He had got married and had two daughters; one was dyslexic and the other suffered from asthma. Paul said that he and his wife mostly agreed over the education of their children. They were having some problems with the youngest daughter; she was stealing things outside the home, but he thought that she would grow out of it since she was just 4 years old. She ran away from home, she was disobedient, this starting when she was 3, destroyed things and she was a bully. Paul said that she should have been born a boy. Both daughters fought with each other because of jealousy. The older daughter was restless and had some sleep disturbance since she was 4 or 5.

Paul liked playing with his children and sometimes when they were naughty he smacked them. He admitted not having spent much time with his children, not as much as he should have done, because he was trying to sort things out, and to find some work. He continuously mentioned that he was a man with plenty of problems, not least being also unable to be in a regular job, but he loved his daughters.

Even though Paul relaxed with the interviewer, the interaction with him was difficult because Paul was vague, inaccurate and showed a general unwillingness or inability to answer the questions directly. This might have been designed to obscure the full extent of his antisociality and deviance, or perhaps was just the result of poor effort on his part, or both. However, some more interesting facts emerged about Paul's armed robbery, his epilepsy, his poor health and his past alcoholism.

Paul recounted his rows with his wife, and admitted that in the last 10 years he hit her once or twice, while she hit him two or three times. His sexual relationship with her was not going all right, and he had some sexual involvements with another 10–15 women besides his wife in the last year. He thought that in the next five years he could still be with her because he did not want to stay away from his children. His wife was very chaotic and pathetic, and both were negatively influencing their children's behaviour.

Paul also mentioned some of the vicious fights he got involved in; somebody threatened him with a gun and Paul went away to find a hammer and return to the site to defend himself. He also admitted being involved in other offences such as handling stolen goods in a stolen car; he did it for money.

When Paul was age 48, he and his family had changed accommodation again, and it was very difficult to trace Paul's new address, and his other family members did not know anything about him. A disabled lady from London, living in the area where Paul used to live, knew Paul's family because she had swapped council houses and lived with them for a while. This lady claimed that the whole family, daughters included, stole from her and in general took advantage of her poor health, so that she and her husband were 'easy to con'. A picture of Paul and his family emerged of a very deviant and dysfunctional family, in which prostitution, child abuse and incest seemed to have prevailed over love, parenthood and caring. It was mentioned that Paul made his eldest daughter pregnant and a son was born. This contributed to Paul's wife divorcing him, although they had another child together, for whom Paul was paying maintenance. Paul's second daughter was, allegedly, taken into care because of her prostitution when she was aged 14. According to the information offered by this lady, Paul sexually abused both daughters and was a quite violent man at home too.

In adulthood, Paul's life showed chronic maladjustment in so many areas of his social functioning, complicated by the influence of alcoholism (CAGE), mental problems (GHQ) and impulsivity. All these problems, embedded into a syndrome of antisociality, contributed substantially to his life failure, and his high level of self-reported offending, violence and drug abuse. His life success level was significantly low, being characterised by continual failures.

After a search for Paul, at age 50, Paul was interviewed; his wife accepted too, even though it was not clear if they were still a couple. They were living in a rented house, with two bedrooms and one bathroom, and he said that he wanted to settle down with his family and keep out of trouble. He was more than usually hopeful about his future, and feeling some warmth for those near him. He was not in contact with his brothers and sisters, apart from two with whom he kept contact about once a year. His social life mainly consisted of meeting, at least once a week, a close friend who visited his house. He mentioned that he had some epileptic fits, suffered from back pain and had some trouble with his hand because of an old fight injury. More than usual, he had lost sleep over worries, and had disturbed nights.

His daughters became a source of a preoccupation, as they manifested some behavioural problems. When the oldest child was age 6, she started bedwetting, having sleep disturbance, fears, some nervous habits, and being bullied, presumably at school. She had some temper tantrums but Paul was not able to remember the age of onset. The problems of his youngest daughter were more intense as they had escalated since the last time he was interviewed. At age 10–11, she started lying, stealing at home and outside, running away from home, truanting, disobeying, getting into fights with other children, being bullied, destroying things, being restless, and having sleep disturbances. Later, at age 15, she started to develop some fears and nervous habits.

Paul reiterated that he had a very good relationship with his wife; however, it was difficult to assess how genuine this affirmation was, given the fact that his wife was next door during the interview. He admitted to having had some rows with her, which included shouting, denigration of each other's families, things thrown or broken, and walking out of the house. Paul was involved in a fight in the last year or so because some people were selling drugs to his daughter.

Paul's criminal career started at age 15 and his last official conviction was at age 46, with a career duration of over 30 years. Paul spent over one year in custody. His criminal career included 15 official offences, including 4 serious motoring offences. His *index variety* was 10, and one offence was violent. His level of psychopathy, measured by the PCL:SV, was 14, with a score of 4 points on the affective/interpersonal factor, and 10 on the irresponsible/antisocial life style. This is a high score.

Paul's life represents most of those aspects that clinical and psycho-criminological manuals describe as problematic and dysfunctional. Moreover, there seems to be intergenerational continuity from Paul's difficulties to his daughters' own maladjustment. Continuity of psychological and social maladjustment can take different forms, either through a person's entire life or between parents and the next generation, or both. This was a case in which the continuity of maladjustment was pervasive and affected the entire family, and each member similarly.

Case 882 – Matthew

Matthew was born in 1953 and was of half Irish origin. The family was composed of two parents and seven children, four boys and three girls, and was regarded as problematic by social services. They had lived for long periods in halfway houses, institutions and furnished rooms. All the older children had been in care, and at the time of one of the first interviews in 1962, they were rehoused. They lived in a working-class four-bedroomed terraced house, which was quite pleasant and was reasonably well furnished. The mother seemed very pleased about it, despite the fact that she did not much like the area because she worried about the antisocial influence of it on the children. The children however were all clean and tidy. Unfortunately, the house did not have a bathroom and hot water, and the mother was quite uneasy about this, given the extra pressure and work that this deficiency caused for her. The family had financial difficulties, and they had struggled with debts before. The father had been evicted from previous furnished places; the mother was quite anxious to remain on an even keel, and keep the home going.

The father had made a bigamous marriage and he was paying money to his first wife. The parents' marital relationship improved in the course of the marriage; the main problem was the husband's drunkenness that his wife looked on with contempt and thought about with disgust.

Matthew's mother

Matthew's mother, who had been convicted, came from a family of eight children, with whom she was on good and warm terms. Her parents were both very much present in her life and loving, and despite the fact that they did not approve of her marriage they reconciled themselves to it and stood by her. She had to get married when she was pregnant with her first child, but she appeared to have regretted that ever since. She admitted that she was the only one of her siblings to have fallen on hard times. She was a quite slim and good-looking lady, very quiet and collaborative. She was surprisingly calm, unhurried and pleasant. She was a very frank informant, though she did not like to come out and say so many negative and bad things. She appeared to be quite fond of her children. She reported that she had left her husband in 1963 because of one of his extremely bad drinking bouts. She took the children away and went to stay with her own mother. Apparently this shook him considerably and it seemed to have straightened him up. Eventually she went back; her husband did not drink subsequently and started to work on a more regular basis.

At times, she was very depressed, and suffered from sleeplessness, headaches and general tiredness. She was unable to show her feelings and kept them to herself. This was also shown by the fact that she did not have any contact with neighbours and did not make any friends. She kept in contact with her own family and her mother who visited regularly, and she did not seem to worry about the social isolation of her life. Having gone through very hard times, occasionally she felt the effects of this. Her considerable strength was seen in her adeptness at putting a sorry story to people in such a convincing and appealing manner that it left any listener helpless. Though superficially cooperative, it was felt by the psychiatric social worker that no true response was ever forthcoming from her. She was quite unable to discipline her children, which for the older children was having the effect of producing a reluctance to face responsibilities. She in fact tended to cover up for the children, and it seemed that she took an almost masochistic enjoyment in seeing the continuation of records of supervision orders. It seemed to the psychiatric social worker, who interviewed her on a few occasions, that behind her compliance she was nevertheless actively encouraging her children in their antisocial attitudes. She tended to rather spoil the children and tried to compensate for the time they spent away from her. She was quite attached to Matthew, who was her eldest son, and was very concerned about Matthew's first offence at age 10.

Matthew's father

Matthew's father was Irish and was one of 14 siblings. He was the third youngest. He had a very unstable job record, drank heavily and had a quick temper but soon calmed down. When he was sober he was very good, but when he was drunk he was quite quarrelsome. His parents were very kind towards him, and probably they had spoilt him a little, especially his father, who was always described in very good terms. Matthew's father was an unkempt small man, who did not look very healthy and who was uneasy and fidgety, though polite and not at all aggressive. He reported some health problems, and had been to the hospital for duodenal ulcers. Even though he had quite frequent spells of unemployment, in 1963 he had kept a maintenance job for one year, and was quite conscientious about it. His parental attitude was difficult to assess; according to his wife, he was strict but never actually ill-treated the children. He had three other children from a previous marriage. He tended to keep the children down, and in any conflict the children tended to side with the mother. He was involved in quite a few problems with the law, having being arrested at various times, and he had five convictions. One burglary was committed with two of his children, one of them being Matthew.

Matthew's siblings

Palena and Lindsay got involved in some small troubles when they helped themselves to something at a big shop. They were discharged at court and since then there had not been another similar occurrence. Their mother admitted it rather shamefacedly. This actually happened when the children were in an institution and were rather demoralized and unhappy. Palena was a pale, rather handsome girl, who was very maternal and kind. She was quite withdrawn and stifled her feelings by focusing upon the problems of her family and friends. Palena, like Matthew later on, also suffered from maternal and emotional deprivation. From an early age, she was aware of parental disharmony and of recriminations associated with her father's overindulgence in alcohol. The family was far from being united, and Palena was often drawn into her parents' rows. The only affective stable figure in her life was her boyfriend, when she was 16 years old, who had a sort of stabilising influence on her. Palena was then charged with stealing a nightdress and two girdles, and she was placed on probation for two years. In 1965, the psychological testing, as a part of her assessment supervision report for the court, placed Palena in a borderline category of intelligence. The psychiatrist who assessed her mentioned that, although Palena did not show signs of frank psychiatric disorder, she was immature and tended to evade difficult situations if possible.

Palena and Lindsay also had poor school records and truanted, but this may be explained by the harsh situation they lived in, where attending school was the least of their worries. The other four children did not have any particular problem or difficulty.

Matthew: childhood

Matthew was very much an unwanted child. The mother had two older daughters and some serious problems with her husband, and had nowhere properly to live to raise children. At the time when Matthew was born the family was settled in a furnished overcrowded room, and the family management was already particularly frustrating.

The first years of Matthew's life were characterised by the experience of loss and continued disappointments, and the lack of parental harmony. The situation between his parents continued to seesaw and his mother began to show some signs of physical distress like fainting, and symptoms of anxiety such as severe headaches, and needed increased support and attention. In between crises his father showed compensatory overanxious reactions with an attempt to please by doing cleaning and cooking to help his wife, but invariably the brief interludes of peace broke down after several weeks, especially when he went binge drinking.

From a very young age, Matthew appeared to be a bit of a problem in regard to being often out and wandering, and most likely being involved with dubious companions. When Matthew was only 3 there was an application for the children to be put into care. Since then there had been several changes of house, usually with changes of school. Matthew spent the next five years in residential care, and was infrequently visited by his mother. The reason was that the family was going to be evicted for arrears of maintenance, while the two older children were sent to some relatives. The psychiatrist who met the family in 1959 mentioned that there were some worries for the children still in care, especially for Matthew who was then just 6.

Matthew resented the fact that two of his sisters and his baby brother were living at home with his mother. Until about the previous Christmas, the children were visited regularly by their mother, until a certain time when the intervals between visits became longer. The children were described as lively and charming, but there was an emphasis on them becoming seriously disturbed. In 1960 all three children had been affected by their mother changing from regular to sporadic visiting, suffering the sense of rejection that became stronger the longer the period was between their mother visiting. Matthew was the one most upset, always remembering that, despite his mother promising to take them back home, they were still in care. Any time their mother went to visit them there was an increase in their hope of going back home, which was regularly disappointed, contributing to an increase in them of a sense of abandonment and despair. In 1961 the mother suffered a health problem which stopped any chance of having the children back home.

Matthew was brought up in a harsh educational regime, which may have been precipitated by the constant marital disharmony. The matrimonial situation of his parents was characterised by severe rows that occurred when Matthew's father had too much to drink. No doubt this atmosphere contributed to the lack of supervision which Matthew needed to contain his emotional instability and distress. The climate in which Matthew and his siblings were reared was poor, not only because of the deprived and neglectful parental attitude, but also because of the disharmony that characterised the family interactions. The father was not involved in Matthew's activities when he was an adolescent. When he first went back home from the children's home, in 1961, Matthew was afraid of the dark and thought that there was a man in his room. He was moody, especially in the morning, and wandered off, to the extent that his mother had to look for him.

From an early age, 8–10, Matthew started showing a daring attitude, a high level of antisociality and impulsiveness, and behavioural problems. However, he was not the only child in the family to have these problems, and his father had a criminal record, having been involved in different criminal activities. When Matthew was aged 11, the psychiatric report indicated that there was no sign of physical disorder nor any evidence of formal illness or severe emotional disturbances, even though he started to manifest some signs of neuroticism (on the NJMI[3]). Matthew was of dull intelligence, his verbal and performance IQs being 87 and 86 respectively on the WISC. Matthew's reading age was 5 years, indicating his continuing need for remedial tuition. Even though Matthew was not recommended for psychiatric treatment then, he was assessed as a quite vulnerable and high-risk child, not least because of his long period of institutionalization.

Matthew hoped to avoid further separation from his family, but the outlook for his future did not appear good.

Matthew was a shy and small boy for his age, and attempted to compensate by fantasising about himself, and by identifying with bigger older boys. Matthew was never at a loss for words, especially when defending his rights or his innocence, but despite his dislike of criticism he was able to listen to reason if it was presented in a friendly manner. He was precocious in becoming a regular smoker at 13 years of age, and his antisociality began to emerge rather early and continued to be high throughout his life development. He had a bullying attitude, and very frequently he used lies to justify his behaviour.

From an early age, Matthew was very interested in animals and chatted at length with exaggerated tales of his animals, when his attitude and demeanour were far less disturbed than formerly. At around age 12, Matthew started to truant from school so he could go to feed pigeons. One of his teachers continued to encourage him and Matthew began to cope with his backwardness at reading.

In 1965, with the help of a very sensitive probation officer, Matthew made excellent progress and he was developing considerable self-confidence. He no longer showed a need to associate with the local delinquents but spent some of his time indoors playing with his brothers or with his classmates. It was evident that Matthew needed a great deal of encouragement and affection from significant adults, and when he felt supported he could disassociate himself from those antisocial activities that became part of his routine in the first 10–11 years of his life. Matthew's progress at school was excellent and he developed considerable self-confidence. He attended school regularly and mastered some subjects that he had found impossible formerly. If he did not associate with the local delinquents and played indoors with his brothers or with class mates, Matthew could have control his behaviour and progressed successfully into a prosocial life.

At age 14, his peers rated him as dishonest and unpopular, though he was attending a school with a high rate of delinquency. He had some concentration difficulties, which might explain why his school attendance record and results were poor. He was often involved in truancy, and wandered around. Matthew failed to achieve expected educational standards. He liked the more practical pursuits. Despite all these problems, thanks to a sensitive teacher who saw his potential, Matthew was encouraged to do the practical things he was interested in, such as looking after some pets. He started to report to his probation officer regularly, and became more relaxed and cheerful.

On only a few occasions did it seem that Matthew and his brother were involved in the father's offences. Matthew had some previous trouble in 1963 when he was just 10 and completed a two-year probation order. He mixed with a particular local group of older boys. Some offences, which involved breaking into a shop, were committed with three of these boys, and handling stolen goods was committed with another one.

At age 14, Matthew was the youngest of the group and he was fascinated by them. He found it very hard to break this association, also because one of the older boys was going out with his sister. Being always the youngest and the smallest member of the delinquent gang that he associated with, he was frequently used as a scapegoat and beaten up by the others. On one occasion, he was found tied to a luggage rack in a railway carriage, but at the time he refused to disclose the names of the boys responsible, because he was terrified of the repercussions.

Matthew: adolescence

During his adolescent years, Matthew started again to truant from school, even though he showed some signs of improvement. It was recognised by the head of the education department that Matthew needed a period of firmness in this very critical period of his life, since he was unlikely to take kindly to activities with an educational flavour. At the end of 1965 Matthew's family underwent another extremely stressful period, with his father drinking continuously and returning home roaring and fighting. Matthew's mother was extremely depressed and she began to show some signs and symptoms of anxiety and severe headaches followed by fainting fits. She was physically exhausted but she tried her best to give the children a good Christmas, working even at nights in the general post office, and doing some extra hours in a foundation. Matthew's mother was so exhausted that she took out a summons in the matrimonial court; however, she did not persist with this because of the dependency that existed between the parents.

Matthew left school at age 15, and subsequently he had some spells of work, constantly interrupted by periods of inactivity. Matthew worked as a metal worker, a packer, a waiter and as a greengrocer's assistant, which was the longest spell of work (six to seven months) until the firm closed. He continued having difficulties in concentrating, and was aggressive and daring, and he failed to settle and lead a more stable life. He developed a strong anti-police attitude, was involved with delinquent friends, started to steal outside home, and self-reported high involvement in delinquency.

When Matthew was 16, he was remanded in a Detention Centre. He was resentful that the other boys involved had not been charged but realised his own guilt. He was severely thrashed by his father, who told him to keep away from the gang, and Matthew did so. During the period on remand, Matthew was very worried and unhappy at the prospect of seeing a psychiatrist, because he felt that this branded him as 'mad'. His mother showed quite an understanding of him, and did all she could to reassure him. His father, on the other hand, made it clear that nothing good could come of his son seeing a psychiatrist because he felt that Matthew's offences were no more than boyish wildness.

The psychologist who met Matthew in 1969 said that Matthew functioned at the low average level of ability, but potentially his ability was within the good average range. His verbal and performance IQs were 89 and 93 respectively on the Wechsler Bellevue Scale for adolescents and adults. Matthew could read for practical purposes, but he came within the dyslexic category when he had to do spelling and written work. According to the psychologist, his poor spelling came from real perceptual difficulties, which had handicapped him during all the school years. His lack of interest in school was evident since primary school, and was closely linked with the difficulties Matthew experienced in learning to read, and when to a limited extent he overcame this difficulty, his much greater handicap was in connection with written work. In test situations, Matthew showed difficulty in reproducing designs, and difficulty in transposing letter symbols from one place to another, and his low score on the picture completion test was related to his poor powers of observation. On the other hand, Matthew was able to perform at a good average level of ability when he was given practical tasks. He was slow and methodical, and he did not rush into trial and error methods of solving problems; he always thought it out carefully and then put the pieces together. The psychologist concluded that Matthew could do a semi-skilled practical training quite well and derive satisfaction from it.

Initially Matthew was unhappy to stay at the Detention Centre, and had plans to abscond, but when he found his plans thwarted and realised the likelihood of getting into further trouble if he did not change his behaviour, he started to settle down into the routine and became accepted by his peers. His behaviour became exemplary; only on one occasion did he lose self-control and truanted, spending all day until evening time with his mates. He joined in all recreational activities, being a very good footballer and table tennis player. He was very energetic and enthusiastic, and needed the release of physical activities to cope with his natural restlessness. Whilst he did not form any strong tie with any particular individual, he had integrated well and he had no problem in living peacefully in a group setting.

Matthew was not a particular problem for the staff, but he was prepared to exploit latitude and he tested the staff to find out what the acceptable limits were and then kept to them. While not actively engaged in disruptive activities he enjoyed being a spectator as long as there was no danger of personal repercussions. It was recognised by the professional people who examined Matthew that he missed being at home, but learned quite well to accept being away, and he was quite philosophical about going away to school. He did not show any particular emotional disturbances, apart from being quite malleable and gullible, and tended to opt out of difficult situations by fantasising about himself. Although these characteristics indicated his susceptibility to be easily led into further trouble, it was also hoped that he could equally be influenced for the better, by receiving continual encouragement via parents, school teachers and probation officers, which might boost his self-confidence.

Mathew: young adulthood

At ages 18 and 32, Matthew's antisociality continued to be high and he had an active and prolific criminal career. He was a consumer of cannabis, drugs and alcohol. He had a high level of neuroticism and held a very aggressive attitude, which was certainly causing him some problems in social situations; hence the easiness with which he got involved in criminal activities.

Matthew got married at age 20 and had a son. Matthew's further and persistent life of crime until adulthood perhaps showed the side effects that his childhood experiences of loss and emotional instability had on him. Matthew got involved in fights, consumed alcohol and drugs, and was assessed as very high in alcoholism on the CAGE test. He had some problems with finding employment. His unemployment was frequent and lasted for long periods, with his longest period of staying in a job being less than two years. He had frequent rows with his wife. At age 32, his level of life failure was extremely high.

Mathew: adulthood

When Matthew was interviewed at age 32, he lived in an up-market council rented maisonette, which was nice, well-kept and well-furnished, without particular problems, and in a nice area. Matthew lived there with his wife and son. Matthew said that some years earlier he moved out of London because of his son's health condition. The boy suffered from croup (which is an inflammation of the voice box and windpipe). This often leads to a barking cough or hoarseness, especially when a child cries. It usually affects children of a very young age between six months and 3 years old, but it could affect older children too. Matthew suffered from it when he was a boy. The doctor advised the family that it would be better for the child to live near the coast. However, when their son was older they decided to move back to the city. Matthew said that there was not a specific pattern of activities he organised with his son. During the week, Matthew spent four or five days with his son; they went out walking to the park, and at times went to the cinema. At weekends, when possible they went to the countryside or to a museum; on Saturdays all the family went shopping together.

Matthew was a serious character who did not give a lot away about himself. Something that stood out was his interest in his son, while he was a bit ambiguous towards his wife, but his relationship with his wife was described in positive terms. Matthew was certainly interested in giving his son the love, warmth and affectionate parental presence that he had never experienced.

Matthew mostly agreed with his wife about their son's education, but some disagreements were present over letting the child play out with other children. His wife was not very keen about it, because she did not want to have trouble with the neighbours. Their child was not a problematic boy but, at times, he was disobedient, got involved in fights and had some temper tantrums. When Matthew and his wife argued, they stopped talking to each other and sleeping in the same bed for a while; during these rows they usually shouted and threw things at each other.

There seemed to be a tinge of sadness about Matthew, but it was very difficult to decipher anything about his inner world, and to suggest what that might be due to. There was no doubt that Matthew's life was very complicated by his antisocial attitude and behaviour, but at the same time it appeared that Matthew felt beaten up and downtrodden by life events. Talking about himself, Matthew mentioned that he was less able than usual to face up to his own problems, and he was feeling nervous and highly strung all the time. However, he was also feeling hopeful about his future, even though he mentioned that he felt less able than usual to face up to his problems.

Matthew's working pattern continued to be unstable, having going through some unemployment periods over the years. He mainly worked as a landscape gardener with his uncle during the summer months. He did not have any formal training, but he learned as he went along. He claimed benefits; he admitted asking his family for some money, and he borrowed money and things from some friends.

At the time of the interview at age 32, Matthew was banned from driving because of a drink driving offence. He admitted having consumed cannabis in the last year, but was trying to give it up. Matthew's health condition seemed good. He talked about his own family with mixed feelings; he met his father every fortnight, but his mother only three times a year.

When Matthew was 49, he was interviewed again. His situation had evolved rather dramatically in the previous 17 years. He was now homeless, and living in friends' houses, sleeping on the floor; his situation was so unstable that he even carried his toothbrush around with him. Matthew had split up with his wife about a year earlier. He did not have a stable occupation, and continued to be self-employed, doing some gardening on request. He had accumulated some debts with some money lenders. He mentioned that he was attending a detox programme to deal with his alcoholism.

The life history of Matthew was characterised by a continuous succession of attempts to stop drinking and abuse of drugs, followed by failures. Matthew was a chronic alcoholic and a drug abuser. His problems stemmed from his childhood, most of which he spent in a children's home. Because of the pain that these memories caused him, Matthew would not and could not answer many of the questions about his childhood or even about his siblings. He freely admitted that he drank to block out the pain of his past. Matthew could not give any detail about his parents and family life with his brothers and sisters because it was too much of a painful subject to discuss.

Contrary to what he said in the previous interview age 32 about his son and his education, Matthew said that, when the boy was young, there was some disagreement with his wife, whom he considered too lenient. About his son, Matthew said that the boy did not have any particular problem, but that at around age 5 the boy started to have fears and show some worries. However, Matthew could not be more precise and give any specific information about this topic. This sounded a failure from his perspective, given the centrality that his son had played in his life.

Matthew was trapped in a vicious circle: the alcohol interfered with his work, the work was sporadic and Matthew's need to drink increased. Matthew admitted that he could fly into a rage: 'a red mist comes into me'. That rage had contributed significantly to destroy his relational world; in some cases it also led to criminal consequences, for instance when he physically destroyed a pub, which ended in a court case. This is just an example of how his life was affected by his mood. He seemed powerless to stop his destructive ways, despite much intervention. He continued to be extremely delinquent in his attitude, and was actively involved in criminal activities. Matthew had, at the time of the interview, a girlfriend but it sounded to be an unstable relationship, which seemed to strengthen his need to drink and reinforce his drinking habit.

Matthew did not have any desire to change; the reasons behind this could be rooted in a life moulded into a chronic antisocial pattern. He was very unwell, and unless he stopped drinking he was unlikely to live much longer. Matthew's criminal career had a long history, which went back to 1963 when he was 10. He continued offending all his life, and was involved in violent acts from an early age. His last offence occurred when he was 51, and his criminal career lasted over 41 years. He spent just over one year in prison. He was a prolific and versatile offender who was convicted for 31 offences, including just two serious motoring offences. He was also a convicted football hooligan. His *variety index* indicates that he was involved in 12 different types of crime, and four of them were violent and sex offences. He died suddenly at age 53 possibly because of a drug overdose and alcohol abuse (according to his wife).

Case 763 – Ralph

Ralph was born in 1953. He came from a working-class family composed of two biological parents, and an older sister. There was another sibling who was born in between who died. From 1962 they lived in a modern detached house in a close, which was beautifully kept and spotless. The children had their own rooms, but Ralph was not very pleased about it because of his fears of the dark and being alone.

The family was very cohesive, and there were warm feelings towards each other. The marital climate was positive, and the parents seemed happy in their relationship. The mother and father got married when they were 18 years old. Both parents were pleased about their home, and they did not want to move ever again. Financially the family seemed quite secure. They had a garden with lots of roses, both front and back, and both parents spent a good deal of time and care in keeping the home nice.

The parents tried to pull together, to ask one another about which decisions to take, and never disagreed in front of the children. The educational attitude in the family was harsh, at times inconsistent, and particularly authoritarian. Both parents cared about their children, and wanted the best for them, especially for Ralph who was the youngest in the family. They were very helpful and collaborative in the interviews.

Ralph's mother

Ralph's mother came from a family of six sisters. She was the middle one, and she used to look after the younger ones. She had an easy and not strict childhood. She was close to her parents, and also to her siblings, even though they were not in touch any more. Her father was a docker. Her mother was a quite cold, not loving, very strict and quite clean person, who remarried after her husband died. She did not see her mother, even though they kept a friendly and harmonious relationship.

Ralph's mother was a nice and well-spoken lady, who was anxious, obsessional and neurotic, and somehow ambivalent in her attitude. She left school at age 14. She started to work in a bookbinding business but she left because her mother did not like it. She then went to work in a factory making deck chairs and ironing boards and kept this job until she got married. She went back to work when Ralph was 3 years old, and she worked in a school canteen, as a cook, and was very satisfied about it. She prepared and served food until the afternoon, and she was free during holidays and school terms.

She complained a great deal about Ralph's difficulties that she had to deal with. However, she spoiled and overprotected him. At the same time, she was vindictive and punitive in her statements, threatening to send him away, and said that he was making her ill. She got irritated with him over small matters, and was rejecting.

The mother was quite moody, easily irritable, often tired and unpredictable. She was a healthy woman, but when Ralph was around 10, she had haemorrhages but tried to hide the problem and did not go to the doctor for a check-up; finally she was diagnosed with a fibroid. She lost a lot of blood, and needed five pints of blood transfused after the operation. She had a full hysterectomy and was in a very low physical state for a while. She was out of work for seven weeks; in the meantime her husband and daughter provided for Ralph and for the management of the house. She used to go out with her husband, especially on Saturday night, and they used to do regular things like visiting relatives, playing bingo or having a drink.

Ralph's father

Ralph's father, who had been convicted, was a dark-skinned and dark-haired man, extremely neat and handsome. He was not particularly thoughtful or over bright. He came from a family of nine, and he had a very hard childhood. The work situation then was very bad, and his father was frequently unemployed. At times, the family did not have enough to eat, and Ralph's father seemed to know well enough, from his own experience, what it meant to live with nothing and without things. His parents were described as very kind, but he was not in contact with them.

Ralph's father was a quite indulgent and tolerant person, who had not many ideas of how to lay down any particular rules or initiate anything. But he was the sort of person who, when he made up his mind, did what he planned to do. He did not worry about his children, because he had an absolute faith in them. However, he was consistent in his attitude and behaviour. He was uncritical of his children, and allowed them to grow up as they pleased. His belief was that, by giving them all the things he himself had missed in his childhood, life would turn out well for them.

Ralph's father was unprepared to run his children's lives and did not spend much time with them, and he did not believe that any parental interference in the way that the children wanted to grow up could be any good for the children. For instance, according to the father, his daughter lived her own life, and he entirely accepted her choice. This was equally true for Ralph, who enjoyed his sports, and pursued boxing and football and many other activities. The father thought that by letting Ralph do all these activities Ralph could outgrow his restlessness. He was devoted to Ralph, even though Ralph never played when his father was around. The father never hit Ralph, but one loud word was very effective.

Ralph's father left school at age 14, and then he did demolition work. He was then called into the Navy, and afterwards he worked in the iron business, but he was badly paid, so he decided to work as a docker, which was very well paid. He liked his job, and wanted to stay in it. He disliked debts, and was particularly strict about that. He was involved in some criminal activities when he was a juvenile.

Ralph's father was in quite good health. He got sometimes very frustrated and preoccupied, but he never suffered from insomnia or anything else. He rarely went out, and he always went out with his wife. They had a car, which was unusual at that time for the parents' generation.

Ralph's sibling

Ralph had an older sister, Marika, who had been a quiet and calm baby, very different from her brother. She worked as a typist, and helped the family both financially and practically with the family maintenance. She left school at age 15, and attended evening classes. She kept herself very neat, had many beautiful clothes and was very loving towards her brother. She used to give him some pocket money. She was the chief confidant of Ralph, who told her everything and spent long times talking to her. She however passed most of this on to her mother, with the loving but at times naïve thought that the family could control him if everything was shared.

Ralph: childhood

Ralph was a much wanted boy. He was born by Caesarian section, and had a very bad infancy. He spent five days in hospital probably with meningitis. He was a difficult baby, demanding constant attention. Hence, he was nursed all the time, and was thoroughly spoiled. Therefore, Ralph was a rather clinging boy, liked to be where his mother was and lived with the constant preoccupation that one day she was going to abandon him. As a child, Ralph was unable to stay in the dark and in his bed for the whole night, and got worried about noises. At least until his teens, he could not sleep the whole night in his own bed and always crept into his parents' bed, causing some uneasiness in the family.

Ralph was unable to sit still, and always twisting and twiddling even when watching TV or reading. Even during his sleep, he was restless. He was very obsessed over the use of the lavatory at school, and he preferred to avoid it, and rushed home in a great hurry in order to go to the toilet at home. It was difficult when Ralph started school; he cried for a fortnight, and his mother had to sit in the class next to him to help him to adjust to the school environment. When he changed school, this ordeal had to be repeated again. At the beginning of school, Ralph did very well; he was a capable child, and behaved properly, without truanting, and came fifth out of 42 in his class. However, it emerged quite early that Ralph was a quite restless child, who liked fighting and was frequently in trouble with other children.

Ralph started to behave antisocially at a very young age. At 8–10, his levels of antisociality and troublesomeness were high; he was quite daring, and he was rated as dishonest by his peers, and was very unpopular amongst them. His teachers found Ralph quite problematic and not easy to discipline, which might have been related to his difficulty in concentrating and his restlessness especially at school, when he had to abide by rules and time schedules. On the physical and athletic side, Ralph was an extremely good swimmer, and he was very keen on football and all sport in general. He kept himself very busy and active, and went to play football every single night.

At age 12–14, Ralph was often involved in fights outside the home. He continued to be highly antisocial, aggressive and daring in his attitude and behaviour; he was a bully and a regular liar, often being involved with delinquent acquaintances. He was a quite nervous and anxious person, and his difficulty in concentration continued to affect his conduct both at home and at school. He truanted often, and developed a strong anti-police attitude. Ralph started smoking at an early age, before 13.

Ralph's mother suffered from his disobedient and defiant attitude, and especially from the disrespect with which Ralph addressed her, shouting or ignoring her requests. However, Ralph still showed a lot of affection towards her, and at time he showed jealousy when his mother was giving attention to her daughter or other children. She tried to be calm and believed that it was just a phase that her son was going through, and it would stop when he matured.

The psychiatric social worker indicated that there had been a complete reversal over discipline in the family. As Ralph got older, he defied his mother more and more, and did not take any notice of her. As a consequence, she left all the disciplinary matters to Ralph's father. Ralph obeyed his father, who was quite strict, because he wanted to avoid punishment.

The major worry of Ralph's mother was that she did not know Ralph's friends and those whom he associated with, especially in the evening. She wanted to have some control over him, but he resented it, and became very secretive over himself and his whereabouts. In retaliation, Ralph's parents stopped giving him pocket money, but this made no difference. The chief punishment for Ralph was keeping him in, which the mother knew hurt him more than anything else.

Initially, the mother shielded Ralph from his father by not telling her husband most of the things Ralph did, and tried to keep bad school reports from him, but when Ralph became an adolescent she had realised that her attitude towards him had made things even worse. Therefore, her only strategy, now that Ralph was older, was to leave his father to deal with him. It was not clear from what she wanted to shield Ralph, since her husband did not seem a very strict disciplinarian or punitive figure. Ralph's father never hit him, but at times his mother reported that when his father was upset he could look at his son with intense eyes as if he were going to hit him. The mother slapped Ralph when she was infuriated, but when he became an adolescent this discipline was not effective whatsoever, because Ralph was bigger and stronger than her.

Ralph: adolescence

Ralph's ambition was to go into the Merchant Navy. His mother encouraged him all along and helped him to look around for some opportunities, as she was glad for him to have some ambitions. Nonetheless, Ralph's attitude to school changed considerably over the years. He disliked school intensely and wanted to leave as soon as he could. He was bored with school, and wanted to have a job. His behaviour improved when he started working two evenings a week and on Saturday at a supermarket for several weeks. However, because he was under age and could not produce an insurance card, he had to give up this job.

In 1965, Ralph was involved in a school fight and he hit a boy so badly that he was taken out from school and then expelled. About Ralph's expulsion from school, his mother tended to minimise it, as if it had occurred because of just a single incident. She regarded the school as the major source of problems, since Ralph always got involved in fights at school and never in the neighbourhood. There was only one instance when Ralph got into a fight with a local boy.

It seemed that Ralph enjoyed fighting, and usually it was the other boys who got hurt. She blamed herself for having sent Ralph to a school not near home, so that it became more difficult for her to supervise her son. However, Ralph's parents appeared to see fighting as not a serious problem, at least not as serious as stealing, so that they were not particularly upset about Ralph's expulsion from school.

In his new school, where he did not know anybody and could start afresh, Ralph was quite happy to start. However, his interest in having more spending money and wanting to earn was putting much pressure on him and his parents, to the extent that the family climate deteriorated, as did his school performance. He even dropped the idea of going into the Merchant Navy. Ralph's troubles at school mainly stemmed from his lack of commitment; several bad reports were written about Ralph's underachievement and bad behaviour; his parents were asked to go and see the headmaster in 1968. Both parents were angry about it because they knew that Ralph had the ability to do well and they wanted him to stay on. The school was prepared to keep him on if Ralph was prepared to work but they, as they put it, could not change his mind.

Ralph's mother was quite indulgent with him, and in the end gave him what he wanted. She felt that, once he had his own job and became seriously involved with a girl, he would become more responsible and serious about his commitments.

Ralph's nervousness was starting to become more evident in adolescence. He cried quite often when he was frustrated over something he wanted and he was refused, such as more pocket money. When Ralph's father spoke severely to him, Ralph often cried. When he was worried about school problems or court cases, he became very nervous, could not sleep, and used to call his mother many times during the night. Ralph's mother believed that smoking was, in the case of Ralph, a nervous habit; he disappeared to go to the lavatory to smoke, only when he was 'on the twitch'. However, he never smoked openly in front of his father.

Ralph left school at age 15. For the next three years he worked, but his employment pattern was disrupted by continuous changes so that Ralph stated that his jobs were too numerous to remember and he could not supply any details. Up to age 21, he worked as a skilled steel fixer for numerous companies.

Ralph committed an offence of assault (grievous bodily harm) at age 15, and it was then that his criminal career took off. He had a high self-reported delinquency measured at ages 14 and 16, and was often associated with delinquent boys with whom he also co-offended.

Ralph: young adulthood

A consistent pattern of antisociality was even more evident when Ralph was between ages 16 and 18. He regularly consumed cannabis and alcohol, and drove after drinking. Ralph started to get involved in gang activities and fights after drinking, accumulated some debts and his anti-police attitude strengthened. He was a heavy smoker and a drug abuser. His self-reported delinquency involvement became more serious, reporting even violence. At age 20, Ralph was single; it was not clear at this stage whether he was still residing with his parents or with a young woman. His files indicated that at age 22 Ralph was still living with his parents, paying them some money for his keep.

Ralph: adulthood

In adulthood, at age 32, Ralph was living with his mother, as his father had died. However, he had also bought a place, which had been improved, and he planned to move to this in the near future. His living conditions were reasonable and quite comfortable. He was going out regularly with a girlfriend, with whom he was going to live. He had a child, but when he was interviewed at age 32 his partner and child were living somewhere else.

Ralph continued to be antisocial in his attitude and behaviour, and was more involved than previously in heavy gambling. He was a consumer of cannabis and alcohol. He spent most evenings out with his friends, and getting into fights. Ralph's working pattern was unsuccessful, irregular and casual. When not working, he claimed supplementary benefits. In his spare time, Ralph went out with friends. He enjoyed staying in bed until late in the morning, and spent his time going to the pub, and played darts and snooker at the pub or at the snooker hall. It was interesting that, while Ralph felt that he was able to concentrate, keep himself busy and make decisions about things in the same way as usual, when he was asked about his difficulties, he mentioned that he felt unable more than usual to overcome them.

Ralph admitted to consuming a large amount of alcohol that included also spirits and vodka. Just before his baby was born, he was caught driving under the influence of alcohol for the second time. In 1985, he was again caught driving while disqualified. He got involved in a serious theft in which a large amount of clothing was stolen, and was given an 18-month prison sentence for this. Ralph did not give out much information about this offence.

At age 47, Ralph was interviewed again at his mother's house. She was now an elderly lady, and was house-bound after a very severe fall. His sister had died of lung cancer. Unsurprisingly, he arrived late for the appointment, and did not show any apologetic attitude. Towards his mother and his partner he was quite dismissive. He kept on smoking during the whole interview. Since the last interview, in 1985, he had managed to buy his own accommodation, and had been living with his partner for many years. Their relationship was going well, and he saw himself still living with her in five years' time. He was now working as a contract driver and was dealing with deliveries.

Ralph's general health condition was fine, but he suffered from an ulcer. He now had three children, all boys, and let his partner deal with them. The children had some behavioural problems. The oldest one started to be disobedient and manifested temper tantrums at age 2; when aged 8 he started lying, and at age 14 he began to steal outside home. The middle one was into frequent lying and temper tantrums as well since age 3; he got involved in fighting and destroying things at age 7, and started to have some nervous habits at age 10. The youngest one was quite disobedient since age 3, and at age 4 he was restless and ran away from home. He was into fights too, since age 5, and started to develop some nervous habits.

In Ralph's social life his friend featured considerably, and he believed that what made a friend was trust and loyalty. He developed a betting habit, and he used to gamble between £200 and £300 per week, but claimed that he usually recouped his bets. In character, Ralph came across as fairly friendly and helpful. However, he seemed to have led a very criminal life style, and was not averse to criminal activities even in adulthood. He admitted gang involvement from his late adolescence and continued until his early adulthood.

Ralph drank, gambled, smoked and did everything else to the extreme. He talked of his sons a little, but seemed to put only one person first: himself. The interviewer felt that Ralph exaggerated some aspects of his life, such as his income and his success at gambling, while underplaying other aspects, such as going to prison for stealing and other unsuccessful incidents. He was assessed as an immature and morally lacking character, who believed that with a little charm he could make anyone see the world through his eyes. What seemed to emerge from his accounts and his family situation was a sort of intergenerational continuity of his childhood problems into his own children.

Talking about his criminal career, Ralph admitted that he mostly offended for money. Ralph's criminal career included 22 official offences, of which three were serious motoring offences. Like many chronic offenders, he had a versatile criminal pattern. The *index variety* of his offending career was 10, which included three violent offences and one sex offence. Ralph committed his first offence when he was 15, and continued to commit crimes over a career duration of 37 years, and served a total of one year in prison. He committed his last offence at age 52. Ralph's level of psychopathy, measured by the PCL:SV, was 12, with a score of 4 points on the affective/interpersonal factor, and 8 on the irresponsible/antisocial life style.

Case 504 – Jeremy

Jeremy was born in 1953. His family was composed of Jeremy's mother and seven children (four boys and three girls), and Jeremy was the fifth oldest child. In 1959, his mother had a miscarriage, a stillborn baby after six months of pregnancy.

The family background in which Jeremy grew up was a difficult one, and very poor. The family lived in a four-bedroom council flat, which was quite spacious and was reasonably well kept and tidy. It was equipped with modern teak furniture, an enormous radiogram, a large TV set, a cocktail cabinet and a modern table with upholstered chairs. However, the home conditions were poor. Two bedrooms were each shared by two boys, and the three girls shared a room. There were eight separate beds in the house. In 1963, after two visits, the description of the family given by the psychiatric social worker was of a family struggling to keep all the pieces together.

The parental attitude in the house, especially when the father was living with them, before the divorce, was particularly harsh, and the situation was aggravated by the fact that the parents were in continuous disagreement even over the children's education, and there was a high level of marital disharmony.

Jeremy's parents divorced around 1963–4. It was an appalling marriage, and very stressful. The father was a violent drinker, irritable, inconsistent, erratic, harsh to his children, giving them many beatings, and was interested in other women and led the whole family a terrible dance. In 1965 Jeremy's mother told the psychiatric social worker that she did not know how she stood so many years with her ex-husband (Jeremy's father) and that she was glad that she could have some peace once he left. Jeremy's father remarried a woman older than himself, who ran a pub and drove an elegant car. It was very painful to her that, when the father saw the children in the street, he completely ignored them. By a court order, he had to pay some money to the family, but maintenance was still a debated issue in the court.

The family seemed to have extremely good close relationships with one another, and there were no complaints about anybody. The children seemed very cheerful. The children were described as good and sensible, concerned for their mother and for each other. The home atmosphere was described as too loving and overcharged with sentimentality.

Jeremy's mother

Jeremy's mother was a tiny little woman who appeared somewhat nervous, anxious and tense, showing signs of strain. However, she was always talking about the good luck she had in having such a wonderful family. She had a happy childhood until her mother died when she was 13. She and her brothers went to a Catholic convent, and she stayed there until she was 16, and they were the happiest years of her life. She left school at age 16, and went into service. She had never heard of her father until she was married and had children. Her father then went to find her. He turned out to be a very nice man, and tried to make up with her for the years that she had been neglected by him. She did not feel bitter about him, and did not regret the experience of being brought up in a convent. When war broke out, she worked as a typist and a duplicator.

Jeremy's mother had three brothers who were all happily married. At the beginning of her marriage, one of the brothers was living with her and her husband, but he left because he could not stand the quarrels between his sister and her husband.

Jeremy's mother was acting as the only parent because her husband deserted the family in 1962 when Jeremy was just 9 years old. On all occasions related to CSDD interview meetings, she was initially ambivalent, being a refuser and forgetting about the appointments, but when the psychiatric social worker arrived, she was always welcoming and pleasant.

Jeremy's mother was a physically feeble lady who suffered from some forms of depression, and was nervous and anxious, which did not help to build up secure emotional stability for her and the children. When Jeremy was around 8 years old, she admitted having taken an overdose of aspirin and was taken to hospital. She was sorry about this act, and said that she would not do anything like that again. In 1963, when Jeremy was 10, she said that she had been living on her nerves for years, and that her nerves were in a state of shock but she refused to go to the doctor. She described herself as full of nervous tics but she was beginning to feel better. Subsequently, in another interview in 1964 she admitted having sleeping problems and having to take sleeping pills.

Despite this, she was always painting a rosy picture of her family, and always underlining how good the children were with her. Jeremy's mother had to struggle a great deal to maintain a climate of affection and love in the family, and was pushed very hard financially, and she just managed to scrape along. Her ex-husband's allowance was now paid directly to the National Assistance Board. She never had a holiday herself, and her children never went away because the girls would refuse to go without their mother. She projected very much a picture of a brave little woman who had battled against all the odds but was supported by the extreme good nature of her children of whom she was very proud. The children received free dinners at school and occasionally got some help with clothing and shoes from a care committee.

She enjoyed staying with her children, towards whom she was overprotective; the children spent their time running around helping her. It may be that, because of the shocking situation of their parents' marriage and the traumatic break up of it, the climate of oversentimentality was what the mother wanted to provide to her children to compensate for the emotional strain they went through with their father. Jeremy's mother spent most of her time at home; she did not like going out or playing bingo. She liked going to the cinema but she could not afford it.

She minimised her sons' troubles, saying that they were 'wonderful' boys. When confronted with Gerald's trouble with the police in 1965, she kept on being very positive, being sure that he had learned his lesson and was not going to commit any illegal activity any more. If, on the one hand, her optimistic attitude encouraged family closeness and affection towards their mother and the other siblings, on the other hand, it did not encourage her children to have a sense of responsibility for their own behaviour and it had some consequences in the family dynamics.

In 1964, when Jeremy was almost 11, his mother was still without a job, and still extremely worried about the divorce from Jeremy's father, who was in arrears with payments to her. He had a preliminary hearing and he pretended not to earn anything, and another hearing was imminent. Jeremy's mother saw the solicitor frequently at that time in the hope of finding some solution. Financially there was still a big strain in the family, which put pressure on everyone in the family. The oldest children contributed to their living but actually all their financial contribution was used for feeding them. At the interview, which took place in 1965, the mother was very cooperative and ready to see the interviewer. On various occasions the mother mentioned that she was unable to work, and that she did not like leaving her children on their own; she needed to be there for them, and especially during school term time she would not leave them unattended.

Jeremy's father

Jeremy's father, who had been convicted, left school at age 14, attaining just the elementary level. He had an unskilled job as a scaffolder, and worked only sporadically. He was a heavy drinker, drinking away a fortune. Apparently, he started drinking at age 14 when his parents took him to the pub. He used to keep his wife extremely short of cash and give her a very small amount of money, keeping the rest (three times more than the amount he gave her to look after the whole family) for himself. The family had to live on benefits and on what the mother managed to obtain from the social services. He used to beat his wife up, and smashed her home up many times. There were frightful rows between him and his wife. When she learnt that her husband had found another woman and gone to live with her, she felt that this event was a godsend and gave him a divorce.

Jeremy's father was a violent and brutal man; in the Army he was a deserter various times. He held the attitude of one who did not care less for anything, and was against any sort of authority or discipline. He was very neglectful towards his children, and used to beat them up when still at home. He was very much against institutions and refused to buy school uniforms for his children. Of course much of this information came from Jeremy's mother, and it could have been biased.

Jeremy's siblings

Redmund, the oldest brother, acted as a father substitute, was very responsible and helped his mother both financially and as a reliable male figure in the family. When he went into the Army, the mother missed him greatly because he was her great standby. He was engaged to get married, but his mother hoped that he was not going to interrupt his Army life; he was in Germany and was doing very well. Of the other brothers, Gerald was a tough hulking lad with, as his mother put it, a rough exterior. Gerald was always involved in fights and minor offences. Fabian left school at age 15, and he started to work part-time soon after.

At the time of the interview in 1963, Linda, Jeremy's oldest sister, was pregnant, and she then gave birth to an illegitimate baby. She had spent six weeks in a Mother and Baby House, having first thought of giving the baby away for adoption, but later she changed her mind and decided to keep the baby, a very attractive child, who was looked after by his grandmother. The family did not know whether Linda refused to say who the father was or simply did not know who he was, given the fact that she had lived a quite promiscuous life. Linda worked in a factory and enjoyed the job; she gave her mother plenty of money to care for the baby.

The two younger girls were doing well. Beatrice had a serious accident falling off a wall at school and fractured her skull, but she fully recovered. Karen was a calm child. Not much more information was available about Jeremy's siblings.

Jeremy: childhood

Jeremy was not a problem; he was quieter than the other siblings and not nearly as tough. He did not mix so well, and although he could stick up for himself, he chose not to fight or get into any kind of difficulties. He was not very keen on school but went regularly, and the only objection he had was that the boys he met at school were rather a rough lot. However, Jeremy had some concentration problems, and he was a restless child. Jeremy had only a dim recollection of his father and for the last eight years he had looked to his mother for support and guidance. His mother had started to work at a local factory.

At age 8–10, Jeremy manifested some antisocial attitudes and behaviour. These problems were not related only to him, given that some of his brothers and one of his sisters were showing some behavioural problems as well. He was a quite daring boy; he was rated dishonest by his peers, and was unpopular amongst them. Jeremy's level of vulnerability was high, especially because of the emotional and social instability of the family situation which did not guarantee a secure, protected, and affective base for a child to grow up in. The family situation did not improve in subsequent years, especially because the financial conditions were very precarious, and the father, after the divorce, continued to ignore the children and did not support them.

Jeremy: adolescence

At age 14, Jeremy started to manifest some symptoms of nervousness and anxiety. He was described by his mother as a worrier over little things. For example, he seemed to be obsessed over checking again and again whether the gas was off, or washing his hands with an excessive frequency. He had a fear of germs and accidents occurring to him.

However, Jeremy's outer behaviour did not seem particularly problematic, and he did not self-report any involvement in antisocial behaviour or violence. Nevertheless, at age 14, Jeremy had a fight with other boys and broke his right hand. He continued to attend school, even though his motivation was low, and he was disinterested in participating in class activities. He left school soon after age 15, without passing any exams. He had the ambition to be a civil airline pilot and was advised to stay at school. If Jeremy had passed his GCE in English he could have sat for a scholarship to train to become a pilot.

Jeremy did not like school, and he wanted to join his brothers at work. After leaving school, he took employment for six months as a spot welder before leaving of his own accord when he moved out of London. Then for two months he worked as a storeman, then for four months was a capstan operator, then he moved to another job as an engineer. When Jeremy returned to London for a short period he resumed his original employment for three months. However, this employment lasted just for a short period of time, and he left the job of his own accord.

During his late adolescent years, after he left school, Jeremy continued to live with his mother and two sisters in a council house where they moved to after he left school. His older brothers and sisters were now married and had left home. The move unsettled him. He was very unhappy to begin with, having lost all his friends, and he went back to London for a while to stay with one of his married sisters. This did not work out and he returned to stay with his mother.

Jeremy's mother mentioned that she never had any trouble with Jeremy until they moved out of London in 1969. Jeremy was described as a very unsettled boy when he was 15, and did not have any friends. However, when he was starting to make friends, his mother felt that he was mixing with the wrong company, and she tried to persuade him to break away from them, but it seemed that he could not and he ended up in court. He had always worked and was never sacked from a job; it is interesting that his mother mentioned that he was the only boy, amongst those he hung around with, who was always in work.

Jeremy had several jobs of an unskilled nature, each of which only lasted a very short period (weeks or months): he was a spot welder, but left for a better job, then he did some engineering work but left after few months for the same reason. Then Jeremy worked as a chain boy but the job finished and he did some heating engineering work, and then moved to become a delivery assistant in a big furniture shop, where he enjoyed working. Jeremy gave his mother money for his keep, and was not a trouble at home.

In 1970, when Jeremy was 17 years old, he was convicted for another burglary, and he said that he was responsible for other numerous breaking and taking offences in the area. Jeremy's mother believed that the cause of Jeremy's problems was the wrong company and being unable to break up from them. His mother always defended her children strongly, and in the probation report, after Jeremy's burglary offence in 1970, it was mentioned that his mother said that nothing similar had happened before to any other member of the family and that she was shocked by her son's crime. She considered Jeremy's behaviour to be quite out of character, a terrible mistake on his part, and never to be repeated. She stated that she could always rely on Jeremy and on the girls to look after the house in her absence when she was out on shift work, and to fend for themselves in a responsible manner.

Jeremy appeared to be also ashamed of himself when he was faced with the fact that he had neglected to pay outstanding fines, and again he was adamant that he was not going to commit any more offences. It was, however, a fact that he kept on offending regularly after 1970.

In the social enquiry report about Jeremy's burglary offence, he could not offer any explanation about his behaviour, and seemed very upset and ashamed of himself, particularly in regard to the effect that his actions had on the rest of the family. He was adamant that it would never happen again. The senior probation officer wrote in his report that, on the evening in question, Jeremy and his co-accused went out with the deliberate intention of coming under the influence of alcohol. They went to several public houses, lied about their ages (the minimum age for drinking being 18), and mixed their drinks. Jeremy stated that they wanted a meal but could not afford the taxi fare to the pub, so they decided to take a vehicle to get there. From that point onwards, the escapade became progressively more serious, and, paradoxically, their misfortune was in avoiding being caught when they stole the first vehicle. The senior probation officer who interviewed Jeremy mentioned that he was impressed by Jeremy being a responsible and stable personality, whose involvement in this offence owed something to his failure to adjust successfully to moving out of London, to his lack of satisfaction and pride in his work, and his need for excitement and adventure.

Jeremy believed, like his mother, that this sort of thing would not occur again. Nevertheless, the probation officer was of the opinion that, given the circumstances in which Jeremy was living, his response to the supervision programme at this stage was only just coping. Jeremy was in fact at considerable risk of relapsing again into offending behaviour, if certain changes in his attitude and life style were not going to follow.

Jeremy spent a few months in a Detention Centre. The Group Officer's Report described Jeremy as a trainee who had accepted his sentence and training, even though with some resentment. In this report, it was suggested that on release Jeremy's chances of success were fair and, unless he made some effort to keep on the straight and narrow, he was going to be in trouble again very soon.

The governor's opinion about Jeremy was quite positive in so far as Jeremy was described as a 'well-made lad, clean and tidy in his turn out'. Jeremy absconded from the centre in his early days, but he deeply regretted this irresponsible action and made more effort during his training to overcome this bad start. It was because of his separation from his mother that Jeremy absconded from the centre. He was punished for the escapade, but he took the punishment, which consisted of extra work, very well. Jeremy was then full of good intentions for his future life. It was clear that he disliked losing his freedom and this was thought to be a deterrent for him, but the most serious problem was his drinking habit that needed to be attended to.

Jeremy seemed to have matured during his time at the Detention Centre. He wrote regularly to his mother, who visited him. Once released, Jeremy went back to work in the furniture store, and he was quite satisfied with his job. However, he was still drinking a lot, and at age 18 he appeared before the Magistrates Court for being drunk and disorderly, and for having committed an indecent act to the annoyance of the people passing by. These offences in themselves were not serious (they were not normally recorded in the Criminal Record Office), but the possible implications for Jeremy were, if a change in his life style had not taken place. The senior probation officer warned him about the serious consequences he was likely to face if he did not give up drinking. Despite all recommendations, Jeremy could not accept this reality, and did not show any intention of reducing his drinking.

Most of the stolen money was spent on drink. Jeremy recounted that he had developed the habit of drinking heavily at weekends in one particular pub, where he drank through the whole weekend until his spare cash was gone. The drinking made him feel good and it appeared to be an attempt to deal with boredom and other dissatisfactions. It was not clear at this stage whether or not Jeremy was becoming addicted to alcohol, but his intake at weekends was considerable, and this was an aspect that the probation officer considered should be monitored. Fortunately, Jeremy's drinking did not affect his work, and his employer spoke very highly of him.

Jeremy: young adulthood

At age 18, Jeremy's level of antisociality was high. He abused cannabis. His sexual life was promiscuous and he was having sexual intercourse without taking any precautions. In adulthood, he was getting out of control and sometimes his drinking habits started to affect his behaviour and attitude towards life. Fortunately, his job ethos seemed to have not altered. However, he started to have some serious debts, which may have led to his gambling problems. When Jeremy was aged 20, he was self-employed. His life turned out to be problematic in many aspects.

Jeremy: adulthood

At age 32, Jeremy was living with his sister and was looking after his young daughter. His intention was to return to live with his partner, if and when she returned home. At age 37, Jeremy was convicted for assaulting his wife after a domestic row. He beat up his wife and dragged her by the hair along the floor and in the garden.

Because Jeremy refused to be interviewed at ages 32 and 48, however, some of the information about his later life is incomplete. Many attempts were made to trace him. The CSDD research team managed to contact one of his sisters in 2002, but she did not have any contact any more with him. She spoke of him as being a 'real charmer', not evil or bad, but just a person who 'wasted himself'. She further said that Jeremy had got seriously into drinking, which had ruined his life. His marriage broke up, and she knew that he was living with someone else. Another sister who seemed to be still in contact with Jeremy was contacted. After much explanation about why Jeremy was needed to be interviewed, she agreed to call him. However, Jeremy refused to take part in further interviewing, and it was impossible to gather more specific and updated information about his life at age 48: no specific details about his job, his family and his life conditions in adulthood were available.

Jeremy's criminal career was characterised by 17 convictions, including three serious motoring offences. His variety index was 6, and his career included two violence and sex offences. His first offence occurred when he was age 10. His last offence was committed when he was 45 years old and his criminal career lasted 35 years, and included time served in prison, which amounted to about six months.

A psycho-criminological perspective on the CSDD chronic offending

> The thing that moves us to pride and shame is not the mechanical reflection of ourselves, but an inputed sentiment, the imagined effect of this reflection upon another's mind.
>
> *(Cooley, 1902/1964, 153)*

These eight cases of chronic offenders were chosen because they represent concrete examples of individuals entrapped in recurrent life 'failures', of which offending was just one element of an antisocial life style that often included drinking, drug abuse, school failure, unemployment, gambling, and sexual promiscuity.

Table 3.1 summarises the criminal careers of these chronic offenders; it shows the ages of the first and last offences, the career duration, the numbers of convictions (offences committed on different days that led to actual convictions), the variety of offence types (out of 18) and the time served in prison. Of course, the last offence is the latest offence up to the search in 2011, and it may not really be the last offence of these men (except in the cases of Jordan and Matthew, who have died). The time served is less than the sentence length. The only offender who served more than ten years in prison was Lachlan, who was sentenced to a total of 27 years in prison for seven separate robbery convictions between ages 17 and 35.

TABLE 3.1 Summary of the criminal career of the eight chronic offenders

Case histories	Age at first offence	Age at last offence	Career duration	Total convictions	Types of offences	Time in prison
590 – Jordan	13.91	46.92	33.01	24	10	5.48
301 – Callum	14.95	58.26	43.32	23	9	1.08
941 – Jasper	15.69	55.85	40.16	15	10	5.56
402 – Lachlan	14.32	54.68	40.36	18	8	15.84
252 – Paul	15.93	46.43	30.51	15	10	1.21
882 – Matthew	10.01	51.43	41.42	31	12	1.13
763 – Ralph	15.00	52.13	37.13	22	10	0.97
504 – Jeremy	10.78	45.75	34.97	17	6	0.53

Note: Types of offences correspond to the different types of offences that the eight chronic offenders committed during their criminal careers. Time in prison is measured in years. The 18 offence types that were taken into account are: (1) burglary, breaking and entering, attempted burglary; (2) theft of vehicle, taking and driving away vehicle; (3) theft from vehicle, theft of parts of vehicle; (4) shoplifting; (5) theft from machines, including parking meters and telephone boxes; (6) theft from work, theft as employee; (7) other theft, including conspiracy to steal and abstracting electricity; (8) fraud, forgery, deception, fare evasion, false pretences, making off without payment; (9) receiving stolen property, handling, unlawful possession; (10) suspected person, equipped to steal, tampering with vehicle, possession of housebreaking implements; (11) robbery, conspiracy to rob, assault with intent to rob; (12) assault causing actual or grievous bodily harm, assault police; (13) insulting or threatening behaviour, breach of peace, obstruct police, violent disorder, affray, interfering with witness; (14) Possession of offensive weapon, possess firearms, possess ammunition, shortening barrel of shotgun; (15) sexual offences: indecent assault, unlawful sexual intercourse, indecent exposure, indecent telephone message, rape, indecent photographs of children, importuning males; (16) drug offences; (17) vandalism, criminal damage, arson; (18) driving while disqualified, drunk driving (these offences were not counted, because of inconsistent recording over time).

> There is no doubt that crime, like many other features, runs in families.
> *(Farrington, 2010)*

In most cases the extent and nature of offending was not necessarily and always the most important feature of their life style. Causes included disrupted families, low income, poor child-rearing, parental neglect, family conflicts and marital disharmony. What was happening in the lives of the chronic offenders (CSDD generation 2 – G2) was that they were recreating the same family background for their own G3 children (see later in this chapter).

Were there, early in these men's lives, some signs of what was likely to happen in their lives? Can a pattern be seen in which some events acted as precursors of what emerged later?

The sense of self-adequacy of these chronic offenders was constantly threatened by clashes in interpersonal relationships, and with the law. The wish to become different from who they had been up to that moment, which they had expressed in many occasions during the age 32 and 48 interviews, had not been a sufficient force to uproot them from their criminogenic paths. The more they were faced with the reality of their maladjustment, the stronger their feelings of the improbability of changing. It was somehow true that the attempt to stop their offending behaviour was of lower importance than a long list of other problematic aspects in their lives that had priority.

The marginalised positions that many ex-offenders occupy in society may be the result of society's prejudice, the effect of offenders' lack of commitment or a combination of both. The former contributes to blocking the activation of a process of *self-change*. The latter reinforces *self-sameness*. Both outcomes have serious repercussions, and it is difficult to establish which one has the most handicapping influence. Self-change implies a forward vision of oneself and one's own life in perspective, in which desisting from offending emerges as a process of a transformed life style and attitude towards society. Self-sameness involves a confirmatory vision, in which the wish to stop offending emerges only if the individual disengages himself from the *delinquent self* that he has always been (Zara, 2005); these aspects are discussed in Chapter 6.

Clinical and treatment studies (Otto & Douglas, 2010) are consistent in suggesting that the steps toward to *how a pattern of maladjustment is (or can be) transformed* primarily require the assessment of the risk factors and dynamic risks (or criminogenic needs) involved, the targeting of the possible familial and social resources available, or lack of them, readiness to change, a strengthened motivation and preparedness to initiate treatment. Any other attempt to reform separated from these crucial issues is likely to fail.

When evaluating cases such as those of Jordan (case 590) or Callum (case 301) or Matthew (case 882) or Jasper (case 941), the assessment of risk should take the main aim not of prediction *per se*, but of *prevention* (see Chapter 4). Once it has been established that certain life conditions or specific individual characteristics or criminogenic needs are significantly involved in enhancing the risk of an antisocial outcome, resources should be targeted to alter, control or remove them.

The early family life of these chronic offenders was characterised by disruption, neglect and, at times, child abuse. Once they were adults a pattern of relationship difficulties emerged in their intimate life, in how they related to their own children and in how they confronted the challenges they encountered. Their social adjustment, measured by employment records, was poor. Their physical and mental well-being was impaired by a life relentlessly fed with alcohol and drugs, aggressiveness, fights and conflicts.

At school, many of these chronic offenders' difficulties in controlling their behaviour became more evident because their attitude towards the people around them, towards authority and towards rules was of a defiant nature and there were many sources of conflict. Also they typically had concentration problems at school, were impulsive and took many risks. Their work pattern mostly consisted of periods of unemployment with some intervals of unskilled and short-term jobs.

Their family life featured marital conflicts, child abandonment and disharmony.

However, a question that comes to mind is: *to what extent could their life have unfolded differently?*

What was required of these offenders was to stop offending. Yet, it is known that this implies desistance from crime or, in psychological terms, change. Systematic change, in personality and behaviour, is likely to occur during transitions into new situations, when the request to behave is not simply expected and necessary, but when previous responses and life choices are actively discouraged, and clear, specific and adequate information about how to behave adaptively is provided (Caspi & Moffitt, 1993), and accompanied by suitable resources and a constant emotional and familial support to embark on a process of change.

Whenever individuals experience profound discontinuities in their social space or crises in their life, as the men involved in the CSDD did, individual idiosyncrasies are likely to be magnified. When people find themselves in ambiguous, stressful, inconsistent, painful, uncertain or consistently tragic circumstances, when the pressure to behave is high, and when no useful and precise structure for how to behave differently is provided, and resources are not available, then it is likely that changes in personality or behaviour will not occur. In these instances, dispositional differences are instead accentuated, because the person would respond to critical, threatening and stressful circumstances by using previously acquired strategies and patterns of reactions already present in their behavioural repertoire. This might help to explain, for instance, behavioural continuity into an antisocial path.

Beyond the individual and dispositional differences that highlight the specificity and uniqueness of each case study described, a pattern of similarity seems, in fact, to be present in all of the chronic offenders studied. As expected, the most maladjusted dimensions were those related to childhood experiences, family, school achievement, working career and health.

Research has shown that the influence and quality of family relationships upon the development of emotional and behavioural disorders in young people is paramount. Adverse family conditions pose a relentless threat to the person's sense of secure attachment (West et al., 1998). Ambivalent parental relationships and unresponsive parents constitute a barrier for the child's development of personal capacity and competence. In contrast, a secure parent–child relationship provides a measure of self-regulation (Rich, 2006), and findings on attachment research suggest that attachment behaviours are designed to ensure stable and regulated internal states, which in turn encourage a successful adaptation to the rearing environment.

Most of the childhood experiences of these chronic offenders were seriously characterised by deprivation and parental disharmony, which contributed to insecure and ambivalent attachment. Attachment has not directly and previously been studied in the CSDD, but the life histories of these chronic offenders accounted for patterns of adaptation within family and social relationships, and for their maladjustment and social difficulties that went back to their childhood. These offenders tended to grow up with an uncertain unaffectional parental presence, in prejudicial family conditions and uncompromised social situations.

Knowledge that the quality of attachment in childhood and adolescence has implications for subsequent social, emotional and mental development and self-control is well established and well recognised. The pathway from infancy to adult adaptation is thought to be mediated by mentalisation and self-regulation functions (Bouchard et al., 2008; Fonagy & Target, 2002). According to attachment theory, individuals create a set of mental models of themselves and others in interaction (*internal working models*) based on repeated interactions with significant others from early childhood (Bowlby, 1980). The stable nature of attachment styles accounts for the development of enduring strategies to regulate emotions and social contacts.

Mentalisation is 'a process of human social functioning and self-regulation, involved in the establishment of robust links between personally meaningful early experiences and their representation' (Bouchard et al., 2008, 48). Reflective function is defined as the capacity to think and envisage mental states both in oneself and in others, to assist the process of building accurate models of why people behave, think, feel and react the way they do (Lyons-Ruth & Block, 1996). The reflective mental state implies that the individual is actively involved in a self-perception and observation of what is experienced or what memory is activated, recalled or modified.

Also for these men, the ways of relating to others and behaving in close relationships, and of incorporating representations of these relationships into one's own mental state, were learned during early childhood, and, using Lorenzini and Fonagy's (2013) terms, they moulded not only the subsequent intimate relationships that these men built up with their romantic partners, children, friends, but also influenced and directed their behaviour. More importantly than any other aspects, the way these chronic offenders related to others and to the world inside and around them appeared to have played a role in altering the equilibrium between their self-regulation and interpersonal regulation of stress and self-frustration.

There is accumulated evidence that maltreatment and a disrupted childhood do impair the child's reflective capacities and sense of self (Beeghly & Cicchetti, 1994; Fonagy & Target, 1997), and this applies more so if abusive behaviour occurs at home. This abusive behaviour may lead the person to maintain the family experiences separately from the public world of school and community, with the consequence that the benefits of a welcoming external world do not influence the child's representation of how to respond to others adequately. Abuse, especially when it is long-lasting, prevents children from testing and modifying their beliefs about the world being cruel, untrustful and threatening, so that the elaboration of different mental representations of caring and supportive mental states could be conceivable. The stable nature of attachment styles accounts for lasting developmental strategies to regulate emotions, integrate cognitions, direct social relationships and adjust social behaviour. A meta-analysis on the significance of insecure attachment and disorganisation in the development of children's externalising behaviour showed that unstable and insecure attachment styles remain relatively stable during life, and that attachment insecurity is significantly associated with externalising behaviours (Fearson et al., 2010). Children rated as insecure showed higher levels of externalising behaviours than children rated as secure. In their analyses, Fearson and colleagues (2010) considered the role of a number of other potentially important moderators, highlighted in the literature, such as socio-economic status (with low-risk individuals anticipated to have larger effects) and gender (with insecure boys expected to show more behaviour problems). Contrary to expectation, attachment insecurity was associated with higher levels of behaviour and externalising problems, even in apparently low-risk psychosocial circumstances, with the magnitude of the association being relatively consistent across high and low SES samples ($d = 0.25$ vs. $d = 0.31$, respectively). However, possible effects of SES should not be ruled out, given the complexity of the variables that are implicated in the socio-economic dimension, and given that a broad division, as employed in the Fearson and colleagues' (2010) meta-analysis, of samples into low versus high or middle class, is clearly limited in precision. As expected, attachment was more strongly associated with externalising behaviour problems in boys than in girls ($d = 0.35$ vs. $d = -0.03$, respectively). The lower rates of externalising problems in girls compared with boys may represent a manifestation of:

a. different aetiological mechanisms that impact upon girls' adjustment to life (Waters *et al.*, 2000);
b. cultural diversities (Bakermans-Kranenburg & van IJzendoorn, 2009);
c. variations in relational and physical aggression (Crick & Grotpeter, 1995), and in covert versus overt antisocial behaviour (Loeber & Schmaling, 1985);
d. biological influences (Vierikko *et al.*, 2003).

Genetic factors are estimated to account for between 23 and 45 per cent of the variance in adult attachment security, 45 per cent for attachment anxiety and 36 per cent for attachment avoidance (Picardi *et al.*, 2011).

The development of attachment relationships, however, can only be of a bidirectional nature as far as children 'co-create' the relationship with their caregivers (Lorenzini & Fonagy, 2013). To the extent that genetic and environmental factors can be separable, 'environmental factors ubiquitously appear to be the most important influence in the development of attachment' (Lorenzini & Fonagy, 2013, 157; see also Fonagy & Target, 2005). Indeed in these cases the family milieu and atmosphere, and the environmental factors, seemed to have substantially and significantly contributed to the *nature and nurture interplay*.

A securely attached child is likely to become a secure and autonomous adult; an avoidantly attached child is likely to become an avoidant and dismissing adult. An anxious and resistant child tends to become an anxious and preoccupied adult. A disoriented and disorganised child tends to become an unresolved and disorganised adult.

An initial personality disorder examination (using the SCID-II; see Spitzer *et al.*, 1990) indicated that many of these men manifested emotional and relational impairments that were pervasive in many areas of their lives and that altered their social functioning. Lachlan (case 402) seemed to fulfil the criteria for an avoidant personality disorder. Jordan (case 590) and Lachlan more likely met the criteria for a schizoid personality disorder. All of these men were antisocially persistent, and Lachlan and Ralph (case 763) fulfilled the criteria for an antisocial personality disorder (see Chapter 5).

As described in detail in Chapter 5, the PCL:SV, used to assess psychopathy in the CSDD sample, is a dimensional measure of the degree to which a person meets the criteria of the prototypical psychopath. The total PCL:SV score provides the rating for the assessment. Despite dimensional ratings being more useful than categorical ones, a categorical diagnosis of psychopathy is contemplated and required in certain settings, such as the forensic one, and for certain applications such as research (Hart et al., 1995). As is discussed in Chapter 5, it is difficult to specify a distinct *best* cut-off score for PCL:SV. Scores of 18 or higher provide robust indication of psychopathy and warrant the use of the PCL-R. Those individuals who score between 12 and 17 may be psychopaths, and it is recommended to use on them the PCL-R for full diagnostic assessment. In the CSDD, 11 per cent of males scored 10 or more on the PCL:SV, and were the most problematic offenders. The vast majority of these chronic offenders scored high (10 or more) on the PCL:SV and were in this very high group. For the CSDD research purposes, a PCL:SV score of 10 or more was a significant cut-off to discriminate the most prolific offenders and those who were chronic and with psychopathic personalities (Farrington, 2007c). The cases of Jordan, Lachlan and Paul (case 252) seemed to fulfil the criteria for a categorical diagnosis of psychopathy (meeting the forensic cut-off of ≥ 13 PCL:SV). Ralph (case 763) also seemed to fulfil the criteria for a categorical diagnosis of psychopathy (meeting the community cut-off of ≥ 12 PCL:SV score). Further assessment would have been necessary to complete the diagnostic examination of psychopathy, and research on the development of psychopathy and its impact on social functioning and adjustment needs to take account of these findings.

Mental health and personality disorders are important components of the individual's functioning in the world, and in the regulation of social behaviour. Their assessments are significant to the extent that they provide specific, focused and individualised information to organise treatment. Empirical and clinical evidence supports a dimensional representation of personality disorder. Livesley (2007) provides an integrated approach to personality disorder, defining it as 'the failure to solve adaptive life tasks relating to identity or self, intimacy and attachment, and prosocial behaviour: in essence, it is the failure to establish coherent representations of self and others and chronic interpersonal dysfunction' (p. 203). A dimensional representation of personality would allow for a complete psychodiagnostic process in which information about the adaptive and maladaptive aspects of personality functioning is essential (Freilone, 2011), and make it possible to distinguish between the diagnosis of general personality disorder and the assessment of individual differences in the form that the disorder takes (Livesley, 2007).

The *DSM 5* (2013) has included some references to the dimensional nature of personality disorders in a specific section (Section III – disorders requiring further study) of the manual related to further development and research (see Chapter 5 in this book). The psycho-criminological utility of a dimensional classification lies in the usefulness of risk assessment and in the accuracy of prediction outcomes. The clinical utility of incorporating a dimensional classification of personality disorders can be seen in treatment planning, and in organising and selecting interventions. The integration of these utilities could make a significant contribution in helping individuals to regain some control over their lives and promote their social functioning.

In these chronic offenders, the representation of their ideas about themselves, their life and their significant others tended to be rigid, maladaptive and defensive, and they almost became disincentivised to take the perspective of others, because of the hostility represented in their mind through the abuse, neglect, abandonment, disappointments, ambivalence and loneliness they experienced. The world was perceived as a place in which they had to be prepared to combat and attack, in order not to be overthrown or defeated.

In all of these eight cases, the experiences of their own parents, and also the experiences that the men had with their own parents, with respect to the intergenerational transmission of family interactions and dynamics, appeared to be central, or at least significant, in the formation and development of the inner- and outerselves (Botbol, 2010). Minuchin (1974) mentioned that family relationships are assimilated into a person's world so that they 'imprint its members with selfhood' (p. 47). It is not infrequently true that dysfunctionality in parenting represents a risk factor for limiting in the child the reflective function, and contributes to social maladjustment. Thus, individuals who come from such an environment and experience different and systematic forms of family difficulties are vulnerable both in terms of adjustment to life and in terms of their 'reduced resilience in the face of it' (Fonagy & Target, 1997, 696).

According to the literature on mental states as a measure of development, in a *reactive mental state* the person is likely to emotionally reject, 'mentally expelled, impulsively discharged, refuse, distort, or inhibit what is currently being activated, thus defending themselves against it' (Bouchard et al., 2008, 49). It was difficult for many of these CSDD men to be committed to a family regime and to provide their partners and children with stability in their affections, with a respectful attitude, and with a consistency in relating to them and in regulating their interpersonal dynamics.

Looking at the life events of these chronic offenders, their adulthood was extremely disturbed, and even if in different forms, an underlying pattern of antisociality and maladjustment (i.e. *population heterogeneity*) represented a sort of existential shadow that shrouded their childhood, adolescence and adulthood. Later life events were also relevant factors in contributing to the observed stability in criminal offending (i.e. *state dependence*) (Nagin & Paternoster, 2000). It was likely that their criminal behaviour had some effects on their subsequent and continual criminality by eroding social and emotional constraints, consolidating self-sameness (being similar to one's own antisocial self in time), and strengthening incentives to crime (Farrington, 2005b; Farrington & Loeber, 2014); or reinforcing a misperception of crime as a short cut to get what they needed (Wikström & Sampson, 2006).

These men appeared to be emotionally and relationally dismissive and shallow individuals; they lacked support and care from parental figures; and they received ambivalent affective and relational messages. Some of them, like Jordan and Lachlan, learned that the way to cope with life events was by denying or dismissing environmental threats. Their interpersonal pattern was characterised by emotional detachment and lack of commitment, and they had difficulties in establishing long-term relationships. They seemed to exhibit what Bowlby (1980) called *compulsive self-reliance* and a higher threshold for experiencing negative emotions (Bennett, 2005). On the other hand, some other men, like Lachlan, developed a preoccupied, avoidant and anxious life style that constantly perceived environmental threats and the need to be on guard (psychologically and socially), and had a lower threshold for stress.

Some men, like Jeremy (case 504) or Paul (case 252), used an aggressive and abusive style of interaction. Jeremy relied on his superficial charm to use people to get what he wanted. Paul vented out his force through promiscuity and the relationship he had with his children. Physical force was a means used by many of these men, from an early age, to relate to the world around them. Ralph (case 763), in one of his school fights at age 14, fractured his opponent's jaw and broke his nose. He was also charged with assaulting a police officer. Lachlan (case 402) went to the victims' home, demanded money with menaces and threatened them. He also threatened a person with a pair of scissors, tied him to a bed and punched him in his face. Matthew (case 882), in a school fight at age 10, used a milk bottle and threw it, injuring the leg of a girl. This style of offensive and aggressive interaction continued to feature in the adult life of most of these men.

In an investigation of the antecedents of intimate partner violence using the CSDD data, Lussier *et al.* (2009) provide evidence that childhood risk factors measured decades earlier predicted later domestic violence. The level of continuity observed between the development of antisociality in children and adolescents and partner violence involvement in adulthood has significant policy implications, especially because of the risk of a chronic pattern of offending. Even though in the CSDD childhood antisociality was not directly linked to later intimate partner violence (IPV) (Piquero *et al.*, 2014), antisociality that started or persisted in adolescence was the main risk factor identified and may be one of the key risk factors that should be targeted for the prevention of later partner violence. Certainly, in predicting IPV, adult risk factors should be considered. These, in fact, would be important, as 'it may be that more proximal adult stressors, such as lost employment, drinking alcohol, or poor relationship quality, could lead to IPV' (Piquero *et al.*, 2014, 298).

To what extent are risk factors for offending similar in different generations?

Some references to the children of these men and their entrance into the social world would be interesting in so far as it would provide some insights into antisocial continuity and discontinuity in the family.

An examination of risk factors for offending in successive generations of males was conducted by Farrington *et al.* (2015) and involved the CSDD males (*generation 2 – G2*) with their biological parents (*generation 1* – G1) and their biological children (*generation 3* – G3). Between 2004 and 2013, efforts were made to interview the biological children of the G2 males (some of whom are described above). There were 691 G3 children whose name and date of birth were known. Only children aged at least 18 (born up to 1995) were targeted, and 551 were interviewed (84 per cent) of the 653 eligible G3 children who were identified. Of the remainder, 39 children refused, 33 parents refused, 13 children could not be traced, 14 were elusive (never being available to interview), and three were aggressive or problematic. Of the 29 children living abroad, 17 were interviewed, usually by telephone.

A convicted G2 father and a convicted G2 mother were significant predictors of G3 children's offending, and unlike the G1 parents, a convicted G2 mother was a stronger predictor than a convicted G2 father. Poor supervision according to the G2 male at age 32 and separation from a G2 parent before age 16 according to the G3 child were significantly related family risk factors. Of the socio-economic risk factors at age 32, low take-home pay of the G2 father, poor housing and low socio-economic status of the G2 father were significantly predictive of G3 offending. Both of the G3 attainment risk factors, together with early risk-taking, suspension and frequent truancy, were related to G3 offending. The results of a logistic regression analysis predicting G3 male offending suggested that the strongest independent predictors of future offending in successive generations were a convicted G2 father (a parental risk factor), low G2 take-home pay (a socio-economic risk factor) and early G3 risk-taking (an impulsiveness risk factor).

Despite these results being limited and only preliminary, they seem to shed some light on the relevance of family and early living conditions for future adjustment to life, and also on a plausible behavioural continuity among successive generations (Farrington *et al.*, 2015).

Studies show that internalising and externalising problems in parents are likely to be associated with a number of problematic consequences in their offspring (Kim *et al.*, 2009; Shankman *et al.*, 2008). Farrington (1994, 1995, 2003, 2012) found that children with an early behavioural conduct problem and an antisocial onset tended to be raised in dysfunctional families, exposed to maladaptive behaviours of their parents who also suffered from mental problems, and involved in criminal careers. Once adults, these children were likely to experience problems in many areas of their personal, psychological, interpersonal and social life (Dutton *et al.*, 2011; Fergusson *et al.*, 2005; Rutter & Quinton, 1984). West and Farrington (1977) termed this *the delinquent way of life*.

Psychiatric studies report that the type and the intensity of exposure to parents' maladjustment can play a role in mediating the effects upon the offspring's psychiatric disorders later in life (Johnson *et al.*, 2001). Other studies (Jaffee *et al.*, 2003) on the impact of a life with (or without) a father have shown interesting findings. Children whose fathers were involved in low level antisociality manifested higher levels of conduct problems the less time their fathers spent with them at home. In contrast those children with highly antisocial fathers, who lived at home with them, were more likely to manifest poor behavioural functioning. Residing with antisocial fathers becomes, for the children, a *double jeopardy* of genetic and environmental risk for conduct problems. Avoiding separation or planning a marriage is unlikely to be an adequate answer for children who live either in malfunctioning or in single-parent families, unless their fathers become a reliable source of emotional, parental, psychological and economic support (Jaffee *et al.*, 2003). It is possible to find dysfunctional results when also residing with multi-problematic, dismissive and antisocial mothers.

Hicks *et al.* (2004) suggested that the probability for parents to pass on to their offspring 'the vulnerability to a heterogeneous and general spectrum of disorders' is not remote, with 'each disorder representing a different expression of this general vulnerability' (Hicks *et al.*, 2004, 926). Retrospective studies of diagnosed children recognise the combination of inheritable and environmental effects from parents. Assuming that little can be done to rectify the inheritable component of the damage, then strong attention should be devoted to the environmental (interactive) components of the impairments, because these need to be carefully assessed and adequately treated (Dutton *et al.*, 2011). Further studies are paramount to explore further these processes, *if* and *to what extent* there exists replicability of risk factors and protective factors over time, places and family generations (Farrington *et al.*, 2015).

Evidence-based research, intertwined with clinical attention, can guarantee that intervention and treatment are planned and implemented based on the characteristics of offenders and their criminogenic needs. This can make a real contribution to crime prevention and offender treatment, in so far as *interventional and treatment quackery* seem instead to have dominated the general practice in too many settings of work with offenders (Latessa *et al.*, 2002). Quackery is dismissive of scientific knowledge, empirical research, training and expertise. 'It embraces the notion that interventions are best rooted in "common sense", in personal experiences, or clinical unstructured and intuitive knowledge' (Latessa *et al.*, 2002, 43). It then follows that interventional and treatment quackery involves the use of treatment interventions that are based neither on existing evidence-based knowledge of the causes of crime and of criminogenic needs that keep offenders under the antisocial spell nor on empirical evidence of what programmes hold the best degree of effectiveness in promoting a change in offending behaviour (see Chapter 7).

Prospective longitudinal studies of offending, as Farrington (2014a) put it, are the best equipped for making assumptions and testing hypotheses about relative continuity and absolute changes in human behaviour; they also have many advantages, including predicting future behaviour, establishing causal order and avoiding retrospective bias. This type of research can have significant implications for prevention or treatment designed to modify living conditions, to change people's attitude and life style, and to interrupt a pattern of disruptive responses to events (Farrington & Loeber, 2014). Interventions can be successful to the extent that the criminogenic needs targeted are manipulable and dynamic, and that appropriate resources are invested to help individuals, like the CSDD chronic offenders, to divert from the pathway to a life of crime.

These eight case histories bring home the reality of people's lives and 'breathe life into dull statistics'. However, as mentioned, many of the statements are subjective opinions. Also, it must be realised that these are the most criminal cases, and that many boys in the CSDD led very successful lives. Many boys came from deprived and criminogenic backgrounds but nevertheless did not offend. It is a pity that we do not have time or space to present other case histories here, but these eight case histories show graphically the intergenerational transmission of an antisocial life style, and how risk factors and criminogenic needs were longitudinally and intensively affecting these boys lives and their adjustment. Chapter 4 focuses on risk assessment and on those instruments that are considered to be the most valid for a risk evaluation and for planning intervention.

Notes

1 He was a sixteenth-century British scientist and naturalist. The original source of the quotation is difficult to trace. It is possible that it is associated with the following reference: William Turner, *Libellus de re herbaria novus* (1538), reprinted in facsimile, with notes, modern names, and a life of the author by B. Jackson (London: Daydon, 1877).
2 All names have been changed, to protect confidentiality. Also, some other details in case histories have been changed to protect anonymity.
3 *The New Junior Maudsley Personality Inventory* (Furneaux & Gibson, 1966).

4
RISK ASSESSMENT

Risk assessment has always been viewed as important but at the same time it has attracted vigorous criticism. There are no settings in which risk assessment has received such an ambivalent welcome as in the criminal justice system, and in the forensic mental health services, correctional facilities and parole boards. Risk assessment has become relevant to a wide range of criminal and civil decisions, such as pre-charge diversion, pre-trial detention, eligibility for alternative measures and suitability for treatment programmes (Hoge et al., 2012), becoming one of the most required professional competences expected of professionals (Elbogen, 2002; Grisso & Tomkins, 1996). It has been mostly employed to predict serious criminal behaviour (Andrews et al., 2006; Bonta, 2002; Maden, 2003), social (Gulotta & Vittoria, 2002a, b; Mulvey & Lidz, 1995) and psychiatric dangerousness (Fornari, 2008; Freilone, 2011), violence (Gray et al., 2011; Maden, 2005), and criminal recidivism (Mulvey & Lidz, 1998; Rice & Harris, 1995; Webster & Hucker, 2007).

The aim of this chapter is to describe the history of risk assessment, to move to the description of the difference between prediction and assessment of criminal recidivism and future violence, and to illustrate the essential nature of risk assessment in practice. Risk assessment is considered here not simply as a scheme to measure the type of risk (historic, stable, dynamic, acute), or to identify the level of risk (dichotomously – yes/no – or dimensionally – high/medium/low), but as a process to evaluate those criminogenic needs that, when appropriately targeted, contribute to aiding and sustaining treatment, so as to produce changes in the level of criminal recidivism risk, in the functioning of the offenders who are treated and in their social adjustment.

This chapter investigates to what extent criminal behaviour can be reliably predicted, depending on the different levels of risk posed by offenders (*risk principle*) and their criminal careers. It will highlight the importance of criminogenic needs in the design of risk instruments (*need principle*), and will describe how intervention might be successfully planned and how treatment should be provided for general reoffending, and specifically, for violent and sexual offenders (*responsivity principle*).

The 'critical zone' of risk assessment in criminological psychology

Risk assessment endured a reversal of fortune during the 1970s and 1980s from which it has not completely recovered (Miller & Brodsky, 2011; Simon, 2005). Some radical fringes in criminology see risk assessment as a *risky business* (Glazebrook, 2010, 88) not least because of society's preoccupation with the ascertainment and avoidance of risk, but especially because of the omnipresent 'language of risk' (Horsefield, 2003, 376) that sees offenders only as consumers (producers) of risk assessments. Some evidence of this trend can be found in current practice where risk assessment is rarely used in prevention policy (Zara, 2013a; Zara & Farrington, 2013).

Various issues are involved. The first focuses on the theoretical construct underlying risk assessment, i.e. prediction or assessment. The second issue is related to which methodology is the best to use and why: clinical, actuarial or integrated. The third issue is concerned with the type of instruments that are most appropriate, with whom, when and in which settings. The fourth issue is about what to do with the risk assessment judgment: is it only a scientific exercise for research purposes? Can scientific evidence be used to influence judgment in court and then treatment and intervention? But the crucial question then becomes whether it is ethical to provide evidence of the future risk of criminal behaviour. The fifth issue focuses on aspects associated with the experts who, at times, find themselves serving three masters: the justice system, the community and the offender. These masters are not necessarily in conflict, because serving the cause of justice implies also consideration for the victims, and for the offenders. Criminal justice professionals provide crime victims with support, and guarantee that the law is working to restore their rights and trust in a proactive justice system, by developing specific preventive protection. Intervening in favour of treating individuals who are involved in long-lasting criminal careers means promoting their desistance and social integration.

The improvement in the accuracy of prediction of reoffending and violence has occurred along with the development and validation of specific instruments that assist the process of risk assessment, and aid in the identification and management of the individual at risk of violence and who persists in offending.

Scientific evidence shows that structured risk assessment instruments provide a level of accuracy significantly greater than chance. Beyond the restraint of imperfection overshadowing measurement performance, research findings show that, when an individual is identified to be at high risk for violent offending, the probability that the person will be violent in the future is quite high, above 80 per cent (Ogloff & Davis, 2005). In other words, 'nothing predicts behavior like *(or better than previous)* behavior' (Kvaraceus, 1966, 53, emphasis added).

Notwithstanding misgivings about giving credit to such an assumption (Soothill, 1999, 119), public concerns over the increase in violence and criminal behaviour by persistent offenders has favoured the use of risk assessment instruments in clinical and forensic practice. Moreover, the admissibility of evidence provided by psychologists in court requires that expert testimony be based upon methods and instruments that have gained recognition and acceptance by the scientific community. Researchers, and mental health and forensic professionals, have responded constructively to the initial distrust in risk assessment. Researchers developed specific instruments and presented new evidence regarding which approach is more valid in assessing criminal recidivism, based on empirical data and meta-analyses. Professionals used the different instruments proved to be more suitable for the individual cases they were called upon to evaluate, and gave expert testimony. Survey data (Archer *et al.*, 2006) showed that the use of structured assessment is widespread: 80 per cent of forensic psychologists in the United States, and 80 and 70 per cent respectively of forensic and general psychiatric hospitals in the United Kingdom, use risk assessment instruments routinely (Higgins *et al.*, 2005; Khiroya, 2009). Other countries in Europe are also adopting risk assessment instruments in forensic psychiatric units or in correctional settings (Zara, 2013a).

Roffey and Kaliski (2012) state that over 400 structured instruments are currently available. A recent meta-review conducted by Singh and Fazel (2010) identified 126 structured professional instruments that are specifically designed to predict violence and recidivism in diverse settings such as prisons, psychiatric units and the community. The concern then is to identify which risk assessment instruments are most valid and helpful in forensic, correctional and treatment settings, and with which types of offenders (males vs. females; adults vs. juveniles; violent vs. non-violent; sex offenders vs. other offenders, to mention just a few), not only to assess their level of risk, but especially to guide intervention, treatment and prevention (Hanson, 2005).

When the past of predicting becomes the prologue of assessing the risk

The scope of risk assessment is germane to the conception of translating scientific knowledge into services for humanity. However, three aspects are relevant to disentangling the process of assessing the risk from the unrealistic expectation of forecasting human behaviour. The first is related to the nature of risk assessment; the second to the dimension of predictability involved; and the third to the scope of assessing risk in practical terms.

Nature of risk assessment

Risk assessment is a method of evaluating the risk of antisocial onset and of persistence, and not an answer for how to reduce onset and persistence. A method implies a process through which factors that enhance and sustain the risk for antisocial behaviour can be successfully identified. Risk assessment is not only about specifying the risk; it is about giving a psychological and behavioural sense to it, because it is about people and their functioning in the world that psychologists, psychiatrists, criminologists, lawyers, public prosecutors, judges and juries deal with professionally. Risk assessment is a method and not an end. It is meant to gather historical and stable factors to assess continuity in time, but it is not simply a reactive process so that 'once a risk, always a risk' (Hanson et al., 2014). It is meant to be, in the scientific evidence-based spirit, a proactive process of identifying and assessing modifiable factors, and of guiding and sustaining change.

Risk assessment should: inform treatment and management decisions; guide and sustain prevention; communicate risk in such a way as to inspire governments to invest in research and intervention with the goal of preventing children from becoming tomorrow's criminals; support parents in coping with the consequences of their familial failures. Successful risk assessment practitioners strongly react to the allegation that it is a practice that makes a person's life restricted within the perimeter of their *zone of risk*. Rather it is a practice that informs intervention and sustains prevention by identifying rewarding alternatives of living. From a public policy perspective, if assessment of the risk of future antisocial behaviour is not based on research findings, it is unsound and fallacious; if it does not inform clinicians it is impractical; if it falls outside the range of application it is unhelpful; if it is not tailored to the individual's criminogenic needs it is unethical.

Predictability

Predictability is defined as understanding the changing manifestations of patterns of adaptation and social functioning over time, and the links between these patterns across situations (Sroufe & Rutter, 1984). A *prediction* is a statement about the future. An *assessment* is a process of figuring out the extent to which someone has learned, achieved, changed or is at risk of doing something, again. Both tasks look to the future, and the interest is on the scientific work carried out to arrive at an assessment that, while emphasizing the risk side of the equation, does not disregard the other side, i.e. protective factors (Rogers, 2000). There are some instances in which the notion of risk is conflated with the notion of prediction: statements of probability are different from statements of prediction, in so far as the former (probability) implies a statement about the likelihood or chance that a specific behaviour will happen, whereas prediction conveys the indication of how likely it is that behaviour will occur within a window of time.

Practice

This aspect concerns the gap between the knowledge of science and effective practice that involves psycho-criminological research and practitioners. Clinical practice is distant from scientific findings, and research has minimal relationship to the actualities of everyday clinical life. Douglas and colleagues (1999) look at risk assessment schemes as calls for collaboration amongst researchers and clinicians, and as beneficial for some convicted individuals, some patients, some children at risk for future maladjustment, and their families and the community. Risk assessment is a process associated with the treatment of convicted offenders and also with prevention policy (Zara & Farrington, 2013). The interest is to arrive not solely at a measurement of risk, but rather to an understanding of how a person, being at a 'certain level of risk of recidivism', could be sustained by an individualised programme that meets their criminogenic needs and their resources for recoverability and treatability. This requires the limitation of the use of clinical discretion and a systematic use of risk evidence, backing up the conclusion with empirical data, so as to make the assessments of risk reliable and generalisable and to abandon the detrimental situation in which, employing the words of Brooks (2010), *the tail wags the dog*.

Most knowledge in psychological criminology is based on observing consequences, seeking antecedents (Dawes, 1993), understanding the past, assessing the present and making decisions about the future, under uncertainties. All these tasks are complicated, not least because of the complexity of human behaviour. A corrective step requires the involvement of a methodology that will help to reduce discretion and systematic errors. This leads to considering the type of risk assessment instruments that might best accompany the evaluation work, guarantee scientific procedure, and improve validity and reliability, while not neglecting the focus that what are being assessed are groups of individuals (in a research setting) and a specific person (in a criminal justice setting). Unfortunately, it seems that 'there is more polemic argument in the risk assessment literature as to what is the best type of approach to risk assessment than there is evidence of concern for public safety' (Boer & Hart, 2009, 27).

The philosophy behind the prediction and assessment of future offending and violence lies mostly in what it is expected to achieve rather than on what risk assessment *is* and *how it works*. The expectation is that risk assessment should inform decisions not only at the level of evaluation of risks and needs of the offenders assessed, but especially at the level of protection and resources available, at the level of case management, and at the level of intervention and prevention. In practical terms, risk assessment has become the process whereby offenders are assessed on several key variables that are empirically known to predict the likelihood of committing an offence. The key issue is the relationship between the appraisal of the offender's risk and the decision-making that follows. Does risk assessment involve only an evaluation of the risk of reoffending that an individual poses to the community? Or is what is really evaluated in this process instead the risk that the Parole Board is willing to take when it makes the decision to transfer an offender to a different risk category institution? Do risk instruments serve to identify the highly dangerous *a priori* or do they simply serve to justify decisions already made (cf. Bonta, 2002, 375)?

The rationale behind risk assessment as a component of prevention and treatment practice is that risk can change as a result of treatment, because of the efficacy of intervention over time, or of the impact of developmental factors and protective factors (Augimeri *et al.*, 2011), or of the context and passage of time (Hoge *et al.*, 2012), or of a combination of all of these aspects.

Risk assessment practice

The pressure of making decisions and predicting what is more likely to happen is a ubiquitous condition of functioning in life. In daily life people resort to heuristics (common sense and rule-of-thumb strategies). On the other hand, within professional settings, making accurate and valid prediction is paramount, and the practice of risk assessment has to be based on science (Swets *et al.*, 2000; Szmukler, 2001). Within the context of professional assessment, any decision has to be documented, scientifically justified, socially accepted, ethical, proven to have integrity and not least has to produce tangible results.

Psychologists, criminologists and experts in mental health are called upon to make decisions and are faced with the responsibility for assessing the likelihood of events occurring or re-occurring, and for establishing the degree of confidence of their predictions, and the accuracy and reliability of them. They are required to know not only how to make good predictions (Grove & Lloyd, 2006), but especially to choose and explain which instruments are likely to be accurate and reliable within the evaluation process, how to use them, and in which cases and circumstances. This does not sound easy, and it is not.

Research findings on *prescriptive assessments* (how professionals should assess risk and which instruments to use) and *descriptive assessments* (how professionals really assess) clearly show that we are still confronted with the problems of accuracy, external validity and reliability. Thus the use of specific and appropriate instruments that accompanies any professional evaluation is fundamental.

Risk assessment terminology

Certainty does not exist in science, and even less in criminological psychology; uncertainty constantly plagues any individual predictions. 'The mother of all uncertainties' is how risk assessment has been referred to (Bailar & Bailer, 1999, 273). Individuals have always tried to emerge victorious from the challenge posed by assessing future behaviour. Making predictions for individuals is recognised as being a problem; hence, the prediction of future criminal behaviour has to coexist with uncertainty and errors: this is a fact. It is not merely a function of the complexity of assessing individual psychological characteristics. It has to do with an uncertainty whose extent is always large, unknown, even perhaps unknowable.

Definition of risk factors

Risk, for Gigerenzer (2008), by definition, is about uncertainty. Risk is a known chance or a measurable probability; it therefore implies a quantified uncertainty.

The term *risk* is used within criminological and forensic settings in varied and at times inconsistent ways (Towl, 2005). Scientists have defined *risk* as a synonym for the concept of dangerousness, or of both a cause and an effect, or as a compound estimate of the likelihood, severity and type of an undesirable and adverse outcome.

Identifying and classifying risk factors, accumulating them and either counting or scoring them in a risk assessment task, does not clarify the mechanism underlying the process that leads to a criminal onset and to its antisocial continuity, nor does it explain which factors are causes and which are only correlates of criminal behaviour, which moderate or mediate the process of risk, and for which individuals and in which situations.

Criminal behaviour has many causes, and no single factor can be identified as the cause of a criminal act. It is more likely that a multitude of risk factors is involved and that the interaction of them contributes to offending. In other words, comprehensive, multi-domain sampling of the factors associated with criminal conduct should be the norm in offender risk assessment. The risk of future offending is indeed proportional to the number of risk factors involved, to the duration of their influence, and to how risk factors operate in a cumulative fashion, the so-called *dose–response relationship* (Loeber et al., 2008a). According to Kraemer and her colleagues (2001), the term *risk* indicates the probability of an outcome, while the term *risk factor* refers to a correlate that precedes the outcome. As Murray et al. (2009) put it, risk factors are naturally occurring predictors of crime, mental health, educational achievement and social welfare, just to mention a few of the most relevant dimensions of human life.

It is important to distinguish risk factors from correlates. The term *correlate* is a measure that is associated with an outcome. All risk factors are correlates but not all correlates are risk factors (Kraemer et al., 2005, 16). The key distinction between correlates and risk factors is the temporal precedence of the factor in relation to the outcome. A risk factor has the ability to predict a consequence and ideally intervention should take place before the outcome occurs. A correlate does not necessarily precede the outcome and is likely to be a symptom or an indicator of an outcome that has already occurred and is associated with it.

A *causal risk factor* is a factor that, when changed, is shown to have changeable impacts on the outcome. In order to establish that a variable is a causal risk factor, Murray et al. (2009) affirm that one needs to demonstrate correlation and precedence, and exposure to the risk factor must be shown to cause an increase in the outcome, i.e. delinquency.

It is reasonable to use the term *causal risk factor* instead of *cause* because the term cause implies deterministic results, and causal relations in social sciences can only be probabilistic (Farrington, 1988; Kraemer et al., 2005). Changes in the factor X are followed by changes in the factor Y with a certain probability (Murray et al., 2009, 4).

The impact of risk factors varies depending on the vulnerability and sensitivity of the individual upon whom they exercise their influence, and on the situation in which they occur which can enhance or attenuate their impact. An individual may be sensitive to certain risk factors but not necessarily vulnerable. An individual may be vulnerable but may not be involved in a situation that encourages the risk impact. The combination of all these aspects has to be taken into account when assessing the risk.

Vulnerability is the state that enhances the susceptibility to a certain condition and weakens the set of protective factors that, if present, would not pose any hazard to the individual. *Sensitivity* is the level of receptiveness of an individual in the face of a certain stimulus (Zara, 2005). For instance, the pressure of antisocial peers is considered a significant risk factor for juvenile delinquency. Social and clinical psychology studies (Emler & Reicher, 1995; Farrington, 2012; Rutter *et al.*, 1998; van Lier & Koot, 2008) suggest that all adolescents are likely to be sensitive to the influence of peers. However not all adolescents are vulnerable to the impact of antisocial associates. An adolescent boy who attends a delinquent school may not become vulnerable to the delinquent influences of his school mates if for instance he comes from a supportive and prosocial family, if he has the possibility of getting involved in recreational activities outside school, if he practises sports with other people who are not interested in antisocial activities or if he has healthy competitive values and alternative socialising conditions to the ones offered to him by his school mates.

With respect to prediction, the concept of dynamic risk draws attention to the fact that risk factors can be of two general types. They can be static or dynamic. *Static factors* do not change or change only in one direction (e.g. age). *Dynamic factors* can change and they include criminogenic needs that are aspects of a person or his or her situation that, when changed, are associated with changes in criminal behaviour (Andrews *et al.*, 1990a). Criminogenic needs are not simply 'any old needs'. They are dynamic risk factors. We stress *dynamic risk* to emphasize, according to Bonta (2002), both prediction and treatment. Furthermore 'there is no reason to think that one type is superior to the other when it comes to predicting recidivism' (Bonta, 2002, 367). Either of them are insufficient, but both are relevant and necessary (Andrews & Bonta, 1998; Andrews *et al.*, 1990b).

The scientific literature is sufficiently robust to offer general suggestions (guidelines) about what should constitute good risk assessment. A risk instrument must be assessed on its power to predict criminal behaviour (Bonta, 2002, 359) and must be based on factors that are empirically related to recidivism (Gendreau *et al.*, 1996).

No risk assessment instrument or checklist will include every possible risk factor or address the issues of all the infinite combinations of circumstances (*the black swan effect*) that can precipitate offending behaviour or violence. Nor is it possible to consider all the strength or protective factors that can buffer the effects or risk factors and enhance resilience. Also neither is it possible to anticipate critical highly improbable events or black swans in Taleb's terms[1] (2007). In practice, risk assessment has become ever more dependent upon a variety of formal and informal data gathering that includes criminal records, self-report information, collateral information from different sources such as family members, friends and colleagues, contacts with law enforcement, school, medical and social service personnel and, in many instances, consultation with colleagues and supervisors. The necessity of an integration of different sources of information is fundamental to guarantee content validity and reliability (Baird & Wagner, 2000; Shlonsky & Wagner, 2005). Understanding how risk factors interrelate and how their interaction may contribute to an increase or a decrease in risk is of fundamental importance for intervention.

From the general to the individual use of assessing the risk

> Our meddling intellect
> Mis-shapes the beauteous forms of things: –
> We murder to dissect.
>
> *(Wordsworth, 1798)*

The use of risk assessment is often criticised because of *its failure to translate group phenomena or outcomes into individual instances*. Social psychology studies have a long tradition of information about predicting human behaviour. It is in fact not a new psychological discovery that it is easier to predict the behaviour of a group of people rather than the behaviour of an individual. Not only scientists, but also poets, such as William Wordsworth as quoted above, and writers such as Conan Doyle, were aware of this.

> Winwood Reade is good on the subject, said Holmes. He remarks that, while the individual man is an insoluble puzzle, in the aggregate he becomes a mathematical certainty. You can, for example, never foretell what any one man will do, but you can say with precision what an average number will add up to. Individuals vary, but percentages remain constant. So says the statistician . . .
>
> *(Doyle, 1890/2001, 84; cited in Webster & Hucker, 2007, 15)*

In discussing predictability, talking about weather forecasting and climate prediction (Gneiting & Katzfuss, 2014) might be useful. These types of forecast take the form of probability distributions over future quantities or events. If the probability of rain is 60 per cent, whether rain or no rain occurs on a particular day does not show that this probability is incorrect. In order to test whether the probability is correct or incorrect, one needs to study, at least, 100 days when the probability of rain is 60 per cent, and investigate whether the actual occurrence of rain in those 100 days was significantly different from the predicted 60 per cent.

It follows that the test of a group prediction is a function of group outcomes, of classes or sequences of events, and it does not convey direct meaning to the probability of a single event. When risk assessment is carried out for research purposes, the accuracy should lie significantly in the greatest number of cases examined. When conducted within the forensic setting, the accuracy of the assessment should refer to the probability, for a particular offender, of reoffending. In both cases greater clarity, not only semantic, but procedural as well, is fundamental to guarantee effective risk assessment. When risk assessment is being used as a statement of predicting future behaviour it is crucial that the types of risk and criminogenic needs are accurately identified and specified. This should be so, independently of the settings in which the assessment is done.

> Such assessment practices are believed to enhance the accuracy of clinical decisions, and allow for targeted interventions, better classification, program evaluations, and resources allocations.
>
> *(Hannah-Moffat, 2005, 32)*

These practices are, nevertheless, often risky, in the sense that decisions may have to be made in spite of incomplete or ambiguous evidence. New ways of understanding risk have revived the assumption that, by knowing the offenders, with their needs and resources, changes in the offending pattern can be encouraged and achieved (from a clinical perspective). It is not important to assess the risk of reoffending by simply getting a risk score *per se*, unless this risk score can be translated into appropriate intervention and preventive measures. If knowledge of criminogenic needs and risks is integrated into assessment procedures, the assertion that offenders can change may become the new focus of intervention governance. Risk should be assessed by specified and systematic criteria, and by an evidence-based methodology that can be shared by professionals, so as to reduce improvisation and subjective intuition. This knowledge requires that researchers and practitioners devote scientific and clinical attention to those factors that are changeable and can encourage modification in how the person behaves and adjusts to prosocial life. As Andrews and Bonta (2010b) suggest, *prediction should provide utility*. Perhaps it should inform the secure containment of risk, to use Rose's words (2002, cited in Hannah-Moffat, 2005, 34), by involving efficient and rational estimation and consideration of the level of risk, dynamic risks and needs. This is the preamble of what is intended by the concept of taking responsibility for doing something *for* and *with* the person.

The clinical and statistical prediction of recidivism

Two kinds of violence predictions are predominant in criminology: (a) those made in emergency situations by frontline police, security officers and staff working in psychiatric settings; (b) those made by mental health, correctional and forensic experts when they are asked to compile risk assessments to provide health units, parole boards or courts with sound and systematic information about the progress made by offenders in regard to compliance to treatment, response to a rehabilitation programme or the level of criminogenic risk that they still pose. In these situations, decisions are taken either under escalating emergencies (the former instance) or under extreme expectancy of preciseness (the latter instance). In both, experts have to be as certain as possible that their responses do not exceed the minimum that is necessary (Webster & Hucker, 2007, 15; see also Webster, 1984).

The current groups of risk assessment instruments involve an actuarial judgement or a structured professional judgement. The former provides a probabilistic estimate of violence risk in a specified time period. The latter permits a professional judgement to be made about risk level (e.g. low, moderate or high) after taking into account the presence or absence of a predetermined set of factors (Fazel et al., 2012). The use of adequate, specific, valid and reliable risk assessment instruments will aid accuracy, thoroughness of information and documentation examination, and reduction of bias and systematic errors.

Expert opinion, however, is divided about which are the most accurate instruments, when to use 'what' and 'with whom'. Some reviews recommend actuarial instruments for their higher predictive accuracy and inter-rater reliability. Some others are in favour of structured professional judgement (SPJ) instruments because of their focus on the individual and for their adherence to the responsivity factor.

Actuarial instruments address historical and static risk: the main interest is on predictive accuracy over time. SPJ instruments take into account dynamic risk: the main interest is in promoting change and assisting treatment. In both cases an excessive number of false positive decisions is the cost to pay in assessing the risk of future criminality and violence (M. A. Campbell et al., 2009; Viljoen et al., 2010; Cooke & Michie, 2012).

The main concerns raised over actuarial instruments are that their assessment may be more illusory than real, or more prejudicial than probative, when applied to individuals (Cooke, 2010; Cooke & Michie, 2010). The concerns over SPJ instruments include their predictive accuracy that has yet to be established: comparatively the validity of SPJ may be exceeded by actuarial instruments. The analysis of types of assessment methods and how they differ or can be integrated is the essential focus of the remainder of this chapter.

Comparing clinical and actuarial risk

The comparison between clinical versus actuarial judgment has a long history, but it now requires to be re-energised if the field of prediction and risk assessment aims to be promoted to a scientific rank. Academic debates often divide risk assessment instruments into three different categories: unstructured professional or clinical judgement (UPJ), actuarial judgement (AJ) and structured professional judgement (SPJ). More recently, this has evolved into a direct introduction of the management of risk into the practice of assessment, in line with the responsivity principle, opening up an avenue for a more comprehensive and integrated approach. This classification is in line with the four-generation evolution (Andrews & Bonta, 2006) that represents a shift from the ideology of simply measuring risk to an intervention model that looks at risk assessment as a scientific utility (e.g. identification of criminogenic needs) to guide individualised treatment and aid case management to address change and promote well-being.

First-generation risk assessment was based on unstructured clinical judgement, which had been prevalent in the first half of the twentieth century. Correctional staff (e.g. probation officers and prison staff) and clinical professionals (e.g. psychologists, psychiatrists and social workers) on the basis of their expertise, professional training and experience, would make judgements about who required enhanced security and supervision (Bonta, 1996; Taxman *et al.*, 2007).

Second-generation risk assessment was based on actuarial and static instruments. At the beginning of the 1970s actuarial judgements, based more on evidence and less on professional intuition, started to gather support because of their predictive superiority in assessing the risk not only of general recidivism (Ægisdóttir *et al.*, 2006; Andrews *et al.*, 2006; Grove *et al.*, 2000), but also of specific groups of offenders, such as mentally disordered offenders (Bonta *et al.*, 1998) and sex offenders (Hanson & Bussière, 1998; Seto, 2005). With actuarial risk assessment instruments, specific and static items were identified and given quantitative scores: the presence of a risk factor may receive a score of one and its absence a score of zero. The scores on the items can then be summed: the higher the score, the higher the risk that the offender will reoffend. An increase of scientific support for the predictive superiority of actuarial risk assessments contributed to the fact that more and more correctional jurisdictions in Canada and the USA adopted this type of assessment for classifying offenders and assigning differential supervision practices.

Third-generation risk assessment was based on instruments that included the consideration of both risks and needs. At the beginning of the 1980s the inclusion of dynamic risk factors in assessment instruments started to be greatly encouraged (Bonta & Wormith, 2007). This generation of risk instruments was sensitive to changes in the offender's life apart from their history.

Fourth-generation risk assessment is based on the integration of case management with risk and need assessment. At the dawn of the twenty-first century this fourth generation of risk assessment instruments was introduced. Risk assessment practice now involves the systematic integration of assessing a broader range of risk factors (dynamic, acute, stable and static), many of which were not previously considered, with intervention, monitoring and treating the offender. The idea of individualised treatment is what has permitted these fourth-generation instruments to receive an encouraging welcome both in the scientific community and in the criminal justice system.

Unstructured clinical judgement

The UCJ approach ('first-generation' approach) leads to decisions that emerge from informal and subjective criteria for establishing which factors seem risky for the particular case under assessment. There are three main limitations of this approach:

1. Clinicians tend to base risk and violence assessment upon their own experience in practice using intuition and judgement alone (Murray & Thomson, 2010).

2. The clinical practice is limited in terms of both accuracy and inter-clinician agreement (Hart et al., 2007).
3. The clinician's focus often tends to be on offending characteristics that are not empirically related to criminal behaviour. For instance, assessment instruments originally developed to predict psychological or psychiatric symptoms simply fail to accurately predict violence and criminal recidivism (Hilton et al., 2006). So an assessment of 'dangerousness' does not equal a prediction of violent recidivism (Murray & Thomson, 2010).

> The assertion sometimes heard from clinicians that 'naturally', clinical prediction, being based on 'real understanding', is superior, is simply not justified by the facts.
>
> *(Meehl, 1954, 119)*

Clinical judgement is not a risk assessment procedure *per se*. Everything is left to the discretion, experience and competence of the clinician. Risk factors are not specified in advance, and neither is the method of combining them into a final evaluation. The adjustment of scores and the incorporation of experience and practice are allowed in the unstructured professional approach and in the clinical approach, but neither yield probabilities of reoffending. The evaluation is unstructured and affected by the clinical background of the professionals. Some psychological tests may be administered within an interview procedure, but the process that leads to a decision is mostly subjective and discretionary. As it exists, this approach is criticised because it lacks reliability, generalizability, validity and replicability of the procedure employed by the clinician to arrive at decisions, and it does not specify which criteria were followed (e.g. Quinsey et al., 2006). The criteria are simply established case by case, because this type of judgement is based on the clinical cases of the clinician, and not on empirical research. Clinical judgements – even if they are made by highly trained and experienced clinicians – 'are relatively poor prognosticators if they fail to attend to empirically defensible risk factors in a structured way' (Andrews & Bonta, 2006, 286).

The many drawbacks of intuitive or clinical judgement that have to be taken into account in evidence-based research and intervention include the following:

1. the lack of structure, transparency, and empirical validation data (Dahle, 2005; Hanson & Morton-Bourgon, 2004, 2007, 2009; Krueger, 2007);
2. the potential for biases in considering risk factors;
3. the inaccuracy in predicting reoffending;
4. the unsystematic, discretionary and subjective procedures.

Clinical intuition is certainly a key factor in a clinical setting (e.g. regarding psychotherapy). Clinical judgement is an indispensable factor of therapeutic engagement within the clinical setting that is necessary for the success of the therapeutic intervention.

In forensic or criminological settings, what is required is a different sort of reasoning and professional engagement, not least because very often the person who is going to be assessed has not chosen the assessment and the intervention that follows, and at best feels obliged to engage in it, often does not feel the need to undertake the assessment, and has strategic interests in covering up or revealing certain aspects and not others of their life, personality and behaviour.

Actuarial judgement (AJ)

Actuarial judgement (the 'second-generation' approach) is considered a real assessment method *per se* because of its role in predicting criminal recidivism, and in evaluating long-term (historical) and short-term (static) risk. In actuarial assessment, the static risk factors are derived from existing data sources such as official records, rather than from a comprehensive theoretical perspective, and the items selected predict recidivism rather than explain it (Spitzer & Maccarone, 2007). In the actuarial approach, risk factors are chosen either on the basis of theoretical assumptions observed, as in the instances of the Acute and the Stable (Hanson *et al.*, 2007a), or on the basis of measured relationships with the outcome, as in the case of the SORAG (Quinsey *et al.*, 1998, 2006) or Static-99 (Hanson & Thornton, 2000). In both cases, explicit statistical rules are provided for combining items into an overall final evaluation of risk. It follows that adjustment of scores is not permitted.

Although actuarial methods are more likely to provide accurate information, there are still a number of difficulties associated with their use. As Wilczynski (1997) points out, risk instruments are better at distinguishing *between* groups than *between* and *within* individuals. According to this assumption, actuarial risk assessment instruments are more useful in categorising individuals, rather than in understanding and resolving their problems (Silver & Miller, 2002). Thus, instead of predicting what will occur, classification of greater or lesser degree of risk simply informs practitioners and agencies about which cases are more likely than others to be at high risk.

Their higher predictive accuracy compared with clinical judgement relies on static risk instruments, whose stability over time provides methodological preciseness. However, this may even be counterproductive in so far as static risk scales portray individuals as 'unchangeable', 'running the risk of diverting offenders away from treatment' (Bonta, 2002, 370).

Where clinical and actuarial judgements meet and don't meet

Meehl (1954) indicated that there are no known cases where clinicians reliably outperformed actuarial methods, even when the statistical models are just linear classification rules. Statistical or actuarial judgements are found to even outperform those clinical experts who have access to the statistical results. The rather surprising result that statistical classifiers significantly outperform human experts is also consistent across disciplines such as medicine, psychology, psychiatry and criminology. Such a result is particularly surprising because it seems to go against the belief amongst social science professionals that clinical perception, intuition and understanding of human needs and problems are essential to accurate diagnoses and prognoses. And yet this may be where the problem lies: clinicians might place too much weight on their own judgments, and not enough consideration on the statistics. The magic touch of human sensitivity in understanding what is happening is, at best, more a 'blissful flair' than a concrete contribution to the assessment. It may be necessary for reinforcing the successful development of intervention, and making the person feel recognised and treated 'humanly', but it may not be specifically influential in the accuracy of predictions.

On the one hand, clinical experts may say that, in order to understand the future behaviour of a known offender it is necessary to explore his or her needs, the psychosocial reality and the dynamic factors involved, in order to come as close as possible to a complete understanding of the offender's criminal career. In other words, their argument is that it is only by humanising the risk assessment that we can evaluate the risk accurately. On the other hand, actuarial experts may advocate a more clear-cut estimation of static risk factors that play a significant impact on the risk of reoffending. In other words, only by rationalising the risk assessment can we control biases and heuristic errors, and perform a more precise risk evaluation.

The idea of clinical versus actuarial judgements can be summarised as follows. Assume that one is interested in diagnosing reoffending in a group of inmates. Usually the clinicians look at criminal files and at the life history of each inmate and state whether the inmate has a risk condition requiring intervention to reduce the risk. This is the clinical approach, which is based on the individual and on the contextualisation of the assessment with the psychosocial reality of the person under assessment. Alternatively, one could ask the experts what features they look for when making their assessment, and then fit a statistical model to those data, trying to predict the outcome or classification based on those features. In this case the intervention of experts is also needed to make an evaluation. This is the actuarial approach, and it is just based on averages of inmates with features x, y and z, and on the calculation of the 'q' percentage that pose a low, medium or high risk of reoffending.

While research findings (Mann, 1996; Quinsey *et al.*, 2006) show that unstructured clinical instruments underperform actuarial measures in general and more so in respect of specifically violent behaviour, research findings are, however, not so clear about which is the best and most accurate approach in criminological psychology. The relative superiority (established in roughly 150 studies starting with the work of Meehl) of statistical prediction rules (SPRs) compared to intuitive judgments, to predict human outcomes (Dawes *et al.*, 1989), leads us to question whether actuarial judgments are still superior when assessing criminal recidivism or whether an integration of the two approaches might be better in criminological settings. Within criminological psychology, is such an amalgamation justifiable? If well-validated actuarial instruments exist, that are accurate and found superior to professional judgment, should professionals use them, totally absenting themselves from the prediction? Or should they still attempt integration? Dawes (2002) raised these issues when he suggested that some professionals use SPRs to refine and complete intuitive judgment, rather than to replace it.

Three areas of theory and research are relevant in the prediction, assessment and treatment of future reoffending. The first consists of identifying risk and protective factors. The second focuses on the recognition of methods and instruments to combine these factors that can guarantee a reliable and valid assessment of risk. The third involves intervention as a way of integrating the previous two areas. Assessing the risk of future criminal behaviour is an essential aspect of intervention and prevention. Risk assessment instruments are in essence risk classification tools rather than offending *prediction* tools (Baird & Wagner, 2000; DePanfilis & Zuravin, 2001; Shlonsky & Wagner, 2005), and most research on risk assessment acknowledges that the use of any kind of risk assessment instrument requires good clinical skills (Doueck et al., 1993). This leads to the introduction of *structured clinical judgements* and of the fourth generation of risk assessments that includes the dimension of treatability.

Structured professional judgement (SPJ)

Doyle and Dolan (2002) note that practitioners are concerned with the clinical reality of assessing and managing risk rather than with the research task of prediction. Consequently, they propose a 'third-generation' approach, referred to as 'empirically validated, structured decision-making' (Douglas et al., 1999) or 'structured clinical judgement' (Hart, 1998). This approach attempts to bridge the gap between the scientific, actuarial approach and the clinical practice of risk assessment. The shift in emphasis is then based on developing evidence-based guidelines and frameworks that promote systematisation and consistency, and yet that are also flexible enough to account for case-specific influences and the context in which assessments are conducted. Such instruments can promote transparency and accountability, encourage the use of professional discretion, and are based on sound scientific knowledge but are practically relevant (Hart, 1998).

Structured professional judgement should not be considered as a risk assessment *per se*, but for reasons different from those of UCJ, SPJ is more a method of evaluating a set of empirically based factors that are known to be associated with recidivism. It requires experts to rate a list of predetermined risk factors, but the final evaluation is left to the professional. This leaves room for a clinically meaningful assessment of the case. Adjustment of scores and incorporation of experience and practice are endorsed in the SPJ approach, but it does not provide probabilities of reoffending. Douglas and Kropp (2002) consider SPJ as a set of guidelines or an *aide-mémoire* (p. 626). This perspective of SPJ allows for a more comprehensive and integrative application in contexts other than the clinical one (e.g. forensic, criminological, preventive services), in which the collaboration of different professionals (e.g. criminologists, psychologists, psychiatrists, police officers, probation officers, social workers, victim personnel and researchers) is expected and necessary. Then, in line with the work of Douglas and Kropp (2002), Melton and colleagues (1997), Otto (2000), and Otto and Douglas (2010), SPJ:

1. reflects current theoretical, clinical, and empirical knowledge about violence;
2. enlightens the *anamnestic approach* in risk assessment so that the identification of significant violent and criminal risk factors and criminogenic needs is done through an accurate examination of the life and criminal career of the individual;
3. provides the minimum set of risk factors that should be taken into account in every case;
4. considers the protective factors available and assesses their possible effects;
5. includes recommendations for information gathering (i.e. the use of different sources and multiple methods), for communicating expert opinions, planning and implementing violence prevention strategies;
6. does not impose restraints for the selection, weighting, or combination of risk and protective factors;
7. entails professional responsibility, discretion, integrity and transparency of risk judgement and management;
8. promotes an analytical and systematic association between risk factors, available resources and most suitable preventive interventions;
9. appraises the degree of intervention, management and action required.

The *Risk-Need-Responsivity* (RNR) model (Andrews & Bonta, 1994) has influenced the way risk factors are seen, assessed and explored. This is particularly relevant in the present context because it promises an integration of work on developmental criminal onsets and the identification of those risks and needs that represent the *active ingredients* on which it seems most appropriate to target intervention (Taxman & Thanner, 2006).

As Andrews and Bonta (2006) stated, people involved in the criminal justice system have many needs that deserve treatment, but not all of these needs are associated with criminal behaviour. The psychological nature of some risk factors has led to the recognition of criminogenic needs as dynamic psychological factors that can change. In this instance, *change* is meant as 'changes in the chances of criminal activity' (Andrews & Bonta, 2010a, 21–2). The idea of integrating risks and needs, in the process of assessment, allows for a better understanding of 'how the past influenced the future' (Taxman & Thanner, 2006, 31). Static risk dimensions, despite being unchangeable, are integrated into the process of risk evaluation because they represent a reliable marker of antisocial continuity. *Risk* is essentially fastened to the past. A possible suggestion is to identify, as early as possible in the life of the individual, how strongly the past is likely to threaten the future prosocial development of an offender. *Need* is an indicator of the extent to which either daily functioning is altered or protective factors are reduced in warding off criminal engagement. If one way to enhance prevention may be to reduce risk factors and to foster protective factors (Augimeri *et al.*, 2010), a way to serve prevention is to concentrate on a reliable methodology to make the process of risk assessment adhere to the criminogenic reality under evaluation.

Research findings show that there exist other factors, called *non-criminogenic needs* by Andrews *et al.* (1990a), because of their lack of significant correlation with criminal behaviour. Nevertheless, they can constitute important components in the functioning of offenders, to the extent that they can hinder treatment and interfere with the possibility for the person of pursuing some significant change in those aspects that cause them suffering and social and personal failures. Some of these non-criminogenic needs are self-esteem, anxiety, poor parenting skills, medical needs, victimization issues and learning disability, to mention but a few. Their inclusion in a RNR assessment may facilitate participation in and compliance with treatment, and this may require addressing them in treatment before or alongside criminogenic needs. As it is with anybody, and in most situations, *happy offenders are more collaborative and more resilient*.

The RNR model is inspired by general personality and social learning theories to explain that criminal behaviour is learned through complex interactions between cognitive, emotional, personality and biological factors and environmental reward–cost contingencies. There are a number of factors or paths that lead to criminal conduct, and some factors are more important than others. Andrews and Bonta (1998) described what they call *the big four* factors of antisocial behaviour: criminal history, antisocial personality, antisocial attitudes and social support for crime. Other variables, less important but nonetheless relevant in the model, are indicators of prosocial conventions, e.g. employment and education, family relationships, facilitators and inhibitors of antisocial and conventional behaviour such as substance abuse (Andrews & Bonta, 1998; Bonta, 2002; Gendreau *et al.*, 1996; see also Bonta *et al.*, 1998, for a review with mentally disordered offenders; Hanson & Bussière, 1998, for a review with sex offenders).

Risk assessment instruments

The tables systematize some of the most well-known risk assessment instruments used in psycho-criminology and forensic settings. The actuarial (AJ) (see Tables 4.1, 4.4, 4.6) and structured professional (SPJ) (see Tables 4.2, 4.3, 4.5, 4.7) judgement instruments included, both for adults and for juveniles, for general criminal recidivism, and for violence and sex offending, are chosen on the basis of their scientific and empirical soundness, their predictive accuracy, and their specificity for targeted groups of offenders (see also Farrington *et al.*, 2008; *Risk Management Authority – RATED*[2] version 3 – 2013, for a review).

Some instruments related to interpersonal partner violence (IPV) are included because of the evidence about their concurrent validity in assessing violence propensity (see Tables 4.4 and 4.5).

The list of instruments used with juvenile offenders (see Tables 4.6–4.7) comprises also some clinical instruments (see Table 4.8) that are not specifically designed to assess the risk of reoffending and violence, but they are often used in forensic

TABLE 4.1 Risk assessment instruments: AJ instruments for assessing the risk of general and sex violence in adults

Instrument	Type	Aims and description	No. items	Author(s)
ACUTE 2007	AJ	Assessing the risk for both sex/violent recidivism, and a total score for general recidivism. It is the acute counterpart of Stable 2007, and it consists of seven acute factors: 　Victim access. 　Hostility. 　Sexual preoccupation. 　Rejection of supervision. 　Emotional collapse. 　Collapse of social supports. 　Substance abuse.	7	Hanson *et al.* (2007a)
STABLE 2007[a]	AJ	Focusing on stable risk factors to predict sexual recidivism or breach. It is a scale organised in two parts, with 12 (+ 1 for child molesters) stable–dynamic risks: 　Significant social influences. 　Capacity for relationship stability. 　Emotional identification with children (<13). 　Hostility towards women. 　General social rejection. 　Lack of concern for others. 　Impulsive. 　Poor problem solving skills. 　Negative emotionality. 　Sex drive/sex preoccupation. 　Sex as coping. 　Deviant sexual preferences. 　Cooperation with supervision.	13	Hanson *et al.* (2007a)

Instrument	Type	Aims and description	No. items	Author(s)
		Static-99 should be used within the first month of supervision; stable assessment should be completed within three months and then every six months thereafter; the acute assessment to be assessed every session (but not more than weekly) (Hanson et al., 2007a). The combination of acute and stable factors incrementally improve the predictive accuracy when added to the static factors assessed in Static-99 (see later). When properly used, these tools showed levels of predictive accuracy as high as other established methods of risk assessment with sexual offenders. Further research is needed particularly: 1. to determine the extent to which the stable and acute variables are related to changes in the recidivism risk; 2. to reliably assess changes of stable factors upon criminal behaviour; 3. to identify rapidly truly acute factors associated with the timing of recidivism (in this last case, more frequent evaluations – daily rather than monthly – would be rather necessary).		
Hare Psychopathy Checklist Revised (PCL-R)[b]	AJ	Assessing psychopathy. While not designed to predict recidivism, it has proven to be a robust predictor of violence and violent recidivism, and it correlates highly with other actuarial risk scales. The PCL-R score provides a dimensional score of the extent to which an individual matches the criteria of a 'prototypical psychopath' (Hare, 2003, 17). Factor 1 is composed of Facet 1 (interpersonal [5 items]) and Facet 2 (affective [4 items]), and Factor 2 is composed of Facet 3 (life style [5 items]) and Facet 4 (antisocial [5 items]). The 20 traits assessed by the PCL-R score are: *F1: Interpersonal* 1. Glibness/superficial charm. 2. Grandiose sense of self-worth. 4. Pathological lying. 5. Conning/manipulative.	20	Hare (1991, 2003)

(Continued)

TABLE 4.1 (continued)

Instrument	Type	Aims and description	No. items	Author(s)
	F2: *Affective*	6. Lack of remorse or guilt. 7. Shallow affect (superficial emotional responsiveness). 8. Callous/lack of empathy. 16. Failure to accept responsibility for own actions.		
	F3: *Life style*	3. Need for stimulation/proneness to boredom. 9. Parasitic life style. 13. Lack of realistic, long-term goals. 14. Impulsivity. 15. Irresponsibility.		
	F4: *Antisocial*	10. Poor behavioral controls. 12. Early behavioral problems. 16. Failure to accept responsibility. 18. Juvenile delinquency. 19. Revocation of conditional release. 20. Criminal versatility.		
	Additional items	11. Promiscuous sexual behaviour. 17. Many short-term marital relationships.		

The PCL-R generally is coded after a detailed semi-structured clinical interview is completed, whenever possible, with the client and a thorough review of case history information, collateral reports, and official records is performed. Up to five items can be omitted, and the total score is then prorated (see Hare, 2003, 6–7). More detailed information is provided in Ch. 5 of this book

TABLE 4.1 (continued)

Instrument	Type	Aims and description	No. items	Author(s)

Hare Psychopathy Checklist Screening Version (PCL:SV)[c]	AJ	Screening for psychopathy in forensic settings and to assess and diagnose psychopathy outside forensic settings. Items can be summed to yield total scores, with scores of 18 or greater on the PCL:SV considered diagnostic of psychopathy, as well as scores reflecting four facets of psychopathy: interpersonal (i.e. arrogant and deceitful interpersonal style), affective (i.e. deficient affective experience), behaviour (i.e. impulsive and irresponsible behavioural style), and antisocial (i.e. delinquency and criminality). The itemised structure of the PCL:SV consists of:
		
		    Adult antisocial behavior.
		    Irresponsible.
		    Impulsive.
		    Adolescent antisocial behavior.
		    Poor behavioural controls.
		    Lacks goals.
		    Superficial.
		    Lacks remorse.
		    Deceitful.
		    Grandiose.
		    Lacks empathy.
		    Doesn't accept responsibility.
		
		Similar to the PCL-R, the PCL:SV was not developed as a risk assessment tool but is a personality assessment. It is however correlated with violence. This version does not rely upon criminal history. Offenders scoring 13–17 should be further assessed using the full version.
			12	Hart et al. (1995)

(Continued)

TABLE 4.1 (continued)

Instrument	Type	Aims and description	No. items	Author(s)
Level of Service[d] Inventory–Revised (LSI-R)	AJ	Predicting parole outcome as well as general and violent recidivism. It is a risk/need assessment instrument. The LSI-R is used by probation and parole officers, correctional officers working in jails and detention facilities. It includes various scales under 10 subheadings: criminal history (10 items), education/employment (10 items), financial (2 items), family/marital (4 items), accommodation (3 items), leisure/recreation (2 items), companions (5 items), alcohol/drug problem (9 items), emotional/personal (5 items), and attitude/orientation (4 items). It may contain more items than is necessary to determine risk of recidivism and the use of it is only necessary if the offender is the focus of service planning.	54	Andrews and Bonta (1995); Andrews et al. (2010)
Level of Service/Case Management Inventory (LSI/CMI)	AJ	Combining risk assessment and case management into one evidence-based system. This instrument was designed for general application and not violence risk assessment *per se*, but it is shown to be related to violence, in so far as all the necessary tools are here in one single application. It is the next step from the LSI-R inventory, and includes 8 sections designed to identify dynamic areas of risk/needs which are specifically relevant to the treatment of offenders. The tool provides a score for the level of risk of reoffending, and it considers factors related to criminogenic potential, responsivity, personal concerns, and the history and nature of perpetration. The instrument contains a professional override to arrive at a final risk/need level between very high and very low.	43	Andrews et al. (2004)
Minnesota Sex Offender Screening Tool (MnSOST)	AJ	Predicting of sexual recidivism. It was developed in response to a call by the Minnesota Dept of Corrections (DOC) for a more formal process for identifying predatory sex offenders. It is a screening tool used on sex offenders by their case managers during their intake period into the corrections system. The score on the MnSOST was then used as a basis for treatment recommendations for civil commitment after the initial sentence.	21	Epperson et al. (1995)

TABLE 4.1 (continued)

Instrument	Type	Aims and description	No. items	Author(s)
Minnesota Sex Offender Screening Tool-Revised (MnSOST-R)	AJ	Screening referral tool for commitment under the state's Sexual Psychopathic Personality and Sexually Dangerous Person Laws, and as part of the state's Community Notification Act. The MnSOST-R is used to implement legal demands that dangerous or predatory sex offenders remain incarcerated to prevent sex reoffending until treatment renders them safe to re-enter society. The 16 variables retained in the MnSOST-R are categorised as either historical/static variables or institutional/dynamic variables. The latter category refers to the offender's period of incarceration for the current or most recent sex offence. *Institutional/Dynamic Variables:* Discipline history while incarcerated Status of chemical dependency treatment Status of sex offender treatment Age at time of release *Historical/Static Variables:* Number of sex-related convictions Length of sexual offending history Commission of sex offences while under correctional supervision Commission of sex offences in public places Force or threat of force in sex offences Multiple acts committed against a single victim Number of age groups victimized Sex offences against a 13- to 15-year-old victim Sex offences against strangers Evidence of adolescent antisocial behaviour Pattern of drug or alcohol abuse Employment history	16	Epperson et al. (1998)

(Continued)

TABLE 4.1 (continued)

Instrument	Type	Aims and description	No. items	Author(s)
		The developers stated that the assessing strategy behind the MnSOST-R is to develop an actuarial tool that can firmly anchor the judgement process, and not simply to make an actuarial score the sole basis of important decisions. It has not yet been validated on a new sample (Hanson, 1998), and some shortcomings are related to its experimental procedures and its ethical standards, so that it cannot support expert testimony in a legal proceeding.		

Minnesota Sex Offender Screening Tool-3 (MnSOST-3)	AJ	Assigning low-, moderate- or high-risk designations to all sexual offenders who are required by law to register. It is a revision of the MnSOST-R, and was developed on a population of adult male incarcerated offenders who were convicted of either a sex or sex-related offence. It is not appropriate for offenders who have never been sentenced for a sex/sex-related offence. It is designed to be scored based upon a file review (paper, electronic or both). Access to official criminal records, including an offender's prior criminal history, is necessary. It is not necessary to interview an offender, but if an offender is interviewed and he provides credible self-report information which subsequently becomes part of the offender's file, this information may be used to score the MnSOST-3.1. It contains 11 predictors, 9 main effects and 2 interaction [x] effects. Of the nine main effects, only three were items derived from the previous version (public place, completion of chemical dependency and sex offender treatment, and age at release). The items retained are:
		    Predatory offence sentences.
		    Sentences with male victims.
		    Public place.
		    Felony sentences.
		    VOFP[e] Harassment/stalking.
		    Disorderly conduct sentence (last 3 years).
		    Completion of sex offender and chemical dependency treatment.
			11	Duwe and Freske (2012)

TABLE 4.1 (continued)

Instrument	Type	Aims and description	No. items	Author(s)
		Age at release. Unsupervised release. [VOFP × Age]. [Disorderly conduct sentence × Age].		
Offender Group Reconviction Scale (OGRS)	AJ	Predicting reoffending only by assessing static risks such as age, gender and criminal history. It allows probation, prison and youth justice staff to produce predictions for individual offenders. It shows a good applicability level to offenders of all ages in both custody and the community. It is based on: Age at the date of the current caution, non-custodial sentence or discharge from custody. Gender. Type of offence for which the offender has currently been cautioned or convicted. Number of times of previous caution orders or convictions. Recorded criminal history (length in years).	6	Copas and Marshall (1998)
Rapid Risk Assessment for Sexual Offense Recidivism (R-RASOR)	AJ	Predicting sexual offender recidivism. The brief risk scale is designed to be used as a screening procedure in settings that require routine assessments of sexual offender recidivism risk. It consists of an actuarial formula and calculates the risk level on the basis of the following static factors: Prior sexual arrests. Age. Ever targeted male victims. Whether any victims unrelated to the offender. R-RASOR does not provide a comprehensive evaluation and should not be used in isolation. It cannot assist in monitoring change over time or during/following treatment; the static factors do not help identify treatment or intervention, so its utility for risk management is limited.	4	Hanson (1997)

(Continued)

TABLE 4.1 (continued)

Instrument	Type	Aims and description	No. items	Author(s)

Sex Offender Needs Assessment Rating (SONAR)	AJ	Assessing sexual reoffending risk among adult sex offenders using a weighted scoring key by clinical staff or case managers. It contributed significantly to the understanding of dynamic risk factors and is best used as a complement to other tools that measure static factors. The items are divided into two areas.
		
		Stable factors:
		  Intimacy deficits.
		  Negative social influences.
		  Attitudes tolerant of sexual offending.
		  Sexual self-regulation.
		  General self-regulation.
		Acute factors:
		  Substance abuse.
		  Negative mood.
		  Anger.
		  Victim access.
			9	Hanson and Harris (2000)

Sex Offender Risk Appraisal Guide (SORAG)	AJ	Assessing the recidivism risk (sexual and violent) of previously convicted sexual offenders. The items are:
		  Lived with biological parents until age 16 (except for death of parent).
		  Elementary school maladjustment.
		  History of alcohol problems.
		  Marital status.
		  Non-violent offence history.
		  Violent offence history.
		  Sexual offence history.
		  Sex and age of index victim.
		  Failure on prior conditional release.
		  Age at index offence.
		  DSM-III criteria for any personality disorder.
		  DSM-III criteria for schizophrenia.
			14	Quinsey et al. (1998, 2006)

TABLE 4.1 (continued)

Instrument	Type	Aims and description	No. items	Author(s)
		Phallometrically measured deviant sexual interests. PCL–R score. The tool is not simple to use; it requires more specific information than many of the other tools, some of which might be difficult to obtain.		
STATIC-99	AJ	Predicting sexual recidivism. It provides explicit probability estimates of sexual reconviction, is easily scored and has been shown to be robustly predictive across several settings using a variety of samples. It demonstrates only moderate predictive accuracy. The items are: Prior sexual offences (same rules as in R-RASOR). Prior sentencing dates (number of distinct occasions on which the offender has been sentenced for criminal offences of any kind). Any conviction for non-contact offences. Index non-sexual violence. Prior non-sexual violence. Any unrelated victims. Any stranger victims. Any male victims. Young. Single.	10	Hanson and Thornton (2000)
STATIC-2002	AJ	Evaluating the risk of sexual and violent recidivism among adult male sexual offenders. It improves the consistency of scoring criteria of Static-99. It can be used by a wide range of evaluators (e.g. psychologists, probation officers, psychiatrists, therapists) using commonly available criminal history information.	14	Hanson and Thornton (2003); A. J. R. Harris et al. (2003); Hanson et al. (2010)

(Continued)

TABLE 4.1 (continued)

Instrument	Type	Aims and description	No. items	Author(s)

		Static-2002 predicts sexual, violent, and any recidivism as well as other actuarial risk tools commonly used with sexual offenders. It is intended to assess some theoretically meaningful characteristics presumed to be the cause of recidivism risk (persistence of sexual offending, deviant sexual interests, general criminality). The items are organised into five subscales:
		
		Age:
		  1. Age at release.
		
		Persistence of sexual offending:
		  2. Prior sentencing occasions for sexual offences.
		  3. Any juvenile arrest for a sexual offence.
		  4. Rate of sexual offending.
		
		Deviant sexual interests:
		  5. Any non-contact sex offences.
		  6. Any male victim.
		  7. Young/unrelated victims.
		
		Relationship to victims:
		  8. Any unrelated victim.
		  9. Any stranger victim.
		
		General criminality:
		  10. Any prior involvement with the criminal justice system.
		  11. Prior sentencing occasions.
		  12. Any community supervision violation.
		  13. Years free prior to index sex offence.
		  14. Any prior non-sexual violence.		

TABLE 4.1 (continued)

Instrument	Type	Aims and description	No. items	Author(s)
Violence Risk Appraisal Guide (VRAG)	AJ	Predicting violent (including violent sexual) recidivism after release to the community. The VRAG is used in a number of capacities including with patients in forensic and non-forensic settings, sex offenders, and offenders in prison. It is used by clinicians, courts, and parole officials. It includes items relating to demographics and childhood history, and involves a psychiatric assessment. The items are: Separation from either biological parent by age 16 (except for death of parent). Elementary school maladjustment. Alcohol problems. Never married. Criminal history score for non-violent offences. Failure on prior conditional release. Age at index offence. Victim injury. Female victim. Meets DSM-III criteria for any personality disorder. Meets DSM-III criteria for schizophrenia. PCL-R score.	12	Quinsey et al. (1998, 2006)

(Continued)

TABLE 4.1 (continued)

Instrument	Type	Aims and description	No. items	Author(s)
		It has been shown to accurately predict intimate partner violence recidivism (Hanson et al., 2007b). One limitation of the VRAG is that it requires a great deal of time, access to offender history and ability to conduct clinical assessments. For a multisite comparison of the RRASOR, SORAG, Static-99, and VRAG see G. T. Harris et al. (2003).		

Notes: AJ = Actuarial Judgement or Statistical Tool. SPJ = Structured Professional Judgement or Structured Clinical Judgement.

a Hanson and Harris have developed a system with both stable and acute risk factors. Originally called SONAR (The Sex Offenders Need Assessment Rating); this system has now been renamed in two parts: STABLE– and ACUTE-2007 (SA07 = total of 20 items) and represents a collaborative long lasting effort by the Canadian Department of Corrections. The STABLE-2007 and the ACUTE-2007 are specialised tools designed to assess and track changes in risk status over time by assessing changeable 'dynamic' risk factors. These assessment tools, when properly used, showed the value of combining static, stable and acute risk factors in the community supervision of sexual offenders and high levels of predictive accuracy in assessing the risk of reoffending.

b PCL-R is not a risk assessment instrument per se. It is a psychometric instrument for psychopathy assessment. It is usually included into a wide battery of instruments as VRAG, HCR-20, and LSI-R with the aim of increasing the level of predictive accuracy of criminal and violent behaviour. In literature PCL-R is often considered a combination of actuarial and clinical evaluations in so far as it implies a process of systematic administration that leads to a final score, still leaving room for a clinical diagnosis. It is used in combination with an interview and it requires collateral information in order to measure personality traits and behaviour related to psychopathy.

c PCL:SV is considered a screening tool (Hart et al., 1995, 1) that could be used both in forensic and non-forensic settings.

d LSI-R is not a risk assessment instrument per se. It contains many dynamic factors and is structured to allow for some adjustment in the final scores, according to the individual's needs. It could be included among the SPJ instruments.

e VOFP: Harassment/stalking/violate order for protection/violate no contact order/violate restraining order.

TABLE 4.2 Risk assessment instruments: 'Atypical' SPJ for assessing the risk of general and sex violence in adults

Instrument	Aims and description	No. items	Author(s)
Self-Assessment Questionnaire (SAQ)*	Assessing and predicting violent and non-violent recidivism. It is designed to help risk managers determine their facility's violence risk level and any improvements or additions needed in their facility's violence prevention programmes. It comprises 72 items, organised into 6 subscales that measure offenders' criminogenic risk/need areas.	72	Loza and Loza-Fanous (2000)
Violence Risk Scale (VRS)*	Predicting and assessing violence risk by integrating the assessment of risk, need, responsivity and treatment change into one tool. The VRS was specifically designed to measure change in risk associated with a change resulting from treatment. It comprises 26 risk items, of which 6 are static and 20 dynamic.	26	Wong and Gordon (2006)
Violence Risk Scale: Sex Offender Version (VRS:SO)*	Predicting sexual recidivism and linking treatment changes to sexual recidivism. This scale is believed to fall into the category of dynamic-actuarial risk assessment. The dynamic items yielded 3 factors that represent sexual deviance, criminality, treatment responsivity. It comprises 26 items, of which 7 are static, 17 dynamic, and 2 responsivity factors.	26	Wong et al. (2003)

Note: 'Atypical' SPJ = Structured Professional Judgement or Structured Clinical Judgement.
*Despite the fact that a clear position does not exist in literature for how to categorise these types of instruments, whether actuarially or clinically structured, in this analysis they are considered SPJ by looking at their structure and considering the presence of both dynamic and responsivity factors, which will also require clinical evaluation.

TABLE 4.3 Risk assessment instruments: SPJ instruments for assessing the risk of general and sex violence in adults

Instrument	Type	Aims and description	No. items	Author(s)

Historical, Clinical, Risk-20 (HCR–20)	SPJ	Assessing violence. The HCR–20 is a structured clinical judgement approach to risk assessment, and was designed for use with mentally disordered adult offenders. It examines historical (H), clinical (C), risk management (RM) dimensions:
		
		H
		  H1 Previous violence.
		  H2 Young age at first violent incident.
		  H3 Relationship instability.
		  H4 Employment problems.
		  H5 Substance abuse problems.
		  H6 Major mental illness.
		  H7 Psychopathy.
		  H8 Early maladjustment.
		  H9 Personality disorder.
		  H10 Prior supervision failure.
		C
		  C1 Lack of insight.
		  C2 Negative attitudes.
		  C3 Active symptoms of major mental illness.
		  C4 Impulsivity.
		  C5 Unresponsiveness to treatment.
		RM
		  R1 Plans lack feasibility.
		  R2 Exposure to destabilizers.
			20	Webster et al. (1997); Douglas et al. (2014)

TABLE 4.3 (continued)

Instrument	Type	Aims and description	No. items	Author(s)

R3 Lack of personal support.
R4 Noncompliance with remediation attempts.
R5 Stress.

The HCR-20 has gathered empirical support across genders, with forensic and psychiatric patients, mentally disorderly offenders, and general offenders in detention (Douglas & Reeves, 2009). HCR-20^{V3} was published in 2013: the general domains of risk covered are similar to those of V2, with some items being dropped, a couple of others being added, the redundancy was reduced, and the distinction between risk management factors was enhanced. A featured of V3 is the addition of sub-items that provide evaluators with specific clues for a more comprehensive view of the items. For the historical item 'problems with violence', three sub-items were included (violence as a child, as an adolescent, as an adult). This inclusion allows not only for an assessment of violence across developmental periods, but also for a consideration of the extent to which violence becomes chronic and fosters a cumulative risk, the longer the duration of its history. The following is a synthesis of the substantive changes. Only the modified items are reported below.

Historical Scale (History of Problems with . . .)

H1. Violence: broadened to include nature and severity of violence, and its developmental trajectory.
H2. Other antisocial behavior: added to reflect nature, severity, developmental trajectory of a history of non-violent AB.
H3. Relationships: broadened to include problems in both intimate and non-intimate relationships.
H7. Personality disorder: broadened to include other personality disorders, not only psychopathy.

(Continued)

TABLE 4.3 (continued)

Instrument	Type	Aims and description	No. items	Author(s)
		H8. Traumatic experiences: broadened to include experiences in all developmental periods, and also those that can disrupt attachment; narrowed because disrupted behaviour is now included in H1/H2. H9. Violent attitudes: added to include information about attitudes that condone violence. H10. Treatment or supervision response: revised to include problems with treatment response. *Clinical Scale (Recent Problems with . . .)* C2. Violent ideation or intent: narrowed to focus on ideation, thoughts, plans and intentions concerning perpetration of violence. C5. Treatment or supervision response: broadened to include problems with response to institutional or community supervision. *Risk Management Scale (Future Problems with . . .)* R1. Professional services and plans: narrowed to focus on difficulties making plans for the evaluee. R2. Living situation: narrowed to focus on difficulties securing a living situation for the evaluee. R4. Treatment or supervision response: broadened to include problems with future treatment response. For a complete overview of the changes included in HCR-20^{V3} see tables in Douglas *et al.* (2014, 98–9).		
Offender Assessment System (OASys)	AJ/SPJ	Assessing the likelihood of reoffending and the risk of serious harm, risks to the individual and other risks. Identifying and classifying offending-related needs. Assisting with management of risk of serious harm. Linking the assessment to the sentence plan, and measuring change during the offender's sentence. OASys is the risk assessment and management system routinely used in the National Offender Management Service (NOMS), the prison and probation service for England and Wales. It is a structured clinical tool used to assess and manage over 250,000 offenders each year in England and Wales. It encompasses the OASys Violent Predictor (OVP) and combines the best actuarial methods with structured professional judgements. This allows for both a standardised evaluation of individual needs and risks, and a management of risk and planning of the intervention. The offending-related factors include 13 sections, covering 12 aspects related to criminal history and offending (first 2 items), assessment of dynamic factors (the other 10 items), and 1 extra control item:	12 + 1	Howard (2009); Howard and Dixon (2012, 2013)

TABLE 4.3 (continued)

Instrument	Type	Aims and description	No. items	Author(s)
		1. Offending information [criminal history].		
		2. [current] Offence analysis.		
		3. Accommodation.		
		4. Education, training and employability.		
		5. Financial management and income.		
		6. Relationships.		
		7. Life style and associates.		
		8. Drug misuse.		
		9. Alcohol misuse.		
		10. Emotional well-being.		
		11. Thinking and behaviour.		
		12. Attitudes.		
		13. Suitability to undertake sentence-related activities (e.g. unpaid work, offending behaviour programmes).		
		Each dynamic risk factor is assessed using between 4 and 10 questions, each scored on a 0/2 or 0/1/2 basis (see Howard & Dixon, 2012). OASys presents risk of harm as Low, Medium, High or Very High.		
Risk Matrix 2000 (RM2000)[a]	SPJ	Predicting the likelihood of reconviction for a sexual or violent offence in the long term (up to 15 years) among adult males convicted of sexual offences. It is used nationally in England and Wales by the Prison, Probation and Police Services. The RM2000 utilises a stepwise approach to risk classification. For assessing risk for sexual aggression the following factors are considered in the first subscale (RM: Sexual): Age at commencement of risk. Sexual appearances. Criminal appearances. Four aggravating factors are examined: Sexual offences against a male.	3 scales RM2000/S RM2000/V RM2000/C	Thornton et al. (2003)

(Continued)

TABLE 4.3 (continued)

Instrument	Type	Aims and description	No. items	Author(s)
		Sexual offences against a stranger. Single. Non-contact sex offence. A second subscale (RM: Violent) is designed to assess risk for violent recidivism and is comprised of three items: Age. Violent appearances. Prior convictions for burglary. The strength of the instruments is based on valid risk factors and explicit rules for combining factors. Robust across settings and samples. The combination of risk categories (both RM: Sexual and RM: Violent) is tabulated to produce an overall level of risk (on a 0–6 scale) intended for predicting sexual or other types of violence (see Kingston et al., 2008).		
Sexual Violence Risk 20 (SVR–20)	SPJ	Predicting the risk of future sexual violence of a particular sexual offender and to guide potential risk management strategies. The items fall within three domains of psychosocial adjustment, sexual offending, future plans: 1. Sexual deviation. 2. Victim of child abuse. 3. Psychopathy (PCL). 4. Major mental illness (DSM-IV). 5. Substance use problems. 6. Suicidal/homicidal ideation. 7. Relationship problems. 8. Employment problems. 9. Past non-sexual violent offences. 10. Past non-violent offences. 11. Past supervision failures.	20	Boer et al. (1997)

TABLE 4.3 (continued)

Instrument	Type	Aims and description	No. items	Author(s)
		12. High density sex offences. 13. Multiple offence types. 14. Physical harm to victim(s) in sex offences. 15. Use of weapons or threats of death in sex offences. 16. Escalation in frequency or severity of sexual offences. 17. Extreme minimization/denial of sex offences. 18. Attitudes that support or condone sex offences. 19. Lacks realistic plans. 20. Negative attitude towards intervention. *Other Considerations*: acute mental disorder, recent loss of social support network, frequent contact with potential victims or poor attitude towards intervention. SVR is useful in assisting the structuring of clinical assessments, and has the advantage of incorporating a 'recent change' score (Douglas *et al.*, 1999).		

Structured Assessment of Risk and Need (SARN)	SPJ	Assessing sexual offenders' risk, need and progress in treatment. It is like a clinical framework to assess the presence of personality characteristics, which research has shown to be significantly associated with reconviction. These can be grouped into four risk domains:
		
		Sexual Interests:
		    Sexual preoccupation.
		    Sexual preference for children.
		    Sexualised violence preference.
		    Other offence related sexual interest.
		Distorted Attitudes:
		    Adversarial sexual beliefs.
		    Child abuse supportive beliefs.
		    Sexual entitlement beliefs.
		    Rape supportive beliefs.
		    View women as deceitful.
			16	Webster *et al.* (2006)

(Continued)

TABLE 4.3 (continued)

Instrument	Type	Aims and description	No. items	Author(s)
		Management of Relationships: Feelings of personal inadequacy. Distorted intimacy balance. Grievance thinking towards others. Lack of emotional intimacy with adults. *Management of Self:* Life style impulsiveness. Poor problem-solving. Poor management of emotions.		
Short Term Assessment of Risk and Treatability (START)	SPJ	Assessing future violent and risk behaviours in the short term, identifying risk to self and others through structured professional judgements, within a mental health context. START is a structured and concise clinical tool to rate offender strengths and risks as they relate to risk assessment and management. It guides the dynamic assessment of short-term (i.e. weeks to months) risk for violence (to self and others) and treatability. START guides clinicians toward an integrated, balanced opinion to evaluate the patient's risk across seven domains: risk to others; self-harm; suicide; unauthorised leave; substance use; self-neglect; being victimized. The items assessed: Social skills. Relationships. Occupational. Recreational. Self-care. Mental state.	20	Webster et al. (2004, 2009)

TABLE 4.3 (continued)

Instrument	Type	Aims and description	No. items	Author(s)
		Emotional state.		
		Substance misuse.		
		Impulse control.		
		External triggers.		
		Material resources.		
		Attitudes.		
		Medication adherence.		
		Rule adherence.		
		Conduct.		
		Insight.		
		Plans.		
		Coping.		
		Social support.		
		Treatability.		
		START allows for a systematic assessment of the individual strengths and vulnerabilities, with the purpose of enhancing mental health.		

Note: When there is the indication of the two risk approaches (AJ/SPJ) it is because in the literature the instrument is often referred to in either category.
a The authors define this instrument *Structured Anchored Clinical Judgment* (SACJ).

TABLE 4.4 Risk assessment instruments: AJ instruments for assessing the risk of domestic violence and Intimate Partner Violence (IPV) in adults

Instrument	Type	Aims and description	No. items	Author(s)
Domestic Violence Risk Appraisal Guide (DVRAG)	AJ	Assessing the risk of IPV recidivism among male offenders with a criminal record for IPV. It was developed to combine the information gathered on scene using the ODARA with an assessment that entails clinical information to produce an instrument better able to predict IPV recidivism. The instruments items: 1. Number of prior domestic incidents (assault on a current or previous female cohabiting partner or her children, recorded in a police occurrence report or criminal record). 2. Number of prior non-domestic incidents (assault on any person other than a current or previous female cohabiting partner or her children, recorded in a police occurrence report or criminal record). 3. Prior correctional sentence of 30 days or more. 4. Failure on prior conditional release. 5. Threat to harm or kill at the index incident (threat of physical harm made towards any person other than himself). 6. Confinement at the index incident (any attempt to physically prevent the female victim from leaving the scene of the incident). 7. Victim concern (concern, fear, worry or certainty about possible future domestic assault, stated at the time of the index incident). 8. Number of children. 9. Victim's number of biological children from a previous partner. 10. Violence against others (any assault on any person other than a current or previous female cohabiting partner or her children). 11. Substance abuse score. 12. Assault on victim when pregnant (index assault or prior).	14	Guo and Harstall (2008); Hilton et al. (2008)

TABLE 4.4 (continued)

Instrument	Type	Aims and description	No. items	Author(s)
		13. Number of barriers to victim support. 14. Psychopathy Checklist-Revised Score.		
		It is recommended that the DVRAG be only used when the assessor has access to detailed clinical, psychosocial history or correctional data of the offender. One limitation of the DVRAG is that its predictive accuracy has not yet been evaluated independently.		
Domestic Violence Screening Inventory (DVSI)	AJ/SPJ	Assessing the likelihood of the occurrence of intimate partner violence recidivism. The DVSI was developed by the Colorado Judicial Department (USA), and was first employed by the Colorado Department of Probation Service. It is used in a number of capacities in the criminal justice system, including at intake, to determine levels of probation supervision, and for case supervision. It includes both static and dynamic factors. The 12 items: Prior non-DV convictions. Prior assault, harassment, menacing. Prior DV treatment. Prior drug or alcohol treatment. History of DV-related restraining orders. History of DV restraining order violation. Object used as weapon in commission of crime. Children present during DV incident. Current employment status (unemployed). Separation from victim in last 6 months. Did victim have restraining order at time of offence? Defendant under community supervision at time of offence.	12	Williams (2012); Williams and Houghton (2004); Williams and Grant (2006); Wong and Hisashima (2008)

(Continued)

TABLE 4.4 (continued)

Instrument	Type	Aims and description	No. items	Author(s)
		The DVSI also includes a psychiatric assessment, intended for forensic use. A modified version of 11 items, DVSI-Revised (DVSI-R), was implemented state wide in Family Services and Connecticut Courts in Connecticut, United States, and includes 7 items which primarily address the behavioural history of perpetrators: Non–family assaults. Arrests or criminal convictions. Family assaults, arrests or criminal convictions. Prior family violence intervention or treatment. Violation of orders of protection or court supervision. Prior or current verbal or emotional abuse. Frequency of violence in past 6 months, and escalation of violence in past 6 months. The other 4 items pertain to: Substance abuse. Objects used as weapons. Children present during prior or current violent incidents. Employment status.		
Domestic Violence Supplementary Report (DVSR)	AJ	Assisting frontline police officers to determine the number of risk factors present when responding to a domestic assault complaint. The DVRS items were chosen both for their relationship to IPV and because they can be coded based on information readily available to frontline police officers. The items: Does the victim fear that the accused will continue the assaults, seriously injure or kill her/him or the children? Has there been a recent escalation in frequency or severity of assaults/threats against the victim? Has there been a recent separation or change in the relationship between the victim and the accused?	19	Ontario Ministry of the Solicitor General (2000)

Instrument	Type	Aims and description	No. items	Author(s)
		Has there been a recent change in the contact between the children and the accused?		
		Has the accused experienced any unusually high stress recently, e.g. financial, loss of job, health problem?		
		Does the accused have any known mental health problems, or exhibit a loss of touch with reality or bizarre behaviour?		
		Has the accused ever demonstrated jealousy or obsessive behaviour towards the victim and/or previous partner?		
		Has the accused demonstrated any stalking behaviour towards (a) the victim? (b) family? or (c) any other person? (e.g. harassing phone calls, watching, threatened or has destroyed the victim's personal property, sending unwanted letters, following/contacting through third party, frequenting workplace, etc.).		
		Does the accused abuse drugs and/or alcohol?		
		Has there been a noticeable increase in the abuse of drugs and/or alcohol?		
		Is the accused more angry or violent when using drugs and/or alcohol?		
		Has the accused ever sexually abused the victim and/or a previous partner?		
		Has the accused threatened/attempted suicide?		
		Has the accused threatened to harm/kill the victim or any other family members/acquaintances?		
		Has the accused threatened to or destroyed any of the victim's personal property?		
		Has the accused injured or killed a pet owned by the victim?		
		Does the accuser's personality feature anger, impulsiveness or poor behaviour control?		
		Does the accused own/have access to firearms or weapons including a licence for the firearm?		
		Has the accused used or threatened the use of firearms or weapons against the victim/children or any other person?		
		The DVSR should be completed based on a victim interview, police investigation and the perpetrator's criminal history (see Nicholls et al., 2013).		

(Continued)

TABLE 4.4 (continued)

Instrument	Type	Aims and description	No. items	Author(s)
Ontario Domestic Assault Risk Assessment (ODARA)	AJ	The ODARA was originally developed for frontline police officers on the scene of an IPV call, but is available for use by victim services, health care workers, probation and correctional services personnel in addition to domestic violence caseworkers in some provinces. This tool assesses risk of future wife assault. Although it was not designed to predict risk of lethality, the authors have found a correlation between higher ODARA scores and more severe assaults in the future. The items: 1. Previous domestic incident. 2. Previous non-domestic incident. 3. Prior correctional sentence of at least 30 days. 4. Failure on previous conditional release. 5. Threat to harm or kill anyone at the index assault. 6. Confinement of the partner during/at the index assault. 7. Victim concerned/fearful of future assaults. 8. Two or more children. 9. Victim has a biological child from a previous partner. 10. Perpetrator's violence against others. 11. Perpetrator's substance abuse. 12. Assault on victim when pregnant. 13. Any barrier to victim support. On an IPV assault scene, this actuarial instrument can be scored and used to make decisions regarding arrest and laying charges. Rice et al. (2010) also recommend that the ODARA can be used to inform decisions and dispositions made by the court such as for bail and conditional release.	13	Hilton et al. (2004); Rice et al. (2010)

Note: AJ = Actuarial Judgement or Statistical Tool.: Actuarial assessment. ODARA is the result of collaborative efforts between the Ontario Provincial Police (OPP) and the Mental Health Centre (MHC) based in Penetanguishene, Ontario. When there is the indication of the two risk approaches (AJ/SPJ) it is because in the literature the instrument is often referred to in either category.

TABLE 4.5 Risk assessment instruments: SPJ instruments for assessing the risk of domestic violence and Intimate Partner Violence (IPV) in adults

Instrument	Type	Aims and description	No. items	Author(s)
Brief Spousal Assault Form for Evaluation of Risk (B-SAFER)	SPJ	Facilitating the work of criminal justice professionals in assessing risk in spousal violence cases, guiding the professionals to obtain relevant information necessary to assess level of risk, assisting victims in safety planning and ultimately working to prevent future harm and more critical incidents, and assisting evaluators to identify risk management strategies. This tool includes a checklist of 10 risk factors and an interview guide. The first 5 risk factors relate to a person's history of intimate partner violence: 1. Violent acts. 2. Violent threat or thoughts. 3. Escalation. 4. Violations of court orders. 5. Violent attitudes. The second section relates to a person's history of psychological (personal) and social (interpersonal) adjustment problems: 6. General criminality. 7. Intimate relationship problems. 8. Employment problems. 9. Substance use problems. 10. Mental health problems. The B-SAFER also includes a Recommended Risk Management Strategies section regarding monitoring/surveillance, control/supervision, assessment/treatment and victim safety planning in addition to a conclusory opinions section regarding case prioritization, life threatening violence, imminent violence and likely victims.	10	Kropp et al. (2005)

(Continued)

TABLE 4.5 (continued)

Instrument	Type	Aims and description	No. items	Author(s)
Danger Assessment (DA)	SPJ	Originally designed for assessing the likelihood of intimate partner homicide by emergency room nurses. Now used for predicting domestic violence recidivism in high-risk violence cases. DA was developed in the USA and is used throughout the USA and Canada. It is used in a number of settings, including for the purposes of victim education and awareness, safety planning and determining the conditions of services. DA is in two parts. The first is a calendar on which the victim specifies the severity and frequency of instances of domestic violence endured during the last 12 months. The second part is a 20-item checklist of risk factors that are related to intimate partner homicide. Both sections are completed in collaboration with the victim. The Revised 20-Item Danger Assessment: 1. Has the physical violence increased in severity or frequency over the past year? 2. Does he own a gun? 3. Have you left him after living together during the past year? 4. Is he unemployed? 5. Has he ever used a weapon against you or threatened you with a lethal weapon? 6. Does he threaten to kill you? 7. Has he avoided being arrested for domestic violence? 8. Do you have a child that is not his? 9. Has he ever forced you to have sex when you did not wish to do so? 10. Does he ever try to choke you? 11. Does he use illegal drugs? By drugs, is meant 'uppers' or amphetamines, 'meth', speed, angel dust, cocaine, 'crack', street drugs or mixtures.	20	Campbell (1986, 1995); J. C. Campbell et al. (2009); Guo and Harstall (2008); Millar (2009)

Instrument	Type	Aims and description	No. items	Author(s)
		12. Is he an alcoholic or problem drinker? 13. Does he control most or all of your daily activities? (For instance: does he tell you who you can be friends with, when you can see your family, how much money you can use, or when you can take the car?) 14. Is he violently and constantly jealous of you? (For instance, does he say 'If I can't have you, no one can'). 15. Have you ever been beaten by him while you were pregnant? 16. Has he ever threatened or tried to commit suicide? 17. Does he threaten to harm your children? 18. Do you believe he is capable of killing you? 19. Does he follow or spy on you, leave threatening notes or messages on answering machine, destroy your property, or call you when you don't want him to? 20. Have you ever threatened or tried to commit suicide?		
Spousal Assault Risk Assessment Guide (SARA)	SPJ	DA is a good tool to use with victims as it allows victims to better understand the risk that the relationship may pose to them and what risk management options are available. It may also serve as a useful instrument when information is difficult to obtain or when the offender cannot be interviewed. DA does not provide the evaluator with a means of assessing the risk level posed by the accused. Helping criminal justice professionals predicting the likelihood of domestic violence, and predicting both intimate partner violence and lethality. SARA includes the following 20 indicators categorised under the following 4 sections: *Criminal History* 1. Past assault of family members. 2. Past assault of strangers or acquaintances. 3. Past violation of conditional release or community supervision.	20	Kropp et al. (1995); Kropp (2008); Kropp and Gibas (2010); Kropp and Hart (2000); Guo and Harstall (2008)

(Continued)

TABLE 4.5 (continued)

Instrument	Type	Aims and description	No. items	Author(s)
		Psychosocial Adjustment		
		4. Recent relationship problems.		
		5. Recent employment problems.		
		6. Victim of and/or witness to family violence in youth.		
		7. Recent substance abuse/dependence.		
		8. Recent suicidal or homicidal thoughts.		
		9. Recent psychotic and/or manic symptoms.		
		10. Personality disorder.		
		Spousal Assault History		
		11. Past physical assault.		
		12. Past sexual assault/sexual jealousy.		
		13. Past use of weapons and/or credible threats of death.		
		14. Recent escalation in frequency or severity of assault.		
		15. Past violation of no-contact orders.		
		16. Extreme minimization or denial of spousal assault history.		
		17. Attitudes that condone spousal assault.		
		Alleged (Current) Offence		
		18. Severe and/or sexual assault.		
		19. Use of weapons or threat of death.		
		20. Violation of no-contact orders.		
		Information for this tool is collected from a number of sources, including the accused, the victim, standardised measures of psychological and emotional abuse, and other records such as police reports. The evaluator considers the items and determines whether the accused is at low, medium or high risk of causing imminent harm to their intimate partner or to another individual. SARA is also used for other purposes, including for determining treatment plans for offenders, intervention strategies and levels of supervision (see Belfrage *et al.*, 2011).		

TABLE 4.5 (continued)

Instrument	Type	Aims and description	No. items	Author(s)
Stalking Assessment and Management (SAM)	SPJ	Aiding systematic assessment and management of risk for stalking, even in complex cases, providing information on violence risk not covered by other tools for violence assessment, assisting an assessor's discretion in making an assessment about arrest, case management, release conditions and charge recommendations. SAM is a structured professional judgment instrument, which includes 3 domains; each of these domains contains 10 factors: *Nature of Stalking Behavior:* N1. Communicates about victim. N2. Communicates with victim. N3. Approaches victim. N4. Direct contact with victim. N5. Intimidates victim. N6. Threatens victim. N7. Violent toward victim. N8. Stalking is persistent. N9. Stalking is escalating. N10. Stalking involves supervision violations. *Perpetrator Risk Factors:* P1. Angry. P2. Obsessed. P3. Irrational. P4. Unrepentant. P5. Antisocial life style. P6. Intimate relationship problems.	30	Kropp et al. (2008a,b; Kropp et al., 2011)

(Continued)

TABLE 4.5 (continued)

Instrument	Type	Aims and description	No. items	Author(s)
		P7. Non-intimate relationship problems. P8. Distressed. P9. Substance use problems. P10. Employment and financial problems. *Victim Vulnerability Factors:* V1. Inconsistent behavior towards perpetrator. V2. Inconsistent attitude towards perpetrator. V3. Inadequate access to resources. V4. Unsafe living situation. V5. Problems caring for dependants. V6. Intimate relationship problems. V7. Non-intimate relationship problems. V8. Distressed. V9. Substance use problems. V10. Employment and financial problems. SAM is not a simple test, does not involve scores or cut-offs, and its use requires judgement. It is evaluated in routine law enforcement and forensic mental health settings, but not in highly specialised settings or populations (e.g. national security, adolescent perpetrators).		

Note: SPJ = Structured Professional Judgement or Structured Clinical Judgement.

settings to provide the courts with a more complete evaluation of the psychological functioning, psychological maturity and mental conditions of the juvenile. This can be useful in as far as the clinical evaluation is the preliminary structure from which to start a more focused assessment of the risk of reoffending and protective resources available, and on which to base a specific treatment intervention. The aim is for an integrated approach in which clinical and risk assessment information assists decision-making about criminal responsibility, social dangerousness, sentencing, alternative measures to detention into youth institutions, release or discharge, and specific community orders, or remits, for admittance to probation programmes.

The choice between AJ or SPJ is beset with reservations, and at best needs prudence. The summary of the instruments proposed in the tables follows certain criteria. When rating a risk assessment instrument, there are at least six significant issues to consider:

1. the theoretical and developmental foundations;
2. the process of construction of the instrument: its history and its established or upcoming pedigree within the scientific community;
3. the identification and inclusion of risk factors that demonstrate predictive validity;
4. the inter-rater reliability level;
5. the accuracy level in predicting the risk of reoffending and error reduction;
6. the significance/usefulness of the instrument in determining the nature, severity and/or likelihood of future risk posed by targeted offenders, and the clinical utility in enabling the specialist to undertake risk formulation and risk management planning.

Empirical grounding involves anchoring theoretical assumptions to measurable events. It implies an examination of the scientific and theoretical underpinning of the risk assessment instruments. Risk assessment instruments based on sound theoretical evidence and on scientific findings from prior research would be considered as having a high level of empirical foundation. It follows that high level of empirical grounding increases the utility of the instrument in assessing the risk posed by the individual.

Validation history is concerned with the existence and quality of validation studies that examine the predictive validity of a risk assessment instrument, and/or its practical usefulness for the assessment and management of risk of harm to others. Ideally, these papers should also describe the perceived strengths and limitations of the tool. The availability of two or more papers written by different authors, in peer-reviewed journals, should be indicated. It is important to distinguish validity in the sample on which the instrument is constructed (*construction sample*) from validity in a different sample (*validation sample*).

General predictive validity refers to the capability of the risk assessment instrument to discern the difference in the risk of reoffending between the recidivist and the

TABLE 4.6 Risk assessment instruments: AJ instruments for assessing the risk of antisocial behaviour in young people

Instrument	Type	Aims and description	No. items	Author(s)
Hare Psychopathy Youth Version (PCL: YV)[a]	AJ	Measuring interpersonal, affective and behavioural domains in juveniles aged 12 to 18. It is a modified version of PCL-R. *Interpersonal*: Impression management. Grandiose sense of self worth. Pathological lying. Manipulation for personal gain. *Affective*: Lack of remorse/guilt. Shallow affect. Callous/lack of empathy. Failure to accept responsibility. *Life style*: Stimulation seeking. Parasitic orientation. Lacks goals. Impulsivity. Irresponsibility. *Antisocial*: Poor anger control. Early behavioral problems. Serious violation of conditional release. Serious criminal behaviour. Criminal versatility. *Unclassified*: Impersonal sexual behavior. Unstable interpersonal relationships.	20	Forth et al. (2003)

TABLE 4.6 (continued)

Instrument	Type	Aims and description	No. items	Author(s)
		It guides experts in the identification of potential patterns of cheating, fighting, bullying and other antisocial acts in young people, in so far as early identification of these traits is critical for their developing adult antisocial behaviour and psychopathy. The PCL:YV emphasizes the need for multidomain and multisource information. Although it modifies the scoring criteria of certain items to focus somewhat more on peer, family and school adjustment, adolescents are presumed to manifest psychopathy in virtually the same way as adults.		
Youth Level of Service/ Case Management Inventory (YLS/ CMI)	AJ	Measuring antisocial risk in young people. It is a combined and integrated risk/needs assessment and a case management instrument, combined into one convenient system derived from the Level of Service Inventory – Revised™ (LSI–R™) for use with general populations of young offenders (ages 12–17). It produces a score and an overall risk categorisation (low-medium-high or very high), and a level of risk or need categorisation in each of the following areas (in parentheses the number of items associated): Prior and current offences/dispositions (5). Family circumstances/parenting (6). Education/employment (7). Peer relations (4). Substance abuse (5). Leisure/recreation (3). Personality/behavior (7). Attitudes/orientation (5). This tool provides clinical assessment, treatment, and case management services to diverse young offender groups.	42	Hoge and Andrews (2002)

Notes: AJ = Actuarial Judgement or Statistical Tool: Actuarial assessment. SPJ = Structured Professional Assessment or Structured Clinical Judgement.
a It is a labour-intensive and complex instrument which requires a lengthy clinical interview and review of records by well-trained clinicians.

TABLE 4.7 Risk assessment instruments: SPJ instruments for assessing the risk of antisocial behaviour in young people

Instrument	Type	Aims and description	No. items	Author(s)
Child Behavior Checklist (CBCL/6–18)	SPJ (CL)	Screening children's competencies and behavioural/emotional problems, covering the child's activities, social relations and school performance. The CBCL is a checklist that parents, other close relatives and/or guardians complete to detect emotional and behavioural problems in children and adolescents, aged 6–18. The CBCL is part of the Achenbach System of Empirically Based Assessment (ASEBA). The CBCL/6–18, revised in 2001, consists of 113 questions, scored on a 3-point Likert scale (0 = absent, 1 = occurs sometimes, 2 = occurs often). The time-frame for item responses is the past 6 months. It is made up of 11 subscales: Delinquent behavior. Aggressive behavior. Withdrawn. Somatic complaints. Anxious/depressed. Social problems. Thought problems. Attention problems. Externalizing problems (includes delinquent and aggressive behaviors). Internalizing problems (includes withdrawn, somatic complaints, and anxiety/depressed problems). Total problems (includes externalizing, internalizing, social, thought, and attention problems).	120	Achenbach (1991a); Achenbach and Rescorla (2001)

TABLE 4.7 (continued)

Instrument	Type	Aims and description	No. items	Author(s)
		The CBCL/6–18 is also scored on (optional) competence scales for activities, social relations, school and total competence. Because of its ease of administration, good psychometric properties and cross-cultural validation, it has been used widely in studies of youths with varying types of psychopathology, behavioural problems and delinquency. However, it is a not an overly positive measure because it seems not to measure strengths in the child, but just deficiencies. There are two other components of the ASEBA: the Teacher's Report Form (TRF) that is to be completed by teachers and the Youth Self-Report (YSR) by the child or adolescent.		
Youth Self-Report (YSR/11-18)	SPJ (CL)	Assessing one's own behaviour problems and socially desirable qualities. The YSR is the self-report counterpart to the CBCL. It is completed by a child or adolescent aged 11–18 to describe his or her own functioning. It scores 8 empirically based syndromes, and provides a summary of total problems along two broadband scales: internalizing (IN) and externalizing (EX): withdrawn, somatic complaints, anxious/depressed (together constituting the IN scale); delinquent behavior, aggressive behavior (together constituting the EX scale); social problems, thought problems, attention problems. The measure assesses *total competency*, which is a scale comprised of competency in activities, social functioning and school performance.	112	Achenbach, (1991b); Achenbach and Rescorla (2001)
Early Assessment Risk List (EARL-20B) (boys)	SPJ	Measuring risk of violence potential in boys under the age of 12. The items are grouped under the headings of Family (F), Child (C), and Responsivity (R) and items are scored on a 0 (not present), 1 (possibly present) or 2 (definitely present) basis. Clinicians offer an overall clinical judgement of risk as Low, Moderate or High. 19 items of the following items are shared with EARL-21:	20	Augimeri et al. (2001)

(Continued)

TABLE 4.7 (continued)

Instrument	Type	Aims and description	No. items	Author(s)
		F1. Household circumstances. F2. Caregiver continuity. F3. Supports. F4. Stressors. F5. Parenting style. F6. Antisocial values and conduct. C1. Development problems. C2. Onset of behavioural difficulties. C3. Abuse/neglect/trauma. C4. Hyperactivity/impulsivity/attention deficits (HIA). C5. Likeability. C6. Peer socialization. C7. Academic performance. C8. Neighbourhood. C9. *Authority Contact (not shared)*. C10. Antisocial attitudes. C11. Antisocial behaviour. C12. Coping ability. R1. Family responsivity. R2. Child responsivity.		
Early Assessment Risk List (EARL-21G) (girls)	SPJ	Measuring risk of violence and antisocial potential in girls under the age of 12. It takes account of gender differences, and the fact that girls often express antisociality and aggressiveness differently from boys. The items: F1. Household circumstances. F2. Caregiver continuity. F3. Supports. F4. Stressors. F5. Parenting style.	21	Augimeri *et al.* (2001)

TABLE 4.7 (continued)

Instrument	Type	Aims and description	No. items	Author(s)
		F6. Caregiver–daughter interaction. F7. Antisocial values and conduct (*extra item*). C1. Developmental problems. C2. Onset of behavioural difficulties. C3. Abuse/neglect/trauma. C4. HIA. C5. Likeability. C6. Peer socialization. C7. Academic performance. C8. Neighbourhood. C9. Sexual development. C10. Antisocial attitudes. C11. Antisocial behaviour. C12. Coping ability. R1. Family responsivity. R2. Child responsivity. The EARLS provide empirical support for identifying early risk differences in aggression and childhood delinquency between genders, and the risk impact posed by family and community influences upon development. They provide a comprehensive understanding from a risk management perspective that encourages preventative intervention.		
Estimate of Risk of Adolescent Sexual Offence Recidivism (ERASOR)	SPJ	Estimating the short-term risk of a sexual re-offence for youth aged 12–18 years. It is an empirically guided checklist designed to assist clinicians, that focuses on 25 domains itemized (16 dynamic risk factors and 9 static) as follows: *Sexual Interests, Attitudes, and Behaviors*	25	Worling (2004)

(Continued)

TABLE 4.7 (continued)

Instrument	Type	Aims and description	No. items	Author(s)
		1. Deviant sexual interests (younger children, violence, or both).		
		2. Obsessive sexual interests/preoccupation with sexual thoughts.		
		3. Attitudes supportive of sexual offending.		
		4. Unwillingness to alter deviant sexual interests/attitudes.		
		Historical Sexual Assaults		
		5. Ever sexually assaulted 2 or more victims.		
		6. Ever sexually assaulted same victim 2 or more times.		
		7. Prior adult sanctions for sexual assault(s).		
		8. Threats of, or use of, violence/weapons during sexual offence.		
		9. Ever sexually assaulted a child.		
		10. Ever sexually assaulted a stranger.		
		11. Indiscriminate choice of victims.		
		12. Ever sexually assaulted a male victim (male adolescents only).		
		13. Diverse sexual-assault behaviours.		
		Psychosocial Functioning		
		14. Antisocial interpersonal orientation.		
		15. Lack of intimate peer relationships/social isolation.		
		16. Negative peer associations and influences.		
		18. Recent escalation in anger or negative affect.		
		19. Poor self-regulation of affect and behaviour.		
		Family/Environmental Functioning		
		20. High-stress family environment.		
		21. Problematic parent–offender relationships/parental rejection.		
		22. Parent(s) not supporting sexual-offence-specific assessment/treatment.		
		23. Environment supporting opportunities to reoffend sexually.		
		Treatment		
		24. No development or practice of realistic prevention plans/strategies.		
		25. Incomplete sexual-offence-specific treatment.		

TABLE 4.7 (continued)

Instrument	Type	Aims and description	No. items	Author(s)
		The instruments aids the formulation of a clinical judgement of low, moderate or high risk.		
Juvenile Sex Offender Assessment Protocol – II (J-Soap–II)[a]	SPJ	Assessing the risk of juvenile sex offenders. J-Soap-II is designed to be used with boys aged 12 to 18 who have been adjudicated for sexual offences, as well as nonadjudicated youths with a history of sexually coercive behaviour. It is a checklist that aids assessing systematically those risk factors that are associated with sexual and criminal offending, that are comprised of four independent subscales. The factors involved in the evaluations are: *Sexual Drive/Preocupation Scale* 1. Prior legally charged sex offences. 2. Number of sexual abuse victims. 3. Male child victim. 4. Duration of sex offence history. 5. Degree of planning in sexual offence(s). 6. Sexualized aggression. 7. Sexual drive and preoccupation. 8. Sexual victimization history. *Impulsive/Antisocial Behavior Scale* 9. Caregiver consistency. 10. Pervasive anger. 11. School behavior problems. 12. History of conduct disorder. 13. Juvenile antisocial behavior. 14. Ever charged or arrested before age 16. 15. Multiple types of offences. 16. History of physical assault and/or exposure to family violence.	28	Prentky and Righthand (2003)

(Continued)

TABLE 4.7 (continued)

Instrument	Type	Aims and description	No. items	Author(s)
		Intervention Scale		
		17. Accepting responsibility for offence(s).		
		18. Internal motivation for change.		
		19. Understands risk factors.		
		20. Empathy.		
		21. Remorse and guilt.		
		22. Cognitive distortions.		
		23. Quality of peer relationships.		
		Community Stability/Adjustment Scale		
		24. Management of sexual urges and desire.		
		25. Management of anger.		
		26. Stability of current living situation.		
		27. Stability in school.		
		28. Evidence of positive support systems.		
Structured Assessment of Violence Risk in Youth (SAVRY)	SPJ	Assessing the risk for violence in adolescents (males and females), aged 12–18. It is a violence risk assessment scheme (24 historical social/contextual individual/clinical variables + 6 protective variables) that evaluates the following factors divided in 4 dimensions: *Historical Risk Factors* History of violence. History of non-violent offending. Early initiation of violence. Past supervision/intervention failures. History of self-harm or suicide attempts. Exposure to violence in the home. Childhood history of maltreatment.	30	Bartel *et al.* (1999); Borum *et al.* (2002)

TABLE 4.7 (continued)

Instrument	Type	Aims and description	No. items	Author(s)
		Parental/caregiver criminality.		
		Early caregiver disruption.		
		Poor school achievement.		
		Social/Contextual Risk Factors		
		Peer delinquency.		
		Peer rejection.		
		Stress and poor coping.		
		Poor parental management.		
		Lack of personal/social support.		
		Community disorganisation.		
		Individual/Clinical Risk Factors		
		Negative attitudes.		
		Risk-taking/impulsivity.		
		Substance use difficulties.		
		Anger management problems.		
		Callous/lacking empathy.		
		Attention deficit/hyperactivity difficulties.		
		Poor compliance.		
		Low interest/commitment to school.		
		Protective Factors		
		Prosocial involvement.		
		Strong social support.		
		Strong attachment and bonds.		
		Positive attitude towards intervention and authority.		
		Strong commitment to school.		
		Resilient personality trait.		

(Continued)

TABLE 4.7 (continued)

Instrument	Type	Aims and description	No. items	Author(s)
		SAVRY is a good predictor of recidivism, has good validity and reliability across settings and countries, pointing to its potential international viability as a risk assessment tool. It helps to categorise those young people who are likely to require more intensive monitoring and targeted interventions. It is not designed to identify potential mental health problems in need of an assessment, does not cover needs that are unrelated to future offending (special education, depression, etc.), and is not appropriate for identifying risk for sexual offending.		

Note: CL = Checklist. It is very difficult to consider the CBCL and YSR a SPJ *tout court*, in so far as scientists consider them respectively a guided checklist to assist parents and guardian's to screen their children's functioning and social competence, and a self-report scale that youths could use to assess their functioning.
a The authors considered J-Soap–II not an actuarial scale. It is an empirically informed guide for systematic review and assessment of a uniform set of items that may increase risk of reoffending.

TABLE 4.8 Structured Personality Scale and Structured Personality Inventory for assessing personality in problematic young people

Instrument	Type	Aims and description	No. items	Author(s)
Adolescent Psychopathology Scale (APS)	SPS	Assessing psychological problems and behaviours that are likely to interfere with an adolescent's psychological adaptation and personal competence, including substance abuse, suicidal behaviour, emotional liability, excessive anger, aggression, alienation, introversion. APS is a multidimensional self-report instrument for juveniles aged 12–19, and measures 3 broad disorder-problem domains: *Clinical Disorders* (20 scales). *Personality Disorders* (5 scales). *Psychosocial Problem Content Areas* (11 scales). The *Response Style Indicator Scales* (4 scales) include indexes of response consistency and infrequency, response veracity and unusual endorsement propensities. The APS is ideal for use when time and circumstance necessitate a brief measure of psychopathology. It addresses issues regarding school safety by assessing excessive anger and propensity for violence towards others. The short form consists of 115-item APS-SF: 12 *Clinical Scales*, 6 of which are associated with the following disorders: conduct disorder, oppositional defiant disorder, major depression, generalized anxiety disorder, post-traumatic stress disorder and substance abuse disorder. 2 *Validity Scales*. The APS-SF is a multidimensional measure of psychopathology and personality.	346	Reynolds (1998, 2000)

Jesness Inventory– Revised (JI-R)	SPI	Assessing personality and behaviour in children and adolescents, aged 8 and above, with severe behavioural problems, and with whom violence potential is a concern. The JI–R is a comprehensive, self-report measure of personality and psychopathology.
		It consists of:
		11 *Personality Scales*:
		  Social maladjustment.
		  Value orientation.
			160	Jesness (1998, 2003)

(Continued)

TABLE 4.8 (continued)

Instrument	Type	Aims and description	No. items	Author(s)
		Immaturity.		
		Autism.		
		Alienation.		
		Asocial index.		
		Manifest aggression.		
		Withdrawal–depression.		
		Social anxiety.		
		Repression.		
		Denial.		
		9 *Personality Subtypes*:		
		Undersocialized, active/undersocialized, aggressive.		
		Undersocialized, passive/unsocialized, passive.		
		Conformist/immature conformist.		
		Group-oriented/cultural conformist.		
		Pragmatist/manipulator.		
		Autonomy-oriented/neurotic, acting-out.		
		Introspective/neurotic, anxious.		
		Inhibited/situational emotional reaction.		
		Adaptive/cultural identifier.		
		DSM-IV Subscales:		
		Conduct disorder.		
		Oppositional defiant disorder.		

TABLE 4.8 (continued)

Instrument	Type	Aims and description	No. items	Author(s)

Millon Adolescent Clinical Inventory (MACI™)	SPI	Evaluating troubled adolescents, and developing diagnosis and treatment plans and as an outcome measure. The MACI™ is a self-report, paper-and-pencil inventory consisting of 160 *true–false* items (organised in 31 scales, divided into 4 sections) designed specifically for adolescents, aged 13–19, in clinical residential and correctional settings. It usually takes 20 to 30 minutes to complete. The MACI™ is distinguished from other clinical instruments primarily by its brevity, its theoretical anchoring, multiaxial format, tripartite construction and validation schema, use of base rate scores, and interpretive depth. It contains:
		3 *Modifying Indexes*, which assess particular response styles:
		    Disclosure.
		    Desirability.
		    Debasement.
		1 *Reliability Scale*.
		12 *Personality Patterns Scales*, intending to parallel the criteria for personality disorders in the DSM-IV:
		    Introversive.
		    Inhibited.
		    Doleful.
		    Submissive.
		    Dramatizing.
		    Egotistic.
		    Unruly.
		    Forceful.
		    Conforming.
		    Oppositional.
		    Self-demeaning.
		    Borderline.
			160	Millon (1993)

(Continued)

TABLE 4.8 (continued)

Instrument	Type	Aims and description	No. items	Author(s)

		8 *Expressed Concerns Scales*, representing potential areas of concern for emotionally disturbed adolescents:
		    Identity diffusion.
		    Self-devaluation.
		    Body disapproval.
		    Sexual discomfort.
		    Peer insecurity.
		    Social insensitivity.
		    Family discord.
		    Childhood abuse.
		7 *Clinical Syndromes Scale*, assessing disorders frequently seen in adolescent populations, corresponding to *DSM–IV* Axis 1 clinical symptoms:
		    Eating dysfunction.
		    Substance abuse.
		    Delinquent.
		    Impulsive.
		    Anxious.
		    Depressive.
		    Suicidal tendency.		

Minnesota Multiphasic Personality Inventory–Adolescent (MMPI-A™)	SPI	Screening personality and psychosocial disorders in adolescents aged 14–18, and evaluating the thoughts, emotions, attitudes and behavioural traits that comprise personality in adolescents. The results of the test reflect an adolescent's personality strengths and weaknesses, and may identify certain disturbances of personality (psychopathologies) or mental deficits caused by neurological problems. The MMPI-A has 478 true/false statements (organised in a set of scales and subscales), takes 45 minutes to an hour to complete, and consists of:	478	Butcher *et al.* (1992)

Instrument	Type	Aims and description	No. items	Author(s)
		8 *Validity Scales*, used to determine whether the test results are actually valid (i.e. if the test taker was truthful, answered cooperatively and not randomly), and to assess the test taker's response style (i.e. cooperative, defensive): Variable response inconsistency. True response inconsistency. Infrequency 1. Infrequency 2. Infrequency. Lie. Correction. ? Cannot Say. 10 *Clinical Scales*, designed to assess potential problems that are associated with adolescence, such as eating disorders, social problems, family conflicts, and alcohol or chemical dependency: Hypochondriasis. Depression. Hysteria. Psychopathic deviate. Masculinity/femininity. Paranoia. Psychasthenia. Schizophrenia. Hypomania. Social introversion. 28 *Harris Lingoes Clinical Subscales*: Subjective depression. Psychomotor retardation. Physical malfunctioning.		

(Continued)

TABLE 4.8 (continued)

Instrument	Type	Aims and description	No. items	Author(s)
		Mental dullness.		
		Brooding.		
		Denial of social anxiety.		
		Need for affection.		
		Lassitude-malaise.		
		Somatic complaints.		
		Inhibition of aggression.		
		Familial discord.		
		Authority problems.		
		Social imperturbability.		
		Social alienation.		
		Self-alienation.		
		Persecutory ideas.		
		Poignancy.		
		Naïveté.		
		Social alienation.		
		Emotional alienation.		
		Lack of ego mastery–cognitive.		
		Lack of ego mastery–conative.		
		Lack of ego mastery–defective inhibition.		
		Bizarre sensory experiences.		
		Anorality.		
		Psychomotor acceleration.		
		Imperturbability.		
		Ego inflation.		
		15 *Content Scales*:		
		Anxiety.		
		Obsessiveness.		
		Depression.		

TABLE 4.8 (continued)

Instrument	Type	Aims and description	No. items	Author(s)
		Health concerns.		
		Alienation.		
		Bizarre mentation.		
		Anger.		
		Cynicism.		
		Conduct problems.		
		Low self-esteem.		
		Low aspirations.		
		Social discomfort.		
		Family problems.		
		School problems.		
		Negative treatment indicators.		
		Content Component Scales:	31	
		Dysphoria.		
		Self-depreciation.		
		Lack of drive.		
		Suicidal ideation.		
		Gastrointestinal symptoms.		
		Neurological symptoms.		
		General health concerns.		
		Misunderstood.		
		Social isolation.		
		Interpersonal scepticism.		
		Psychotic symptomatology.		
		Paranoid ideation.		

(Continued)

TABLE 4.8 (continued)

Instrument	Type	Aims and description	No. items	Author(s)
		Explosive behavior.		
		Irritability.		
		Misanthropic beliefs.		
		Interpersonal suspiciousness.		
		Acting-out behaviors.		
		Antisocial attitudes.		
		Negative peer group influence.		
		Self-doubt.		
		Interpersonal submissiveness.		
		Low achievement orientation.		
		Lack of initiative.		
		Introversion.		
		Shyness.		
		Family discord.		
		Familial alienation.		
		School conduct problems.		
		Negative attitudes.		
		Low motivation.		
		Inability to disclose.		
		5 *(PSY-5) Personality Psychopathology Scales:*		
		Aggressiveness.		
		Psychoticism.		
		Disconstraint.		
		Negative emotionality/neuroticism.		
		Introversion/low positive emotionality.		
		3 *Social Introversion Subscales:*		
		Shyness/self-consciousness.		

TABLE 4.8 (continued)

Instrument	Type	Aims and description	No. items	Author(s)
		Social avoidance. Alienation – self and others. *6 Supplementary Scales:* MacAndrew-alcoholism revised. Alcohol/drug problem acknowledgement. Alcohol/drug problem proneness. Immaturity. Anxiety. Repression. There is also a short form of the test that is comprised of the first 350 items from the long-form of the MMPI-A. Some studies have employed the original MMPI to investigate the characteristics of juvenile delinquents (Hathaway & Monachesi, 1963); more recently internal psychometric properties of the MMPI-A and external correlates of scores on its scales were established in forensic evaluations (Handel et al., 2011). Within the juvenile justice system the request for psychological assessments is increasing (Glaser et al., 2002; Grisso, 1998; Mulvey & Iselin, 2008) to assist the court in making decisions related to dispositional decisions prior to adjudication or appropriate sentencing, and/or adequate treatment to reduce the risk of antisocial relapsing.		
Personality Inventory for Youth (PIY)	SPI	Assessing emotional and behavioural adjustment, family interaction, neurocognitive and attention-related academic functioning. PIY is a valid and reliable self-report measure, appropriate for children and adolescents aged 9–19 years. It is composed of 270 items covering (organised in 9 scales and 24 subscales):	270	Lachar and Gruber (1995)

(Continued)

TABLE 4.8 (continued)

Instrument	Type	Aims and description	No. items	Author(s)
		9 *non-overlapping Clinical Scales*: Cognitive impairment. Impulsivity/distractibility. Delinquency. Family dysfunction. Reality distortion. Somatic concern. Psychological discomfort. Social withdrawal. Social skill deficits. 24 *non-overlapping Subscales*, which reveal specific clinical content, making it a valid diagnostic tool. 4 *Validity Scales*, which help determine whether the respondent is uncooperative or is exaggerating, malingering, responding defensively, carelessly, or without adequate comprehension: Validity. Inconsistency. Dissimulation. Defensiveness. *Critical Items* are sorted into 8 problem-categories.		

Note: SPS = Structured Personality Scale. SPI = Structured Personality Inventory.

non-recidivist populations. Validity is, therefore, the meaningfulness of the instrument: it is not a property of a test, but of the use of the test; it is a measure of the appropriateness and usefulness of the test (Anastasi, 1982). It involves sensitivity, discriminatory capacity and applicability. *Sensitivity* refers to how well the instrument enables the assessor to attribute the right level of risk to the right group of offenders, which should lead to a higher true positive rate and a lower false positive rate. *Discriminatory capacity* refers to what extent the ability of the assessor to differentiate between offenders and the risk level they pose is enhanced by using the instrument. *Applicability* refers to the validity of the risk assessment instrument for different populations. 'The closer the *fit* between a given individual and the population and situation of those in the validation research, the more confidence can be expressed in the applicability of the results' (Heilbrun, 1992, 226).

Given that many risk assessment instruments were developed and validated on samples of predominantly male offenders, the applicability of these instruments to different populations, i.e. female offenders, ethnic minority offenders, mentally disordered offenders, learning disability offenders, young offenders, cannot be assumed.

Inter-rater reliability is the degree to which two or more independent raters/assessors are consistent in their ratings/evaluations of the risk posed by an individual when using the same instrument. It is desirable for a risk assessment tool to have high inter-rater reliability whereby assessors score the items similarly when using the same instruments. Researchers should be able to demonstrate inter-rater consistency of the instrument in judgements about individual risk factors and overall risk classifications. Inter-rater reliability is easier to achieve on instruments that measure static risk.

Test-retest reliability refers to the consistency of an instrument; it is the degree to which an instrument is consistent with its results over time. Establishing that the risk assessment instruments are reliable is essential, since without reliability the risk assessment performance cannot be replicated and validation cannot be attained. Actuarial instruments that base the risk assessment on solely static risk factors may report a higher reliability level. A risk assessment instrument which evaluates dynamic risk cannot calculate reliability exactly, but it can be estimated in a number of different ways. Reliability is necessary, but it is not sufficient. For a test to be reliable, it also needs to be valid.

Validity refers to whether or not an instrument really measures what it is purported to measure. Reliability is a measure of precision. Validity is a measure of accuracy. In some cases, a test might be reliable, but not valid. For example, if a clock is behind by 15 minutes, it shows the time with a reliable and constant (*im*)-preciseness every day, but it is not valid because it has taken away (removed) 15 minutes from the correct time.

Criterion-related validity is concerned with the relationship between individuals' performance on two measures tapping the same construct. It typically is estimated by correlating scores on a new measure with scores from an acknowledged criterion measure (Salkind, 2010). There are two forms of criterion-related validity: concurrent validity and predictive validity. *Concurrent validity* of risk assessment instruments is a measure of agreement between the results obtained by the given risk assessment instrument under investigation, and the results attained for the same population by using another accredited risk assessment instrument (the *gold standard*). Concurrent validity is also quantified by the correlation coefficient between the two sets of measurements gathered for the same target population: the measurement performed by the evaluating instrument and the measurement by the standard instrument. *Predictive validity* of risk assessment instruments is a measure of agreement between results attained by the evaluated instrument and those obtained from more direct measurements. Predictive validity answers the question whether a specific risk assessment measures what it is intended to measure, and whether the results obtained could be used to predict recidivism in offenders. It addresses how well a specific tool *predicts* future behaviour and is quantified by the correlation coefficient between the two sets of measurements obtained for the same target population.

Research findings show that the process of risk assessment is less than perfect in terms of *sensitivity*[3] (i.e. correct identification of true and false positives) and *specificity*[4] (i.e. correct identification of true and false negatives). Errors in *sensitivity*[5] lead to overestimating the likelihood of an offender relapsing into violence and reoffending. Errors in *specificity*[6] contribute to underestimating future harm to potential victims and to society. Evidence of valid and specific instruments used to aid professional assessment and judgements contributes considerably to the reduction of systematic errors.

Table 4.9 shows a 2 × 2 table to indicate the subdivision of true positives and false positives that emerges in any prediction task, and to what extent a risk assessment instrument is *sensitive* and *specific*.

Sensitivity is the proportion of offenders *with* high level of risk, who recidivate; in probability notation: TP/(TP + FN). *Specificity* is the proportion of offenders *without* high level of risk and who do not recidivate; in probability notation: TN/(TN + FP). Sensitivity and specificity describe how well the risk assessment instrument discriminates between offenders who are likely to recidivate and who are not.

Predictive value of a positive risk assessment is the proportion of offenders with *high risk* who recidivate. *Predictive value of a negative risk assessment* is the proportion of offenders with *low risk* who do not recidivate.

TABLE 4.9 2 × 2 prediction table

Recidivism predicted	Actual		
	High risk	Low risk	
Y	TP	FP	Total positive
N	FN	TN	Total negative
	Total recidivists	Total non-recidivists	Grand total

Note: TP = true positives, FP = false positives, FN = false negative, TN = true negatives.

The *significance and usefulness* of risk instruments in determining the risk posed by targeted offenders, and their *clinical utility* in managing the risk, depend on a close scrutiny both of the way the identification of the risk factors has been completed, of its adherence to accepted legal and scientific standards, of their respect for ethical and procedural matters, and of the way the treatment has been guided. Follow-up findings indicate how a specific instrument conceivably aids the containment of the risk of future violence and criminality.

Identification of risk factors refers to the sensitivity of the instrument in recognising risk factors and criminogenic needs significantly related to criminal behaviour and its persistence. This is achieved by gathering empirical evidence in follow-up studies and treatment programmes that target these factors. Evidence of judgement concordance about risk formulation and risk management planning between evaluators adds to the quality of the identification risk level, especially in the risk of serious harm.

Predictive power of the instrument refers to the accuracy in predicting risk of reoffending, with the positive predictive value (PPV) which is the proportion of participants classified as at risk who reoffend, and the negative predictive value (NPV) which is the proportion of those classified as not at risk who do not reoffend (see Table 4.9). Where data are available, it is useful to consider the area under the curve (AUC) measure (i.e. the ROC method). The area under the ROC curve (AUC) (Zweig & Campbell, 1993) is recognised as the best measure of predictive efficiency in an $N \times 2$ table because AUCs are less dependent on the base rate of the outcome variable in the sample and are unaffected by changes in sample size (see Farrington *et al.*, 2008). It is however important to bear in mind that AUCs are influenced by the variability in the risk scores (see Humphreys & Swets, 1991; Zara & Farrington, 2013). The maximum value for the AUC is 1.0, indicating that there is a perfect separation of the values of the two groups under investigation (i.e. 100 per cent *sensitivity* and 100 per cent *specificity*). An AUC value of 0.5 indicates no discriminative value (i.e. 50 per cent sensitivity and 50 per cent *specificity*) and it is represented by a straight, diagonal line extending from the lower left corner to the upper right. An AUC value of 0.75 (i.e. 75 per cent chance of being correct) and above, indicates high predictive accuracy, demonstrating discriminatory power and, therefore potential utility as a 'diagnostic test' in determining those offenders who are likely to recidivate.

The ROC curve plots the probability of a true positive ('hit') (e.g. the fraction of recidive offenders identified at each cut-off point) against the probability of a false positive ('false alarm') (e.g. the fraction of non-recidive offenders identified at each cut-off point). Where such measures are not available, the assessment of an instrument's predictive accuracy is based on narrative evidence in the literature and discussions with authors, other academics, and practitioners who use the instruments in real-life situations.

When assessing risk, more research and policy attention is paid to *true and false positives* than to *false negatives*; more on what people *do* rather than on why people *don't* (Zara & Farrington, 2013). This assumption leaves room for two statistical performance indicators which are considered in the practice of violence and criminal recidivism risk assessment: NND and NSD.[7] Despite their limitations, these indicators contribute to measuring different facets of predictive validity.

The *number needed to be detained* (NND) is a measure of the effectiveness of assessment (Fleminger, 1997) and, in some ways, also of intervention and treatment, because this indicator (like NSD) is based on the *number needed to treat* (NNT) statistics, which is a measure of treatment effect in the medical literature (Cook & Sackett, 1995). It is the number of people who would have to be detained in order to prevent one person from being convicted (Buchanan & Leese, 2006). It is the inverse of positive predictive value and can only be calculated when the prevalence of the behaviour to be prevented is known. The *number safely discharged* (NSD) is a measure of the number of individuals assessed to be at low risk and who could be discharged prior to a single new violent incident occurring (Fazel et al., 2012).

> These prospectively-oriented statistics are useful in that they simulate clinical decision making by providing estimates of the number of individuals who may be either unnecessarily detained or discharged prior to necessary risk reduction when relying on the results of a risk assessment tool.
>
> (Singh, 2013, 12)

These estimates have their own limitations. There are no specific standardised guidelines for their interpretation and for when to use these indicators. Both indicators are base-rate dependent and vary depending on the population, time at risk and outcome of interest (DeClue & Campbell, 2013). Moreover, they constitute a moral choice rather than a statistical matter. DeClue and Campbell (2013) report on their prediction analysis based on the Static-99R assessment of sexual violent recidivism (Helmus et al., 2012). With such an instrument, it would be predicted that an offender with a score of 7 or more would sexually reoffend. If a decision were made based on the fact that 22 per cent of them actually sexually reoffended, the number of people scoring 7 or higher that would have to be detained in order to prevent one sexual re-offence is five (NND). On the other hand, an offender with a score below 7 would be unlikely to reoffend. If a decision were made based on the fact that 94 per cent of them did not reoffend, then 18 people (NSD) could be released prior to one act of sexual recidivism occurring within five years. In such a situation, the moral pulls which decision-makers could find themselves *in-between*, using Singh's (2013) description, can be divided into those that prefer to err in favour of safety and those who err in favour of liberty. Some may consider the unnecessary detention of five people to prevent the occurrence of a sixth violent behaviour the preferable measure to ensure public safety, and consider it a sacrifice to make. This so-called *precautionary principle* (Kemshall, 1998) is the attempt by professionals to avoid failures in assessing the risk of violence: the consequences of missing a true positive (e.g. when a high-risk offender is not identified) are direr than when making false positive decisions (e.g. when a low-risk offender is wrongly identified as high-risk).

Others may feel that the civil rights of those five unnecessarily detained individuals should instead be always safeguarded first.

It is desirable to assess the social costs and benefits of the four possible outcomes: TP, FP, TN, FN. Then it could be specified where the cut-off should be to maximise expected utility.

The risk assessment instruments introduced and briefly described in the tables are those which have been widely used in clinical and criminal justice settings; their predictive accuracy is well established for the majority, while for others it varies depending on how, with whom, in which context, and with which purposes they were used (Hanson & Morton-Bourgon, 2007). The vast majority of them are included in RATED; some are awaiting validation.

Public concerns about the increase of violence in society (Brundtland, 2002), about the escalation of criminal careers among persistent and chronic offenders (Cale & Lussier, 2012; Camp et al., 2013; Loeber & Farrington, 1998a, b), and about the assessment of risk in violent mentally ill patients (Peterson et al., 2014; Singh et al., 2014) have encouraged the use of scientific-based risk assessment instruments among psychiatrists and psychologists. The criminal justice system in the USA, the UK and in many Northern European countries has started to demand more and more expert reports to assist the court in assessing criminal responsibility, sentencing judgements, indeterminate sentencing, social dangerousness evaluations, release, parole, revocation decisions and treatment planning approvals (Harcourt, 2007; Harrison, 2010; Simon, 2010; Zara & Freilone, 2014). These reports, more and more, are required to be evidence-based and in line with scientific standards in structure and content.

As an example, in 1993, in *Daubert v. Merrell Dow Pharmaceuticals, Inc.*, the US Supreme Court ruled that judges must act as 'gatekeepers' in the courtroom, determining if the scientific evidence introduced is relevant and reliable. The *Daubert* decision has had a tremendous impact on how science is used (and misused) in courts, opening an important debate that has also affected psychological and psychiatric expertise. This implies that much attention should be given to the methodology, the validity and specificity of the instruments used for a particular context of application. Though a discussion on what makes evidence scientific is not the focus of this work, and to what extent this has promoted change in the practice of assessing risk in criminological psychology and in forensic psychiatry, nevertheless it can offer some food for thought.

Research in this field has developed rapidly in the last 20 years; what is more important is that risk assessment is no longer only an academic topic (if this were ever the case), but it is more than ever seen as a scientific method that gets life from its practice. It has become a core component of the work of professionals, and accuracy in the procedure and methodology, scientific validity of the instruments, and ethical standards are just a few of the criteria to meet when submitting evidence to the criminal justice system or to the mental health authority.

The debate over the appropriateness in conducting risk assessment of violence and criminal recidivism using AJ and SPJ instruments has involved researchers for many years. The advantage of AJ instruments resides in their accuracy of prediction. The advantage of SPJ instruments is based on their utility to guide change and sustain treatment.

The limitations associated with clinical and unstructured judgements are their reliance on informal, impressionistic, intuitive, subjective conclusions (Grove & Meehl, 1996). This type of judgement involves an informal and unsystematic way of looking at risk factors that is not based on empirical work, but on the belief that they increase the risk of criminal recidivism. Distrust in unstructured clinical judgments has a long history, the essence of which can be found in Monahan's words 'psychiatrists and psychologists are accurate in no more than one out of 3 predictions of violent behavior over a several year period among institutionalized populations that had both committed violence in the past (and thus had high base rates for it) and who were diagnosed as mentally ill' (1981, 47–9).

The limitations associated with actuarial judgements are their inability to predict rare occurrences or first-time offences or risk in young people, when and for whom there is less historical information available, to show statistical accuracy for individual assessments, to address violence from mental health disorders or to ascertain prevention (Bullock, 2011; Sjöstedt & Grann, 2002). Furthermore, actuarial risk assessment measures are insensitive to change, and do not establish whether the individual being specifically assessed falls into the recidivist or non-recidivist group.

For some, combining actuarial science with clinical judgement obscures transparency, accountability and consistency that is necessary for guaranteeing the reliability and validity of risk assessment. Furthermore, this combination may lessen the standards of relevancy and admissibility in court (Abbott, 2011). For others, combining actuarial and clinical judgements provides guidelines for assessing risk in a systematic, evidence-based and structured manner, especially when judgements involve sexually violent and dangerous people (Sreenivasan et al., 2010). SPJ practice is also seen as flexible and sensitive to individual differences (Hanson & Morton-Bourgon, 2009; Hart et al., 2007).

However, more work is necessary to improve the clinical practice of risk assessment procedures and decision-making both in forensic and mental health settings (Borum, 1996; Borum et al., 1993; Gottfredson & Moriarty, 2006). Despite the fourth-generation development of risk assessment achieving an extensive recognition, research should continue to offer evidence of the incremental improvement in the accuracy of criminal recidivism prediction, when clinical, specialised training, and professional experience are combined with algorithmic procedures and actuarial science (Hanson, 2009).

The improvement that researchers aspire to is to be able to develop risk assessment instruments that integrate the strengths of both clinical and actuarial approaches and promote an assessment practice that includes the evaluation of risk, its management, intervention and prevention.

- It is the method of selection rather than the risk factors included that distinguishes clinical from statistical predictions: the unspecified combination-rule

and clinical intuition for the former; the specified combination-rule based on empirically derived item-weights for the latter (Hilton et al., 2006).
- The comparison between actuarial and clinically based instruments has not always reported consistent findings and concordant conclusions. This may also depend on the heterogeneity of the studies reviewed, the different purposes of the risk assessments, the different settings where the assessment takes place and the instruments used to aid risk assessments.
- Some meta-analyses found that actuarial instruments are superior in their predictive accuracy to structured clinical instruments (Hanson & Morton-Bourgon, 2007); however, in some meta-analyses, the clinical judgements were not differentiated into unstructured and structured professional judgements (Ægisdóttir et al., 2006; see Singh & Fazel, 2010, for a meta-review). Others found that the superiority attributed to actuarial judgement over SPJ instruments is uncertain and that there is empirical support for the validity of the SPJ instruments in assessing the risk of violence to others (Guy, 2008).
- Many risk factors and processes that are central in optimising the evaluation of the risk of violence and criminal recidivism are clinical constructs (e.g. psychopathy, antisocial personality disorders, impulsivity, conduct disorder, early childhood aggression) and they are included in numerous risk instruments. While clinical skills are required to measure and accurately appraise violence and recidivism, the place for the clinical judgement is *within* (Hilton et al., 2006) or *integrated with* (Zara, 2013a), rather than *outside* or *parallel to* actuarial instruments.
- Farrington et al. (2008) found that SPJ instruments were promising for identifying accurately high risk of violence and recidivism, and for addressing those evidence-based risk factors, detected as significant, through intervention and treatment.
- Fazel et al. (2012), in their meta-analysis on the use of risk assessment to predict violence and antisocial behaviour in 73 samples involving 24,827 individuals, from 13 countries, found that risk assessment instruments designed to assess violence and antisocial behaviour perform well when used to aid treatment and management decisions, while their predictive accuracy in identifying offenders at high risk of violence or criminal recidivism seems to diminish when used as exclusive determinants for sentencing and court decisions.

Some conclusions can be reached from this analysis.

- The accuracy of actuarial and structured professional judgements in predicting violence consistently exceed chance, so that research should aid risk assessment practice with accurate and precise information, and validated instruments.
- There is impressive development of instruments to assess the risk of violence and criminal recidivism.
- There is also a counter-response in criticizing the promotion of a *culture of risk*.

- Risk assessment is something more than a simplistic measure of risk. Risk management is more than detaining people. Both require the ability to:

  1. identify dynamic risk;
  2. address change;
  3. plan treatment;
  4. anticipate dangerous situations;
  5. prevent the circumstances from recurring (Buchanan, 2008).

- Whereas human behaviour at an individual level may be very difficult to predict, the assessment of risk is an assimilated practice that professionals cannot avoid. Hence, it has to be addressed skilfully; the methodology has to be sound and scientifically oriented; the instruments used have to be evidence-based.
- The identification of risk alone is a static procedure, especially when it does not lead to prevention. Clients' risk should be translated into plans for treatment and care.
- Risk instruments that are largely based on assessments done for research purposes do not necessarily perform as well in clinical or in forensic settings.
- Risk instruments should not be used on their own and with the simplistic aim of assessing the individual risk. They should be part of a more comprehensive evaluation of the person and of their psychological functioning, and their social adjustment, so that the passage from classifying individuals at the group level into the individual level becomes more precise for aiding treatment and management. The accuracy of a diagnostic instrument depends on how well it can identify a present state or a current condition (Fazel et al., 2012). The PCL-R was designed to assess psychopathy and as part of a comprehensive clinical evaluation of personality; it was not designed to assess the risk for someone to become psychopathic or to reoffend. Subsequently research findings show that, although it was not originally developed as a risk assessment instrument, psychopathy, as measured by the PCL-R, is a strong predictor of violence and criminal recidivism and it was integrated into the VRAG assessment criteria (see Table 4.1). When used along with other risk assessment instruments in the assessment of risk, it increases the level of accuracy of the assessment (Coid et al., 2010). However, when compared with other risk assessment instruments the PCL-R produced the lowest rates of predictive validity for future offending (Singh et al., 2011a,b).
- Risk assessment instruments that have been widely tested within the criminal justice systems or in correctional settings to predict the risk of violence and criminal recidivism should be extensively tested for the purpose of risk management in clinical practice. The completion of a risk assessment by clinicians rather than researchers or forensic professionals may affect not only the quality (Vojt et al., 2013) but also the results of the completed assessments (Zara, 2013a). The same postulation also applies to those instruments designed and developed for clinical purposes; they should also be tested in other settings

too, especially when the aim is not therapeutic but to assess the risk, as in the case of forensic expert reports.

An example of a broadly tested instrument is the HCR-20. Research studies using both retrospective and prospective data have established that the HCR-20 is predictive of future violence, including violent and non-violent recidivism (de Vogel et al., 2004). The HCR-20 is also used in clinical practice, for decisions to transfer patients from high to lower levels of security in the UK (Dolan & Blattner, 2010), in decisions to discharge male forensic psychiatric patients from medium secure units in the UK (Gray et al., 2008), and in guiding treatment and managing violence risk in a forensic psychiatric setting (Pedersen et al., 2012). Vojt and colleagues (2013) consider it important that the validity of the HCR-20 continues to be tested in different settings, and with the HCR-20V3 (2013) the opportunity to use it to inform risk management, and not merely for making predictions, has become more feasible.

- Risk assessment instruments are valid also to the extent that they can accurately identify the risk differently depending on the populations to be assessed (e.g. males vs. females; adults vs. children; ethnic characteristics; etc.). The closer the demographic characteristics of the tested sample are to those of the original one used for constructing the instrument, the higher the predictive validity (Singh et al., 2011a).

The main aim is to assess the risk of reoffending, violence and sex abuse with method, systematicity and reduced error, so as to intervene quickly enough to prevent offenders becoming persistent offenders, and especially to stop persistent offenders from wasting away their potential to change, and ending up leading marginalised, unsuccessful, and painful lives similar to those described by the chronic offenders in Chapter 3. This can only be achieved by rendering the practice of risk assessment better and more effective. A way of making this improvement is if it is guided by science and by professionals who are inspired by research findings and evidence. But this is only part of a bigger picture that also involves the evaluation of the effect of risk management on risk reduction and protection enhancement, and of the impact of personality disorders that contribute significantly to social maladjustment.

The next chapter addresses psychopathy as a multifaceted construct that significantly contributes to increase the likelihood of antisociality and violence.

Notes

1 A *Black Swan* is an event with three features: (1) it is an outlier, which conveys rarity; (2) it carries an extreme impact; (3) it encourages retrospective predictability. The 'highly expected *not happening* is also a Black Swan. Note that, by symmetry, the occurrence of a highly improbable event is the equivalent of the nonoccurrence of a highly probable one' (Taleb, 2007, p. xviii; *emphasis* as in the original).

2 RATED – Risk Assessment Tools Evaluation Directory (Aug. 2013) is an online tool directory that facilitates periodic reviews and updates. It aims to provide a summary of the empirical evidence to offer a balanced approach to assessment and to contribute to effective and ethical practice. RATED also provides relevant research information on each assessment tool included in the directory, which comprises (but is not limited to) validation evidence. It is also possible to have access to a *Risk Tools tab*, to find those risk instruments that have been evaluated and those awaiting validation for all the categories of interests (e.g. general recidivism, violence, sexual violence, domestic violence, youth assessment, female offenders, internet, stalking, learning disabilities, diagnostic personality assessment). Currently (May 2014) there are more than 61 tools evaluated, and others awaiting validation. There is also a tab which permits the submission of a new instrument for evaluating whether it meets the standards for the inclusion in RATED. There is also a section, related to the authors of risk assessment instruments, inviting them to provide up-to-date information of studies, developments, and any corrections or additions of their tools. RATED is available at: http://rated.rmascotland.gov.uk.

3 Also called *True Positive Rate* (TPR) = TP ÷ (TP + FN).

4 It is calculated as: TN ÷ (TN + FP).

5 Type I error is also known as a 'false positive'.

6 Type II error is also known as a 'false negative'.

7 NND = 1 ÷ PPV. NSD = [1 ÷ (1 − NPV)] − 1. PPV = TP ÷ (TP + FP).

5
PSYCHOPATHY

Introduction

Psychopathy is perhaps, as Neumann and colleagues (2007) put it, the earliest and the most documented and studied personality disorder. Being a multifaceted construct (Farrington, 2006), it is marked by a pattern of maladaptive personality traits that include explanatory components such as high emotionality, impulsiveness, low empathy and callousness, as well as behavioural aspects, such as antisociality and an irregular life style.

The aim of this chapter is twofold. First, to examine the nature, the history and the diagnostic criteria and assessment of psychopathy. Second, to explore whether, and to what extent, psychopathy and antisociality share (or do not share) some of the core psychological and behavioural dimensions. The key questions to address are: *What is the significance of psychopathy for recidivism? What is the impact that psychopathy has upon social and behavioural functioning? Does psychopathy contribute to increasing the likelihood of criminal and violent behaviour?*

The following analysis will contribute to shedding some light on these aspects and on their implications within the criminal justice system.

Psychopathy: a word full of meanings

Psychopathic literally means *psychologically damaged*, but currently it is frequently employed with the meaning of *antisocial* or *socially damaging* (Blackburn, 1988, 2007). Extensive descriptions of psychopathic personalities are generally based on psychiatric-forensic, offending and, more recently, on civil community samples. The prevalence of psychopathy is estimated at approximately 0.6–1 per cent in the general population (Coid *et al.*, 2009; Hare, 2003) and 3.5 per cent in the business world (Babiak & Hare, 2006). Even though some studies (Babiak, 1995, 1996) suggest that psychopathic personality traits may be functional to life success and to climbing the professional ladder, others (Gao & Raine, 2010; Ullrich et al., 2008) reveal that psychopaths are less likely to have records of accomplishment in their personal life (e.g. successful intimate relationships) and in their social behaviour (e.g. status and wealth). Gao and Raine (2010) drew attention to the difficulties in researching successful psychopathy, as the majority of studies have focused on incarcerated male offenders, leaving our knowledge of successful psychopaths limited and incomplete. Researchers find a significant proportion of psychopathic personality traits among individuals involved in antisocial, criminal and violent behaviour (DeLisi, 2009; Freilone, 2011; Hare & Neumann, 2010; Tuvblad et al., 2013; Vaughn & DeLisi, 2008; Vaughn et al., 2008).

In US federal correctional settings, psychopaths comprise about 15–25 per cent of offenders (Hare, 1998a), while estimates of prevalence rates of psychopathy among severely mentally ill (SMI) persons vary between 1 per cent and 25 per cent (Crocker et al., 2005), with forensic populations having higher prevalence rates than general psychiatric populations (Hare, 1996a).

Analyses carried out across different countries, with large samples of adults and youths, in penitentiary or forensic-psychiatric institutions, and in the general community, illustrate that psychopathy can be represented by four dimensions. The multifaceted nature of the disorder involves failures: *to relate* to other people in a trustworthy, reliable and truthful manner (the interpersonal facet); *to participate* emotionally in a relationship, and *to experience* empathy, guilt, love, tenderness, concern or sympathy for other people's distress or joy (the affective facet); *to adopt* a prosocial attitude to life, take responsibility and accept to share social norms (the life-style facet); *to abide* by the law (the antisocial facet). These dimensions reflect the dissocial characteristics of psychopathy, are significantly (moderately to strongly) intercorrelated, and there is empirical evidence to suggest that they are indicators of a super-ordinate factor (Hare & Neumann, 2005, 2006). The existence of a *psychopathy super factor* (Neumann et al., 2007, 106) may provide insights into the understanding of the unified nature of the construct.

This hierarchical nature of psychopathy, which entails interpersonal, affective, life-style and antisocial factors, does not imply that all psychopaths are incapable of interpersonal relationships, but that their interactions reflect relational disturbances, and are marked by cunning, pathological lying, manipulation and self-grandiosity. As Hare (1993) formulated in a quite distinguished narrative description, 'some psychopaths earned reputations for being fearless fighter pilots during World War II, staying on their targets like terriers on an ankle. Yet, these pilots often failed to keep track of such unexciting details as fuel supply, altitude, location, and the position of other planes' (p. 77).

Not all psychopaths are affectively flat, but they are callous, superficially charming, morbidly egocentric, unempathetic and irresponsible. A hint of it can be found in the lecture on moral insanity by Kitching (1857) when he explained that:

> '[a] man may have intellectual abilities of the first order, and yet be deficient in those qualities which go to the composition of a good subject in his social,

domestic, and moral relations. These latter faculties do not appear to hold any definite relation to the development or strength of the former. The circle of our own acquaintance may supply us with examples of men conspicuous for the zeal and success with which they cultivate science, commerce, or the arts, or the ability with which they follow out any favourite pursuit, who are, nevertheless, greatly deficient in those moral perceptions and sensibilities which are necessary for the formation of a great and useful character. How much has the history of the world and the peace of nations been disturbed by the unregulated ambition and unscrupulous daring of clever and gifted men, in whom Nature had implanted excellent powers of mind, but left them unfurnished, or scantily provided, with the controlling and humanising faculties of an equally powerful moral constitution. Had the moral faculties of such men been equal to their intellects, how differently would the history of a Caesar or a Napoleon, or a Nicholas, have been written. Instead of being traced with a pen dipped in blood, and guided by the light of a thousand fires of sacked and burning villages and towns, inspired by the drum of war and the thunder of cannon, it would have beamed with the light of love to human kind, and would have formed, each in its time, an epoch in the advancement of the human race in the arts of civilisation, literature, commerce, and peace.

(p. 336)

The life style of psychopaths is impulsive and parasitic, their behaviour is lacking in control, and it reflects persistent, serious, heterogeneous and antisocial conducts. Early conceptualisations of antisociality in individuals who were diagnosed as psychopaths are found in Cleckley (1976):

Not only is the psychopath undependable, but also in more active ways he cheats, deserts, annoys, brawls, fails, and lies without any apparent compunction. He will commit theft, forgery, adultery, fraud, and other deeds for astonishingly small stakes, and under much greater risks of being discovered than will the ordinary scoundrel.

(p. 343)

Cleckley (1976) always emphasised the personality dimensions of the disorder, and clearly believed that most psychopaths were not violent. While acknowledging that a considerable proportion of incarcerated individuals displayed psychopathic traits, Cleckley (1976) asserted that the majority of psychopaths were not criminals (see Andrade, 2008).

It is true that a considerable proportion of prison inmates show indications of such a disorder. It is also true that only a small proportion of typical psychopaths are likely to be found in penal institutions, since the typical patient, as will be brought out in subsequent pages, is not likely to commit major crimes

that result in long prison terms. He is also distinguished by his ability to escape ordinary legal punishments and restraints. Though he regularly makes trouble for society, as well as for himself, and frequently is handled by the police, his characteristic behavior does not usually include committing felonies which would bring about permanent or adequate restriction of his activities. He is often arrested, perhaps one hundred times or more. But he nearly always regains his freedom and returns to his old patterns of maladjustment.
(Cleckley, 1976, 19)

Nevertheless 'the qualities of the psychopath become manifest only when he is connected into the circuits of full social life' (Cleckley, 1976, 22).

They [psychopaths] do not necessarily land in jail every day (or every month) or seek to cheat someone else during every transaction. If so, it would be much simpler to deal with them. This transiently (but often convincingly) demonstrated ability to succeed in business and in all objective affairs makes failures more disturbing to those about them.
(Cleckley, 1976, 340)

This does not mean that psychopaths are incapable of social behaviour. What is relevant is the pervasiveness of these features across time and situations, and the persistence of dissocial traits that distinguish psychopaths from the rest of the population. What is crucial is not just what *is present* in their personality (e.g. poor moral reasoning) that makes them extensively irresponsible and manipulative, but what *is absent* (e.g. they are unhampered by remorse, regret or guilt) and to what extent that absence (e.g. lack of empathy, lack of consideration for others) influences their disregard for social values and moral norms. Clinically and socially, it is important to consider not only the behaviour of psychopaths, but also *what they do not* and yet *should do* in certain circumstances.

Psychopathy is a significant construct especially in psycho-criminological research and forensic settings. The exploration of psychopathic traits is important to the extent that it can assist risk assessment, prevention, and to a certain degree intervention. This chapter investigates not only the personality constructs underlying psychopathy, but also how these aspects are integrated within larger systems of personality development (e.g. biological, familial, social) to exercise causal effects upon the development of psychopathy, and its influence on criminal recidivism.

A historical look at the evolution of the psychopathy construct

The concept of *psychopathy*, defined as the *convincing mask of sanity* (Cleckley, 1976), and the psychopaths as *flowers without scent* (Hill, 1954) or as *Amyciaea lineatipes* (Patrick, 2007), a genus of crab spiders that mimics ants and targets and kills them, has evolved considerably over the last century. It has changed from a mere assembly of mental disorders, otherwise undistinguishable and unclassifiable, to a more defined and yet complex personality condition. In psychiatric settings, it seems to have evolved from other concepts such as *manie sans délire* (mania without delirium or insanity without delusions) (Pinel, 1809), *moral insanity* (Prichard, 1835) and *moral imbecility* (Maudsley, 1874). The reason why the concepts of *mania without delirium* or of *moral insanity* are always introduced in psychopathy studies is because of their early adherence to the definition of what psychopathy was considered to be. Pinel (1809) is recognised as the first to highlight that in certain disorders it was the emotions that were primarily involved, leaving the intellectual functions unscathed.

James Cowles Prichard (1835), a Bristol physician, is credited with being the first to recognise the class of people for whom the current diagnosis of psychopathy is intended (Hill, 1954). With the concept of moral insanity was meant any form of insanity that involved 'feelings, affections, inclinations, temper, habits [. . .], without any remarkable disorder or defect of the interest or knowing and reasoning faculties, [. . .] without any insane illusion or hallucinations' (Prichard, 1835, 6; also quoted in Sass & Felthous, 2008, 13). Even though this psychopathological condition may be, even today, not so straightforward to diagnose, because it requires a longitudinal study of the life history of the person, Prichard's intention was first to emphasise that the disorder of behaviour was persistent and lifelong, and that it was independent of any mental deficiency or intellectual disorder. Secondly he promoted the idea, within the juridical system, that insanity was not 'coextensive with mental illusion' (Ward, 2010, 8): such individuals know the difference between 'right and wrong' (Cima *et al.*, 2010) but it is as if they were compelled to act antisocially and aggressively by an underlying deficit (Toch, 1998), even though those insane impulses should not exempt a person from criminal responsibility (Fornari, 2008, 2013; Maibom, 2005). The salient characteristic of moral insanity was for Prichard the absence of intellectual delusion, initially in line with the famous Parisian 'mad-doctor' Jean Etienne Dominique Esquirol (1772–1840) (Goldstein, 1987). Prichard, in 1835, wrote that '[t]here is a form of mental derangement in which the intellectual faculties [are uninjured], while the disorder is manifested principally or alone in the state of feelings, temper, or habits [. . .]. The moral . . . principles of the mind . . . are depraved or perverted, the power of self-government is lost or greatly impaired, and the individual is . . . incapable . . . of conducting himself with decency and propriety in the business of life' (quoted in Ozarin, 2001, 21). In 1842, Prichard observed that the term *monomania* (a concept that was attributed to Esquirol, 1839) could not be applicable to a disorder that was not characterised by any particular errors or delusions (Augstein, 1996).

Much research has been carried out since then, and yet Prichard's arguments about responsibility and mental problems seem as fresh as ever (Blair, 2007; Fox *et al.*, 2013; Gao *et al.*, 2009; Glannon, 2008; Hare & Neumann, 2009; Kiehl & Sinnott-Armstrong, 2013; Morse, 2008; Raine, 2013; Vincent, 2008; Zara, 2013b).

Henry Maudsley's work (1874) focused mostly on moral insanity and responsibility. He conceived the former not as a discrete disease but rather as a syndrome that could occur as a phase of several different conditions such as *folie circulaire* (similar to bipolar disorder) and general paralysis of the insane (known now as neurosyphylis) (see Ward, 2010, 10), but which could also occur on its own. Although he initially defined moral insanity in a similar vein to Prichard, he placed more emphasis on those emotional features that characterised the morally insane person, who showed such insensibility from an early age. Maudsley (1874) did not accept the vague and judgemental coinage of *moral insanity*, which became almost a *waste basket* for unclassifiable conditions (Holmes, 1991, 79), and believed that a more scientific approach should be employed in the study of individuals who displayed alterations in their character and moral insensibility. He gathered together cases of general paralysis of the insane, directly observed prisoners and worked as a private practitioner for young people whose families consulted him. This clinical material helped him construct a category of insanity which profoundly challenged the legal views of responsibility and made an ambitious case for medical authority over criminal justice. Maudsley (1874) believed that emotions and impulses alone, without any disturbance of reason, could drive a person to commit a crime. He resisted many legal figures and lawyers who simply considered moral insanity as a 'groundless medical invention' (Maudsley, 1874, 68, quoted in Sass & Felthous, 2008, 14), and argued for the acceptance of the concept of diminished responsibility in English law.

The term *psychopathic personalities* was first employed by von Feuchtersleben (1845), by which he meant psychological defect, psychosis or illness of personality, while the term *psychopathic inferiority*, first used by J. L. A. Koch in Germany in 1888, replaced moral insanity as a diagnosis, and later in 1891 he employed the term psychopathy.

Schneider (1923) defined *psychopathic personalities* (a concept already introduced by Kraepelin in 1904), as abnormal, who either suffered personally because of their abnormality or made the community suffer because of it. However, differently from Kraepelin, who held a mainly socially judgemental opinion about the concept, Schneider did not consider psychopathy as a mental illness because, according to his idea, illnesses were necessarily related to injury or diseases. Schneider (1923), going through the nine editions of his book, between 1923 and 1950, developed a typology which differentiated ten types of psychopathic personalities, based on his clinical work: the hyperthymic and depressive psychopaths, with their deviations of mood and activity; the insecure psychopaths, with their subgroups of sensitive and anankastic (obsessive or compulsive) psychopaths; the fanatics; the self-assertive psychopaths; the emotionally unstable psychopaths; the explosive; the callous; the weak-willed; the asthenic (feeble and lacking in strength) psychopaths. His work on psychopathy is still influencing the current classification systems of the DSM-IV and ICD-10 for personality disorders.

For Henderson (1939, 1955) psychopathic states apply to individuals 'who conform to a certain intellectual standard but who throughout their lives exhibit disorders of conduct of an antisocial or asocial nature'. This classification differentiated: (1) those who were predominantly self-aggressive and aggressive towards others, including drug-addicts and alcoholics; (2) those who were predominantly passive or inadequate; (3) those who were predominantly creative. Henderson (1939) assumed that psychopathic conditions exerted a special influence over the prognosis of mental problems in general and he believed that it was the psychopathic state that constituted 'a rock on which our prognosis and treatment in relation to many psychoneurotic and psychotic states becomes shattered' (p. 37, quoted in Sass & Felthous, 2008, 14).

In 1948 Karpman attracted the world's psychiatric attention when stating that 'the concept of psychopathic personality is at present in a transitional state'. His work was based on carefully studied material that offered a diagnosis of psychopathic personality divided into two main groups: the *primary*, *essential*, or *idiopathic* psychopath who does not exhibit signs of underlying anxiety, or retain fear conditioning responses or mental conflicts, and the *symptomatic* or *secondary* psychopath who displays an over-reactive attitude, a high degree of emotional reactivity, anxiety, and strong antisocial and delinquent aspects. Primary and secondary psychopaths may differ in their aetiology: the former being genetically predisposed; and the latter being influenced by environmental and life circumstances such as parental dysfunction, abuse and poor socialisation.

Modern roots of the concept of psychopathy

The term 'psychopathy' became accepted in America early in the twentieth century, and included in various textbooks of the period (e.g. the fourteenth edition of *Outlines of Psychiatry* by William A. White, 1935; Strecker, 1944; Edward Strecker and Franklin G. Ebaugh included the term in *Practical Clinical Psychiatry for Students and Practitioners,* 1925). The first psychiatric nomenclature was prepared in 1917 by the National Committee for Mental Hygiene in collaboration with the American Medical Psychological Association (forerunner of APA) (Ozarin, 2001). The proposal included the rubric 'psychosis with constitutional psychopathic inferiority', while the 1934 eighth revision used the term 'psychopathic personality', and included pathological sexuality and emotionality subtypes, with asocial or amoral tendencies.

Burt (1944) preferred to employ the term *temperamental deficiency* instead of *moral imbecility* and proposed the following criterion: 'a temperamental defective is one who, without being defective also in intelligence, exhibits, permanently, and from birth or from an early age, less emotional control than would be exhibited by an average child of half his chronological age; or, in the case of an adult, of the age of seven or less' (p. 513). Using this criterion, about 9 per cent of Burt's delinquent cases would be classified as temperamentally defective compared with under 1 per cent of the law-abiding population. Burt (1923, 1944) believed that the American medical acceptance of the term psychopathy was to 'cover almost all mental conditions that are classifiable neither as insanity on the one hand, nor as intellectual dullness or deficiency on the other' (pp. 595–6, quoted in Ward, 2010, 16).

Lunbeck (1994) recognised that, beyond the usefulness of the concept, there was the danger of its elusiveness: 'a rubric that encompassed incarcerated criminals and dissipated high-livers, promiscuous girls and lazy men, deficiencies so vague, so numerous and, in the end so elusive that some wondered whether it referred to anything at all' (Lunbeck, 1994, 65; quoted in Ward, 2010, 16).

Beyond the mask of sanity

In 1941 Hervey Cleckley, a psychiatrist at the University of Georgia Medical School, published *The Mask of Sanity*, which went through five editions, the last one published in 1976. This work described cases of patients who were characterised by dissocial behaviour, which could not be replaced by any clear motivation and which was caused neither by mental impairment nor by psychosis. Cleckley strove for clarification over a condition that he believed was a true illness, having the kernel of psychosis that had not manifested itself. In 1976 Cleckley developed a clinical profile of the individual psychopath, who is emotionally shallow and superficial, egocentric and socially insensitive, opportunistic, unable to engage empathetically with others, or to be socially respectful and responsible. Sixteen major features were considered to be characteristic of psychopathy:

1. Superficial charm and good intelligence.
2. Absence of delusions and other signs of irrational thinking.
3. Absence of nervousness or psychoneurotic manifestations.
4. Unreliability.
5. Untruthfulness and insincerity.
6. Lack of remorse or shame.
7. Inadequately motivated antisocial behaviour.
8. Poor judgement and failure to learn by experience.
9. Pathologic egocentricity and incapacity for love.
10. General poverty in major affective reactions.
11. Specific loss of insight.
12. Unresponsiveness in general interpersonal relations.
13. Fantastic behaviour with drink and sometimes without.
14. Suicide rarely carried out.
15. Sex life impersonal, trivial and poorly integrated.
16. Failure to follow any life plan.

Some of these features are still included in subsequent work on psychopathy, even though the concept of antisociality seems to have for a long time overlapped with or overshadowed it. The DSM-IV^{TM}'s and the DSM-IV-TR's concept of *antisocial personality disorder*[1] (ASPD) (American Psychiatric Association, 1994, 2000) includes most of Cleckley's criteria. In the current International Classification of Mental Disorders (ICD-10, World Health Organization, 2010[2]), the closest diagnostic condition is *dissocial personality disorder*.[3]

The *Psychodynamic Diagnostic Manual*[4] (2006) includes psychopathic personality among the personality disorders it contemplates (PDM P axis). The PDM P axis considers each personality disorder in terms of temperamental, thematic, affective, cognitive and defence patterns; it does not consider disorders as artificially isolated and distinct:

> P103. Psychopathic (Antisocial) Personality Disorders encompasses:
> P103.1 Passive/Parasitic.
> P103.2 Aggressive.

The *passive/parasitic subtype* comprises the more dependent, less aggressive, usually non-violent, manipulator and con artist individuals, while the *aggressive subtype* includes actively predatory and often violent individuals.

The PDM uses the term 'psychopathic' to relate to the personality, and not just the symptoms. The psychopathic (antisocial) personality for example has aggressiveness and a high threshold for emotional stimulation as part of the temperamental or contributing constitutional-maturational factors. The main thematic or central tension/preoccupation is manipulating/being manipulated. The central affects are rage and envy. The characteristic pathogenic belief about the self is 'I can make anything happen', while the characteristic pathogenic belief about others is 'Everyone is selfish, manipulative and dishonest'. The central way of defending is reaching for omnipotent control over others (Gordon, 2010).

Kernberg (2004) believed psychopathy should, in fact, fall under a continuum spectrum of *pathological narcissism* that ranged from narcissistic personality on the low end, *malignant narcissism* in the middle, and *psychopathy* at the high end.

The fifth edition of the *Diagnostic and Statistical Manual of Mental Disorders* (or DSM-5) (APA, 2013) offers new criteria for personality disorders (*dimensional method*), and despite its importance historically and contemporarily, psychopathy continues not to be specifically included in the medical and psychological community of the DSM-5. Some of the previously psychopathic traits are included under antisocial personality disorder,[5] despite the two diagnoses actually measuring different traits. ASPD focuses on criminality and social deviance, while psychopathy loads on the interpersonal and affective shallowness. Thus, in spite of the fact that the definition of ASPD in the DSM-5 (APA, 2013) may correct some of the disparity between the two disorders by including more personality-oriented criteria, such as the individual's identity and self-functioning (Tufts, 2013), equating ASPD and psychopathy will only contribute to inflate the diagnosis of psychopathy within the criminal justice system (Hare, 1996b; Ogloff, 2006). A diagnosis of ASPD encompasses a substantially higher percentage of offenders than the percentage of those who qualify for a diagnosis of psychopathy. Research findings suggest that ASPD has a prevalence rate of 50–80 per cent in prison populations (Ogloff, 2006, 522), and yet only approximately 15 per cent of prisoners would be expected to be psychopathic, as assessed by the PCL-R. Although a majority of psychopaths do 'meet the criteria for ASPD, *most individuals with ASPD are not psychopaths*' (Hare, 1996b, 2). A systematic review by Fazel and Danesh (2002) examined 62 prison studies covering more than 23,000 prisoners worldwide. Their findings show that 65 per cent of the male inmates had a personality disorder, with 47 per cent of them fulfilling the criteria for antisocial personality disorder. Among women, 42 per cent of them had a personality disorder, including 21 per cent who suffered from antisocial personality disorder. In other words, about one in two male prisoners and about one in five female prisoners have antisocial personality disorders. In a study carried out in Denmark, personality disorder was observed in 30 per cent of the prison inmates, with a significant proportion of psychopathy related to psychiatric comorbidity. The prevalence of psychopathy was, however, lower in European than in North American prisons, and medium to high scores of psychopathy were related to higher psychiatric comorbidity.

Black and colleagues (2010) conducted a random sample of 320 newly incarcerated offenders. ASPD was present in 113 inmates (35.3 per cent), and there was no gender-based prevalence difference. The offenders who met the criteria for a diagnosis of ASPD were younger, had a higher suicide risk and had higher rates of mood, anxiety, substance use, psychotic, somatoform disorders, borderline personality disorder and ADHD. Their quality of life was worse, and their LSI-R scores were higher, indicating a greater risk for recidivism.

These findings have several implications. First, the risk of having psychiatric disorders seems noticeably higher in prisoners than in the general population. Second, the presence of antisocial personality disorder is a high risk for developing mental illness (Andersen, 2004) and suicide (Verona *et al.*, 2001). Third, it is assumed that treating mental disorder in prisoners is particularly problematic, not only because the lack of a clinical setting makes it very cumbersome to engage the inmates in a treatment programme and foster a therapeutic alliance, but also because of the lack of resources available for mental health care within the correctional system (Fazel & Danesh, 2002).

Despite the ambiguity and the confusion related to such a condition, the most widely used definition of psychopathy is the one which includes a reference to antisocial behaviour, that is, behaviour that does not imply always and certainly a violation of the law. As Sass and Felthous (2008, 26) suggested, 'it is behavior that is offensive to others and violates social norms. It may, but it does not have to be, the result of a disorder. The behavior itself, not its cause, is indicated by the term.' Following this assumption, it emerges that the differentiation of psychopathy from antisocial personality disorders and from dissocial or antisocial behaviour is fundamental, especially in psycho-criminological and forensic settings (Sass, 1987).

Psychopaths

Psychopaths are those individuals who show a clear and persistent disposition towards antisocial, deviant and delinquent behaviour without psychopathologically relevant abnormalities that impair their functioning. Later descriptions of psychopathy also tended to identify a heterogeneous group of offenders who shared only an antisocial history (Karpman, 1948). McCord and McCord (1964) described psychopaths as lacking guilt, remorse and lasting bonds with others, while possessing high levels of impulsivity. They are assumed to show emotional detachment, guiltlessness and an inability to experience deeper feelings of love.

Psychopathy, as defined by Hare (1991, 2003), describes a specific subgroup of antisocial personality disorder (ASPD) that is characterised by emotional detachment and antisocial behaviour. Emotional detachment emphasises the abnormal emotional responsiveness in psychopathy and distinguishes psychopathy from antisocial personality disorder (Hare et al., 2000; Herpertz & Sass, 2000). Within the affective domain, psychopaths are described as fearless, shallow and callous. Empathy and remorse are found to be lacking and psychopaths are indifferent to the feelings and needs of others. As a function of deficient emotional reactivity, criminal psychopaths are unable to learn from negative experiences such as punishment. Thus, their forensic prognosis is poor (Hare, 1991, 2003).

However, any agreement on the descriptive characteristics of the psychopath would mean 'little unless it can be shown that the features define a valid clinical construct capable of reliable identification' (Hare, 1996a, 28). According to Hart et al. (1995) four issues should be acknowledged with the aim to describe and understand the nature of psychopathy: (1) its two-structure set-up; (2) its chronicity; (3) its association with criminality; (4) its link with deceitfulness. Analysing these issues is relevant, as the specialised literature suggests:

1. Two dimensions are both essential and reasonably adequate to provide a comprehensive description of psychopathic symptomatology. Research findings and clinical work support strongly a two-factor structure (Benning et al., 2003; Hare & Neumann, 2006; Harpur et al., 1989).
2. Psychopathy is a chronic disorder. Research findings show that the onset of the disorder emerges early in childhood and is likely to persist into adulthood (Lindberg, 2012; Pardini & Byrd, 2013; Pardini et al., 2006; Pardini & Loeber, 2007; Salekin, 2007; Shaw & Porter, 2012).
3. Psychopathy and criminality are distinct but interrelated constructs. Criminological studies are consistent in finding a higher base rate of psychopathy among the antisocial and criminal population than in the civil community and in the psychiatric population. This is not surprising given that features such as impulsivity, callousness, lack of empathy and remorse, and so forth, are considered robust risk factors for antisocial and violent behaviour (Blair, 2010; Douglas et al., 2007; Rice & Harris, 2013).
4. Deceitfulness – lying, deception, manipulation – is closely linked with psychopathy. There is empirical evidence that psychopaths are likely to engage in fraudulent, cunning, false and dishonest behaviours that do not necessarily drive them into social failure (Francis Smith & Lilienfeld, 2013; Hancock et al., 2011) but, in some situations, may lead to high social and professional positions (Babiak, 2007; Babiak et al., 2010).

Assessing psychopathy

The most widely used instrument available for assessing psychopathy is the *Psychopathy Checklist-Revised* (PCL-R) (Hare, 1991) and its variants, the *Psychopathy Checklist: Screening Version* (PCL:SV) (Hart et al., 1995), and the *Psychopathy Checklist: Youth Version* (PCL:YV) (Forth et al., 2003). The structural reliability and predictive validity of the construct of psychopathy has received rigorous scientific, clinical and research attention since the development of the Psychopathy Checklist (PCL) (Hare, 1980), and its revision in 1991 with the Psychopathy Checklist-Revised (PCL-R), and the Psychopathy Checklist: Screening Version (PCL:SV) (Hart et al., 1995). These empirical instruments are conceptually and methodologically related measures of psychopathy, and have shown a robust ability to predict reoffending (Meloy, 1988), violent recidivism (Freilone, 2011; Harris et al., 1991; Hemphill et al., 1998), social dangerousness (Salekin et al., 1996), emotional dysregulation (Fowles & Dindo, 2006; Grieve & Mahar, 2010), forensic patients' adjustment (Chakhssi et al., 2010; Hare & Neumann, 2009), responsivity level to treatment (Polaschek & Daly, 2013), correctional adjustment (Hare et al., 1988).

The PCL-R is a 20-item clinical rating scale with total scores ranging from 0 to 40. Scores of 30 or more generally meet the threshold for a psychopathy diagnosis. The PCL-R appears to have a two-factor structure: the interpersonal/affective dimensions and the life-style/antisocial dimensions (Hare, 2003). *Factor 1* comprises characteristics such as callousness, guiltlessness, affective shallowness, egocentricity and lack of empathy. *Factor 2* includes items assessing poor behaviour control, impulsivity, juvenile delinquency, criminal versatility and irresponsible life style.

The PCL:SV is a 12-item clinical rating scale with a total score from 0 to 24. Even though is impossible to 'specify the "best" single cut-off score for the PCL:SV, one that maximises every facet of predictive efficiency with respect to every criterion' (Hart et al., 1995, 22), a score of 18 or higher generally meets the threshold for diagnostic purposes of psychopathy, and warrants further assessment with the comprehensive PCL-R, while a score of 13 indicates potential psychopathy (see Chapter 3 for psychopathy in chronic offenders). The factor structure of the PCL:SV is conceptually, psychometrically and empirically related to the PCL-R. Research evidence suggests that the pattern of external correlates is highly similar between the two measures (Hare & Neumann, 2006).

Taxon versus dimension

Given the moral, political and legal implications of psychopathy as a construct and as a diagnosis in history, the concern over the consideration of psychopathic disorder as *a category mistake* (Holmes, 1991) was raised.

Do psychopaths differ from other individuals in kind or in degree?

While some scholars emphasise the dimensional nature of the disorder, others support a categorical view, focusing on the latent taxon in relation to some aspects of psychopathy. Blackburn and Coid (1998), exploring the dimensions of personality disorder in violent offenders, found some evidence for considering psychopathy as a dimensional disorder, albeit at the extreme end of the continuum, rather than a categorical one. Other researchers (Cooke & Michie, 2001; Cooke et al. 2004; McHoskey et al., 1998) advocate a dimensional view of personality and personality disorders, especially when taking into account, as Murphy and Vess (2003) state, the considerable overlap among narcissistic, antisocial, borderline and histrionic personality disorders that constitute a recurring pattern of covarying traits in the assessment of psychopathic personality[6] (Blackburn & Coid, 1999; Hart & Hare, 1997). And, as Hare and Neumann (2008) indicate, 'because there are no exclusion criteria for its use, it is possible to investigate PCL-R comorbidity with other disorders, but its dimensional nature suggests that a likely scenario is overlap of symptoms' (p. 220).

Morey (1988) stressed the categorical representation of personality disorder. Harris and colleagues (1994) analysed 653 PCL-R scores of male forensic patients, through different taxonometric methods, and reached the conclusion that psychopaths are a discrete class. Their methodology allowed them to identify two groups of individuals: one within the psychopathic category (with a cut-off score of about 25 that optimised the prediction of criminal and violent recidivism, which in their study identified 24 per cent of their sample),[7] and the other outside it.

There is disagreement over whether psychopathy constitutes a dimensional disorder (as a sort of an extreme continuum of antisocial, self-serving, Machiavellian activities) or a discrete psychopathological category that does not permit a precise identification of persistent, self-serving, manipulative, violent and serious antisocial behaviour that can be qualitatively distinct from other forms of behaviour. Whereas the former, as Lilienfeld (1998) suggests, seeks to uncover the underlying psychopathic dimension of behaviour, the latter pursues the assumption of the psychopathic taxon, defined by Meehl and Golden (1982, 127) as 'an entity, type, syndrome, species, disease, or more generally, a nonarbitrary class'.

'Psychopathy may not be pathology as it is usually understood: the characteristics associated with the taxon could have contributed to Darwinian fitness under a variety of conditions such as those in which life is *nasty, brutish, and short*' (Harris et al., 1994, 396, emphasis of the authors). It is as if the view of psychopathy as a disorder (Quinsey, 2010) should be substituted by it being the result of a heritable life strategy, a sort of an adaptive functional process (Buss, 2005). Psychopaths seem to have developed an extraordinarily powerful camouflage mechanism, which is useful in social contexts where they approach, charm, control and use their victims. In other words, would psychopathy be the result of a degeneration from *Homo sapiens* into *Homo ferox*? (Pietrini & Bambini, 2009, 260).

Does antisocial behaviour play a relevant part in psychopathy?

Understanding the latent structure of a construct has important implications for conceptualisation, measurement and intervention. A growing body of research shows that psychopathy (Edens *et al.*, 2006; Guay *et al.*, 2007; Marcus *et al.*, 2004; Walters *et al.*, 2007b), antisocial personality, and criminality are dimensional in nature (Walters *et al.*, 2007a). While exploring the methodology behind this finding is beyond the scope of this chapter, it certainly constitutes a central aspect of this investigation.

> One of our subjects, who scored high on the Psychopathy Checklist, said that while walking to a party he decided to buy a case of beer, but realized that he had left his wallet at home six or seven blocks away. Not wanting to walk back, he picked up a heavy piece of wood and robbed the nearest gas station, seriously injuring the attendant.
>
> *(Hare, 1993, 58–9)*

A great debate as to whether antisocial or criminal behaviour is essential to psychopathy is at the core of recent empirical studies. It seems that antisocial behaviour and violence play an influential role in the modern conceptualisation of psychopathy and in its assessment. The PCL-R and the PCL:SV include antisocial behaviour, in a broad spectrum of its meaning, as important dimensions of psychopathy. However as Blackburn (2007) suggests, it is possible to account for criminality in terms of personality, but the converse is not true. Findings from his correlational study, though, indicated that antisocial behaviour, in its broad spectrum, is a characteristic feature of psychopathy: an aggressive way of relating to others and a self-interest at the expense of others 'belong more clearly to the universe of personality than that of criminality or morality' (Blackburn, 2007, 157). This discussion is relevant to this book only to the extent that it helps clarify the relationship between the emotional and interpersonal facets of psychopathy, and the behavioural facet. It also helps to establish the extent to which psychopathy or psychopathic traits could be assessed by longitudinal data. In the CSDD longitudinal data presented here, the psychopathy findings are from the PCL:SV measure.

The antisocial nature of psychopathy

The upstream (core) and downstream (manifestation) features of psychopathy are far from clear. This division seems as important as ever, given that psychopathy and antisocial behaviour have been considered, by some scholars, intertwined (Hare, 1991, 2003) and, by others, independent (Cooke & Michie, 2001).

Some consider antisocial behaviour as part of the core construct of psychopathy and advocate that it should be included in the assessment of psychopathy (Hare & Neumann, 2010). Others focus more on the clinical manifestations of psychopathy, and see aggressive and criminal behaviour and violence as consequences that are neither diagnostic nor specific features of psychopathy. They argue that it is tautological to say that psychopathy causes antisocial behaviour if antisocial behaviour is included in the definition of psychopathy (Skeem & Cooke, 2010a). Hare and Neumann (2010) regard antisocial (broadly defined, so as to encompass what Farrington, 1997, defined as a 'syndrome of antisociality') and persistent problematic behaviour (Hare & Neumann, 2005) as integral parts of psychopathy. Personality traits that are relevant to psychopathy are inferred from behaviour. Hare and Neumann (2006) argue that, until the scientific community achieve a complete understanding of 'relevant biopsychological processes we will have to rely on inferences of these processes from behaviors, some of which are antisocial in nature' (p. 60).

It is not criminal behaviour *per se* that is a key feature of psychopathy, but the motivation or (lack of) explanation for it that becomes relevant. Blackburn (2007) claimed that, even though specific acts are not the same as personality traits, traits or dispositions are defined by *regularities* in behaviour. *Continuity* over time and the *frequency* of criminal acts can be an indication of underlying dispositions. Thus, even though the extent to which psychopathy contributes to criminal behaviour 'is an empirical question that can be only answered if the two are identified independently' (Blackburn, 1988, 507), the 'antisocial facet of the PCL-R is a further disposition, i.e. criminality. It is a more specific disposition of *social rule-breaking*, but is another disposition nonetheless' (Blackburn, 2007, 145).

Lilienfeld argued (1994) that a model of psychopathy based on two dimensions, which collectively includes the emotional/interpersonal and the deviant/antisocial life style, may be under-inclusive of certain psychopathic individuals who, so far, have not displayed antisocial conduct, and over-inclusive of some non-psychopathic individuals who are criminal. The under-inclusivity of the model might then miss a significant proportion of successful psychopaths who are considered socially functioning (Babiak & Hare, 2006). The over-inclusivity has a similar inverted problem in so far as it might include persistent offenders, who are psychologically heterogeneous and not necessarily influenced by a psychopathic personality. Moreover, Skeem and Cooke (2010a,b) also state that, at the construct level, such a model of psychopathy may be under-inclusive because of the exclusion of traits such as anxiety, which seem central to psychopathy, and over-inclusive because of criminal behaviour being included in the diagnosis of psychopathy.

However, traditional conceptualisations of anxiety have produced mixed findings on the role of anxiety in psychopathy, and research findings have not always been able to reconcile models of anxious and fearful temperaments with psychopathy and antisocial behaviour. In a recent study, Dolan and Rennie (2007) examined the relationship between self-reported anxiety and fear and psychopathy in a group of 110 adolescent male offenders, who exhibited conduct disorder. Their findings showed differential associations of anxiety and fearfulness with the different psychopathic dimensions. Trait anxiety was negatively correlated with the affective components of psychopathy, while fearfulness was negatively correlated with the more antisocial components of the construct. In a previous study by Frick and colleagues (1999), on 143 clinically referred children, it was found that measures of trait anxiety and low fearfulness had divergent correlations with psychopathic dimensions: whereas conduct problems were positively correlated with trait anxiety, callous and unemotional traits were negatively correlated with trait anxiety.

Other researchers (Caspi *et al.*, 1995; Kagan *et al.*, 1993; McBurnett *et al.*, 1991; Schwartz *et al.*, 2003) have devoted considerable attention to the role of anxiety, nervousness and temperamental characteristics in the expression of disruptive and antisocial behaviour, and also because of its neurobiological foundation (Gray, 1976, 1987). Gray's (1973) conceptualization of behavioural activation and inhibition systems has been applied to understanding various forms of psychopathology (Meyer *et al.*, 1999; Mineka *et al.*, 1998), including internalising (Kagan *et al.*, 1987) and externalising problems (Arnett *et al.*, 1997; Carver & White, 1994). His theory suggests that two distinct neurobiological systems operate in opposition to one another: one seems to be involved in the expression of aggressive behaviour (the *Behavioral Activation System* or *BAS*); the other is implicated in the production of anxious behaviour (the *Behavioral Inhibition System* or *BIS*). It is likely that higher levels of activity in the BAS, accompanied by a parallel increase in the activity in the BIS, should result in less severe behavioral manifestations of conduct disturbance.

Despite various studies providing contrasting findings (Anderson *et al.*, 1987; Verhulst & van der Ende, 1993), it is suggested that a weak behavioural inhibition system (BIS), measured by electrodermal hypo-reactivity (Fowles, 2000), is associated with a single dimension of temperament involving both low anxiety and behavioural disinhibition, and, possibly, with poor control of emotions. These findings have also demonstrated that electrodermal hypo-reactivity appears to relate to an impulsivity dimension among psychopaths rather than emotional difficulties. Other studies emphasise the role of mitigating psychological factors on externalizing behaviour (Ollendick *et al.*, 1999).

As suggested by Frick *et al.* (1999) these research findings required a distinction between fearfulness and anxiety. Fearfulness is defined as sensitivity to signals of impending danger, and the inhibitory system is likely to respond by increasing attention, arousal and inhibition of behaviour. Depue and Spoont (1987) indicated that fearfulness is likely to load on a higher-order personality dimension of constraint. Fear can vary in its manifestations that physiologically take the forms of freezing, startle, heart rate and blood pressure changes, and increased vigilance; it is a functionally adaptive behavioural and perceptual response elicited during threat that facilitates appropriate defensive reactions (e.g. escape and avoidance) that can reduce danger. Anxiety can take the form of an exaggerated fear state, and it is likely to be generated by impending threat, aversive stimuli or wrong predictions, whose consequences are perceived as unavoidable. In anxious situations a higher-order personality dimension of negative affectivity is likely to be involved.

Genetic investigations can help to elucidate the aetiological boundaries of psychopathy, and reveal the complex relationships between internalising and externalising problems and psychopathic traits. The genetic basis of psychopathic traits has received little empirical attention, and only recently has genetic research identified a genetic factor that can explain the covariation between psychopathic personality and antisocial behaviour, reflecting a genetic vulnerability to externalising psychopathology (Larsson *et al.*, 2007). Larsson and colleagues found that a common genetic factor loaded on both psychopathic personality traits and antisocial behaviour, whereas a common shared environmental factor loaded exclusively on antisocial behaviour. The genetic overlap, found in this study, between psychopathic personality traits and antisocial behaviour may reflect a genetic vulnerability to externalising psychopathology. It is interesting that their finding of shared environmental influences exclusively in antisocial behaviour seems to suggest an aetiological distinction between psychopathic personality dimensions and antisocial behaviour. Larsson and colleagues (2007) stress the significance of knowledge about the temperamental correlates of antisocial behaviour for the identification of susceptibility genes, as well as for possible prevention through identification of at-risk children early in life.

Blonigen and colleagues (2005) have shown the presence of different genetic influences on the distinct psychopathic pattern of fearless dominance and impulsive antisociality. Their study was designed to examine the aetiological connections between psychopathic traits, as measured by the Multidimensional Personality Questionnaire (MPQ), and the broad psychopathological domains of internalising (mood and anxiety) and externalising (antisocial behaviour, substance abuse) behaviours in a sample of 626 pairs of male and female twins at age 17 from the Minnesota Twin-Family Study (MTFS).[8] The findings revealed a significant genetic influence on distinct psychopathic traits defined as *fearless dominance and impulsive antisociality*: whereas the former was associated with reduced genetic risk for internalising psychopathology, impulsive antisociality was associated with increased genetic risk for externalising psychopathology (Blonigen et al., 2005).

Previous studies (Frick et al., 2000; Harpur et al., 1989; Patrick, 1994, 1995) show evidence of an inverse relationship between the interpersonal-affective facet of psychopathy and self-reported anxiety. Empirical findings suggest that a temperamental lack of fearful inhibition and high novelty-seeking seem to play a significant role in predisposing to psychopathic behaviour (Cloninger, 1987), while high levels of anxiety are often present in antisocial individuals (Rosen & Schulkin, 1998). Walker and colleagues (1991) found that anxiety buffered or counterbalanced the effects of conduct disturbances, in the sense that children with comorbid conduct disorders, who were also anxious, later reported fewer police contacts and were rated by peers as less aggressive than children with only conduct disorders.

A study of Zara and Farrington (2010) suggests that, other things being equal, a nervous, anxious, shy and timid temperament tended to protect a boy from becoming an early offender (antisocial onset before age 20). However the shielding effect exerted by psychological factors seems to be a 'negative protective' influence in so far as they seem to delay the impact (Elander et al., 2000; Kerr et al., 1997) and encourages late onset offending at age 21 and thereafter (Zara & Farrington, 2007, 2009). These findings can find explanation in the fact that these internalising factors, in the long run, may leave the individual vulnerable and unprepared to deal with external, stressful and antisocial influences (Rutter, 2003a,b). Clinical findings suggest that resistance to hazards may derive from controlled exposure to risk, rather than from risk avoidance (Rutter, 2006).

A current exploration of the CSDD (see Chapter 2 for a full description of the study) has analysed how adult onset offending could be related to psychopathy at age 48. Scores on the 12-item PCL:SV ranged from 0 to 12 for late onset offenders (M = 4.0; SD = 2.9), and from 0 to 16 for early onset offenders (M = 6.7; SD = 4.3).[9] *Factor 1* was based on a combination of ADI and DAE to create an affective interpersonal dimension (AI), while *factor 2* included IIB and ANT, so as to create a broad impulsive and antisocial dimension (IA). Not surprisingly, high levels of psychopathy were related to early onset offending (Odds Ratio or OR = 5.5); 32 per cent of early onset offenders in the CSDD were high on psychopathy versus 8 per cent of late onset offenders. Table 5.1 also shows relationships between high scores on the two factors, and the four facets and the onset of offending.

In those individuals who showed high impulsivity and antisocial features, the risk of becoming an early offender was 5.1 times higher than for those who were lower on this factor. Late onset offending, at age 21 or thereafter, was better characterised by a high risk of affective deficiency rather than by impulsivity or antisociality, suggesting that affective and emotional difficulties play a significant role in influencing antisocial involvement at some later point in life. Previous multivariate analyses are concordant with this result: emotional and psychological difficulties are likely to put an individual at a delayed risk for offending, acting early in life as inhibitory factors against antisociality. It is interesting to note that anxiety at ages 12–14 was the only psychological problem that was significantly correlated with the affective/interpersonal factor of psychopathy ($r = .276$, $p < .002$).

TABLE 5.1 PCL:SV scores versus the onset of offending in the CSDD

Scores	% Late onset offenders	% Early onset offenders	Risk	
	High	High	OR	CI 95%
Total PCL:SV	7.7	31.6	5.5★	1.23–24.97
Factor 1: AI	7.7	23.2	3.6	.792–16.52
Factor 2: IA	11.5	40.0	5.1★	1.43–18.22
Facet 1: ADI	7.7	26.3	4.3	944–19.46
Facet 2: DAE	19.2	33.7	2.1	.736–6.18
Facet 3: IIB	11.5	33.7	3.9★	1.09–13.95
Facet 4: ANT	15.4	48.4	5.2★	1.65-16.12

Notes: OR: Odds Ratios (all $p < .05$). In this analysis, PCL:SV scores for all facets and factors were dichotomized. *Factor 1 – AI*: Affective/interpersonal factor. *Factor 2 – IA*: Impulsive/antisocial factor. Facet 1 – ADI: Arrogant, Deceitful Interpersonal Style. Facet 2 – DAE: Deficient Affective Experience. Facet 3 – IIB: Impulsive and Irresponsible Behaviour. Facet 4 – ANT: Antisocial Behaviour.
High score on PCL:SV = 10 or more out of 24; high score on ADI, DAE and IIB = 2 or more out of 6; high scores on ANT = 4 or more out of 6. High score on the affective and interpersonal factor = 3 or more out of 12. High score on impulsive and antisocial factor = 6 or more out of 12.
For total PCL:SV, area under ROC curve = .692, SE = .055, $p < .003$. For the *AI* factor, area under ROC curve = .628, SE = .057, $p < .045$. For the *IA* factor, area under ROC curve = .700, SE = .057, ★$p < .05$.

Casey and colleagues (2011) indicate that adolescence is a period of increased rates of anxiety, which may affect the way that anxious adolescents experience their emotions and relate to people. Given the pivotal role of psychological factors such as fear and anxiety in antisocial behaviour, and in psychopathy, these distinctions are necessary not only conceptually but especially empirically, when the aim is prevention and treatment. Zara (2013b) suggests that anxiety may act as a moderator of antisocial manifestations in adolescence, and yet it may put individuals at risk of future affective deficiency, which seems to be a significant component of psychopathy. Undoubtedly, the proposition that there may be a link between affective and interpersonal deficiency and late onset offending is one that needs to be tested.

Psychopathy in the CSDD

Early life experiences and exposure to undesirable family conditions are hypothesised to be instrumental in affecting future development, and shaping social functioning and later behaviour. Longitudinal data permit the complexity of the linkage to be explored. The significance of the experience, its intensity, the developmental timing of its occurrence and the duration of its impact seem to be crucial variables to take into account. Certainly the earlier and the longer the impact of family factors, the more intense the effect. Prospective longitudinal data on psychopathy from the CSDD have made it possible to investigate the potential links between psychopathic features and life adjustment, and the intergenerational continuity of psychopathy by investigating the possible link between psychopathic parents and psychopathic children.

The CSDD data have helped put into perspective the complex interdependency between personality features and the behavioural manifestations that are the hallmark of psychopathy. As Farrington (2007b) emphasised, there are unfortunately very few prospective longitudinal surveys that specifically investigate the development of psychopathy from childhood to adulthood. '[T]hese surveys are more relevant than retrospective studies of psychopathy, especially since psychopathy is highly correlated with persistent, serious and violent offending' (Farrington, 2007b, 320).

The remainder of this chapter reviews findings from the Cambridge longitudinal data on criminal behaviour. The aim of this section is to explore the extent to which high scores on psychopathy are associated with a persistent and chronic criminal career. Given that many childhood factors are strong predictors of future criminality, and that the earlier their influence the more likely is antisocial involvement and a long criminal career, psychopathy scores were also explored in relation to the criminal careers of the sample. Individual, family and social variables were analysed to study the extent to which they could be robust predictors of psychopathy.

At age 48, 365 CSDD men out of the 394 still alive completed a social interview, and 304 of them (83 per cent) also completed a medical interview that included the PCL:SV (Hart *et al.*, 1995) and the SCID-II (Farrington, 2007b).

TABLE 5.2 Descriptive PCL:SV scores for the entire CSDD sample

	PCL:SV	Factor 1: AI	Factor 2: IA	*Facet 1: ADI*	*Facet 2: DAE*	*Facet 3: IIB*	*Facet 4: ANT*
Mean	3.5	1.2	2.3	.5	.7	.6	1.7
Std Deviation	3.8	1.6	2.6	.8	1.0	1.1	1.8
Median	2.0	1.0	1.0	0.0	0.0	0.0	1.0
Minimum	0	0	0	0	0	0	0
Maximun	17	8	11	4	5	5	6

The scores on the 12-item PCL:SV ranged from 0 to 17 (out of a possible maximum score of 24), with a mean of 3.5 and a standard deviation of 3.8. Table 5.2 reports the descriptive PCL:SV scores. Although psychopathy was measured at age 48, it refers to the adult life from age 18 to age 48. The proportion of those CSDD men scoring 10 or more on the PCL:SV was 11 per cent (or 33 out of 304 men). Nearly half (45.5 per cent) of the men scoring 10 or more were chronic offenders, compared with 2 per cent of the remainder (see later in this chapter).

Psychopathy and antisocial personality in the CSDD

The DSM-IV and DSM-IV-TR (American Psychiatric Association, APA, 1994, 2000) criteria for antisocial[10] personality disorder (ASPD) requires both the syndrome of antisociality (deceitfulness, impulsivity, irritability and aggressiveness, lack of remorse, fighting, truancy, stealing) since age 15, and conduct disorder (CD) before age 15 (Goldstein et al., 2010). With the DSM-5 (APA, 2013), significant, stable, and across time and situations, impairments in *personality* and interpersonal *functioning*, along with the presence of pathological personality traits, must be present in order to allow for an ASPD diagnosis in adults (see nn. 1 and 5 for the reference to the DSM).

Farrington (1997) has shown that ASPD is also characterised by a constellation of adverse familial (e.g. poverty, family size, harsh and erratic parental discipline, marital disharmony, parental criminality) and individual (e.g. low IQ, being unpopular) features that are likely to lead to a pattern of antisocial behaviour that persists. Throughout antisocial personality is indicated by a full spectrum of attitudes and life style that involves being troublesome, difficult to discipline and unpopular in childhood; being impulsive and daring in adolescence; holding an anti-establishment attitude, self-reporting delinquency and violence, and being sexually promiscuous in young adulthood; having a poor relationship with parents and a partner, having a child living elsewhere, drinking, gambling, using drugs and being unemployed in adulthood.

The continuity of such patterns from childhood to adulthood is evident, implying *heterotypic continuity*, but it is not absolute. Robins (1978) assumed that all types of antisocial behaviour in childhood predict high level of antisocial behaviour in adulthood, [. . .] indicating that adult and childhood antisocial behaviour both form syndromes and that these syndromes are closely interconnected. [. . .] Moreover the variety of antisocial behaviour in childhood is a better predictor of adult antisocial behaviour than is any particular behaviour.

(p. 611)

However, 'relative stability is not incompatible with absolute change. [. . .] In any case, if only half of antisocial children become antisocial adults, while only half of antisocial adults were antisocial children, a considerable amount of relative change is occurring' (Farrington, 1991a, 393–4).

The last part of this chapter explores the connection between psychopathy and antisocial personality in the CSDD.

TABLE 5.3 Antisocial personality scales

Antisocial Personality (AP) Scales

Age 10	*Age 14*
Troublesome (TP)	Convicted (R)
Conduct problem (M)	SR delinquency (B)
Difficult to discipline (T)	Steals outside home (M)
Dishonest (P)	Regular smoking (B)
Has stolen (B)	Had sex (B)
Gets angry (B)	Bully (B)
Daring (M, P)	Lies frequently (T, M)
Lacks concentration/restless (T)	Lacks concentration/restless (T)
Impulsive (B)	Daring (T)
Truant (T)	Disobedient frequently (T)
	Hostile to police (B)
	Truant (T)
Age 18	*Age 32*
Convicted (R)	Convicted (R)
SR delinquency (B)	SR delinquency (B)
SR violence (B)	Involved in fights (B)
Antisocial group (B)	Heavy drinking (B)
Taken drug (B)	Taken drug (B)
Heavy smoker (B)	Poor relationship with wife (B)
Heavy drinker (B)	Poor relationship with parents (B)
Drunk driver (B)	Divorced/child elsewhere (B)
Irresponsible sex (B)	High unemployment (B)
Heavy gambler (B)	Tattooed (B)
Unstable job record (B)	Impulsive (B)
Anti-establishment (B)	
Tattooed (B)	
Impulsive (B)	

Notes: R = Records. B = Boy/Man. T = Teacher. P = Peer. M = Mother. SR = Self-report.

Antisocial personality risk scores at different ages (10, 14, 18 and 32) are based on the scales devised by Farrington (1991a). Originally, the scales were operationalised by including measures of personality as well as behaviours. The variables included in each scale are reported in Table 5.3.

The variables included in each risk scale emerged in preliminary analyses (Farrington, 1991a) as independent predictors of antisocial and criminal behaviour. These variables comprise personality and behavioural features, and are closely related to the psychopathic features and antisociality as diagnosed by DSM-IV. The following general principles were applied in devising the AP scales:

1. Each risk variable included was dichotomised, as far as possible, into the *worst quarter* versus the remainder. As Farrington (1991a) suggested, 'it is difficult to summarise relationships between variables that identify less than 5 per cent of the sample and, conversely, if half or more are identified by a variable, it is hard to argue that the variable is a measure of antisocial behavior' (p. 391).

2. The rationale behind dichotomisation is dependent on the nature of the variables studied. Many variables involved are inherently dichotomous: e.g. having a criminal parent, criminal conviction. Many explanatory variables were not normally distributed but skewed. Dichotomisation helps to isolate those cases that are mostly affected by the variable under investigation, and the relative influence of all variables can be assessed by direct comparisons (Farrington & Loeber, 2000; Loeber *et al.*, 1998).

3. The use of dichotomous variables to create risk measures promotes a focus on individuals rather than on variables. As Loeber and colleagues (1998) point out, the percentage of individuals influenced by a variable or a combination of variables is a rather meaningful and clear statistic. Knowledge based on individuals and on their adjustment to life, depending on the presence or absence of a certain condition, or on the accumulation of risks, is particularly relevant for preventive interventions.

4. Those variables that reflected an underlying pattern of antisocial personality risk over time, though conceptually distinct, were included.

5. The variables in each scale were included only if they were significantly correlated to at least half of the other variables in that scale. When two variables were too closely intercorrelated, they were not both included because they were not theoretically distinct. Based on the study of Farrington (1991a), the decision about which variables to exclude depended on the significance of the correlations with convictions at different ages (14, 18 and 32), and with troublesome behaviour at age 10 according to peer and teacher rating. A variable was dropped when it did not correlate with convictions or troublesomeness, independently of a second variable, provided that the second variable correlated with convictions independently of the first one (Farrington, 1991a, 391).

6. The variables were drawn from different sources (self-reported, parents, teachers, peers and records) to control for measurement bias.

7. Each scale at each age was devised independently of knowledge of variables at any other age. This was done in order to avoid the risk of procedurally minimising or maximising the continuity of constructs between different ages.
8. A variable was not included if more than 10 per cent of the data were missing.

The tables show relationships between the four facets of psychopathy and antisocial personality at different ages of development (ages 10, 14, 18 and 32). Scores on all facets were dichotomised. Nearly half (15 out of the 33 men, or 45.5 per cent) of those scoring 10 or more on the PCL:SV at age 48, were high on the antisocial personality score measured at age 10 compared with 34 out of 271 (12.5 per cent), who scored low on the PCL:SV. When antisocial personality, measured at age 10, was analysed in relation to psychopathy, the four facets were moderately related with ANT (OR = 4.96) and ADI (OR = 4.25) having the strongest associations and IIB (OR = 3.50) and DAE (OR = 2.44) the weakest (Table 5.4).

Of the 33 males high on psychopathy (scores 10 plus) 15 (45.5 per cent) were also high on antisocial personality (OR = 5.81). The significance of the association between antisocial personality at age 10 and psychopathy at age 48 indicates the continuity of antisociality over long time periods.

When psychopathy was related to antisocial personality at age 14, the ANT (OR = 15.47) and IIB (OR = 7.82) facets had the strongest associations, and DAE (OR = 4.66) and ADI (OR = 3.29) the weakest (Table 5.5).

TABLE 5.4 PCL:SV scores versus antisocial personality at age 10

Scores	% Antisocial personality at age 10			
	High risk	Low risk	OR	(CI 95%)
Total PCL:SV	45.5	12.5	5.8	2.68–12.59
Factor 1: AI	32.7	12.4	3.4	1.74–6.73
Factor 2: IA	37.8	12.4	4.3	2.12–8.74
Facet 1: ADI	38.5	12.8	4.3	2.03–8.89
Facet 2: DAE	27.8	13.6	2.4	1.22–4.90
Facet 3: IIB	34.0	12.8	3.5	1.73–7.09
Facet 4: ANT	37.9	11.0	5.0	2.55–9.63

Notes: OR: Odds Ratios (all $p < .05$). In this analysis, PCL:SV scores for all facets and factors were dichotomised. Factor 1 – AI: Affective/interpersonal factor. Factor 2 – IA: Impulsive/antisocial factor.
Facet 1 – ADI: Arrogant and Deceitful Interpersonal. Facet 2 – DAE: Deficient Affective Experience. Facet 3 – IIB: Impulsive and Irresponsible Behaviour. Facet 4 – ANT: Antisocial Behaviour.
High score on PCL:SV = 10 or more out of 24. High score on ADI, DAE and IIB = 2 or more out of 6. High scores on ANT = 4 or more out of 6. High score on the AI = 3 or more out of 12. High score on IA = 6 or more out of 12. The Antisocial Personality (AP) at age 10 variable was dichotomised. Low score = 0–4 risks out of 10. High score = 5 or more risks out of 10. 10 items at age 10.

TABLE 5.5 PCL:SV scores versus antisocial personality at age 14

Scores	% Antisocial personality at age 14			
	High risk	Low risk	OR	(CI 95%)
Total PCL:SV	57.6	10.7	11.3	5.14–24.97
Factor 1: AI	36.4	11.2	4.5	2.29–8.86
Factor 2: IA	55.6	8.9	12.8	6.20–25.54
Facet 1: ADI	33.3	13.2	3.3	1.54–6.99
Facet 2: DAE	37.0	11.2	4.7	2.37–9.19
Facet 3: IIB	46.8	10.1	7.8	3.87–15.77
Facet 4: ANT	53.4	6.9	15.5	7.58–31.56

Notes: OR: Odds Ratios (all $p < .05$). In this analysis, PCL:SV scores for all facets and factors were dichotomised. *Factor 1 – AI*: Affective/interpersonal factor. *Factor 2 – IA*: Impulsive/antisocial factor.
Facet 1 – ADI: Arrogant and Deceitful Interpersonal. Facet 2 – DAE: Deficient Affective Experience. Facet 3 – IIB: Impulsive and Irresponsible Behaviour. Facet 4 – ANT: Antisocial Behaviour.
High score on PCL:SV = 10 or more out of 24. High score on ADI, DAE and IIB = 2 or more out of 6. High scores on ANT = 4 or more out of 6. High score on the AI = 3 or more out of 12. High score on IA = 6 or more out of 12. The Antisocial Personality (AP) variable at age 14 was dichotomised. Low score = 0–4 risks out of 12. High score = 5 or more risks out of 12. 12 variables at age 14.

The impulsive and antisocial dimension (IA) that corresponds to *factor 2* of psychopathy (OR = 12.8) was significantly associated with antisocial personality at age 14. This is not unusual given the rise in irresponsible, risky and antisocial behaviours during the adolescent years. Of the 33 males who scored high (10 or more) on psychopathy 19 (57.6 per cent) were also high on antisocial personality at age 14 (OR = 11.3).

When antisocial personality at age 18 was related to psychopathy, the strongest association was with the facet of ANT (OR = 17.8). Of the 58 men scoring high on psychopathy (10 or more), 70.7 per cent scored high on antisocial personality at age 18. Being high on AP at age 18 increases the odds of scoring high (10 or more) on psychopathy at age 48 by 25.5 times. 81.8 per cent (27 out of 33) of these men were high on psychopathy as measured here (Table 5.6).

Of those high on psychopathy 71.9 per cent (23 out of 32) were also high on antisocial personality at age 32 (OR = 29.9). Not surprisingly, the impulsive and antisocial facets of psychopathy, which, as previously indicated, when combined reflect *factor 2* (IA), were strongly associated with antisocial personality (OR = 30.9). *Factor 1*, which combines the affective and interpersonal facets, was weakly, though still significantly, associated with antisocial personality at age 32 (Table 5.7).

In line with previous studies (Farrington, 1991a), the AP scales at the four ages were all significantly intercorrelated, with stronger correlations between those time periods that were closer to each other, and with the weakest correlations between

TABLE 5.6 PCL:SV scores versus antisocial personality at age 18

Scores	% Antisocial personality at age 18			
	High risk	Low risk	OR	(CI 95%)
Total PCL:SV	81.8	15.5	24.5	9.55–63.05
Factor 1: AI	58.2	14.9	8.0	4.20–15.11
Factor 2: IA	73.3	13.9	17.0	8.06–36.01
Facet 1: ADI	56.4	17.7	6.0	2.96–12.17
Facet 2: DAE	51.9	16.4	5.5	2.92–10.31
Facet 3: IIB	59.6	16.0	7.8	3.97–15.19
Facet 4: ANT	70.7	11.4	18.9	9.43–37.39

Notes: OR: Odds Ratios (all $p < .05$). In this analysis, PCL:SV scores for all facets and factors were dichotomised. *Factor 1 – AI*: Affective/interpersonal factor. *Factor 2 – IA*: Impulsive/antisocial factor.

Facet 1 – ADI: Arrogant and Deceitful Interpersonal. Facet 2 – DAE: Deficient Affective Experience. Facet 3 – IIB: Impulsive and Irresponsible Behaviour. Facet 4 – ANT: Antisocial Behaviour.

High score on PCL:SV = 10 or more out of 24. High score on ADI, DAE and IIB = 2 or more out of 6. High scores on ANT = 4 or more out of 6. High score on the AI = 3 or more out of 12. High score on IA = 6 or more out of 112.

The Antisocial Personality (AP) variable at age 18 was dichotomised. Low score = 0–4 risks ot of 14. High score = 5 or more risks out of 14. 14 variables at age 18.

TABLE 5.7 PCL:SV scores versus antisocial personality at age 32

Scores	% Antisocial personality at age 32			
	High risk	Low risk	OR	(CI 95%)
Total PCL:SV	71.9	7.9	29.9	12.29–72.91
Factor 1: AI	42.6	8.6	7.9	3.93–15.95
Factor 2: IA	65.9	5.9	30.9	13.72–69.73
Facet 1: ADI	35.9	11.5	4.3	2.01–9.15
Facet 2: DAE	45.3	8.1	9.4	4.61–18.99
Facet 3: IIB	58.7	6.7	19.7	9.17–42.43
Facet 4: ANT	54.4	5.4	21.0	9.78–45.10

Notes: OR: Odds Ratios (all $p < .05$). In this analysis, PCL:SV scores for all facets and factors were dichotomised. *Factor 1 – AI*: Affective/interpersonal factor. *Factor 2 – IA*: Impulsive/antisocial factor.

Facet 1 – ADI: Arrogant and Deceitful Interpersonal. Facet 2 – DAE: Deficient Affective Experience. Facet 3 – IIB: Impulsive and Irresponsible Behaviour. Facet 4 – ANT: Antisocial Behaviour.

High score on PCL:SV = 10 or more out of 24. High score on ADI, DAE and IIB = 2 or more out of 6. High scores on ANT = 4 or more out of 6. High score on the AI = 3 or more out of 12. High score on IA = 6 or more out of 12.

The Antisocial Personality (AP) variable at age 32 was dichotomised. Low score = 0–4 risks out of 11. High score = 5 or more risks out of 11. 11 variables at age 32.

TABLE 5.8 Correlations of antisocial personality at four ages and PCL:SV scores

	AP 10	AP 14	AP 18	AP 32	Total PCL:SV	Factor 1: AI	Factor 2: IA	Facet 1: ADI	Facet 2: DAE	Facet 3: IIB	Facet 4: ANT
AP 10	—										
AP 14	.50	—									
AP 18	.38	.58	—								
AP 32	.30	.42	.55	—							
Total PCL:SV	.37	.53	.62	.69	—						
Factor 1: AI	.27	.35	.44	.50	.86	—					
Factor 2: IA	.38	.56	.64	.71	.95	.65	—				
Facet 1: ADI	.26	.31	.34	.33	.65	.80	.48	—			
Facet 2: DAE	.20	.27	.39	.50	.76	.87	.61	.41	—		
Facet 3: IIB	.24	.41	.40	.60	.80	.55	.84	.38	.53	—	
Facet 4: ANT	.41	.57	.69	.68	.90	.62	.95	.46	.57	.63	—

Notes: Correlations all significant at $p < .001$. All scores continuous.

the most widely separated ages of 10 and 32. Moreover, the total score of psychopathy was significantly intercorrelated with antisocial personality at every age, with increasing correlations over time: at age 18 ($r = .62$) and 32 ($r = .69$) the correlations were highest. Table 5.8 shows these correlations.

More studies are certainly needed to explore the superordinate dimension of psychopathy that seems to pervade several personality disorders rather than a distinct category being the antisocial dimension of psychopathy.

Not everybody in the CSDD became offenders, not every offender was high on psychopathy and not every psychopathic offender shared the same life experiences. Nonetheless, there were individual, family and social consistencies in the development of these individuals.

Psychopathy as a risk factor for violence and criminal recidivism

Over recent decades, research on psychopathy and its causes and treatment has proliferated. In line with this scientific focus, an intense course of investigation has focused on the efficacy of the measure of psychopathy in predicting violence and criminal behaviour, and their continuation over time. Many studies in criminological psychology advocate that psychopathic personality disorder is a significant factor in recidivism and relapse in violence. The importance of reviewing to what extent and why psychopathy is a risk factor for relapsing into violence and crime is paramount for various reasons.

In the remainder of this chapter we will examine two issues: risk assessment and prevention. The strength and the consistency of scientific findings have encouraged professionals, researchers and institutions to include an evaluation of psychopathy in the risk assessment procedure. Longitudinal studies show that early antisocial tendencies predict the stability of psychopathic traits prior to adulthood in non-institutionalised youths (Frick et al., 2003). Their findings show that the level of conduct problems in childhood, the quality of parenting the child received and the familial socio-economic status were the most consistent predictors of the stability of psychopathic traits. Impulsive and aggressive manifestations are likely to characterise the social interactions of these children, who are also likely to come from a particularly deprived family background, with lack of affection and emotional support from parents.

A systematic review and meta-analysis by Jolliffe and Farrington (2009) suggests that measures of impulsiveness taken in childhood (as early as age 5) were significantly related to later violence (official and self-reported). However, the magnitude of this relationship depended on a number of factors, with one of the most important being how violence and impulsiveness were measured. In those studies in which impulsiveness was measured by poor concentration, along with more global measures (e.g. an ADHD diagnosis), the preliminary findings show that the mean effect size produced was significantly smaller than the mean effect size of studies that compared daring/risk-taking to later self-reported violence. Jolliffe and Farrington (2009) explain their findings by suggesting that

[t]his is not necessarily surprising given the behavioural nature of daring and risk-taking. In fact, many daring and risk-taking behaviours might be closely linked with violence. It might be that this daring and risk-taking type of impulsiveness is an indication of a direct pathway linking early impulsiveness and later violence, whereas poor concentration may have diminished (but still significant) effects because it is operating more through indirect pathways such as disrupting education or influencing the parenting that the child receives.

(p. 57)

Longitudinal studies (Frick *et al.*, 2003; Larsson *et al.*, 2007) suggest that early antisocial tendencies predict the stability of and covary with the expression of other psychopathic traits later in life (Hare & Neumann, 2010). Behaviour genetic studies on children (Baker *et al.*, 2007; Viding *et al.*, 2005; Viding *et al.*, 2007), adolescents (Taylor *et al.*, 2003) and adults (Blonigen *et al.*, 2005), all suggest that the overlap of antisociality with psychopathic traits can also be explained by common genetic factors (Hare & Neumann, 2010). Neuroscientific and clinical studies have shown that exposure to early untoward experiences, like physical (Pollak *et al.*, 1998), emotional (Heim & Nemeroff, 2001) and sexual (Cleverley & Boyle, 2010; Neigh *et al.*, 2009), abuse and neglect, and caregiver inconsistency and disruption (McCord, 2001), is likely to alter the neurobiology of the brain, especially in the amygdala, and contribute to the affective and interpersonal deficits that are recognised in psychopaths (Daversa, 2010). The quality of the environment where the child is brought up has been found to be just as significant as genetic influences, with factors such as the age of onset of the abuse, the duration and the frequency of the episodes playing a key role. As Champagne (2010, 566) states, *epigenetic* means 'over or above' genetics, and this concerns the factors that influence the structure of DNA to regulate the level of gene expression. Central questions still remain to be answered such as how different types of adversity affect psychobiological and personality development, what events are more likely to lead to long-term alterations of the neural system and how these alterations will vary depending on the developmental period (*individual vulnerability*), on the individuals affected (*individual differences*) and on the milieu involved (*nature and nurture interplay*) (Pollak, 2005; Moffitt *et al.*, 2006; Rutter, 2003a).

The *shared environmental* influences (e.g. those that are likely to exert the same effect on children growing up in the same family, such as socio-economic status) and the *nonshared environmental* influences (e.g. those that include experiences and life events unique to each individual within the home, such as different parental interaction and treatment) are those variables that strengthen the complexity of this interplay. The shared environment promotes behavioural similarities between individuals within families, while highlighting the differences between individuals across families. The nonshared environment promotes individual differences within and between families.

Predictors of adult psychopathy in the CSDD

The best method of establishing that an individual or a family factor predicts psychopathy is through a prospective longitudinal study. It has already been established that these types of studies 'avoid retrospective bias' (e.g. where the recollection of parents about their child-rearing methods are biased by the knowledge that their child has become a psychopath) and help in establishing causal order (Farrington, 2007b, 229). The strength of a longitudinal investigation consists in providing knowledge about the order of events, and about how and when they are likely to influence individual development.

It has been speculated that psychopathy may be a component of behavioural responses to early adverse conditions and a distressing environment (Daversa, 2010; Farrington, 2007a, b; Grisolia, 2001). Studies (Lynam & Gudonis, 2005) examining the psychosocial reality and family life of psychopaths reveal that these individuals generally suffered parental inconsistency and erratic discipline, though the consequences for behaviour have not always been clear and homogeneous (Kagan, 1994). Parental discipline and the way parents respond to the behaviour of their child affect the quality of the child's development. A history of parental inconsistency and physical punishment has been suggested as playing a contributory role in antisocial development. A parent's inconsistency may result in an inconsistent attitude towards the child's misbehaviour, some days turning a blind eye to a disruptive behaviour and other days punishing it severely; this erratic or inconsistent discipline also predicts delinquency (West & Farrington, 1973). On a similar note, previous studies (Daversa, 2010; Paris, 1998) suggest that psychopathy is more likely to develop when families are disrupted and when the social structure outside the home does not provide the necessary support for children at risk. Parental disinterest towards the child's good behaviour, physical neglect and emotional detachment, such as a lack of praise and support, may strengthen antisocial reactions in the child.

In the CSDD, physical neglect measured at age 8 significantly predicted high psychopathy scores – 10 or more – at age 48 (OR = 5.1); 34.3 per cent of the boys who were neglected at age 8, because their parents were not providing the necessary care to look after their health and security, were high on psychopathy, against 8.1 per cent of the remainder. Interestingly, physical neglect also predicted all four facets of psychopathy. A father not interested and uninvolved in the activities of his child was predictive of high psychopathy (OR = 6.5); strangely it was not predictive of the affective and deceitful interpersonal facet. Table 5.9 shows the results of this analysis of the CSDD.

Poor parental supervision was predictive of high psychopathy at age 48 (OR = 3.6), and of the impulsive and antisocial facets. Parental supervision was a combined variable and was rated according to vigilance (e.g. watchfulness, concern and closeness of supervision) and rules (e.g. whether parents were rigid or lax in their application of rules and in exerting penalties for not respecting them) (West, 1969; West & Farrington, 1973); 23.6 per cent of boys with under-vigilant parents and those with parents who were negligent in behavioural rules were likely to become

TABLE 5.9 Early predictors of psychopathy at age 48

Childhood risk factors (ages 8–10)	PCL:SV	ADI	DAE	IIB	ANT
Parental educational style					
Poor supervision	3.6★	1.0	1.4	2.6★	3.4★
Harsh discipline	2.6★	1.7	1.6	1.6	2.6★
Father uninvolved	6.5★	1.5	2.6★	2.0★	3.1★
Physical neglect	5.9★	2.7★	2.4★	4.7★	4.0★
Parental disagreement	3.0★	1.9★	1.6	2.1★	2.9★
Family milieu					
Young mother	2.4★	1.0	2.1★	1.5	1.9★
Depressed mother	2.7★	1.0	1.7	2.1★	2.0★
Disrupted family	4.3★	1.5	1.7	2.8★	2.9★
Large family size	3.5★	1.7	2.4★	2.6★	2.8★
Poor housing	3.0★	1.4	2.0★	2.6★	2.2★
Low social class	3.1★	2.0★	1.6	2.0★	2.3★
Low family income	4.6★	1.9★	2.7★	3.6★	3.2★
Family criminality					
Convicted father	5.1★	2.1★	3.1★	2.9★	4.0★
Convicted mother	4.5★	1.8	2.2★	2.2★	3.3★
Delinquent sibling	4.0★	2.6★	3.3★	2.9★	4.7★
Psychological factors					
High daring	3.6★	1.5	2.3★	2.3★	2.9★
Poor concentration	3.6★	2.7★	2.5★	1.9★	3.0★
High impulsivity	2.4★	1.2	1.6	1.6	1.9★
Unpopular	1.9	2.0★	1.4	1.2	2.0★
Dishonest	4.1★	2.0★	2.3★	2.7★	3.5★
Troublesome	3.4★	2.2★	1.7	1.8★	3.5★
Scholastic factors					
Delinquent school	3.9★	2.4★	2.1★	2.2★	3.0★
Low non-verbal IQ	2.4★	1.8	2.0★	2.1★	2.6★
Low verbal IQ	2.7★	1.9★	2.0★	1.9★	2.6★
Low junior attainment	1.7	1.5	2.0★	1.6	3.0★
Low school track record	3.0★	2.4★	2.6★	1.5	2.9★

Notes: This table is based on Table 19.1 of Farrington (2007b, 323) and we are very grateful to John Wiley & Sons, Ltd. for giving permission to use the figures in the original table. As in the original analysis, all risk factors are dichotomised, unless otherwise stated, and are compared with dichotomised scores. PCL:SV = total PCL:SV score; ADI = arrogant, deceitful interpersonal style; DAE = deficient affective experience; IIB = impulsive or irresponsible behavioural style; ANT = antisocial behaviour.
★$p < .05$, one-tailed.
Non-significant predictors: authoritarian parents, depressed father.

psychopathic, in comparison with the 8 per cent of the remainder. In a previous analysis, boys who were poorly supervised were more likely to become delinquents than those who were assessed as receiving adequate supervision (Farrington, 2007b).

Of the family milieu variables, which concern the living climate of the child, only low family income was predictive of high psychopathy (OR = 4.6) and of all the four facets of psychopathy. The other variables, disrupted family (separation from a natural parent before age 10 for reasons other than death or hospitalisation) (OR = 4.3), large family size (number of children in the family: five or more siblings) (OR = 3.5), low social class (based on occupational prestige) (OR = 3.1), poor housing (dilapidated premises, neglected accommodation, poor decoration and interiors, inadequate and old furniture) (OR = 3.0), a depressed (psychiatrically treated) (OR = 2.7) or young mother (given birth for the first time as a teenager) (OR = 2.4), were all significantly and independently predictive of high psychopathy. Having a convicted father (OR = 5.1), a convicted mother (OR = 4.5) or a delinquent sibling (OR = 4.0) by the tenth birthday were also predictive of high psychopathy, and also predicted all four facets.

Of the psychological factors measured at age 8–10, poor concentration or restlessness (OR = 3.6) and high dishonesty (rated by peers) (OR = 4.1) were significant predictors of high psychopathy, and of all the four facets. Troublesomeness (rated by teachers and peers) also significantly predicted high psychopathy scores, especially for ADI and ANT, but it was not significantly predictive of DAE. High impulsivity moderately predicted psychopathy (OR = 2.4) and more specifically the ANT facet of it (OR = 1.9). Attending a high delinquency rate school (OR = 3.9) and low verbal IQ (OR = 2.7) were robust predictors of high psychopathy, and were significantly related to all four facets.

Certainly, more studies are necessary to deepen our understanding of the development of psychopathic personality. The personality structure of psychopathy – an arrogant and deceitful interpersonal style, deficient affective experiences and an irresponsible life style – is significantly manifested in antisocial behaviour, even though, as these results suggest, it also influences other aspects of the social functioning and life adjustment of the individual. There is a great need to carry out prospective longitudinal analysis within high-risk community samples to investigate the development of psychopathy, the link between psychopathic parents and psychopathic children, and the likelihood that psychopathic individuals may be more frequently involved in persistent antisocial, manipulative and socially disruptive behaviours.

Psychopathy and convictions in the CSDD

Up to age 50, 167 men (41 per cent) of the sample were convicted out of 404 men who were at risk, after excluding seven men who emigrated permanently before age 21 and therefore could not be searched for convictions. Convictions were only considered for the more serious standard list offences: motoring and other minor offences were omitted. As mentioned in Chapter 2 of this book, most offences were of burglary, drug use, fraud, theft, vandalism and violence.

In the CSDD, when PCL:SV scores were compared with the number of convictions, significant differences emerged between those scoring 10 or more on the

TABLE 5.10 PCL:SV scores versus convictions

Score	% Convicted offenders				% Chronic offenders			
	High	Low	OR	(95% CI)	High	Low	OR	(95% CI)
Total	97.0	33.0	65.1	8.75–483.99	45.5	1.9	44.2	14.42–135.24
ADI	69.2	35.6	4.1	1.97–8.402	28.2	3.4	11.1	4.25–29.17
DAE	68.5	33.7	4.3	2.27–8.04	22.2	3.2	8.6	3.32–22.32
IIB	74.5	33.6	5.8	2.85–11.67	29.8	2.3	17.7	6.35–49.16
ANT	86.2	29.0	15.3	6.91–33.94	32.8	0.4	118.9	15.47–913.36

Notes: OR = Odds Ratio (all $p < .05$). ADI = arrogant, deceitful interpersonal style; DAE = deficient affective experience; IIB = impulsive or irresponsible behavioural style; ANT = antisocial behaviour. % Convicted and % Chronic among low versus high scorers. Chronic offenders = 10 or more convictions. High scores on total PCL:SV = 10 or more out of 24; high scores on ADI, DAE, and IIB = 2 or more out of 6; high scores on ANT = 4 or more out of 6.

PCL:SV and the remainder: all except one (97 per cent) of the 33 men scoring 10 or more (11 per cent of the sample) were convicted, compared with 46 out of 73 men scoring 4–9 (63 per cent) and only 43 out of 197 men scoring 0–3 (22 per cent). Nearly half (45 per cent) of the men scoring 10 or more were chronic offenders, compared with 2 per cent of the remainder (see Table 5.10).

Of the convicted men, 118 were recidivists (almost 71 per cent of the offending group), who incurred two or more convictions. For the purpose of this analysis, the recidivist group was divided into two levels: those who were convicted for two or more offences versus the one-timers; those who were convicted for at least three offences versus the remainder. The rationale behind this distinction lies on the nature of recidivism. Technically those who are convicted for two offences are recidivists; however, this definition does not allow for a specific identification of those individuals who pose a greater risk for offending. Using a more restrictive measure of recidivism (three or more convictions) allows for a more selective identification of those offenders who are truly persistent. Moreover, of the convicted men, 28 (almost 17 per cent of the offending group) were defined as chronic offenders because their criminal career involved 10 or more convictions. These chronic offenders were responsible for 52 per cent of all offences resulting in a conviction.

An in-depth analysis of the distribution of PCL:SV scores within this sample indicates that 33 males were the 'most psychopathic' at age 48 according to their total scores.

This is the first longitudinal study that has related childhood risk factors to measures of psychopathy or antisocial personality 40 years later.

Scores on all four facets were dichotomised. As reported in a previous study (Farrington, 2007b), the findings show (see Table 5.4) that 39 men (13 per cent) scored 2 or more out of 6 on ADI; 54 men (18 per cent) scored 2 or more out of 6 on DAE; 47 men (15 per cent) scored 2 or more out of 6 on IIB; and 58 men

(19 per cent) scored 4 or more out of 6 on ANT. Not surprisingly, ANT was most strongly related to convictions (Odds Ratio or OR = 15.3). ADI (OR = 4.1) and DAE (OR = 4.3) were rather similarly related to convictions, and IIB (OR = 5.8) had a stronger relationship.

The vast majority of chronic offenders who completed the medical interview (15 out of 20) scored 10 or more on the PCL:SV (OR = 44.2). ANT (OR = 118.9) was strongly related to chronic offending; 19 out of 20 chronic offenders were high on ANT (7 per cent of the sample). Of the other three facets, IIB (OR = 17.7) was the most significantly related to chronic offending, with 14 out of 20 chronic offenders scoring 2 or more on the impulsive and irresponsible behavioural style.

Nearly all (96.9 per cent) of the offenders with two or more convictions were high on psychopathy (OR = 21.1) versus 59.6 of the one-time offenders (Table 5.11).

Furthermore, nearly all (90.6 per cent) of the recidivist offenders, who committed at least three offences for which they were convicted, were high on psychopathy (OR = 16.4), and were especially high on the impulsive and antisocial dimensions (IA) (OR = 20.4).

Chronic offending was significantly related to high psychopathy (OR = 14.8), with almost half of the chronic sample (46.9 per cent) having high scores. Factor 2, characterised by impulsivity and antisociality (IA), was strongly related to chronic offending. Factor 1, characterised by affective and interpersonal deficits (AI), was modestly related to chronic offending (Table 5.12).

TABLE 5.11 PCL:SV scores versus offending

Scores	Offenders			
	Recidivists	% One-timer	OR	(95%CI)
Total PCL:SV	96.9	59.6	21.06	2.75–161.26
Factor 1: AI	92.1	59.0	8.09	2.30–28.47
Factor 2: IA	97.6	55.0	32.7	4.29–249.84
Facet 1: ADI	96.3	61.7	16.1	2.10–124.13
Facet 2: DAE	86.5	61.9	3.9	1.39–11.15
Facet 3: IIB	97.1	58.1	24.5	3.20–187.18

Notes: OR: Odds Ratios (all $p < .05$). In this analysis, PCL:SV scores for all facets and factors were dichotomised. Factor 1 – AI: Affective/interpersonal factor. Factor 2 – IA: Impulsive/antisocial factor.

Facet 1 – ADI: Arrogant, Deceitful Interpersonal Style. Facet 2 – DAE: Deficient Affective Experience. Facet 3 – IIB: Impulsive and Irresponsible Behaviour. Facet 4 – ANT: Antisocial Behaviour.

High score on PCL:SV = 10 or more out of 24; high score on ADI, DAE and IIB = 2 or more out of 6; high scores on ANT = 4 or more out of 6. High score on AI = 3 or more out of 12. High score on IA = 6 or more out of 12. Recidivists = 2 + convictions; One-timer = 1 conviction only. This analysis involves a less restrictive measure of recidivism.

TABLE 5.12 PCL:SV scores versus criminal recidivism

Scores	% Recidivist offenders				% Chronic offenders			
	High	Low	OR	(95% CI)	High	Low	OR	(95% CI)
Total PCL:SV	90.6	37.1	16.4	4.63–58.07	46.9	5.6	14.8	4.75–46.28
Factor 1: AI	81.6	37.3	7.4	2.92–18.88	36.8	7.2	7.5	2.59–21.62
Factor 2: IA	90.2	31.3	20.4	6.54–63.30	39.0	5.0	12.2	3.72–39.78
Facet 1: ADI	85.2	41.5	8.1	2.60–25.31	40.7	9.6	6.5	2.32–18.20
Facet 2: DAE	73.0	41.7	3.8	1.62–8.80	32.4	9.5	4.6	1.67–12.42
Facet 3: IIB	91.4	34.9	19.9	5.63–70.46	40.0	7.0	8.9	3.05–25.92
Facet 4: ANT	88.0	25.4	21.6	7.89–59.10	38.0	1.4	42.9	5.50–334.89

Notes: OR: Odds Ratios (all $p < .05$). In this analysis, PCL:SV scores for all facets and factors were dichotomised. *Factor 1 – AI*: Affective/interpersonal factor. *Factor 2 – IA*: Impulsive/antisocial factor.
Facet 1 – ADI: Arrogant and Deceitful Interpersonal. Facet 2 – DAE: Deficient Affective Experience. Facet 3 – IIB: Impulsive and Irresponsible Behaviour. Facet 4 – ANT: Antisocial Behaviour.
High score on PCL:SV = 10 or more out of 24; high score on ADI, DAE and IIB = 2 or more out of 6; high scores on ANT = 4 or more out of 6. High score AI = 3 or more out of 12. High score on IA = 6 or more out of 12. Recidivism = 3 + convictions. This analysis involves a more restrictive measure of recidivism.

The one non-offender who had a high PCL:SV score was certainly not less 'psychopathic' than those who had similarly high PCL:SV scores but were convicted; he simply showed a different set of antisocial, aggressive, callous and irresponsible behaviours. Man 421 came from a working-class Irish Catholic family, and grew up in a family with a nervous mother who was psychiatrically treated. At age 8 he had a low IQ, socially he had few if any friends, and was rated unpopular by his peers. At age 10 he manifested a high level of impulsiveness and clumsiness. His impulsiveness seemed to constitute a stable feature of his character as it remained high in the course of his development when impulsivity was measured at age 18 and again at age 32. When he reached adolescence (ages 14–16) he self-reported episodes of delinquency, and was involved with delinquent friends. At age 14 he had a low verbal IQ, lacked concentration and frequently truanted, both self reported and rated by teachers. He was a quite aggressive adolescent, also involved in bullying. He continued to be aggressive as an adult, being frequently involved in fights during youth and adulthood. At age 18 he had high level of antisociality, high gambling and had debts; he was a cannabis user and a heavy smoker, and consumed a considerable quantity of alcohol. This may explain why he was involved in fights after drinking, and was a drunk driver. His level of antisociality continued to be high at age 32, when he also self-reported drug use and delinquency involvement. Nevertheless he did not have a high score on life failure nor a high level of unemployment, though he often stole from work. He was never arrested or convicted. Figure 5.1 shows the continuity of antisocial, aggressive, impulsive and socially inadequate attitudes of man 421 along his life.

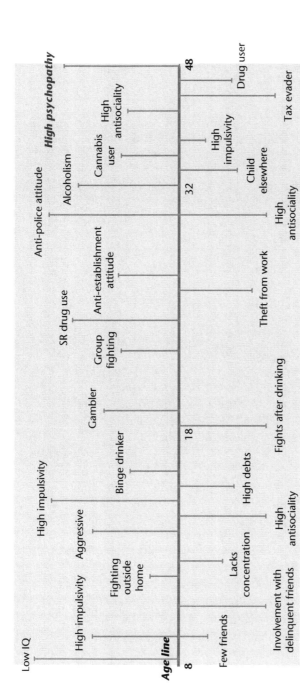

FIGURE 5.1   The life-course of man 421

Psychopathy has been regarded a 'socially devastating disorder' (Hare, 1998b). Even though criminality does not represent the core feature of psychopathy, and there is evidence of psychopaths climbing successfully the social ladder (Babiak & Hare, 2006; Caponecchia et al., 2011; Pardue et al., 2013a, b; Smith & Lilienfeld, 2013), psychopathy is recognised as a significant risk factor for antisociality. The likelihood that psychopathic individuals will harm others, violate the rights of other people, will manipulate and use them, and will resort to violence and criminal behaviour to achieve their goals is not only possible but highly probable. The assessment of criminal recidivism will benefit in accuracy and reliability if psychopathic traits are also added to the practice of risk assessment and risk management.

A number of studies (Hemphill et al., 1998) have shown that psychopaths are more likely to relapse into criminality than nonpsychopaths, even among young violent offenders (Långström & Grann 2002). Other studies (Myers & Monaco, 2000) found a significant negative association between scores on a scale that measures control of aggression and psychopathy scores on the PCL-R. Aggression is distinguished into *instrumental aggression*, i.e. intentional, planned and directed to a specified target; and *reactive aggression*, i.e. spontaneous, impulsive and driven by emotions (Gulotta, 2005; Woodworth & Porter, 2002). Woodworth and Porter (2002) found that homicides perpetrated by psychopathic offenders were more likely to be instrumentally compelled, while homicides committed by nonpsychopaths were often the results of crimes of passion.

It is interesting to note that in a study carried out by Laurell and Dåderman (2005) in Sweden, with a sample of men prosecuted for homicides, there was not a significant association between psychopathy and a social relationship with the victim. Their results showed that there was no difference in PCL-R scores between those who murdered persons known to them and those who murdered strangers.

Research should continue to investigate the predictive validity of psychopathy in civil psychiatric settings, forensic settings, non-offenders, community samples, samples of females and young people, ethnic and racial minority groups (Douglas et al., 2007). Treatment will gain from an accurate and comprehensive assessment of the risk processes, variables and criminogenic needs involved in reinforcing and sustaining psychopathy.

Raine and Yang (2006, 203) concluded that:

> there are some similarities between the neural system underlying moral decision making in normal individuals, and brain mechanisms thought to be impaired in delinquent, criminal, violent, and psychopathic populations. We suggest that this is not a chance association but instead represents a neural insight into the etiology of antisocial behavior.

Furthermore, DeLisi and Vaughn (2008, 164) offered a quite insightful description of the relational, social, and legal implications of psychopathy and psychopaths in society:

There is a synergy between the violent criminals' personality traits, life style, and observed behavior that dovetails so exquisitely that it is as if their criminality is wrapped up in a box. That box is psychopathy.

It is believed that only by scientific research and clinical studies can we gather new evidence to unwrap that box. Research has shown that a significant contribution to unpack the 'psychopathy box' can also be made by neurocriminology. The final section of this chapter will focus on neurocriminology, concentrating attention on how and to what extent this specific knowledge could indirectly assist criminal justice in the evaluation and attribution of criminal responsibility, and could directly serve the sentencing process in which psychologists and criminologists are mostly involved in planning and providing treatment.

The contribution of neurocriminology

Violence does, in truth, recoil upon the violent, and the schemer falls into the pit which he digs for another.[11]

Neurocriminology (Nordstrom *et al.*, 2011; Zara, 2013b) is the study of the neurobiological and neuropsychological structures and functions implicated in aggressive and antisocial behaviour, and in its escalation. The cognitive and emotional expressions of antisociality are central to neurocriminology (Blair, 2003). It follows that a biopsychosocial model satisfies a comprehensive view not only of what criminal behaviour is, but also of how it could be controlled, modified and treated in a multidimensional perspective.

Despite the importance and interest of these aspects in psycho-criminological studies and especially for recidivism research, an analysis of psychophysiology, neuropsychology, brain imaging, genetics and hormones goes beyond the scope of this book. This section includes a synthetic examination of the research findings.

The starting point here, following also from the above quotation, is that the behavioural phenotype of those who criminally offend, and do so persistently or chronically and/or violently, consistently differs from those who are not offenders. Furthermore, significant differences also emerge between persistent offenders and occasional or one-time offenders. It is likely that, in addition to the variety in the behavioural phenotype, there would also be variation in biological, psychological and psychopathological phenotypes.

There is not a unique and standard criterion to diagnose who is an offender and which is the criminal phenotype that the law recognises as liable to be tried, assessed, judged and punished. The law looks at the individual case on the basis of impartiality and the principles of equality, justice and just trial and punishment. Research focuses on samples who can be representative of groups in the offending population; psycho-criminology assimilates scientific information into the risk assessment process; clinical-forensic psychology carries clinical and individual analysis of the person by adhering to sound knowledge and treatment plans. Ideally, these different approaches should inform the law and should assist the process of justice administration. This section will review how neurocriminology could play a significant role in reducing recidivism by adding another level of knowledge to the puzzle of criminality.

The law recognises the mental state of the offender as important in a criminal defence. Criminal law holds people always accountable for their behaviour, and hence responsible for a crime unless they have acted under severe and external duress (e.g. in self-defence, with a gun pointed at the head of the person) or they suffer a serious defect of rationality (e.g. being unable to distinguish right from wrong). It was in the seventeenth century that Sir Edward Coke referred to the maxim that 'an act does not make a person guilty of a crime, unless that person's mind is also guilty' (McSherry, 2003). This is certainly so in the Model Penal Code (American Law Institute, 1962; see also Glenn & Raine, 2014a) which requires the cognitive capacity for rationality. The general principle for imposing liability in English criminal law is that the defendant must be proved to have committed the act whilst having a guilty state of mind. The physical elements that constitute a crime are collectively called the *actus reus* (guilty act). The accompanied mental state is named *mens rea* (guilty mind). Under the *M'Naghten Rule* 'every man is to be presumed to be sane'. This means that people are presumed to be sane and to have a sufficient degree of reason to be responsible for their crimes, until the contrary is proved. Given this, in order to establish a defence on the ground of insanity, it must be clearly proved that, at the time of the committed act, 'the party accused was labouring under such a defect of reason, from disease of the mind, as not to know the nature and the quality of the act he was doing; or if he did know it, that he did not know he was doing what was wrong' (Gazzaniga, 2011, 188).

There may be room, within criminal law, for also considering, in theory, the concepts of emotional capacity and the capacity for self-determination. Emotional knowledge is certainly relevant in translating knowledge about 'right and wrong' into behaviour. In some European countries (e.g. Italy) emotional knowledge is considered relevant, but only when its alteration is grounded in or is the result of a mental disorder that is causally relevant for the offensive act to take place. In the light of the growing neuroscientific evidence regarding moral judgement and antisocial behaviour, many researchers (Glenn & Raine, 2014b; Morse, 2008; Zara, 2013b) have argued that certain individuals, who suffer from serious antisocial and psychopathic disorders, may not be completely and always responsible for their criminal and violent behaviour. Some others researchers (Fornari, 2012; Freilone, 2011; Hare, 2013) instead claim that these mental conditions should not be considered as a reason for discounting, for instance, psychopathic offenders from criminal liability and punishment.

Legal systems serve as a social mediator of dealings between people (Gazzaniga, 2011, 186). This requires considering how the law can guarantee community protection, how it can meet the rights of the victims, but also how it can make punishment beneficial for the offenders. Hence, taking either position (i.e. severe psychopaths as less responsible vs. fully responsible), and adopting neither a specific theoretical nor an empirical assumption, a step forward to the sentencing stage of legal administration implies considering the mental and personality conditions of these offenders to serve the threefold aims of the criminal law: punishment of the culprit; protection of society and victims; treatment of the offenders.

As mentioned before, the reference to a 'guilty criminal mind' as a requirement to make a person responsible is what still influences criminal law. The prosecution bears the legal burden of proving not only that the criminal conduct was voluntary, but also that the accused possessed the relevant fault elements that constitute the four major parts of *mens rea*. These parts can be identified with: *intention* (acting with the conscious purpose of engaging in a specific conduct that causes a specific result); *knowledge* (being aware that a particular conduct of a specific nature is legal or illegal); *recklessness* (disregarding the risk involved); and *negligence* (contributing to a substantial and known risk that could have been avoided if the duty of care by the person had been fulfilled). Furthermore, these parts are relevant not in an abstract sense, but in their mental mechanisms that govern their manifestations in action. Intention and purposefulness involve the brain's intentional systems; knowledge and awareness involve the emotional systems; recklessness involves the reward systems; negligence involves the joy-seeking systems (Gazzaniga, 2011). Current empirical findings can explain to what extent an impairment in any of these mechanisms and in their connectivity alters social and moral behaviour, and how the individual is able (or unable) to direct, control, modify or halt this behaviour.

However, while biological, neuropsychological, cognitive and emotional features are not inevitable causes, they are multicausal factors in the determination of criminal behaviour. Open-mindness towards this evidence could permit building up a channel for bringing new scientific findings into the evaluation of criminal behaviour, along with the more traditional psychiatric and clinical assessments. Ignoring the neuroscientific evidence may lead to an altered and incomplete understanding of who humans really are, how they function, how we can prevent criminal behaviour and violence, and how we can treat those who act criminally.

There is disagreement among researchers and scholars about what scientific evidence and clinical evidence actually tell us about the nature of persistent, chronic and criminal behaviour and violence. Furthermore a second debate includes 'the extent to which the legal system will be, or should be, influenced by what science says about psychopathy and culpability' (Hare, 2013, p. vii). There is no doubt that some violent, persisting and psychopathic criminal behaviour is associated with functional and structural brain mechanisms that in these individuals may be altered or simply may work differently. It is important to always differentiate correlation from causation.

The assumption is not that the brains of persistent offenders *are per se* different from those of non-offenders or other offenders (impaired or abnormal), but that the brain functions differently when criminal and violent persisting offending is the behavioural manifestation. As Glenn and Raine (2014a) suggest '[t]he functioning of the brain reflects the culmination of a variety of genetic and environmental influences and their interaction' (p. 106). Moreover, research findings that show differences between, for instance, psychopaths and nonpsychopaths in their brain functioning, do not claim that all individuals with psychopathic tendencies are the same.

People plan and then modify their behaviour for different reasons; they can constrain an action because of an external instruction or because of their own decision or because of an alteration in some of the brain areas deputised to regulate behavioural control. The understanding of how individuals can intentionally control their own behaviour has always had some interest for psychologists, psychiatrists, criminologists, judges, lawyers and neuroscientists (Brass & Haggard, 2008). The region of the dorsomedial prefrontal cortex (dmPFC) serves a significant role in disengaging from current needs and impulses, so that self-control could be exerted across a wide range of situations and in various forms (Brass & Haggard, 2007), not only behavioural (Isoda & Noritake, 2013). It seems that that connectivity between the dmPFC and the motor preparation areas suggests that self-control is achieved by modulating brain areas involved in motor preparation (Kühn et al., 2009). Brass and Haggard (2008) propose the WWW model that distinguishes three components: a component related to the decision about which action to execute (*what component*); a component that is related to the decision about when to execute an action (*when component*); a component associated to the decision about whether to execute an action or not (*whether component*).

Recent evidence suggests that the dorsal fronto-median cortex (dFMC) is involved not only in the cancellation of motor responses, but also in the inhibitory control of more abstract internal states such as emotions or desires that have no immediate behavioural output (Lynn et al., 2014). The WWW model of intentional action is an example of top-down processing, in which a mental state of, for instance, the intention to behave, influences the next mental state of performing or inhibiting the action. Intentional inhibition refers to the ability to cancel or suppress, even at the last moment, ongoing behaviour on the basis of decisions that are generated internally (Brass & Haggard, 2008). A lesion along the path from intention to action can alter behaviour, and a claim can be made about whether a person is functioning adequately or not, and whether he or she could have acted otherwise. Hence, dysfunctions in the dFMC could alter intentional inhibition, and therefore affect the organisation of behaviour.

Another area of interest is the ventromedial region of the prefrontal cortex (vmPFC) that serves numerous functions that are important for decision-making, guiding social behaviour and processing emotional information (Fellows & Farah, 2007). It has been proved that the vmPFC encodes social stimuli, ponders the different options on the basis of the social contexts and serves the association between stimuli, and between reward and punishment feedbacks (Blair, 2008; Glenn & Raine, 2014b). Damages in the vmPFC seem to contribute to impairments in real-world competencies (Anderson et al., 2006). Patients with damage to the vmPFC resemble individuals involved in persistent antisocial behaviour and with psychopathic traits, and this is what led researchers to speak about 'acquired psychopathy' (Eslinger & Damasio, 1985).

Social encounters are activated by the median prefrontal cortex (mPFC), which also modulates social reactions. In a study conducted by Harris and Fiske (2006), different emotions were elicited in a sample of American participants involved in viewing some pictures illustrating various individuals. Emotions such as envy were experienced when viewing rich people, pity was experienced when seeing the elderly and pride was experienced when looking at American Olympic athletes. These emotions were all associated with activity in the mPFC. Different brain responses, however, were elicited with the emotion of disgust (e.g. looking at photos of drug addicts). For such photos their activation pattern was similar to that involved in the experience of seeing an inanimate and insignificant object such as a rock. These results suggested that, if extreme out-groups can prompt a dehumanising response in normally functioning individuals, it might be that, in those individuals with psychopathic traits, the influence from this *unconscious bias* could be augmented and could lead to extreme acts and violence. In a world inhabited not only by oneself but also by others, it is essential to understand the emotional states of oneself and of others (Shamay-Tsoory et al., 2005), to regulate emotions adequately (Ochsner et al., 2002) and to engage in moral behaviours or to recoil upon violent events (Gazzaniga, 2005, 2011; Mendez, 2009). The orbitofrontal region is involved in these social functions, and a malfunctioning of it can alter the emotional interactions of people. Human social interactions entail individuals exerting a control to override overwhelming or conflictual or utilitarian social-emotional responses stimulated by dilemmas (see also Moll & de Oliveira-Souza, 2007). Individuals are capable of calculating reasoning (e.g. cost-benefit analyses) (see Greene et al., 2004), and also of generating other-aversive emotions (e.g. anger, frustration or moral disgust) (see Greene et al., 2001) when there is restraint in situations that alert their defensive or aggressive mechanisms. When individuals attempt to make sense of other people's behaviour and make judgements about it, they also rely on inferences about their beliefs and intentions. The ventromedial prefrontal cortex (vmPFC) seems to be implicated in generating social emotions (Anderson et al., 2006), in making moral judgements and in processing and assessing harmful intent for moral judgements, i.e. 'the ability to blame those who intend harm, even when they fail to cause harm' (Young et al., 2010, 849). Koenigs and colleagues (2007) suggest that focal bilateral damage of the vmPCF seems to produce an abnormally utilitarian pattern of judgements on moral dilemmas that oppose choices for aggregate welfare against emotionally aversive behaviours. The right dorsolateral prefrontal cortex (dlPFC) is involved when judgements about punishment are made (Glenn et al., 2009b).

Morality, that represents the 'traffic light regulator' of social interactions, can be described as composed of three distinct aspects: (1) a person's moral orientations and principles; (2) a person's competence to act accordingly (Lind, 2008); (3) a recognition of the mental states of other people, and acting, if not accordingly to other people's expectations, at least to acknowledge them. This distinction points out the role of individual differences within the moral domain. Moral judgement competence is the ability to apply moral orientations and principles in a consistent and differentiated manner in varying social situations.

A striking feature of much of the antisocial behaviour shown by psychopaths is that it is mostly instrumental in nature, i.e. goal-directed towards achieving money, sexual opportunities or increased status (Cornell *et al.*, 1996), disregarding any sort of moral standards apart from their own. This suggests that the pathology associated with psychopathy interferes with socialisation. In other words, 'the emotional impairment found in individuals with psychopathy interferes with socialisation such that the individual does not learn to avoid antisocial behaviour' (Blair, 2003, 5). It is likely that the neural circuitry of sociality reinforces the psychopathic traits and that individuals who may also come from a disrupted emotional family and conflictual social context, are more likely to react callously, unempathically and instrumentally in those social situations where their personal interests are at stake.

Emotions such as guilt and shame are complex social emotions. They are also moral emotions, because they occur in response to social and moral violations. These emotions inhibit the transgression of social rules, and motivate reparative behaviour. The impaired mental states of these emotions may lead to inappropriate behaviours as observed in early brain-damaged individuals (Anderson *et al.*, 1999), in autism (Baron-Cohen *et al.*, 1999; Frith, 2001) and also in those individuals affected by antisocial personality disorders (Brower & Price, 2001).

Following Johnson-Laird's mental model framework (1983), Bucciarelli and colleagues (2008) introduce the *principle of independent systems*, according to which emotions and moral evaluations are based on independent systems operating in parallel. A person may experience emotions in many circumstances that have no moral components. Conversely, when people establish that a moral (or a social) rule is broken, they may not experience any emotional reaction. Consistent with this assumption, some situations may elicit an emotional response prior to a moral evaluation, some may elicit a moral evaluation prior to an emotional response, and some may elicit both reactions at the same time. Some of the current theories on moral judgement account for moral judgement in psychopaths. Some scholars argued that psychopaths are emotionally shallow, superficial in their social interactions and therefore morally insensitive (Blair, 1995). Other scholars argued that psychopaths are more likely to rely on cold and calculating reasoning processes when dealing with moral and social situations, disregarding or not responding to the emotional components that the situation might elicit (e.g. Glenn *et al.*, 2011). These accounts are based on the assumption that emotions do not concur to influence moral judgements and to motivate moral behaviour in psychopathic individuals. It may then be plausible to hypothesise that psychopathic individuals rely more on calculating, self-serving and utilitarian reasoning processes to determine whether specific actions are appropriate according to societal standards. Thus, as Cima and colleagues (2010) suggested, although psychopaths are cognitively able to distinguish the difference between right and wrong (i.e. the moral judgement), they may not have the feeling of what is right and wrong (Glenn *et al.*, 2009b) and they may lack the motivation and the gratification to translate their moral judgements into appropriate moral behaviour Koenigs et al., 2012. Psychopaths seem to fail the recognition between conventional rules and moral rules (Blair, 1997), to be impaired in social exchange reasoning (e.g. insensitive to cues that govern cooperative relationships and exchanges) (Reis et al., 2007) and in precautionary reasoning (e.g. impulsivity, risk-taking and insensitivity to cues for when to enact appropriate precautions) (Ermer & Kiehl, 2010). The role of the prefrontal cortex (PFC) in social behaviour likely depends in large part on its interaction with the areas outside the PFC. Alterations and lesions in these areas can be potentially relevant to persistent antisocial behaviour. Therefore, future studies of the PFC functional, structural connectivity, cortical thickness and corresponding functional connectivity will contribute to a major comprehension of the neurobiological mechanisms of social and moral behaviour (Glenn & Raine, 2014a; Koenigs et al., 2012; Pascual et al., 2013). Another area of the PFC, the anterior cingulate cortex (ACC), is found to be relevant in mediating a number of social and affective decision-making functions including reward, punishment, pain, negative affect, empathy, error detection, performance monitoring and cognitive control (Koenigs, 2012; for further information on specific research development see also the GCS fMRI – Research Group[12]). Gregory and colleagues (2012) explored whether the structural grey matter (GM) differed between persistent violent offenders who met both criteria for antisocial personality disorder and the syndrome of psychopathy (ASPD+P), and those offenders who met only the criteria for ASPD (ASPD−P). Their findings pointed to the presence of a reduced GM volume within areas implicated in empathic processing, moral reasoning and processing of prosocial emotions, such as guilt and embarrassment among those offenders who displayed antisocial behaviour and exhibited psychopathy. In other words, offenders with ASPD+P displayed reduced GM volumes bilaterally in the anterior rostral prefrontal cortex and temporal poles in comparison with ASPD−P and non-offenders. Gregory and colleagues (2012) also found that these reductions were not attributable to substance use disorders. On the other hand, offenders with ASPD−P exhibited GM volumes similar to the non-offenders.

The shallowness and relational superficiality that characterises psychopathic behaviour, along with manipulativeness and disempathy that direct their social interactions, may also result from some impairment in what is often called the emotional brain (LeDoux, 1996).

The amygdala, located in the brain's temporal area, has received considerable attention in so far as numerous studies have associated psychopathy with abnormal size, shape or activity of this subcortical structure (Birbaumer et al., 2005; Boccardi et al., 2011). The amygdala is involved in aversive conditioning and instrumental learning (LeDoux, 2007), and its reduced activity was associated with psychopathy during emotional stimuli processing (Kiehl et al., 2001), moral decisions about emotional moral dilemmas (Glenn et al., 2009a) and during fear conditioning (Birbaumer et al., 2005).

The amygdala plays a role in both recognition and recall of fearful facial expressions. Studies show that bilateral amygdala damage in humans compromises the recognition of fear in facial expressions (Adolphs *et al.*, 1995); this compromised ability has been found in young people with conduct disorder and with callous and unemotional traits (Jones *et al.*, 2009). This impairment appears to result from an insensitivity to the intensity of fear expressed by faces, while leaving intact the recognition of face identity, lending support to the idea that the recognition of fear in facial expressions and the recognition of face identity are served in part by anatomically separate neural systems (Adolphs, 2006b). Moreover, developmental neuroscience studies indicate that the amygdala plays a significant role not just in fear processing, but also in attention and in detecting relevance (Pessoa & Adolphs, 2010). Patients who report damage to the amygdala share many characteristics with psychopathic individuals such as a less pronounced sense of danger and remaining dispassionate and emotionally flat when asked to recount highly emotional or traumatic experiences (Tranel *et al.*, 2006). They also exhibit fearlessness in the face of very risky and dangerous situations (Baskin-Sommers *et al.*, 2011).

Preliminary studies show that psychopaths display less amygdalar activation (i.e. a brain region implicated in fear processing) than nonpsychopaths during aversive conditioning, moral decision-making, social interaction and cooperation, and memory for emotionally salient words (Glenn *et al.*, 2009a; Glenn & Raine, 2014a; Yang *et al.*, 2009). Conversely, a study by Muller and colleagues (2003) shows that the amygdala is hyper-reactive when psychopaths view certain emotionally salient scenes. Despite the research advancement of neuroscience applied to criminology (Glenn & Raine, 2014b; Zara, 2013b), Baskin-Sommers and Newman (2012) suggest that knowledge of the association of the amygdala with social behaviour and emotional processing is still incomplete and further examination is needed to explain conflicting results.

It is interesting to note that amygdala and orbitofrontal cortex dysfunctions may mean that emotional information about threat, risk or harm to others, that signal cues from the amygdala to cortical areas, may not inform decision-making, so that callousness, lack of empathy, instrumental aggression, and irresponsibility are the most likely manifestations (Marsh *et al.*, 2011).

There are additional areas that seem to be implicated in antisocial personality and psychopathy: the *hippocampus*, which is essential for the retrieval of emotional memories and is involved in fear conditioning (Boccardi *et al.*, 2010; LeDoux, 1996); the *insula* (Ly *et al.*, 2012), especially its anterior part, which is involved in emotions, saliency detection and emotion recognition, such as the processing of the visceral emotion of disgust (Phillips *et al.*, 1998; Wicker *et al.*, 2003[13]); the *striatum*, which was found to be associated with reward sensitivity, reward seeking and impulsivity (Cohen *et al.*, 2009; Glenn *et al.*, 2012); and *angular gyrus*, which is implicated in the experience of guilt and embarrassment (Takahashi *et al.*, 2004).

THE BRAIN is wider than the sky.

(Dickinson, 1924)

This brief description of some brain regions and their implication for social functioning does not exhaustively cover the topic. The aim here was not to achieve completeness, given the vastness of the human brain, but to highlight that social behaviour is not the result of forces and influences external to the individual, but depends on the complexity of internal and external variables, in action and reaction. Assessing the totality of these influences may not be foreseeable, but to ignore some and not others on the basis of theoretical sympathy or one's preferences involves disrespect towards scientific procedure.

The debate about how relevant neuroscience is in the understanding of criminal behaviour emerges from the argument between those who hold that human behaviour cannot be reduced to a process of firing neurons and neurotransmitters, and the brain chemicals that communicate information throughout our brain and body, and those who hold that human behaviour cannot be understood only within a social perspective, and influenced only by social and cultural forces.

The evidence of robust structural and functional brain differences between persistent and chronic offenders, with and without psychopathy, adds to the evidence that these offenders represents a distinct phenotype that needs to be acknowledged in prevention, in treatment and in risk assessment. The assessment of dangerousness and the risk of future violence is central in criminal justice, and with the evidence offered by neuroscience some concepts such as criminal liability and responsibility seem to have acquired a new perspective, at least in how they can be evaluated, presented and argued and debated in court. The emergence of forensic neuroscience and neurocriminology is however rejected by some people because of the idea that introducing these concepts within the criminal justice system may lead to another humiliation – *the neuroscientific humiliation* – that humanity is likely to endure in the twenty-first century (Schleim, 2012; Zara, 2013b). It is misleading to equate neuroscience with determinism. If our brain is to be blamed for criminal behaviour, then it is argued that the very foundation of the legal system, based on free will and voluntary choices is at stake. Putting it differently, using Gazzaniga's words (2011, 198), 'with determinism there is not blame, and, with not blame, there should be no retribution and punishment'. However, the question is not whether neuroscience is relevant in our understanding of criminal behaviour, but how to integrate its evidence in such a way as to avoid reductionism and to see the individual who offends as a total person.

Research evolution cannot be stopped. Neuropsychology is becoming ever more relevant in the study of criminal behaviour and in the rehabilitation of the offender; risk assessment procedures have started to include neuropsychological knowledge; brain scan results are now invited into the courtroom. The problem, in fact, does not reside in the course that scientific development is taking, but in how research findings are instrumentally used. There is 'something in modern culture that believes more about scans than the scientist does himself' (Gazzaniga, 2011, 190); if there is something that our social and legal system should be careful of, it is certainly not neuroscience or neurocriminology, but the misinterpretation and misuse of its findings.

For instance, neuroscientists, or at least the majority of them, do not claim that, when reading a brain scan, a particular area is noted and can be pointed out as related to a specific function. Moreover, a person with an abnormal brain scan does not necessarily exhibit abnormal behaviour; a person with an abnormal brain is not automatically incapable of acting responsibly. An abnormal brain does not imply that a person cannot follow rules (Gazzaniga, 2011).

It is argued here that determinism is one thing and neuroscience another. Neuroscience is not the answer to anything, nor even the response to a specific and complex aspect of human functioning such as criminal behaviour. However, neuroscience is a method of investigation, and in combination with other approaches, can aid our understanding of how humans function and malfunction, and which aspects play a relevant role in it (Zara, 2013b). Neuroscience analyses are not required in every criminal evaluation, but they should be requested and performed in those situations and for those offenders who exhibit consistent and 'remarkable' impairment in their functioning. In such situations, neuroscience evidence will be relevant and essential along with other evidence, in the same way that psychiatric assessment is requested for those offenders who manifest significant mental disorders. Responsibility is not located in any specific region in the brain (Gazzaniga, 2005).

In the case of schizophrenia, which involves an abnormal neurotransmitter disorder, there is no higher incidence of violence in people affected by the disorder if they take their medication. They are then able to follow rules and obey them. On the other hand, people with acquired left frontal lobe damage can act in a strange way, and changes in their behaviour can contribute to an increase in violence (from 3 to 13 per cent) (Gazzaniga, 2011). As Gazzaniga (2011) suggests, a frontal lobe lesion is not a predictor of violent behaviour, in so far as one case cannot become the generalisation point for another case.

The scan does not show what was happening at the time of the crime but what is measured at the time of the scan. Brains are sensitive to many factors that can alter a scan: fatigue, alcohol, drugs, caffeine, tobacco, the menstrual cycle, concomitant disease and so on. Moreover, performances are not constant, but can vary. Every brain is slightly different, in the same way as fingerprints are. An individual's brain has a unique configuration, size and shape, and responds to stimuli differently and solves problems in diverse ways. Moreover, there is variation also in how our brains are connected; the white matter consists of a network of fibres that connects neural structures: these connections can be modulated at a synaptic level. The brain processes information differently depending on these connections.

Neuroscientific evidence is more probative or is prejudicial?

Neuropsychological and biological evidence, like other types of information, such as psychological, social and familial, is enlightening and helpful in so far as it contributes to the complete picture, and it can be used when relevant and present. Neuroscientific analyses contribute to the incremental validity of the evidence and offer data on how humans function neuropsychologically and biologically. They should be read in integration with other data, and not in isolation. Paraphrasing

Andrew Lang,[14] experts should not use neuroscientific evidence and risk assessment in the way that a drunkard uses lamp posts, for support rather than for illumination.

This is why it is believed that the study of criminal careers that are characterised by persistence and chronicity could benefit from the contribution of neurocriminology not only in assessing the risk of criminal recidivism, but especially in evaluation and assessing responsivity. Neurocriminology could assist in deciding what can be done given a particular type of offending, given the precise criminal and clinical history, given the specific criminogenic needs implicated, and given the cognitive and emotional functioning of that specific offender. If the offender, for instance, has an alteration in their circuitry of morality, the treatment cannot ignore knowledge about this matter. If an offender is also coming from a disrupted and criminogenic family, the treatment should be organised to attenuate the impact of abusive family members upon the person's life adjustment. Only the future will tell how important and successful an integrative approach to criminal recidivism is, how it contributes to our understanding of violent and sex offending, and how relevant it is for prevention and intervention. The next chapter focuses on sex offending and on how to assess and manage it accurately and effectively.

Notes

1   According to the DSM-IV-TR (APA, 2000), a synthesis of the DSM-IV-TR Diagnostic Criteria for Antisocial Personality Disorder (301.7) indicates the following features as being crucial for an accurate diagnosis: a pervasive pattern of disregard for the rights of others occurring since age 15; adulthood (the individual should be aged at least 18); evidence of CD with onset before age 15; the occurrence of antisocial behaviour is not exclusively during the course of schizophrenia or a manic episode. The pattern of disregard for and violation of people's needs and rights should include three (or more) of the following:

   1. Failure to respond adequately to social norms and abide by the law, and repeatedly committing deeds that constitute grounds for arrest and prosecution.
   2. Deceitfulness, characterised by recurring lying, falseness in attitude, use of aliases, or conning people for personal profit or pleasure.
   3. Impulsivity or inability to plan ahead.
   4. Irritability and aggressiveness, which is shown by recurrent involvement in provoking behaviours, fights or assaults.
   5. Careless behaviour and disrespect for the safety of self or of other people.
   6. Irresponsibility, as indicated by a reckless attitude towards work commitment, and disinterest in meeting financial obligations.

   The last point also leads to a lack of remorse and any sense of guilt or shame for one's own behaviour, as shown by being indifferent to or excusing having offended, mistreated, or stolen from others.

2   ICD-11 is planned for 2015.
3   According to the ICD-10 (World Health Organization, 2010), Dissocial personality disorder (F60.2) comprises the general criteria of disorders of adult personality and behaviour (F60-F69) that are required for an accurate diagnosis. These criteria encompass: a variety of conditions and behaviours of clinical significance, which are likely to persist and be the manifestation of the individual's characteristic life style and mode of

relating to themselves and other people. Some of these conditions have an early onset, which could be explained by both genetic and biological factors, and by social experiences. Some other conditions and behavioural patterns develop only later in life. Specific personality disorders (F60.-), which also comprise the *dissocial personality disorder*, are ingrained in the individual way of functioning, and are pervasive patterns of behaviour in so far that they are inflexible responses to a broad range of personal and social situations. They represent extreme or substantial deviations from the way in which the average individual in a particular culture would perceive, think, feel, and behave. Such behavioural patterns are likely to be stable across multiple domains and situations. They are frequently, but not always, associated with various degrees of personal distress and problems of a social nature.

Specific personality disorders constitute a severe disturbance in the personality and behavioural tendencies of the individual. They do not directly result from disease, damage, or other brain impairments, or from other psychiatric disorders. They typically involve numerous areas of the personality, and are, almost always, associated with considerable personal distress and social inadequacy. Usually their manifestation occurs early on in childhood or adolescence, and continues throughout adulthood.

Dissocial personality disorder (F60.2). This personality disorder is characterised by a pattern of disregard for social obligations, callousness and lack of concern for other people's feelings. There is gross incongruence between behaviour and the prevailing social norms. Moreover behaviour is not readily changeable by experiences, however intense these might be in terms of their impact, whether adverse or pleasant. There is a low tolerance to frustration and a low threshold for releasing aggression, and for acting out violence. A tendency to blame others for one's own misdeeds is prevalent. Furthermore there is a penchant to formulate plausible and rational explanations for those behaviours that made the person in conflict with social norms and expectations.

The disorder includes: amoral, antisocial, asocial, psychopathic and sociopathic personality disorders. It excludes: conduct disorders (F91.-); emotionally unstable personality disorders (F60.3).

4 The *Psychodynamic Diagnostic Manual* (2006) is the first psychological diagnostic classification system that considers the whole person in various stages of development (Gordon, 2010), their overall emotional, cognitive, social functioning and subjective experiences, and ways of engaging in the therapeutic process. Three dimensions are considered. The dimension of personality patterns and disorders (*dimension I*) has been placed first in the PDM system because of the accumulating evidence that problems or symptoms cannot be analysed, understood, assessed, or treated in the absence of an understanding of the mental life of the person who is affected by them. The dimension of mental functioning (*dimension II*) offers a description of the emotional functioning that contributes to an individual's personality and to the overall level of psychological health or pathology. The dimension of manifest symptoms and concerns (*dimension III*) refers to the patient's *personal experience* of their prevailing difficulties.

5 Diagnosing disorders in the DSM-IV edition (APA, 1994, 2000) involved two aspects. The first was defining what a personality disorder was. A personality disorder (PD) was defined as a pervasive pattern of inner experience and behaviour that diverges extremely from the cultural norms of the person, and involves consistent and stable deviations in thoughts, emotions, impulse and self-control, and interpersonal relatedness that ought to be present at least since adolescence, and should not be the result of substances or another mental disorder. These ways of thinking, feeling, or behaving are substantially distressful and problematical for the person. The second aspect was defining what types of personality disorders were present. The DSM-IV (APA, 2013) listed 10 PDs: paranoid, schizoid, schizotypal, narcissistic, antisocial, borderline, histrionic, avoidant, dependent, obsessive-compulsive and a 'not otherwise specified' category. However, as Krueger and colleagues (2011) pointed out, to assume that PDs could be listed in ten categories is a flaw, not least because of the lack of substantial evidence that PDs

represent categories in nature. This may be one reason to have pursued a reconceptualisation of PDs in the DSM-5. '[. . .] the preponderance of the evidence demonstrates that PD variation is more continuous than discrete [. . .]. Many of the limitations of the *DSM–IV–TR* model (e.g. low reliability, artificial thresholds for diagnosis, high comorbidity) stem from assuming that the discreteness of entities are continuous' (Krueger et al., 2011, 325–6). Moreover, despite the definition of personality disorder remaining unchanged in the DSM-5 (APA, 2013), the construct of *identity*, that involves a process of *self-sameness* and *self-consistency* over time, has been integrated as a central diagnostic criterion for personality disorders (Schmeck et al., 2013).

The DSM-5 (APA, 2013) proposes a revised definition of personality disorders. A personality disorder reflects *adaptive failure* that involves an impaired sense of self-identity or failure to develop effective interpersonal functioning. It was decided to retain the DSM-IV PD system (*categorical method*) for DSM-5 in section II, which lists all formal clinical diagnoses. Hence, none of the criteria for personality disorders have changed in the DSM-5, and a hybrid personality model (*dimensional-categorical method*) was introduced in the DSM-5's section III (*disorders requiring further study*). Section III includes evaluation of impairments in personality functioning (how an individual typically experiences themselves as well as others) and five broad areas of pathological personality traits (APA, 2013; Skodol, 2014). The DSM-5 proposes five PDs, plus one type that is 'trait specified': *T 00* – Borderline Personality Disorder; *T 01* – Obsessive-Compulsive Personality Disorder; *T 02* – Avoidant Personality Disorder; *T 03* – Schizotypal Personality Disorder; *T 04* – Antisocial Personality Disorder (Dyssocial Personality Disorder); *T 05* – Narcissistic Personality Disorder; *T 06* – Personality Disorder Trait Specified. In the new model of the *DSM-5* (see section III, *Emerging Measures and Models*), a configuration of trait facets can be used to define one of the six proposed PDs. Clinicians would assess personality and diagnose a personality disorder based on an individual's particular difficulties in personality functioning and on specific patterns of those pathological traits. Impairment in personality functioning could be rated along a continuum, with a moderate or greater impairment being required for diagnosis of PD: 0 = little to no impairment. 1 = some impairment. 2 = moderate impairment. 3 = severe impairment. 4 = extreme impairment. The four elements of personality functioning are explained with descriptive charts to evaluate the degree of impairment: *identity*; *self-direction*; *empathy*; *intimacy*. Clinicians would rate on a 1–5 scale how much a patient meets a particular PD (with 4 or 5 being a threshold for diagnosis). The scale is derived from the *5-factor Model of Personality* (FFM) and *Personality Psychopathology Five* (PSY-5). The five comprehensive trait domains, that contain 25 specific personality trait facets, are named: *negative affectivity* (vs. emotional stability); *detachment* (vs. extraversion); *antagonism* (vs. agreeableness); *disinhibition* (vs. conscientiousness); *psychoticism* (vs. lucidity). These domains can be assessed with several psychometric tests. For instance, for a diagnosis of Antisocial PD, elevations on trait facets from the domains of *antagonism* (callousness, deceitfulness, manipulativeness, hostility) and *disinhibition* (impulsivity, irresponsibility, risk-taking) are required in addition to impairments in both self- and interpersonal functioning (Skodol, 2012). With this new dimensional method, it is possible to diagnose a personality disorder based on traits (PD-Trait Specified). The presence of both section II and section III in the DSM-5 provides possibilities in terms of examining the optimal method to recognise these disorders, so as to foster the assessment, clinical utility, and most importantly, the external validity of the method. As Paris (2014) suggests, further research that includes multivariable studies in which psychological, biological and social factors are not only considered, but also examined in interactions, are necessary.

The definition of ASPD has changed with every edition of the DSM. The DSM-5 (APA, 2013) does not require any childhood or adolescent manifestation of symptoms in order to meet the requirements for an ASPD diagnosis. However, the exclusion of this criterion may only intensify social concerns, as individuals may be diagnosed with ASPD as a result of serious, though temporary, behaviours. In order to make a diagnosis of *antisocial personality disorder* – 301.7 (F60.2) with the DSM-5 (APA, 2013) the following criteria must be met:

A. Significant impairments in *personality functioning* affecting *self functioning* AND *interpersonal functioning*.
B. Pathological *personality traits* in the domains of *antagonism* and *disinhibition*.
C. The impairments in personality functioning and the expression of personality trait expression are relatively stable across time and situations.
D. These impairments are not better understood as normative for the individual's developmental stage or sociocultural environment.
E. These impairments are not exclusively due to the direct physiological effects of a substance (e.g. a drug of abuse or a medication) or a general medical condition (e.g. severe head trauma).
F. The individual is at least aged 18.

Regarding criteria A:

- *Self functioning impairments* affect (a or b):
    a. *Identity*: Ego-centrism; self-esteem built up through personal gain, power, or pleasure.
    b. *Self-direction*: Goal-setting based on personal gratification; absence of prosocial internal ethical standards and values.

AND

- *Interpersonal functioning impairments* affect (a or b):
    a. *Empathy*: Lack of concern for the rights, feelings, needs, or suffering of other people; lack of remorse after hurting or mistreating another person.
    b. *Intimacy*: Incapacity for reciprocation in intimate relationships; exploitation of the partner as the primary means of relationships; easiness in using deceitfulness and coercion, dominance or intimidation, to control other people.

Regarding criteria B, pathological personality traits involve the following domains:

- *Antagonism*, which includes:
    a. *Manipulativeness*: Frequent use of stratagems to deceive or control other people; resorting to seduction, charm, glibness, or ingratiation to satisfy one's own interests.
    b. *Deceitfulness*: Untruthfulness and dishonesty; self-manufacture; embellishment of self and events.
    c. *Callousness*: Lack of concern and respect for other people; lack of remorse for one's own negative impact on others; aggressiveness; sadism.
    d. *Hostility*: Recurrent resentment moods; anger or irritability in response to minor scorns; malicious, vindictive, or rancorous behaviour.
- *Disinhibition*, which involves:
    a. *Irresponsibility*: Disregard for obligations or commitments, and failure to honour them; disinterest in meeting agreements and promises.
    b. *Impulsivity*: Acting on impulse in response to instantaneous stimuli; inability to plan and to establish future projects; lack of consideration for the outcomes.
    c. *Risk taking*: Engagement in dangerous, daring, and risky activities; acting out of boredom, and disregarding the consequences of one's own limitations; denial of the reality of personal danger.

6 'The psychopath's symptoms have for a long time been regarded as primarily sociopathic. It is true that all, or nearly all, psychiatric disorder is in an important sense sociopathic, in that it affects adversely interpersonal relations' (Cleckley, 1976, 21).
7 This cut-off is lower that the score of 30 recommended for research purposes (see Hare, 1996a, 36; also Hare, 1991).
8 The MTFS is 'an ongoing epidemiological-longitudinal study which explores genetic and environmental factors that empirically and clinically have been recognized to increase the likelihood of substance abuse and related psychopathology in reared together, same-sex twins and their parents' (Blonigen *et al.*, 2005, 4).
9 For the whole CSDD sample, the scores on the 12-item PCL:SV ranged from 0 to 17 (out of a possible maximum of 24), with a mean of 3.5 and a standard deviation of 3.8. See Farrington (2007b) for a complete analysis of the social origins of psychopathy.
10 As reviewed earlier in this chapter, research findings are concordant in considering criminality as neither a necessary nor a sufficient condition of psychopathy. Nonetheless, antisociality, in its heterogeneous manifestations, constitutes a significantly related construct to psychopathy. Antisociality can be defined as a pattern which involves a persistent and pervasive manifestation of aggressiveness, impulsivity, irresponsibility, which may or may not lead to criminality. It consists of personality factors and behaviour, and it is what the scientific community recognised as antisocial personality disorder (ASPD).
11 'The Adventure of the Speckled Band', in Doyle (1892).
12 www.gcs-fmri.unito.it
13 Cf. note 12 for research activities of the GCS-fMRI Group: www.gcs-fmri.unito.it. See also Cauda *et al.* (2012).
14 Andrew Lang, 1844–1912. Scottish poet, novelist, and literary critic, and contributor to anthropology. Quoted in Knowles (2009).

6
SEX OFFENDING

Sex offending is considered to be one of the most offensive crimes in our society. The assumption that sex offenders are very dangerous individuals, more likely than other offenders to recidivate, and especially to recidivate sexually, is rooted in social preoccupation, rather than in scientific evidence.

This chapter will discuss the progress of science in the understanding of sexual offending, with particular attention to sexual recidivism. It starts by discussing the many misconceptions relating to sex offending and by exploring the probability of a sex offender committing another sex offence in their criminal career. It then moves on to look at the extent to which the seriousness of crimes should really be taken into account for assessing offenders as being at high risk of reoffending. The Western criminal justice responses to sex offending will also be explored.

The naïve psychology of sex offending

Cognitive psychology studies provide the explanations of why the common perception of sex offending recidivism is, more than other forms of criminal recidivism, likely to be biased.

Human reasoning is of limited power (Johnson-Laird, 2008, 73). Without us having any intention of undermining professional competence and expertise, much research on how humans reason and the *ipse dixit*[1] *spell* shows that experts are not immune from biasing their thinking, especially when dealing with cases that impact the already complicated intertwine of *fast and slow thinking* (Kahneman, 2011) and elicit intuitive predictions. Most individuals cope with daily problems, and succeed in many professional and career endeavours, but make egregious errors in tests of rationality both in the laboratory and in real life too. The *fundamental paradox of rationality* concerns the discrepancy between knowledge and performance (Johnson-Laird & Oatly, 2000). The natural tendency of human judgement is to overvalue vivid, evocative or emotionally loaded information. Evaluation of this sort inhibits the objectivity of general, but also, of specialised, opinion (Prentky et al., 2006; Puddu, 2002). Suggestive and emotional events have a potent psychologically biasing effect that is explained by what Kahneman and Tversky (1973) called the *availability heuristic*. An availability heuristic is a mental short cut or rule of thumb that gives importance to immediate examples that come to the forefront of our thoughts. If knowledge makes a possibility available to us, then we tend to think that it has a higher probability of occurring than events that are less available. It follows that disturbing and evocative news of sexual abuse can encourage an *overattribution* (or *correspondence bias*) of predictive accuracy that incites erroneous opinions. The likelihood of the recurrence of sex crimes is perceived to be very high, and the risk attributed is of a threat that persists indefinitely and without variation.

Risk assessment studies (Zara, 2010a, 2013a) report that, while the seriousness of crime is a predominant consideration in juridical thinking (though it does not determine either the type or length of conviction), in psycho-criminological thinking, it is one of the many variables to consider when assessing the criminal career of offenders, and certainly not the most significant one when predicting recidivism. According to scientific evidence, the reality is that the likelihood of sexual recidivism is low (Hanson, 2002; McCann & Lussier, 2008; Smallbone & Cale, 2015).

Other fallacies that can influence the sex offender profile emerge as a consequence of the *representativeness heuristic* that relies on stereotyping to attribute category membership, when ignoring base rate information (Kahneman & Tversky, 1972) and when focusing on the recognition details of the information gathered (*recognition bias*). People need to classify things; when something or someone does not fit precisely into a 'comparable known' category, they will approximate with the nearest class available. The fallacy is in assuming that similarity in one aspect leads to similarity in other aspects.

Research on the impact of heuristics on risk assessment evidence reveals that 'no matter how much a person may fit the stereotype for a particular social category, one cannot accurately judge the likelihood that the person actually falls into that category without knowing the base rate of members of that category in the population' (Davis & Follette, 2002, 135). Edward is a single man in his sixties; he enjoys the company of young people with whom he is often seen strolling in the park. Some concerns are spread in the village, and people have become suspicious about his 'dubious' past of which little is known though. The doubt is that he may be a . . . 'paedophile'. However, how correct is this assumption?

Classifying people was considered by Toch 'a grim business which channelizes destinies and determines fate. [. . .]. Classifications are attractive because [. . .] they convert ambiguity and complexity into neat packages that can be handled and processed' (Toch, 1970, 15). Without dismissing this critical opinion, the view on taxonomies and differential categories held is that they provide researchers, professionals and policy-makers with single understandings of those features, characteristics and aspects that are not only pervasive, but that are constantly and systematically present in the most criminogenic realities of sex offences and the perpetrators. And because, according to Fredrickson (2013, 7), 'science, at its best, self corrects', and is always temporary, further research will always contribute to the falsification of those assumptions that have become inappropriate, obsolete or inadequate.

Another fallacy to consider is the *regression fallacy*. *Regression towards the mean* or the *regression artefact*, the inevitable fluctuations of a random process, is a natural statistical correction that is observed across all areas of human performance. We know that observations at the extreme end of a distribution are rare (Johnson-Laird, 2008). They represent only a minimal proportion of the offenders who are exceptionally persistent. Hence, the chance that among the criminal population there is an exceptionally persistent high-risk and dangerous sex offender is low. 'The concept of regression to the mean is tricky. It is a piece of technical knowledge from statistics. We can understand when it is explained to us. But its instances aren't so easy for us to identify. Instead, our propensity to create explanations leads us to violate the norms of probability' (Johnson-Laird, 2008, 184). Failure to take regression towards the mean into account is a major source of error in assessing violence (Monahan, 1981; Monahan *et al.*, 2001).

As Kahneman (2011) suggests, the fact that one observes regression when one predicts a later sex offence from an earlier sex offence should help convince one that regression does not have a causal explanation. However, in Kahneman and Tversky's (1973) terms, the representativeness heuristic explains that we tend to make nonregressive predictions that highly unusual events will continue as if they were a part of an 'average trend'. Reoffending sexually is a relatively unusual outcome, whereas not reoffending sexually is the typical outcome. People are inclined, however, to make nonregressive predictions that suggest the opposite (i.e. that sexual reoffending is likely to happen; it becomes the predicted average outcome).

Being aware of these mental processes helps to make the best use of knowledge about reasoning and judgement results: risk assessment is an example of increasing professional reasoning accuracy leading to an assessment not exempt from errors, but an assessment in which systematic and casual errors are reduced. An assessment is a professional explanation which gathers the best possible information to arrive at the most accurate and valid judgement. According to Johnson-Laird (2008), an explanation in fact 'doesn't just increase the information in the observations: it can eliminate observations as erroneous' (p. 196).

Affective responses versus rational responses to sex offending

The outcry of society about sex offending is overshadowed by the emotional impact that such a crime has on the victims and on the community as a whole. Science is explicative, but its message suffers when it does not meet the idea of protection demanded by the community. Two levels of institutional responses are expected: the obligation of governments to impose punishment, serious restrictions and restorative practices on sex offenders, and the duty to protect victims and society. Thus, the responsibility of experts to intervene with the aim of treating and rehabilitating sex offenders is limited by two forces: the Scylla of severely punishing sex offenders in an attempt to stop them from reoffending, and the Charybdis of seeing everything as a risk for sex reoffending, despite the high number of false positives.

Assumptions regarding the criminal careers of sex offenders are based on the view that these offenders are of a different type (Lieb et al., 1998), who specialise in sex-related offences (Lussier, 2005), are more likely to relapse into sex offences (Harris et al., 2009), commit crimes frequently (Miethe et al., 2006), deserve unique and more severe sentencing by the criminal justice system (Tewksbury et al., 2011), should be enforced into community registration and notification (Zgoba & Levenson, 2012), should face post-conviction polygraph testing (Rosky, 2012), and should undergo treatment (Burdon & Gallagher, 2002). It follows that the growing public concern over sex offenders puts pressure on governments and policy-makers to prioritise confinement responses over prevention and treatment programmes.

Some legal efforts to protect society from sex offenders have been adopted around the Western world by putting in motion special provisions for sex offenders, particularly implemented after release from detention or as alternatives to confinement that are more far-reaching than for any other types of criminals (Hebenton, 2009; Petrunik, 2003). In the USA, the Sexually Violent Predator (SVP) commitment laws use a mental health commitment model to address recidivist sex offenders and to lock up the 'most dangerous' ones after their prison sentences expire (Janus, 2000). All these laws claim is that the deprivation of liberty that they authorise is *civil* rather than criminal. There are three criteria for confinement, which were established by the US Supreme Court in *Kansas v. Hendricks* (1997): (1) a history of sexually harmful behaviour; (2) a mental abnormality that produces an impairment of control over sexually harmful behaviour; (3) a prediction of future sexually dangerous behaviour. The SVP laws permit the state to confine a person indefinitely under procedures that lack the fundamental protections commonly associated with major deprivations of liberty (Janus, 2013, 330). These schemes have survived constitutional scrutiny on the grounds that they serve the ends of protecting society and offering treatment for violent sex offenders, which are both outside the spectrum of criminal punishment (King, 1999).

The following pages will present some of the most significant sex offender schemes and rulings that are prescribed in various countries and intended to manage sex offenders and reduce their risk of sexual recidivism. Despite the differences in their jurisprudence, governments across continents share the common duty of punishing sex offenders appropriately, and aim for the same goal of rehabilitating sex offenders into society.

US rulings

The political and social involvement of the law in the fight against sexual violence is markedly noticeable since the Community Protection Act adopted by the Washington State legislature in 1990 (Prentky, 2003). The Violence against

Women Act (VAWA) was passed in 1994, and was expanded with the Violence Against Women Act of 2000. The Jacob Wetterling Act, passed by the US Congress in 1994, established requirements that sex offenders must register addresses and personal information with law enforcement agencies. Megan's Law (1994) allowed for the public disclosure of registry information, and subsequent amendments to the Wetterling Act required states to post information about convicted sex offenders on internet websites. The Federal Rules of Evidence were revised in 1995, allowing the admissibility of previous sexual offences (Rule 413(a)). In a criminal case in which the defendant is accused of sexual assault, evidence of any prior offence committed by the defendant, including sexual assault, is admissible and may be considered as relevant evidence.

In 2006, the Adam Walsh Act enhanced sex offender registration and notification (SORN) requirements by lengthening the duration of sex offender registration and increasing penalties for sex offenders who fail to register. Failure to register is upgraded to a felony offence with a penalty of one to ten years in prison (Adam Walsh Child Protection and Safety Act of 2006). Policy-makers in the US have also turned to zoning laws to control where sex offenders live, putting some restrictions on where they can circulate and reside (Duwe et al., 2008). This form of supervision also includes the use of electronic monitoring in order to follow the offenders' movements in the community, and the use of polygraph equipment to verify an offender's location and liability (Vess, 2011).

UK orders

With the 2003 Criminal Justice Act, the Multi-Agency Public Protection Arrangements (MAPPA) were formalised in the UK (Kemshall et al., 2005). The Sexual Offences Act 2003 makes new provision about sexual offences, their prevention and the protection of children from harm from other sexual acts, and for connected purposes. In brief, this Act clearly defines *consent* in terms of a person who agrees by choice, has the freedom and the capacity to make that choice; it sets the age of a *child* at 18, amending the Protection of Children Act 1978, and provides a defence for all sexual offences when the child is 16 or over and the relationship is consensual; it creates a new offence of assault by penetration, the insertion of a body part or foreign object, such as a bottle, into the anus or vagina without consent; it redefines sexual assault as an intentional sexual touching without consent; and it classifies any sexual intercourse with a child aged 12 or younger as rape. The offence of rape is reclassified as the penetration by the penis of somebody's vagina, anus or mouth, without consent. The Sexual Offences Act 2003 stated that a sex offender who is sentenced to imprisonment for a term of 30 months or more will be subject to notification requirements (i.e. placed on the sex offenders' register) for life. However, a decision of the Supreme Court declared that the provision about indefinite notification requirements was incompatible with Article 8 of the European Convention of Human Rights (on respect for private and family life) European Convention of Human Rights and Fundamental Freedoms (1950).

In 2012 a statutory guidance was issued. Persons will not come off the register automatically, and qualifying offenders will be required to submit an application to the police seeking a review of their indefinite notification requirements. This will occur once they have completed a minimum period of time subject to the notification requirements (15 years from the point of first notification following release from custody for the index offence for adults, and 8 years for juveniles). Currently the main orders used in the UK are the Sexual Offences Prevention Order, Risk of Sexual Harm Order, Foreign Travel Orders, and the Notification Requirements (The Sexual Offences Act 2003, Part Two). Moreover, the Child Sex Offender Disclosure Scheme, known as Sarah's Law 2001 (Lipscombe, 2012) was brought in following a campaign when Sarah, an 8-year-old girl, was murdered by a convicted child molester in 2000. This scheme acts as a modified sex offenders' register where parents can enquire for information about a named individual.

There are many other countries which hold a sexual offence system that has provisions for review mechanisms, including Australia, Canada, France, Ireland, Italy and South Africa. These mechanisms differ, however. A number of systems include a review undertaken by a court, while in France the review is undertaken by the prosecutor. In Italy the reviewing mechanisms are under the specific judicial authority of the Surveillance Tribunal that can also grant benefits such as the re-entry into the community, the return to detention or the referral to a mental unit facility or therapeutic community.

To confine people for a certain period of time in order to prevent future crime implements a type of preventive detention policy that seems to undermine notions of justice, constitutional principles and ethics. Despite controversy, these schemes are accepted in many countries as a means to provide treatment and promote desistance from sex violence.

Risk assessment in the service of humanity and justice

Risk assessment, in the prediction of sexual recidivism, has become a very active and crucial part of evaluations in which sex crimes are involved, because of the acknowledgement of its utility in criminal justice and in the public health sector (Janus & Prentky, 2003). If risk assessment is gaining more recognition in this field, science should be in the foreground of the service of humanity and the improvement of human well-being.

Prentky and colleagues (2006) were adamant when stating that the adjudication of sexual violent offenders places demands on science. Primarily the pressure is for experts to provide sound information on the influence of mental impairments and abnormality on the criminal act committed, which can assist judgements about criminal responsibility. Secondly the pressure continues, via the requests of courts and parole boards, to provide precise evidence of the likelihood that a sex offender will reoffend again. This risk information is then used for deciding about the commitment schemes that are appropriate for a very narrow group of the most 'challenging' offenders: recidivist sex offenders.

Base rate of sexual recidivism

General public opinion endorses the idea that sex offenders are lifelong predators (La Fond, 2005), are the most likely to reoffend, sexually and violently (Lieb *et al.*, 1998), and the least likely to change. These views contrast with those held by scientists, and at times predominate over expert views, reinforcing the gap between research findings, the criminal justice system and intervention policies.

Criminal statistics show that the rates of sexual recidivism are overall lower than for other crimes (Hanson *et al.*, 2003, 2014). This finding is counterintuitive for two reasons. The first is that the likelihood of relapsing into another sex crime in the short and medium term is low, typically being around 14 per cent after five years (Hanson & Bussière, 1998), suggesting that there is always a period of antisocial latency before committing another serious and violent offence (Zara, 2005). This is in line with the *criminal career paradigm* (Farrington, 2003; Piquero *et al.*, 2003) that individuals involved in a long, prolific and active antisocial career are mostly heterogeneous, and rarely specialise in sex or violent crimes.

The second is that the likelihood of persisting into a sex offending career diminishes with time, and after reaching its peak between ages 18 and 30 years (Hanson, 2005), it starts decreasing, waning substantially after age 60. Although cumulative recidivism rates increase with time, the chances that an offender will recidivate decrease the longer the offender remains offence-free in the community.

The vast literature in psychology, psychiatry and medicine has addressed the accuracy with which low base rate behaviours (such as sexual violence) can be predicted or diagnosed from individual assessments (Swets *et al.*, 2000). For a low base rate such as sex reoffending, even when using the most accurate assessment instruments, the rate of false positives usually exceeds the rate of true positives. This information is particularly relevant to reduce biases: the fact that the individual fits the intuitive or stereotypical profile of a person who would commit a sex offence should not thereby *postdict* (predict after the fact) that the person *did* (*prejudicial impact*) or *will* (*risk assessment impact*) commit that crime.

Davis and Follette (2002) argued that specific assessments are no more than a response to *intuitive profiling,* i.e. matching of a sex offender's characteristics or behaviours to formal profiles of the typical perpetrator of the crime in question. Intuitive profiling 'is presented [. . .] with the assumption that such evidence is *probative* (providing useful diagnostic information) of the likelihood of either past (such as a crime) or future (such as future violence) behavior' (p. 134). The term *probative* refers to evidence which, if true, leads to a conclusion more likely than if the evidence were false.

Davis and Follette (2002) continued emphasising that the degree of error of this assumption varies predictably with the base rates within the population of both the behaviour and the profiling characteristic (the pre- or post- 'dictor' variable) in question. Specifically related to sex offending, the greater the discrepancy between the base rate of the predictor variable (the risk profiling characteristic) and the sex offending, the greater the likelihood of false positives (i.e. that the predicted person will not relapse into another sex offence). Intuitive profiling is dependent on the base rates of the predictors (profiling characteristics and behaviours) and the criterion (material fact or sex offence). In the former instance, a single profiling predictor is more probative as its base rate becomes lower; in the latter instance, a predictor is more probative as the base rate of the criterion (material fact or sex offence) becomes higher (Davis & Follette, 2002, 148).

The base rate is the proportion of a group of sex offenders who will reoffend within a specified temporal period that follows any custodial conviction. The assumption that, while in detention, sex offenders are not able to reoffend, is certainly not always correct, and yet it represents a clear-cut point from where to start assessing the base rate of sexual violence. The US Department of Justice reported that the sexual recidivism rate, measured by arrests for a new sex crime, was 5.3 per cent over a three-year period (Langan et al., 2003). The proportion of those reconvicted for another sex offence in England and Wales was relatively low: less than 10 per cent, even amongst those who could be followed up for six years (Hood et al., 2002).

When talking about the base rate two problems emerge. The first is related to what Koehler (1996, 1) said: 'the ambiguous, unreliable, and unstable base rates of the real world'. The second highlights the variance in base rates of a specific population, i.e. sex offenders. For instance, Barbaree (1997) reported that base rates for adult sex offenders generally range from 10 to 40 per cent. This range variance leads to another complication that emerges when the attention is focused on different types of sex offenders. Some base rates may be even lower than 10 per cent when studying specific types of sex offenders, i.e. exclusive incest offenders or elderly offenders. Other base rates may be higher than 40 per cent, when studying persistent sex offenders involved in many offences spanning many years.

Hanson and colleagues (2003) carried out one of the major meta-analyses on this topic and showed that recidivism base rates for sex offenders decline with time, as happens with many other types of violent crime. Overall, the observed rates of recidivism in the studies meta-analysed were between 10 and 15 per cent after five years; 20 per cent after ten years; and between 25 and 40 per cent after 20 years, which suggested that the longer a sex offender has gone straight, the lower the likelihood that they will reoffend. However, how to interpret these results is difficult, not least because many sexual offences never appear in official records.

What might be plausible to assume in statistical terms might also be so in criminological evidence. The *hazard rate*, that is the theoretical measure of the risk of occurrence of an event (e.g. sexual violence) at a point in time, suggests that the probability of, for instance, sexual offending by those who have not yet reoffended, may shed some more light on the extent of reoffending risk posed by sex offenders. In a study conducted by Howard (2011), patterns of reoffending were studied in terms of their hazards, i.e. the chances of reoffending for a given quarter were the probability of reoffending in that quarter, given that reoffending had not occurred in an earlier quarter. Survival analysis was used to trace proven reoffending rates in successive quarters of the follow-up, based on the date when re-offences were committed. A sample of *Offender Assessment System* (OASys) assessments, completed at the start of community supervision dating from January 2002 to March 2007, were divided into six groups on the basis of their criminal history and OGP and OVP scores:[2] sexual offenders, low-risk, non-violent specialists, violent specialists, versatile high-risk, and versatile. Hazards were calculated for different types of reoffending, and were highest in the first few months following sentence or discharge, and some types of reoffending were more persistent than others. As expected, the findings showed that *low-risk offenders* had the lowest likelihood of all groups of violent and non-violent reoffending. *Non-violent specialists* were less likely than the high-risk versatile group to commit violent re-offences. *Violent specialists* were consistently more likely to commit violent than non-violent re-offences, though their absolute level of violent reoffending was only around two-thirds that of versatile offenders and two-fifths that of high-risk versatile offenders. The *high-risk versatile offenders* had very large hazards of both violent and non-violent reoffending and were offenders who pose a risk that was both immediate and enduring. *Versatile offenders* had the second-highest violent re-offence risk. *Sexual offenders*, who were older than offenders in all other groups and in 99 per cent of cases were males, had low but non-negligible hazards of violent and non-violent reoffending, which however remained greater than the hazard of sexual or compliance[3] reoffending. It is interesting to note that sexual reoffending hazards were moderately persistent but, on the four-year timescale available in this research, were not exceptionally persistent compared with other offences (Howard, 2011). These results tie in with other studies.

A series of empirical studies has examined the continuation of reoffending among juvenile sex offenders in adulthood (Caldwell, 2010; McCann & Lussier, 2008). Research findings suggest that juvenile offenders, when they reoffend, they do so more likely during adolescence and primarily for non-sex crimes (Burke et al., 2002). Moreover, other investigations (Caldwell, 2002) point to the fact that those juveniles who reoffend sexually in adolescence constitute only a small proportion of them. Empirical studies indicate that these juveniles who persist in reoffending sexually until adulthood represent a minor part (5–10 per cent) (Zimring, 2004) and, as with adult sex offenders, their likelihood of reoffending increases with a longer time of follow-ups (Lussier et al., 2010).

Hargreaves and Francis (2014) examined the long-term sexual recidivism risk of juvenile sex offenders in England and Wales, and compared their risk to the risk posed by a first-time sexual offence committed by non-convicted juveniles. In their study the England and Wales Offenders Index was used to extract birth cohort data, while life table methods were used to estimate cumulative recidivism risk. Moreover, discrete time hazard models were used to compare hazard functions. Their findings showed that, after a five-year-period, 7 per cent of juvenile sexual offenders, who committed their first sex crime before age 21, were reconvicted of another sexual offence; at the end of a 35-year follow-up, 13 per cent of sex offenders had a sexual reconviction. The reconviction hazard analysis indicated that the hazard of juvenile sexual offenders converged with the hazard of first sexual conviction of a non-convicted comparison group after 17 years. These findings have interesting implications for the sex offender register, which allows further monitoring of sexual offenders and protection of the public. The reconviction hazard analysis by Hargreaves and Francis (2014) suggested that the sexual reoffend risk in juvenile sex offenders became so low that it was similar to the risk of a first sexual offence by someone with no convictions.

However, what emerges as significant from these studies is that most juveniles who are involved in sex crimes do not become adult sex offenders (Lussier et al., 2015).

Hanson and Morton-Bourgon (2005) suggested that most sex offenders were more likely to recidivate with a non-sex offence than with a sex offence. Over 15 years, 24 per cent of known adult male sex offenders were rearrested for another sex crime, with the subgroup of child molesters, with boys as victims, sexually reoffending most frequently: 35 per cent over 15 years (Harris & Hanson, 2004).

In the prospective longitudinal Cambridge Study of Delinquent Development, sex offending was rare, with less than 3 per cent of males being convicted for sex offences to age 50 (Piquero et al., 2012). Further, there was no continuity in sex offending from the juvenile to adult years and very few recidivists were sex offenders.

Looking at data on criminal careers, it emerged that sex offenders were proportionately more likely than other criminals to commit another sex crime, even though the vast majority of new sex crimes were not committed by registered sex offenders (Langan et al., 2003).

In a study conducted by Hanson and colleagues (2003) sex offenders with an adult victim and child molesters were similar in their sexual recidivism rates. However, in line with meta-analysed findings from Hanson and Bussière (1998), rapists had higher recidivism rates than child molesters for other nonsexual violent offences. Among child molesters, those who were more likely to recidivate sexually were those who offended against unrelated girls, followed by those who offended against unrelated boys, and incest offenders.

Frequent sex offenders were not only more likely to commit more offences but also more likely to be detected and convicted. It is then plausible to assume that if a sex offender commits many offences then the recorded rates of offending should be close to the actual rates: this depends on the probability of detection being close to 100 per cent. On the other hand, if a typical sex offender commits only a few offences (e.g. five or fewer), then the observed recidivism rates would be expected to underestimate the actual rates given the high rate of undetected sex offences. There is an agreement among experts on the fact that recorded rates represent underestimates. To specify the extent of underestimation is particularly difficult. Hanson and colleagues (2003) advocate that, if the estimates of actual sexual recidivism are, over a 20-year period, at least 10–15 per cent higher than the recorded recidivism, then it is likely that the actual sexual recidivism may lie between 35 and 55 per cent. Their calculation is based on the assumption that 60 per cent or fewer of sex offenders commit five (or fewer) new offences over a period of 20 years, and that the probability of detection for each offence is 15 per cent.

Harris and colleagues (2011) examined the offending records of a sample of sex offenders referred for civil commitment, whose criminal careers were already observed in a previous study (Harris et al., 2009). Their findings suggested that committed offenders were more likely than other offenders to reoffend and to reoffend sexually. Rapists were more likely than child molesters to reoffend and to reoffend violently, but no difference was found between different types of offenders on sexual recidivism. Child molesters were more likely than rapists to specialise in sex offences after release. Versatile offenders were more prolific than specialist offenders, and were more likely to reoffend and to reoffend violently, but the groups did not differ in their likelihood of sexual recidivism. Hanson and Bussière (1998) reviewed 61 follow-up studies and found that the strongest predictor of sexual recidivism was a compiled measure of sexual deviancy, with sexual interest in children, as measured by phallometric assessment, as the strongest independent predictor. A criminal life style and antisocial personality, which are significant criminogenic needs, were better predictors of violent and general recidivism than of sexual recidivism. The failure to complete treatment was a moderate predictor of sexual recidivism, while psychological problems (e.g. self-esteem, anxiety) and psychological maladjustment (e.g. denial, lack of remorse, lack of victim empathy, low motivation for treatment and negative mood) had little or no relationship with recidivism.

Hanson and Morton-Bourgon (2005) pointed out that the same major recidivism predictors were found for adolescent sex offenders as for adult sexual offenders. For adolescent sex offenders, sexual recidivism was predicted by sexual deviance[4] and an antisocial orientation.[5] An antisocial orientation also predicted violent nonsexual recidivism,[6] any violent recidivism[7] and any recidivism[8] among adolescent sex offenders. Davis and Follette (2002) pointed out that 'base rates representing averages across an entire population [. . .] may seriously misestimate the likelihood of violence' (p. 149). This does not mean that aggregate base rates from meta-analyses convey nothing. Aggregate base rates of 13 or 14 per cent tell us that, as a group, the known sexual recidivism rates of sexual offenders are quite low. Given these base rates, it is certainly more accurate to predict that no one will reoffend sexually, than to try to predict who specifically will reoffend (Quinsey et al., 1995), but despite its accuracy, this prediction is not of any use whatsoever.

Although many offences are not discovered, and many offenders are never convicted, it is likely that these findings identify important predictors of sex offending recidivism, not least because these findings come from sufficiently large and diversified samples. However, meta-analyses can be criticised because putting together the diverse methods of data collection, data calculation and data reporting in 61 (Hanson & Bussière, 1998) or 82 (Hanson & Morton-Bourgon, 2005) separate studies inevitably results in a high degree of methodological variability (Prentky et al., 1997). Thus, further research is needed to continue to monitor recidivism rates, and to attempt to resolve the problem that many sex offenders do not appear in official records, so that the extent to which the undetected offences influence the observed recidivism rates is still a matter of debate (Hanson et al., 2003, 156).

Age and sex offending

How does the inevitable process of ageing influence sex offending?

This is a question that has kept researchers busy for decades, and the responses to it play a crucial role in how older sex offenders are assessed, treated, and considered amenable not only to treatment but to change. The *age-crime curve* unveils some noteworthy aspects. The age-crime curve is one of the *most consistent* findings in criminology, so that Goring (1913) referred to it as a 'law of nature', following what Quételet (1831/1984) presented as a statistically derived creature: the 'average individual', that is the product of systematic, accurate and ample observations. The age-crime curve is also one of the *most contended* and least understood areas in developmental criminology (Farrington, 1986a, 2005a; Shulman et al., 2013a, b).

The age-crime curve consistently shows that offending is most prevalent during adolescence, reaching its peak between ages 16 to 20, and then decreases with age, in adulthood. Gottfredson and Hirschi (1990), advancing what is defined as the *inexplicability hypothesis* (Sweeten et al., 2013), argued that age has a direct effect on crime, and cannot be accounted for by any variable or combination of variables that are provided by criminological and psychological sciences. For them the similarity of the age-crime distribution was remarkable, virtually identical, through time, across places and among nationalities (see also Hirsch & Gottfredson, 1983). What has emerged as significant is that the age-crime curve seems to remain the same at all ages (the *non-interactive hypothesis*) and stays constant across different time periods, amongst different populations and even between sexes (the *invariance hypothesis*).

The age-crime curve is a contentious topic when the offending distribution over time and across age groups is not quite as straightforward as it seems. Brown and Males (2011) claimed that the age-crime curve is illusory, not least because it underscores the danger of drawing inferences about individual behaviour from analysis of aggregate data.

However, the aggregate age-crime curve could in fact be the sum of different trajectories of offending (Farrington, 2003; Piquero et al., 2010).

Despite the apparent similarities, this well-known curve actually varies extensively in some specific aspects of criminal careers (McVie, 2005): the slope may be more to the left or right depending on the age of onset (i.e. early vs. late); the peak of the distribution may be more or less sharp depending on the type of data (i.e. official vs. self-report); the peak age may be higher or lower depending on types of crimes (e.g. theft vs. burglary vs. violence).

Criminal career studies have explored the relationship between age and crime, and completed the analysis by taking into account that antisocial onset emerges before the age of criminal responsibility and before the police can record the behaviour as an offence. This leads to the fact that much of the age-crime curve is made up by official events, so that the decline in antisocial and criminal behaviour after age 20 may be balanced by a significant rise in antisocial behaviour early in life, sometimes as early as age 7 (Loeber et al., 1989; Moffitt, 1993; West & Farrington, 1973), which is not shown in official records of offending. Moreover, the emergence of a *delayed criminal career*, that is, a criminal onset at age 21 and later, makes it conceptually and methodologically unsustainable to aggregate everyone aged 21 and over into one group of adult offenders (Zara & Farrington, 2010).

There may also be some variation in the peak of the distribution depending both on whether self-reported delinquency data are available, and on the seriousness of crimes involved. For instance, the highest risk lies in a subgroup of offenders whose violent crime seems to continue into old age but who represent a very small percentage of the whole criminal population; these offenders correspond to what Moffitt (1993, 2006) calls *life-course persistent offenders* or what Wolfgang and colleagues (1987) define as *chronic offenders* (see Chapter 2).

Criminological descriptions tend to present the age-crime curve as a count of the total number of offences committed within a specific period. McVie (2005) indicates that it may also be presented in terms of the prevalence of offending, which is a count of the number of people within the population who have offended (or been cautioned or convicted). The shape of these two curves tends to be approximately similar. The aggregate age-crime curve combines prevalence and frequency of offending.

Blumstein *et al.* (1988b) revealed that the distinction between participation or prevalence (i.e. the distinction between those who engage in crime and those who do not), and frequency, is crucial. They claim that the decline in the aggregate offending rate after a teenage peak does not necessarily lead to a decline in the offending frequency (λ). Piquero and colleagues (2007) suggest that it is possible that the decline in the aggregate age-crime curve could be entirely attributable to the termination of criminal careers and that the average value of λ could stay constant (or increase or decrease) with age for those offenders who continue to be active after that peak. This ultimately, of course, is an empirical question in so far as participation in offending, and not frequency, is the key dimension that varies with age (Blumstein *et al.*, 1988a).

While cross-sectional studies can only study between-subject differences, longitudinal studies allow for the analysis of both between- and within-subject changes, and it is this latter type of analysis that frames the criminal career focus on participation, frequency and termination (Piquero *et al.*, 2007). Thus the criminal career paradigm focuses not only on participation, but also highlights the significance of the frequency of active offenders, which reflects an interest in systematic differences in offending frequencies and in changes in offending frequency during active criminal careers.

Farrington (1986b), in the CSDD, found that the peak number of convictions was primarily affected by prevalence rather than frequency. Regarding what Farrington (2005b) defines as *long-term antisocial potential*, longitudinal data support the assumption that people can be ordered on a continuum from low to high, with the distribution of antisocial potential in the population at any age being highly skewed. A few people have relatively high levels of antisocial potential, and are more likely to commit many different types of antisocial acts, including different types of offences. Thus, offending behaviour seems to be versatile rather than specialised. While the relative ordering of people on antisocial potential (long-term between-individual variation) tends to be consistent over time, absolute levels of antisocial potential vary with age, peaking in the teenage years, because of changes within individuals in those risk factors that influence long-term antisocial potential.

This ordering of people along the age-crime curve seems to also follow a similar trend when looking at dangerous, high-risk or chronic offenders. Research findings show that even persistent and chronic offenders reduce their offending participation and frequency with age. A sort of criminal *burnout process* (Coid, 2003) seems to influence the trend of the most active and prolific criminal career offenders. This is certainly not the same as talking about desistance from crime, which implies a choice of pursuing a path free from any crime. It is more in line with what Farrington (1997, 2005a) and Walters (1990) describe as a reduction in criminal involvement during the maturity stage of life. Many individuals may continue to remain on the fringes of society, behaving irresponsibly, even though their conduct is no longer so explicitly criminal.

This is why Laws and Ward (2011, 93) consider that there is no reason to suppose that the classical age-crime curve does not apply to sex offenders. Apart from some sex offenders who have some special criminogenic needs and suffer from paraphilias, the majority of sex offenders follow an age-crime trend similar to other offenders, except without a particular concentration of sex crimes in any particular temporal stage. Their involvement in sex crimes mostly occurs along the whole criminal career, with a subsequent decrease in offending according to the decline in the general offending frequency and participation (see also Francis *et al.*, 2015).

The key point is to understand how it could be possible to activate a process of criminal desistance in sex offenders and, if this is feasible, how it could be encouraged as early as possible. There are many differentiated mechanisms and promotive processes for flattening the crime peak in adolescence or for accelerating the decline in crime in adulthood. As Sweeten and colleagues (2013) advocate, this is quite a promising criminological story, 'as one need not simply wait for age to have its effect, but can pursue strategies to accelerate desistance from crime' (p. 935). The remainder of this chapter will explore these aspects.

Ageing out from sex offending

Findings across criminal career research (Blumstein *et al.*, 1986; Farrington, 2003; Sampson & Laub, 2003), and especially on sexual offending (Hanson, 2006; Långström & Hanson, 2006), show that age is a significant predictor of recidivism. Risk assessment instruments include age in the list of items to predict sexual violent recidivism among sex offenders. Little is known about whether or how much the risk of reoffending diminishes because of ageing. The main limitations of these risk instruments is that they are based on unchangeable factors and do not adjust the risk for older offenders with other factors that influence change (Barbaree & Blanchard, 2008). Rice and Harris (2014) conducted two studies to explore whether, to what extent and how age is related to sexual recidivism. First, using three non-overlapping samples of violent offenders, they examined the sexual and violent recidivism of 113 sex offenders who were over age 50 on release. The age at first offence (or having been arrested under age 16), the age at the index offence and the age at release contributed incremental validity in the prediction of violent recidivism to scores on a brief static actuarial tool (Quinsey et al., 1995). The results obtained suggest that almost all of the statistical effects of age on violent recidivism were related to age at first offence, with very little attributable to the passage of time since that first offence and, hence, to age at release. The three age variables exhibited, however, considerable collinearity. Rice and Harris (2014) reached the conclusion in their studies that age at release and the amount an offender has aged are likely to be the better indexes of the dynamic effects of ageing than age at the time of the offence. These results suggest that the dynamic effects of ageing are quite small in comparison with the static effects of an enduring antisocial potential. However, more studies are necessary to explore further the impact of changes in age and sexual recidivism.

In their second study (Rice & Harris, 2014), using the same three samples combined, found violent-offence-free years after release was related to violent recidivism, measured with the actuarial instrument Violence Risk Appraisal Guide (VRAG). The age at release and the passage of time did not significantly and independently contribute to the lowering of VRAG recidivism risk estimates based on extended periods of violent-offence-free behaviour while at risk to reoffend. This was so as long as the offender was not in the three highest VRAG categories. The adjustment, however, was based on the measured association among VRAG scores, time spent offence-free and violent recidivism. Hence, the adjusting correction factor was as actuarial as was the original VRAG, and not a clinical adjustment.

A study conducted by Hanson (2005) on older sexual offenders from eight samples ($n = 3,425$) drawn from Canada, the United States, and the United Kingdom, and followed up after prison release for an average of seven 7 years, indicated that, when controlling for Static-99 scores (Hanson & Thornton, 2000), the average recidivism rates steadily declined with age: from 14.8 per cent for offenders under age 40 to 8.8 per cent for offenders in their forties, to 7.5 per cent for offenders in their fifties, and to 2 per cent for offenders aged 60 or older. As Prentky and colleagues (2006) pointed out, referring to the above study, among offenders aged 60 or older, sexual recidivism rates were low even for those who scored within the moderate-high range and the high range on the Static-99.

Another approach in investigating the likelihood of sexual reoffending is to adjust recidivism risk downwards after age 40. Hazard rates (or escape rates) reflect the decline in recidivism rates as a proportion of the recidivism rate in Year x, in Year x + 1, etc. According to Duerden (2009), a hazard is the rate at which events happen, for those who have not yet reoffended. The probability of an event happening in an interval of time (e.g. one year) is the length of the time interval multiplied by the hazard. If we assume a linear decrease in the recidivism rate after age 40, adjustments to actuarially derived risk could be made depending on two additional factors: the number of years the individual's age at release exceeds 40 and the rate of the decline in recidivism rates per year. Barbaree and colleagues (2003) reported a hazard rate of .95 when controlling for actuarial risk. Hanson (2005) and Thornton (2006) reported hazard rates of .98 when controlling for risk using the Static-99 and the number of previous offences. Therefore, the most conservative adjustment would use a hazard rate of .98, indicating a reduction in the recidivism risk of approximately 2 per cent per year after age 40.

Thornton (2006) examined the relationship between the age on release and sexual recidivism in a sample of 752 male sexual offender detainees followed up for ten years. Sexual offenders released at a younger age were more involved in general crimes, while those released at an older age tended to be sexual specialists. When two aspects of their criminal career (sexual deviance and general criminality) were controlled, the age on release was found to make a significant contribution to the prediction of a sexual reconviction. Overall, the odds of being sexually reconvicted declined by about 0.02 with each year of increasing age. It could be assumed then that the likelihood of being reconvicted for a new sexual offence decreases by 2 per cent per year. Those offenders who were convicted for sexual offences on at least two prior occasions showed a high sexual recidivism rate when released between the ages of 18 and 24 (80 per cent). For those aged between 25 and 59 their sexual reconviction rate was consistently just under 50 per cent regardless of age. For the small group who were aged 60 plus no further sexual reconvictions were found.

Studies show that the prior history of offending appears to be the best predictor of sexual recidivism, in so far as the more sex crimes an offender has committed, the more likely the offender will continue to offend (Berliner et al., 1995; Coxe & Holmes, 2009; Dempster & Hart, 2002; Harris & Hanson, 2004).

Studies on sex recidivism look only at conviction records, to assess whether or not offenders are rearrested or reconvicted for new sex offences. For instance, in a study by Langan et al. (2003), which involved 9,691 convicted sex offenders, 71.5 per cent of them had only one reconviction. The underestimation of sex offence occurrences which lead to an official record within a specific and limited time period after release directly influences recidivism data. Patterson and Campbell (2010) suggest that this underestimation is particularly likely among rapists, because rape is one of the most underreported crimes, which results in a low rate of subsequent arrests and convictions. While research studies have found that a younger age at the time of release predicts a higher likelihood of reoffending (Barbaree et al., 2009; Dickey et al., 2002), they also show that rapists are usually younger than child molesters when released, while incest-only offenders are older and the least likely to reoffend after an initial arrest (Freeman, 2007; Hanson, 2002). This finding, however interesting, should be interpreted in combination with other evidence. Studies show that rapists are more likely to exhibit more general antisocial features (Robertiello & Terry, 2007), including some psychopathic traits (Serin et al., 2001), so that when they are rearrested it is more likely that the charge would be for a violent rather than a sexual offence.

Barbaree and colleagues (2009) reported some counterintuitive findings on antisocial measures as predictors of recidivism. While all reoffending decreases as a person ages, and this may be more so for those crimes that require physical strength, energy, sexual arousal and duress, other offensive behaviours may actually increase with age. An example could be offenders with sexual paraphilias, who are more likely than antisocial rapists to reoffend as they age. As Laws and Ward (2011) openly worded it, to reoffend sexually *an erect penis* is not necessary or required. *Age* describes the passage of time, which does not occur in a social or psychological vacuum; it is, instead, connected to a variety of situations and combines many variables: physical vitality, emotional maturity, impulsivity, anger and self-control. These variables may have a dramatic impact on how sexual arousal and sexual needs are expressed, but they do not necessarily suppress sexual fantasies, which, on the contrary, may be reinvigorated by alternative attempts to achieve gratification. Woessner (2010) classified sexual 'fantasist' offenders as *socially and mentally unremarkable*, who usually commit their offences under extreme life stressors.

From who they are to what works with sex offenders

If it is agreed that sex offending is not only a criminal act, but also a public health problem (Robertiello & Terry, 2007) that elicits concerns primarily about how to protect victims and also about how to intervene with offenders, then understanding the mental, interpersonal, psychological and emotional characteristics of those who perpetrate sex abuse, and the extent to which deviant sexuality is entrenched in their abusive behaviour, is paramount for outlining effective measures to control this behaviour in the future and to reduce the risk.

When the focus is on both the offenders and the victims, there is a primary distinction between sex offenders: rapists and child molesters; when the focus is on the offenders the distinction is made between males and females, or between adults (with the sub-differentiation of elderly people not only as offenders but also as victims) and juveniles; when the focus is also on the setting where the abuse occurs the differentiation recognises intrafamiliar and extrafamiliar offenders; when the interest is on the offence, an interesting distinction is made between physical and cyber abuse, and also between *hands on* and *hands off* offences. Research and clinical studies offer an opportunity to delve into the psychosocial and mental reality of sex offenders. It is essential to take into account this knowledge in any treatment plan, because it can lead to more specific intervention, more appropriate assessment of the risk, and more effective supervision and management of the person. It follows that understanding the needs and criminogenic features of sex offenders serves prevention and intervention aims. Rapists and child molesters can be seen as 'similar' when they are merged into the same offence type (i.e. sex crime), but they differ substantially, not just because of the victims involved in their crimes, but in their mental, psychological, emotional and relational way of functioning in the world.

Who sex offenders are

Rapists are grouped as follows:

- *Compensatory*, who look for power reassurance (Groth, 1979), may have courtship disorder (Freund, 1990), and use force only to be able to achieve sexual gratification. With compliant victims they may also offer some sort of 'pillow talk' after the assault; they are also called *gentlemen rapists* (Robertiello & Terry, 2007).
- *Assertive*, who exert aggressiveness and control over the victims in order to restore their sense of masculinity. They tend to be opportunistic, use drugs and alcohol before the abuse, are geographically mobile and like to leave their victims in a state of shock. Because of their impulsiveness they often attack their victims without planning, and are unlikely to use weapons. Their sex abuse is recreational and the expression of a life style in which they aim for the recognition of their power by others. This type is similar to the opportunistic offenders of Knight and Prentky (1990).
- *Retaliator and power controllers*, whose abuse has the character of a pseudo-sexual act; the manifestation of anger and dominance is aimed at humiliating and degrading their victims. As Groth (1983, 165, cit. in Robertiello & Terry, 2007, 510) explained, these offenders convey the 'sexual expression of aggression rather than the aggressive expression of sexuality'. They are motivated by anger and hatred and also tend to use violence whether the victim resists or not. They are similar to the pervasively angry offenders of Knight and Prentky's (1990) typology.
- *Sadistics*, who are sexually excited by the pain and suffering that they cause to their victims. It is likely that these offenders have high psychopathy levels and do not show any sign of empathy or remorse. Their abuse is highly planned and the majority of victims are unfamiliar to them. It is likely that the abuse leads to sexual murders.
- *Vindictive rapists*, who are those who use power, control and hatred on their victims, but unlike the opportunistic or assertive rapists they do not have a criminal and impulsive life style. They could be differentiated further on the basis of their high or low level of social competence (Knight & Prentky, 1990; Robertiello & Terry, 2007).

Child molesters represent a complex offending cluster, and are grouped as follows:

- *Fixated offenders* are characterised by a persistent, continual and compulsive attraction to children. Often a diagnosis of paedophilia is reported, while in other cases these offenders manifest recurrent, intense, sexually arousing fantasies of at least six months in duration involving pre-pubescent children (American Psychiatric Association, 1999; Hall & Hall, 2007, 2009). What is specific about them is that fixated offenders are often unable to attain any degree of

psycho-sexual maturity, and are not likely to have appropriate sexual relationships, not even in adulthood (Douglas et al., 2013). They are likely to develop relationships with vulnerable children, whom they recruit and groom with the desire to get involved in a sexual relationship with them (Conte, 1991).
- *Regressed offenders* tend to emerge in adulthood, are situationally influenced and precipitated by external stressors, such as unemployment, marital problems and substance abuse. Negative affective states such as loneliness, social exclusion and isolation can, according to Schwartz (1995), undermine their self-confidence and encourage feelings of self-inadequacy. Regressed offenders tend to abuse children who are easy to access, such as their own children; the abusive behaviour is often limited to a temporary period in their life.
- *Female sex offenders* can be differentiated into teacher/lover, male coerced/male accompanied, and predisposed, depending on whether they are seeking a loving and intimate relationship, or are influenced by a partner who abuses and coerces them to act out sexual acts with children, or are inclined to abuse and seek control and power after a history of being personally victimised sexually and physically (Terry, 2006).

Even when assessing juvenile sex offenders, differentiations could be made by focusing on types of victims, and reasons for the offences, intrusiveness, criminogenic needs and psychopathological factors (O'Brien & Bera, 1986; Prentky et al., 2000; Zara, 2012).

In the light of these research findings and of pivotal studies on sex offending, the essential question is whether sex offenders could be treated, and the extent to which the effectiveness of treatment contributes to a reduction in the risk of general or sexual recidivism, or to a reduction in both types of recidivism.

What is likely to work with sex offenders?

It is important to consider that ending sex reoffending does not necessarily imply reducing offending, in so far as someone could continue committing other types of crime. The effectiveness of sexual treatment was limited by the uncertain state of scientific knowledge about the causes of deviant sexuality and the complex linkage between violence and sexual impulses (Laws & O'Donohue, 2008; Zara, 2005). Almost two decades later, the progress made on *what works* with sex offenders is tempered by the importance of moving beyond the *ipse dixit* (i.e. *it is just how it is*) factor, and paralleling intervention with scientific evidence that requires not only assessing the accuracy and integrity of treatment and rehabilitative programmes, but also needs monitoring their continuing efficacy over time.

The claim that sex offenders cannot be treated and that they will all invariably reoffend once allowed back into the community is quite widespread among the general public. However, Zara and Farrington (2014) argue that programmes specifically designed to treat sex offenders may be effective in reducing sexual recidivism. Research evidence (Hanson et al., 2009; Schmucker & Lösel, 2008) and treatment data (Lösel, 2012; Yates, 2013) suggest that appropriate treatment leads to a reduction of sexual recidivism and to an increase in the protection of victims and in the promotion of well-being.

Cognitive-behavioural approaches (Craig et al., 2008; Mann & Marshall, 2009) seem to be the most promising in so far as they are set up to move sex offenders towards a process of changing their internal (cognitive and emotive) functioning, as well as their overt behaviour, and their social adjustment to others and to life. When examining the general effect sizes of sex offending treatment it is notable that they are not particularly large, but not necessarily smaller than the treatment effect sizes obtained with other types of intervention with other types of offenders (Hood et al., 2002; Ireland et al., 2009).

A meta-analysis conducted by Hanson and colleagues (2002), which included few true randomized studies, involved a vast range of treatment programs and a total of over 9,000 sex offenders. The findings indicated that the rate of sex offending was lower for treated offenders (12.3 per cent) in comparison with untreated groups (16.8 per cent). Significantly, those studies that employed a cognitive-behavioural or systemic treatment approach had a reduction in recidivism ranging from 9.9 per cent to 17.4 per cent.

This approach consists mostly of teaching sex offenders to reorganise their attitudes towards their sexual behaviour, to develop an ability to empathise with the victims, to appreciate the consequences of their sexually abusive behaviour, even though it may not be explicitly aggressive or violent, and to learn how to control their sexual obsessiveness and their sexual needs in order to avoid further offending.

If the assumption of cognitive programmes is that the way a person thinks affects the way that the person behaves, then the aim is to increase offender's self-control over their offending patterns and to build up a set of strategies to readdress their needs. This requires a complete understanding of the antecedents of their offences, to identify the mechanisms that made them switch to sexual offending and to reframe their sexually deviant fantasies into sexual and not abusive desires.

Distorted thinking in sex offending

Research findings show that, at the basis of sex offending, there are various risk factors, of which procriminal attitudes constitute one significant set of criminogenic needs that precipitate sexual violence and promote its maintenance over time.

Distorted thinking (Andrews & Bonta, 2010a), combined with *emotional dysregulation* (Davidson et al., 2000; Loeber & Pardini, 2008), contribute to preserve an antisocial orientation, and evidence of this has also been identified in young violent offenders (Beauchaine et al., 2007; Miller et al., 2012). Distorted thinking is the difficulty in seeing or recognising that other people have mental states and independent thoughts and needs. Emotional dysregulation is the difficulty in modulating and controlling emotions in response to other people such as victims. These cognitive distortions have at their roots some maladaptive thoughts, beliefs or implicit theories that can be elicited at different points in time and in different contexts to sustain, explain, and justify violent acts thereafter (Brown, 2005).

Procriminal attitudes or distorted thoughts do not act as crime reinforcers in the same fashion for all sex offenders. A meta-analysis of 46 samples ($n = 13,782$) conducted by Helmus and colleagues (2013) explored to what extent attitudes supportive of sex offending are psychologically meaningful risk factors for assessing offenders. Findings showed that sex offending attitudes had a small, but consistent, relationship with sexual recidivism. Some differences emerged when types of offenders were compared: attitudes better predicted recidivism for child molesters than for rapists. While pro-rape and pro-child-molesting attitudes predicted recidivism for child molesters, pro-child-molesting attitudes appeared unrelated to recidivism for rapists.

Denying the offence or minimising its seriousness or its consequences can be explained differently. In some cases there is a distorted view of one's own behavioural accountability, while in other cases there is the belief that one is not completely responsible because one has been provoked or found oneself involved in a course of action started by the victim. It is possible that some sex offenders, despite admitting the sexual nature of their behaviour, do not recognise the abusive nature of it or they attribute responsibility to the victim. In some cases, the explanation lies in the idea that the victim has not really suffered any trauma or negative consequences, or even that the sexual action was performed for the good of the victim. These explanations are based on distorted and biased thinking (Gannon et al., 2007; Nunes & Jung, 2012) and often on a difficulty in deciphering the emotions of others, such as the victims (Marsh & Blair, 2008).

The understanding of people's emotions to encourage an appropriate social behaviour requires empathy. Empathy is recognised as a multidimensional process that involves a recognition and understanding of a person's subjective experience, perspective taking and a vicarious sharing of emotional states in response to another's affective cues. This results in feelings of concern or compassion or worry for this person (sympathy), although it also can lead to self-oriented preoccupations (personal distress) (Davis, 1983; Decety & Jackson, 2004; Jackson & Decety, 2004; Zara & Mosso, 2014). Furthermore, empathy does not simply imply perceiving and sharing the sufferance or joy of a person experiencing that emotional state (*affective empathy*), but it also implies the recognition and the understanding of it at a cognitive level (*cognitive empathy*): *knowing what the other person is experiencing*; at an emotional level: *feeling what the other person is feeling*. In doing so, individuals become able to tune their behaviour accordingly to what they are feeling in interacting or just observing somebody else (Jolliffe & Farrington, 2004; Zara & Mosso, 2014).

Many studies show that deficits or difficulties in empathy or some facets of it are often significant precursors of violent offending (Jolliffe & Farrington, 2004), including sex offending (Covell & Scalora, 2002; Marshall et al., 2009).

The assumption is that empathy, like other mental states or emotions, can be represented as distributed on a bell curve (Baron-Cohen, 2011), with at one extreme those who have a very low degree of empathy and at the other extreme those who have a very high empathy. Despite the central role of empathy in directing human relationships, and in modulating the emotional tone of them, empirical research on empathy in sex offenders conducted during the last three decades has yielded inconsistent findings (Geer et al., 2000; Mann et al., 2010; Marshall et al., 1995). Some studies reported lower levels of generalised empathy or of some of its components (e.g. empathic concern, perspective taking) in sex offenders compared with non-sex offenders (Lindsey et al., 2001; Lisak & Ivan, 1995; Rice et al., 1994) or their non-offending counterparts (Burke, 2001). Other studies have found no differences between sex offenders and other groups of participants (Hanson & Scott, 1995; Langevin et al., 1988), or showed empathy deficits in sex offenders only in specific situations or towards their own victims (Fernandez & Marshall, 2003; Pithers, 1999).

It is plausible to assume that sex offenders have some impairments more of the affective facet of empathy that also includes the relational dimension of emotional sharing, than of cognitive empathy, that includes perspective taking and sympathy (empathy concern), which may summarise the *knowing without caring attitude* described by Cima et al. (2010).

Barnett and Mann (2013) suggest that empathy processes can be altered by the influence of implicit theories that support offensive and violent behaviour, by theory of mind deficits and by intense emotion dysregulation. It may be that these could constitute impediments to the experience of empathy for a potential victim in a sexual offence situation. These impediments seem to differ across and within individuals, in so far as what may be an obstacle for one offender to empathise will not explain somebody else's *dis*empathic attitude during their offending (Barnett & Mann, 2013). Lack of empathy at the time of offending may differ from the lack of empathy necessary to cope with the consequences of the offending and with the experience of social accusation. It could also be that child molesters have high empathy because they need empathy to make friends with children, and lure them into their offending. Certain offences, such as sexual crimes against children, would be expected to involve a greater degree of victim contact than other offences considered 'victimless'. A greater degree of victim contact would in fact be expected to facilitate empathy by facing the immediate expression of victim emotions.

In a meta-analysis carried out by Jolliffe and Farrington (2004), a common measure of effect size (the standardized mean difference) in 35 studies, 21 of cognitive empathy and 14 of affective empathy, was calculated. It was found that cognitive empathy had a stronger negative relationship with offending than had affective empathy. The relationship between low empathy and offending was relatively strong for violent offenders, but relatively weak for sex offenders. An important finding of their meta-analysis was that the empathy differences between offenders and non-offenders disappeared when intelligence and SES was controlled for in the non-offending and offending populations. Moreover, Jolliffe and Farrington (2004) specifically identified studies that used sex offenders exclusively as the offending group, or where sex offenders were separable from other offenders. A subset of 18 studies covering 1,752 participants, with a mean number of 52 offenders and

45 non-offenders per study were gathered. Contrary to expectations, low empathy was more strongly related to mixed offending than to sex offending. When the mean effect size of these 18 studies was compared to that of the remaining 19, a significant between-groups difference was found (Q between groups = 4.33, P < .04). However, it was the mixed offender group that demonstrated the higher mean effect size at −0.31 (P < .0001) compared to −0.18 (P < .0005) for sex offenders. This result shows that the disparity in empathy between mixed offenders and controls was greater than between sex offenders and controls. The suggestion that sex offenders may have particular deficits in concordant emotional responses (affective empathy) compared to other types of offenders was not supported.

Empathy in sex offenders needs further investigation, and interventions that target it require a different focus depending on which specific dimensions of empathy are addressed (e.g. perspective taking or emotional recognition or compassion) and, also, on what types of offenders and offending are investigated.

Offenders who perform violent and sex crimes seem to lack a recognition and an understanding of other people's emotions, especially when these are negative ones, and also seem to have some difficulties in attributing social meanings to other people's emotions, which is what conveys direction to relationships. For instance, if a social partner shows fear or surprise as a reaction to what another person is doing, it is likely that one's behaviour needs to be modified both in kind and degree in order to take into account the other person's emotional state.

Studies on emotions provide a comprehensive understanding of how individuals behave in the way they do, and of how their actions are always conditioned and directed by their emotions. Research findings (Hudson et al., 1993) show that sex offenders might be less accurate than controls or non-sex offenders in recognising the emotional states of others. In Hudson and colleagues' study (1993) sexually aggressive men (child molesters and rapists) were less accurate than violent non-sex offenders in recognising emotional expressions, with confusion between fear and surprise on the one hand, and disgust and anger on the other hand. Confusion between fear and surprise has been hypothesised to cause sex offenders to have difficulties in recognising distress in others (Adolphs, 2006a; Phillips et al., 2004).

Research findings by Gery and colleagues (2009) support the view that sex offenders might have impairments in the decoding of some emotional cues conveyed by the conspecifics' face (relating to the same species), which could have an impact on affective empathy. Furthermore, a recent study on emotional recognition in a sample of Scottish offenders (Robinson et al., 2012) suggests that sex offenders showed a 'relative' deficit in the emotion of *surprise*, and some superiority in recognising *sadness*; this result differs from the 'typical' antisocial pattern. The findings also demonstrate that all offenders, in comparison with age, sex and IQ-matched controls, displayed some impairments in recognising sadness, anger, disgust and fear. In addition, within the group of convicted prisoners, a deficit in fear recognition was associated with a history of previous prison sentences. It is interesting that deficits in fear recognition have been associated, in particular, with antisociality, especially violent behaviour, and that accurate recognition of fearful faces has been demonstrated experimentally to predict prosocial behaviour (Marsh et al., 2007).

While these distortions are considered by some researchers to be causally linked to offending (Abel et al., 1984), others see them as *post-hoc* rationalisations that serve to diminish responsibility and protect the offender's sense of self-worth (Anderson & Dodgson, 2002). As Blumenthal and colleagues (1999) suggested, the question of whether these dysfunctions are aetiological or consequential still remains unanswered. Nevertheless, treatment research suggests that reducing cognitive and emotional distortions is the primary positive outcome in preventive treatment (Ware & Mann, 2012), in therapeutic interventions, and it may provide an indicator of the risk of recidivism (Hanson & Morton-Bourgon, 2005).

The psychological dimension of denial in sex offending

Cognitive and emotional deficits are present in different degrees in sex offenders. Sex offenders vary in their level of empathy and of denial or vary in the way they hold distorted beliefs about their sexual needs and the victims' consent to sexual interactions. Much evidence (Barbaree, 1991; Jung & Daniels, 2012; Schneider & Wright, 2004) points to denial as a complex, multifaceted process involving many forms or types, and of various degrees, with each type running on a continuous dimension from *full admission* to *complete denial*. There may be the case of an offender who admits the sexual abuse against the victim but who also claims that the victim was not harmed and has in fact benefited from the experience.

Definitions of denial vary depending on whether it is operationalised as a *dichotomous* or as a *dimensional* variable, in which various levels of minimisation and of responsibility are also included (Barbaree, 1991): denial of the offence, denial of responsibility, denial of intent, extent or planning, thinking errors, not attributing responsibility, externalising blame and refusing to recognise the presence and/or the persistence of a sexual problem (Schneider & Wright, 2004).

Knight and Thornton (2007) showed some diverging trends between the acceptance of responsibility and recidivism. When rapists took no responsibility, and manifested extreme levels of denial and minimisation, there was a higher rate of sexual recidivism. The admission of their sex offence could represent for these sex offenders high emotional, social and cognitive pain and would not be worth the gain (e.g. avoiding another conviction). For child molesters the effect was the opposite: the more responsibility they took, the higher their level of recidivism. When extreme denial and minimisation were clearly present, their level of sexual recidivism was low. The admission of their sex offences may represent for child molesters the overcoming of two taboos: the incest taboo, and the social disgracefulness and self-humiliation taboo. Denying the abuse or minimising the effects of its consequences may act as a moral buffer against reoffending: it shows that the offender recognises the negative social value of the act (*external pressure*) or has internal ethics (*internal pressure*), even though there is no admission.

The assumption that denial in all its forms (from complete refutation of the fact to minimisation of the consequences on the victims) exacerbates the risk of recidivism has been challenged in many studies. Denial is indirectly associated with sexual recidivism in so far as it is a factor of significance in how to maximise the effectiveness of individualised sex offending treatment.

Clinical and forensic knowledge has prejudiced the practice of assessing the risk of sex offending recidivism to the extent that sex offenders who deny their offences and responsibility are deemed not compliant or not amenable to change. Even though some treatment programmes accept sex offenders who exhibit some forms of denial, when they persist in their denial offenders are asked to leave (Brown, 2005). This perspective seems to be paradoxical: sex offenders are expected to be out of denial before entering treatment, which seems similar to requiring patients 'to (at least partially) cure themselves before they can receive treatment' (Schneider & Wright, 2004, 7).

The association of denial and the risk of recidivism is considered by Beech and Fisher (2002) a *logical fallacy*: in their study fixated paedophiles, who were at high risk of reoffending, were also quite open and willing to speak about their offending, reporting a low level of denial and minimisation. Differences were found when comparing them to incest offenders, who were quite high on denial, but had a low risk of recidivism.

Recent studies have also explored the extent to which denial interacts with the risk level. Harkins et al. (2010) examined denial, motivation and risk in a sample of 180 offenders and observed an opposite pattern between high- and low-risk offenders. High-risk offenders in absolute denial reoffended at a lower rate than their admitting peers. However low-risk offenders in absolute denial reoffended more, even though the results were not statistically significant. Nunes and colleagues (2007) found that sex offenders who admitted their offences, and those who denied their offences, reoffended sexually at the same rate (10–15 per cent after five years). Denial was associated with higher rates of sexual recidivism for low-risk incest offenders, while lower rates of sexual recidivism were found for high-risk sex offenders. Denial was associated with higher rates of sexual recidivism for familial sex offenders, while no consistent relationship emerged between denial and recidivism for non-familial offenders.

Langton and colleagues (2008) followed up on a group of 436 sex offenders to examine the effect of denial and minimisation upon recidivism, while controlling for psychopathic traits, sex offender type, failure to complete specialised treatment and the actuarial risk of sexual reoffending. When dichotomous denial and minimisation were present they failed to predict sexual recidivism in the full sample and in the subsets of distinct types of sex offenders. For a subset of 102 sex offenders who only participated in an initial treatment, the interaction between actuarial risk and scores on a continuous measure of minimisation predicted sexual recidivism in 17.8 per cent of cases. These results should be read with caution, as suggested by the researchers, because the high risk was measured by other variables (e.g. psychopathy, treatment failure) that may have moderated the association.

Jung and Nunes (2012) explored the extent to which denial was related to treatment perceptions among sex offenders. Their findings showed that most aspects of denial and minimisation were significantly correlated with treatment perceptions: greater denial was associated with greater treatment rejection and less treatment readiness.

'Denial is not simply lying, but a defense mechanism fueled by shame, guilt, threat to self-esteem, cognitive dissonance, and fear of consequences' (Levenson, 2011, 348). These defensive functions seem to contribute to the *syndrome of the rear-view mirror* (Zara, 2005), which binds the individual's cognitions and emotions to the past, so that a new self-appraisal would be retrospective, and a complete self-vision would be impaired. It follows that denial should become a central target of any sex offender treatment.

It is not sufficient to offer just any cognitive-behavioural programmes to any group of offenders who manifest cognitive deficits, denial responses or relational and sexual incompetence. The design and delivery of the treatment play a crucial role in its effectiveness. As Andrews (2006) stated, the implementation of effective interventions and human services is not just a matter of selecting the best evidence-based programme off the shelf. Even well researched and *blueprint* programmes may fail to achieve the expected and desired results if the above aspects are not considered. For treatments to be effective in reducing recidivism they have also to be clinically relevant, i.e. 'to maintain respect for and attention to diversity in both people and programming' (Andrews *et al.*, 1990a, 20). The clinical nature of individualised intervention includes the importance of efforts designed for readiness to change (Zara, 2010a), to assess the psychological and individual dimension of risk factors (Hart *et al.*, 2007), to bolster motivation (Marshall *et al.*, 2001) and to prepare them for initiating treatment (Theodosi & McMurran, 2006). It may be that society will benefit more from offenders who stop abusing victims, even if the process of admitting and taking responsibility for their offences will only follow behavioural change, rather than anticipating it.

The assessment and treatment of sex offenders should include addressing risk levels, responding to the type of needs and adhering to responsivity. Thus, every effort should be made to offer treatment to higher risk sex offenders exhibiting high levels of denial and minimisation. Such sex offenders also require more intense efforts to engage them in treatment, in so far as various reviews show that treated offenders are likely to have a decrease in their recidivism rate in comparison with controls (Lösel & Schmucker, 2005).

Interventions designed to evaluate rather than eliminate denial could be effective because they can provide specific knowledge about which psychological dimensions are relevant for which types of sex offenders (Andrews & Bonta, 2010a) and at which stage of their criminal careers. If an acceptance of denial in sex offenders is seen as a *treatment need*, then treatment will not only be organised in *responsive terms*, but will be more effective. If denial is assessed as a 'failure to accept responsibility for their offenses' (ATSA, 2001, 63), then treatment will be based on the judgement of an ineptitude, and it is likely to fail.

It is not just a matter of repairing the broken things in life or fixing the damage, but also building positive perspectives, amplifying and nurturing them, and making change possible and conceivable. Being a sex offender does not make one an eternal offender, just as being at high risk does not mean being at high risk forever (Hanson et al., 2014). It is a fundamental challenge for researchers to keep on working for improving risk assessment instruments to use for evaluating the criminogenic needs of sex offenders. It is also an ethical responsibility for clinicians to use such specialised instruments in their practice. It is a duty of the criminal justice system to recognise that the use of risk assessment is done to prevent further violence from occurring and more individuals from becoming victims. It is a goal of researchers to keep on studying the criminal careers of sex offenders because it will benefit prevention efforts by providing explanations for the link between sexual and nonsexual offending, and for understanding whether sexual and nonsexual abusive behaviours spring from a common set of risk factors and criminogenic needs (Blokland & Lussier, 2015).

The importance of a multifactorial approach to the explanation of sex offending over and above any single-factor model becomes even more relevant when longitudinal research findings highlight the different impacts of childhood risk factors upon adolescent-onset and adult-onset of sex offending (Lussier et al., 2015).

As discussed previously, scientific evidence is quite strong in emphasising the importance of specific and individualised assessment and intervention (see Chapter 4), especially for those offenders who have criminogenic needs that affect their social functioning (see Chapter 7) and who may also suffer from a personality disorder such as psychopathy, that increases the risk for antisociality (see Chapter 5).

Evidence-based intervention and policies seem not only more successful but also more encouraging, in so far as they offer a more complete and sound scientific perspective to a very complex and often misunderstood area of criminal careers that is 'when offending goes sexually'. Chapter 7 discusses what works in reducing reoffending and criminal recidivism.

Notes

1 Latin for 'He, himself, said it' is an expression used to convey an arbitrary dogmatic statement which the speaker expects the listener to accept as valid. In other words, it is the fallacy of distorting an issue by asserting that something is 'just how it is'. See Whitney and Smith (1906).
2 OASys General reoffending Predictor (OGP); OASys Violence Predictor (OVP).
3 Compliance reoffending involves breaching reporting requirements of a sentence for sex offending (e.g. providing incorrect address details to police) or criminal breaches of civil orders related to sexual offending.

4 Specifically: $d. = .36 \pm .24$, 7 studies; $n = 734$. For a complete description of all the meta-findings see Hanson and Morton-Bourgon (2005, 1157).
5 $d. = .19 \pm .17$, 14 studies; $n = 1,958$.
6 $d. = .33 \pm .19$, 5 studies; $n = 825$.
7 $d. = .46 \pm .26$, 3 studies; $n = 559$.
8 $d. = .41 \pm .13$, 10 studies; $n = 1,400$.

7
EVIDENCE-BASED INTERVENTION AND TREATMENT

The aim of this chapter is to provide an outline of *what works*, with whom, how, when and for how long, in an attempt to gather informed knowledge on assessing and reducing criminal recidivism.

The starting point is that without treatment all persistent offenders, and especially the high-risk and high-need ones, will be more likely to reoffend. This chapter presents an analysis of the principles and structures of those programmes that are effective in reducing recidivism. The evaluation of their effectiveness goes beyond the aim of this chapter and the scope to this book. However, it will be relevant to explore (a) whether programmes for recidivist and chronic offenders differ from those for other types of offenders and, if yes, how; (b) whether programmes should take account of type of offending (e.g. sex offences) or personality disorder (e.g. psychopathy), or both; (c) to what extent the success of a treatment depends on responsivity; (d) whether knowledge about neurocriminology could inform responsivity plans apart from assessing the risk and identifying the criminogenic needs of the offenders.

Scientific evidence for prevention and intervention

Welsh and Farrington (2012b) point out that crime prevention means many different things to many different people, depending on their roles, their professional responsibilities and on whether they work in research, in the criminal justice system or in a public or clinical setting. The actions of a police officer who intervenes to arrest a suspect, or a judge and jury who sentenced an offender to detention, refer more accurately to the concept of *crime control*; their societal actions are motivated by an offence that has already occurred and by an offender who is likely to be already known by the criminal justice system (Lejins, 1967). Those actions that take place to anticipate offending at any level constitute *prevention*. If those strategies that operate outside the criminal justice system represent an alternative, perhaps, even a 'socially progressive way to reduce crime' (Welsh & Farrington, 2012b, 4), then treatment becomes important as an intervention to serve the promotion of well-being, the improvement of mental health, the development of relational competencies and the restoration of the individual personal and social functioning.

The principle that *Every Offender Matters*[1] is relevant in a book on criminal recidivism and chronic offending in so far as it aids the notion that crime intervention should not be discretionary, but should be a mandatory response in terms of treatment and prevention. In other words, assisting and serving the process of changing behaviour through treatment is the scope of crime intervention.

Treatment is required when addressing persistent and chronic offending in order to prevent offenders pursuing their criminal careers.

Prevention is essential, especially, with primary offending, when antisociality is beginning, and has not yet taken the course of being acted upon, but it is also pertinent with criminal recidivism because treatment, when it is effective, reinforces the potential to reduce further offending, and its continuity in time.

The prevention of antisocial behaviour and youth violence is crucial in interrupting violent development. According to Dodge (2001), 'prevention science has provided a bridge between an understanding of how chronic violence develops and how prevention programs can interrupt that development' (p. 63, cited in Welsh & Farrington, 2012c, 510).

It follows that the fundamental purpose of intervention is to reduce criminal recidivism. In order to achieve this, it is necessary to directly intervene with those criminogenic aspects and life conditions that maintain, aggravate and reinforce the offenders' antisocial potential. The main conclusion of a systematic analysis of crime prevention is that imprisonment does not generally have an effective crime reduction effect (Chapter 1), especially if it is not followed by individualised and effective rehabilitation programmes (Farrington, 2015b). Taking into account the fact that the 'one size fits all' approach has proved to be utterly inappropriate, treatment programmes should be tailored to offenders' criminogenic risks, should adapt the intervention to the intensity of risk exposure and should meet the needs, readiness, cognitive style and learning ability of the offender. The most significant factor leading to a reduction in reoffending is addressing criminogenic needs, which are directly and strongly associated with antisocial potential.

However, intervention occurs within a social structure and takes shape alongside the task of applying research to policy, i.e. strengthening the bridge between academic research and the application of its findings to the 'real world'. Research has consistently established that longitudinal studies (Chapter 2) are better equipped to provide evidence on causes, on within-individual and between-individual differences, on continuity and change, and on the most significant risk and protective factors for offending. Individual differences account for specific variables, needs and protective factors that are significantly related to the lives of specific offenders (Chapter 3), their criminal careers and also to their potential for rehabilitation and change.

Randomised experiments are designed to evaluate the efficacy and effectiveness of prevention programmes (Welsh & Farrington, 2012c). This knowledge is fundamental in terms of understanding how to plan individualised treatment, and to make it effective and appropriate for the person to whom it is delivered. Hence, assessing risk should be accompanied by the process of also assessing protective factors that mitigate the impact of adverse conditions, and that serve risk management and promotive interventions (Chapter 4). The joint scope of science and professional responsibility is to target serious and persistent offenders, who pose a high risk for society as a whole, and to guarantee the rights of citizens to have a safe life in the community, by protecting them from becoming victims or reducing their risk of being victimised once again by violence and abuse.

Sex offenders (Chapter 6) are not necessarily at high risk of persisting in sexually abusive behaviour but, nevertheless, research findings and clinical studies show that they require specialised responses in terms of: responsibility (how to make the sentence have a 'responsibilising' impact upon their behaviour); metacognition (how to recognise their own behaviour as having undesirable effects on others, and how to accept that other people have rights, different opinions, and personal needs); treatment (how to treat); prevention (who to treat to stop further victimisation and sustain desistance); and resilience (how to promote the capacity to withstand and rebound from disrupting life conditions and their adverse consequences). In a similar vein, offenders who are also psychopathic or report marked psychopathic features (Chapter 5) require special scientific, clinical and criminological attention.

Farrington (2015a,b) argues that criminological research typically concentrates on either the development of criminal persons or the occurrence of criminal events, but rarely on both. The focus of treatment should primarily be on offenders rather than offences. Offenders are predominantly versatile rather than specialised; they are likely to commit a variety of offences, and the typical offender who commits violence, vandalism or drug abuse also tends to commit theft or burglary. Findings from the CSDD (Chapters 2 and 3) suggest that violent offenders usually also have convictions for non-violent offences. It follows that, according to Farrington (2015b, forthcoming), when studying offenders, it is unnecessary to develop a different theory for each different type of offence. However, in trying to explain why offences occur, the situations are so diverse and specific to particular crimes that it is probably necessary to have different explanations for different types of offences.

The psychology of persistent and recidivist offenders

> The persistent criminal, like the madman, is not the man who has lost his reason. The persistent criminal is the man who has lost everything except his reason.
>
> *(Adapted from G. K. Chesterton, 1908)*

Within a single chapter it is impossible to explore exhaustively the science of treatment. The focus of this section is on the evidence-based findings that suggest which offenders are considered at high risk for criminal continuity (persistent offenders); who are assumed to be more in need of mental health support (mentally disordered and personality disordered offenders), even though not necessarily insane in front of the law (as mentioned in the Chesterton quote); who are considered to be especially socially dangerous (sexual and violent offenders); and who are assessed as not amenable for treatment (psychopathic offenders); who are evaluated as not motivated or uninterested in treatment (violent and sex offenders) or even not entitled to treatment (denial sex offenders).

Personality describes and accounts for consistent and relatively enduring patterns of thoughts, feelings and emotions, and behaviours that distinguish one individual from others (Kluckhohn & Murray, 1953; Roberts et al., 2008). The complexity of personality development in offending (Oliver et al., 2008) comprises three major topics: human nature and individual differences (Buss, 1984); the dimensional nature of a personality disorder (Livesley, 2007); and the way in which psychopathy, personality disorders and antisocial and/or criminal behaviour are interrelated and influence each other (Blackburn 2007). Personality is relevant in the study of criminal careers because criminal and violent deeds are often not accessories or additional components of the individual behaviour, but are systematic ways of relating to others and to the world, and of functioning in social settings. It was Allport (1937) who saw personality traits as possessing causal force, but, even without crediting personality with such a pivotal impact, it is maintained that personality and its disorders could contribute to the explanation of the criminogenic dynamics influencing persisting and chronic offending, and could provide useful information about how to intervene, with whom and when.

The DSM-5 (2013) emphasises the enduring pattern of inner experience and behaviour underlying a personality disorder that diverges prominently from the individual's culture and social standards, that is pervasive and inflexible, that has an onset in adolescence or early adulthood, that is stable over time, and that alters the social and relational functioning of the person, leading to distress or impairment.

According to Hogue (2010) the concept of personality disorder is laden with an evaluative edge, which becomes even more germane within the criminal justice system. This is because of the importance of a complete and accurate assessment of those aspects that are significant criminogenic needs, and that are necessary to address, especially in the executive phase of the sentence when convicted offenders are placed in a position to start their process of an *active self-responsibilisation* focusing on what can be done, starting from the offence committed, in order to work towards community re-entry. Despite personality being crucial for a complete risk assessment and for intervention planning, not much information is available about personality disorder and its assessment in criminal, forensic and detention populations.

'Accurate assessment is always an issue' (Hogue, 2010, 270). The offending population presents additional challenges and risks. Again the DSM-5 (2013) explicitly mentions that in forensic settings 'there is a risk that diagnostic information will be misused or misunderstood' (p. 25), and that the use of clinical and specialised knowledge 'should be informed by an awareness of the risks and limitations of its use in forensic settings' (p. 25). '[N]onclinical decision makers should be cautioned that a diagnosis does not carry any implications regarding the etiology . . . of the individual's mental disorder or . . . of control over behaviors' (APA, 2013, 25). It follows that, despite an assessment of diminished behavioural control representing a feature of the disorder, its diagnosis does not necessarily imply that an individual is incapable of self-control and behavioural control.

To understand why offending has become continuous and pervasive, it is necessary to move *from* the behaviour (what the person did) *to* the person (who the person is and how he or she functions). Findings from the CSDD are consistent across analyses in suggesting that those CSDD individuals who were persistent and recidivist in offending were heterogeneous, started with a complicated family life, had experienced an adverse childhood, were likely to have personality problems, had major difficulties in achieving life success (this either being for family stability or professional satisfaction), were highly aggressive, antisocial, impulsive, and daring, and likely filled their day with alcohol and drugs. Criminality was only a feature, however important, of their social functioning.

The remainder of this chapter will look first at what research evidence shows about effective treatment, and which programmes are most accurate in assessing the level of risk and most effective in reducing criminal recidivism. Second, the focus will be on those psychopathic, sexually deviant, familial or socially dysfunctional conditions that play an important role in how offenders adjust, do not adjust or adjust poorly along their life-course.

Setting the stage for an effective prevention policy

Welsh and Farrington (2012b) propose a new crime prevention policy. Among its central characteristics, one emerges as especially relevant for the principles of intervention presented here, which is 'the need to overcome "the short-termism" politics of the day; to ensure that the highest quality scientific research is at center stage in political and policy decisions; and to strike a greater balance between crime prevention and crime control' (Welsh & Farrington, 2012b, 14).

One of the reasons for emphasising the importance of scientific evidence is because preventing offending and reducing recidivism has been hampered by rhetoric and ideology, rather than being driven by evidence-based research (Visher & Weisburd, 1998; Welsh & Farrington, 2012a). The declaration that *nothing works* by Martinson (1974), because most rehabilitation programmes up to that time were assessed as not having any significant effect on recidivism, has made it clear that crime interventions ought to be guided by evidence-based research.

Since then, numerous studies have been interested in unveiling the findings of the 'what works?' approach (McGuire, 1995). Others argue that any intervention may be better than no intervention. Some, however, may cautiously propose that the magnitude of the specific effects of different crime prevention programmes should be strictly scrutinised and methodologically guided in order to avoid the *Dodo Bird verdict*[2] that all crime prevention programmes are about equal in efficacy because any intervention breaks the pessimistic spell of *nothing can be done* to reform offenders (Zara & Farrington, 2014).

Criminological research findings indicate that offenders should be separated for treatment based on their level of risk (Andrews & Bonta, 2010a; Andrews *et al.*, 1990b; Andrews *et al.*, 2006; Lowenkamp *et al.*, 2006a,b; Latessa *et al.*, 2014). As Ainsworth and Taxman (2013) synthetise, the risk of placing high-risk and low-risk offenders together in the same treatment plan may have a contagion effect of increasing recidivism for low-risk offenders (Lowenkamp & Latessa, 2005; Lowenkamp *et al.*, 2006a). Some claim that intervention with low- to medium-risk offenders may make things worse (Andrews & Dowden, 2006), while intervention with high-risk and persistent offenders could significantly reduce reoffending (Andrews & Bonta, 2010a).

Addressing the issue of *what works and what is promising* in preventing crime is not only a scientific challenge, but it is a professional responsibility for researchers, criminologists and psychologists, practitioners, policy-makers and politicians involved in the task of protecting and enhancing the well-being of individuals and their community. The psychology that assists the courts, justice agencies and the decision-making in detention and by parole boards has two main tasks. The first is to help keep low-risk offenders low-risk and not interfere with their existing strengths and resources. The second is to identify moderate and higher-risk offenders and arrange crime-prevention activities consistent with ethical and legal knowledge, and also in adherence with the *Risk-Need-Responsivity* principles (Andrews & Dowden, 2007; see later in this chapter). Intervention plans and treatment programmes must be designed and implemented to facilitate the effective application of criminological knowledge.

Crime reduction and prevention results from effective intervention programmes and it 'is therefore defined not by its intentions, but by its consequences' (Sherman *et al.*, 2002, 3). Effective treatment should lead to the reduction of criminal events within a high-risk population, the prevention of criminal recidivism, the lessening of criminal harm and the prevention of antisocial and criminal onsets in problematic and vulnerable children. These are requirements for an effective and evidence-based prevention policy: acknowledging the pattern of risk for these offenders, and which criminogenic needs influence their behaviour; assessing how risks and needs combine with each other and contribute to the level of the offending vulnerability; and recognising which resources are available to design programmes aiming to reduce the likelihood of relapsing once more into a criminal path.

Research has shown that punishment and formal variations in punishment or diversion, deterrence and 'scared straight' responses are ineffective in reducing criminal recidivism (Latessa *et al.*, 2014; Lösel, 2001; McGuire, 2002, Petrosino *et al.*, 2003, 2013; Wilson & MacKenzie, 2006; Zara & Farrington, 2014), while different findings are found when talking about boot camps (Lipsey, 2009; Wilson *et al.*, 2005) or High Intensive Treatment (HIT) programmes (Jolliffe *et al.*, 2013). Classical psychotherapy, low-structured milieu therapy, psychodynamic and counselling approaches, and self-enhancement interventions such as fostering positive self-regard, self-actualisation and self-esteem, have little or no desirable effects on recidivism rates, even though they may be effective in improving other aspects of the psychological well-being of the offenders (Lipsey & Cullen, 2007; Lipsey *et al.*, 2007; Zara & Farrington, 2014).

This does not mean that clinical values are irrelevant or dismissed in psycho-criminological settings. The message is that, when certain treatment factors are combined and clinical principles are respected, the impact upon reoffending is considerably enhanced. For example, a boot camp combined with cognitive-behavioural and pre-release employment programmes was effective in reducing reoffending and further convictions in the research of Jolliffe and colleagues (2013, see later in this chapter). However, effectiveness in reducing recidivism is directly related to how many and how specifically criminogenic needs are targeted: they are the active ingredients for significant desirable outcomes. If they are not treated, it is very unlikely that even small reductions in recidivism risk can be achieved, however clinically adherent the *unspecific* intervention might be.

What is promising

The *Risk-Need-Responsivity* (RNR) model (Andrews & Bonta, 2010a, 46–7; see also Chapters 1 and 4 of this book) is promising because it provides an overarching structure on which intervention can be focused and offenders become central in treatment programmes *for* and with *them*. Key factors are:

- Respect for the person and the normative context. Interventions are offered with recognition of the personal autonomy of the individual, and coherently according to the setting in which they are delivered.
- Psychological theory: programmes should be based upon an empirically solid psychological theory. Scientific evidence indicates that the general personality and cognitive social learning approach is *what works and works best* within the detention and criminological settings.
- Promotion and enhancement of crime prevention services: the reduction of criminal recidivism and victimisation can be seen as a legitimate objective of the community as a whole, and of service agencies, both within and outside justice and corrections.

Hence, it is essential to consider that the characteristics of the offenders are relevant not in an abstract psychological sense but in terms of the level of risk, the type of needs and their responsivity. The person is where the intervention should start from in order to move back to their psychosocial reality and then to the larger social context in which the person is meant to operate and adjust. The *risk principle* states that recidivism can be reduced if the level of treatment provided to the offender is proportional to the offender's risk of reoffending. The *need principle* calls for the focus of treatment to be on criminogenic needs.

Criminogenic risks or *dynamic (psychological) risk factors* are those factors that, when present, increase the risk of reoffending, and on the other hand, when they are directly addressed, reduce the likelihood of reoffending. *Criminogenic needs* (e.g. antisocial personality patterns, personality disorders, pro-criminal attitudes, social supports for crime, substance abuse, family/marital relationships, school/work, prosocial recreational activities) are dynamic as opposed to static risk factors (such as age of onset). Static variables are unidirectional in nature in so far as they are unable to be reduced, and can only increase as offenders have more criminal justice events that add to their criminal history (Ainsworth & Taxman, 2013).

Offenders have many needs that deserve treatment but not all of these needs are associated with their criminal behaviour. *Non-criminogenic needs* may include, for instance, shaky self-esteem, vague feelings of personal distress, major mental disorders such as schizophrenia or manic depression, and physical health problems.

Higher risk offenders are likely to have a broader range of needs and problems than lower risk offenders, and generally the former respond more successfully to treatment (Andrews & Dowden, 2006). What is important is to match treatment to risk and to address those criminogenic needs which are directly linked to offending. Treatments focusing on non-criminogenic needs appear to either slightly increase offending rates or not contribute to their reduction. More studies are necessary to investigate the mechanisms which, by increasing the psychological well-being or mental health of the offenders, may reduce reoffending.

Research evidence indicates that treatment should be delivered responsively. This means that the general structure of the programme should be explicit and that it should be delivered in adherence to its rationale according to its design.

The *responsivity principle* refers to how to treat the offender. *General responsivity* sets up the intervention to respond to the style and mode that is consistent with the ability and learning style of the offender. Appropriate monitoring systems and professional training of staff assist the maintenance of the integrity of the programme. The general responsivity principle states that cognitive-behavioural and social learning methods work best with offenders, and that they are the most effective way of teaching people new behaviours. Effective cognitive social learning strategies operate according to the following two principles: the *relationship principle* (establishing a warm, respectful and collaborative working alliance with the offender) and the *structuring principle* (influencing the direction of change towards prosocial attitudes, which can be addressed through modelling, reinforcement, problem-solving, etc.).

Specific responsivity considers offender characteristics such as interpersonal sensitivity, anxiety, verbal intelligence, cognitive maturity, cognitive distortion, and emotional dysfunction, so as to match them to the appropriate mode and style of treatment. The specific responsivity principle states that interventions should take into account people's different cognitive abilities, personalities, biosocial (e.g. gender, race, mental health) characteristics, motivations and background experiences.

As with the CSDD men, a set of clinically relevant factors are life style and social stabilisers and destabilisers influencing life adjustment, and although not directly related to offending behaviour, they can significantly impact an offender's amenability and responsiveness to treatment and supervision. Some of these factors include living conditions such as housing; life-style factors such as education, employment and financial means; affective factors such as family support and friends; social network factors such as antisocial associates (see Chapter 3). These factors are not criminogenic themselves, but constitute those extrapersonal circumstances that need to be assessed in offenders under supervision or on probation. As Ainsworth and Taxman (2013) advocate, a failure to comply with these conditions can lead to a technical violation or a failure to successfully complete the supervision process. These variables can also act as stabilisers in an offender's life in the sense that they may serve to reinforce prosocial features that facilitate the offender's access to new opportunities and social integration.

The offender is central to treatment because treating an offender appropriately leads to an effective reduction in the risk of recidivism, which specifically means less risk of victimisation. As Andrews (2006) stated, the implementation of effective interventions and human services is not just a matter of selecting the best evidence-based programme off the shelf. Even well-researched and *blueprint* programmes may fail to achieve the expected and desired results if the above aspects are not considered. Further investigations have suggested that the success of cognitive-behavioural programmes may be related to their adherence to the psychosocial reality of offending populations. Andrews *et al.* (1990a, 20) suggested that, for treatments to be effective in reducing recidivism, they have also to be clinically relevant, i.e. 'to maintain respect for and attention to diversity in both people and programming'.

Treatment studies show that reoffending is influenced not only by the efficacy of treatment, but also by the motivation to be involved in a treatment programme (McMurran, 2002) and by its completion (Andrews & Bonta, 2010b; McMurran *et al.*, 2008). McMurran and Theodosi (2007) found that treatment completers were least likely to reoffend, while treatment noncompleters offended at a higher rate than did those not given treatment. These findings are significant in so far as they suggest that some relevant aspects should be addressed in treatment planning (McMurran, 2010):

a. treatment works; *however*
b. treatment seems to fail in engaging high-risk offenders; *and*
c. treatment non-completion may exacerbate risk.

The motivation to change (McMurran & Ward, 2004; Newman, 1994) and the readiness to change (West, 2005) are the result of an interaction between the offender, with their needs and the programme structure with the personnel involved in the professional dynamics, and the conditions within which the interaction occurs and how it occurs. As McMurran (2010) advocates, '[t]he readiness to change model has the potential to broaden the study of offender treatment engagement and behaviour change by addressing intrapersonal, interpersonal and contextual factors and their interactions. The utility of this model remains to be evidenced' (p. 121). Both the internal (e.g. thinking pattern, self-perception, cognitive, affective and relational distortions, denial, minimisation, and attributional style) and the external (e.g. type of treatment programme offered, when, where, how, by whom) conditions for readiness are important.

Towards an integration of the 'what' we know about

> People have a great deal of difficulty appreciating statistical contingency in the absence of a causal story that makes the contingency reasonable.
> *(Dawes, 1999, 29)*

Zara and Farrington (2014) suggest that, despite the reliable human prediction that past behaviour is the most robust and significant predictor of future behaviour, reducing the risk of future offending by intervening with past criminogenic behaviour is not straightforward. The finding that 'everybody does *it*', where the 'it' stands for crime (Gabor, 1994) should not either reduce scientific investment in discovering the multiple, early or widespread causes of offending or increase social and political discouragement over the fact that nothing more can be done to control offending. While many males commit minor crimes infrequently, the criminal justice system has to focus on the minority of people who commit severe or frequent crimes.

The social, economic and environmental causes of criminal violence generally have received more acceptance in the social policy domain because they are not perceived as judgemental, deterministic or blaming individual offenders, or as deterministic as the psychological or individual causes.

The roles of personality and of criminogenic needs in offending were seen as deterministic and blaming the individual was considered by some people to be partial and biased. However, the attempt to shift the focus especially to the social causes of offending often resulted in an impoverished understanding of the complexity of persisting in a life of crime for those offenders embedded in a criminal career. According to Andrews and Bonta (2010a), for much of the twentieth century, criminology theory neglected the evidence of a possible and significant link of personality, especially antisocial personality traits, with criminal behaviour. 'Criminology's favorite explanatory variable, social class, had to be protected' (Andrews & Bonta, 2010a, 222). This ideological stance was the expression of a protective mechanism maintained in criminology to avoid being labelled as deterministic, and of being perceived as a 'serving' science under the spell of psychiatry and neuroscience. The new risk to avoid was of reducing criminal behaviour to pathology, and the offender to a mentally insane person. If something was to blame it had to be the system.

However, in the last 20 years or so, research has provided consistent evidence for the rediscovery of the *nature and nurture* dynamic in offending. A social variable is not less deterministic than a biological one, if it is considered as the sole variable that causes offending. Causes are not deterministic; causes are probabilistic.

Farrington (1988) and Zara (2010a) suggest that to understand behaviour we need to appreciate the psychology of individuals, gathering knowledge about their personality traits, about the situation in which individuals behave, and about the way they encode and decode the context, and give meaning to it. In the absence of a 'causal' story (as worded by Dawes, 1999), it is meaningless to attempt to understand human development. In the interplay between 'individual x environment', there exists an *inversely proportional relationship* between the individual's vulnerability and the environmental factors (Zara, 2013b). The more criminogenic the environment, the less relevant are the personality components. The more striking the personality components and traits, the less significant or relevant are the environmental factors.

Psychological criminology research does not disregard any of these dimensions, and works to strengthen the integration of them, which already exists and cannot be dismissed: the individual is the expression of this integration and of this 'absolute' interdependence. Moreover, a general personality and a cognitive social psychology approach (Andrews & Bonta, 2010a) and a syndrome of antisociality (Farrington, 2005b) may be more relevant than social factors to serve as responsivity targets for planned interventions. Treatment becomes a possibility, personality disorders become criminogenic needs, psychopathic and antisocial traits become risk dimensions to be taken into consideration, and they can be controlled and influence intervention plans.

As Mills and his colleagues (2011) suggest, assessing the risk and conveying risk estimates is unsatisfactory *per se*; to place them in the context of a story that explains them is what is necessary to direct intervention and plan treatment. The risk assessment process is what makes the story unfold. Dawes (1999, 39) argued that we do not appreciate probability, base rate, risk levels or the combination of criminogenic needs, without the story which can temporally, contextually and psychologically convey a structure to the information. Offending behaviour does not occur within a psychological and social vacuum; offenders arrive at a behaviour following different paths (*equifinality principle*), and a similar starting point can lead to different outcomes (*multifinality principle*).

The approach proposed by Mills *et al.* (2011) is structured to tell the individual's story (see Chapter 3), in which what the person did (i.e. a criminal offence) is not where we start to understand them but where we arrive at, given their story:

- Why is he or she here? (Evaluation Setting).
- Where did he or she come from? (Psychosocial Background).
- What has he or she done? (Criminal Career History).
- What can be done about it? (Risk Assessment and Risk Management).
- Which treatment is the most appropriate and How can it be conveyed? (Treatment Plan and Responsivity) (see Chapter 4).

The 'when' aspect of intervention

Never too early, never too late is the most insightful catchphrase in criminology (Loeber & Farrington, 1998c); it is promising to the extent that it serves to prevent antisocial onset and to assist treatment in interrupting criminal continuity. When concentrating on developmental risk factors, the focus is on the large population of children and adolescents, and their families, who are at risk of behavioural problems, relational and social difficulties. The earlier the support is offered, the more probable is the interruption of any externalised forms of malfunctions and/or of dysfunctional manifestations. Preventing antisocial onset is different from preventing criminal recidivism. Intervention at the beginning of a criminal career has much potential to succeed because it works to interrupt a pattern of behaviours which *is going to become* systematic, rather than working to modify it when it has already become chronic.

When concentrating on the small segment of the population (i.e. chronic, persistent and recidivist offenders) who are responsible for 50 to 71 per cent of recurrent offending and criminal violence (Loeber & Farrington, 1998a; Hodgins, 1994, 2007; Hodgins *et al.*, 2009; Kratzer & Hodgins, 1999; Moffitt *et al.*, 2002), it is common to find enduring individual and psychological difficulties, family disruption, personality disorders, alcohol and drug abuse, mental problems, neuropsychological impairments, social marginality, erratic employment status and economic troubles. This segment of the offending population is the focus of the remainder of the chapter.

Treating violent and persistent offenders as homogeneous can lead to faults in interpreting the aetiology, pathology, clinical aspects, prognosis and social influences of criminal behaviour, and to the misinterpretation of individual differences (Elliott, 1999).

Persistent and chronic offenders (*who to treat*) are more likely than other offenders to have specific criminogenic needs, personality features, and family and social milieus that facilitate, sustain and aggravate, in the life-course, their antisocial outcomes. Acknowledging and assessing the dimensions that characterise their offending provides experts with deepened knowledge of what areas to consider in planning intervention (*what to treat*). This requires consideration of the circumstances in which these risk processes are embedded (family and social background), and the importance of distinguishing the static elements of the criminal career, from the dynamic and changeable dimensions (*criminogenic needs*), and from the critical aspects of their conditions (*acute risk*) that is the basis of *how to treat*.

In his meta-analytic overview, Lipsey (2009) outlines those factors that are significantly related to intervention effectiveness, and which programmes, aimed to reduce criminal recidivism, adhere to them. Early interventions on reducing the risk of recidivism in serious juvenile offenders are essential for interrupting the continuation pattern of reoffending. According to Andrews and Bonta (2010a,b) those programmes that conform to the risk, need and responsivity (*RNR*) principles can achieve a recidivism reduction of around 50 per cent. Lipsey (2009) suggests that intervention effects are dependent on: the *type of treatment*, which involves intervention approach and modality; the *intensity of treatment*, which encompasses quantity and quality of treatment provided; the *characteristics of the offenders* receiving the treatment. His analysis was based on 548 independent study samples, and information was extracted from 361 primary research reports. Lipsey's (2009) meta-analysis shows that intervention effectiveness was not significantly associated with the level of supervision applied by the juvenile justice system *per se*, when characteristics of the offenders and the level of risk were controlled. In fact, most of the interventions were about equally effective irrespective of whether the juvenile was under probation supervision, custodial facility, diversion or no official supervision. Two interesting and opposite results, that deserve mentioning, are: reduced effectiveness of counselling approaches within incarceration; and increased effectiveness of skill-building approaches within the community without juvenile justice supervision. Lipsey (2009) explained that the relative robustness of intervention effects across various levels of juvenile justice system supervision provides reassurance over the fact that treatment effectiveness is not absolutely dependent on the context. On the other hand, Lipsey also suggested that quality programmes could, in fact, be effective even within institutional settings where there is more potential for iatrogenic and adverse effects. Programmes that embodied therapeutic approaches such as counselling (with a mentoring and a group angle rather than an individual or a peer slant) and skill training (especially those with a behavioural and cognitive-behavioural orientation, in comparison to the job-related one) were more effective in reducing recidivism in comparison with those that were inspired by control, coercion, surveillance or discipline. Those juveniles who were at higher level of delinquency risk benefited more from intervention, especially from those programmes which were: well organised and accurately implemented, which targeted those juvenile offenders at higher risk for reoffending, and were delivered by professionals who were trained and supervised. It was interesting to note that intervention, when organised to meet the *therapeutic* (Lipsey, 2009) or *clinically relevant* (Andrews et al., 1990a) or the *RNR principles* (Andrews & Bonta, 2010a) can have effective effects for younger and older juveniles, males and female, minorities and whites. It is evident that some approaches are more effective than others, others are more responsive and more ethically sound, and some are more long-lasting in their effects; however, it is important to remember that to some (and perhaps to a significant!) extent, the effectiveness of treatment depends on the individual it is offered to. In other words, what seems to work with reoffenders and to work more effectively echoes Lipsey's (2009) observation, '[i]t does not take a magic bullet program to impact recidivism, only one that is well made and well aimed' (p. 145).

The extensive literature on what works in reducing offending and criminal recidivism should also be extended to include questions such as 'how long does it last?' (Jolliffe et al., 2013, p. 519). Jolliffe and colleagues (2013) explored the effects on recidivism of high intensity training (HIT) for young offenders aged 18–21 at Thorn Cross Young Offenders Institution in England and followed the reduction in the number and cost of reconvictions after a follow-up of ten years compared with the control group. The results show that those offenders from HIT were less likely to be reconvicted after one year of release (56 per cent) in comparison with the control group (73.6 per cent) (chi-squared = 8.48, $p < .002$; Odds Ratio = 2.21), and that this significant difference persisted over time, up to year 5 (83.2 per cent compared to 91.2 per cent; chi-squared = 3.58, $p < .03$; Odds Ratio = 2.11) (Jolliffe et al., 2013, 522). No significant differences were found between the cumulative prevalence of reconvictions of the two groups beyond year 5, and this could be explained by the ceiling effects having already reached its influence, but still the decrease in the frequency of offending in years 3–4 led to a decrease in the cumulative number of convictions and in the cumulative costs of offending. From two to ten years, the number of offences saved increased significantly from 169 (1.35 per young offender) to 419 (3.35 per young offender). Jolliffe and Farrington (2013) suggested that the *benefit:cost ratio* for HIT programme was about 4 after ten-year follow-up. Based on the costs of offences in 2010 (Home Office, 2011), the overall cumulative crimes saved corresponded to 419 less convictions of the HIT group that cost £1,342,714 less, over the decade period, with a cumulative cost savings per young offender of £10,742 for the entire ten-year follow-up period (Jolliffe & Farrington, 2013).

Intensive treatment programmes, such as those mentioned above, can be successful if they blend rehabilitative components with RNR principles, placing emphasis on counselling, cognitive-behavioural intervention, social skill training and drug treatment, with some of the principles of stability, order and to a certain extent inevitability of the 'military paradigm' (Duwe & Kerschner, 2008; MacKenzie, 2012; MacKenzie et al., 2007; Wilson et al., 2005). Moreover, any intervention that can be organised as an alternative to traditional incarceration or correctional or 'scared straight' and disciplinary programmes can have important effects, in so far as the offender's levels of risk and needs are taken into account in the design of the intervention, and are recognised as a contribution to the integrity of the programme (see also Taxman & Pattavina, 2013). It follows that what seems to be relevant in reducing recidivism is the attention to the offenders (e.g. criminogenic needs) and the treatment characteristics; the intensity and duration of treatment (e.g. longer duration and more meaningful contact); the type of treatment based upon cognitive-behaviour and skill oriented programmes; the focus on extrapersonal circumstances (e.g. family); the ethical nature of the programme, with its explicit timing, criteria and rules, and the competence of the staff involved are found to be the active ingredients contributing to the robustness of the outcomes. These last components remind one of what Caspi and Moffitt (1993) considered as a *strong* situation, similar to the one found in the military, where firmness and decisiveness in adhering to a system that provides disambiguated norms and principles are likely to promote change in the life-course of individuals. It includes pressure towards a new way of behaving, while providing clear information about how to behave adaptively.

Three features of the military experience could perhaps promote psychological change, and prove beneficial when transposed into rehabilitating programmes. The first one is the *knifing off* of past experiences, which means separation from the immediate influence of the criminogenic environment where the offenders were embedded, and the involvement in basic social skills training and respect of other people's rights. The second feature is a *legitimate time-out*, by releasing the offenders from unconventional expectations and immersing them in new interactional and prosocial opportunities in which to develop a new identity. The third feature is the broadened range of perspective, social knowledge and basic interpersonal skills that lead to a greater awareness of self, a recognition and tolerance of diversity, and new skills that are encouraged to be applied in new situations upon re-entry into the community (Caspi & Moffitt, 1993, 266). Berger and Luckman (1966) seemed to have understood the deep impact of childhood experiences upon psychological development when they observed that 'it takes severe biographical shocks to disintegrate the massive reality internalized in early childhood' (p. 142).

Many of the CSDD men, and in particular the chronic offenders examined in Chapter 3, needed emotional stability, social guidance and a coherent education along with clear rules to accompany their social behaviour. These are basic elements of social functioning that individuals learn early in life, with their parents, at school and interacting with others in the world. Many of these men grew up bereft of the emotional and educational support that a child needs in order to build a secure base to count on for protection and comfort, some were deprived of any parental affection and family stability, and most of them were left to rely on themselves to survive in a world that they perceived as threatening and unfair.

Targets of specialised treatment

In Chapter 1 the differences between persistence and criminal recidivism were presented, and in Chapter 3 the criminal careers of chronic offenders were explored. When talking about chronic and persistent offenders the image that jumps to mind is of those offenders who commit continuously the most heinous and serious crimes, and who are specialised in that type of offending for the length of their criminal careers. This is not always the case. Sexually aggressive offenders, violent offenders, murderers, are more likely to be involved in a versatile pattern of crimes, which sees an escalating and an aggravating process (Loeber & Farrington, 2011). Moreover, even when persistent they do not commit crimes, especially violent ones, every day in the week. The more violent the crime committed by chronic offenders the more likely that there will occur a latency period between crimes (Zara, 2005). Criminal latency encompasses a period of 'cooling off', in which the offender may try to abscond, or to make sense of how to reorganise his or her life after the offence. This applies particularly if the previous act involved the death of or violence against a family member. In such cases, the offender may need some time to try to control the events around them and to avoid raising suspicion about them. Even when persistent and recidivist, offenders do not always react insensitively and automatically to their misdeeds, transgressions or crimes.

The criminal careers of CSDD chronic offenders (Chapter 3) are a unique example of a multiple interaction of risk causes, moderators and criminogenic needs that contributed directly and indirectly to their life in crime. Planning intervention means also taking into account that biology is as important as culture, that mental health is as significant as community stability in the algorithm of offending, and that the brain is as relevant in regulating the individual's behavioural choices as the social and external influences are.

The remainder of this chapter will focus on specific subgroups of offenders (sex offenders and psychopathic offenders), who more than other offenders may have specific criminogenic needs, personality disorders and might require a more specific responsivity plan for what, how and when to choose the best and most adequate treatment possible.

Zooming in on the sex offending risk

Already in Chapter 6, it was shown that sex offenders are all different, and when persistent, they have versatile criminal careers. Heterogeneity refers to the diversity of offences committed, that are not necessarily all against the person and not all violent ones. Some of the CSDD chronic offenders who were also sex offenders, displayed many of the difficulties that other serious offenders had, and came from a very problematic background as disruptive as the one in which many other chronic offenders were raised. These aspects complicate the scenario because the focus of the law is on the illegal act committed, while the focus of science is on the criminogenic process behind it, and that led to it. While researchers in the field of criminological psychology are mostly interested in the causes of offending, they cannot pretend that the two aspects are separate within the criminal justice system. Thus, it is fair to say that the seriousness of the outcome is not always the phenotypic expression of a criminogenic pattern and a psychopathological process. At times other factors, such as opportunities for crime, a disinterest for social rules and utilitarian choices, are the drive to offend. Science has the duty to inform the law and to offer reliable and valid evidence of the different impacts that criminogenic needs and risk factors exert upon human behaviour. This knowledge about causes should certainly have a use in how to plan treatment, while sentencing the offenders for the crime committed.

Beyond the matter of looking at psychopathy as a mitigation or as an aggravation (Luna, 2013), the call to scientists is to propose strategies to respond as effectively as possible to the psychopathic and antisocial threat of persistent offenders. In some instances, it could be claimed that their capability for instrumental reasoning and transformation of reality into a practical matter does not justify the plea of insanity defence or of diminished responsibility.

If, on the one hand, Welsh and Farrington (2011) found that the US public preferred youth treatment programmes to imprisonment, showing a great deal of tolerance towards juvenile offenders, on the other hand, pressure to punish and to enact statutes focusing on the civil commitment of sexually violent predators and violent psychopathic offenders arises from the conviction that they constitute an irremediable danger to society and pose great risk for future crimes (Prentky *et al.*, 2006; Schlank & Cohen, 1999). The public demands longer and more severe sentences (La Fond, 2005; Lippke, 2008), and the legal argument is to guarantee protection both by punishment and by governing the offender's release through the path of the statutory category of, for instance, sexually violent predators (Lieb *et al.*, 1998). It follows that an offender is allowed to be civilly committed after the completion of a criminal sentence (see Chapter 6). In the midst of this crossfire of interests, psychopathy and antisocial personality disorders continue to rest on a controversial stand. Punishing the guilty offender, who is also diagnosed with a mental disorder, requires the consideration of what to do with and for them, especially in light of making community protection certain, and not wasting the financial resources and professional investment used in keeping them out of society.

Appreciating specific responsivity features becomes essential in the practice of risk assessment and treatment planning for: addressing aspects such as personality disorders, so as to provide responsive services; serving those needs specific to disordered or disabled offenders; offering developmentally adequate services depending on the age of the offender; and designing interventional plans to compensate for the lack of family and social support of the offenders.

Clinical evidence suggests that, when sex crimes are a feature of the criminal careers of persistent offenders, it is likely that cognitive distortions, denial and minimisation represent ways in which offenders recount their sex offences, in which they explain their involvement and justify their responsibility and the consequences of their acts.

Some of these clinical factors, though non-criminogenic needs, may well be specific responsivity factors (Andrews & Dowden, 2007). For instance, a self-aggrandising attitude and a self-belittling attitude are not a contradiction in terms, in so far as they serve different offending aims and satisfy different criminogenic needs. A self-aggrandising attitude is typical in individuals who have a grandiose sense of themselves and a hypertrophic self-worth; their superficial charm helps them to manipulate people. This attitude can facilitate also those who offend sexually against adults, who do not have difficulties in social relationships, but who end up in using force when their target does not respond positively to their requests, and does not fall under the spell of their charm. A self-belittling attitude is the façade acquired by many child molesters, who are likely to attract their young victims by enhancing pretextual concerns for them and their needs, even at the price of showing humbleness, hyper-social sensitivity and timidity, which eases the initial trust that children and, often, their family members, have in them.

Furthermore, offenders with a low self-esteem may first need to gain reassurance over their potential before being able to respond effectively to treatment. On the other hand, some offenders may be so self-confident that they would not recognise that anything needs to change in themselves or in their life style. For some sex offenders in denial, it may be necessary first to work on their denial before they actively are involved in any treatment; some child molesters, despite their denial, may not be at risk of reoffending, because denying their offence, the seriousness of it or the consequences of it, plays the role of a dual psychological restraint. In these circumstances, denial is an expression, however indirect or masqueraded or disguised, that these child molesters sense that something awesome motivated their behaviour, be that either the incest taboo or social shame, or both. Working to eradicate denial might have, in these offenders, opposite consequences, because making an admission could represent removing the inner restraint, and hence increasing the risk of reoffending. For some others, recognising that their intimacy with children is harmful for the victim may cause a collapse of the scaffolding that sustains their self-image and well-being, so some preliminary work towards mentalisation may be required before they are ready for treatment (see Chapters 3 and 6).

Zooming in on personality disorders and on the psychopathic risk

> In following him, I follow but myself;
> Heaven is my judge, not I for love and duty,
> But seeming so, for my peculiar end [. . .]
> *(Othello, Act 1, scene 1, 58–60)*

Antisocial personality disorders and psychopathic features are likely to be more prevalent in the persistent and chronic offending population. These are high-risk and high-need offenders; it is also likely that they have some personality traits and psychological processes that make sense of their social functioning, and have a developmental history that ensnared them into a criminal career. Table 7.1 synthesises predictors of the risk of persistent and chronic offending within the scope of the RNR model.

Callous-unemotional traits in childhood and psychopathic traits in adulthood often characterise the population of persistent and chronic offenders. In the case of these offenders, it may be that some emotional impairments, problems in self-control and difficulties in thinking about the future, when facing or anticipating the possible consequences of their actions, take preference over rational control, and alter an adequate reading of the social situation and a transference of this acknowledgment into behaviour.

While the core of antisocial personality disorder is behavioural, and is itself displayed in systematic and continuous disruptiveness, aggressiveness, delinquency and violence, the crux of psychopathy, as Glenn and Raine (2014a) put it, is not the commission of antisocial or criminal behaviour, 'per se, but rather the distinctive personality traits, including emotional deficits' (p. 3).

A large literature, before scientific and clinical evidence was available, offered a window into the vast valley of what psychopathy is and how it is manifest. Shakespeare in *Othello* presents Iago as a perfect example of a villain, or in modern terms, of a psychopath. Iago holds in his mind a clear picture of what he is doing. He charms people. His life is entrenched in deceit. His social relationships are based on manipulation. His communication is ingrained in an unfolding lie. His insensitiveness shouts out when he kills his wife for a practical reason and not out of hate. It was just that Iago needed to eliminate an obstacle in his path. Psychopathic features and manifestations are complex to describe and easy to misinterpret because the rationality of psychopaths seems lucid, and even Shakespeare needed an extended literary plot to give space to Iago's immoral behaviour: this is the longest part in the play with over 1,000 lines.

As Luna (2013, 365) stresses in his comparative synthesis, differently from the paranoid schizophrenic who distorts the world, the psychopath abides by a morally disputable and reprehensible command: 'Only I count' (Pillsbury, 2009, 159).

As indicated in Chapter 5, understanding how the minds and the brains of psychopaths work (e.g. neurocriminology) is not an opportunity to excuse psychopaths or persistent antisocial offenders, but to diminish the space and degree of opportunity within which they can *act* in the way they do. Understanding psychopathological and neuropsychological factors, in addition to social, cultural and environmental influences, contributes to the incremental validity of any risk assessment and may help to address successfully the problem of criminal recidivism especially posed by these individuals. Once it is established which criminogenic needs

TABLE 7.1 Predictors of the risk of persisting and chronic offending based on the RNR model

Static risk: criminal career
Antisocial onset
Childhood behavioural problems
Criminal versatility
Family criminality
History of abuse
Juvenile delinquency
Neuropsychological (structural) impairments

Dynamic and psychological risk: criminogenic needs
Affective shallowness
Cognitive distortions
Disempathy
Failure in responsibility acceptance
Impulsivity
Interpersonal unreliability
Lack of remorse
Neuropsychological (functional) impairments
Procriminal attitudes
Self-aggrandising attitude
Self-belittling attitude
Self-control
Sexual deviance
Sexual promiscuity
Unrealistic projects
Victimistic attitude

Responsivity
Age (juvenile or adult offenders)
Attributional style (internal *vs* external locus of control)
Gender (female or male offenders)
Glibness/superficial charm/superficiality/deception
Inattention to others and to situations
Insincerity
Manipulation of others
Minimisation of responsibility
Relational superficiality

Note: Andrews and Bonta (2010a, 221) presented a similar table related to the PCL-R items based on *The Psychology of Criminal Conduct* perspective.

are most relevant in criminal recidivism, and what risk factors augment the likelihood of antisocial continuation, and that it is likely to be a diagnosis of a mental or personality disorder, the subsequent step is to know to what extent a mental or a personality disorder causes the behavioural disturbance, and has psychological repercussions.

Can a leopard change its spots?

This question leads to reconsideration of matters of continuity and discontinuity of criminal behaviour. While a criminal career can be defined as the pattern of within-individual changes in antisocial and criminal behaviour across the life-course (Piquero et al., 2007), the nature and structure of this patterning cannot be understood by 'simply' observing offending frequency and type over time. What appeared to be significant in the lives of the persistent and recidivist offenders analysed in this book is, in fact, their consistent way of (mal)functioning in their lives, of being in their family setting with their family members, with their partners and children, at work or in social situations with friends. Behavioural continuity and discontinuity in the CSDD offenders were analysed over a time span that included 50 years of their lives. Continuity in their criminal behaviour was not the most important and problematic aspect of their social and interpersonal lives, and it has emerged as less substantial than their consistency in responding inefficiently, impulsively, aggressively, destructively to many of the personal, family, scholastic, professional, social and relational events in which they were involved.

This does not mean that change, or some changes in some aspects of life, could not be possible in the lives of persistent offenders. Some have in fact made some choices that have favoured their desistence from their criminal careers. However, those who instead had chronically persisted into a life of crime were those who came from the most disrupted and dysfunctional family situations of the CSDD, who suffered the most terrible emotional neglect and deprivation when they were children and adolescents, who grew up without a parental figure who guided, supervised and supported them, who abandoned school very early, who could not find a stable and satisfactory job. These persistent offenders manifested signs of aggressiveness, antisociality, daringness and impulsivity very early in their lives; these signs continued to feature in their personalities and life style once adults.

Paraphrasing Welsh and Farrington (2012c, 517), it can be said, without much hesitation, that without a sound focus on crime prevention and early intervention in the lives of children and family at risk, 'any crime policy will not be worth the paper it is written on'.

Longitudinal studies, such as the CSDD (West & Farrington, 1973, 1977; Farrington, 2003); the Montréal Sample of Adjudicated Youths (Le Blanc & Fréchette, 1989); the Denver Youth Study (DYS) (Elliott et al., 1985); the Dunedin Multidisciplinary Health and Human Development Study (Moffitt et al., 2001; Silva & Stanton, 1996); the Montréal Longitudinal and Experimental Study (MLES) (Tremblay et al., 1987, 2003); the Pittsburgh Youth Study – PYS (Loeber et al.,

2003); the Project on Human Development in Chicago Neighborhoods (PHDCN) (Earls & Visher, 1997); the Project on Individual Development and Environment (Stattin et al., 1989); the Rochester Youth Development Study (RYDS) (Thornberry & Krohn, 2003), have provided substantial evidence that persistent antisociality, recidivist criminality and chronic offenders are likely to have an onset in childhood; that moderating and mediating factors affect and redirect the offending trajectories all along the life-course; that proximal factors are recurrent in reinforcing the acting out of criminal behaviour since any event or situation can be influenced by several variables depending on the level of vulnerability and sensibility of the person to their influence.

The encouraging message of these longitudinal results is that it is *never too late to intervene* and to intervene efficiently. This takes one on to what Farrington (2014b) defines as developmental prevention, i.e. interventions designed to prevent the development of criminal potential in individuals, especially those targeting risk and protective factors discovered in longitudinal studies of human development. Devoting specific and empirical attention to protective factors is essential because much more research is needed to discover direct protective factors that contribute to predict a low probability of reoffending and violence, and also to ascertain those buffering protective factors that predict a low probability of reoffending and violence in the presence of risk (and that often interact with risk factors) (Lösel & Farrington, 2012).

As Welsh et al. (2015) suggest, to invest in prevention is more cost-beneficial than investing in imprisonment, both monetarily and in terms of health and life quality. A conjunction of multiple perspectives (e.g. research findings, scientific evidence, public policy interest and community awareness) moving towards a similar direction is an opportunity that in itself has an *omen* of success: the time is ripe for major investment to improve the lives of disadvantaged children. This cannot and should not be ignored.

Policy implications

According to Loeber et al. (2008b) there is a direct connection between safety and criminal behaviour, and this is particularly true in the case of persisting offending by recidivists. Persistent offending contributes not only to shaking the trust in the criminal justice system, but also to building up a biased image of who these offenders are: a threat to a civilised society, not amenable to treatment, and hence incapable of changing. It follows that intervention policies for preventing recidivism are often perceived as a waste of public money.

This book is concerned with criminal recidivism, and with expanding our knowledge of the causes, risk factors and criminogenic needs involved in persisting offending. This knowledge has important policy implications for prevention strategies and treatment. Crime prevention strategies should always be based on sound, empirical, broad and multidisciplinary evidence about crime problems, their multiple causes and promising and proven practices.

Most recidivist and chronic offenders manifest some extreme psychological, family and social difficulties from childhood (e.g. impulsivity, aggressiveness, daring, anxiety, lack of concentration, unpopularity, poor social skills, poor family background, broken homes, poor parental supervision, parent's hostility, family conflicts, social isolation, etc.) that sustain their developmental maladjustment. In adolescence and adulthood, these offenders continue to be influenced by more proximal risk factors that mostly reinforce, as in a *cumulative effect*, the pattern of antisociality (Farrington, 1995, 1997; Loeber & Farrington, 1998a; Pardini et al., 2006; Theobald et al., 2013). As indicated in Chapters 2 and 3, research shows that in the long run recidivist offenders, compared with other offenders and especially with non-offenders, are less healthy, worse educated, having unsteady employment, having an unstable family life, and holding a less responsible view of their parental role (Farrington, 2012; Lussier et al., 2009; Piquero et al., 2014; Theobald et al., 2014).

Most persistent offenders start their criminal careers early in their lives; an early onset almost triples the likelihood of becoming a violent, serious and chronic offender, making it almost certain that the criminal career becomes a long one (Loeber & Farrington, 2001, 2011). Recidivist offenders are more likely than other offenders and non-offenders to be affected by internalising and psychological problems, such as personality disorders, so that it is more difficult for them to function in a prosocial manner (Auty et al., 2015; Blonigen et al., 2005; Blonigen & Krueger, 2007; Pollak, 2005). Recidivist offenders are also more likely to be socially inept, tend to accumulate more social failures than other individuals, have a higher risk of suffering from addiction problems (Flannery et al., 2007; Jennings et al., 2015), and of dying younger from violent accidents (Richardson et al., 2013).

Understanding the potential impact that risk factors, criminogenic needs and promotive factors exert on individual development, and on the emergence of persistent criminal behaviour at an early age, can have vast implications for designing effective, comprehensive and adequate preventive and treatment strategies. We make the following recommendations:

- *Scientific research should be increased*, especially longitudinal studies that look at human development from a prospective lens, and that see the patterning of changes and stability of risk and protective factors, and criminogenic needs, over time. Randomised experiments should be encouraged in so far as they allow the evaluation of the most effective and promising interventions for investing public money and professional attention.
- *Risk assessment practice should be expanded*, and the use of specific assessment instruments when dealing with high-risk offenders should be developed, so that the process of planning interventions meets also the responsivity principle of treatment. Screening and assessment should take place in various health agencies, care organisations and local authorities working with offenders, so that only effective evidence-based interventions are selected and implemented.
- *Early and sequential screening and interventions* should take place in order to promote public health, to provide parental support where needed, to identify early

the highest risk children, to supply opportunities to motivate and encourage changes in both parents and children, to sustain teachers in how to deal with the most difficult cases, and to stimulate in the public the idea that offending, especially when persisting, is a community responsibility that needs a shared effort to tackle and reduce it.

Research findings, to support evidence-based decisions of practitioners, policy-makers and legal authorities, are extremely important because local, national and EU governments need now, more than ever, to enact legislation that can make a real and effective difference to the safety of the community, to the sense of trust of the crime victims and to the possibility of turning round the lives of recidivist and persistent offenders.

It is likely that substantial financial savings to the government and taxpayers will be achieved, if developmental and community prevention programmes are supported (Lee et al., 2012). Welsh et al. (2015) have examined various developmental prevention studies and show that the types of benefits achieved from their implementation are wide-ranging, and include substantial savings to the criminal justice system, education, health care, social services, correction, employment and, especially, savings to crime victims.

More research on the most cost-beneficial programmes in different settings should be conducted and encouraged. Cost-benefit evidence is extremely powerful in persuading policy-makers to invest in effective programmes. As Welsh and colleagues (2015) would say, that would be in everyone's interest.

Notes

1   This principle is similar to the strategic objectives of *Every Child Matters*, a major government policy document (Chief Secretary to the Treasury, 2003; www.everychildmatters.gov.uk). See also Farrington (2014a).
2   This is named after the Dodo Bird in *Alice in Wonderland* who argued that 'all have won and all must have prizes' (Shadish & Sweeney, 1991).

8
CONCLUSIONS

Criminal recidivism refers to reoffending within a particular follow-up period. As the time period increases, the probability of recidivism also increases. Recidivism can be measured by self-reports of offending or by official measures such as rearrest, reconviction or reincarceration. Recidivism is often measured as a dichotomous variable, but it is also useful to measure the time to reoffending, the number of re-offences, and the types and financial costs of re-offences. For some purposes (e.g. in studying sex offenders), it is useful to define recidivism according to the commission of similar types of re-offences. Recidivism is defined according to the commission of a subsequent offence during a certain follow-up period, but often there is more interest in a small minority of persistent or chronic offenders who account for the majority of offences.

Recidivism can sometimes be long delayed. For example, in the research of Soothill and Gibbens (1978), one-third of recidivist sex offenders were not reconvicted until at least ten years after their sex offence. Therefore, it is important to study recidivism in long-term longitudinal studies, preferably including frequent interviews and measuring self-reported as well as official offending (see e.g. Brame et al., 2014). Very long follow-up periods are needed to study true desistance, defined as the complete termination of offending. Ideally, comparable measures of recidivism should be regularly published in all countries.

The probability of recidivism decreases with age and is lower for females than for males. It is generally higher after custodial sentences than after non-custodial sentences. This result holds up in quasi-experimental analyses that control for pre-existing differences between the two categories of offenders, for example, using propensity score matching. There have been very few randomised experiments comparing custodial and non-custodial sentences, but these do not generally show that the probability of recidivism is higher after custodial sentences (Villetaz et al., 2014). More randomised experiments should be carried out in which offenders who would normally receive a short custodial sentence are randomly assigned to receive a non-custodial sentence.

The most relevant theories that explain recidivism are developmental and life-course theories of offending (Farrington, 2005a). In particular, the theory of Moffitt (1993) distinguishes between adolescence-limited and life-course-persistent offenders. The life-course-persistent offenders start offending early (typically before age 14) and continue offending for a long time, whereas the adolescence-limited offenders start later and give up offending by their early twenties. The main causes of life-course-persistent offending are neuropsychological deficits in childhood, including a difficult temperament, low self-control, impulsiveness, hyperactivity and cognitive deficits, and a poor family background, including low family income, poor parenting, harsh discipline, parental conflict and disrupted families. Also, their antisocial behaviour increases the probability of escalating into more serious crimes in a process of cumulative continuity. In contrast, the adolescence-limited offenders are influenced by delinquent peers and are trying to achieve adult goals such as money and status in their teenage years. They give up offending by their early twenties, when they can achieve these goals legitimately.

As mentioned, theories of recidivism need to be tested in longitudinal studies. The Cambridge Study in Delinquent Development (CSDD) is a prospective longitudinal study of the development of offending and antisocial behaviour in over 400 males from age 8. These London males have been followed up to age 48 in face-to-face interviews and up to age 56 in criminal records. Up to age 50, 167 (41 per cent) were convicted of criminal offences, and 118 of these (71 per cent) were recidivists, because they had two or more convictions. Generally, the males who offended at the earliest ages tended to have long criminal careers with many convictions. Interestingly, 28 chronic offenders (7 per cent of the sample), each with at least ten convictions, accounted for 52 per cent of all convictions. These chronic offenders had an average criminal career duration of over 21 years up to age 50.

In the CSDD, the best predictors at age 8–10 of whether a boy would become a one-time offender or a recidivist were family factors such as low praise by the parents, low parental interest in education, harsh parental attitude and discipline, parental disharmony, low family income and large family size. Individual factors such as troublesomeness, dishonesty and daring, which were among the best predictors of convicted compared with unconvicted males, did not discriminate so well between recidivists and one-time offenders.

Case histories of offenders can provide insightful information about human development, and Chapter 3 presented detailed case histories of the eight most highly chronic offenders in the CSDD. Generally, these males came from deprived backgrounds, showed problematic behaviour in childhood and adolescence, and continued in an antisocial life style in adulthood. Their offending was only one element of a much larger syndrome of antisocial behaviour which persisted from childhood to adulthood. However, it should be realised that development often appears almost inevitable and preordained when looking backwards but not when looking forwards. By definition, these males were highly persistent offenders. However, our statistical analyses show that there were many other males who came from similar backgrounds but who did not become chronic offenders. Therefore, the backward view is a little misleading. This is one reason why prospective longitudinal studies are essential, in order to tell us about forward probabilities (e.g. the percentage of males coming from disrupted families who were convicted) as well as backward probabilities (e.g. the percentage of convicted males who came from disrupted families). It is important to study people from criminogenic backgrounds who nevertheless lead successful and prosocial lives as well as those from criminogenic backgrounds who live antisocial lives.

There is no doubt that recidivism can be predicted with a greater than chance accuracy, and many useful risk assessment instruments are reviewed in detail in Chapter 4. Actuarial instruments predict recidivism quite accurately but are of limited use in guiding intervention, treatment and management decisions, because they focus on risk factors that cannot be changed. The fourth-generation instruments, that include risk/needs assessment, structured professional judgement and case management, are the most useful at present. Future instruments should ideally include protective factors as well as risk factors, and should ideally include causal factors, as specified by Murray et al. (2009). Also, future instruments should be more closely linked to and based on the results of major prospective longitudinal studies. There would then be a closer linkage between assessment and successful treatment.

In evaluating any prediction instrument, it is important to measure true positives, false positives, true negatives and false negatives. The ROC curve is extremely useful in specifying how these quantities vary as different selection criteria are used. In setting an optimum cut-off point, it is desirable to take account of the social and financial costs and benefits of the four possible outcomes. With very serious offences, for example, the cut-off point could be set low, in order to minimise the number of recidivists who are not identified. However, when the consequences of selection are severe (e.g. imprisonment), the cut-off point could be set high, in order to minimise the number of non-recidivists who are unnecessarily detained.

Psychopathy is an important factor that is related to recidivism and chronic offending and that can influence risk assessment and treatment. In the CSDD, high antisocial personality scores at ages 10, 14, 18 and 32 (in the top quarter) were related to high psychopathy scores at age 48 (in the top 10 per cent), and especially to the irresponsible/antisocial factor 2 scores. For example, 82 per cent of those who were high on antisocial personality at age 18 were high on psychopathy at age 48, showing the continuity over time of antisocial personality and behaviour. Almost all of the males with high psychopathy scores were convicted, and three-quarters of the chronic offenders had high psychopathy scores.

In the CSDD, the best childhood predictors of high psychopathy scores were low involvement of the father with the boy, physical neglect of the boy, a convicted father or mother, a disrupted family, low family income and high dishonesty. These factors may explain and predict the development of an 'affectionless character', in the terms of Bowlby (1951), and the development of a persistent and chronic offender. However, in addition to family factors, neurobiological factors, and especially mechanisms in the prefrontal cortex, are implicated in the development of psychopathy.

Sex offending is statistically unusual. In the CSDD, for example, only 3 per cent of a community sample of males were convicted for a sex offence up to age 50. Similarly, the sexual recidivism (recidivating by committing a sex offence) rate of sex offenders is low, typically around 10 per cent (Hargreaves & Francis, 2014). This low base rate makes it difficult to predict sexual recidivism, and false positive rates are often high. It is more common for sex offenders to recidivate by committing a non-sex offence than by committing a sex offence. This applies more to rapists, who tend to be versatile offenders, than to child molesters, who tend to be more specialised.

Sexual recidivism is predicted by sexual deviancy, such as a sexual interest in children, especially for child molesters. An antisocial personality and a criminal life style predict general recidivism but not specific sexual recidivism. Sexual recidivism can be understood and predicted by understanding different types of sex offenders, including different types of rapists and child molesters. Meta-analyses show that sex offender treatment (especially cognitive-behavioural treatment targeting thinking skills) is effective in reducing sexual recidivism.

It is evident from the persisting antisocial life style of the highly chronic offenders in the CSDD that it is not always easy to deflect people from a criminal trajectory. Many programmes have been shown to be ineffective, especially deterrence-based interventions such as 'scared straight' and boot camps. However, meta-analyses show that many other programmes are effective in reducing recidivism. This is especially true of cognitive-behavioural programmes and those that conform to the Risk-Need-Responsivity principles. In other words, programmes need to be tailored to the risk level of the offender, to the offender's needs and to the offender's responsivity or willingness to change. It is essential to accurately assess the personality features of the offender in order to understand why that person offends. It is particularly important to target psychopathic features such as impulsiveness, low empathy and a callous-unemotional personality.

Methods of reducing recidivism should be based not only on the best knowledge and theories but also on the best evaluation of evidence. Ideally, all interventions should be evaluated in randomised trials, or at least in high-quality quasi-experimental analyses. Ideally, there should be a long-term follow-up to investigate the persistence of desirable changes. Ideally, the financial benefits of the treatment should be compared with the financial costs; cost-benefit analyses are especially powerful in persuading policy-makers to invest in intervention programmes.

The main implications for policy-makers are as follows. Assess the strengths and weaknesses of offenders using the most modern and dynamic risk/needs assessment instruments that include protective factors as well as risk factors. Use these instruments to guide the management and treatment of offenders. Use the most effective cognitive-behavioural interventions with the most suitable and responsive offenders. Measure the financial costs and benefits of treatment, taking account of the reduction in offending (see Farrington & Koegl, in press).

This book has tried to summarise the best knowledge about the explanation, prediction and prevention of recidivism. We have studied recidivism from a variety of perspectives (psychological, criminological, neurocriminological, juridical and clinical) and we have presented theories, research findings and different methodological approaches. We conclude that a great deal has been learned about recidivism and about persistent offending. To advance knowledge still further, we need more prospective longitudinal studies to investigate the development of offending and antisocial behaviour, and more randomised experiments to investigate the effectiveness of intervention programmes.

REFERENCES

Abbott, B. R. (2011) 'Throwing the baby out with the bath water: Is it time for clinical judgment to supplement actuarial risk assessment?', *Journal of the American Academy of Psychiatry and the Law*, 39: 222–30.

Abel, G. G., Becker, J. V., and Cunningham-Rathner, J. (1984) 'Complications, consent, and cognitions in sex between children and adults', *International Journal of Law and Psychiatry*, 7: 89–103.

Achenbach, T. (1991a) *Manual for the Child Behavior Checklist/4–18 and 1991 Profile*. Burlington, VT: University of Vermont, Dept of Psychiatry.

Achenbach, T. (1991b) *Manual for the Youth Self Report and 1991 Profile*. Burlington, VT: University of Vermont, Dept of Psychiatry.

Achenbach, T. M., and Rescorla, L. A. (2001) *Manual for the ASEBA School-Age Forms and Profiles*. Burlington, VT: University of Vermont, Research Center for Children, Youth, and Families.

Adam Walsh Child Protection and Safety Act of 2006 (H.R. 4472, 42 USC 16901 note) (2006) Public Law 109-248, 109th Congress. United States.

Adolphs, R. (2006a) 'How do we know the minds of others? Domain-specificity, simulation, and inactive social cognition', *Brain Research*, 1079: 25–35.

Adolphs, R. (2006b) 'Perception and emotion: How we recognize facial expressions', *Current Directions in Psychological Science*, 15: 222–6.

Adolphs, R., Tranel, D., Damasio, H., and Damasio, A. (1995) 'Fear and the human amygdala', *Journal of Neuroscience*, 75: 5879–91.

Ægisdóttir, S., White, M. J., Spengler, P. M., Maugherman, A. S., Anderson, L. A., Cook, R. S., et al. (2006) 'The meta-analysis of clinical judgment project: Fifty-six years of accumulated research on clinical versus statistical prediction', *Clinical Psychology Review*, 34: 341–82.

Ainsworth, S. A., and Taxman, F. S. (2013) 'Creating simulation parameter inputs with existing data sources: Estimating offender risks, needs, and recidivism', in F. S. Taxman and A. Pattavina (eds), *Simulation Strategies to Reduce Recidivism: Risk Need Responsivity (RNR) Modeling for the Criminal Justice System* (pp. 115–42). New York: Springer.

Allport, G. W. (1937) *Personality: A Psychological Interpretation*. New York: Holt, Rinehart, & Winston. American Law Institute (1962) *Model Penal Code*. Philadelphia, PA: American Law Institute.
American Law Institute (1962) *Model Penal Code*. Philadelphia: American Law Institute.
American Psychiatric Association (1994) *Diagnostic Manual of Mental Disorder (DSM-IV^{TM})*. Washington, DC: American Psychiatric Association.
American Psychiatric Association (1999) *Dangerous Sex Offenders: A Task Force Report of the American Psychiatric Association*. Washington, DC: APA.
American Psychiatric Association (2000) *Diagnostic Manual of Mental Disorder Text Revision (DSM-IV-TR)*. Washington, DC: American Psychiatric Association.
American Psychiatric Association (2013) *Diagnostic and Statistical Manual of Mental Disorders* (5th edn). Arlington, VA: American Psychiatric Association.
Anastasi, A. (1982) *Psychological Testing* (5th edn). New York: Macmillan.
Andersen, H. (2004) 'Mental health in prison populations: A review with special emphasis on a study of danish prisoners on remand', *Acta Psychiatrica Scandinavica*, 110: 5–59.
Anderson, D., and Dodgson, P. G. (2002) 'Empathy deficits, self-esteem, and cognitive distortions in sexual offenders', in Y. M. Fernandez (eds), *In their Shoes: Examining the Issue of Empathy and its Place in the Treatment of Offenders* (pp. 73–90). Oklahoma City, OK: Wood 'N' Barnes Publishing.
Anderson, J. C., Williams, S., McGee, R., and Silva, P. A. (1987) 'DSM–III disorders in preadolescent children', *Archives of General Psychiatry*, 44: 69–76.
Anderson, S. W., Bechara, A., Damasio, H., Tranel, D., and Damasio, A. R. (1999) 'Impairment of social and moral behavior related to early damage in human prefrontal cortex', *Nature Neuroscience*, 2: 1032–7.
Anderson, S. W., Barrash, J., Bechara, A., and Tranel, D. (2006) 'Impairments of emotion and real-world complex behavior following childhood- or adult-onset damage to ventromedial prefrontal cortex', *Journal of International Neuropsychological Society*, 12: 224–35.
Andrade, J. T. (2008) 'The inclusion of antisocial behavior in the construct of psychopathy: A review of the research', *Aggression and Violent Behavior*, 13: 323–35.
Andrews, D. A. (2006) 'Enhancing adherence to risk-need-responsivity: Making quality a matter of policy', *Criminology and Public Policy*, 5: 595–602.
Andrews, D. A., and Bonta, J. (1994) *The Psychology of Criminal Conduct*. Cincinnati, OH: Anderson Press.
Andrews, D. A., and Bonta, J. (1995) *The LSI-R: The Level of Service Inventory – Revised*. Toronto: Multi-Health Systems.
Andrews, D. A., and Bonta, J. (1998) *The Psychology of Criminal Conduct* (2nd edn). Cincinnati, OH: Anderson Press.
Andrews, D. A., and Bonta, J. (2006) *The Psychology of Criminal Conduct* (4th edn). Cincinnati, OH: Anderson Press.
Andrews, D. A., and Bonta, J. (2010a) *The Psychology of Criminal Conduct* (5th edn). Cincinnati, OH: Anderson.
Andrews, D. A., and Bonta, J. (2010b) 'Rehabilitating criminal justice policy and practice', *Psychology, Public Policy, and Law*, 16: 39–55.
Andrews, D. A., and Dowden, C. (2006) 'Risk principle of case classification in correctional treatment: A meta-analytic investigation', *International Journal of Offender Therapy and Comparative Criminology*, 50: 88–100.

Andrews, D. A., and Dowden, C. (2007) 'The Risk-Need-Responsivity model of assessment and human service in prevention and corrections: Rehabilitative jurisprudence', *Canadian Journal of Criminology and Criminal Justice*, 49: 439–64.

Andrews, D. A., Bonta, J., and Hoge, R. D. (1990a) 'Classification for effective rehabilitation: Rediscovering psychology', *Criminal Justice and Behavior*, 17: 19–52.

Andrews, D. A., Zinger, I., Hoge, R., Bonta, J., and Cullen, F. (1990b) 'Does correctional treatment work? A psychologically informed meta-analysis', *Criminology*, 28: 269–404.

Andrews, D. A., Bonta, J., and Wormith, J. S. (2004) *LS/CMI: The Level of Service/Case Management Inventory: An Offender Assessment System*. Toronto: Multi-Health Systems.

Andrews, D. A., Bonta, J., and Wormith, J. S. (2006) 'The recent past and near future of risk and/or need assessment', *Crime and Delinquency*, 52: 7–27.

Andrews, D. A., Bonta, J., and Wormith, J. S. (2010) 'The Level of Service (LS) assessment of adults and older adolescents', in R. K. Otto and K. S. Douglas (eds), *Handbook of Violence Risk Assessment* (pp. 199–225). New York: Routledge.

Archer, R. P., Buffington-Vollum, J. K., Stredny, R. V., and Handel, R. W. (2006) 'A survey of psychological test use patterns among forensic psychologists', *Journal of Personality Assessment*, 87: 84–94.

Arnett, P. A., Smith, S. S., and Newman, J. P. (1997) 'Approach and avoidance motivation in psychopathic criminal offenders during passive avoidance', *Journal of Personality and Social Psychology*, 72: 1413–28.

ATSA Professional Issues Committee (2001) *Practice Standards and Guidelines for Members of the Association for the Treatment of Sexual Abusers*. Beaverton, OR: ATSA.

Augimeri, L. K., Koegl, C. J., Webster, C. D., and Levene, K. (2001) *Early Assessment Risk List for Boys: EARL-20B, Version 2*. Toronto: Earlscourt Child and Family Centre (now called Child Development Institute).

Augimeri, L. K., Enebrink, P., Walsh, M. M., and Jiang, D. (2010) 'Gender-specific childhood risk assessment tools: Early assessment risk lists for boys (EARL-20B) and girls (EARL-21G)', in R. K. Otto and K. S. Douglas (eds), *Handbook of Violence Risk Assessment* (pp. 43–62). Oxford: Routledge, Taylor & Francis.

Augimeri, L. K., Walsh, M. M., Liddon, A. D., and Dassinger, C. R. (2011) 'From risk identification to risk management: A comprehensive strategy for young children engaged in antisocial behavior', in D. W. Springer and A. Roberts (eds), *Juvenile Justice and delinquency* (pp. 117–40). Sadbury, MA: Jones & Bartlett.

Augstein, H. F. (1996) 'J C Prichard's concept of moral insanity: A medical theory of the corruption of human nature', *Medical History*, 40: 311–43.

Auty, K. M., Farrington, D. P., and Coid, J. W. (2015) 'Intergenerational transmission of psychopathy and mediation via psychosocial risk factors', *British Journal of Psychiatry*, 206: 26–31.

Babiak, P. (1995) 'When psychopaths go to work: A case study of an industrial psychopath', *Applied Psychology: An International Review*, 44: 171–88.

Babiak, P. (1996) 'Psychopathic manipulation in organizations: Pawns, patrons, and patsies', *Issues in Criminological and Legal Psychology*, 24: 12–17.

Babiak, P. (2007) 'From darkness into the light: Psychopathy in industrial and organizational psychology', in H. Hervé and J. C. Yuille (eds), *The Psychopath: Theory, Research, and Practice* (pp. 411–28). Mahwah, NJ: Erlbaum.

Babiak, P., and Hare, R. (2006) *Snakes in Suits: When Psychopaths Go to Work*. New York: Regan Books.

Babiak, P., Neumann, C. S., and Hare, R. D. (2010) 'Corporate psychopathy: Talking the walk', *Behavioral Sciences and the Law*, 28: 174–93.

Babinski, L. M., Hartsough, C. S., and Lambert, N. M. (1999) 'Childhood conduct problems, hyperactivity-impulsivity, and inattention as predictors of adult criminal activity', *Journal of Child Psychology and Psychiatry and Allied Disciplines*, 40: 347–55.

Bailar, J. C., and Bailer, A. J. (1999) 'Risk assessment – The mother of all uncertainties: Disciplinary perspectives on uncertainty in risk assessment'. *Annals of the New York Academy of Sciences*, 895: 273–85.

Baird, C., and Wagner, D. (2000) 'The relative validity of actuarial and consensus based risk assessment systems', *Children and Youth Services Review*, 22: 839–71.

Baker, L. A., Jacobson, K. C., Raine, A., Lozano, D. I., and Bezdjian, S. (2007) 'Genetic and environmental bases of childhood antisocial behavior: A multi-informant twin study', *Journal of Abnormal Psychology*, 116: 219–35.

Bakermans-Kranenburg, M. J., and van IJzendoorn, M. H. (2009) 'The first 10,000 Adult Attachment Interviews: Distributions of adult attachment representations in clinical and non-clinical groups', *Attachment and Human Development*, 11: 223–63.

Barbaree, H. E. (1991) 'Denial and minimization among sex offenders: Assessment and treatment outcome', *Forum on Corrections Research*, 3: 30–3.

Barbaree, H. E. (1997) 'Evaluating treatment efficacy with sexual offenders: The insensitivity of recidivism studies to treatment effects', *Sexual Abuse: A Journal of Research and Treatment*, 9: 111–28.

Barbaree, H. E., and Blanchard, R. (2008) 'Sexual deviance over the life span: Reduction in deviant sexual behaviour in the aging sex offender', in D. R. Laws and W. T. O'Donohue (eds), *Sexual Deviance: Theory, Assessment, and Treatment* (2nd edn, pp. 37–60). New York: Guilford Press.

Barbaree, H. E., Blanchard, R., and Langton, C. M. (2003) 'The development of sexual aggression through the life span: The effect of age on sexual arousal and recidivism among sex offenders', in R. Prentky, E. Janus, and M. Seto (eds), *Understanding and Managing Sexually Coercive Behavior* (pp. 59–71). Annals of the New York Academy of Sciences, vol. 989. New York: New York Academy of Sciences.

Barbaree, H. E., Langton, C. M., Blanchard, R., and Cantor, J. M. (2009) 'Aging versus stable enduring traits as explanatory constructs in sex offender recidivism: Partitioning actuarial prediction into conceptually meaningful components', *Criminal Justice and Behavior*, 36: 443–65.

Barnett, A., Blumstein, A., and Farrington, D. P. (1989) 'A prospective test of a criminal career model', *Criminology*, 27: 373–88.

Barnett, G., and Mann, R. E. (2013) 'Empathy deficits and sexual offending: A model of obstacles to empathy', *Aggression and Violent Behavior*, 18: 228–39.

Baron-Cohen, S. (2011) *Zero Degrees of Empathy: A New Theory of Human Cruelty*. London: Penguin UK.

Baron-Cohen, S., Ring, H. A., Wheelwright, S., Bullmore, E. T., Brammer, M. J., Simmons, A., and Williams, S. C. (1999) 'Social intelligence in the normal and autistic brain: An fMRI study', *European Journal of Neuroscience*, 11: 1891–8.

Bartel, P., Borum, R., and Forth, A. (1999) *Structured Assessment for Violence Risk in Youth (SAVRY)*. Consultation Edition.

Baskin-Sommers, A. R., and Newman, J. P. (2012) 'Cognition–emotion interactions in psychopathy: Implications for theory and practice', in H. Häkkänen-Nyholm and J.-O. Nyholm (eds), *Psychopathy and Law: A Practitioner's Guide* (pp. 79–97). Chichester: Wiley-Blackwell.

Baskin-Sommers, A. R., Curtin, J. J., and Newman, J. P. (2011) 'Specifying the attentional selection that moderates the fearlessness of psychopathic offenders', *Psychological Science*, 22: 226–34.

Beauchaine, T. P., Gatzke-Kopp, L., and Mead, H. (2007) 'Polyvagal theory and developmental psychopathology: Emotion dysregulation and conduct problems from preschool to adolescence', *Biological Psychology*, 74: 174–84.

Beech, A. R., and Fisher, D. D. (2002) 'The rehabilitation of child sex offenders', *Australian Psychologist*, 37: 206–15.

Beeghly, M., and Cicchetti, D. (1994) 'Child maltreatment, attachment, and the self system: Emergence of an internal state lexicon in toddlers at high social risk', *Development and Psychopathology*, 6: 5–30.

Belfrage, H., Strand, S., Storey, J. E., Gibas, A. L., Kropp, P. R., and Hart, S. D. (2011) 'Assessment and management of risk for intimate partner violence by police officers using the spousal assault risk assessment guide', *Law and Human Behavior*, 36: 60–77.

Bennett, C. S. (2005) 'Attachment theory and research applied to the conceptualization and treatment of pathological narcissism', *Clinical Social Work Journal*, 34: 45–60.

Benning, S. D., Patrick, C. J., Blonigen, D. M., Hicks, B. M., and Iacono, W. G. (2003) 'Estimating facets of psychopathy from normal personality traits: A step toward community-epidemiological investigations', *Psychological Assessment*, 15: 340–50.

Berger, P., and Luckman, T. (1966) *The Social Construction of Reality*. New York: Doubleday.

Berliner, L., Schram, D., Miller, L. L., and Milloy, C. D. (1995) 'A sentencing alternative for sex offenders: A study of decision making and recidivism', *Journal of Interpersonal Violence*, 10: 487–502.

Birbaumer, N., Veit, R., Lotze, M., Erb, M., Hermann, C., Grodd, W., and Flor, H. (2005) 'Deficient fear conditioning in psychopathy: A functional magnetic resonance imaging study', *Archives of General Psychiatry*, 62: 799–805.

Black, D. W., Gunter, T., Loveless, P., Allen, J., and Sieleni, B. (2010) 'Antisocial personality disorder in incarcerated offenders: Psychiatric comorbidity and quality of life', *Annals of Clinical Psychiatry*, 22: 113–20.

Blackburn, R. (1988) 'On moral judgments and personality disorders: The myth of psychopathic personality revisited', *British Journal of Psychiatry*, 153: 505–12.

Blackburn, R. (2007) 'Personality disorder and antisocial deviance: Comments on the debate on the structure of the psychopathy checklist-revised', *Journal of Personality Disorder*, 21: 142–59.

Blackburn, R., and Coid, J. W. (1998) 'Psychopathy and the dimensions of personality disorder in violent offenders', *Personality and Individual Differences*, 25: 129–45.

Blackburn, R., and Coid, J. W. (1999) 'Empirical clusters of DSM-III personality disorders in violent offenders', *Journal of Personality Disorders*, 13: 18–34.

Blair, R. J. R. (1995) 'A cognitive developmental approach to morality: Investigating the psychopathy', *Cognition*, 57: 1–29.

Blair, R. J. R. (1997) 'Moral reasoning and the child with psychopathic tendencies', *Personality and Individual Differences*, 27: 135–45.

Blair, R. J. R. (2003) 'Neurobiological basis of psychopathy', *British Journal of Psychiatry*, 182: 5–7.

Blair, R. J. R. (2007) 'Aggression, psychopathy and free will from a cognitive neuroscience perspective', *Behavioral Sciences and the Law*, 25: 321–31.

Blair, R. J. R. (2008) 'The amygdala and ventromedial prefrontal cortex: Functional contributions and dysfunction in psychopathy', *Philosophical Transactions of the Royal Society London B: Biological Sciences*, 363: 2557–65.

Blair, R. J. R. (2010) 'Neuroimaging of psychopathy and antisocial behavior: A targeted review', *Current Psychiatry Reports*, 12: 76–82.

Blokland, A. A. J., and Lussier, P. (2015) 'The criminal career paradigm and its relevance to studying sex offenders', in A. A. J. Blokland and P. Lussier (eds), *Sex Offenders: A Criminal Career Approach* (pp. 19–34). Chichester: John Wiley & Sons.

Blonigen, D. M., and Krueger, R. F. (2007) 'Personality and violence: The unifying role of structural models of personality', in D. J. Flannery, A. T. Vazsonyi, and I. D. Waldman (eds), *The Cambridge Handbook of Violent Behavior and Aggression* (pp. 288–305). New York: Cambridge University Press.

Blonigen, D. M., Hicks, B. M., Krueger, R. F., Patrick, C. J., and Iacono, W. G. (2005) 'Psychopathic personality traits: Heritability and genetic overlap with internalizing and externalizing psychopathology', *Psychological Medicine*, 35: 637–48.

Blumenthal, J. A., Babyak, M. A., Moore, K. A., Craighead, W. E., Herman, S., Khatri, P., Waugh, R., Napolitano, M. A., Forman, L. M., Appelbaum, M., Murali Doraiswamy, P., and Krishnan, K. R. (1999) 'Effects of exercise training on older patients with major depression', *Archives of Internal Medicine*, 159: 2349–56.

Blumstein, A., and Nakamura, K. (2009) 'Redemption in the presence of widespread criminal background checks', *Criminology*, 47: 327–59.

Blumstein, A., Cohen, J., and Hsieh, P. (1982) *The Duration of Adult Criminal Careers*. Final report submitted to National Institute of Justice, Aug. Pittsburgh, PA: School of Urban and Public Affairs, Carnegie-Mellon University.

Blumstein, A., Farrington, D. P., and Moitra, S. (1985) '*Delinquency careers: Innocents, desisters, and persisters*', in M. Tonry and N. Morris (eds), *Crime and Justice: An Annual Review of Research*, 6: 187-219. Chicago, IL: University of Chicago Press.

Blumstein, A., Cohen, J., Roth, J. A., and Visher, C. A. (eds) (1986) *Criminal Careers and 'Career Criminals'* (vol. 2). Panel on Research on Career Criminals, Committee on Research on Law Enforcement and the Administration of Justice, Commission on Behavioral and Social Sciences and Education, National Research Council. Washington, DC: National Academy Press.

Blumstein, A., Cohen, J., and Farrington, D. P. (1988a) 'Criminal career research: Its value for criminology', *Criminology*, 26: 1–35.

Blumstein, A., Cohen, J., and Farrington, D. P. (1988b) 'Longitudinal and criminal career research: Further classifications', *Criminology*, 26: 57–74.

Boccardi, M., Ganzola, R., Rossi, R., Sabattoli, F., Laakso, M. P., and Repo-Tiihonen, E. (2010) 'Abnormal hippocampal shape in offenders with psychopathy', *Human Brain Mapping*, 31: 438–47.

Boccardi, M., Frisoni, G. B., Hare, R. D., Cavedo, E., Najt, P., Pievani, M., Rasser, P. E., Laakso, M. P., Aronen, H. J., Repo-Tiihonen, E.,Vaurio, O., Thompson, P. M., and Tiihonen, J. (2011) 'Cortex and amygdala morphology in psychopathy', *Psychiatry Research: Neuroimaging*, 193: 85–92.

Boer, D. P., and Hart, S. D. (2009) 'Sex offender risk assessment: Research, evaluation, "best-practice" recommendations and future directions', in J. L. Ireland, C. A. Ireland, and P. Birch (eds), *Violent and Sexual Offenders: Assessment, Treatment, and Management* (pp. 27–42). Cullompton, Devon: Willan Publishing.

Boer, D. P., Hart, S. D., Kropp, P. R., and Webster, C. D. (1997) *Manual for the Sexual Violence Risk – 20: Professional guidelines for assessing risk of sexual violence*. Vancouver, BC: The Mental Health, Law, and Policy Institute.

Bonta, J. (1996) 'Risk-needs assessment and treatment', in A. T. Harland (ed.), *Choosing Correctional Options that Work: Defining the Demand and Evaluating the Supply* (pp. 18–32). Thousand Oaks, CA: Sage.

Bonta, J. (2002) 'Offender risk assessment: Guidelines for selection and use', *Criminal Justice and Behavior*, 29: 355–79.

Bonta, J., and Wormith, J. S. (2007) 'Risk and need assessment', in G. McIvor and P. Raynor (eds), *Developments in Social Work with Offenders* (pp. 131–52). London and Philadelphia, PA: Jessica Kingsley Publishers.

Bonta, J., Law, M., and Hanson, R. K. (1998) 'The prediction of criminal and violent recidivism among mentally disordered offenders: A meta-analysis', *Psychological Bulletin*, 123: 123–42.

Borum, R. (1996) 'Improving the clinical practice of violence risk assessment: Technology, guidelines and training', *American Psychologist*, 51: 945–56.

Borum, R., Otto, R., and Golding, S. (1993) 'Improving clinical judgement and decision making in forensic evaluation', *Journal of Psychiatry and Law*, 21: 35–76.

Borum, R., Bartel, P., and Forth, A. (2002) *Manual for the Structured Assessment of Violence Risk in Youth (SAVRY)*, consultation edn, version 1. Tampa, FL: University of South Florida.

Botbol, M. (2010) 'Towards an integrative neuroscientific and psychodynamic approach to the transmission of attachment', *Journal Physiology Paris*, 104: 263–71.

Bottoms, A., Shapland, J., Costello, A., Holmes, D., and Muir, G. (2004) 'Towards desistance: Theoretical underpinnings for an empirical study', *Howard Journal of Criminal Justice*, 43: 368–89.

Bouchard, M.-A., Target, M., Lecours, S., Fonagy, P., Tremblay, L.-M., Schachter, A., and Stein, H. (2008) 'Mentalization in adult attachment narratives: Reflective functioning, mental states, and affect elaboration compared', *Psychoanalytic Psychology*, 25: 47–66.

Bowlby, J. (1951) *Maternal Care and Mental Health*. Geneva: World Health Organization.

Bowlby, J. (1980) *Attachment and Loss*, vol. 3, *Loss, Sadness and Depression*. London: Hogarth Press/Institute of Psychoanalysis.

Brame, R., Mulvey, E. P., Piquero, A. R., and Schubert, C. A. (2014) 'Assessing the nature and mix of offences among serious adolescent offenders', *Criminal Behaviour and Mental Health*, 14: 254–64.

Brand, S., and Price, R. (2000) *The Economic and Social Costs of Crime*. Home Office Research Study, 217. London: Research, Development and Statistics Directorate, Home Office.

Brass, M., and Haggard, P. (2007) 'To do or not to do: The neural signature of self-control', *Journal of Neuroscience*, 27: 9141–5.

Brass, M., and Haggard, P. (2008) 'The what, when, whether model of intentional action', *Neuroscientist*, 14: 319–25.

Brody, S. R. (1976) *The Effectiveness of Sentencing: A Review of the Literature*. Home Office Research Study, 35. London: HMSO.

Brooks, W. M. (2010) 'The tail still wags the dog: The pervasive and inappropriate influence by the psychiatric profession on the civil commitment process', *North Dakota Law Review*, 86: 259–318.

Brower, M. C., and Price, B. H. (2001) 'Neuropsychiatry of frontal lobe dysfunction in violent and criminal behaviour: A critical review', *Journal of Neurology, Neurosurgery, and Psychiatry*, 71: 720–6.

Brown, E., and Males, M. (2011) 'Does age or poverty level best predict criminal arrest and homicide rates? A preliminary investigation', *Justice Policy Journal*, 8: 1–30.

Brown, S. (2005) *Treating Sex Offenders: An Introduction to Sex Offender Treatment Programmes*. Cullompton, Devon: Willan Publishing.

Brundtland, G. H. (2002) 'Violence prevention: A public health approach', *JAMA*, 288: 1580.

Bucciarelli, M., Khemlani, S., and Johnson-Laird, P. N. (2008) 'The psychology of moral reasoning', *Judgment and Decision Making*, 3: 121–39.

Buchanan, A. (2008) 'Risk of violence by psychiatric patients: Beyond the "actuarial versus clinical" assessment debate', *Psychiatric Services*, 59: 184–90.

Buchanan, A., and Leese, M. (2006) 'Quantifying the contributions of three types of information to the prediction of criminal conviction using the receiver operating characteristic', *British Journal of Psychiatry*, 188: 472–8.

Budd, T., Sharp, C., and Mayhew, P. (2005) *Offending in England and Wales: First results from the 2003 Crime and Justice Survey*. Home Office Research Study No. 275. London: Home Office.

Bullock, K. (2011) 'The construction and management of risk management technologies in contemporary probation practice', *British Journal of Criminology*, 51: 120–35.

Burdon, W. M., and Gallagher, C. A. (2002) 'Coercion and sex offenders controlling sex-offending behavior through incapacitation and treatment', *Criminal Justice and Behavior*, 29: 87–109.

Burke, D. (2001) 'Empathy in sexually offending and non-offending adolescent males', *Journal of Interpersonal Violence*, 16: 222–33.

Burke, J. D., Loeber, R., and Birhamer, B. (2002) 'Oppositional defiant disorder and conduct disorder: A review of the past 10 years, part II', *Journal of the American Academy of Child and Adolescent Psychiatry*, 41: 1275–93.

Burt, C. (1923) 'Delinquency and mental defect', *British Journal of Medical Psychology*, 3: 168–78.

Burt, C. (1944) *The Young Delinquent*. London: University of London.

Bushway, S. D., Thornberry, T. P., and Krohn, M. D. (2003) 'Desistance as a developmental process: A comparison of static and dynamic approaches', *Journal of Quantitative Criminology*, 19: 129–53.

Buss, D. M. (1984) 'Evolutionary biology and personality psychology: Toward a conception of human nature and individual differences', *American Psychologist*, 39: 1135–47.

Buss, D. M. (2005) *The Murderer Next Door: Why the Mind is Designed to Kill*. New York: Penguin Press.

Butcher, J. N., Williams, C. L., Graham, J. R., Archer, R. P., Tellegen, A., Ben-Porath, Y. S., and Kaemmer, B. (1992) *Minnesota Multiphasic Personality Inventory – Adolescent*. Minneapolis, MN: University of Minnesota Press.

Calaprice, A. (2011) *The Ultimate Quotable Einstein*. Princeton, NJ: Princeton University Press and Hebrew University of Jerusalem.

Caldwell, M. (2002) 'What we do not know about juvenile sexual reoffense risk', *Child Maltreatment*, 7: 291–302.

Caldwell, M. (2010) 'Study characteristics and recidivism base rates in juvenile sex offender recidivism', *International Journal of Offender Therapy and Comparative Criminology*, 54: 197–212.

Cale, J., and Lussier, P. (2012) 'Merging developmental and criminal career perspectives: Implications for risk assessment and risk prediction of violent/sexual recidivism in adult sexual aggressors of women', *Sexual Abuse: Journal of Research and Treatment*, 24: 107–32.

Camp, J. P., Skeem, J. L., Barchard, K., Lilienfeld, S. O., and Poythress, N. G. (2013) 'Psychopathic predators? Getting specific about the relation between psychopathy and violence', *Journal of Consulting and Clinical Psychology*, 81: 467–80.

Campbell, J. C. (1986) 'Nursing assessment for risk of homicide with battered women', *Advances in Nursing Science*, 8: 36–51.

Campbell, J. C. (1995) 'Prediction of homicide of and by battered women', in J. C. Campbell (ed.), *Assessing Dangerousness: Violence by Sexual Offenders, Batterers and Child Abusers* (pp. 96–113). Thousand Oaks, CA: Sage.

Campbell, J. C., Webster, D. W., and Glass, N. (2009) 'The danger assessment: Validation of a lethality risk assessment instrument for intimate partner femicide', *Journal of Interpersonal Violence*, 24: 653–74.

Campbell, M. A., French, S., and Gendreau, P. (2009) 'The prediction of violence in adult offender: A meta-analytic comparison of instruments and methods of assessment', *Criminal Justice Behavior*, 36: 567–90.

Cann, J., Falshaw, J., and Friendship, C. (2004) 'Sexual offenders discharged from prison in England and Wales: A 21-year reconviction study', *Legal and Criminological Psychology*, 9: 1–10.

Caponecchia, C., Sun, A. Y. Z., and Wyatt A. (2011) '"Psychopaths" at work? Implications of lay persons' use of labels and behavioural criteria for psychopathy', *Journal of Business Ethics*, 107: 399–408.

Carver, C. S., and White, T. L. (1994) 'Behavioral inhibition, behavioral activation, and affective responses to impending reward and punishment: The BIS/BAS scales', *Journal of Personality and Social Psychology*, 67: 319–33.

Casey, B. J., Jones, R. M., and Somerville, L. H. (2011) 'Braking and accelerating of the adolescent brain', *Journal of Research on Adolescence*, 21: 21–33.

Caspi, A., and Moffitt, T. E. (1993) 'When do individual differences matter? A paradoxical theory of personality coherence', *Psychological Inquiry*, 4: 247–71.

Caspi, A., and Silva, P. A. (1995) 'Temperamental qualities at age 3 predict personality traits in young adulthood: Longitudinal evidence from a birth cohort', *Child Development*, 66: 486–98.

Caspi, A., Henry, B., McGee, R. O., Moffitt, T. E., and Silva, P. A. (1995) 'Temperamental origins of child and adolescent behavior problems: From age three to age fifteen', *Child Development*, 66: 55–68.

Catalano, R. F., and Hawkins, J. D. (1996) 'The social development model: A theory of antisocial behaviour', in J. D. Hawkins (ed.), *Delinquency and Crime: Current Theories* (pp. 149–97). Cambridge: Cambridge University Press.

Cauda, F., Costa, T., Torta, D. M., Sacco, K., D'Agata, F., Duca, S., Geminiani, G., Fox, P. T., and Vercelli, A. (2012) 'Meta-analytic clustering of the insular cortex: Characterizing the meta-analytic connectivity of the insula when involved in active tasks', *Neuroimage*, 62: 343–55.

Chakhssi, F., de Ruiter, C., and Bernstein, D. (2010) 'Change during forensic treatment in psychopathic versus nonpsychopathic offenders', *Journal of Forensic Psychiatry and Psychology*, 21(5): 660–82.

Chambers Dictionary of Etymology (1988) New York: H. W. Wilson Co.

Champagne, F. A. (2010) 'Early adversity and developmental outcomes: Interaction between genetics, epigenetics, and social experiences across the life span', *Perspectives on Psychological Science*, 5: 564–74.

Champion, D. J. (1994) *Measuring Offender Risk: A Criminal Justice Sourcebook*. Westport, CT: Greenwood Publishing Group.

Chen, X., and Adams, M. (2010) 'Are teen delinquency abstainers social introverts? A test of Moffitt's theory', *Journal of Research in Crime and Delinquency*, 47: 439–68.

Chesterton, G. K. (1908) *Orthodoxy*. The Project Gutenberg EBook. www.gutenberg.org/files/16769/16769-h/16769-h.htm. Accessed 19 Jan. 2014.

Chief Secretary to the Treasury (2003) *Every Child Matters*. Presented to Parliament by the Chief Secretary to the Treasury by Command of Her Majesty. www.education.gov.uk/publications/eOrderingDownload/CM5860.pdf. Accessed 26 Mar. 2015.

Child Sex Offenders Disclosure Scheme (Sarah's Law) (2001) London: Home Office.

Christiansen, K. O., Elers-Nielsen, M., Le Maire, L., and Sturup, G. K. (1965) 'Recidivism among sexual offenders', *Scandinavian Studies in Criminology*, 1: 55–85. London: Tavistock.

Cicchetti, D., and Cohen, D. J. (1995) 'Perspectives on developmental psychopathology', in D. Cicchetti and D. J. Cohen (eds), *Developmental Psychopathology: Theory and Methods* (vol. 1, pp. 3–20). New York: John Wiley & Sons.
Cima, M., Tonnaer, F., and Hauser, M. D. (2010) 'Psychopaths know right from wrong but don't care', *Social Cognitive and Affective Neuroscience*, 5: 59–67.
Clarke, S. (2013) 'Trends in crime and criminal justice, 2010', *Eurostat: Statistics in Focus*, 18. Brussels: European Union.
Cleckley, H. (1976) *The Mask of Sanity* (5th edn). St Louis, MO: Mosby.
Cleverley, K., and Boyle, M. H. (2010) 'The individual as a moderating agent of the long-term impact of sexual abuse', *Journal of Interpersonal Violence*, 25: 274–90.
Cloninger, C. R. (1987) 'A systematic method for clinical description and classification of personality variants', *Archives of General Psychiatry*, 44: 573–88.
Cohen, J. (1986) 'Research on criminal careers: Individual frequency rates and offense seriousness', in A. Blumstein, J. Cohen, J. A. Roth, and C. A. Visher (eds), *Criminal Careers and 'Career Criminals'* (vol. 2, pp. 292–418). Washington, DC: National Academy Press.
Cohen, M. X., Schoene-Bake, J.-C., Elger, E. C., and Weber, B. (2009) 'Connectivity-based segregation of the human striatum predicts personality characteristics', *Nature Neuroscience*, 12: 32–4.
Coid, J. (2003) 'Formulating strategies for the primary prevention of adult antisocial behaviour: "High risk" or "population" strategies?', in D. P. Farrington and J. W. Coid (eds), *Early Prevention of Adult Antisocial Behaviour* (pp. 32–78). Cambridge: Cambridge University Press.
Coid, J., Yang, M., Ullrich, S., Roberts, A., and Hare, R. D. (2009) 'Prevalence and correlates of psychopathic traits in the household population of Great Britain', *International Journal of Law and Psychiatry*, 32: 65–73.
Coid, J., Yang, M., Ullrich, S., Zhang, T., Sizmur, S., Farrington, D. P., and Rogers, R. D. (2010) 'Most items in structured risk assessment instruments do not predict violence', *Journal of Forensic Psychiatry and Psychology*, 22: 3–21.
Community Protection Act (1990) Washington, DC: Washington State Legislature.
Conte, J. R. (1991) 'The nature of sexual offences against children', in C. R. Hollin and K. Howells (eds), *Clinical Approaches to Sex Offenders and their Victims* (pp. 11–34). Chichester: John Wiley & Sons.
Cook, R. J., and Sackett, D. L. (1995) 'The number needed to treat: A clinically useful measure of treatment effect', *British Medical Journal*, 310: 452–4.
Cooke, D. J. (2010) 'More prejudicial than probative?', *The Journal*. www.journalonline.co.uk/Magazine/55-1/1007437.aspx. Accessed 30 Apr. 2014.
Cooke, D. J., and Michie, C. (2001) 'Refining the construct of psychopathy: Toward a hierarchical model', *Psychological Assessment*, 13: 171–88.
Cooke, D. J., and Michie, C. (2010) 'Limitations of diagnostic precision and predictive utility in the individual case: A challenge for forensic practice', *Law and Human Behavior*, 34: 259–74.
Cooke, D. J., and Michie, C. (2012) 'Violence risk assessment: From prediction to understanding – or From what? To why?', in C. Logan and L. Johnstone (eds), *Managing Clinical Risk: A Guide to Effective Practice* (Issues in Forensic Psychology) (pp. 3–25). London: Routledge.
Cooke, D. J., Michie, C., Hart, S. D., and Clark, D. A. (2004) 'Reconstructing psychopathy: Clarifying the significance of antisocial and socially deviant behavior in the diagnosis of psychopathic personality disorder', *Journal of Personality Disorders*, 18: 337–57.
Cooley, C. H. (1902/1964) *Human Nature and the Social Order*. New York: Charles Scribner's Sons.

Cooper, C., and Roe, S. (2012) *An Estimate of Youth Crime in England and Wales: Police Recorded Crime Committed by Young People in 2009/2010.* Home Office Research Report, 64. London: Home Office.

Copas, J., and Marshall, P. (1998) 'The Offender Group Reconviction Scale: The statistical reconviction score for use by probation officers', *Journal of the Royal Statistical Society, Series C*, 47: 159–71.

Cornell, D. G., Warren, J., Hawk, G., Stafford, E., Oram, G., and Pine, D. (1996) 'Psychopathy in instrumental and reactive violent offenders', *Journal of Consulting and Clinical Psychology*, 64: 783–90.

Covell, C. N., and Scalora, M. J. (2002) 'Empathic deficits in sexual offenders: An integration of affective, social and cognitive constructs', *Aggression and Violent Behavior*, 7: 251–71.

Coxe, R., and Holmes, W. (2009) 'A comparative study of two groups of sex offenders identified as high and low risk on the Static-99', *Journal of Child Sexual Abuse*, 18: 137–53.

Craig, L. A., Browne, K. D., and Beech, A. R. (2008) *Assessing Risk in Sex Offenders.* Chichester: John Wiley.

Crick, N. R., and Grotpeter, J. K. (1995) 'Relational aggression, gender, and social-psychological adjustment', *Child Development*, 66: 710–22.

Criminal Justice Act of 2003 (c.44) (2003) London: HMSO.

(The) Criminal Justice Act 2003 (Categories of Offences) Order 2004. no. 3346. London: Stationery Office and Queen's Printer of Acts of Parliament.

Crocker, A. G., Mueser, K. T., Drake, R. E., Clark, R. E., McHugo, G. J., Ackerson, T. H., and Alterman, A. I (2005) 'Antisocial personality, psychopathy, and violence in persons with dual disorders: A longitudinal analysis', *Criminal Justice and Behavior*, 32: 452–76.

Cunliffe, J., and Shepherd, A. (2007) *Reoffending of Adults: Results from the 2004 Cohort.* London: Home Office Statistical Bulletin.

Dahle, K. P. (2005) *Psychologische Kriminalprognose: Wege zu einer integrativen Beurteilung der Rückfallwahrscheinlichkeit von Strafgefangenen* [Psychological prediction of criminal reoffence: Toward an integrated method for the assessment of risk of reoffence of prisoners]. Herboltzheim: Centaurus.

Daversa, M. (2010) 'Early environmental predictors of the affective and interpersonal constructs of psychopathy', *International Journal of Offender Therapy and Comparative Criminology*, 54: 6–21.

Davidson, R. J., Putnam, K. M., and Larson, C. L. (2000) 'Dysfunction in the neural circuitry of emotion regulation: A possible prelude to violence', *Science*, 289: 591–4.

Davis, D., and Follette, W. C. (2002) 'Rethinking the probative value of evidence: Base rates, intuitive profiling, and the "postdiction" of behavior', *Law and Human Behavior*, 26: 133–58.

Davis, M. H. (1983) 'Measuring individual differences in empathy: Evidence for a multidimensional approach', *Journal of Personality and Social Psychology*, 44: 113–26.

Dawes, R. M. (1993) 'The prediction of the future versus an understanding of the past: A basic asymmetry', *American Journal of Psychology*, 106: 1–24.

Dawes, R. M. (1999) 'A message from psychologists to economists: Mere predictability doesn't matter like it should (without a good story appended to it)', *Journal of Economic Behavior and Organization*, 39: 29–40.

Dawes, R. M. (2002) 'The ethics of using or not using statistical prediction rules in psychological practice and related consulting activities', *Philosophy of Science*, 69: S178–S184.

Dawes, R. M., Faust, D., and Meehl, P. E. (1989) 'Clinical vs actuarial judgement', *Science*, 243: 1668–74.

DeClue, G., and Campbell, T. W. (2013) 'Calibration performance indicators for the Static-99R: 2013 update', *Open Access Journal of Forensic Psychology*, 5: 82–8.

Decety, J., and Jackson, P. L. (2004) 'The functional architecture of human empathy', *Behavioral and Cognitive Neuroscience Reviews*, 3: 71–100.

Delaware Executive Department (1984) *Recidivism in Delaware: A Study of Rearrest After Release from Incarceration*. Dover, DE: Delaware Executive Department Statistical Analysis Center.

DeLisi, M. (2009) 'Psychopathy is the unified theory of crime', *Youth Violence and Juvenile Justice*, 7: 256–73.

DeLisi, M., and Vaughn, M. G. (2008) 'Still psychopathic after all these years', in M. DeLisi and P. J. Conis (eds), *Violent Offenders: Theory, Research, Public Policy, and Practice* (pp. 155–68). Boston, MA: Jones & Bartlett.

Dempster, R. J., and Hart, S. D. (2002) 'The relative utility of fixed and variable risk factors in discriminating sexual recidivists and nonrecidivists', *Sexual Abuse: A Journal of Research and Treatment*, 14: 121–38.

DePanfilis, D., and Zuravin, S. J., (2001) 'Assessing risk to determine the need for services', *Children and Youth Services Review*, 23: 3–20.

Depue, R. A., and Spoont, M. R. (1987) 'Conceptualizing a serotonin trait: A dimension of behavioral constraint', in J. Mann and M. Stanley (eds), *The Psychobiology of Suicidal Behavior* (pp. 47–62). New York: New York Academy of Sciences.

de Vogel, V., de Ruiter, C., Hildebrand, M., Bos, B., and van de Ven, P. (2004) 'Type of discharge and risk of recidivism measured by the HCR-20: A retrospective study in a Dutch sample of treated forensic psychiatric patients', *International Journal of Forensic Mental Health*, 3: 149–65.

Dickey, R., Nussbaum, D., Chevolleau, K., and Davidson, H. (2002) 'Age as a differential characteristic of rapists, pedophiles, and sexual sadists', *Journal of Sex and Marital Therapy*, 28: 211–18.

Dickinson, E. (1924/1960) 'THE BRAIN is wider than the sky', in *The Complete Poems of Emily Dickinson*, ed. Thomas H. Johnson (Part One: Life CXXVI). Boston, MA: Little, Brown & Co.

Dodge, K. A. (2001) 'The science of youth violence prevention: Progressing from developmental epidemiology to efficacy to public policy', *American Journal of Preventive Medicine*, 20: 63–70.

Dolan, M., and Blattner, R. (2010) 'The utility of the Historical Clinical Risk-20 Scale as a predictor of outcomes in decisions to transfer patients from high to lower levels of security: A UK perspective', *BMC Psychiatry*, 10: 76.

Dolan, M., and Rennie, C. E. (2007) 'Is juvenile psychopathy associated with low anxiety and fear in conduct-disordered male offenders?', *Journal of Anxiety Disorders*, 21: 1028–38.

Doueck, H. J., English, D. J., DePanfilis, D., and Moore, G. T. (1993) 'Decision making in child protective services: A comparison of selected risk-assessment systems', *Child Welfare*, 72(5): 441–53.

Douglas, J., Burgess, A. W., Burgess, A. G., and Ressier, R. K. (2013) *Crime Classification Manual* (3rd edn). Hoboken, NJ: Wiley-Blackwell.

Douglas, K. S., and Kropp, P. R. (2002) 'A prevention-based paradigm for violence risk assessment: Clinical and research applications', *Criminal Justice and Behavior*, 29: 617–58.

Douglas, K. S., and Reeves, K. (2009) 'The HCR-20 violence risk assessment scheme: Overview and review of the research', in R. K. Otto and K. S. Douglas (eds), *Handbook of Violence Risk Assessment* (pp. 147–86). Oxford: Routledge.

Douglas, K., Cox, D., and Webster, C. (1999) 'Violence risk assessment: Science and practice', *Legal and Criminological Psychology*, 4: 149–84.
Douglas, K. S., Vincent, G. M., and Edens, J. F. (2007) 'Risk for criminal recidivism', in C. Patrick (ed.), *Handbook of Psychopathy* (pp. 533–54). New York: Guilford Press.
Douglas, K. S., Hart, S. D., Webster, C. D., Belfrage, H., Guy, L. S., and Wilson, C. M. (2014) 'Historical-Clinical-Risk Management-20, version 3 (HCR-20^{V3}): Development and overview', *International Journal of Forensic Mental Health*, 13: 93–108.
Doyle, A. C. (1890/2001) *The Sign of Four*. London: Penguin Classics.
Doyle, A. C. (1892/2007) *The Adventures of Sherlock Holmes*. London: Penguin Classics.
Doyle, M., and Dolan, M. (2002) 'Violence risk assessment: Combining actuarial and clinical information to structure clinical judgements for the formulation and management of risk', *Journal of Psychiatric and Mental Health Nursing*, 9: 649–57.
Dubourg, R., Hamed, J., and Thorns, J. (2005) *The Economic and Social Costs of Crime Against Individuals and Households 2003/04*. Home Office Online Report 30/05. London: Research, Development and Statistics Directorate, Home Office.
Duerden, M. (2009) *What are Hazard Ratios?* www.whatisseries.co.uk. Accessed 10 Jan. 2014.
Dugan, E. (2008) 'Re-offending rates rise as the prison population expands', *Independent*, 20 July. www.independent.co.uk/news/uk/crime/reoffending-rates-rise-as-the-prison-population-expands-872411.html. Accessed 20 Dec. 2013.
Dutton, D. G., Denny-Keys, M. K., and Sells, J. R. (2011) 'Parental personality disorder and its effects on children: A review of current literature', *Journal of Child Custody*, 8: 268–83.
Duwe, G., and Freske, P. J. (2012) 'Using logistic regression modeling to predict sexual recidivism: The Minnesota Sex Offender Screening Tool-3 (MnSOST-3)', *Sexual Abuse: A Journal of Research and Treatment*, 24: 350–77.
Duwe, G., and Kerschner, D. (2008) 'Removing a nail from the boot camp coffin: An outcome evaluation of Minnesota's Challenge Incarceration Project', *Crime and Delinquency*, 54: 614–43.
Duwe, G., Donnay, W., and Tewksbury, R. (2008) 'Does residential proximity matter? A geographic analysis of sex offense recidivism', *Criminal Justice and Behavior*, 35: 484–504.
Earls, F. J., and Visher, C. A. (1997) *Project on Human Development in Chicago Neighborhoods: A Research Update*. Washington, DC: National Institute of Justice, Office of Justice Program, US Department of Justice.
Edens, J. F., Marcus, D. K., Lilienfeld, S. O., and Poythress, N. G. (2006) 'Psychopathic, not psychopath: Taxometric evidence for the dimensional structure of psychopathy?', *Journal of Abnormal Psychology*, 115: 131–44.
Eggleston, E. P., and Laub, J. H. (2002) 'The onset of adult offending: A neglected dimension of criminal career', *Journal of Criminal Justice*, 30: 603–22.
Elander, J., Rutter, M., Simonoff, E., and Pickles, A. (2000) 'Explanations for apparent late onset criminality in a high-risk sample of children followed up in adult life', *British Journal of Criminology*, 40: 497–509.
Elbogen, E. B. (2002) 'The process of violence risk assessment: A review of descriptive research', *Aggression and Violent Behavior*, 7: 591–604.
Elliott, D. S., Huizinga, D., and Ageton, S. (1985) *Explaining Delinquency and Drug Use*. Beverly Hills, CA: Sage Publications.
Elliott, F. A. (1999) 'A neurological perspective', in V. B. Van Hasselt and M. Hersen (eds), *Handbook of Psychological Approaches with Violent Offenders: Contemporary Strategies and Issues* (pp. 417–37). USA: Kluwer Academic/Plenum Publishers.

Ellis, L. (1988) 'The victimful–victimless crime distinction, and seven universal demographic correlates of victimful criminal behaviour', *Personality and Individual Differences*, 3: 525–48.
Emler, N., and Reicher, S. (1995) *Adolescence and Delinquency*. Oxford: Blackwell Publishers.
Epperson, D. L., Kaul, J. D., and Huot, S. (1995) 'Predicting risk of recidivism for incarcerated sex offenders'. Paper presented at the annual ATSA conference in New Orleans.
Epperson, D. L., Kaul, J. D., and Hesselton, D. (1998) 'Final report on the development of the Minnesota Sex Offender Screening Tool–Revised (MnSOST-R)'. Paper presented at the 17th Annual Conference of the Association for the Treatment of Sexual Abusers, Vancouver.
Ermer, E., and Kiehl, K. A. (2010) 'Psychopaths are impaired in social exchange and precautionary reasoning', *Psychological Science*, 21: 1399–1405.
Eslinger, P. J., and Damasio, A. R. (1985) 'Severe disturbance of higher cognition after bilateral frontal lobe ablation: Patient EVR', *Neurology*, 35: 1731–41.
Esquirol, E. (1839) *Des Maladies Mentales Considérées sous les Rapports Médical, Hygiénique et Médico-Legal* [Mental Diseases under Medical, Hygienic and Medico-Legal Aspects]. Paris: Bailliéré.
EUICS Report (2005) *The Burden of Crime in the EU: A Comparative Analysis of the European Survey of Crime and Safety* (EUICS).
European Convention of Human Rights and Fundamental Freedoms (1950) Protocols Nos. 11 and 14, 4 November 1950, ETS 51950. Council of Europe.
Farrell, G. (2013) 'Five tests for a theory of the crime drop', *Crime Science*, 2: 5.
Farrell, G., Tilley, N., Tseloni, A., and Mailley, J. (2008) 'The crime drop and the security hypothesis', *British Society of Criminology Newsletter*, 62: 17–21.
Farrell, G., Tseloni, A., Mailley, J., and Tilley, N. (2011) 'The crime drop and the security hypothesis', *Journal of Research in Crime and Delinquency*, 48: 147–75.
Farrington, D. P. (1973) 'Self-reports of deviant behaviour: Predictive and stable?', *Journal of Criminal Law and Criminology*, 64: 99–110.
Farrington, D. P. (1982) 'Longitudinal analyses of criminal violence', in M. E. Wolfgang and N. A. Weiner (eds), *Criminal Violence* (pp. 171–200). Beverly Hills, CA: Sage.
Farrington, D. P. (1985) 'Predicting self-reported and official delinquency', in D. P. Farrington and R. Tarling (eds), *Prediction in Criminology* (pp. 150–73). Albany, NY: State University of New York Press.
Farrington, D. P. (1986a) 'Age and crime', in M. Tonry and N. Morris (eds), *Crime and Justice: An Annual Review of Research*, 7: 189–250. Chicago, IL: University of Chicago Press.
Farrington, D. P. (1986b) 'Stepping stones to adult criminal careers', in D. Olweus, J. Block, and M. R. Yarrow (eds), *Development of Antisocial and Prosocial Behavior: Research, Theories and Issues* (pp. 359–84). New York: Academic Press.
Farrington, D. P. (1988) 'Studying changes within individuals: The causes of offending', in M. Rutter (ed.), *Studies of Psychosocial Risk: The Power of Longitudinal Data* (pp. 158–83). Cambridge: Cambridge University Press.
Farrington, D. P. (1989) 'Self-reported and official offending from adolescence to adulthood', in M. W. Klein (ed.), *Cross-National Research in Self-Reported Crime and Delinquency* (pp. 399–423). Dordrecht: Kluwer.
Farrington, D. P. (1991a) 'Antisocial personality from childhood to adulthood', *The Psychologist*, 4: 389–94.
Farrington, D. P. (1991b) 'Childhood aggression and adult violence: Early precursors and later life outcomes', in D. J. Pepler and K. H. Rubin (eds), *The Development and Treatment of Childhood Aggression* (pp. 5–29). Hillsdale, NJ: Lawrence Erlbaum.

Farrington, D. P. (1992) 'Criminal career research: Lessons for crime prevention', *Studies on Crime and Crime Prevention*, 1: 7–29.

Farrington, D. P. (1994) 'Interactions between individual and contextual factors in the development of offending', in R. K. Silbereisen and E. Todt (eds), *Adolescence in Context: The Interplay of Family, School, Peers and Work in Adjustment* (pp. 366–89). New York: Springer-Verlag.

Farrington, D. P. (1995) 'The development of offending and antisocial behaviour from childhood: Key findings from the Cambridge Study in Delinquent Development', *Journal of Child Psychology and Psychiatry*, 36: 929–64.

Farrington, D. P. (1997) 'Human development and criminal careers', in M. Maguire, R. Morgan, and R. Reiner (eds), *The Oxford Handbook of Criminology* (2nd edn, pp. 361–408). Oxford: Oxford University Press.

Farrington, D. P. (1998) 'Predictors, causes and correlates of male youth violence', in M. Tonry and M. H. Moore (eds), *Crime and Justice: An Annual Review of Research, Youth Violence*, 24: 421–75. Chicago, IL: University of Chicago Press.

Farrington, D. P. (1999) 'A criminological research agenda for the next millennium'. *International Journal of Offender Therapy and Comparative Criminology*, 43: 154–67.

Farrington, D. P. (2002a) 'Multiple risk factors for multiple problem violent boys', in R. R. Corrado, R. Roesch, S. D. Hart, and J. K. Gierowski (eds), *Multi-Problem Violent Youth: A Foundation for Comparative Research on Needs, Interventions, and Outcomes* (pp. 23–34). Amsterdam: IOS Press.

Farrington, D. P. (2002b) 'Developmental criminology and risk-focused prevention', in M. Maguire, R. Morgan, and R. Reiner (eds), *Oxford Handbook of Criminology* (3rd edn, pp. 657–701). Oxford: Oxford University Press.

Farrington, D. P. (2003) 'Key results from the first 40 years of the Cambridge Study in Delinquent Development', in T. P. Thornberry and M. D. Krohn (eds), *Taking Stock of Delinquency: An Overview of Findings from Contemporary Longitudinal Studies* (pp. 137–83). New York: Kluwer/Plenum.

Farrington, D. P. (ed.) (2005a) *Integrated Developmental and Life-Course Theories of Offending*. Advances in Criminological Theory, 14. New Brunswick, NJ: Transaction.

Farrington, D. P. (2005b) 'The Integrated Cognitive Antisocial Potential (ICAP) theory', in D. P. Farrington (ed.), *Integrated Developmental and Life-Course Theories of Offending*. Advances in Criminological Theory, 14 (pp. 73–92). New Brunswick, NJ: Transaction.

Farrington, D. P. (2006) 'Family background and psychopathy', in C. J. Patrick (ed.), *Handbook of Psychopathy* (pp. 229–50). New York: Guilford Press.

Farrington, D. P. (2007a) 'Childhood risk factors and risk-focussed prevention', in M. Maguire, R. Morgan, and R. Reiner (eds), *The Oxford Handbook of Criminology* (4th edn, pp. 602–40). Oxford: Oxford University Press.

Farrington, D. P. (2007b) 'Social origins of psychopathy', in A. Felthous (ed.), *The International Handbook of Psychopathic Disorders and the Law: Laws and Policies* (pp. 319–24). Chichester: John Wiley & Sons.

Farrington, D. P. (2007c) 'Advancing knowledge about desistance', *Journal of Contemporary Criminal Justice*, 23: 125–34.

Farrington, D. P. (2010) 'Family influences on delinquency', in D. W. Springer and A. R. Roberts (eds), *Juvenile Justice and Delinquency* (pp. 203–22). Sudbury, MA: Jones & Bartlett.

Farrington, D. P. (2012) 'Childhood risk factors for young adult offending: Onset and persistence', in F. Lösel, A. Bottoms, and D. P. Farrington (eds), *Young Adult Offenders: Lost in Transition?* (pp. 48–64). Abingdon, Oxon: Routledge.

Farrington, D. P. (2014a) 'Reflections on a life course of developmental criminology', in R.

M. Lerner, A. C. Petersen, R. K. Silbereisen, and J. Brooks-Gunn (eds), *The Developmental Science of Adolescence: History through Autobiography* (pp. 150–66). New York: Psychology Press.

Farrington, D. P (2014b) 'Encouraging policy makers and practitioners to make rational choices about programs based on scientific evidence on developmental crime prevention', *Criminology and Public Policy*, 12: 295–301.

Farrington, D. P. (2015a) 'The developmental evidence base: Prevention', in G. Towl and D. Crighton (eds), *Forensic Psychology* (2nd edn). Oxford: Blackwell (in press).

Farrington, D. P. (2015b) 'The developmental evidence base: Psychosocial research', in G. Towl and D. Crighton (eds), *Forensic Psychology* (2nd edn). Oxford: Blackwell (in press).

Farrington, D. P., and Hawkins, J. D. (1991) 'Predicting participation, early onset, and later persistence in officially recorded offending', *Criminal Behaviour and Mental Health*, 1: 1–33.

Farrington, D. P., and Koegl, C. J. (in press) 'Monetary benefits and costs of the Stop Now And Plan program for boys aged 6-11, based on the prevention of later offending', *Journal of Quantitative Criminology*, (in press).

Farrington, D. P., and Loeber, R. (2000) 'Some benefits of dichotomization in psychiatric and criminological research', *Criminal Behaviour and Mental Health*, 10: 100–122.

Farrington, D. P., and Loeber, R. (2014) 'Establishing causes of offending in longitudinal and experimental studies', in G. J. N. Bruinsma and D. Weisburd (eds), *Encyclopedia of Criminology and Criminal Justice*. New York: Springer-Verlag.

Farrington, D. P. and Moitra, S. (1985) 'Delinquency careers: Innocents, desisters, and persisters', in M. Tonry and N. Morris (eds), *Crime and Justice: An Annual Review of Research* (vol. 6, pp. 187–222). Chicago, IL: University of Chicago Press.

Farrington, D. P., and Welsh, B. C. (2005) 'Randomized experiments in criminology: What have we learned in the last two decades?', *Journal of Experimental Criminology*, 1: 9–38.

Farrington, D. P., and Welsh, B. C. (2006) 'A half-century of randomized experiments on crime and justice', in M. Tonry (ed.), *Crime and Justice* (vol. 34, pp. 55–132). Chicago, IL: University of Chicago Press.

Farrington, D. P., and Welsh, B. C. (2007) *Saving Children from a Life of Crime*. Oxford: Oxford University Press.

Farrington, D. P., and West, D. J. (1993) 'Criminal, penal and life histories of chronic offenders: Risk and protective factors and early identification', *Criminal Behaviour and Mental Health*, 3: 492–523.

Farrington, D. P., Gallagher, B., Morley, L., St Ledger, R. J., and West, D. J. (1988a) 'A 24-year follow-up of men from vulnerable backgrounds', in R. L. Jenkins and W. K. Brown (eds), *The Abandonment of Delinquent Behaviour: Promoting the Turnaround* (pp. 155–73). New York: Praeger.

Farrington, D. P., Snyder, H. N., and Finnegan, T. A. (1988b) 'Specialization in juvenile court careers', *Criminology*, 26: 461–87.

Farrington, D. P., Jolliffe, D., Hawkins, J. D., Catalano, R. F., Hill, K. G., and Kosterman, R. (2003) 'Comparing delinquency careers in court records and self-reports', *Criminology*, 41: 933–58.

Farrington, D. P., Coid, J. W., Harnett, L., Jolliffe, D., Soteriou, N., Turner, R., and West, D. J. (2006) *Criminal Careers up to Age 50 and Life Success up to Age 48: New Findings from the Cambridge Study in Delinquent Development*. Home Office Research Study, 299. London: Home Office.

Farrington, D. P., Jolliffe, D., and Johnstone, L. (2008) *Assessing Violence Risk: A Framework for Practice*. Edinburgh: Risk Management Authority Scotland.

Farrington, D. P., Coid, J. W., and West, D. J. (2009) 'The development of offending from age 8 to age 50: Recent results from the Cambridge Study in Delinquent Development'. *Monatsschrift für Kriminologie und Strafrechtsreform*, 92: 160–73.

Farrington, D. P., Auty, K. M., Coid, J. W., and Turner, R. E. (2013) 'Self-reported and official offending from age 10 to age 56', *European Journal of Criminal Policy and Research*, 19: 135–51.

Farrington, D. P., Ttofi, M. M., Crago, R. V., and Coid, J. W. (2015) 'Intergenerational similarities in risk factors for offending', *Journal of Developmental and Life-Course Criminology*, 1: 48–62.

Fazel, S. and Danesh, J. (2002) 'Serious mental disorder in 23,000 prisoners: A systematic review of 62 surveys', *Lancet*, 359: 545–50.

Fazel, S., Singh, J. P., Dool, H., and Grann, M. (2012) 'Use of risk assessment instruments to predict violence and antisocial behaviour in 73 samples involving 24,827 people: Systematic review and meta-analysis', *British Medical Journal*, 345: 1–12.

Fearson, R., Bakermans-Kranenburg, M. J., van Ijendoorn, M. H., Lapsley, A., and Roisman, G. I. (2010) 'The significance of insecure attachment and disorganization in the development of children's externalizing behavior: A meta-analytic study', *Child Development*, 8: 435–56.

Fellows, K. L., and Farah, M. J. (2007) 'The role of ventromedial prefrontal cortex in decision making: Judgment under uncertainty or judgment per se?', *Cerebral Cortex*, 17: 2669–74.

Fergusson, D. M., Horwood, L. J., and Riddle, E. M. (2005) 'Show me the child at seven: The consequences of conduct problems in childhood for psychosocial functioning in adulthood', *Journal of Child Psychology and Psychiatry*, 46: 837–49.

Fernandez, Y., and Marshall, W. L. (2003) 'Victim empathy, social self-esteem and psychopathy in rapists', *Sexual Abuse: Journal of Research and Treatment*, 15: 11–26.

Feuchtersleben, E. von (1845) *Lehrbuch der ärztlichen Seelenkunde* [Textbook of Medical Mental Science]. Vienna: Gerold.

Flannery, D. J., Singer, M. I., van Dulmen, M., Kretschmar, J. F., and Belliston, L. M. (2007) 'Exposure to violence, mental health, and violent behavior', in D. J. Flannery, A. T. Vazsonyi, and I. D. Waldman (eds), *The Cambridge Handbook of Violent Behavior and Aggression* (pp. 306–21). New York: Cambridge University Press.

Fleminger, S. (1997) 'Number needed to detain', *British Journal of Psychiatry*, 171: 287.

Fonagy, P. (2003) 'Towards a developmental understanding of violence', *British Journal of Psychiatry*, 183: 190–2.

Fonagy, P., and Target, M, (1997) 'Attachment and reflective function: Their role in self-organization', *Development and Psychopathology*, 9: 679–700.

Fonagy, P., and Target, M, (2002) 'Early intervention and the development of self–regulation', *Psychoanalytic Inquiry*, 22: 307–35.

Fonagy, P., and Target, M. (2005) 'Bridging the transmission gap: An end to an important mystery of attachment research?', *Attachment Human Development*, 7: 333–43.

Fornari, U. (2008) *Trattato di psichiatria forense* [Treatise of forensic psychiatry] (4th edn). Turin: UTET.

Fornari, U. (2012) *Al di là di ogni ragionevole dubbio: Ovvero sulla cosiddetta prova scientifica nelle discipline psicoforensi* [Beyond any reasonable doubt: The scientific proof in the psychoforensic disciplines]. Turin: Espress Publisher.

Fornari, U. (2013) *Trattato di psichiatria forense* [Treatise of forensic psychiatry] (5th edn). Turin: UTET.

Forth, A., Kosson, D., and Hare, R. (2003) *The Hare Psychopathy Checklist: Youth Version, Technical Manual*. New York: Multi-Health Systems.

Fowles, D. C. (2000) 'Electrodermal hyporeactivity and antisocial behavior: Does anxiety mediate the relationship?', *Journal of Affective Disorders*, 61: 177–89.

Fowles, D. C., and Dindo, L. (2006) 'A dual-deficit model of psychopathy', in C. J. Patrick (ed.), *Handbook of the Psychopathy* (pp. 14–34). New York: Guilford Press.

Fox, A., Kvaran, T., and Fontaine, R. (2013) 'Psychopathy and culpability: How responsible is the psychopath for criminal wrongdoing?', *Law and Social Inquiry*, 38: 1–26.

Francis, B., Hargreaves, C., and Soothill, K. (2015) 'Changing prevalence of sex offender convictions: Disentangling age, period and cohort effects over time', in A. A. J. Blokland and P. Lussier (eds), *Sex Offenders: A Criminal Career Approach* (pp. 199–218). Chichester: John Wiley & Sons.

Francis Smith, S., and Lilienfeld, S. O. (2013) 'Psychopathy in the workplace: The knowns and unknowns', *Aggression and Violent Behavior*, 18: 204–18.

Fredrickson, B. L. (2013) 'Updated thinking on positivity ratios', *American Psychologist*. Advance online publication. DOI:10.1037/a0033584.

Freeman, N. J. (2007) 'Predictors of rearrest for rapists and child molesters on probation', *Criminal Justice and Behavior*, 34: 752–68.

Freilone, F. (2011) *Psicodiagnosi e disturbi di personalità: Assessment clinico e forense* [Psychodiagnosis and Personality Disorders: Clinical and Forensic Assessment]. Genoa: Fratelli Frilli Publisher.

Freund, K. (1990) 'Courtship disorder', in W. L. Marshall, D. R. Laws, and H. E. Barbaree (eds), *Handbook of Sexual Assault: Issues, Theories and Treatment of the Offender* (pp. 195–207). New York: Plenum Press.

Frick, P. J., Lilienfeld, S. O., Ellis, M., Loney, B., and Silverthorn, P. (1999) 'The association between anxiety and psychopathy dimensions in children', *Journal of Abnormal Child Psychology*, 27: 383–92.

Frick, P. J., Lilienfeld, S. O., Edens, J. F., Poythress, N. G., and McBurnett, K. (2000) 'The association between anxiety and antisocial behavior', *Primary Psychiatry*, 7: 52–7.

Frick, P. J., Kimonis, E. R., Dandreaux, D. M., and Farell, J. M. (2003) 'The 4 year stability of psychopathic traits in non-referred youth', *Behavioral Sciences and the Law*, 21: 713–36.

Friendship, C., and Thornton, D. (2001) 'Sexual reconviction for sex offenders discharged from prison in England and Wales: Implications for evaluating treatment', *British Journal of Criminology*, 6: 121–9.

Friendship, C., Thornton, D., Erikson, M., and Beech, A. R. (2001) 'Reconviction: A critique and comparison of two main data sources in England and Wales', *Legal and Criminological Psychology*, 6: 121–9.

Friendship, C., Beech, A. R., and Browne, K. D. (2002) 'Reconviction as an outcome measure in research', *British Journal of Criminology*, 42: 442–4.

Frith, U. (2001) 'Mind blindness and the brain in autism', *Neuron*, 32: 969–79.

Furneaux, W. D., and Gibson, H. B. (1966) *The New Junior Maudsley Personality Inventory*. London: University of London Press.

Gabor, T. (1994) *Everybody Does It: Crime by the Public*. Toronto: University of Toronto Press.

Gannon, T. A., Ward, T., and Collie, R. (2007) 'Cognitive distortions in child molesters: Theoretical and research developments over the past two decades', *Aggression and Violent Behavior*, 12: 402–16.

Gao, Y., and Raine, A. (2010) 'Successful and unsuccessful psychopaths: A neurobiological model', *Behavioral Sciences and the Law*, 28: 194–210.

Gao, Y., Glenn, A. L., Schug, R. A., Yang, Y., and Raine, A. (2009) 'The neurobiology of psychopathy: A neurodevelopmental perspective', *Canadian Journal of Psychiatry*, 54: 813–23.

Gazzaniga, M. S. (2005) *The Ethical Brain*. New York: Dana Press.
Gazzaniga, M. S. (2011) *Who's in Charge? Free Will and the Science of the Brain*. New York: HarperCollins Publishers.
Geer, J. H., Estupinan, L. A., and Manguno-Mire, G. M. (2000) 'Empathy, social skills, and other relevant cognitive processes in rapists and child molesters: Issues, theories, and treatment of the offender', *Aggression and Violent Behavior*, 5: 99–126.
Gendreau, P., Little, T., and Goggin, C. (1996) 'A meta-analysis of the predictors of adult offender recidivism: What works!', *Criminology*, 34: 575–607.
Gery, I., Miljkovitch, R., Berthoz, S., and Soussignan, R. (2009) 'Empathy and recognition of facial expressions of emotion in sex offenders, non-sex offenders and normal controls', *Psychiatry Research*, 16: 252–62.
Gigerenzer, G. (2008) *Rationality for Mortals*. Oxford: Oxford University Press.
Giordano, P. C., Cernkovich, S. A., and Rudolph, J. L. (2002) 'Gender, crime, and desistance: Toward a theory of cognitive transformation', *American Journal of Sociology*, 107: 990–1064.
Glannon, W. (2008) 'Moral responsibility and the psychopath', *Neuroethics*, 1: 158–166.
Glaser, B. A., Calhoun, G. B., and Petrocelli, J. V. (2002) 'Personality characteristics of male juvenile offenders by adjudicated offenses as indicated by the MMPI-A', *Criminal Justice and Behavior*, 29: 183–201.
Glazebrook, J. S. (2010) 'Risky business: Predicting recidivism', *Psychiatry, Psychology and Law*, 17: 88–120.
Glenn, A. L., and Raine, A. (2014a) *Psychopathy: An Introduction to Biological Findings and their Implications*. New York: New York University Press.
Glenn, A. L., and Raine, A. (2014b) 'Neurocriminology: Implications for the punishment, prediction and prevention of criminal behaviour?', *Nature Reviews Neuroscience*, 15: 54–63.
Glenn, A. L., Raine, A., and Schug, R. A. (2009a) 'The neural correlates of moral-decision making psychopathy', *Molecular Psychiatry*, 14: 5–6.
Glenn, A. L., Raine, A., Schug, R. A., Young, L., and Hauser, M. (2009b) 'Increased DLPFC activity during moral decision-making in psychopathy', *Molecular Psychiatry*, 14: 909–11.
Glenn, A. L., Raine, A., and Laufer, W. S. (2011) 'Is it wrong to criminalize and punish psychopaths?', *Emotion Review*, 3: 301–4.
Glenn, A. L., Yang, Y., and Raine, A. (2012) 'Neuroimaging in psychopathy and antisocial personality disorder: Functional significance and a neurodevelopmental hypothesis', in J. R. Simpson (ed.), *Neuroimaging in Forensic Psychiatry: From the Clinic to the Courtroom* (pp. 81–98). Chichester: Wiley-Blackwell.
Gneiting, T., and Katzfuss, M. (2014) 'Probabilistic forecasting', *Annual Review of Statistics and its Application*, 1: 125–51.
Goldberg, D. P. (1978) *Manual of the General Health Questionnaire*. Windsor: NFER Publishing.
Goldstein, J. (1987) *Console and Classify: The French Psychiatric Profession in the Nineteenth Century*. Cambridge: Cambridge University Press.
Goldstein, R. B., Dawson, D. A., and Grant, B. F. (2010) 'Conditions follow-up: Results from wave 2 of the National Epidemiologic Survey on alcohol and related conditions', *Journal of the American Psychiatric Nurses Association*, 16: 212–26.
Gordon, R. M. (2010) 'The Psychodynamic Diagnostic Manual (PDM)', in I. Weiner and E. Craighead (eds), *Corsini's Encyclopedia of Psychology* (4th edn, vol. 3, pp. 1312–15), Hoboken, NJ: John Wiley & Sons.
Goring, C. (1913) *The English Convict*. Montclair, NJ: Patterson Smith.

Gottfredson, D. M., and Hirschi, T. (1990) *A General Theory of Crime*. Stanford, CA: Stanford University Press.

Gottfredson, S. D., and Moriarty, L. J. (2006) 'Clinical versus actuarial judgments in criminal justice decisions: Should one replace the other?', *Federal Probation*, 70: 15–18.

Gray, J. A. (1973) 'Causal theories of personality and how to test them', in J. R. Royce (ed.), *Multivariate Analysis and Psychological Theory* (pp. 409–63). New York: Academic Press.

Gray, J. A. (1976) 'The behavioural inhibition system: A possible substrate for anxiety', in M. P. Feldman and A. Broadhurst (eds), *Theoretical and Experimental Bases of the Behaviour Therapies* (pp. 3–41). London: Wiley.

Gray, J. A. (1987) *The Psychology of Fear and Stress* (2nd edn). Cambridge: Cambridge University Press.

Gray, N. S., Taylor, J., and Snowden, R. J. (2008) 'Predicting violent reconvictions using the HCR-20', *British Journal of Psychiatry*, 192: 384–7.

Gray, N. S., Taylor, J., and Snowden, R. J. (2011) 'Predicting violence using structured professional judgment in patients with different mental and behavioral disorders', *Psychiatry Research*, 187: 248–53.

Greene, J. D., Sommerville, R. B., Nystrom, L. E., Darley, J. M., and Cohen, J. D. (2001) 'An fMRI investigation of emotional engagement in moral judgment', *Science*, 293: 2105–8.

Greene, J. D., Nystrom, L. E., Engell, A. D., Darley, J. M., and Cohen, J. D. (2004) 'The neural bases of cognitive conflict and control in moral judgment', *Neuron*, 44: 389–400.

Greenfeld, L. A. (1985) *Examining Recidivism*. Washington, DC: US Dept of Justice, Bureau of Justice Statistics.

Gregory, S., Ffytche, D., Simmons, A., Kumari, V., Howard, M., Hodgins, S., and Blackwood, N. (2012) 'The antisocial brain: Psychopathy matters: A structural MRI investigation of antisocial male violent offenders', *Archives of General Psychiatry*, 69: 962–72.

Grieve, R., and Mahar, D. (2010) 'The emotional manipulation psychopathy nexus: Relationships with emotional intelligence, alexithymia, and ethical position', *Personality and Individual Differences*, 48: 945–50.

Grisolia, J. S. (2001) 'Neurobiology of the psychopath', in A. Raine and J. Sanmartin (eds), *Violence and Psychopathy* (pp. 79–90). New York: Kluwer Academic/Plenum.

Grisso, T. (1998) *Forensic Evaluation of Juveniles*. Sarasota, FL: Professional Resources Press.

Grisso, T., and Tomkins, A. (1996) 'Communicating violence risk assessments', *American Psychologist*, 51: 928–30.

Groth, A. N. (1979) *Men Who Rape: The Psychology of the Offender*. New York: Plenum Press.

Groth, A. N. (1983) 'Treatment of the sexual offender in a correctional institution', in J. G. Greer and I. R. Stuart (eds), *The Sexual Aggressor: Current Perspectives on Treatment* (pp. 160–76). New York: Van Nostrand Reinhold Co.

Grove, W. M., and Lloyd, M. (2006) 'Meehl's contribution to clinical versus statistical prediction', *Journal of Abnormal Psychology*, 115: 192–4.

Grove, W. M., and Meehl, P. E. (1996) 'Comparative efficiency of informal (subjective, impressionistic) and formal (mechanical, algorithmic) prediction procedures: The clinical–statistical controversy', *Psychology, Public Policy, and Law*, 2: 293–323.

Grove, W. M., Zald, D. H., Lebow, S., Snitz, B. E., and Nelson, C. (2000) 'Clinical versus mechanical prediction: A meta-analysis', *Psychological Assessment*, 12: 19–30.

Guay, J. P., Ruscio, J., Hare, R. D., and Knight, R. A. (2007) 'A taxometric analysis of the latent structure of psychopathy: Evidence for dimensionality', *Journal of Abnormal Psychology*, 116: 701–16.

Guilford, J. P. (1936) 'Unitary traits of personality and factor theory', *American Journal of Psychology*, 48: 673–80.

Gulotta, G. (2005) 'I volti dell'aggressività e dell'aggressione: Predatori, strumentali e affettivi' [Types of aggression and aggressors: Instrumental and affective predators], in G. Gulotta and I. Merzagora Betsos (eds), *L'omicidio e la sua investigazione* [Homicide and its investigation] (pp. 1–89). Milan: Giuffrè.

Gulotta, G. and Vittoria, D. (2002a) 'La pericolosità sociale' [Social dangerousness], in G. Gulotta et al. (eds), *Elementi di psicologia giuridica e di diritto psicologico* [Elements of juridical psychology and psychological law] (pp. 401–9). Milan: Giuffrè.

Gulotta, G., and Vittoria, D. (2002b) 'La predizione di pericolosità sociale verso gli altri' [Prediction of social dangeruousness], in G. Gulotta et al. (eds), *Elementi di psicologia giuridica e di diritto psicologico* [Elements of juridical psychology and psychological law] (pp. 412–29). Milan: Giuffrè.

Guo, B., and Harstall, C. (2008) *Spousal Violence Against Women: Preventing Recurrence*. Alberta, Canada: Institute of Health Economics. www.ihe.ca/documents/SpousalViolence_1.pdf. Accessed 28 Apr. 2014.

Guy, L. (2008) 'Performance indicators of the structured professional judgment approach for assessing risk for violence to others: A meta-analytic survey' (Master's thesis). http://ir.lib.sfu.ca/handle/1892/10581. Accessed 10 May 2014.

Haas, H., Farrington, D. P., Killias, M., and Sattar, G. (2004) 'The impact of different family configurations on delinquency', *British Journal of Criminology*, 44: 520–32.

Hall, R. C. W., and Hall, R. C. W. (2007) 'A profile of pedophilia: Definition, characteristics of offenders, recidivism, treatment outcomes, and forensic issues', *Mayo Clinic Proceedings*, 82: 457–71.

Hall, R. C. W., and Hall, R. C. W., (2009) 'A profile of pedophilia: Definition, characteristics of offenders, recidivism, treatment outcomes, and forensic issues', *Focus: The Journal of Lifelong Learning in Psychiatry*, 7: 522–37.

Hancock, J. T., Woodworth, M. T., and Porter, S. (2011) 'Hungry like the wolf: A word-pattern analysis of the language of psychopaths', *Legal and Criminological Psychology*, 18: 102–14.

Handel, R. W., Archer, R. P., Elkins, D. E., Mason, J. A., and Simonds-Bisbee, E. C. (2011) 'Psychometric properties of the Minnesota Multiphasic Personality Inventory–Adolescent (MMPI–A): Clinical, content, and supplementary scales in a forensic sample', *Journal of Personality Assessment*, 9: 566–81.

Hannah-Moffat, K. (2005) 'Criminogenic risk and the transformative risk subject: Hybridizations of risk/need in penality', *Punishment and Society*, 7: 29–51.

Hanson, R. K. (1997) *The Development of a Brief Actuarial Risk Scale for Sexual Offense Recidivism*. Ottawa: Solicitor General of Canada.

Hanson, R. K. (1998) 'What do we know about sexual offender risk assessment', *Psychology, Public Policy, and Law*, 4: 50–72.

Hanson, R. K. (2002) 'Recidivism and age', *Journal of Interpersonal Violence*, 17: 1046–62.

Hanson, R. K. (2005) 'Twenty years of progress in violence risk assessment', *Journal of Interpersonal Violence*, 20: 212–17.

Hanson, R. K. (2006) 'Does Static-99 predict recidivism among older sexual offenders?', *Sex Abuse*, 18: 343–55.

Hanson, R. K. (2009) 'The psychological assessment of risk for crime and violence', *Canadian Psychology*, 50: 172–82.

Hanson, R. K., and Bussière, M. T. (1998) 'Predicting relapse: A meta-analysis of sexual offender recidivism studies', *Journal of Consulting and Clinical Psychology*, 66: 348–62.

Hanson, R. K., and Harris, A. J. R. (2000) 'Where should we intervene? Dynamic predictors of sex offense recidivism', *Criminal Justice and Behavior*, 27: 6–35.

Hanson, R. K., and Morton-Bourgon, K. E. (2004) *Predictors of Sexual Recidivism: An Updated Meta-Analysis* (Research Report, 2004–02). Ottawa: Public Safety and Emergency Preparedness Canada.

Hanson, R. K., and Morton-Bourgon, K. E. (2005) 'The characteristics of persistent sexual offenders: A meta-analysis of recidivism studies', *Journal of Consulting and Clinical Psychology*, 73: 1154–63.

Hanson, R. K., and Morton-Bourgon, K. E. (2007) *The Accuracy of Recidivism Risk Assessments for Sexual Offenders: A Meta-Analysis*. Ottawa: Public Safety and Emergency Preparedness Canada.

Hanson, R. K., and Morton-Bourgon, K. E. (2009) 'The accuracy of recidivism risk assessments for sexual offenders: A meta-analysis of 118 prediction studies', *Psychological Assessment*, 21: 1–21.

Hanson, R. K., and Scott, H. (1995) 'Assessing perspective-taking among sexual offenders, nonsexual criminals, and nonoffenders', *Sexual Abuse: Journal of Research and Treatment*, 7: 259–77.

Hanson, R. K., and Thornton, D. (2000) 'Improving risk assessments for sex offenders: A comparison of three actuarial scales', *Law and Human Behavior*, 24: 119–36.

Hanson, R. K., and Thornton, D. (2003) *Notes on the Development of Static-2002* (Corrections Research User Report, 2003-01). Ottawa: Dept of the Solicitor General of Canada.

Hanson, R. K., Gordon, A., Harris, A. J. R., Marques, J. K., Murphy, W., Quinsey, V. L., and Seto, M. C. (2002) 'First report of the Collaborative Outcome Data Project on the effectiveness of psychological treatment of sex offenders', *Sexual Abuse: A Journal of Research and Treatment*, 14: 169–94.

Hanson, R. K., Morton, K. E., and Harris, A. J. R. (2003) 'Sexual offender recidivism risk: What we know and what we need to know', *Annals of the New York Academy of Science*, 989: 154–66.

Hanson, R. K., Harris, A. J., Helmus, L., and Thornton, D. (2014) 'High-risk sex offenders may not be high risk forever', *Journal of Interpersonal Violence*, 29: 2792–813.

Hanson, R. K., Harris, A. J., Scott, T.-L., and Helmus, L. (2007a) *Assessing the Risk of Sexual Offenders on Community Supervision: The Dynamic Supervision Project*. Ottawa: Public Safety Canada.

Hanson, R. K., Helmus, L., and Bourgon, G. (2007b) *The Validity of Risk Assessments for Intimate Partner Violence: A Meta-Analysis*. Ottawa: Public Safety Canada.

Hanson, R. K., Bourgon, G., Helmus, L., and Hodgson, S. (2009) 'The principles of effective correctional treatment also apply to sexual offenders: A meta-analysis', *Criminal Justice and Behavior*, 36: 865–91.

Hanson, R. K., Helmus, L., and Thornton, D. (2010) 'Predicting recidivism amongst sexual offenders: A multi-site study of Static-2002', *Law and Human Behavior*, 34: 198–211.

Harcourt, B. (2007) *Against Prediction: Profiling, Policing, and Punishing in an Actuarial Age*. Chicago, IL: University of Chicago Press.

Hare, R. D. (1980) 'A research scale for the assessment of psychopathy in criminal populations', *Personality and Individual Differences*, 1: 111–19.

Hare, R. D. (1991) *The Hare Psychopathy Checklist-Revised (PCL-R)*. Toronto: Multi-Health Systems.

Hare, R. (1993) *Without Conscience: The Disturbing World of Psychopaths among us*. New York: Pocket Books.

Hare, R. (1996a) 'Psychopathy: A clinical construct whose time has come', *Criminal Justice and Behavior*, 23: 25–54.

Hare, R. D. (1996b) 'Psychopathy and antisocial personality disorder: A case of diagnostic confusion', *Psychiatric Times* (1 Feb.): 2–3.

Hare, R. D. (1998a) 'Psychopathy, affect, and behavior', in D. Cooke, A. Forth, and R. Hare (eds), *Psychopathy: Theory, Research, and Implications for Society* (pp. 105–37). Dordrecht: Kluwer.

Hare, R. D. (1998b) 'Psychopaths and their nature: Implications for the mental health and criminal justice systems', in T. Millon, E. Simonson, M. Burker-Smith, and E. David (eds), *Psychopathy: Antisocial, Criminal, and Violent Behavior* (pp. 188–212). New York: Guilford Press.

Hare, R. D. (2003) *Manual for the Revised Psychopathy Checklist* (2nd edn). Toronto: Multi-Health Systems.

Hare, R. D. (2013) 'Foreword', in K. A. Kiehl and W. P. Sinnott-Armstrong (eds), *Handbook on Psychopathy and Law* (pp. vii–ix). New York: Oxford University Press.

Hare, R. D., and Neumann, C. S. (2005) 'Structural models of psychopathy', *Current Psychiatry Reports*, 7: 57–64.

Hare, R. D., and Neumann, C. S. (2006) 'The PCL-R assessment of psychopathy: Development, structural properties, and new directions', in C. Patrick (ed.), *Handbook of Psychopathy* (pp. 58–90). New York: Guilford Press.

Hare, R. D., and Neumann, C. S. (2008) 'Psychopathy as a clinical and empirical construct', *Annual Review of Clinical Psychology*, 4: 217–46.

Hare, R. D., and Neumann, C. S. (2009) 'Psychopathy: Assessment and forensic implications', *Canadian Journal of Psychiatry*, 54: 791–802.

Hare, R., and Neumann, C. (2010) 'The role of antisociality in the psychopathy construct: Comment on Skeem and Cooke (2010)', *Psychological Assessment*, 22: 446–54.

Hare, R. D., McPherson, L. M., and Forth, A. E. (1988) 'Male psychopaths and their criminal careers', *Journal of Consulting and Clinical Psychology*, 56: 710–14.

Hare, R. D., Clark, D., Grann, M., and Thornton, D. (2000) 'Psychopathy and the predictive validity of the PCL-R: An international perspective', *Behavioral Sciences and the Law*, 18: 623–45.

Hargreaves, C., and Francis, B. (2014) 'The long term recidivism risk of young sexual offenders in England and Wales: Enduring risk or redemption?', *Journal of Criminal Justice*, 42: 164–72.

Harkins, L., Beech, A. R., and Goodwill, A. M. (2010) 'Examining the influence of denial, motivation, and risk on sexual recidivism', *Sexual Abuse: A Journal of Research and Treatment*, 22: 78–94.

Harpur, T. J., Hare, R. D., and Hakstian, A.R. (1989) 'Two-factor conceptualization of psychopathy: Construct validity and assessment implications', *Psychological Assessment*, 1: 6–17.

Harris, A. J. R., and Hanson, R. K. (2004) *Sex Offender Recidivism: A Simple Question*. Ottawa: Solicitor General of Canada.

Harris, A. J. R., Phenix, A., Hanson, R. K., and Thornton, D. (2003) *Static-99 Coding Rules: Revised 2003*. Ottawa: Dept of the Solicitor General of Canada.

Harris, D., Smallbone, S., Dennison, S., and Knight, R. (2009) 'Specialization and versatility in sexual offenders referred for civil commitment', *Journal of Criminal Justice*, 37: 37–44.

Harris, D., Knight, R., Dennison, S., and Smallbone S. (2011) 'Postrelease specialization and versatility in sexual offenders referred for civil commitment', *Sexual Abuse: A Journal of Research and Treatment*, 23: 243–59.

Harris, G. T., Rice, M., and Cormier, R. (1991) 'Psychopathy and violent recidivism', *Law and Human Behaviour*, 15: 626–37.

Harris, G. T., Rice, M. E., and Quinsey, V. L. (1994) 'Psychopathy as a taxon: Evidence that psychopaths are a discrete class', *Journal of Consulting and Clinical Psychology*, 62: 387–97.

Harris, G. T., Rice, M. E., Quinsey, V. L., Lalumière, M. L., Boer, D., and Lang, C. (2003) 'A multi-site comparison of actuarial risk instruments for sex offenders', *Psychological Assessment*, 15: 413–25.

Harris, L. T., and Fiske, S. T. (2006) 'Dehumanizing the lowest of the low: Neuroimaging responses to extreme out-groups', *Psychological Science*, 17: 847–53.

Harrison, K. (2010) 'Dangerous offenders, indeterminate sentencing, and the rehabilitation revolution', *Journal of Social Welfare and Family Law*, 32: 423–33.

Hart, S. D. (1998) 'The role of psychopathy in assessing risk for violence: Conceptual and methodological issues', *Legal and Criminological Psychology*, 3: 121–37.

Hart, S. D., and Hare, R. D. (1997) 'Association between psychopathy and narcissism: Theoretical views and empirical evidence', in E. Ronningstam (ed.), *Disorders of Narcissism: Theoretical, Empirical, and Clinical Implications* (pp. 415–36). Washington, DC: American Psychiatric Press.

Hart, S. D., Cox, D. N., and Hare, R. D. (1995) *The Hare Psychopathy Checklist: Screening Version*. Toronto: Multi-Health Systems.

Hart, S. D., Michie, C., and Cooke, D. J. (2007) 'Precision of actuarial risk assessment instruments: Evaluating the "margins of error" group v. individual predictions of violence', *British Journal of Psychiatry*, 49: s60–s65.

Hathaway, S. R., and Monachesi, E. D. (1963) *Adolescent Personality and Behavior: MMPI Patterns of Normal, Delinquent, Dropout, and Other Outcomes*. Minneapolis, MN: University of Minnesota Press.

Hebenton, B. (2009) 'Comparative analysis of the management of sexual offenders in the USA and UK', in J. L. Ireland, C. A. Ireland, and P. Birch (eds), *Violent and Sexual Offenders: Assessment, Treatment and Management* (pp. 257–83). Cullompton, Devon: Willan Publishing.

Heilbrun, K. (1992) 'The role of psychological testing in forensic assessment', *Law and Human Behavior*, 16: 257–72.

Heim, C., and Nemeroff, C. B. (2001) 'The role of childhood trauma in the neurobiology of mood and anxiety disorders: Preclinical and clinical studies', *Biological Psychiatry*, 49: 1023–39.

Heisenberg, W. (1962) *Physics and Philosophy: The Revolution in Modern Science*. New York: Harper & Row Publishers.

Helmus, L., Hanson, R. K., Thornton, D., Babchishin, K. M., and Harris, A. J. R. (2012) 'Absolute recidivism rates predicted by Static-99R and Static-2002R sex offender risk assessment tools vary across samples: A meta-analysis', *Criminal Justice and Behavior*, 39: 1148–71.

Helmus, L., Hanson, R. K., Babchishin, K. M., and Mann, R. E. (2013) 'Attitudes supportive of sexual offending predict recidivism: A meta-analysis', *Trauma, Violence, and Abuse*, 14: 34–53.

Hemphill, J., Hare, R., and Wong, S. (1998) 'Psychopathy and recidivism: A review', *Legal and Criminal Psychology*, 3: 139–70.

Henderson, D. K. (1939) *Psychopathic States*. New York: W. W. Norton.

Henderson, D. K. (1955) 'Psychopathic states', *British Journal of Delinquency*, 6: 5–11.

Herpertz, S. C., and Sass, H. (2000) 'Emotional deficiency and psychopathy', *Behavioral Sciences and the Law*, 18: 567–80.

Hicks, B. M., Krueger, R. F., Iacono, W. G., McGue, M., and Patrick, C. J. (2004) 'Family transmission and heritability of externalizing disorders: A twin family study', *Archives of General Psychiatry*, 61: 922–8.

Higgins, N., Watts, D., Bindman, J., Slade, M., and Thornicroft, G. (2005) 'Assessing violence risk in general adult psychiatry', *Psychiatry Bulletin*, 29: 131–3.

Hill, D. (1954) 'Psychopathic personality', *Postgraduate Medical Journal*, 399–403.

Hilton, N. Z., Harris, G. T., Rice, M. E., Lang, C., Cormier, C. A., and Lines, K. J. (2004) 'A brief actuarial assessment for the prediction of wife assault recidivism: The Ontario Domestic Assault Risk Assessment', *Psychological Assessment*, 16: 267–75.

Hilton, N. Z., Harris, G. T., and Rice, M. E. (2006) 'Sixty-six years of research on the clinical versus actuarial prediction of violence', *The Counseling Psychologist*, 34: 400–9.

Hilton, N. Z., Harris, G. T., Rice, M. E., Houghton, R. E., and Eke, A. W. (2008) 'An in depth actuarial assessment for wife assault recidivism: The Domestic Violence Risk Appraisal Guide', *Law and Human Behavior*, 32: 150–63.

Hirschi, T., and Gottfredson, M. (1983) 'Age and the explanation of crime', *American Journal of Sociology*, 89: 552–84.

Hodgins, S. (1994) 'Status at age 30 of children with conduct problems', *Studies on Crime and Crime Prevention*, 3: 41–62.

Hodgins, S. (2007) 'Persistent violent offending: What do we know? Editorial', *British Journal of Psychiatry*, 190: s12–s14.

Hodgins, S., de Brito, S., Simonoff, E., Vloet, T., and Viding, E. (2009) 'Getting the phenotypes right: An essential ingredient for understanding aetiological mechanisms underlying persistent violence and developing effective treatment', *Frontiers in Behavioural Neuroscience*, 3: 1–10.

Hoge, R. D., and Andrews, D. A. (2002) *Youth Level of Service/Case Management Inventory: User's Manual*. Toronto: Multi Health Services.

Hoge, R. D., Vincent, G. M., and Guy, L. S. (2012) 'Prediction and risk/needs assessments', in R. Loeber and D. P. Farrington (eds), *From Juvenile Delinquency to Adult Crime: Criminal Careers, Justice Policy, and Prevention* (pp. 150–83). Oxford: Oxford University Press.

Hogue, T. E. (2010) 'Personality disorder classification in forensic settings', in J. M. Brown and E. A. Campbell (eds), *The Cambridge Handbook of Forensic Psychology* (pp. 267–75). Cambridge: Cambridge University Press.

Holmes, C. A. (1991) 'Psychopathic disorder: A category mistake?', *Journal of Medical Ethics*, 17: 77–85.

Home Office (2011) *Revisions Made to the Multipliers and Unit Costs of Crime Used in the Integrated Offender Management Value for Money Toolkit*. London: Home Office.

Hood, R., Shute, S., Feilzer, M., and Wilcox, A. (2002) *Reconviction Rates of Serious Sex Offenders and Assessments of their Risk*. Findings, 164. London: Home Office.

Horsefield, A. (2003) 'Risk assessment: Who needs it?', *Probation Journal*, 50: 374–9.

House of Commons Justice Committee (2008) *Towards Effective Sentencing*. London: The Stationery Office.

Howard, P. (2009) *Improving Prediction of Reoffending Using the Offender Assessment System (OASys)*. Ministry of Justice Research Summary, 02/09. London: Ministry of Justice.

Howard, P. (2011) *Hazards of Different Types of Reoffending*. Ministry of Justice Research Series, 3/11. London: Ministry of Justice.

Howard, P. D., and Dixon, L. (2012) 'The construction and validation of the OASys violence predictor: Advancing violence risk assessment in the English and Welsh correctional services', *Criminal Justice and Behavior*, 39: 287–307.

Howard, P., and Dixon, L. (2013) 'Identifying change in the likelihood of violent recidivism: Causal dynamic risk factors in the OASys violence predictor', *Law and Human Behavior*, 37: 163–74.

Hudson, S. M., Marshall W. L., Wales D., McDonald E., Bakker L. W., and McLean A. (1993) 'Emotional recognition skills in sex-offenders', *Annals of Sex Research*, 6: 199–211.

Humphreys, L. G., and Swets, J. A. (1991) 'Comparison of predictive validities measured with biserial correlations and ROCs of signal detection theory', *Journal of Applied Psychology*, 76: 316–21.

Ireland, J. L., Ireland, C. A., and Birch, P. (eds) (2009) *Violent and Sexual Offenders: Assessment, Treatment, and Management*. Cullompton, Devon: Willan Publishing.

Isoda, M., and Noritake, A. (2013) 'What makes the dorsomedial frontal cortex active during reading the mental states of others?', *Frontiers in Neuroscience*, 7: 1–14.

Jackson, P. L., and Decety, J. (2004) 'Motor cognition: A new paradigm to study self–other interactions', *Current Opinion in Neurobiology*, 14: 259–63.

[The] Jacob Wetterling Act. Crimes against Children and Sexually Violent Offender Registration Act (Title XVII – Crimes Against Children, Subtitle A) (1994). Washington, DC: Federal Sex Offender Legislation.

Jaffee, S. R., Moffitt, T. E., Caspi, A., and Taylor, A. (2003) 'Life with (or without) father: The benefits of living with two biological parents depend on the father's antisocial behavior', *Child Development*, 74: 109–26.

Janus, E. S. (2000) 'Sexual predator commitment laws: Lessons for law and the behavioral sciences', *Behavioral Sciences and the Law*, 18: 5–21.

Janus, E. S. (2013) 'Preventive detention of sex offenders: The American experience versus international human rights norms', *Behavioral Sciences and the Law*, 31: 328–43.

Janus, E. S., and Prentky, R. A. (2003) 'Forensic use of actuarial risk assessment with sex offenders: Accuracy, admissibility and accountability', *American Criminal Law Review*, 40: 9–59.

Jennings, W. G., Piquero, A. R., Farrington, D. P., Ttofi, M. M., Crago, R. V., and Theobald, D. (2015) 'The intersections of drug use continuity with non-violent offending and involvement in violence over the life-course: Findings from the Cambridge Study in Delinquent Development', *Youth Violence and Juvenile Justice*, (in press). DOI: 10.1177/1541204014559524.

Jesness, C. F. (1998) 'The Jesness Inventory classification system', *Criminal Justice and Behavior*, 15: 78–91.

Jesness, C. F. (2003) *Jesness Inventory: Revised*. North Tonowanda, NY: Multi-Health Systems.

Johnson, J. G., Cohen, P., Kasen, S., Smailes, E., and Brook, J. S. (2001) 'Association of maladaptive parental behavior with psychiatric disorder among parents and their offspring', *Archives of General Psychiatry*, 58: 453–60.

Johnson-Laird, P. N. (1983) *Mental Models: Towards a Cognitive Science of Language, and Consciousness*. Cambridge: Cambridge University Press.

Johnson-Laird, P. (2008) *How we Reason*. Oxford: Oxford University Press.

Johnson-Laird, P. N., and Oatly, K. (2000) 'The cognitive and social construction of emotions', in M. Lewis and J. Haviland (eds), *Handbook of Emotions* (2nd edn, pp. 458–75). New York: Guilford.

Jolliffe, D., and Farrington, D. P. (2004) 'Empathy and offending: A systematic review and meta-analysis', *Aggression and Violent Behavior*, 9: 441–76.

Jolliffe, D., and Farrington, D. P. (2009) 'A systematic review of the relationship between childhood impulsiveness and later violence', in M. McMurran and R. C. Howard (eds), *Personality, Personality Disorder and Violence: An Evidence Based Approach* (pp. 41–60). Chichester: John Wiley & Sons.

Jolliffe, D., and Farrington, D. P. (2014) 'Self-reported offending: Reliability and validity', in G. J. N. Bruinsma and D. Weisburd (eds), *Encyclopedia of Criminology and Criminal Justice*. New York: Springer-Verlag.

Jolliffe, D., Farrington, D. P., and Howard, P. (2013) 'How long did it last? A 10-year reconviction follow-up study of high intensity training for young offenders', *Journal of Experimental Criminology*, 9: 515–31.

Jones, A. P., Laurens, K. R., Herba, C. M., Barker, G. J., and Viding, E. (2009) 'Amygdala hypoactivity to fearful faces in boys with conduct problems and callous-unemotional traits', *American Journal of Psychiatry*, 166: 95–102.

Jonkman, H., Yperen, T. van, and Prinsen, B. (2008) 'Prevention', in R. Loeber, N. W. Slot, P. van der Laan, and M. Hoeve (eds), *Tomorrow's Criminals: The Development of Child Delinquency and Effective Interventions* (pp. 179–96). Aldershot: Ashgate Publishing.

Jung, S., and Daniels, M. (2012) 'Conceptualizing sex offender denial from a multifaceted framework: Investigating the psychometric qualities of a new instrument', *Journal of Addictions and Offender Counseling*, 33: 2–17.

Jung, S., and Nunes, K. L. (2012) 'Denial and its relationship with treatment perceptions among sex offenders', *Journal of Forensic Psychiatry and Psychology*, 23: 485–96.

Kagan, J. (1994) *Galen's Prophecy: Temperament in Human Nature*. New York: Basic Books.

Kagan, J., Reznick, J. S., and Snidman, N. (1987) 'The physiology and psychology of behavioral inhibition in children', *Child Development*, 58: 1459–73.

Kagan, J., Snidman, N., and Arcus, D. (1993) 'On the temperamental categories of inhibited and uninhibited children', in K. H. Rubin and J. B. Asendorpf (eds), *Social Withdrawal, Inhibition, and Shyness in Childhood* (pp. 19–28). Hillsdale, NJ: Lawrence Erlbaum Associates.

Kahneman, D. (2011) *Thinking, Fast and Slow*. New York: Penguin Books.

Kahneman, D., and Tversky, A. (1972) 'Subjective probability: A judgment of representativeness', *Cognitive Psychology*, 3: 430–54.

Kahneman, D., and Tversky, A. (1973) 'On the psychology of prediction', *Psychological Review*, 80: 237–51.

Kansas v. Hendricks, 521 U.S. 346 (1997).

Karpman, B. (1948) 'The myth of the psychopathic personality', *American Journal of Psychiatry*, 104: 523–34.

Kazemian, L. (2007) 'Desistance from crime: Theoretical, empirical, methodological and policy considerations', *Journal of Contemporary Criminal Justice*, 23: 5–27.

Kazemian, L., and Farrington, D. P. (2010) 'The developmental evidence base: Desistance', in G. J. Towl and D. A. Crighton (eds), *Forensic Psychology* (pp. 133–47). Oxford: Blackwell.

Kemshall, H. (1998) 'Defensible decisions for risk: Or "it's the doers wot get the blame"', *Probation Journal*, 45. 67–72.

Kemshall, H., Mackenzie, G., Wood, J., Bailey, R., and Yates, J. (2005) *Evaluating the Effectiveness of the Criminal Justice and Court Services Act 2000 in Strengthening Multi Agency Public Protection Arrangements*. Leicester: De Montfort University.

Kernberg, O. F. (2004) *Aggressivity, Narcissism, and Self-Destructiveness in the Psychotherapeutic Relationship: New Developments in the Psychopathology and Psychotherapy of Severe Personality Disorders*. New Haven, CT: Yale University Press.

Kerr, M., Tremblay, R. E., Pagani, L., and Vitaro, F. (1997) 'Boys' behavioral inhibition and the risk of later delinquency', *Archives of General Psychiatry*, 54: 809–16.

Khiroya, R., Weaver, T., and Maden, T. (2009) 'Use and perceived utility of violence risk assessments in English medium secure forensic units', *Psychiatrist*, 33: 129–32.

Kiehl, K. A., and Sinnott-Armstrong, W. P. (eds) (2013) *Handbook on Psychopathy and Law*. New York: Oxford University Press.

Kiehl, K. A., Smith, A. M., Hare, R. D., Mendrek, A., Forster, B. B., and Brink, J. (2001) 'Limbic abnormalities in affective processing by criminal psychopaths as revealed by functional magnetic resonance imaging', *Biological Psychiatry*, 50: 677–84.

Kim, H. K., Capaldi, D. M., Pears, K. C., Kerr, D. C. R., and Owen, L. D. (2009) 'Intergenerational transmission of internalising and externalising behaviours across three generations: Gender-specific pathways', *Criminal Behaviour and Mental Health*, 19: 125–41.

King, C. A. (1999) 'Fighting the devil we don't know: Kansas v. Hendricks. A case study exploring the civilization of criminal punishment and its ineffectiveness in preventing child sexual abuse', *William and Mary Law Review*, 4: 1427–69.

Kingston, D. A., Yates, P. M., Firestone, P., Babchishin, K., and Bradford, J. M. (2008) 'With the Static-99 and the Sex Offender Risk Appraisal Guide', *Sex Abuse: A Journal of Research and Treatment*, 20: 466–84.

Kitching J. (1857) 'Lectures on moral insanity', *British Medical Journal*, 1: 334–6, 389–91, 435–56.

Kluckhohn, C., and Murray, H. A. (1953) 'Personality formation: The determinants', in C. Kluckhohn, H. A. Murray, and D. M. Schneider (eds), *Personality in Nature, Society, and Culture* (2nd edn, pp. 53–67). New York: Knopf.

Knight, R. A., and Prentky, R. A. (1990) 'Classifying sex offenders: The development and corroboration of taxonomic models', in W. L. Marshall and H. E. Barbaree (eds), *Handbook of Sexual Assault: Issues, Theories, and Treatment of the Offenders* (pp. 23–52). New York: Plenum Press.

Knight, R. A., and Thornton, D. (2007) *Evaluating and Improving Risk Assessment Schemes for Sexual Recidivism: A Long-Term Follow-up of Convicted Sexual Offenders* (Document No. 217618). Washington, DC: US Dept of Justice.

Knowles, E. M. (2009) *The Oxford Dictionary of Quotations* (7th edn). Oxford: Oxford University Press.

Koehler, J. J. (1996) 'The base rate fallacy reconsidered: Normative, descriptive, and methodological challenges', *Behavioral and Brain Sciences*, 19: 1–53.

Koenigs, M. (2012) 'The role of prefrontal cortex in psychopathy', *Reviews in the Neurosciences*, 23: 253–62.

Koenigs, M., Young, L., Adolphs, R., Tranel D., Cushman, F., Hauser, M., and Damasio, A. (2007) 'Damage to the prefrontal cortex increases utilitarian moral judgements', *Nature*, 446: 908–11.

Koenigs, M., Kruepke, M., Zeier, J., and Newman, J. P. (2012) 'Utilitarian moral judgment in psychopathy', *SCAN*, 7: 708–14.

Kraemer, H. C., Stice, E., Kazdin, A., Offord, D., and Kupfer, D. (2001) 'How do risk factors work together? Mediators, moderators, and independent, overlapping, and proxy risk factors', *American Journal of Psychiatry*, 158: 848–56.

Kraemer, H. C., Lowe, K. K., and Kupfer, D. J. (2005) *To your health: How to Understand What Research Tells us about Risk*. New York: Oxford University Press.

Kraepelin, E. (1904) *Psychiatrie: Ein Lehrbuch für Studirende und Ärzte* [Psychiatry: A Textbook for Students and Physicians] (7th edn). Canton, MA: Science History Publications.

Kratzer, L., and Hodgins, S. (1999) 'A typology of offenders: A test of Moffitt's theory among males and females from childhood to age 30', *Criminal Behaviour and Mental Health*, 9: 57–73.

Kropp, P. R. (2008) 'Intimate partner violence risk assessment and management', *Violence and Victims*, 23: 202–22.

Kropp, P. R., and Gibas, A. (2010) 'The Spousal Assault Risk Assessment Guide (SARA)', in R. K. Otto and K. S. Douglas (eds), *Handbook of Violence Risk Assessment* (pp. 227–50). New York: Routledge/Taylor & Francis.

Kropp, P. R., and Hart, S. D. (2000) 'The Spousal Assault Risk Assessment (SARA) Guide: Reliability and validity in adult male offenders', *Law and Human Behavior*, 24: 101–18.

Kropp, P., Hart, S., Webster, C., and Eaves, D. (1995) *The Spousal Assault Risk Assessment (SARA)*. Vancouver: British Columbia Institute Against Family Violence.

Kropp, P. R., Hart, S. D., and Belfrage, H. (2005) *Brief Spousal Assault Form for the Evaluation of Risk (B-SAFER): User Manual*. Vancouver, Canada: Proactive Resolutions.

Kropp, P. R., Hart, S. D., and Lyon, D. R. (2008a) *Guidelines for Stalking Assessment and Management (SAM)*. Vancouver: ProActive ReSolutions.

Kropp, P. R., Hart, S. D., Webster, C. D., and Eaves, D. (2008b) *Manual for the Spousal Assault Risk Assessment Guide* (2nd edn). Vancouver: British Columbia Institute Against Family Violence.

Kropp, P. R., Hart, S. D., Lyon, D. R., and Storey, J. E. (2011) 'The development and validation of the guidelines for stalking assessment and management', *Behavioral Science and the Law*, 29: 302–16.

Krueger, J. (2007) *Clinical and Structured Assessment of Sex Offenders*. New York: New York State Division of Probation and Correctional Alternatives.

Krueger, R. F., Eaton, N. R., Derringer, J., Markon, K. E., Watson, D., and Skodol, A. E. (2011) 'Personality in DSM-5: Helping delineate personality disorder content and framing the metastructure', *Journal of Personality Assessment*, 93: 325–31.

Kühn, S., Haggard, P., and Brass, M. (2009) 'Intentional inhibition: How the veto-area exerts control', *Human Brain Mapping*, 30: 2834–43.

Kurlychek, M. C., Brame, R., and Bushway S. D. (2006) 'Scarlet letters and recidivism: Does an old criminal record predict future offending?', *Criminology and Public Policy*, 5: 483–504.

Kurlychek, M. C., Brame, R., and Bushway, S. D. (2007) 'Enduring risk? Old criminal records and predictions of future criminal involvement', *Crime and Delinquency*, 53: 64–83.

Kvaraceus, W. C. (1966) *Anxious Youth: Dynamics of Delinquency*. Columbus, OH: Charles E. Merrill.

Lachar, D., and Gruber, C. P. (1995) *Personality Inventory for Youth*. Los Angeles, CA: Western Psychological Services.

La Fond, J. Q. (2005) *Preventing Sexual Violence: How Society Should Cope with Sex Offenders*. Washington, DC: American Psychological Association.

Langan, P. A., Schmitt, E. L., and Durose, M. R. (2003) *Recidivism of Sex Offenders Released in 1994*. (No. NCJ 198281). Washington, DC: US Dept of Justice, Bureau of Justice Statistics.

Langevin R., Write P., and Handy L. (1988) 'Empathy, assertiveness, and defensiveness among sex-offenders', *Annals of Sex Research*, 1: 533–47.

Långström, N., and Grann, M. (2002) 'Psychopathy and violent recidivism among young criminal offenders', *Acta Psychiatrica Scandinavica*, 106: 86–92.

Långström, N., and Hanson, R. K. (2006) 'High rates of sexual behavior in the general population: Correlates and predictors', *Archives of Sexual Behavior*, 35: 37–52.

Langton, C. M., Barbaree, H. E., Harkins, L., Arenovich, T., McNamee, J., Peacock, E. J., Dalton, A., Hansen, K. T., Luong, D., and Marcon, H. (2008) 'Denial and minimization among sexual offenders: Posttreatment presentation and association with sexual recidivism', *Criminal Justice and Behavior*, 35: 69–98.

Larsson, H., Tuvblad, C., Rijsdijk, F. V., Andershed, H., Grann, M., and Lichtenstein, P. (2007) 'A common genetic factor explains the association between psychopathic personality and antisocial behavior', *Psychological Medicine*, 37: 15–26.

Latessa, E. J., and Lowenkamp, C. (2005) *What are criminogenic needs and why are they important?* For the Record 4th Quarter 2005, 15. http://ojj.la.gov/ojj/files/What_Are_Criminogenic_Needs.pdf.

Latessa, E. J., Cullen, F. T., and Gendreau, P. (2002) 'Beyond correctional quackery: Professionalism and the possibility of effective treatment', *Federal Probation*, 66: 43–9.

Latessa, E. J., Listwan, S. J., and Koetzle, D. (2014) *What Works (and Doesn't) in Reducing Recidivism*. Waltham, MA, USA: Anderson Publishing Elsevier.

Laub, J. H., and Sampson, R. J. (2001) 'Understanding desistance from crime', in M. Tonry (ed.), *Crime and Justice: A Review of Research* (vol. 28, pp. 1–70). Chicago, IL: University of Chicago Press.

Laub, J. H., and Sampson, R. J. (2007) *Shared Beginnings, Divergent Lives: Delinquent Boys to Age 70*. Cambridge, MA: Harvard University Press.

Laurell, J., and Dåderman, A. M. (2005) 'Recidivism is related to psychopathy (PCL-R) in a group of men convicted of homicide', *International Journal of Law and Psychiatry*, 28: 255–68.

Laws, D. R., and O'Donohue, W. (2008) *Sexual deviance: Theory, assessment, and treatment* (2nd ed). New York, NY: Guilford Press.

Laws, D. R., and Ward, T. (2011) *Desisting from Sex Offending: Alternatives to Throwing away the Keys*. New York: Guilford Press.

Le Blanc, M., and Fréchette, M. (1989) *Male Criminal Activity, from Childhood through Youth: Multilevel and Developmental Perspectives*. New York: Springer-Verlag.

LeDoux, J. E. (1996) *The Emotional Brain*. New York: Simon & Schuster.

LeDoux, J. (2007) 'The amygdala', *Current Biology*, 17: R868–R874.

Lee, S., Aos, S., Drake, E. K., Pennucci, A., Miller, M. G., and Anderson, L. (2012) *Return on Investment: Evidence-Based Options to Reduce Statewide Outcomes*. Olympia, WA: Washington State Institute for Public Policy.

Leete, R., and Fox, J. (1977) 'Registrar General's social classes: Origins and uses', *Population Trends*, 8: 1–7.

Lejins, P. P. (1967) 'The field of prevention', in E. W. Amos and C. F. Wellford (eds), *Delinquency Prevention: Theory and Ppractice* (pp. 1–21). Englewood Cliffs, NJ: Prentice-Hall.

Levenson, J. S. (2011) '"But I didn't do it!": Ethical treatment of sex offenders in denial', *Sexual Abuse: A Journal of Research and Treatment*, 23: 346–64.

Lieb, R., Quinsey, V., and Berliner, L. (1998) 'Sexual predators and social policy', in M. Tonry (ed.), *Crime and Justice: A Review of Research*, 23: 43–114. Chicago, IL: University of Chicago Press.

Lilienfeld, S. O. (1994) 'Conceptual problems in the assessment of psychopathy', *Clinical Psychology Review*, 14: 17–38.

Lilienfeld, S. O. (1998) 'Methodological advances and developments in the assessment of psychopathy', *Behavior Research and Therapy*, 36: 99–125.

Lind, G. (2008) 'The meaning and measurement of moral judgment revisited: A dual aspect model', in D. Fasko and W. Willis (eds), *Contemporary Philosophical Perspectives on Moral Development and Education* (pp. 185–220). Creskill, NJ: Hampton.

Lindberg, N. (2012) 'Psychopathic features in adolescence', in H. Häkkänen-Nyholm and J.-O. Nyholm (eds), *Psychopathy and Law: A Practitioner's Guide* (pp. 127–38). Chichester: Wiley-Blackwell.

Lindsey, R. E., Carlozzi, A. F., and Eells G. T. (2001) 'Differences in the dispositional empathy of juvenile sex-offenders, non-sex offending delinquent juveniles, and nondelinquent juveniles', *Journal of Interpersonal Violence*, 16: 510–22.

Lippke, R. L. (2008) 'No easy way out: Dangerous offenders and preventive detention', *Law and Philosophy*, 27: 383–414.
Lipsey, M. W. (2009) 'The primary factors that characterize effective interventions with juvenile offenders: A meta-analytic overview', *Victims and Offenders*, 4: 124–47.
Lipsey, M. W., and Cullen, F. T. (2007) 'The effectiveness of correctional rehabilitation: A review of systematic reviews', *Annual Review of Law and Social Science*, 3: 297–320.
Lipsey, M. W., Landenberger, N. A., and Wilson, S. J. (2007) 'Effects of cognitive-behavioral programs for criminal offenders', *Campbell Systematic Reviews*, 6: 1–27.
Lipscombe, S. (2012). *Sarah's law: the child sex offender disclosure scheme.* Standard Note: SN/HA/1692. House of Commons Library. Available at: http://www.parliament.uk/business/publications/research/briefing-papers/SN01692/sarahs-law-the-child-sex-offender-disclosure-scheme. Accessed 25 June 2014.
Lisak, D., and Ivan, C. (1995) 'Deficits in intimacy and empathy in sexually aggressive men', *Journal of Interpersonal Violence*, 10: 296–308.
Livesley, W. J. (2007) 'A framework for integrating dimensional and categorical classifications of personality disorder', *Journal of Personality Disorders*, 21: 199–224.
Lloyd, C., Mair, G., and Hough, M. (1994) *Explaining Reconviction Rates: A Critical Analysis.* Home Office research Study, 136. London: Home Office.
Loeber, R., and Farrington, D. P. (eds) (1998a) *Serious and Violent Juvenile Offenders: Risk Factors and Successful Interventions.* Thousand Oaks, CA: Sage.
Loeber, R., and Farrington, D. P. (1998b) 'Conclusions and the way forward', in R. Loeber and D. P. Farrington (eds), *Serious and Violent Juvenile Offenders: Risk Factors and Successful Interventions* (pp. 405–27). Thousand Oaks, CA: Sage.
Loeber, R., and Farrington, D. P. (1998c) 'Never too early, never too late: Risk factors and successful interventions for serious and violent juvenile offenders', *Studies on Crime and Crime Prevention*, 7: 7–30.
Loeber, R., and Farrington, D. P. (eds) (2001) *Child Delinquents.* Thousand Oaks, CA: Sage.
Loeber, R., and Farrington, D. P. (2011) *Young Homicide Offenders and Victims: Risk Factors, Prediction, and Prevention from Childhood.* New York: Springer.
Loeber, R., and LeBlanc, M. (1990) 'Toward a developmental criminology', in M. Tonry and N. Morris (eds), *Crime and Justice: A Review of Research* (vol. 12, pp. 375–473). Chicago, IL: Chicago University Press.
Loeber, R., and Pardini, D. (2008) 'Neurobiology and the development of violence: Common assumptions and controversies', *Philosophical Transactions of the Royal Society B: Biological Sciences*, 363: 2491–503.
Loeber, R., and Schmaling, K. B. (1985) 'Empirical evidence for overt and covert patterns of antisocial conduct problems: A meta-analysis', *Journal of Abnormal Child Psychology*, 13: 337–53.
Loeber, R., Stouthamer-Loeber, M., van Kammen, W. B., and Farrington, D. P. (1989) 'Development of a new measure of self-reported antisocial behaviour for young children: Prevalence and reliability', in M. W. Klein (eds), *Cross-National Research in Self-Reported Crime and Delinquency* (pp. 203–25). Dordrecht: Kluwer.
Loeber, R., Farrington, D. P., Stouthamer-Loeber, M., and Van Kammen, W. B. (1998) *Antisocial Behavior and Mental Health Problems: Explanatory Factors in Childhood and Adolescence.* Mahwah, NJ: Lawrence Erlbaum.
Loeber, R., Farrington D. P., Stouthamer-Loeber, M., Moffitt, T. E., Caspi, A., White, H. R., Wei, E. H., and Beyers, J. M. (2003) 'The development of male offending: Key findings from fourteen years of the Pittsburgh Youth Study', in T. P. Thornberry and M. D. Krohn (eds), *Taking Stock of Delinquency: An Overview of Findings from Contemporary Longitudinal Studies* (pp. 93–136). New York: Kluwer Academic/Plenum Publishers.

Loeber, R., Slot, N. W., and Stouthamer-Loeber, M. (2008a) 'A cumulative developmental model of risk and protective factors', in R. Loeber, N. W. Slot, P. van der Laan, and M. Hoeve (eds), *Tomorrow's Criminals* (pp. 133–61). Aldershot: Ashgate Publishing.

Loeber, R., van der Laan, P. H., Slot, N. W., and Hoeve, M. (2008b) 'Conclusions and recommendation', in R. Loeber, N. W. Slot, P. van der Laan, and M. Hoeve (eds), *Tomorrow's Criminals* (pp. 261–84). Aldershot: Ashgate Publishing.

Lorenzini, N., and Fonagy, P. (2013) 'Attachment and personality disorders: A short review', *Focus: The Journal of Lifelong Learning in Psychiatry*, 11: 155–66.

Lösel, F. (2001) 'Evaluating the effectiveness of correctional programs: Bridging the gap between research and practice', in G. A. Bernfeld, D. P. Farrington, and A. W. Leschied (eds), *Offender Rehabilitation in Practice* (pp. 67–92). Chichester: Wiley.

Lösel, F. (2011) 'What works in correctional treatment and rehabilitation for young adults?', in F. Lösel, A. E. Bottoms, and D. P. Farrington (eds), *Young Adult Offenders: Lost in Transition?* (pp. 74–113). Abingdon, Oxon: Routledge.

Lösel, F. (2012) 'Offender treatment and rehabilitation: What works?', in M. Maguire, R. Morgan, and R. Reiner (eds) *The Oxford Handbook of Criminology* (5th edn, pp. 986–1016). Oxford: Oxford University Press.

Lösel, F., and Bender, D. (2003), 'Protective factors and resilience', in D. P. Farrington and J. Coid (eds), *Prevention of Adult Antisocial Behaviour* (pp. 130–204). Cambridge: Cambridge University Press.

Lösel, F., and Farrington, D. P. (2012) 'Direct protective and buffering protective factors in the development of youth violence', *American Journal of Preventive Medicine*, 43: S8–S23.

Lösel, F., and Schmucker, M. (2005) 'The effectiveness of treatment for sexual offenders: A comprehensive meta-analysis', *Journal of Experimental Criminology*, 1: 117–46.

Lowenkamp, C. T., and Latessa, E. J. (2005) 'Increasing the effectiveness of correctional programming through the risk principle: Identifying offenders for residential placement', *Criminology and Public Policy*, 4: 263–90.

Lowenkamp, C. T., Latessa, E. J., and Holsinger, A. M. (2006a) 'The risk principle in action: What have we learned from 13,676 offenders and 97 correctional programs?', *Crime and Delinquency*, 52: 77–93.

Lowenkamp, C. T., Latessa, E. J., and Smith, P. (2006b) 'Does correctional program quality really matter? The impact of adhering to the principles of effective intervention', *Criminology and Public Policy*, 5: 575–94.

Loza, W., and Loza-Fanous, A. (2000) 'Predictive validity of the Self-Appraisal Questionnaire', *Journal of Interpersonal Violence*, 15: 1183–91.

Luna, E. (2013) 'Psychopathy and sentencing', in K. A. Kiehl, and W. P. Sinnott-Armstrong (eds), *Handbook on Psychopathy and Law* (pp. 358–88). New York: Oxford University Press.

Lunbeck, E. (1994) *The Psychiatric Persuasion: Knowledge, Gender and Power in Modern America*. Princeton, NJ: Princeton University Press.

Lussier, P. (2005) 'The criminal activity of sexual offenders in adulthood: Revisiting the specialization debate', *Sexual Abuse: A Journal of Research and Treatment*, 17: 269–92.

Lussier, P., Farrington, D. P., and Moffitt, T. E. (2009) 'Is the antisocial child father of the abusive man? A 40-year prospective longitudinal study on the developmental antecedents of intimate partner violence', *Criminology*, 47: 741–80.

Lussier, P., Tzoumakis, S., Cale, J., and Amirault, J. (2010) 'Criminal trajectories of adult sex offenders and the age effect: Examining the dynamic aspect of offending in adulthood', *International Criminal Justice Review*, 20: 147–68.

Lussier, P., Blokland, A. A. J., Mathesius, J., Pardini, D., and Loeber, R. (2015) 'The childhood risk factors of adolescent-onset and adult-onset of sex offending: Evidence from a prospective longitudinal study', in A. A. J. Blokland and P. Lussier (eds), *Sex Offenders: A Criminal Career Approach* (pp. 91–118). Chichester: John Wiley & Sons.

Ly, M., Motzkin, J. C., Philippi, C., Kirk, G. R., Newman, J. P., Kiehl, K. A., and Koenigs, M. (2012) 'Cortical thinning in psychopathy', *American Journal of Psychiatry*, 169: 743–9.

Lynam, D. R. (1996) 'Early identification of chronic offenders: Who is the fledgling psychopath?', *Psychological Bulletin*, 120: 209–34.

Lynam, D. R., and Gudonis, L. (2005) 'The development of psychopathy', *Annual Review of Clinical Psychology*, 1: 381–407.

Lynn, M. T., Muhle-Karbe, P. S., and Brass, M. (2014) 'Controlling the self: The role of the dorsal frontomedian cortex in intentional inhibition', *Neuropsychologia*. DOI: 10.1016/j.neuropsychologia.2014.09.009 (in press).

Lyons-Ruth, K., and Block, D. (1996) 'The disturbed caregiving system: Relations among childhood trauma, maternal caregiving, and infant affect and attachment', *Infant Mental Health Journal*, 17: 257–75.

McBurnett, K., Lahey, B. B., Frick, P. J., Risch, C., Loeber, R., Hart, E. L., *et al.*, (1991) 'Anxiety, inhibition, and conduct disorder in children: II. Relation to salivary cortisol', *Journal of the American Academy of Child and Adolescent Psychiatry*, 30: 192–6.

McCann, K., and Lussier, P. (2008) 'Antisociality, sexual deviance and sexual reoffending in juvenile sex offenders: A meta-analytical investigation', *Youth Violence and Juvenile Justice*, 6: 363–85.

McCollister, K. E., French, M. T., and Fang, H. (2010) 'The cost of crime to society: New crime-specific estimates for policy and program evaluation', *Drug Alcohol Depend*, 108: 98–109.

McCord, J. (2001) 'Psychosocial contributions to psychopathy and violence', in A. Raine and J. Sanmartin (eds), *Violence and Psychopathy* (pp. 141–69). New York: Kluwer Academic/Plenum.

McCord, W., and McCord, J. (1964) *The Psychopathy: An Essay on the Criminal Mind*. Oxford: D. Van Nostrand.

McGuire, J. (ed.) (1995) *What Works: Reducing Reoffending*. Chichester: Wiley.

McGuire J. (2002) 'Criminal sanctions versus psychologically-based intervention with offenders: A comparative empirical analysis', *Psychology, Crime, and Law*, 8: 183–208.

McHoskey, J. W., Worzel, W., and Szyarto, C. (1998) 'Machiavellianism and psychopathy', *Journal of Personality and Social Psychology*, 74: 192–210.

MacKenzie, D. L. (2012) 'Challenges of conducting field experiments in correctional settings: Boot camp prison study as an example', *Journal of Experimental Criminology*, 8: 289–306.

MacKenzie, D. L., Bierie, D., and Mitchell, O. (2007) 'An experimental study of a therapeutic boot camp: Impact on impulses, attitudes, and recidivism', *Journal of Experimental Criminology*, 3: 221–46.

MacLeod, J. F., Grove, P. G., and Farrington, D. P. (2012) *Explaining Criminal Careers*. Oxford: Oxford University Press.

McMurran, M. (ed.) (2002) *Motivating Offenders to Change: A Guide to Enhancing Engagement in Therapy*. Chichester: Wiley.

McMurran, M. (2010) 'Theories of change', in J. M. Brown and E. A. Campbell (eds), *The Cambridge Handbook of Forensic Psychology* (pp. 118–25). Cambridge: Cambridge University Press.

McMurran, M., and Theodosi, E. (2007) 'Is offender treatment non-completion associated with increased reconviction over no treatment?', *Psychology, Crime and Law*, 13: 333–343.

McMurran, M., and Ward, T. (2004) 'Motivating offenders to change in therapy: An organising framework', *Legal and Criminological Psychology*, 9: 295–311.

McMurran, M., Theodosi, E., Sweeney, A., and Sellen, J. (2008) 'What do prisoners want? Current concerns of adult male prisoners', *Psychology, Crime, and Law*, 14: 267–74.

McSherry, B. (2003) 'Voluntariness, intention, and the defence of mental disorder: Toward a rational approach', *Behavioral Sciences and the Law*, 21: 581–99.

McVie, S. (2005) 'Patterns of deviance underlying the age-crime curve: The long term evidence', *British Society of Criminology E-Journal*, 7.

Maden, A. (2003) 'Standardised risk assessment: Why all the fuss?', *Psychiatry Bulletin*, 27: 201–4.

Maden, A. (2005) 'Violence risk assessment: The question is not whether but how', *Psychiatry Bulletin*, 29: 121–2.

Maguire, M. (1997) 'Crime statistics, patterns and trends: Changing perceptions and their implications', in M. Maguire, R. Morgan, and R. Reiner (eds), *The Oxford Handbook of Criminology* (pp. 135–88). Oxford: Clarendon Press.

Maibom, H. L. (2005) 'Moral unreason: The case of psychopathy', *Mind and Language*, 20: 237–57.

Maltz, M. D. (1984) *Recidivism*. Orlando, FL: Academic Press.

Mann, R. D. (1996) 'A critique of P. E. Meehl's *Clinical versus Statistical Prediction*', *Behavioral Science*, 1: 224–30.

Mann, R. E., and Marshall, W. L. (2009) 'Advances in the treatment of adult incarcerated sex offenders', in A. R. Beech, L. A. Craig, and K. D. Browne (eds), *Assessment and Treatment of Sex Offenders: A Handbook* (pp. 329–47). Chichester: John Wiley.

Mann, R. E., Hanson, R. K., and Thornton, D. (2010) 'Assessing risk for sexual recidivism: Some proposals on the nature of psychologically meaningful risk factors', *Sexual Abuse: A Journal of Research and Treatment*, 22: 191–217.

Marcus, D. K., John, S. L., and Edens, J. F. (2004) 'A taxometric analysis of psychopathic personality', *Journal of Abnormal Psychology*, 113: 626–35.

Marsh, A. A., and Blair, R. J. R. (2008) 'Deficits in facial affect recognition among antisocial populations: A meta-analysis', *Neuroscience and Neurobehavioral Reviews*, 32: 454–65.

Marsh, A. A., Kozak, M. N., and Ambady, N. (2007) 'Accurate identification of fear facial expressions predicts prosocial behavior', *Emotion*, 7: 239–51.

Marsh, A. A., Finger, E. C., Fowler, K. A., Jurkowitz, I. T. N., Schechter, J. C., Yu, H. H., Pine, D. S., and Blair, R. J. R. (2011) 'Reduced amygdala-orbitofrontal connectivity during moral judgments in youths with disruptive behavior disorders and psychopathic traits', *Psychiatry Research: Neuroimaging*, 194: 279–86.

Marshall, W. L., Hudson S. M., Jones R., and Fernandez Y. M. (1995) 'Empathy in sex offenders', *Clinical Psychology Review*, 15: 99–115.

Marshall, W. L., Thornton, D., Marshall, L. E., Fernandez, Y. M., and Mann, R. (2001) 'Treatment of sexual offenders who are in categorical denial: A pilot project', *Sexual Abuse: Journal of Research and Treatment*, 13: 205–15.

Marshall, W. L., Marshall, L. E., Serran, G. A., and O'Brien, M. D. (2009) 'Self-esteem, shame, cognitive distortions and empathy in sexual offenders: Their integration and treatment implications', *Psychology, Crime and Law*, 15: 217–34.

Martinson, R. (1974) 'What works? Questions and answers about prison reform', *The Public Interest*, 35: 22–54.

Maruna, S. (2001) *Making Good: How Ex-Convicts Reform and Rebuild their Lives*. Washington, DC: American Psychological Association.

Maruna, S., and Roy, K. (2007) 'Amputation or reconstruction? Notes on the concept of "knifing off" and desistance from crime', *Journal of Contemporary Criminal Justice*, 23: 104–24.

Maudsley, H. (1874) *Responsibility in Mental Disease*. London: H. S. King.

Maughan, B., and Rutter, M. (2001) 'Antisocial children grown up', in J. Hill and B. Maughan (eds), *Conduct Disorders in Childhood and Adolescence* (pp. 507–52). Cambridge: Cambridge University Press.

Mayfield, D., McLeod, G., and Hall, P. (1974) 'The CAGE questionnaire: Validation of a new alcoholism screening instrument', *American Journal of Psychiatry*, 131: 1121–3.

Meehl, P. (1954) *Clinical versus Statistical Prediction: A Theoretical Analysis and a Review of the Evidence*. Minneapolis, MN: University of Minnesota Press.

Meehl, P. E., and Golden, R. (1982) 'Taxometric methods', in P. Kendall and J. Butcher (eds) *Handbook of Research Methods in Clinical Psychology* (pp. 127–81). New York: Wiley.

Megan's Law 1994 (H.R. 2137, 42 USC 13701 note) (1996). Public Law 104-145, 104th Congress. United States.

Meloy, J. R. (1988) *The Psychopathic Mind*. Northvale, NJ: Jason Aronson.

Melton, G. B., Petrila, J., Poythress, N. G., and Slobogin, C. (1997) *Psychological Evaluations for the Courts: A Handbook for Mental Health Professionals and Lawyers* (2nd edn). New York: Guilford.

Mendez, M. F. (2009) 'The neurobiology of moral behavior: Review and neuropsychiatric implications', *CNS Spectrum*, 14: 608–20.

Meyer, B., Johnson, S. L., and Carver, C. S. (1999) 'Exploring behavioral activation and inhibition sensitivities among college students at risk for bipolar spectrum symptomatology', *Journal of Psychopathology and Behavioral Assessment*, 21: 275–92.

Miethe, T., Olson, J., and Mitchell, O. (2006) 'Specialization and persistence in the arrest histories of sex offenders: A comparative analysis of alternative measures and offense types', *Journal of Research in Crime and Delinquency*, 43: 204–29.

Millar, A. (2009) *Inventory of Spousal Violence Risk Assessment Tools Used in Canada*. Ottawa: Dept of Justice Canada. http://canada.justice.gc.ca/eng/pi/rs/rep-rap/2009/rr09_7/index.html. Accessed 28 Apr. 2014.

Miller, D. J., Vachon, D. D., and Aalsma, M. C. (2012) 'Negative affect and emotion dysregulation: Conditional relations with violence and risky sexual behavior in a sample of justice-involved adolescents', *Criminal Justice and Behavior*, 39: 1316–27.

Miller, S. L., and Brodsky, S. L. (2011) 'Risky business: Addressing the consequences of predicting violence', *Journal of the American Academy of Psychiatry and the Law*, 39: 396–401.

Millon, T. (1993) *Millon Adolescent Clinical Inventory Manual*. Minneapolis, MN: National Computer Systems.

Mills, J. F., Kroner, D. G., and Morgan, R. D. (2011) *Clinician's Guide to Violence Risk Assessment*. New York: Guilford Press.

Mineka, S., Watson, D., and Clark, L. A. (1998) 'Comorbidity of anxiety and unipolar mood disorders', *Annual Review of Psychology*, 49: 377–412.

Ministry of Justice (2007) *Statistical Bulletin: Offender Management Caseload Statistics 2006*. London: The Stationery Office.

Ministry of Justice (2010a) *Reoffending of Adults: Results from the 2008 Cohort*. London: Ministry of Justice Statistics Bulletin.

Ministry of Justice (2010b) *Reoffending of Juveniles: Results from the 2008 Cohort*. London: Ministry of Justice Statistics Bulletin.

Ministry of Justice (2010c) *Compendium of Reoffending Statistics and Analysis*. London: Ministry of Justice Statistics Bulletin.

Ministry of Justice (2011) *Compendium of Reoffending Statistics and Analysis*. London: Ministry of Justice Statistics Bulletin.

Ministry of Justice (2013) *Compendium of Reoffending Statistics and Analysis*. London: Ministry of Justice Bulletin.

Minuchin, S. (1974) *Families and Family Therapy*. Cambridge, MA: Harvard University Press.

Moffitt, T. E. (1993) 'Life-course-persistent and adolescence-limited antisocial behaviour: A developmental taxonomy', *Psychological Review*, 100: 674–701.

Moffitt, T. E. (2006) 'A review of research on the taxonomy of life-course persistent versus adolescence-limited antisocial behavior', in F. T. Cullen, J. P. Wright, and K. R. Blevins (eds), *Taking Stock: The Status of Criminological Theory* (vol. 15, pp. 277–311). Brunswick, NJ: Transaction Publications.

Moffitt, T. E., and Caspi, A. (2001) 'Childhood predictors differentiate life-course persistent and adolescence-limited antisocial pathways among males and females', *Development and Psychopathology*, 13: 355–75.

Moffitt, T. E., and Caspi, A. (2007) 'Evidence from behavioral genetics for environment contributions to antisocial conduct', in P.-O. H. Wilkström and R. J. Sampson (eds), *The Explanation of Crime: Context, Mechanisms and Development* (pp. 108–52). Cambridge: Cambridge University Press.

Moffitt, T. E., Caspi, A., Rutter, M., and Silva, P. A. (2001) *Sex Differences in Antisocial Behaviour*. Cambridge: Cambridge University Press.

Moffitt, T. E., Caspi, A., Harrington, H., and Milne, B. J. (2002) 'Males on the life-course-persistent and adolescence-limited antisocial pathways: Follow-up at age 26 years', *Developmental Psychopathology*, 14: 179–207.

Moffitt, T. E., Caspi, A., and Rutter, M. (2006) 'Measured gene–environment interactions in psychopathology: Concepts, research strategies, and implications for research, intervention, and public understanding of genetics', *Perspectives on Psychological Science*, 1: 5–27.

Moll, J., and de Oliveira-Souza, R. (2007) 'Moral judgments, emotions and the utilitarian brain', *Trends in Cognitive Science*, 11: 319–21.

Monahan, J. (1981) *Predicting Violent Behavior: An Assessment of Clinical Techniques*. Newbury Park, CA: Sage.

Monahan, J., Steadman, H., Silver, E., Appelbaum, P., Robbins, P., Mulvey, E., Roth, L., Grisso, T., and Banks, S. (2001) *Rethinking Risk Assessment: The MacArthur Study of Mental Disorder and Violence*. New York: Oxford University Press.

Morey, L. C. (1988) 'The categorical representation of personality disorder: A cluster analysis of DSM-III-R personality features', *Journal of Abnormal Psychology*, 3: 314–21.

Morse, S. J. (2008) 'Psychopathy and criminal responsibility', *Neuroethics*, 1: 205–12.

Mulheirn, I., Gough, B., and Menne, V. (2010). *Prison Break: Tackling Recidivism, Reducing Costs*. London: Social Market Foundation.

Muller, J. L., Sommer, M., Wagner, V., Lange, K., Taschler, H., Roder, C. H., Schuierer, G., Klein, H. E., and Hajak, G. (2003) 'Abnormalities in emotion processing within cortical and subcortical regions in criminal psychopaths: Evidence from a functional magnetic resonance imaging study using pictures with emotional content', *Biological Psychiatry*, 54: 152–62.

Mulvey, E. P., and Iselin, A. R. (2008) 'Improving professional judgments of risk and amenability in juvenile justice', *The Future of Children*, 18: 35–57.

Mulvey, E., and Lidz, C. (1995) 'Conditional prediction: A model for research on dangerousness to others in a new era', *International Journal of Law and Psychiatry*, 18: 129–43.

Mulvey, E. P., and Lidz, C. W. (1998) 'The clinical prediction of violence as a conditional judgment', *Social Psychiatry and Psychiatric Epidemiology*, 33: S107–S113.

Murphy, C., and Vess, J. (2003) 'Subtypes of psychopathy: Proposed differences between narcissistic, borderline, sadistic, and antisocial psychopaths', *Psychiatric Quarterly*, 74: 11–29.

Murray, J., and Thomson, M. E. (2010) 'Clinical judgement in violence risk assessment', *Europe's Journal of Psychology*, 1: 128–49.

Murray, J., Farrington, D. P., and Eisner, M. P. (2009) 'Drawing conclusions about causes from systematic reviews of risk factors: The Cambridge Quality Checklists', *Journal of Experimental Criminology*, 5: 1–23.

Myers, W. C., and Monaco, L. (2000) 'Anger experience, style of anger expression, sadistic personality disorder and psychopathy in juvenile sexual homicide offenders', *Journal of Forensic Sciences*, 45: 698–701.

Nagin, D., and Paternoster, R. (2000) 'Population heterogeneity and state dependence: State of the evidence and directions for future research', *Journal of Quantitative Criminology*, 16: 117–44.

Nagin, D. S., Farrington, D. P., and Moffitt, T. E. (1995) 'Life-course trajectories of different types of offenders', *Criminology*, 33: 111–39.

Neigh, G. N., Gillespie, C. F., and Nemeroff, C. B. (2009) 'The neurobiological toll of child abuse and neglect', *Trauma Violence Abuse*, 10: 389–410.

Neumann, C. S., Hare, R. D., and Newman, J. P. (2007) 'The super-ordinate nature of the psychopathy checklist-revised', *Journal of Personality Disorders*, 21: 102–17.

Newman, C. F. (1994) 'Understanding client resistance: Methods for enhancing motivation to change', *Cognitive and Behavioral Practice*, 1: 47–69.

Nicholls, T. L., Pritchard, M. M., Reeves, K. A., and Hilterman, E. (2013) 'Risk assessment in intimate partner violence. A systematic review of contemporary approaches', *Partner Abuse*, 4: 76–168.

Nordstrom, B. R., Gao, Y., Glenn, A. L., Peskin, M., Rudo-Hutt, A. S., Schug, R. A., Young, Y., and Raine, A. (2011) 'Neurocriminology', *Advances in Genetics*, 75: 255–83.

Nunes, K. L., and Jung, S. (2012) 'Are cognitive distortions associated with denial and minimization among sex offenders?', *Sexual Abuse: A Journal of Research and Treatment*, 25: 166–88.

Nunes, K. L., Hanson, R. K., Firestone, P., Moulden, H. M., Greenberg, D. M., and Bradford, J. M. (2007) 'Denial predicts recidivism for some sexual offenders', *Sexual Abuse: A Journal of Research and Treatment*, 19: 91–105.

O'Brien, M., and Bera, W. H. (1986) 'Adolescent sexual offenders: A descriptive typology', *Preventing Sexual Abuse: A Newsletter of the National Family Life Education Network*, 1: 2–4.

Ochsner, K. N., Bunge, S. A., Gross, J. J., and Gabrieli, J. D. E. (2002) 'Rethinking feelings: An fMRI study of the cognitive regulation of emotion', *Journal of Cognitive Neuroscience*, 14: 1215–29.

Ogloff, J. R. (2006) 'Psychopathy/antisocial personality disorder conundrum', *Australia and New Zealand Journal of Psychiatry*, 40: 519–28.

Ogloff, J. R., and Davis, M. (2005) 'Assessing risk for violence in the Australian context', in D. Chappell and P. Wilson (eds), *Issues in Australian Crime and Criminal Justice* (pp. 301–338). Chatswood: Lexis Nexis Butterworths.

Oliver, P. J., Robins, R. W., and Pervin, L. A. (eds) (2008) *Handbook of Personality: Theory and Research* (3rd edn). New York: Guilford Press.

Ollendick, T. H., Seligman, L. D., and Butcher, A. T. (1999) 'Does anxiety mitigate behavioral expression of severe conduct disorder in delinquent youth?', *Journal of Anxiety Disorders*, 12: 565–74.

Ontario Ministry of the Solicitor General (2000) *A Guide to the Domestic Violence Supplementary Report Form.* Toronto: Police Services Division.
OPCS (1980) *Classification of Occupations 1980.* London: HMSO.
OPCS (1991) *Standard Occupational Classification* (vol. 3). London: HMSO.
Otto, R. K. (2000) 'Assessing and managing violence risk in outpatient settings', *Journal of Clinical Psychology*, 56: 1239–62.
Otto, R. K., and Douglas, K. S. (eds) (2010) *Handbook of Violence Risk Assessment.* New York: Routledge/Taylor & Francis.
Ozarin, L. (2001) 'Moral insanity: A brief history', *Psychiatric News*, 36: 21.
Pajer, K. A. (1998) 'What happens to "bad" girls? A review of the adult outcomes of antisocial adolescent girls', *American Journal of Psychiatry*, 155: 862–70.
Pardini, D. A., and Byrd, A. L. (2013) 'Developmental conceptualizations of psychopathic features', in K. A. Kiehl and W. P. Sinnott-Armstrong (eds), *Handbook on Psychopathy and Law* (pp. 61–77). New York: Oxford University Press.
Pardini, D. A., and Loeber, R. (2007) 'Special section: Interpersonal and affective features of psychopathy in children and adolescents: Advancing a developmental perspective', *Journal of Clinical Child and Adolescent Psychology*, 36: 269–75.
Pardini, D., Obradovic, J., and Loeber, R. (2006) 'Interpersonal callousness, hyperactivity/impulsivity, inattention, and conduct problems as precursors to delinquency persistence in boys: A comparison of three grade-based cohorts', *Journal of Clinical Child and Adolescent Psychology*, 35: 45–59.
Pardue, A. D., Robinson, M. B., and Arrigo, B. A. (2013a) 'Psychopathy and corporate crime: A preliminary examination, part 1', *Journal of Forensic Psychology Practice*, 13: 116–44.
Pardue, A. D., Robinson, M. B., and Arrigo, B. A. (2013b) 'Psychopathy and corporate crime: A preliminary examination, part 2', *Journal of Forensic Psychology Practice*, 13: 145–69.
Paris, J. (1998) 'A biopsychosocial model of psychopathy', in T. Millon, E. Simonsen, M. Birket-Smith, and R. D. Davis (eds), *Psychopathy: Antisocial, Criminal, and Violent Behavior* (pp. 277–87). New York: Guilford Press.
Paris, J. (2014) 'After DSM-5: Where does personality disorder research go from here?', *Harvard Review of Psychiatry*, 22: 216–21.
Parker, T. (1983) *The People of Providence.* London: Hutchinson.
Pascual, L., Rodrigues, P., and Gallardo-Pujol, D. (2013) 'How does morality work in the brain? A functional and structural perspective of moral behavior', *Frontiers in Integrative Nerusocience*, 7: 1–8.
Paternoster, R., Brame, R., and Farrington, D. P. (1997) 'On the relationship between adolescent and adult offending frequencies', *Journal of Quantitative Criminology*, 17: 201–25.
Patrick, C. J. (1994) 'Emotion and psychopathy: Startling new insights', *Psychophysiology*, 31: 319–30.
Patrick, C. J. (1995) 'Emotion and temperament in psychopathy', *Clinical Science*, 5–8.
Patrick, C. J. (2007) 'Preface', in C. Patrick (ed.), *Handbook of Psychopathy* (pp. xiii–xvi). New York: Guilford Press.
Patterson, D., and Campbell, R. (2010) 'Why rape survivors participate in the criminal justice system', *Journal of Community Psychology*, 38: 191–205.
Patterson, G. R. (1982) *Coercive Family Interactions.* Eugene, OR: Castalia Press.
Patterson, G. R., Reid, J. B., Jones, R. R., and Conger, R. E. (1975) *A Social Learning Approach to Family Intervention: Families with Aggressive Children* (vol. 1). Eugene, OR: Castilia.
Patterson, G., DeBaryshe, B., and Ramsey, E. (1989) 'A developmental perspective on antisocial behaviour', *American Journal of Psychology*, 44: 329–35.

Patterson, G. R., DeGarmo, D. S., and Forgatch, M. S. (2004) 'Systematic changes in families following prevention trials', *Journal of Abnormal Child Psychology*, 32: 621–33.

Pedersen, L., Rasmussen, K., and Elsass, P. (2012) 'HCR-20 violence risk assessments as a guide for treating and managing violence risk in a forensic psychiatric setting', *Psychology, Crime and the Law*, 18: 733–43.

Pessoa, L., and Adolphs, R. (2010) 'Emotion processing and the amygdala: From a "low road" to "many roads" of evaluating biological significance', *Nature Reviews Neuroscience*, 11: 773–82.

Petersilia, J. M. (1987) *Expanding Options for Criminal Sentencing*. Santa Monica, CA: Rand.

Peterson, J. K., Skeem, J., Kennealy, P., Bray, B., and Zvonkovic, A. (2014) 'How often and how consistently do symptoms directly precede criminal behavior among offenders with mental illness?', *Law and Human Behavior*, 38: 439–49.

Petrosino, A., Turpin-Petrosino, C., and Buehler, J. (2003) 'Scared straight and other juvenile awareness programs for preventing juvenile delinquency: A systematic review of the randomized experimental evidence', *Annals of the American Academy of Political and Social Science*, 589: 41–62.

Petrosino, A., Turpin-Petrosino, C., Hollis-Peel, M. E., and Lavenberg, J. G. (2013) *Scared Straight and Other Juvenile Awareness Programs for Preventing Juvenile Delinquency: A Systematic Review*. Oslo: Campbell Collaboration.

Petrunik, M. (2003) 'The Hare and the Tortoise: Dangerousness and sex offender policy in the United States and Canada', *Canadian Journal of Criminology and Criminal Justice*, 45: 43–72.

Phillips, M. L., Young, A. W., Scott, S. K., Calder, A. J., Andrew C., Giampietro, V., Williams, S. C. R., Bullmore, E. T., Brammer, M., and Gray, J. A. (1998) 'Neural responses to facial and vocal expressions of fear and disgust', *Proceedings Biological Sciences*, 265: 1809–17.

Phillips, M. L., Williams, L. M., Heining, M., Herba, C. M., Russell, T., Andrew, C., Bullmore, E. T., Brammer, M. J., Williams, S. C., Morgan, M., Young, A. W., and Gray, J. A. (2004) 'Differential neural responses to overt and covert presentations of facial expressions of fear and disgust', *Neuroimage*, 21: 1484–96.

Picardi, A., Fagnani, C., Nistico, L., and Stazi, M. A. (2011) 'A twin study of attachment style in young adults', *Journal of Personality*, 79: 965–91.

Pietrini, P., and Bambini, V. (2009) 'Homo ferox: The contribution of functional brain studies to understanding the neural bases of aggressive and criminal behavior', *International Journal of Law and Psychiatry*, 32: 259–65.

Pillsbury, S. H. (2009) 'Misunderstanding provocation', *Michigan Journal of Law Reform*, 43: 143–73.

Pinel, P. (1809) *Traité Médico-Philosophique sur L'aliénation Mentale* [Medico Philosophical Treatise on Mental Derangement] (2nd edn). Paris: Brosson.

Piquero, A. R., Farrington, D. P., and Blumstein, A. (2003) 'The criminal career paradigm', *Crime and Justice*, 30: 359–506. Chicago, IL: University of Chicago Press.

Piquero, A. R., Brezina, T., and Turner, M. G. (2005) 'Testing Moffitt's account of delinquency abstention', *Journal of Research in Crime and Delinquency*, 42: 27–54.

Piquero, A. R., Brame, R., Fagan, J., and Moffitt, T. E. (2006) 'Assessing the offending activity of criminal domestic violence suspects: Offense specialization, escalation, and de-escalation evidence from the Spouse Assault Replication Program', *Public Health Reports*, 121: 409–18.

Piquero, A. R., Farrington, D. P., and Blumstein, A. (2007) *Key Issues in Criminal Career Research*. Cambridge: Cambridge University Press.

Piquero, A. R., Farrington, D. P., Nagin, D. S., and Moffitt, T. E. (2010) 'Trajectories of offending and their relation to life failure in late middle age: Findings from the Cambridge

Study in Delinquent Development', *Journal of Research in Crime and Delinquency*, 47: 151–73.
Piquero, A. R., Farrington, D. P., Jennings, W. G., Diamond, B., and Craig, J. (2012) 'Sex offenders and sex offending in the Cambridge Study in Delinquent Development: Prevalence, frequency, specialization, recidivism and (dis)continuity over the life-course', *Journal of Crime and Justice*, 35: 412–26.
Piquero, A. R., and Moffitt, T. E. (2005) 'Explaining the facts of crime: How the developmental taxonomy replies to Farrington's invitation', in D. P. Farrington (ed.), *Integrated Developmental and Life-Course Theories of Offending*. Advances in Criminological Theory, 14 (pp. 51–72). New Brunswick, NJ: Transaction.
Piquero, A. R., Theobald, D., and Farrington, D. P. (2014) 'The overlap between offending trajectories, criminal violence, and intimate partner violence', *International Journal of Offender Therapy and Comparative Criminology*, 58: 286–302.
Pithers, W. D. (1999) 'Empathy: Definition, enhancement, and relevance to the treatment of sex abusers', *Journal of Interpersonal Violence*, 14: 257–84.
Pogarsky, G. (2004) 'Projected offending and contemporaneous rule-violation: Implications for heterotypic continuity', *Criminology*, 42: 111–36.
Polaschek, D. L. L., and Daly, T. E. (2013) 'Treatment and psychopathy in forensic settings', *Aggression and Violent Behavior*, 18: 592–603.
Pollak, S. D. (2005) 'Early adversity and mechanisms of plasticity: Integrating affective neuroscience with developmental approaches to psychopathology', *Development and Psychopathology*, 17: 735–52.
Pollak, S., Cicchetti, D., and Klorman, R. (1998) 'Stress, memory, and emotion: Developmental considerations from the study of child maltreatment', *Development and Psychopathology*, 10: 811–28.
Prentky, R. A. (2003) 'A 15-year retrospective on sexual coercion: Advances and projections', *Annual New York Academy of Science*, 989: 13–32.
Prentky, R., and Righthand, S. (2003) *Juvenile Sex Offender Assessment Protocol II: Manual*. Washington, DC: Office of Juvenile Justice and Delinquency Prevention.
Prentky, R., Lee, A., Knight, R., and Cerce, D. (1997) 'Recidivism rates among child molesters and rapists: A methodological analysis', *Law and Human Behavior*, 21: 635–59.
Prentky, R., Harris, B., Frizzell, K., and Righthand, S. (2000) 'An actuarial procedure for assessing risk in juvenile sex offenders', *Sexual Abuse: A Journal of Research and Treatment*, 12: 71–93.
Prentky, R. A., Janus, E., Barbaree, H., Schwartz, B. K., and Kafka, M. P. (2006) 'Sexually violent predators in the courtroom: Science on trial', *Psychology, Public Policy, and Law*, 12: 357–93.
Prichard, J. C. (1835) *Treatise on Insanity*. London: Sherwood, Gilbert, & Piper.
Prime, J., White, S., Liriano, S., and Patel, K. (2001) *Criminal Careers of Those Born between 1953 and 1978*. London: Home Office Statistical Bulletin 4/01.
Protection of Children Act 1978 (c. 37) (1978) London: The Stationery Office.
Psychodynamic Diagnostic Manual (PDM) (2006) Washington, DC: Alliance Psychoanalytic Organization.
Puddu, L. (2002) 'Abusi sessuali e minori: Errori diagnostici, giustizia e verità processuali' [Sexual abuse and minors: Diagnostic errors, justice, and the criminal procedural realities], in G. Gulotta and S. Pezzati (eds), *Sessualità, diritto e processo* [Sexuality, Law and the Criminal Trial] (pp. 669–92). Milan: Giuffrè.
Quételet, A. (1831/1984) *Research on the Propensity for Crime at Different Ages* (tr. S. F. Sylvester). Cincinnati, OH: Anderson.

Quinsey, V. L. (2010) 'Evolutionary theory and criminal behaviour', *Legal and Criminological Psychology*, 7: 1–13.

Quinsey, V. L., Rice, M. E., and Harris, G. T. (1995) 'Actuarial prediction of sexual recidivism', *Journal of Interpersonal Violence*, 10: 85–105.

Quinsey, V. L., Harris, G. T., Rice, E. M., and Cormier, A. C. (1998) *Violent Offenders: Appraising and Managing Risk*. Washington, DC: American Psychological Association.

Quinsey, V. L., Harris, G. T., Rice, M. E., and Cormier, C. A. (2006) *Violent Offenders: Appraising and Managing Risk* (2nd edn). Washington, DC: American Psychological Association.

Raine, A. (2013) *The Anatomy of Violence: The Biological Roots of Crime*. New York: Pantheon Books.

Raine, A., and Yang, Y. (2006) 'Neural foundations to moral reasoning and antisocial behavior', *Social Cognitive and Affective Neuroscience*, 1: 203–13.

Reis, D. L., Brackett, M. A., Shamosh, N. A., Kiehl, K. A., Salovey, P., and Gray, J. R. (2007) 'Emotional intelligence predicts individual differences in social exchange reasoning', *NeuroImage*, 35: 1385–91.

Reiss, A. J., and Farrington, D. P. (1991) 'Advancing knowledge about co-offending: Results from a prospective longitudinal survey of London males', *The Journal of Criminal Law & Criminology*, 82: 360–95.

Reynolds, W. M. (1998) *Adolescent Psychopathology Scale*. Odessa, FL: Psychological Assessment Resources.

Reynolds, W. M. (2000) *Adolescent Psychopathology Scale – Short Form: Professional Manual*. Odessa, FL: Psychological Assessment Resources.

Rice, M. E., and Harris, G. T. (1995) 'Violent recidivism: Assessing predictive validity', *Journal of Consulting and Clinical Psychology*, 63: 737–48.

Rice, M. E., and Harris, G. T. (2013) 'Psychopathy and violent recidivism', in K. A. Kiehl and W. P. Sinnott-Armstrong (eds), *Handbook on Psychopathy and Law* (pp. 231–49). New York: Oxford University Press.

Rice, M. E., and Harris, G. T. (2014) 'What does it mean when age is related to recidivism among sex offenders?', *Law and Human Behavior*, 38: 151–61.

Rice, M. E., Chaplin, T. C., Harris, G. T., and Coutts, J. (1994) 'Empathy for the victim and sexual arousal among rapists and non rapists', *Journal of Interpersonal Violence*, 9: 435–49.

Rice, M. E., Harris, G. T., and Hilton, N. Z. (2010) 'The Violence Risk Appraisal Guide and Sex Offender Risk Appraisal Guide for violence risk assessment and the Ontario Domestic Assault Risk Assessment and Domestic Violence Risk Appraisal Guide for wife assault risk assessment', in R. K. Otto and K. S. Douglas (eds), *Handbook of Violence Risk Assessment* (pp. 99–120). New York: Routledge/Taylor & Francis.

Rich, P. (2006) *Attachment and Sexual Offending: Understanding and Applying Attachment Theory to the Treatment of Juvenile Sexual Offenders*. Chichester: John Wiley & Sons.

Richardson, J. B., Brown, J., and Van Brakle, M. (2013) 'Pathways to early violent death: The voices of serious violent youth offenders', *American Journal of Public Health*, 103: e5–e16.

Robertiello, G., and Terry, K. J. (2007) 'Can we profile sex offenders? A review of sex offender typologies', *Aggression and Violent Behavior*, 12: 508–18.

Roberts, B. W., Wood, D., and Caspi, A. (2008) 'The development of personality traits in adulthood', in P. J. Oliver, R. W. Robins, and L. A. Pervin (eds), *Handbook of Personality: Theory and Research* (pp. 375–98). New York: Guilford Press.

Robins, L. N. (1978) 'Sturdy childhood predictors of adult antisocial behaviour: Replications from longitudinal studies', *Psychological Medicine*, 8: 611–22.

Robins, L. N. (1979) 'Sturdy childhood predictors of adult outcomes: Replications from longitudinal studies', in J. E. Barrett, R. M. Rose, and G. L. Klerman (eds), *Stress and Mental Disorder* (pp. 219–35). New York: Raven Press.

Robinson, L., Spencer, M. D., Rhomson, L. D. G., Sprengelmeyer, R., Owens, D. G. C., Stanfield, A. C., Hall, J., Baig, B. J., MacIntyre, D. J., McKechanie, A., and Johnstone, E. C. (2012) 'Facial emotion recognition in Scottish prisoners', *International Journal of Law and Psychiatry*, 35: 57–61.

Roffey, M., and Kaliski, S. Z. (2012) 'To predict or not to predict – that is the question: An exploration of risk assessment in the context of South African forensic psychiatry', *African Journal of Psychiatry*, 15: 227–33.

Rogers, R. (2000) 'The uncritical acceptance of risk assessment in forensic practice', *Law and Human Behavior*, 24: 595–605.

Rose, N. (2002) 'At risk of madness', in T. Baker and J. Simon (eds), *Embracing Risk: The Changing Culture of Insurance and Responsibility* (pp. 209–37). Chicago, IL: University of Chicago Press.

Rosen, J. B., and Schulkin, J. (1998) 'From normal fear to pathological anxiety', *Psychological Review*, 105: 325–50.

Rosky, J. W. (2012) 'The (f)utility of post-conviction polygraph testing', *Sexual Abuse: A Journal of Research and Treatment*, 20: 1–23.

Russell, B. (1916/2000) *Autobiography*. London: Routledge.

Rutter, M. (2003a) 'Crucial paths from risk indicators', in B. B. Lahey, T. E. Moffitt, and A. Caspi (eds), *Causes of Conduct Disorder and Juvenile Delinquency* (pp. 3–24). New York: Guilford Press.

Rutter, M. (2003b) 'Categories, dimensions, and the mental health of children and adolescents', *Annals of the New York Academy of Sciences*, 1008: 11–21.

Rutter, M. (2006) 'Implications of resilience concepts for scientific understanding', *Annals of the New York Academy of Sciences*, 1094: 1–12.

Rutter, M., and Quinton, D. (1984) 'Parental psychiatric disorder: Effects on children', *Psychological Medicine*, 14: 853–80.

Rutter, M., Giller, H., and Hagell, A. (1998). *Antisocial Behavior by Young People*. Cambridge: Cambridge University Press.

Salekin, R. T. (2007) 'Psychopathy in children and adolescents', in C. Patrick (ed.), *Handbook of Psychopathy* (pp. 389–414). New York: Guilford Press.

Salekin, R. T., Rogers, R., and Sewell, K. W. (1996) 'A review and meta-analysis of the Psychopathy Checklist and Psychopathy Checklist-Revised: Predictive validity of dangerousness', *Clinical Psychology: Science and Practice*, 3: 203–15.

Salkind, N. J. (2010) *Encyclopedia of Research Design*. Thousand Oaks, CA: Sage.

Sampson, R. J., and Laub, J. H. (2003) 'Life-course desisters? Trajectories of crime among delinquent boys followed to age 70', *Criminology*, 41: 555–92.

Sampson, R. J., and Laub, J. H. (2005) 'A general age-graded theory of crime', in D. Farrington (ed.), *Integrated and Developmental and Life-Source Theories of Offending* (pp. 165–81). Palo Alto, CA: Transaction Publishers.

Sass, H. (1987) *Psychopatie – Soziopaties – Dissozialität: Zur Differentialtypologie der persönlichkeitsstörungen* [Psychopathy – Sociopathy – Dissociality: The Differential Typology of Personality Disorder]. Berlin: Springer.

Sass, H., and Felthous, A. R. (2008) 'History and conceptual development of psychopathic disorders', in A. R. Felthous and H. Sass (eds), *The International Handbook of Psychopathic Disorders and the Law* (pp. 9–30). Chichester: John Wiley & Sons.

Schlank, A., and Cohen, F. (1999) *The Sexual Predator: Law, Policy, Evaluation, and Treatment*. Kingston, NJ: Civic Research Institute.

Schleim, S. (2012) 'Brains in context in the neurolaw debate: The examples of free will and "dangerous" brains', *International Journal of Law and Psychiatry*, 35: 104–11.

Schmeck, K., Schlüter-Müller, S., Foelsch, P. A., and Doering, S. (2013) 'The role of identity in the DSM-5 classification of personality disorders', *Child and Adolescent Psychiatry and Mental Health*, 7: 1–11.

Schmucker, M., and Lösel, F. (2008) 'Does sexual offender treatment work? A systematic review of outcome evaluations', *Psicothema*, 20: 10–19.

Schneider, K. (1923/1950) *Die Psychopathischen Persönlichkeiten* [Psychopathic Personalities]. London: M. W. Hamilton Cassell.

Schneider, S. L., and Wright, R. C. (2004) 'Understanding denial in sexual offenders: A review of cognitive and motivational processes to avoid responsibility', *Trauma, Violence, and Abuse*, 5: 3–20.

Schwartz, B. K. (1995) 'Characteristics and typologies of sex offenders', in B. K. Schwartz and H. R. Cellini (eds), *The Sex Offender: Corrections, Treatment and Legal Practice* (vol. 3, pp. 3.2–3.31). Kingston, NJ: Civic Research Institute.

Schwartz, C. E., Wright, C. I., Shin, L. M., Kagan, J., and Rauch, S. L. (2003) 'Inhibited and uninhibited infants "grown up": Adult amygdalar response to novelty', *Science*, 300: 1952–3.

Scott, S. (2004) 'Childhood antecedents of juvenile delinquency', in S. Bailey and M. Dolan (eds), *Adolescent Forensic Psychiatry* (pp. 97–111). London: Arnold.

Scott, S. (2005) 'Do parenting programmes for severe child antisocial behaviour work over the longer term, and for whom? One year follow-up of a multi-centre controlled trial', *Behavioural and Cognitive Psychotherapy*, 33: 403–21.

Scott, S. (2010) 'National dissemination of effective parenting programmes to improve child outcomes', *British Journal of Psychiatry*, 196: 1–3.

Scott, S., Spender, Q., Doolan, M., Jacobs, B., and Aspland, H. (2001) 'Multicentre controlled trial of parenting groups for child antisocial behaviour in clinical practice', *British Medical Journal*, 323: 194–7.

Scott, S., Sylva, K., Doolan, M., Price, J., Brain, J., Crook, C., and Landau, S. (2010) 'Randomised controlled trial of parent groups for child antisocial behaviour targeting multiple risk factors: the SPOKES project', *Journal of Child Psychology and Psychiatry*, 51: 48–57.

Serin, M. C., Mailloux, D. L., and Malcolm, P. B. (2001) 'Psychopathy, deviant sexual arousal, and recidivism among sexual offenders', *Journal of Interpersonal Violence*, 16: 234–46.

Seto, M. C. (2005) 'Is more better? Combining actuarial risk scales to predict recidivism among adult sex offenders', *Psychological Assessment*, 17: 156–67.

Sexual Offences Act 2003 (c. 42) (2003) London: The Stationery Office.

Shadish, W. R., and Sweeney, R. B (1991) 'Mediators and moderators in meta-analysis: There's a reason we don't let dodo birds tell us which psychotherapies should have prizes', *Journal of Consulting and Clinical Psychology*, 59: 883–93.

Shamay-Tsoory, S. G., Tomer, R., Berger, B. D., Goldsher, D., and Aharon-Peretz, J. (2005) 'Impaired "affective theory of mind" is associated with right ventromedial prefrontal damage', *Cognitive Behavioral Neurology*, 18: 55–67.

Shankman, S. A., Klein, D. N., Lewinsohn, P. M., Seeley, J. R., and Small, J. W. (2008) 'Family study of subthreshold psychopathology in a community sample', *Psychological Medicine*, 38: 187–98.

Shaw, J., and Porter, S. (2012) 'Forever a psychopath? Psychopathy and the criminal career trajectory', in H. Häkkänen-Nyholm and J.-O. Nyholm (eds), *Psychopathy and Law: A Practitioner's Guide* (pp. 201–20). Chichester: Wiley-Blackwell.

Sherman, L. W., Farrington, D. P., Welsh, B. C., and MacKenzie, D. L. (eds) (2002) *Evidence-Based Crime Prevention*. London: Routledge.

Shlonsky, A., and Wagner, D. (2005) 'The next step: Integrating actuarial risk assessment and clinical judgment into an evidence–based practice framework in CPS case management', *Children and Youth Services Review*, 27: 409–27.

Shulman, E., Steinberg, L., and Piquero, A. (2013a) 'A mistaken account of the age-crime curve: Response to Males and Brown (2013)', *Journal of Adolescent Research*, 29: 25–34.

Shulman, E., Steinberg, L., and Piquero, A. (2013b) 'The age-crime curve in adolescence and early adulthood is not due to age differences in economic status', *Journal of Youth and Adolescence*, 42: 848–60.

Silva, P. A., and Stanton, W. (eds) (1996) *From Child to Adult: The Dunedin Multidisciplinary Health and Development Study*. Oxford: Oxford University Press.

Silver, E., and Miller, L. L. (2002) 'A cautionary note on the use of actuarial risk assessment tools for social control', *Crime and Delinquency*, 48: 138–61.

Simon, J. (2005) 'Reversal of fortune: the resurgence of individual risk assessment in criminal justice', *Annual Review of Law and Social Science*, 1: 397–421.

Simon, R. I. (2010) *Preventing Patient Suicide: Clinical Assessment and Management*. Arlington, VA: American Psychiatric Pub.

Sinclair, M., and Taylor, C. (2008) *The Cost of Crime*. London: Tax Payer Alliance.

Singh, J. (2013) 'Predictive validity performance indicators in violence risk assessment: A methodological primer', *Behavioral Sciences and the Law*, 31: 8–22.

Singh, J. P., and Fazel, S. (2010) 'Forensic risk assessment: A metareview', *Criminal Justice Behavior*, 37: 965–88.

Singh, J. P., Grann, M., and Fazel, S. (2011a) 'A comparative study of violence risk assessment tool: A systematic review and metaregression analysis of 68 studies involving 25,980 participants', *Clinical Psychology Review*, 31: 499–513.

Singh, J. P., Serper, M., Reinharth, J., and Fazel, S. (2011b) 'Structured assessment of violence risk in schizophrenia and other disorders: A systematic review of the validity, reliability, and item content of 10 available instruments', *Schizophrenia Bulletin*, 37: 899–912.

Singh, J. P., Fazel, S., Gueorguieva, R., and Buchanan, A. (2014) 'Rates of violence in patients classified as high risk by structured risk assessment instruments', *British Journal of Psychiatry*, 204: 180–7.

Sjöstedt, G., and Grann, M. (2002) 'Risk assessment: What is being predicted by actuarial prediction instruments?', *International Journal of Forensic Mental Health*, 1: 179–83.

Skeem, J. L., and Cooke, D. J. (2010a) 'Is criminal behavior a central component of psychopathy? Conceptual directions for resolving the debate', *Psychological Assessment*, 22: 433–45.

Skeem, J. L., and Cooke, D. J. (2010b) 'One measure does not a construct make: Directions toward a reinvigorating psychopathy research – Reply to Hare and Neumann', *Psychological Assessment*, 22: 455–9.

Skodol, A. E. (2012) 'Personality disorders in DSM-5', *Annual Review of Clinical Psychology*, 8: 317–44.

Skodol, A. E. (2014) 'Personality disorder classification: Stuck in neutral, how to move forward?', *Current Psychiatry Reports*, 16: 1–10.

Smallbone, S., and Cale, J. (2015) 'An integrated life-course developmental theory of sexual offending', in A. A. J. Blokland, and P. Lussier (eds), *Sex Offenders: A Criminal Career Approach* (pp. 51–72). Chichester: John Wiley & Sons (in press).

Smith, S. F., and Lilienfeld, S. O. (2013) 'Psychopathy in the workplace: The knowns and unknowns', *Aggression and Violent Behavior*, 18: 204–18.

Social Exclusion Unit (2002) *Reducing Re-offending by Ex-Prisoners*. London: Social Exclusion Unit.

Soothill, K. (1999) *Criminal Conversation: An Anthology of the Work of Tony Parker*. London and New York: Routledge.

Soothill, K., and Gibbens, T. (1978) 'Recidivism of sexual offenders: A re-appraisal', *British Journal of Criminology*, 18: 267–76.

Soothill, K. L., Jack, A., and Gibbens, T. C. N. (1976) 'Rape: A 22-year cohort study', *Medicine, Science, and the Law*, 16: 62–9.

Soothill, K., Ackerley, E., and Francis, B. (2008) 'Criminal convictions among children and young adults: Changes over time', *Criminology and Criminal Justice*, 8: 297–315.

Soothill, K., Fitzpatrick, C., and Francis, B. (2009) *Understanding Criminal Careers*. Cullompton, Devon: Willan Publishing.

Spitzer, E., and Maccarone, R. (2007) *Research Bulletin: Clinical and Structured Assessment of Sex Offenders*. New York: New York State Division of Probation and Correctional Alternatives. www.dpca.state.ny.us/pdfs/somgmtbulletinmay2007.pdf. Accessed 10 May 2014.

Spitzer, R. L., Williams, J. B. W., Gibbon, M., and First, M. B. (1990) *The Structured Clinical Interview for DSM-III-R Axis II Disorders (SCID-II)*. Washington, DC: American Psychiatric Press.

Sreenivasan, S., Weinberger, L. E., Frances, A., and Cusworth-Walker, S. (2010) 'Alice in actuarial land: Through the looking glass of changing Static-99 norms', *Journal of the American Academy of Psychiatry and the Law*, 38: 400–6.

Sroufe, L. A., and Rutter, M. (1984) 'The domain of developmental psychopathology', *Child Development*, 55: 17–29.

Stagner, R. (1937) *Psychology of Personality*. New York: McGraw-Hill.

Stattin, H., Magnusson, D., and Reichel, H. (1989) 'Criminal activity at different ages: A study based on a Swedish Longitudinal Research population', *British Journal of Criminology*, 29: 368–85.

Storm-Mathisen, A., and Vaglum, P. (1994) 'Conduct disorder patients 20 years later: A personal follow-up study', *Acta Psychiatria Scandinavica*, 89: 416–20.

Strecker, E. A. (1944) *Fundamentals of Psychiatry* (2nd edn). Philadelphia: J. B. Lippincott Co.

Strecker, E., and Ebaugh, F. G. (1925) *Practical Clinical Psychiatry for Students and Practitioners*. Philadelphia, PA: P. Blakiston's Son & Co.

Sweeten, G., Piquero, A. R., and Steinberg, L. (2013) 'Age and the explanation of crime, revisited', *Journal of Youth and Adolescence*, 42: 921–38.

Swets, J. A., Dawes, R. M., and Monahan, J. (2000) 'Better decisions through science', *Scientific American*, 283: 82–7.

Szmukler, G. (2001) 'Violence risk prediction in practice', *British Journal of Psychiatry*, 78: 84–8.

Takahashi, H., Yahata, N., Koeda, M., Matsuda, T., Asai, K., and Okubo, Y. (2004) 'Brain activation associated with evaluative processes of guilt and embarrassment: An fMRI study', *NeuroImage*, 23: 967–74.

Taleb, N. N. (2007) *The Black Swan: The Impact of the Highly Improbable*. London: Penguin Books.

Tavares, C., and Thomas, G. (2009) 'Crime and criminal justice: Statistics in focus, population and social conditions', *Eurostat*, 36: 1–12.

Taxman, F. S., and Pattavina, A. (eds) (2013) *Simulation Strategies to Reduce Recidivism: Risk Need Responsivity (RNR) Modeling for the Criminal Justice System*. New York: Springer.

Taxman, F. S., and Thanner, M. (2006) 'Risk, need, and responsivity (RNR): It all depends', *Crime and Delinquency*, 52: 28–51.

Taxman, F. S., Cropsey, K. L., Young, D. W., and Wexler, H. (2007) 'Screening, assessment, and referral practices in adult correctional settings', *Criminal Justice and Behavior*, 34: 1216–34.

Taylor, J., Loney, B. R., Bobadilla, L., Iacono, W. G., and McGue, M. (2003) 'Genetic and environmental influences on psychopathy trait dimensions in a community sample of male twins', *Journal of Abnormal Child Psychology*, 31: 633–45.

Terry, K. J. (2006) *Sexual Offenses and Offenders: Theory, Practice and Policy*. Belmont, CA: Wadsworth.

Tewksbury, R., Mustaine, E. E., and Payne, B. K. (2011) 'Community corrections professionals' views of sex offenders, sex offender registration and community notification, and residency restrictions', *Federal Probation*, 75: 45–50.

Theobald, D., and Farrington, D. P. (2009) 'Effects of getting married on offending: Results from a prospective longitudinal survey of males', *European Journal of Criminology*, 6: 496–516.

Theobald, D., and Farrington, D. P. (2011) 'Why do the crime-reducing effects of marriage on offending vary with age?', *British Journal of Criminology*, 51: 136–58.

Theobald, D., and Farrington, D. P. (2012) 'The effects of marital breakdown on offending: Results from a prospective longitudinal survey of males', *Psychology, Crime and Law*, 19: 391–408.

Theobald, D., Farrington, D. P., and Piquero, A. R. (2013) 'Childhood broken homes and adult violence: An analysis of moderators and mediators', *Journal of Criminal Justice*, 41: 44–52.

Theobald, D., Farrington, D. P., and Piquero, A. (2014) 'Does the birth of a first child reduce the father's offending?', *Australian and New Zealand Journal of Criminology*, 48: 3–23.

Theodosi, E., and McMurran, M. (2006) 'Motivating convicted sex offenders into treatment: A pilot study', *British Journal of Forensic Practice*, 8: 28–35.

Thornberry, T. P., and Krohn, M. D. (2003) 'The development of panel studies of delinquency', in T. P. Thornberry and M. D. Krohn (eds), *Taking Stock of Delinquency: An Overview of Findings from Contemporary Longitudinal Studies* (pp. 1–9). New York: Kluwer Academic/Plenum Publishers.

Thornberry, T. P., and Krohn, M. D. (2005) 'Applying interactional theory to the explanation of continuity and change in antisocial behavior', in D. P. Farrington (ed.), *Integrated Developmental and Life Course Theories of Offending*. Advances in Criminological Theory, 14: 183–209. New Brunswick, NJ: Transaction.

Thornton, D. (2006) 'Age and sexual recidivism: A variable connection', *Sexual Abuse: A Journal of Research and Treatment*, 18: 123–35.

Thornton, D., Mann, R., Webster, S., Blud, L., Travers, R., Friendship, C., and Erikson, M. (2003) 'Distinguishing and combining risks for sexual and violent recidivism', in R. Prentky, E. Janus, M. Seto, and A. W. Burgess (eds), *Understanding and Managing Sexually Coercive Behavior* (vol. 989, pp. 225–35). New York: Annals of the New York Academy of Sciences.

Toch, H. (1970) 'The care and feeding of typologies and labels', *Federal Probation*, 34: 15–19.

Toch, H. (1998) 'Psychopathy or antisocial personality disorder in forensic settings', in T. Millon, E. Simonsen, M. Birket-Smith, and R. D. Davis (eds), *Psychopathy: Antisocial, Criminal, and Violent Behavior* (pp. 144–58). New York: Guilford.

Tonry, M. (2008) 'Learning from the limitations of deterrence research', in M. Tonry (ed.), *Crime and Justice: A Review of Research* (vol. 37, pp. 279–311). Chicago, IL: University of Chicago Press.

Towl, G. (2005) 'Risk assessment', *Evidence Based Mental Health*, 8: 91–3.

Tranel, D., Gullickson, G., Koch, M., and Adolphs, R. (2006) 'Altered experience of emotion following bilateral amygdala damage', *Cognitive Neuropsychiatry*, 11: 219–32.

Tremblay, R. E., Desmarais-Gervais, L., Gagnon, C., and Charlebois, P. (1987) 'The Preschool Behavior Questionnaire: Stability of its factor structure between cultures, sexes, ages and socio-economic classes', *International Journal of Behavioral Development*, 10: 467–84.

Tremblay, R. E., Vitaro, F., Nagin, D., Pagano, L., and Séguin, J. R. (2003) 'The Montreal Longitudinal and Experimental Study', in T. P. Thornberry and M. D. Krohn (eds), *Taking Stock of Delinquency: An Overview of Findings from Contemporary Longitudinal Studies* (pp. 205–54). New York: Kluwer Academic/Plenum Publishers.

Tufts, A. (2013) 'Born to be an offender? Antisocial personality disorder and its implications on juvenile transfer to adult court in federal proceedings', *Lewis and Clark Law Review*, 17: 333–59.

Turner, W. (1538) *Libellus de re herbaria novus* (reprinted in 1877 in facsimile, with notes, modern names, and a life of the author) by B. Jackson. London: Daydon.

Tuvblad, C., Bezdjian, S., Raine, A., and Baker, L. A. (2013) 'Psychopathic personality and negative parent-to-child affect: A longitudinal cross-lag twin study', *Journal of Criminal Justice*, 41: 331–41.

Ullrich, S., Farrington, D. P., and Coid, J. W. (2008) 'Psychopathic personality traits and life-success', *Personality and Individual Differences*, 44: 1162–71.

Van Kesteren, J. P., Mayhew, P., and Nieuwbeerta, P. (2000) *Criminal Victimization in Seventeen Industrialized Countries: Key Findings from the 2000 International Crime Victims Survey*. The Netherlands: Ministry of Justice.

Van Lier, P. A. C., and Koot, H. M. (2008) 'Peer relationships and the development of externalising problem behaviour', in R. Loeber, N. W. Slot, P. van der Laan, and M. Hoeve (eds), *Tomorrow's Criminals: The Development of Child Delinquency and Effective Interventions* (pp. 103–20). Aldershot: Ashgate Publishing.

Vaughn, M. G., and DeLisi, M. (2008) 'Were Wolfgang's chronic offenders psychopaths? On the convergent validity between psychopathy and career criminality', *Journal of Criminal Justice*, 36: 33–42.

Vaughn, M. G., Howard, M. O., and DeLisi, M. (2008) 'Psychopathic personality traits and delinquent careers: An empirical examination', *International Journal of Law and Psychiatry*, 31: 407–16.

Verhulst, F. C., and van der Ende, J. (1993) 'Comorbidity in an epidemiological sample: A longitudinal perspective', *Journal of Child Psychology and Psychiatry*, 34: 767–83.

Verona, E., Patrick, C. J., and Joiner, T. E. (2001) 'Psychopathy, antisocial personality, and suicide risk', *Journal of Abnormal Psychology*, 110: 462–70.

Vess, J. (2011) 'Ethical practice in sex offender assessment: Consideration of actuarial and polygraph methods', *Sexual Abuse: A Journal of Research and Treatment*, 23: 381–96.

Viding, E., Blair, R. J. R., Moffitt, T. E., and Plomin, R. (2005) 'Evidence for substantial genetic risk for psychopathy in 7-year-olds', *Journal of Child Psychology and Psychiatry*, 46: 592–7.

Viding, E., Frick, P. J., and Plomin, R. (2007) 'Aetiology of the relationship between callous-unemotional traits and conduct problems in childhood', *British Journal of Psychiatry*, 190: s33–s38.

Vierikko, E., Pulkkinen, L., Kaprio, J., Viken, R., and Rose, R. J. (2003) 'Sex differences in genetic and environmental effects on aggression', *Aggressive Behavior*, 29: 55–68.

Viljoen, J. L., McLachlan, K., and Vincent, G. M. (2010) 'Assessing violence risk and psychopathy in juvenile and adult offenders: A survey of clinical practices', *Assessment*, 17: 377–95.

Villetaz, P., Gillieron, G., and Killias, M. (2014) *The Effects on Reoffending of Custodial versus Non-Custodial Sanctions*. Stockholm: National Council for Crime Prevention.

Vincent, N. A. (2008) 'Responsibility, dysfunction and capacity', *Neuroethics*, 1: 199–204.
[The] Violence against Woman Act (1994) (Title IV, sec. 40001-40703). Washington, DC: Dept of Justice.
Visher, C., and Weisburd, D. (1998) 'Identifying what works: Recent trends in crime prevention strategies', *Crime, Law and Social Change*, 28: 223–42.
Vojt, G., Thomson, L. D. G., and Marshall, L. A. (2013) 'The predictive validity of the HCR-20 following clinical implementation: Does it work in practice?', *Journal of Forensic Psychiatry and Psychology*, 24: 371–85.
Walker, J. L., Lahey, B. B., Russo, M. F., Frick, P. J., Christ, M. A., McBurnett, K., Loeber, R., Stouthamer-Loeber, M., and Green, S. (1991) 'Anxiety, inhibition, and conduct disorder in children: I. Relations to social impairment', *Journal of the American Academy of Child and Adolescent Psychiatry*, 30: 187–91.
Walters, G. D. (1990) *The Criminal Lifestyle: Patterns of Serious Criminal Conduct*. Newbury Park, CA: Sage.
Walters, G. D., Diamond, P. M., Magaletta, P. R., Geyer, M. D., and Duncan, S. A. (2007a) 'Taxometric analysis of the antisocial feature Scale of the Personality Assessment Inventory in Federal Prison Inmates', *Assessment*, 14: 351–60.
Walters, G. D., Duncan, S. A., and Mitchell-Perez, K. (2007b) 'The latent structure of psychopathy: A taxometric investigation of the Psychopathy Checklist-Revised in a heterogeneous sample of male prison inmates', *Assessment*, 14: 270–8.
Ward, T. (2010) 'Psychopathy and criminal responsibility in historical perspective', in L. Malatesti and J. McMillan (eds), *Responsibility and Psychopathy* (pp. 7–24). Oxford: Oxford University Press.
Ware, J., and Mann, R. E. (2012) 'How should "acceptance of responsibility" be addressed in sexual offending treatment programs?', *Aggression and Violent Behavior*, 17: 279–88.
Wartna, B., and Nijssen, L. (2006a) *National Studies on Recidivism: An Inventory of Large-Scale Recidivism Research in 33 European Countries*. Research and Documentation Centre (WODC): WODC-Studies on Recidivism Fact Sheet, 11: 1–10.
Wartna, B., and Nijssen, L. (2006b) 'National reconviction rates: Making international comparisons', *Newsletter of the European Society of Criminology*, 5: 3–14.
Waters, E., Merrick, S., Treboux, D., Crowell, J., and Albersheim, L. (2000) 'Attachment security in infancy and early adulthood: A twenty-year longitudinal study', *Child Development*, 71: 684–9.
Webster, C. D. (1984) 'How much of the clinical predictability of dangerousness issue is due to language and communication difficulties? Some sample courtroom questions and some inspired but heady answers', *International Journal of Offender Therapy and Comparative Criminology*, 28: 159–67.
Webster, C. D., and Hucker, S. J. (2007) *Violence Risk Assessment and Management*. Chichester: Wiley.
Webster, C. D., Douglas, K. S., Eaves, S. D., and Hart, S. D. (1997) 'Assessing risk of violence to others', in C. D. Webster and M. A. Jackson (eds), *Impulsivity: Theory, Assessment, and Treatment* (pp. 251–77). New York: Guilford Press.
Webster, C., Martin, M., Brink, J., Nicholls, T., and Middleton, C. (2004) *The Short Term Assessment of Risk and Treatability (START)*. British Columbia: Forensic Psychiatric Services Commission.
Webster, C. D., Martin, M. L., Brink, J., Nicholls, T. L., and Desmarais, S. (2009) *Manual for the Short-Term Assessment of Risk and Treatability (START)* (version 1.1). Port Coquitlam, BC: Forensic Psychiatric Services Commission and St Joseph's Healthcare.

Webster, S. D., Mann, R. E., Carter, A. J., Long, J., Milner, R. J., O'Brien, M. D., Wakeling, H. C., and Ray, N. L. (2006) 'Inter-rater reliability of dynamic risk assessment with sexual offenders', *Psychology, Crime and Law*, 12: 439–52.

Welsh, B. C., and Farrington, D. P. (2011) 'The benefits and costs of early prevention compared with imprisonment: Toward evidence-based policy', *Prison Journal*, 91: 120–37.

Welsh, B. C., and Farrington, D. P. (eds) (2012a) *The Oxford Handbook of Crime Prevention*. New York: Oxford University Press.

Welsh, B. C., and Farrington, D. P. (2012b) 'Crime prevention and public policy', in B. C. Welsh and D. P. Farrington (eds), *The Oxford Handbook of Crime Prevention* (pp. 3–19). New York: Oxford University Press.

Welsh, B. C., and Farrington, D. P. (2012c) 'The science and politics of crime prevention: Toward a new crime policy', in B. C. Welsh and D. P. Farrington (eds), *The Oxford Handbook of Crime Prevention* (pp. 509–20). New York: Oxford University Press.

Welsh. B. C., Farrington, D. P., and Gowar, B. R. (2015) 'Benefit-cost analysis of crime prevention programs', in M. Tonry (ed.) *Crime and Justice: A Review of Research*, 44. Chicago, IL: University of Chicago Press.

West, D. J. (1969) *Present Conduct and Future Delinquency*. London: Heinemann.

West, D. J., and Farrington, D. P. (1973) *Who Becomes Delinquent? Second Report of the Cambridge Study in Delinquent Development*. London: Heinemann Educational Books.

West, D. J., and Farrington, D. P. (1977) *The Delinquent Way of Life: Third Report of the Cambridge Study in Delinquent Development*. London: Heinemann Educational Books.

West, M., Rose, M. S., Spreng, S., Sheldon-Lerre, A., and Adam, K. (1998) 'Adolescent attachment questionnaire: A brief assessment of attachment in adolescence', *Journal of Youth and Adolescence*, 27: 661–73.

West, R. (2005) 'Time for a change: Putting the transtheoretical (stages of change) model to rest', *Addiction*, 100: 1036–9.

White, W. A. (1935) *Outlines of Psychiatry: Nervous and Mental Disease* (14th edn). New York: Publishing Co.

Whitney, W. D., and Smith, B. E. (1906) *The Century Dictionary and Cyclopedia: A Work of Universal Reference in All Departments of Knowledge with a New Atlas of the World*. New York: The Century Co.

Wicker, B., Keysers, C., Plailly, J., Royet, J.-P., Gallese, V., and Rizzolatti, G. (2003) 'Both of us disgusted in my insula: The common neural basis of seeing and feeling disgust', *Neuron*, 40: 655–64.

Wikström, P.-O. (2005) 'The social origins of pathways in crime: Towards a developmental ecological action theory of crime involvement and its changes', in D. P. Farrington (ed.), *Integrated Developmental and Life Course Theories of Offending*. Advances in criminological theory, 14: 211–45. New Brunswick, NJ: Transaction.

Wikström, P.-O. H., and Sampson, R. J. (2006) 'Introduction: Toward a unified approach to crime and its explanation', in P.-O. H. Wikström and R. J. Sampson (eds), *The Explanation of Crime: Context, Mechanisms and Development* (pp. 1–7). Cambridge: Cambridge University Press.

Wilczynski, A. (1997) *Child Homicide*. London: Greenwich Medical Media.

Williams, K. R. (2012) 'Family violence risk assessment: A predictive cross-validation study of the Domestic Violence Screening Instrument-Revised (DVSI-R)', *Law and Human Behavior*, 36: 120–9.

Williams, K. R., and Grant, S. R. (2006) 'Empirically examining the risk of intimate partner violence: The Revised Domestic Violence Screening Instrument (DVSI-R)', *Public Health Reports*, 121: 400–8.

Williams, K. R., and Houghton, A. B. (2004) 'Assessing the risk of domestic violence reoffending: A validation study', *Law and Human Behavior*, 24: 437–355.

Wilson, D. B., and MacKenzie, D. L. (2006) 'Boot camps', in B. C. Welsh and D. P. Farrington (eds), *Preventing Crime: What Works for Children, Offenders, Victims, and Places* (pp. 73–86). Dordrecht: Springer.

Wilson, D. B., MacKenzie, D. L., and Mitchell, F. N. (2005) 'Effects of correctional boot camps on offending', *Campbell Collaboration Reviews*, 2005: 6. www.campbellcollaboration.org. Accessed 26 Sept. 2013.

Woessner, G. (2010) 'Classifying sexual offenders', *International Journal of Offender Therapy and Comparative Criminology*, 54: 327–45.

Wolfgang, M. E., Figlio, R. M., and Sellin, T. (1972) *Delinquency in a Birth Cohort*. Chicago, IL: University of Chicago Press.

Wolfgang, M. E., Thornberry, T. P., and Figlio, R. M. (1987) *From Boy to Man, from Delinquency to Crime*, Chicago, IL: University of Chicago Press.

Wong, S. C. P., and Gordon, A. (2006) 'The validity and reliability of the Violence Risk Scale: A treatment-friendly violence risk assessment tool', *Psychology, Public Policy and Law*, 12: 279–309.

Wong, S., Olver, M. E., Nicholaichuk, T. P., and Gordon, A. (2003) *The Violence Risk Scale: Sexual Offender Version (VRS-SO)*. Saskatoon: Regional Psychiatric Centre and University of Saskatchewan.

Wong, T., and Hisashima, J. (2008) *State of Hawaii, 2003–2007: Domestic Violence Exploratory Study on the DVSI and SARA. Interagency Council on Intermediate Sanctions Technical Report #1*. Hawaii: Hawaii State Dept of Health. http://icis.hawaii.gov/wp-content/uploads/2013/07/SARA-DVSI-Exploratory-Study-Oct-2008.pdf. Accessed 22 Oct. 2014.

Woodworth, M., and Porter, S. (2002) 'In cold blood: Characteristics of criminal homicides as a function of psychopathy', *Journal of Abnormal Psychology*, 111: 436–44.

Wordsworth, William (1798) 'The tables turned; an evening scene, on the same subject', in *The Complete Poetical Works of William Wordsworth, 1798–1800* (vol. 2, pp. 53–4). New York: Cosimo Classics.

World Health Organization (2010) *International Statistical Classification of Diseases and Related Health Problems* (10th edn, ICD-10). New York: World Health Organization.

Worling, J. R. (2004) 'The estimate of risk of adolescent sexual offense recidivism (ERASOR): Preliminary psychometric data', *Sex Abuse*, 16: 235–54.

Yang, Y., Raine, A., Narr, K. L., Colletti, P., and Toga, A.W. (2009) 'Localization of deformations within the amygdala in individuals with psychopathy', *Archives of General Psychiatry*, 66: 986–94.

Yates, P. M. (2013) 'Treatment of sexual offenders: Research, best practices, and emerging models', *International Journal of Behavioral and Consultation Therapy*, 8: 89–96.

Young, L., Bechara, A., Tranel, D., Damasio, H., Hauser, M., and Damasio, A. (2010) 'Damage to ventromedial prefrontal cortex impairs judgment of harmful intent', *Neuron*, 65: 845–51.

Zara, G. (2005) *Le Carriere Criminali* [Criminal Careers]. Milan: Giuffrè.

Zara, G. (2006) *La Psicologia Criminale Giovanile* [Juvenile Criminal Psychology]. Rome: Carocci.

Zara, G. (2010a) 'Persistenza e recidivismo criminale: Il risk-assessment in psicologia criminologica' [Criminal persistence and recidivism: Risk assessment in criminological psychology], in G. Gulotta and A. Curci (eds), *Mente, Società e Dirittto* [Mind, Society and the Law] (pp. 555–603). Milan: Giuffrè.

Zara, G. (2010b) 'Farrington, David P.: The integrated cognitive antisocial potential theory', in F. T. Cullen and P. Wilcox (eds), *Encyclopedia of Criminological Theory* (pp. 313–22). Thousand Oaks, CA: Sage.

Zara, G. (2012) 'Adult onset offending: Perspectives for future research', in R. Loeber and B. C. Welsh (eds) *The future of criminology* (pp. 85–93). New York: Oxford University Press.

Zara, G. (2013a) 'La validità incrementale della psico-criminologia e delle neuroscienze in ambito giuridico' [Incremental validity of psychological criminology and neuroscience in the forensic setting], *Sistemi Intelligenti*, 2: 311–38.

Zara, G. (2013b) 'Neurocriminologia e giustizia penale' [Neurocriminology and criminal justice], *Cassazione Penale*, 2: 822–40.

Zara, G., and Farrington, D. P. (2006) 'Later criminal careers: Psychological influences', in J. Obergfell-Fuchs and M. Brandenstein (eds), *Nationale und Internationale Entwicklungen In Der Kriminologie* [National and International Developments in Criminology] (pp. 109–36). Frankfurt: Verlag fur Polizeiwissenschaft.

Zara, G., and Farrington, D. P. (2007) 'Early predictors of late onset offenders', *International Annals of Criminology*, 45: 37–56.

Zara, G., and Farrington, D. P. (2009) 'Childhood and adolescent predictors of late onset criminal careers', *Journal of Youth and Adolescence*, 38: 287–300.

Zara, G., and Farrington, D. P. (2010) 'A longitudinal analysis of early risk factors for adult onset offending: What predicts a delayed criminal career?', *Criminal Behaviour and Mental Health*, 20: 257–73.

Zara, G., and Farrington, D. P. (2013) 'Assessment of risk for juvenile compared with adult criminal onset: Implications for policy, prevention and intervention', *Psychology, Public Policy and Law*, 19: 235–49.

Zara, G., and Farrington, D. P. (2014) 'Cognitive-behavioral skills training in preventing offending and reducing recidivism', in E. M. Jiménez González and J. L. Alba Robles (eds), *Criminology and Forensic Psychology* (pp. 55–102). Charleston, S. C.: Criminology and Justice Publisher.

Zara, G., and Freilone, F. (2014) 'Insanity defense (and GBMI verdicts)', in A. A. Bruce and G. J. Geoffrey (eds), *Encyclopedia of Criminal Justice Ethics*. Thousand Oaks, CA: Sage.

Zara, G., and Mosso, C. (2014) 'Empathy', in A. A. Bruce and G. J. Geoffrey (eds), *Encyclopedia of Criminal Justice Ethics*. Thousand Oaks, CA: Sage.

Zgoba, K. M., and Levenson, J. (2012) 'Failure to register as a predictor of sex offense recidivism: The big bad wolf or a red herring?', *Sexual Abuse: A Journal of Research and Treatment*, 24: 328–49.

Zimring, F. (2004) *An American Travesty: Legal Responses to Adolescent Sexual Offending*. Chicago, IL: University of Chicago Press.

Zweig, M. H., and Campbell, G. (1993) 'Receiver-operating characteristic (ROC) plots: A fundamental evaluation tool in clinical medicine', *Clinical Chemistry*, 39: 561–77.

INDEX

Abbott, B. R. 226
Abel, G. G. 305
Achenbach, T. M. 202–3
Adam Walsh Child Protection and Safety Act of 2006 286
Adams, M. 34
Adolphs, R. 274, 304
Ægisdottir, S. 227
Age: age crime curve 25, 293–5; age of criminal responsibility 19, 70, 293; ageing 24–5, 293, 295–6
Ainsworth, S. A. 315, 317–18
Allport, G. W. 313
American Law Institute 268
American Psychiatric Association 238, 250, 299
Anastasi, A. 221
Andersen, H. 339
Anderson, D. 305
Anderson, J. C. 246
Anderson, L. A. 270, 271
Anderson, S. W. 272
Andrade, J. T. 233
Andrews, D. A. 148, 155, 157, 158, 159–60, 164–5, 170, 201, 301, 307, 315–17, 318–20, 326, 328
Antisociality: antisocial behaviour (ANT) 1–2, 31, 34, 36–7, 39, 53–4, 58, 67, 92, 109, 133, 141, 151, 165, 171, 200–2, 204–5, 227, 238, 240–1, 243–51, 254–5, 260–4, 267–8, 270–4, 277, 293, 311, 334, 337; antisocial escalation 24, 30–2, 38, 92, 325; *see also* aggravation; antisocial facet 232, 245, 254, 259; antisocial onset 19, 32, 37, 49–50, 53, 62, 68, 145, 150, 247, 293, 320–1, 328; antisocial orientation 292, 301; antisocial potential 12, 23, 27, 29, 31, 34, 37–8, 56, 165, 204, 211, 284, 294–6, 311, 333, 377; *see also* antisocial propensity, violence propensity
Antisocial personality (AP): antisocial personality disorder (ASPD) 141, 227, 238–41, 272–3, 277, 279–81, 326–7
Archer, R. P. 150
Arnett, P. A. 246
ATSA Professional Issues Committee 308
Augimeri, L. K. 153, 164, 203–4
Augstein, H. F. 235
Auty, K. M. 331

Babiak, P. 231, 241, 263, 266
Babinski, L. M. 58
Bailar, J. C. 153
Bailer, A. J. 153
Baird, C. 156, 163
Baker, L. A. 258
Bakermans-Kranenburg, M. J. 141
Bambini, V. 243
Barbaree, H. 289, 295, 297–8, 305
Barnett, A. 27
Barnett, G. 303
Baron-Cohen, S. 202, 303
Bartel, P. 208
Base rate: base rate of sexual recidivism 288; cumulative recidivism rates 288; hazard rate 289, 297
Baskin-Sommers, A. R. 274

Beauchaine, T. P. 301
Beech, A. R. 306
Beeghly, M. 140
Belfrage, H. 196
Bender, D. 27
Bennett, C. S. 144
Benning, S. D. 241
Bera, W. H. 300
Berger, P. 324
Berliner, L. 297
Birbaumer, N. 273
Black, D. W. 240
Blackburn, R. 231, 243–5, 313
Blair, R. J. R. 235, 241, 267, 270, 272, 273, 302
Blanchard, R. 295
Blattner, R. 229
Block, D. 140
Blokland, A. A. J. 308
Blonigen, D. M. 247, 258, 281, 331
Blumenthal, J. A. 305
Blumstein, A. 26, 30, 31, 58, 294, 295
Boccardi, M. 273, 274
Boer, D. 152, 184
Bonta, J. 148, 152, 155, 157–61, 164–5, 170, 301, 307, 315–16, 318–19, 320–2, 328
Borum, R. 208, 226
Botbol, M. 143
Bottoms, A. 27
Bouchard, M.-A. 140, 143
Bowlby, J. 140, 144, 336
Boyle, M. H. 258
Brame, R. 333
Brand, S. 19–20
Brass, M. 270
Brodsky, S. L. 149
Brody, S. R. 8–9
Brooks, W. M. 152
Brower, M. C. 272
Brown, E. 293
Brown, S. 302, 306
Brundtland, G. H. 225
Bucciarelli, M. 272
Buchanan, A. 224, 228
Budd, T. 19
Burdon, W. M. 285
Burke, D. 303
Burke, J. D. 290
Burt, C. 237
Bushway, S. D. 28
Buss, D. M. 243, 313
Bussière, M. T. 159, 165, 288, 291–2
Butcher, J. N. 214
Byrd, A. L. 241

Calaprice, A. 18
Caldwell, M. 290
Cale, J. 225, 283
Cambridge Study Delinquency Development Study (CSDD) 44–5, 48–51, 54–5, 58–9, 62, 65–6, 68, 70, 75, 101, 130, 136–7, 139, 142–4, 146–7, 244, 248–51, 257, 259, 261, 281, 294, 312, 314, 317, 324–5, 329, 334–6; case histories 2–3, 43, 60, 67–8, 137, 139, 147, 334; *see also* life histories, life stories; case 252 – Paul 101, 137, 142, 144; adolescence 107; adulthood 110; childhood 106; young adulthood 110; father 103; mother 101; siblings 105; case 301 – Callum 80, 137–8; adolescence 84; childhood 83; adulthood 85; father 82; mother 81; siblings 83; young adulthood 84; case 402 – Lachlan 95, 141, 137, 144; adolescence 98; adulthood 100; childhood 97; young adulthood 100; Lachlan's father 96; Lachlan's mother 95; Lachlan's siblings 97; case 504 – Jeremy 129, 137, 144; adolescence 133; adulthood 135; childhood 132; young adulthood 135; father 131; mother 130; siblings 132; case 590 – Jordan 72, 137–8, 141; childhood 74; adolescence 75; adulthood 78; young adulthood 77; father 73; mother 72; siblings 74; stepmother 74; case 763 – Ralph 123, 137, 141–2, 144; adolescence 126; adulthood 127; childhood 124; young adulthood 127; father 123; mother 122; siblings 124; case 882 – Matthew 113, 137–8, 144; adolescence 118; adulthood 120; childhood 115; young adulthood 119; father 114; mother 113; siblings 115; case 941– Jasper 87, 137–8; adolescence 90; adulthood 93; childhood 89, young adulthood 91; father 88; mother 88; siblings 89
CAGE questionnaire 69–70, 86, 100, 112, 120
Camp, J. P. 225
Campbell, G. 223
Campbell, J. C. 194
Campbell, M. A. 158
Campbell, R. 297
Campbell, T. W. 224
Cann, J. 23
Caponecchia, C. 266
Carver, C. S. 246
Casey, B. J. 249
Caspi, A. 28, 35, 36, 139, 246, 323–4

Catalano, R. F. 37
Cauda, F. 281
Chakhssi, F. 242
Champagne, F. A. 258
Champion, D. J. 7–8
Chen, X. 34
Chesterton, G. K. 312–13
Chief Secretary to the Treasury 332
Child Sex Offenders Disclosure Scheme (Sarah's Law) 287
Christiansen, K. O. 12
Cicchetti, D. 58, 140
Cima, M. 235, 272, 303
Clarke, S. 22
Cleckley, H. 233–4, 238, 281
Cleverley, K. 258
Cloninger, C. R. 247
Cognitive: cognitive-behavioural approaches 301; cognitive-behavioural programmes or interventions 301, 307, 323, 336–7; cognitive deficits 305; cognitive distortion(s) 305, 307, 334; cognitive shifts 27; cognitive transformation 27; fundamental paradox of rationality 282; principle of independent systems 272
Cognitive psychology: availability heuristic 283; bias 5–6, 9, 39, 146, 158, 252, 259, 271, 283; bias of impunity 6; black swan 71, 155, 22; correspondences bias; distorted and biased thinking 302; distortions 208, 301, 305, 318, 326, 328; distorted thinking 301–2; dodo bird verdict 314; fast and slow thinking 282; heuristics 153, 162, 283–4; *see also* availability heuristic, representativeness heuristic; human reasoning 282; implicit theories 302–3; intuitive predictions 282; intuitive profiling 288–9; ipse dixit 282, 300; logical fallacy 306; mentalisation 140, 327; precautionary principle 224; recognition bias 283; regression artefact 284; regression fallacy 284; representativeness heuristic 283–4; unconscious bias 271
Cohen, D. J. 58
Cohen, F. 325
Cohen, J. 61
Cohen, M. X. 274
Coid, J. 38, 228, 231, 243, 295
Community Protection Act 285
Conte, J. R. 300
Continuity: absolute change 142, 251; cumulative continuity 34, 334; heterotypic continuity 34, 56, 58, 250; homotypic continuity 56, 58; population heterogeneity 143; relative stability 4, 34, 251; state dependence 143
Cook, R. J. 224
Cooke, D. J. 158, 243–5
Cooley, C. H. 136
Cooper, C. 18, 19
Copas, J. 173
Cornell, D. G. 272
Covell, C. N. 302
Coxe, R. 297
Craig, L. A. 301
Crick, N. R. 141
Crime: crime against property 61; crime against the person 61; crime prevention 315; crime reduction 315
Criminal Justice Act of 2003 61, 286
Criminal law: Actus reus 268; criminal liability 8, 268, 275; *see also* responsibility; criminal responsibility 8, 70, 199, 225, 235, 267–8, 275, 286–7, 293; *see also* liability; duty to protect 284; English criminal law 286; (U.S.) Federal Rules of Evidence 286; guilt 8, 21, 44, 69, 86, 98, 109–10, 118, 168, 200, 208, 232, 234, 241, 272–4, 277, 307; guilty criminal mind 269; intention 269; Jacob Wetterling Act 286; knowledge 269; legal system 269, 275; Megan's Law 286; Mens rea 268–9; *see also* intention, knowledge, negligence, recklessness; M'Naghten Rule 268; (U.K.) Ministry of Justice 9–13, 15, 17, 20, 28–9; Model Penal Code 268; negligence 269; recklessness 269; Safety Act of 2006 286; US rulings 285; Violence Against Women Act (VAWA) 285
Criminal career paradigm: research 3–4, 6, 8, 13–15, 18–19, 21–6, 28, 30, 32, 34–7, 40, 43, 54, 58, 61, 67–8, 71, 136, 139, 142, 146, 149–53, 156–7, 160, 162–5, 167, 185, 199, 221–3, 225–30, 232, 234–5, 239, 241–3, 245–6, 257, 266–71, 273–5, 279, 281–4, 288, 290, 292–3, 295, 297–8, 300–5, 307–8, 310–12, 314–21, 330–3, 337; criminological psychology research 67; deterrence research 24
Criminal careers: aggravation 1, 24, 30–2, 34, 38, 92, 185, 190, 193, 196, 206, 225, 267, 325; *see also* escalation; co-offending 33; chronicity 58–60, 62–4, 66, 241, 277; delayed criminal career 294; desistance 1, 3, 5, 24–30, 49, 58, 139, 149, 287, 295, 312, 333;

duration 30, 32, 45, 47, 49–52, 60, 62, 112, 129, 136–7, 154, 181, 207, 249, 258, 286, 299, 323, 334; de-escalation 1, 30; de-celeration 24–6, 30; escalation 30–2, 34, 38, 185, 190, 193, 196, 206, 255, 267; *see also* aggravation; false desistance 48; intermittent desistance 30; onset 1, 19, 21, 28, 30–5, 37, 39, 45, 47, 49–51, 53, 58–64, 68, 71, 100, 104, 112, 145, 150, 154, 164, 204–5, 241, 247–9, 258, 277–8, 293–4, 308, 313, 315, 317, 320–1, 328, 330–1; adolescent onset 308; adult onset 308; late onset 34–5, 247–9; early onset 32, 53, 58, 60, 62–4, 248, 278, 331; residual career length (RCL) 49; residual number of offences (RNO) 31; true desistance 26–7, 333; versatile criminal careers 61; Variety Index (VI) 62–4, 122, 136
Criminal Record Office (CRO) 44–5, 70, 135
Crocker, A. G. 232
Cullen, F. 316
Cunliffe, J. 20

Dåderman, A. M. 266
Dahle, K. P. 160
Daly, T. E. 242
Damasio, A. 271
Danesh, J. 239, 240
Daniels, M. 305
Daversa, M. 258, 259
Davidson, R. J. 301
Davis, D. 283, 288–9, 292
Davis, M. 149
Davis, M. H. 302
Dawes, R. M. 152, 162–3, 319, 320
de Oliveira-Souza, R. 271
de Vogel, V. 229
Decety, J. 302
DeClue, G. 224
Delaware Executive Department 8
DeLisi, M. 232, 266
Dempster, R. J. 297
DePanfilis, D. 163
Depue, R. A. 246
Developmental and life course theories: integrated cognitive antisocial potential theory 23
Diagnostic and Statistical Manual of Mental Disorders 69; *DSM-IV-TR* 238, 250, 277, 279; *DSM 5* 142, 239, 250, 279–80, 313
Dickey, R. 297

Dickinson, E. 274
Dindo, L. 242
Dixon, L. 182–3
Dodge, K. A. 311
Dodgson, P. G. 305
Dolan, M. 163, 229, 245
Doueck, H. J. 163
Douglas, J. 300
Douglas, K. 151, 163, 185
Douglas, K. S. 138, 163–4, 180–2, 266
Dowden, C. 315, 317, 326
Doyle, A. C. 156, 281
Doyle, M. 163
Dubourg, R. 21
Duerden, M. 296
Dugan, E. 21
Dutton, D. G. 145–6
Duwe, G. 172, 286, 323

Earls, F. J. 330
Ebaugh, F. G. 237
Edens, J. F. 244
Eggleston, E. P. 35
Elander, J. 247
Elbogen, E. B. 148
Elliott, D. S. 329
Elliott, F. A. 321
Ellis, L. 54
Emler, N. 155
Emotion(s): emotion dysregulation 303; emotional brain 273; emotional deficits 305, 327; emotional distortion 305; emotional dysregulation 242, 301; emotional knowledge 268; emotional system 269
Empathy: affective empathy 302–4; cognitive empathy 303; disempathic attitude 303
Epperson, D. L. 170–1
Ermer, E. 273
Eslinger, P. J. 271
Esquirol, E. 235
EUICS Report 22
European Convention of Human Rights and Fundamental Freedoms 286

Farah, M. J. 270
Farrell, G. 22
Farrington, D. P. 9, 18, 23, 25–8, 32–5, 37–9, 44–8, 51–4, 58–9, 61–2, 66–7, 69–70, 86, 98, 137, 142–6, 149, 152, 154–5, 165, 223, 225, 227, 231, 244, 247, 249–52, 254, 257, 259–60, 262, 281, 288, 293–5, 300, 302–3, 310–12, 314, 315–16, 319–21, 323–5, 329–32, 334, 337

Fazel, S. 150, 158, 224, 227–8, 239–40
Fearson, R. 140, 141
Fellows, K. L. 270
Felthous, A. R. 235–7, 240
Fergusson, D. M. 145
Fernandez, Y. 303
Feuchtersleben, E. 236
Fiske, S. T. 271
Flannery, D. J. 331
Fleminger, S. 224
Follette, W. C. 283, 288–9, 292
Fonagy, P. 68, 140–1, 143
Fornari, U. 148, 235, 268
Forth, A. 200, 242
Fowles, D. C. 242, 246
Fox, A. 235
Fox, J. 66
Francis Smith, S. 241
Francis, B. 290–1, 295, 336
Fréchette, M. 329
Fredrickson, B. L. 284
Freeman, N. J. 297
Freilone, F. 67, 142, 148, 225, 232, 242, 268
Freske, P. J. 172
Freund, K. 299
Frick, P. J. 245–7, 257–8
Friendship, C. 8, 23, 34
Frith, U. 272
Furneaux, W. D. 147

Gabor, T. 319
Gallagher, C. A. 285
Gannon, T. A. 302
Gao, Y. 232, 235
Gazzaniga, M. S. 268–9, 271, 275–6
Geer, J. H. 303
Gendreau, P. 155, 165
General Health Questionnaire GHQ 66, 70, 79
Gery, I. 304
Gibas, A. 195
Gibbens, T. 11, 12, 25, 333
Gibson, H. B. 147
Gigerenzer, G. 153
Giordano, P. C. 27
Glannon, W. 235
Glaser, B. A. 219
Glazebrook, J. S. 149
Glenn, A. L. 268–4, 327
Gneiting, T. 156
Goldberg, D. P. 66, 70
Golden, R. 243
Goldstein, J. 235
Goldstein, R. B. 250
Gordon, A. 179

Gordon, R. M. 239, 278
Goring, C. 293
Gottfredson, D. M. 25, 32, 293
Gottfredson, M. 293
Gottfredson, S. D. 226
Grann, M. 226, 266
Grant, S. R. 189
Gray, J. A. 246
Gray, N. S. 148, 229
Greene, J. D. 271
Greenfeld, L. A. 7
Gregory, S. 273
Grieve, R. 242
Grisolia, J. S. 259
Grisso, T. 148, 219
Groth, A. N. 299
Grotpeter, J. K. 141
Grove, W. M. 153, 159, 226
Gruber, C. P. 219
Guay, J. P. 244
Gudonis, L. 259
Guilford, J. P. 30
Gulotta, G. 148, 266
Guo, B. 188, 194, 195
Guy, L. 227

Haas, H. 54
Haggard, P. 270
Hall, R. C. W. 299
Hancock, J. T. 241
Handel, R. W. 219
Hannah-Moffat, K. 157
Hanson, R. K. 150–1, 159–61, 165–7, 172–5, 178, 225–7, 283, 288–9, 291–2, 295–7, 300, 301, 303, 305, 308–9
Harcourt, B. 225
Hare, R. 167–8, 231–2, 235, 239, 241–5, 258, 266, 268–9, 281
Hargreaves, C. 290–1, 336
Harkins, L. 306
Harpur, T. J. 241, 247
Harris, A. J. R. 175, 291, 297
Harris, D. 285, 292
Harris, G. T. 148, 178, 241–3, 295–6
Harris, L. T. 271
Harrison, K. 225
Harstall, C. 188, 194, 195
Hart, S. 70, 142, 152, 160, 163, 169, 178, 195, 226, 241–3, 249, 297, 307
Hathaway, S. R. 219
Hawkins, J. D. 28, 37
Hebenton, B. 285
Heilbrun, K. 221
Heim, C. 258
Heisenberg, W. 4

Helmus, L. 224, 302
Hemphill, J. 242, 266
Henderson, D. K. 236–7
Herpertz, S. C. 241
Hicks, B. M. 146
Higgins, N. 150
Hill, D. 234, 235
Hilton, N. Z. 160, 188, 192, 227
Hirschi, T. 25, 32, 293
Hisashima, J. 189
Hodgins, S. 32, 321
Hoge, R. 148, 153, 201
Hogue, T. E. 313
Holmes, C. A. 236, 242
Holmes, W. 297
Home Office 323
Hood, R. 289, 301
Horsefield, A. 149
Houghton, A. B. 189
House of Commons Justice Committee 20
Howard, P. 182, 183, 289–90
Hucker, S. J. 148, 156, 158
Hudson, S. M. 304
Humphreys, L. G. 223

Individual: individual differences 23, 31, 34, 53, 68–9, 226, 258, 272, 311, 313, 321; individual risk 221, 228; individual vulnerability 258; individualised assessment 308; individualised intervention 68, 159, 312
Ireland, J. L. 301
Iselin, A. R. 219
Isoda, M. 270
Ivan, C. 303

Jackson, P. L. 302
Jaffee, S. R. 145, 146
Janus, E. 285, 287
Jennings, W. G. 331
Jesness, C. F. 211
Johnson-Laird, P. N. 272, 282, 284, 344
Johnson, J. G. 145
Jolliffe, D. 9, 257, 302, 303, 315–16, 322–3
Jones, A. P. 274
Jonkman, H. 65
Jung, S. 302, 305, 307

Kagan, J. 246, 259
Kahneman, D. 282–4
Kaliski, S. Z. 150
Kansas v. Hendricks 285
Karpman, B. 237, 241
Katzfuss, M. 156

Kazemian, L. 25, 27–8
Kemshall, H. 224, 286
Kernberg, O. F. 239
Kerr, M. 247
Kerschner, D. 323
Khiroya, R. 150
Kiehl, K. A. 235, 273
Kim, H. K. 145
King, C. A. 285
Kingston, D. A. 184
Kitching, J. 232
Kluckhohn, C. 313
Knight, R. 299, 305
Knowles, E. M. 281
Koch, M. 236
Koegl, C. J. 337
Koehler, J. J. 289
Koenigs, M. 271, 273
Koot, H. M. 155
Kraemer, H. C. 154
Kraepelin, E. 236
Kratzer, L. 321
Krohn, M. D. 32, 330
Kropp, P. 163–4, 193, 195, 197
Krueger, J. 160
Krueger, R. F. 278, 279, 331
Kühn, S. 270
Kurlychek, M. C. 26
Kvaraceus, W. C. 149

La Fond, J. Q. 288, 325
Lachar, D. 219
Langan, P. A. 289, 291, 297
Langevin R. 303
Långström, N. 266, 295
Langton, C. M. 306
Larsson, H. 246, 247, 258
Latessa, E. J. 68, 146, 315
Laub, J. H. 27–8, 32, 35, 37, 67, 295
Laurell, J. 266
Laws, D. R. 295, 298, 300
Le Blanc, M. 329
LeBlanc, M. 25
LeDoux, J. E. 273, 274
Lee, S. 332
Leese, M. 224
Leete, R. 66
Lejins, P. P. 310
Levenson, J. 285, 307
Lidz, C. 148
Lieb, R. 285, 288, 325
Life histories: life stories 2, 67–8, 139
Lilienfeld, S. O. 241, 243, 245, 266
Lind, G. 271
Lindberg, N. 241

Lindsey, R. E. 303
Lippke, R. L. 325
Lipscombe, S. 287
Lipsey, M. W. 315–16, 321–2
Lisak, D. 303
Livesley, W. J. 142, 313
Lloyd, C. 9
Lloyd, M. 153
Loeber, R. 18, 25, 28, 32, 37, 141, 143, 146, 154, 225, 241, 252, 293, 301, 320–1, 324, 329, 330–1
Longitudinal research: longitudinal study(ies) 1, 3, 34, 53, 146, 235, 257–8, 259, 262, 281, 311, 329–31, 333–5, 337; prospective longitudinal study 1, 3, 146, 259, 335, 337
Lorenzini, N. 140, 141
Lösel, F. 27, 300–1, 307, 315, 330, 352
Lowenkamp, C. 68, 315
Loza-Fanous, A. 179
Loza, W. 179
Luckman, T. 324
Luna, E. 325, 327
Lunbeck, E. 237, 238
Lussier, P. 34, 67, 144, 225, 283, 285, 290–1, 308, 331
Ly, M. 274
Lynam, D. R. 28, 259
Lynn, M. T. 270
Lyons-Ruth, K. 140

Maccarone, R. 161
MacKenzie, D. L. 315, 323
MacLeod, J. F. 25
Maden, A. 148
Maguire, M. 9
Mahar, D. 242
Maibom, H. L. 235
Males, M. 293
Maltz, M. D. 6
Mann, R. D. 162
Mann, R. E. 301, 303, 305
Marcus, D. K. 244
Marsh, A. A. 274, 302, 305
Marshall, P. 173
Marshall, W. L. 301–3, 307
Martinson, R. 314
Maruna, S. 27, 28
Maudsley, H. 235, 236
Maughan, B. 67
Mayfield, D. 69
McBurnett, K. 246
McCann, K. 283, 290
McCollister, K. E. 67
McCord, J. 241, 258

McCord, W. 241
McGuire, J. 314–15
McHoskey, J. W. 243
McMurran, M. 307, 318
McSherry, B. 268
McVie, S. 293–4
Meehl, P. 160–1
Meehl, P. E. 226, 243
Megan's Law 286
Meloy, J. R. 242
Melton, G. B. 164
Mendez, M. F. 271
Meyer, B. 246
Michie, C. 158, 243–4
Middleton, C. 385
Millar, A. 194
Miller, D. J. 301
Miller, L. L. 161
Miller, S. L. 149
Millon, T. 213
Mills, J. F. 320
Mineka, S. 246
Ministry of Justice 9–13, 15, 17, 20, 28, 29
Minuchin, S. 143
Moffitt, T. E. 28, 32–6, 67, 139, 258, 293–4, 321, 323–4, 329, 334
Moitra, S. 28
Moll, J. 271
Monachesi, E. D. 219
Monaco, L. 266
Monahan, J. 226, 284
Morality: moral behaviour 269, 272–3; moral emotions 272; moral imbecility 235, 237; moral insanity 232, 235–6; moral judgments 271–3
Morey, L. C. 243
Moriarty, L. J. 226
Morse, S. J. 235, 268
Morton-Bourgon, K. E. 160, 225–7, 291–2, 305, 309
Mosso, C. 302
Mulheirn, I. 20, 21
Muller, J. L. 274, 373
Multifinality principle 320
Mulvey, E. 148, 219
Murphy, C. 243
Murray, H. A. 313
Murray, J. 154, 159, 160, 335
Myers, W. C. 266

Nagin, D. S. 27, 143
Nakamura, K. 26
Neigh, G. N. 258
Nemeroff, C. B. 258
Neumann, C. S. 231–2, 235, 241–5, 258

Neuroscience: amygdala 258, 273–4; angular gyrus 274; anterior cingulate cortex (ACC) 273; brain 97, 258, 266–7, 269–76, 278, 324, 328; *see also* brain scan; brain scan 275–6; behavioural activation system (BAS) 246; behavioural inhibition system (BIS) 246; developmental neuroscience 274; dorsal fronto-median cortex (dFMC) 270; dorsomedial prefrontal cortex (dmPFC) 270; prefrontal cortex (PFC) 273, 336; hippocampus 274; insula 274; intentional inhibition 270; frontal lobe lesion 276; GCS fMRI – Research Group 273; medial prefrontal cortex (mPFC) 270–1; neurocriminology 3, 267–8, 275, 277, 310; neuropsychology 275; neuroscientific humiliation 275; orbitofrontal region 271; reward system 269; right dorsolateral prefrontal cortex (dlPFC) 271; striatum 274; structural grey matter (GM) 273; ventromedial region (vmPFC) 270

Newman, C. F. 318
Newman, J. P. 274
Nicholls, T. 191
Nijssen, L. 13–17
Nordstrom, B. R. 267
Noritake, A. 270
Nunes, K. L. 302, 306–7

O'Brien, M. 300
Oatly, K. 282
Offenders: abstainers 34, 35; adolescent delinquents (AL) 33; adolescent limited offenders 27, 32, 334; chronics 1–2, 30, 32, 49–50, 52, 58–64, 66–71, 87, 100, 129, 136–40, 142–3, 146, 225, 229, 242, 250, 262–3, 275, 294–5, 310, 321, 324–5, 327, 330–1, 333–6; *see also* chronic offenders; chronic offenders xiv, 1–2, 32, 49–50, 52, 58–64, 66–71, 136–143, 146, 225, 229, 250, 262–4, 275, 294–5, 310, 321, 324–5, 327, 330–1, 333–6; early onset offenders 248; desisters 26, 52; incest offenders 289, 291, 306; incest only offenders 297; intrafamiliar offenders 298; late onset offenders 34–5, 248; late starters 35; life course persistent offenders (LPC) 2, 33, 334; Offender index (OI) 8; one-timers 50, 52, 60, 62–4, 262; opportunistic offenders 299; persisters 59; recidivists 1–2, 4–7, 25–6, 30, 46–57, 199, 221–2, 226, 262–4, 285, 287, 291, 310, 312, 314, 321, 324, 329–35; *see also* recidivist offenders; recidivist offender(s) xiii, 1, 26, 46, 49–50, 263–6, 312, 321, 324, 329, 331; versatile offenders 290, 292, 336; violent specialists 290

Ochsner, K. N. 271
Ogloff, J. R. 149, 239
Oliver, P. J. 313
Ollendick, T. H. 246
Ontario Ministry of the Solicitor General 190
Otto, R. 130, 164
Ozarin, L. 235, 237

Pajer, K. A. 58
Pardini, D. 241, 301, 331
Pardue, A. D. 266
Paris, J. 259, 279
Parker, T. 41
Pascual, L. 273
Paternoster, R. 37, 143
Patrick, C. J. 234, 247
Pattavina, A. 323
Patterson, D. 297
Patterson, G. 54
Pedersen, L. 229
Persistence 1–2, 5–6, 24, 28, 31–2, 34, 36, 38–9, 49, 53–4, 150, 176, 223, 234, 277, 305, 324, 336
Personality disorders: dissocial behaviour 238; dissocial personality disorder 238, 277–8; pathological narcissism 239; personality functioning 142, 279–80
Personality assessment: Adolescent Psychopathology Scale (APS) 211; Jesness Inventory-Revised (JI-R) 211; Millon Adolescent Clinical Inventory (MACI™) 213; Minnesota Multiphasic Personality Inventory-Adolescent (MMPI-A™) 214; Personality Psychopathology Five (PSY 5) 218, 279
Pessoa, L. 274
Petersilia, J. M. 8
Peterson, J. K. 225
Petrosino, A. 315
Phillips, M. L. 274, 304
Picardi, A. 141
Pietrini, P. 243
Pillsbury, S. H. 327
Pinel, P. 235
Piquero, A. 19, 30, 33–5, 41–2, 59, 61–3, 65, 67, 69, 144, 288, 291, 293–4, 329, 331
Pithers, W. D. 303
Pogarsky, G. 58
Polaschek, D. L. L. 242

Police National Computer (PNC) 8, 19, 44–5
Pollak, S. 258, 331
Porter, S. 241, 266
Predictability: false negative(s) 2, 222–3, 230, 335; false positive(s) 2, 158, 221–4, 230, 285, 288, 335–6; general predictive validity 119; negative predictive value (NPV) 223; number needed to be detained (NND) 224, 230; number needed to treat (NNT) 224; number safely discharged (NSD) 224, 230; positive predictive value (PPV) 223, 230; prediction 2–3, 53, 71, 138, 142, 148–9, 151–8, 160, 162–3, 222, 224, 226, 243, 285, 287, 292, 296–7, 319, 335, 337; predictive accuracy 158, 161, 165, 167, 175, 178, 189, 223, 225, 227, 283; predictive power 223; predictive validity 199, 221–2, 224, 228–9, 242, 266; predictive value of a positive risk assessment 222; sensitivity 2, 53, 154–5, 162, 214, 221–3, 246, 273–4; specificity 2, 139, 165, 222–3, 225; true positive(s) 221, 223–4, 230, 288; true negative(s) 222, 335
Prentky, R. 207, 283, 285, 287, 292, 296, 299, 300, 325
Price, B. H. 272
Price, R. 19, 20
Prichard, J. C. 235
Prime, J. 45, 51
Propensity: antisocial propensity 27, 37; violence propensity 165
Protection of Children Act 1978 286
Protective factors 27, 66, 146, 151, 153, 155, 163–4, 209, 311, 330–1, 335–6
Psychodynamic Diagnostic Manual (PDM) 238, 239, 278
Psychopathy: affective and emotional difficulties 248; affective facet 232, 247, 303; affective interpersonal dimension (AI) 248; affective responses 284; arrogant and deceitful interpersonal style (ADI) 248, 250, 253–6, 260–4; callousness 3, 231, 241–2, 274, 278–80; deceitfulness 3, 241, 250, 277, 279–80; deficient affective experience (DAE) 169, 248, 253–5, 260, 262–4; psychopath(s) 2, 105, 129, 142, 167, 232–4, 236–42, 245–6, 258–9; idiopathic psychopath 237; interpersonal facet 232, 259; impulsive and irresponsible behaviour (IIV) 169, 248, 253–5, 263–4; impulsive/antisocial (IA) 207, 248, 253–5, 263–4; life-style facet 232; mask of sanity 234, 238; negative affectivity 246, 279; personality structure of psychopathy 261; primary psychopath 237; psychopathic individuals 245, 261, 266, 272, 274; psychopathic inferiority 236–7; psychopathic offender(s) 257, 268, 313, 325; psychopathic personalities 142, 231, 236; psychopathic risk 327; psychopathic traits 233–4, 239, 244, 246–7, 258, 266, 271–2, 297, 306, 327; psychopaths 232–4, 236, 237, 239–43, 245–6, 258–9, 266, 268, 270, 272–4, 327–8; Psychopathy Checklist – Revised Scale (PCL – R) 142, 167–8, 175, 177–8, 200, 228, 239, 242–5, 266, 328; Psychopathy Checklist Screening Version (PCL:SV) 69–70, 80, 95, 100, 113, 129, 142, 169, 178, 242, 244, 248–50, 253–6, 260–4, 281; Psychopathy Checklist Youth Version (PCL:YV) 200–1, 242; successful psychopaths 232, 245
Puddu, L. 283

Quételet, A. 293
Quinsey, V. L. 160–2, 174, 177, 243, 292, 296
Quinton, D. 145

Raine, A. 67, 232, 235, 266, 268–70, 273–4, 327
RATED 165, 225, 230
Reeves, K. 181
Recidivism: re-arrest 1, 6–8, 333; re-conviction 1, 5–12, 14–15, 17, 20–1, 23, 28, 173, 175, 183, 185, 290–1, 297, 332–3, 333; re-incarceration 1, 5–8, 333; re-offending 1–2, 4, 6–9, 12–13, 15, 17–21, 23–4, 27–8, 45, 54, 65, 149, 152, 157, 160, 162–3, 165, 170–1, 173–4, 178, 182, 199, 210, 229, 242, 282, 284–5, 288–90, 295–8, 300, 306, 308, 311, 315–18, 321–2, 326, 330, 333; criminal life style 128, 292, 336; criminal recidivism 2–5, 13, 18, 23–5, 28, 31–2, 36, 38, 49, 55, 66, 148, 150, 160–2, 225–8, 234, 257, 264, 266, 277, 308, 310–11, 314–16, 321–2, 324, 328–30, 333; general recidivism 159, 166, 230, 292, 336; recidivism probability 25, 65
Reicher, S. 155
Reis, D. L. 273
Reiss, A. J. 33
Reliability: inter-rater reliability 158, 199, 221

Rennie, C. E. 245
Rescorla, L. A. 202–3
Reynolds, W. M. 211
Rice M. E. 192, 241, 295, 296, 303
Rich, P. 139
Richardson, J. B. 331
Righthand, S. 207
Risk: risk focused approach 53; risk instrument 155; risk management 165, 173, 180–2, 184, 193, 195, 199, 205, 223, 228–9, 266, 312, 320; risk of criminal recidivism 38, 226, 277; risk of reoffending 23, 54, 152, 157, 162, 165, 170, 178, 199, 210, 229, 282, 295, 306, 316, 326; risk principle 3, 148, 316; risk processes 6, 15, 28, 31, 71, 266, 321; risk taking 280
Risk Assessment: actuarial judgement (AJ) 176; actuarial instrument(s) 158, 162, 192, 221, 227, 296, 335; clinical assessment 201; clinical judgement (CJ) 2, 146, 158–60, 187, 226–7; see also unstructured clinical judgement (UCJ); clinical practice 160, 163, 226, 228–9; first generation risk assessment 159; fourth generation risk assessment 159, 163; professional structured judgement 163, 197; second generation risk assessment 159, 161; structured anchored clinical judgement (SACJ) 187; structured assessment 150, 185, 208; structured clinical judgement 163, 176, 179–80, 198, 201; structure professional judgement assessment (SPJ) 158, 163–5, 178–80, 182–9, 192–9, 201–5, 207–8, 210, 225–7; risk assessment impact 288; risk assessment instrument 2–3, 149–50, 152, 155, 158–9, 163, 165–6, 178–80, 190, 193, 199–200, 202, 221–2, 225, 227–30, 295, 308, 335; risk assessment practice 26, 153, 159, 227, 331; risk assessment studies 283; third generation risk assessment 159, 163; unstructured clinical judgement (UCJ) 159
Risk assessment instruments: ACUTE 2007 166, 167, 174, 178; Brief Spousal Assault Form for Evaluation of Risk (B-SAFER) 193; CBCL 210; Child Behavior Checklist (CBCL/6–18) 202–3; Danger Assessment (DA) 194–5; Domestic Violence Risk Appraisal Guide (DVRAG) 188–9; Domestic Violence Screening Inventory (DVSI) 189–90; Domestic Violence Supplementary Report (DVSR) 190–1; Early Assessment Risk List (EARL-20B) 203; Early Assessment Risk List (EARL-21G) 204; Estimate of Risk of Adolescent Sexual Offense Recidivism (ERASOR) 205; Historical, Clinical, Risk-20 (HCR-20) 39, 151, 158, 161, 171, 178, 180–2, 206, 208, 226, 229, 234; see also HCR-20V3; Historical, Clinical, Risk-20 Version 3 (HCR-20V3) 181–2, 229; see also HCR-20; Juvenile Sex Offender Assessment Protocol-II (J-Soap-II) 207, 210; Level of Service Inventory–Revised (LSI-R) 170, 178, 240; Level of Service/Case Management Inventory (LSI/CMI) 170; Minnesota Sex Offender Screening Tool (MnSOST) 170–2; Minnesota Sex Offender Screening Tool-Revised (MnSOST-R) 171–2; Minnesota Sex Offender Screening Tool-3 (MnSOST-3) 172; Ontario Domestic Assault Risk Assessment (ODARA) 188, 192; Offender Assessment System (OASys) 182–3, 290, 308; Offender Group Reconviction Scale (OGRS) 173; Rapid Risk Assessment for Sexual Offense Recidivism (R-RASOR) 173, 175; Risk Matrix 2000 (RM2000) 183; Stalking Assessment and Management (SAM) 197–8; Self-Assessment Questionnaire (SAQ) 179; Spousal Assault Risk Assessment Guide (SARA) 195–6; Structured Assessment of Risk and Need (SARN) 185; Structured Assessment of Violence Risk in Youth (SAVRY) 208, 210; Sex Offender Needs Assessment Rating (SONAR) 174, 178; Sex Offender Risk Appraisal Guide (SORAG) 161, 174; STABLE 2007 166, 178; Short Term Assessment of Risk and Treatability (START) 186–7; STATIC – 2002 175–6; STATIC – 99 161, 167, 175, 296–7; Sexual Violence Risk 20 (SVR-20) 184; Violence Risk Appraisal Guide (VRAG) 177–8; Violence Risk Scale (VRS) 179; Violence Risk Scale: Sex Offender Version (VRS:SO) 179; Youth Level of Service/Case Management Inventory (YLS/CMI) 201; Youth Self-Report (YSR) 203; Youth Self-Report (YSR/11–18) 203

Risk factors: acute risk 178, 321; causal risk factor 154; childhood risk factors 144, 260, 262, 308; dynamic factors 2, 155, 158–9, 174, 183, 205, 221, 228, 336; dynamic psychological risk factors 164; dynamic risk factors 2, 155, 159, 174, 183, 205; static risk factors 161–2, 221, 317

Risk-Need-Responsivity: criminogenic need(s) 3, 15, 66, 68, 138, 146–8, 151–2, 155, 157–8, 164–5, 223, 266, 277, 292, 295, 308, 311, 313, 315–16, 319–21, 323–6, 328, 330–1; general responsivity 317; need(s) 3, 25, 146, 148, 159, 164, 170, 178–9, 185, 201, 210, 216, 295, 307, 310, 314–16, 321, 324, 326–7, 336; need principle 3, 148, 316; risk principle 3, 148, 316; responsivity principle 3, 149, 158, 317, 331; RNR model 165, 321–3, 327–8; RNR principles 321–3; specific responsivity 317, 325–6

Robertiello, G. 297, 298, 299
Roberts, B. W. 313
Robins, L. N. 53, 58, 250
Robinson, L. 304
Roe, S. 18, 19
Roffey, M. 150
Rogers, R. 151
Rose, N. 157
Rosen, J. B. 247
Rosky, J. W. 285
Roy, K. 27
Rutter, M. 18, 67, 145, 151, 155, 247, 258

Sackett, D. L. 224
Salekin, R. T. 241–2
Salkind, N. J. 221
Sampson, R. J. 27–8, 32, 37, 67, 143, 295
Sass, H. 235–7, 240–1
Scalora, M. J. 302
Schlank, A. 325
Schleim, S. 275
Schmaling, K. B. 141
Schmeck, K. 279
Schmucker, M. 300, 307
Schneider, K. 236
Schneider, S. L. 305–6
Schulkin, J. 247
Schwartz, B. K. 300
Schwartz, C. E. 246
Scott, H. 303
Scott, S. 54
Serin, M. C. 297

Seto, M. C. 159
Sex crimes: Adam Walsh Act 286; Community Protection Act 285; Denial 87, 105, 144, 185, 196, 212, 216, 280, 292, 302, 305–8, 313, 318, 326; *see also* denying; Denying 302, 305, 326; Hands off offences 298; Hands on offences 298; Multi-Agency Public Protection Arrangements (MAPPA) 286; Sarah's Law 287; sex offending 3, 12, 165, 277, 282, 284, 288, 291–3, 295, 298, 300–2, 304–6, 308, 325, 336; sex offending attitudes 302; sex offending risk 325; sexual assault 10, 22, 196, 206, 286; sex offences 23, 59, 122, 136, 171, 176, 185, 207, 283, 285, 291–2, 297–8, 305, 310, 326; *see also* hands off offences, hands on offences; Sexual Offences Act 2003 (U.K.) 286–7; Sexual Offences Prevention Order 287; Sexual Violent Predator (SVP) 285

Sex offenders: child molester(s) 166, 287, 291–2, 297–9, 302–5, 326, 336; rapist(s) 12, 291–2, 297–9, 302, 304–5, 326; female sex offenders 300; fixated offenders 299; fixated paedophiles 306; gentlemen rapists 299; vindictive rapists 299

Sexual Offences Act 2003 286–7
Shadish, W. R. 332
Shakespeare, W. 40, 327
Shamay-Tsoory, S. G. 27
Shankman, S. A. 145
Shaw, J. 241
Shepherd, A. 20
Sherman, L. W. 105, 315
Shlonsky, A. 156, 163
Shulman, E. 293
Silva, P. A. 35, 329
Silver, E. 161
Simon, J. 149
Simon, R. I. 225
Sinclair, M. 20
Singh, J. 150, 224–5, 227–9
Sinnott-Armstrong, W. P. 235
Sjöstedt, G. 226
Skeem, J. 244–5
Skodol, A. E. 279
Smallbone, S. 283
Smith, B. E. 308
Smith, S. F. 241, 266
Social Exclusion Unit 21
Soothill, K. 11–12, 25, 150, 333
Spitzer, E. 161

Spitzer, R. L. 141
Spoont, M. R. 246
Sreenivasan, S. 226
Sroufe, L. A. 151
Stagner, R. 67
Stanton, W. 329
Stattin, H. 330
Storm-Mathisen, A. 58
Strecker, E. 237
Sweeney, R. B. 332
Sweeten, G. 293, 295
Swets, J. A. 153, 223, 288
Syndrome: antisocial behaviour 1–2, 31, 34, 36–7, 39, 53–6, 58, 67, 74, 77, 79, 83, 86, 90, 92, 99, 107–9, 111–12, 116–17, 119, 125–7, 133, 135, 141, 144–5, 151, 165, 171, 200–2, 204–5, 227, 229, 231, 233, 238, 240–1, 243–55, 260–4, 267, 270, 272–3, 277, 281, 293, 305, 308, 311, 320, 329–31, 334, 337; *see also* antisociality; the rear-view mirror 325
Szmukler, G. 153

Takahashi, H. 274
Taleb, N. N. 71, 155, 229
Target, M. 140–1, 143
Tavares, C. 18
Taxman, F. S. 159, 164, 315, 317–18, 323
Taylor, C. 20
Taylor, J. 258
Terry, K. J. 297–300
Tewksbury, R. 285
Thanner, M. 164
[The] *Jacob Wetterling Act* 286
Theobald, D. 27, 54, 67, 331
Theodosi, E. 307, 318
[The] *Violence against Woman Act* 285
Thomas, G. 18
Thomson, M. E. 159–60
Thornberry, T. P. 32, 330
Thornton, D. 23, 161, 175, 183, 296–7, 305
Toch, H. 235, 283
Tomkins, A. 148
Tonry, M. 24
Towl, G. 154
Tranel, D. 274
Treatment 3, 7, 23, 29, 53, 68, 138, 142–3, 146, 148–9, 150–2, 155, 157–9, 161, 164–5, 171, 223–9, 237, 242, 266–7, 277, 300–1, 305–7, 310–31, 335–7
Treatment programme(s) 25, 148, 240, 285
Tremblay, R. E. 329

Tufts, A. 239
Turner, M. G. 71, 147
Tuvblad, C. 232
Tversky, A. 283–84

Ullrich, S. 232

Vaglum, P. 58
Validity: concurrent validity 165, 221–2; criterion related validity 221; predictive validity 199, 221–2, 224, 228–9, 242, 266
van der Ende, J. 246
Van Kesteren, J. P. 22
Van Lier, P. A. C. 155
Vaughn, M. G. 232, 266,
Verhulst, F. C. 246
Verona, E. 240
Vess, J. 243, 286
Viding, E. 258
Vierikko, E. 141
Viljoen, J. L. 158
Villetaz, P. 333
Vincent, N. A. 235
Violence: domestic violence 67, 144, 188–90, 192–5, 230; interpersonal partner violence (IPV) 165
Visher, C. 314, 330
Vittoria, D. 148
Vojt, G. 228, 229
Vulnerability 31, 53–4, 71, 98, 132, 146, 154–5, 198, 246–7, 258, 315, 330

Wagner, D. 156, 163
Wagner, V. 156, 163
Wales, D. 16
Walker, J. L. 247
Walters, G. D. 244, 295
Ward, T. 235–8, 295, 298, 318
Ware, J. 305
Wartna, B. 13–17
Waters, E. 141
Webster, C. 148, 156, 158, 180, 186
Webster, S. 185
Weisburd, D. 314
Welsh, B. C. 18, 28, 310–12, 314, 325, 329–30, 332
West, D. J. 38, 40, 54, 58, 69, 98, 145, 259, 293, 329
West, M. 139
West, R. 318
White, T. L. 246
White, W. A. 237
Wicker, B. 274
Wikström, P.-O. 37, 143
Wilczynski, A. 161

Williams, K. R. 189
Wilson, D. B. 315, 323
Woessner, G. 298
Wolfgang, M. E. 35, 49, 58, 294
Wong, S. 179
Wong, T. 189
Woodworth, M. 266
Wordsworth, W. 156
World Health Organization (ICD-10) 238
Worling, J. R. 205
Wormith, J. S. 159
Wright, R. C. 305–6

Yang, Y. 266, 274
Yates, P. M. 301
Young, L. 271

Zara, G. 18, 35, 138, 149, 150, 152, 155, 223, 225, 227–8, 235, 247, 249, 267, 268, 274–6, 283, 288, 292, 294, 300, 302, 305, 307, 315–16, 319–20, 324
Zgoba, K. M. 285
Zimring, F. 290
Zuravin, S. J. 163
Zweig, M. H. 223

eBooks
from Taylor & Francis
Helping you to choose the right eBooks for your Library

Add to your library's digital collection today with Taylor & Francis eBooks. We have over 50,000 eBooks in the Humanities, Social Sciences, Behavioural Sciences, Built Environment and Law, from leading imprints, including Routledge, Focal Press and Psychology Press.

Choose from a range of subject packages or create your own!

Benefits for you
- Free MARC records
- COUNTER-compliant usage statistics
- Flexible purchase and pricing options
- All titles DRM-free.

Benefits for your user
- Off-site, anytime access via Athens or referring URL
- Print or copy pages or chapters
- Full content search
- Bookmark, highlight and annotate text
- Access to thousands of pages of quality research at the click of a button.

Free Trials Available
We offer free trials to qualifying academic, corporate and government customers.

eCollections

Choose from over 30 subject eCollections, including:

Archaeology	Language Learning
Architecture	Law
Asian Studies	Literature
Business & Management	Media & Communication
Classical Studies	Middle East Studies
Construction	Music
Creative & Media Arts	Philosophy
Criminology & Criminal Justice	Planning
Economics	Politics
Education	Psychology & Mental Health
Energy	Religion
Engineering	Security
English Language & Linguistics	Social Work
Environment & Sustainability	Sociology
Geography	Sport
Health Studies	Theatre & Performance
History	Tourism, Hospitality & Events

For more information, pricing enquiries or to order a free trial, please contact your local sales team:
www.tandfebooks.com/page/sales

www.tandfebooks.com